HAUNTED SKIES

PRESERVING THE SOCIAL HISTORY OF UFO RESEARCH

VOLUME THREE   1970-1975

REPLACING EARLIER VOLUME REMOVED FROM SALE
NOW IN COLOUR: REVISED AND EXPANDED

**JOHN HANSON
DAWN HOLLOWAY
V. J. HYDE**

HAUNTED SKIES VOLUME 3 Revised 1970-1975
First paperback edition printed 2017 in the United Kingdom.
A catalogue record for this book is available from the British Library.

ISBN 978-09956428-3-6

Published by
Haunted Skies Publishing

For more copies of this book, please email: johndawn1@sky.com

Telephone: 0121 445 0340

Designed and typeset by Bob Tibbitts ~ (iSET)

Printed in Great Britain

FOREWORD

By HOWARD HUGHES

I HAVE been fascinated by UFOs and aliens from the days when I made myself tired for school by staying up late to watch 'The Invaders' on Granada television. I wondered what might have inspired the story of David Vincent – aka Roy Thinnes – who parked up at a 'deserted diner' to grab some sleep on a long drive only to witness an alien craft land. He had seen the unpalatable truth and he had to live – and occasionally cheat death – with it. 'They' were here and 'they' were doing much more than merely observing us.

At my Liverpool Comprehensive school I was a founder member of a short-lived 'UFO Society', but I was disappointed to discover a photo we submitted to a local paper may have been faked with a Frisbee. My briefly-sparked interest waned. I got interested in radio broadcasting – and look where that led, but I continued to be intrigued by the question: 'in a universe so enormous, how can we be alone?' It has always seemed to me to be statistically unlikely.

In the late 1960s, my wonderful Liverpool grandmother, Edna, who lived in a cobbled street in Waterloo, swore she'd seen a metallic 'saucer' languidly hovering over the main Liverpool railway track behind her small terraced home. She drew it. It was the classic domed UFO – lights at the bottom and apparent 'windows' at the top. She was not prone to fantasy. She was a down-to-earth 'Nan'. She bought me sweets and took me on days out to Southport. She did not suffer fools gladly but was capable of enormous empathy and love. Edna did not have a television and she did not watch sci-fi films but, until the end of her life, she swore that is what she had seen hovering close to a cloud not long after dawn, one sunny morning.

Howard's grandmother, Edna

How many people do you know who have seen something similar or know someone who has? Perhaps more than governments, politicians and military planners care to admit.

At the end of the day – in the absence of revelation or 'disclosure' – there is only belief. Either you believe there is something out there or you don't, and the process of making a decision is assisted by evidence. Perhaps it's something you've seen or something you've been told. It's unlikely, but it might be something you read in a tabloid newspaper. Maybe you have read a book on the subject. Maybe you think you have been abducted by the 'Greys'. Evidence is the key to belief or dismissal.

The *'Haunted Skies'* series of books is the best researched series of its kind. I have worked on news-desks all my life, but I have never seen research so thorough – documents, photographs, statements, witness accounts, and many, many of them.

I urge you to read and digest this new edition and let it help you come to an informed decision. Are the claimed craft 'theirs' or 'ours'? Do governments know more than they tell us, and is there a big truth that has yet to be revealed? This book will help you come to a view.

John, Dawn, V J and the team deserve great success for their hard work and the frequent wearing out of old-fashioned shoe leather in the quest for detail. The boy who loved *'The Invaders'* and went on to be a broadcaster and journalist is impressed.

Howard with Steve Bassett while on a recent tour in the UK

Today the big buzzword is "Disclosure." There is an active campaign for an end to the so-called "truth embargo" that has, it is asserted, kept information the public needs to know deeply secret. As I write these words American Disclosure advocate Steve Bassett is in the UK – touring Europe to raise the profile of the issue. In my view, and that is all it can be, there are details of incidents like Roswell and Rendlesham Forest that have been denied to the public. We can only guess why that might be. Whether any of these details amount to a "smoking gun" is unclear. There may be many reasons why secrecy has been maintained. But I may be wrong. And it's possible we already know all there is to know.

Are "UFOs" and "ETs" from beyond our planet, beneath the surface of our planet or from a different dimension? Are they, perhaps, our mental manifestations of something somehow generated by another "intelligence?" Maybe there are aspects of our consciousness that need much more exploration. We'll only get answers to the questions if our leaders and the media take the issues more seriously. But therein lies a problem. If there were free public Hearings aimed at getting to the core of the matter, would they reach any useful conclusions? If there were conclusions and those conclusions rubbished what we now call Ufology they would never be totally accepted and would probably be denounced as a coverup – which may or may not turn out to be true. We'd be little further on. The big truth is we have come to trust politicians and the mainstream media less and less about more and more.

So what is the way forward? We must carry on questioning witnesses and documenting cases. It's too late now to do anything else. This genie is out of the bottle. But perhaps any truth that is "out there" will not be found down here but will come out as we continue exploring planets beyond our own. I will be watching the future Mars missions with extreme interest.

INTRODUCTION

IN 2017, we learnt of a 40th Anniversary reunion to be held at Broad Haven Village Hall on the 4th February, organised by the South Wales UFO Society. We spoke to Emlyn Williams – head of the group, and told him of our interest with regard to a forthcoming book about the UFO events that had occurred around the locality. He kindly invited us to attend and I (John) spoke about the *Haunted Skies* book to the packed hall. A *BBC* film crew from the *'One Show'* arrived and I took part in a 20 minutes interview, in which I was asked whether I had come across any other examples of similar phenomena around the Welsh area, to which I replied in the affirmative and outlined the nature of a number of investigations into those matters. Not surprisingly, I later received an email instructing me that they would not be using any of the film, as someone had complained they had been caught on the film during the interview outside – which I regarded as suspicious, to say the least.

Further developments

On the 29th August 2017, I was contacted by Jonathan Hurdiss of *One Tribe TV*, in Bath, who told me that they were producing a five minutes film for the *BBC One Show* about the Rendlesham Forest UFO encounter of 1980, and wanted me to put him in touch with any civilian witnesses. I suggested that he should speak to Colonel Halt, but he said his company could not afford to pay for him to come over. I then suggested he ring/Skype Charles Halt – read the *Halt Perspective* and also gave him permission to use any of the film taken of Colonel Halt currently on the *Haunted Skies* website, and then get back to me. Taking into consideration that Jonathan did not have a copy of the book itself, I asked our book designer and typesetter – Bob Tibbitts – to let him have access to the PDF, which was done, but at the time of writing this text we have not heard anything more and can only wish him the best of luck with his endeavors.

Many people whom we came across over the intervening years felt frustrated with the *apparent* indifference adopted by the MOD, who have always declined to be drawn into any discussion over sightings of UFOs brought to their attention, and seek to convince us the majority of UFO sightings can be explained and that as they are of no Defence significance, they are of no interest.

Closure of Air Desk 2A

In December 2009, the authors learned of the closure of Air Desk 2a, at the MOD, as part of a cost cutting exercise, which may give the impression UFOs are no longer of any importance to the authorities. This is puzzling, knowing the many occasions involving what appear to have been attempts to intercept UFOs by the RAF, and of the irrefutable fact that so many people have described seeing what appears to be structured craft of unknown origin in our skies.

However, common sense dictates *they are of interest* and always have been. How can they not be of interest? Our *apparent* inability to determine the nature of what UFOs represent, and where they come from, should not prevent us asking questions about something we deserve an answer to.

UFO Disclosure

Many people ask us *"when will UFO disclosure take place?"* We tell them that we do not know, but feel it is not likely to happen for many years.

Over the last 60 years there has been a concerted effort, by many, to force official disclosure on the UFO subject by the authorities, following the tremendous weight of testimonial evidence from people, who optimistically believed that eventually Governments were going to 'come clean' – which, of course, never happens. Sadly, those thousands, if not millions, of sightings have faded into history, mostly unforgotten … until now.

Sporadically, over the last twenty 25 years, there has been considerable excitement generated by the media in an attempt to convince us that startling new files are going to be released into the public domain – invariably nothing of the sort ever happens. Likewise, we occasionally hear of claims that NASA is going to release a major announcement about Mars or the Moon, which is interpreted by naïve activists as official disclosure that we are in contact with an extraterrestrial intelligence over a period of the last 60 years. How often have we heard rumours that unsettling disclosures are expected from our Government within the next few days? Common sense dictates that serious secret scientific investigations on this subject will have been carried out by the authorities into identifying the nature of what exactly it is that confronts us, the findings of which have never been made public.

One of the reasons why investigations like this have taken place is that whatever the UFO phenomenon represents, it involves technological objects which can metamorphose and move at tremendous speed, materialize and dematerialize at will, and on occasion, communicate with the observer.

Military black projects, classified under national security, will never be discussed in open hearings. One has to also consider that if the knowledge was made public, then people would ask why we have been lied to for decades and what 'Flying Triangles' are – which go back to the turn of the 20th Century – never mind crop circles, cattle mutilations, alien interaction with people, and other paranormal events. Disclosure!? No way is this going to ever happen.

Is there a block on *Haunted Skies* books in the media?

We contacted veteran journalist Michael Hellicar of the *Daily Mail*, in 2009, and asked him for his views as to why we had been unable, despite sending *Haunted Skies* to various newspapers, to get anybody interested in reviewing the books.

Michael replied:

> *"I appreciate your dilemma: It is difficult to get anyone in the mainstream media to take much notice of a serious study of UFO activity. Although most national newspapers, including my own – the Daily Mail – do report credible UFO sightings, (and indeed we even report foreign sightings on Mail Online, which is the most visited newspaper web site in the world), there is rarely much follow-up. This is for the obvious reason that there usually is nothing more to report; a UFO is here one minute, gone the next… and in many cases, if not the majority, trained observers such as police and military witnesses are reluctant to be publicly identified.*
>
> *In addition to that, it is a sad and uncomfortable fact that serious researchers, such as yourselves, are often undermined by an obsessive minority - crackpots, unfortunately, who flood us with wild theories and unverifiable 'facts' and irrelevant history whenever a sighting is reported. I don't know why your books have had such little media attention, but I can tell you that literally dozens, if not hundreds, of books are published every week, and book editors of newspapers don't have the time to read all of them. Indeed, they tend to only be able to concentrate on the books that are brought to their attention by PRs employed by the publishers. This isn't a firm policy, by any means, but it isn't a case of the media willfully ignoring books such as yours; it is a matter of going with what has*

been deliberately, if not aggressively, targeted at them. I can only urge you to keep up the good work. Going on local radio and TV is an effective way of promoting your work. All local media outlets welcome stories in their own area, and national newspapers often pick up their stories that way. I would suggest, too, that simply sticking to the facts of a reported sighting will add to credibility. The mistake so many investigators make, (not including your good selves, I am sure), is to add their own theories as to where the craft came from and what the purpose was. This then takes the sighting into the realms of fantasy. So, too, do theories that governments are covering up sightings."

The demise of *Haunted Skies* Volumes 1 to 6

Sadly due to a disagreement with our ex-publisher all six volumes of *Haunted Skies* books were removed from sale in 2014, which meant we lost a great deal of time and money. Undaunted we set about replacing them. Here is the cover of Volume 4 to set the background to what we regard as one of the greatest unsolved phenomena's of modern day time.

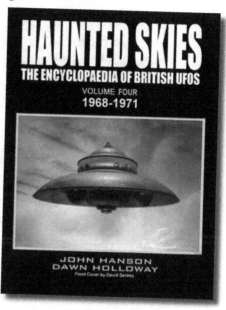

In this book you will read about many spectacular sightings, some involving the appearance of what appears to be interactions between the occupants of the UFOs by people (many women) that allege some frightening experiences. It is always difficult to know what to make of these, but without doubt the ones that we have come across are genuine people who have a lot to lose and nothing to gain by having the courage to come forward and simply tell what they witnessed. One wonders whether any association can be made with an observation made by the late Brad Steiger, who, after having received a number of letters from women that alleged to have been sexually molested by the occupants of these 'craft', noticed

"...a pattern that may have meant nothing – but may mean everything. After having obtained the birth data of many of the witnesses concerned, I discovered all the young women were born in March, April and May of 1948."

Brad speculated of the fact that the women were born nine months later, after major UFO activity in June 1947, and wonders how many of their mothers and grandmothers had similar experiences – food for thought, now 40 years on...?

Brad Steiger

Was born as Eugene E. Olson on February 19, 1936, at the Fort Dodge Lutheran Hospital during a blizzard. He grew up on a farm in Bode, Iowa. He identified as Lutheran until the age of eleven, when a near-death experience changed his religious beliefs. His parents encouraged him to become a teacher. He graduated from Luther College (Iowa) in 1957 and the University of Iowa in 1963. He taught high school English before teaching Literature and Creative Writing at his former college from 1963 to 1967.

Steiger claims to have written his first book at age seven. His first book, *Ghosts, Ghouls and Other Peculiar People*, was published in 1965. He became a full-time writer by 1967. He has authored/co-authored almost 170 books, which have sold 17 million copies. He has written biographies on Greta Garbo, Judy Garland, and Rudolph Valentino, the latter of which was adapted as a film in 1977.

With his wife Sherry Hansen Steiger, he is the author of *Four-legged Miracles: Heart-warming Tales of Lost Dogs' Journeys Home*

Steiger has appeared as a radio guest on 'Coast to Coast AM' and the 'Jeff Rense Program'. Steiger has written that he believes Atlantis was a real place. In his book *Atlantis Rising* he argued that Atlantis was the home of an all-powerful civilization with sophisticated technological achievement He also declared the tracks at Paluxy River to be evidence for an ancient civilization of giant humans.

He is a proponent of the ancient astronauts' idea. Steiger has stated that many humans descend from alien beings. He refers to these beings as "star people". Steiger has been married to Sherry Hansen Steiger, an author and minister, since 1987. They have five children and nine grandchildren. (**Source: Wikipedia**)

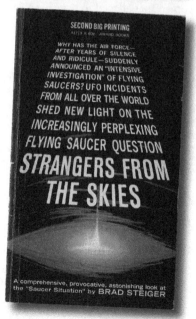

CHAPTER 1 – 1970

THE REAL UN-SENSATIONALISED FACTS!

JANUARY

2nd January 1970 – UFOs over London (three objects)
6th January 1970 – Cigar-shaped object sighted over Watford,
14th January 1970 – UFO over Stratford-upon-Avon, Warwickshire
18th January 1970 – Triangular UFO over Cradle Hill
26th January 1970 – Unidentified object over the sea

FEBRUARY

2nd February 1970 – Glowing UFO under the sea
3rd February 1970 – Boomerang-shaped UFO seen by children
3rd t February 1970 – Diamond UFO, Birmingham
4th February 1970 – Flattened bell-shaped UFO seen over London
9th February 1970 – Birmingham couple sight UFO
10th February 1970 – UFO encounter on Elm Hill, Warminster
11th February 1970 – Bright lights in the sky over London
13th February 1970 – Cigar-shaped UFO over London
25th February 1970 – Dull orange object over London

MARCH

3rd March 1970 – UFO hovers over Alexandra Palace, London
4th March 1970 – Red 'ball of light' in the sky over Derbyshire
9th March 1970 – Bright orange object over Leicester
12th March 1970 – Rotating UFO over Leicester
13th March 1970 – Strange behaviour from UFO over Woking, Surrey
24th March 1970 – Dronfield, Derbyshire
27th March 1970 – Three black lines, followed by UFO 'fountain', Southampton

APRIL

11th April 1970 – Pulsing, orange UFO over Bournemouth
22nd April 1970 – UFO over Arkansas, USA

MAY

1st May 1970 – Eight UFOs sighted over Glastonbury Tor
12th May 1970 – Mexican hat-shaped UFO over ancient site,
18th May 1970 – Three objects sighted over Devon,
25th May 1970 – Yellow 'disc' seen in sky over Leicestershire
29th May 1970 – Square UFO sighted over sea
May 1970 – Motorist encounters green cigar
Spring 1970 – Were RAF jets scrambled?
Early 1970 – 'Flying Saucer' over Reading Atomic Power Station, witnesses threatened

JUNE

5th June 1970 – Mysterious 'light' in the sky
8th June 1970 – UFOs over Yorkshire
12th June 1970 – Schoolchildren sight UFO over Buckinghamshire
16th June 1970 – Blinding light over Leicestershire
18th June 1970 – Strange 'light' over West Yorkshire
19th June 1970 – UFO hovers over Army base, Hampshire
26th June 1970 – Black 'star' reported over Hertfordshire
29th June 1970 – Glowing object paces family car at Apopka, Orlando, USA
June 1970 – Three lights, forming a triangle, seen by police officer
June 1970 – Passenger train paced by a UFO
Summer 1970 – Close encounter, followed by medical ailments
Summer 1970 – Strange 'beings' seen in house

JULY

1st July 1970 – Triangular UFO over Illinois, USA
2nd July 1970 – 'Flying cigar' over Gloucestershire
3rd July 1970 – UFO formations over Kent,
18th July 1970 – UFO Lecture, Kensington Library, London,
26th July 1970 – Dazzling UFO over Bedfordshire
28th July 1970 – Bright yellow 'light' over Bedfordshire
29th July 1970 – Shield-shaped object over Devon
30th July 1970 – UFO over Middlesex

AUGUST

1st August 1970 – UFOs over Kent
10th August 1970 – Unusual object over the sea, Isle of Wight
12th August 1970 – Deep black UFO over Essex
12th August 1970 – Motorist encounters red glowing object
12th August 1970 – Black UFO over Essex
14th August 1970 – Cylindrical object falls into a Lancashire river
19th August 1970 – Oval UFO over Leicestershire

21st August 1970 – Police officers sight UFO over London
22nd August 1970 – Object over Heathrow Airport, London
26th July 1970 – Orange 'light' over Bedfordshire
28th August 1970 – Cigar-shaped UFO over Leicestershire
31st August 1970 – Red and white lights over Illinois, USA
Summer 1970 – UFOs over Birmingham
August 1970 – Dr. Joseph Allen Hynek visits the UK

SEPTEMBER

2nd September 1970 – Police Officers sight UFO over Essex
5th September 1970 – Mysterious 'light' seen over grain bins, Illinois, USA
7th September 1970 – Cigar-shaped UFO over Southampton
8th September 1970 – UFO display over Wisconsin, USA
12th September 1970 – Red 'lights' seen over Cannock Chase, Staffordshire
15th September 1970 – Flashing 'lights' over London,
20th September 1970 – Four orange lights sighted over Staffordshire
September 1970 – Mr Arthur Shuttlewood, Paul Devereux,
September – Landed UFO, Norfolk
September 1970 – 'Silver ball' over Filey – RAF scrambled?
28th September 1968 – UFO landing, Warminster
29th September 1970 – UFO over Bournemouth
Close encounter over Norwich

OCTOBER

2nd October 1970 – Silver sphere over Manchester
4th October 1970 – Metallic object in the sky over Hampshire
UFO over Bolton, Lancashire
9th October 1970 – Shining 'disc' over Derbyshire
11th October 1970 – Motorist sights two UFOs
14th October 1970 – UFOs sighted over Colorado, USA
11th-18th October 1970 – Incredible account of UFO activity around a Scottish BBC TV mast
19th October 1970 – UFO over Eastern Counties
20th October 1970 – Motorist encounters UFO over Isle of Wight

21st October 1970 – Bright 'light' over Essex
October 1970 – Did a 'Vulcan' Bomber try and intercept UFO?
27th October 1970 – UFOs over Northampton
28th October 1970 – Mysterious lights over Northampton

NOVEMBER

5th November 1970 – Glowing 'light' in the sky over Swindon, Wiltshire
9th November 1970 – Fluttering object over Northamptonshire
10th November 1970 – Flash of light seen
13th November 1970 – UFOs over Lincolnshire
14th November 1970 – Spinning object in the sky over Northampton
15th November 1970 – Strange red line seen in the sky
16th November 1970 – UFO over Lincolnshire
20th November 1970 – Domed UFO seen
21st November 1970 – UFO over London … Police seen to take photographs
24th November 1970 – UFO over North Walsham
24th November 1970 – UFO over Illinois, USA
25th November 1970 – Silver cigar-shaped UFO seen over Cornwall
28th November 1970 – 'Flying Saucer' over London
28th November 1970 – 'Flying Saucer' over Matlock
30th November 1970 – Orange light seen over Dorset

DECEMBER:

1st December 1970 – Brilliant flashes light up the sky
6th December 1970 – Motorist encounters UFO over Warwickshire
7th December 1970 – Motorist encounters landed UFO
8th December 1970 – UFO hovers over football ground
8th December 1970 – Landed UFO seen by motorist in Berkshire
12th December 1970 – Strange 'light' in the sky over Coventry
14th December 1970 – Not UFOs this time over an Atomic Power Station!

JANUARY 1970

2nd January 1970 – UFOs over London (three objects)

At 2.35pm, UFO enthusiast David Prockter from Mornington Road, Leytonstone, sighted *"three banana-shaped objects"* in the sky.

Reacting quickly, he picked up a camera and took four photographs.

> *"The sighting lasted about eight minutes – ample opportunity to note their movements, which consisted of a 'falling leaf action' as they swung in the air. After the first object moved away, disappearing behind a house, the remaining objects became more oval in shape – the size of a match head, at arm's length. I estimated them to be a hundred feet in width. A couple of minutes later, the remaining two also moved off at high speed."*

We saw no reason to disbelieve these photos (which were declassified by the MOD) were none other than 100 per cent genuine.

From left to right: Mike Perryman, Roy Lake, Unidentified, Kevin B. Hall and David Prockter

By LIZ GILL

FLYING saucers, great balls of fire, little green men from outer space — those are the images that usually spring to mind whenever the term UFO is mentioned.

But David Prockter, 21, of Leytonstone, is more cautious — he takes them seriously but he shies away from sensationalism.

"We know they exist but what they are or where they come from we don't know yet."

David who works in the Government bookshop and edits the quarterly journal UFO News from his home in St Augustine's Court, first got interested in UFOs after he saw one.

"I was only about 13 at the time and I was waiting at the bus stop to come home after school. I saw what looked like a meteor but this was during the daytime.

It appeared to enter the earth. The whole experience only lasted a couple of seconds. Some of my friends saw it too, others didn't.

"It was the kind of thing where if you'd sneezed you'd have missed it," he said.

It was from that brief encounter that David's fascination with the subject was born. He purposely went UFO spotting.

"On another occasion I saw two cigar shapes with a square shape behind them over Wanstead Flats. This was during the day too and they were high up and seemed quite a distance away so I couldn't tell their size."

But his most spectacular sighting came during a trip to Warminster in Wiltshire which for some reason is a good source of UFO sightings and has become a Mecca for enthusiasts.

Mystery of UFOs — checks made by experts

David Proctor ... telescope at the ready.

A damski cigar-shaped UFO. The authenticity of this picture has never been proven nor disproven.

Satellites

"I saw something there that looked like a plastic bag full of water. It had that kind of rolling movement. It was about ten feet off the ground and about 50 yards at first. It passed over the top of me and disappeared behind some trees. As it came past it seemed to give off heat."

Despite his experiences — "I was a bit frightened. They're pretty awe inspiring to say the least," David retains an open mind on many other reports.

Along with other members of the Essex UFO Study Group he goes out to check on witnesses who claim to have seen UFOs.

"If the person does not want to talk about it then we don't push it, but if they are prepared to help us we give them about 30

These include lists of meteor showers, details of artificial satellites, reports of shooting stars, checks on aircraft routes, even flight paths of wild

Scientific

"They could be all or any of these," David. "At the moment we don't have enough information. Our job now should be to collect this information. If one ever got near enough perhaps some sort of scientific evaluation could be made."

At the moment ufology — as the study of UFOs is called — suffers from internal squabbles between rivals groups and of course the occasional crank and sensation seeker.

Neither do they have access to classified information and though paranoia about Government secrecy is not obvious in Britain as it is in the States, many UFO observers believe that many reports never become known to the public.

David does not know what is going to happen in the future but feels that a lot of evidence is being ignored – ostrich-like – by too many people.

Incidents

Sightings of Unidentified Flying Objects seem to be on the increase. And they don't just happen in exotic places. Here are two incidents from the files of David Prockter and they're all from London.

November 1970. Two schoolboys out at 10 on a Walthamstow cricket field claim they saw a silver light racing across the sky at high speed. At one stage it was brighter than the brightest star. Similar reports came in from Hackney, Clapham, Redbridge and Hyde Park.

Array of lights

December 1973. A woman reports seeing a mysterious array of lights moving across the night sky. It started off as a red pulsating ball

---

Dan Goring, editor of *Earth-link*:

"I knew David for 30 years and met him after joining the Essex UFO Study Group, when I found out he was producing his own magazine titled UFO News *which was published between 1970 and 1976. He was a lifelong friend of Edward Harris, who produced* Cosmology News Link. *David was regarded with the greatest of respect. Unfortunately he was in bad health and had to use walking sticks. He*

EARTHLINK 60p

UFOs and Related Subjects

passed away at aged 49 from a heart attack on 25th May 2002. He was buried on the 12th August 2002 at Manor Park Cemetery, London, because the coroner was unable to trace the two surviving relatives."

1,St. Augustines Court,
Mornington Road,
Leytonstone,
LONDON,
E.11 3BQ.

Phone:–01–556–6616

8.1.71.

Dear Mr. Tibbetts,

Today I recieved your latest issue of SYNTONIC, which I read with enthusiasm. The new cover was very striking I must admit-I feel that the cover of the magazine you edit(speaking on general terms not personally) should be presented in a striking way so as to impress.

I have done this to UFO News and only one person has objected and called it 'too gaudly'. Your cover designer Miss D. Harpley,must be congratulated. A most impresive design with the UFO shadow coming out just right.

Your editorial was very sensible. The printing costs these days are ridiculous and I hope to secure a litho and plate maker in the not too distant future,then I will be able to run UFO News and any others from my own home, and this will save an abundance of time. A price increase is the only possible way out at the mo, at least if you do this you will be able to come out on time as you have been doing,with up to daye news and events. Witness Spacelink-a magazine like that is very expensive to produce,and I know of several people who have cancelled their subscriptions because of its irregularity. Despite the fact that it is supposed to be quarterly,it has never had more than two issues per year. The price of SK is 3/6 so it is poss than Lionel may raise his price. SK 4/-, I would say is the highest price I would pay for a UFO magazine,and I would not do this for SK. I no longer buy my own copies of FSR as I find that most of these mags produce foriegn news when at the mo I would like to concentrate on England.

I would like to see more pages in SYNTONIC,and another three or four sides would allow you to charge a higher price without feeling any guilt. But I fear that all UFO mags still going today all need new blood,as ideas are getting stale in a lot of cases,and groups like S.I.U.F.O.P. and M.U.F.O.B. like to do nothing but attack other ufologists in their respective newsletters. That is something which I feel should not have to be tolerated.

One day in the future I will come down to a C.U.F.O.R.G. meeting and see what you do. I don't have any idea about your opinion of sky watching but I believe that watching the night sky you will only see a UFO by accident. I have never seen a UFO on a sky watch and the most I haveever got from one has been colds and wet feet. However a lot of my friends **have** seen aerial phenomena during an organised watch so continuation of them must be justified. I wold like to attend one of yours. Do you co-ordinate with any other groups such as B.U.F.O.R.A. or COS-MOS who do a lot of this activity?

Yours Very Sincerely,

David Prockter

Dan Goring and Margaret Fry

Edward Harris:

    "I and David were involved in the production of Cosmology News-link *which was published in colour and had segments on its front page. Some bright spark suggested we called it* Cosmic Orange. *I knew David for 40 years since he was aged 12. I was shocked to learn of his death."*

Another popular UFO magazine was *Space-link*, run by Lionel Beer.

Edward Harris

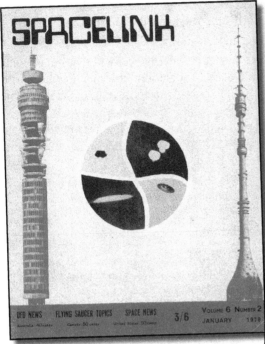 

6th January 1970 – Cigar-shaped object sighted over Watford

At 8.53am, Derek Murphy – employed by *Ind Coope Brewery*, in Watford – was looking out of the work's restroom window, when he saw a bright cigar-shaped object, high in the clear morning sky, towards Watford Gasworks.

Mr Murphy called his colleague – Roger Coultham – to come and have a look. Both men then watched the vivid yellow 'bar of light', which remained clearly visible, despite passing clouds, and was last seen heading slowly away towards the direction of the M1 Motorway, where it was seen to change from horizontal to vertical before being lost from view.

(Source: South-West Unidentified Aerial Phenomena Investigation Group)

At 5.15 pm, also on 6th January 1970, *Southampton Echo* photographer – Dick Patience, was travelling home by bus when he saw a *'fiery cross'* shaped object, motionless in the sky, between Marchonwood and Hythe area.

> *"It seemed to be at a height of less than ten thousand feet. I could see small lights at the front and rear, with a blinding light near amidships. The whole thing was surrounded by a faint glow. After a few minutes, it moved away towards the south."*

(Source: Nicholas Maloret, 'WATSUP')

14th January 1970 – UFO over Stratford-upon-Avon, Warwickshire

At 8.20am, a cone-shaped object, trailing red and yellow sparks, was seen crossing the sky at an estimated height of only 600 feet, over Stratford-upon-Avon, by many schoolchildren – a matter later brought to the attention of John D. Llewellyn, a local UFO investigator from the town.

Enquiries made by him into the incident revealed that two children saw what they described as *'a doughnut shaped object'*, showing three to four flashing square lights, an outline of a door, and a transparent dome (through which they could see the stars), heading westwards, accompanied by a whirring noise, at 8.25am. As it flew past, the whirring noise increased, the lights went out, and it vanished.

Forty-five minutes later, a similar object was seen passing over the town.

Mr Llewellyn considered the children may have seen a meteorite, after he was told that some multi-coloured pieces were seen to fall away from the object while in mid-flight, although enquiries made with other organisations, such as the British Astronomical Association, appear to rule this out as a possible explanation.

Could this have been the same object seen by Reginald Duncombe – a Security Guard at a factory in Old Birmingham Road, Stratford – who was unlocking the gates, at 8.30am, during mid-January 1970, when a passer-by stopped and directed his attention upwards into the sky?

> *"I saw this cone-shaped object, illuminated at its front by a brilliant searchlight, moving slowly through the sky at about 500 feet above the gasometer, heading towards Alcester. I later discovered a similar object was seen in Reading later that afternoon."*

(Source: Bob Tibbitts, CUFORG/*Stratford-upon-Avon Herald*, 16.1.1970)

18th January 1970 – Triangular UFO over Cradle Hill

At 9.30pm, Arthur Shuttlewood and John Roseweir, B.Sc., (Chairman of Contact UK), were on Cradle Hill when, according to Arthur:

> *"...a golden ellipsoid silently glided into view from the south-west and hovered about 50 feet above the ground, between Cop Heap and Warminster Downs, edged by West Wiltshire Golf Club greens, for 20 seconds, almost due south of where we were positioned on the hill by the now familiar white metal gates. Over the sun-disc aero form was a silvery plume, which in spite of the stiff breeze from the south-east was motionless and unwavering. From the bottom could be seen a dark triangle or pyramidal shape, about 30 feet overall dimension."*

According to John there were, in fact, two other witnesses to this phenomenon, who were living in a house on Boreham Road.

(Source: *Flying Saucer Review*, Volume 16, No. 4, July/August 1970)

26th January 1970 – Unidentified object over the sea

Shipyard workers at Southampton watched an unidentified 'light' hovering over Southampton Water, at 11.20pm, before splitting into two and heading off towards the Isle of Wight.

At 9pm, a similar object was seen over Balsall Heath, Birmingham, travelling towards Five Ways Island, leaving a red trail in the sky. At 7.40am on 6th February 1970, schoolboy – Roy Allingham (15), from Wanstead, London E11 – was with another boy, when they sighted a reddish/yellow/white oval shaped object in the south-west, hovering behind some trees, 500 yards away, over Hollow Ponds.

FEBRUARY 1970

2nd February 1970 – Glowing UFO under the sea

Mr P. Glover was walking along the promenade at Shoreham, at 8pm, looking due south, when he saw:

> *"...a glowing red and orange object, about the size of pea, hovering above the surface of the sea approximately three miles away; fifteen seconds later it disappeared from sight, followed by a strange glow under the water. A few seconds later it moved westwards, about half a mile, before stopping – then moved northwards and stopped again. The glow increased in illumination and faded away from view."* **(Source UFOSIS)**

3rd February, 1970 – Boomerang-shaped UFO seen by children

On the early morning, five schoolchildren from Stratford-upon-Avon, Warwickshire, were left shaken after watching a 'noisy' boomerang-shaped object, with a bar of red flashing light on its base, surmounted by three red, three green and yellow lights, cross the sky, heading westwards. **(Source: John D. Llewellyn)**

3rd February, Diamond UFO Birmingham

At 6.25pm on 3rd February 1970, Mrs J. Hayward from Stirchley (South of Birmingham) was getting ready for work, when she noticed what she took to be a star in the sky – until it gradually increased in size,

> "... *like a gigantic diamond in the sky, giving off this intense buzzing noise – then it appeared to shrink and go behind a cloud. I told the Police and received a visit, later, from an MOD man, who interviewed me*". **(Source: UFOSIS)**

At 7.10pm, the same day, Nigel Carey of Avon Road, Whitnash, Leamington Spa, was in his back bedroom when he noticed a bright yellow object in the sky. As a result of his excited call, his mother – Barbara, ran to the window.

> "*I lined my eyes up with the window frame and saw what looked like two huge cat's eyes in the sky, slowly moving upwards. All of a sudden they jumped across the sky, at terrific speed, crossing the golf course and then the Lockheed works. I was so excited I telephoned my local councillor, who advised me to contact the local newspaper and tell them what I had seen. I was annoyed to later discover, when they published the story, that someone suggested I had seen a Comet!*"

Another witness was Miss Enid Edmonds, who was in the back garden of her house, at 7pm, when she saw:

> "*...a bright orange/yellow star, stationary in the sky; after a few seconds, it moved over the town. To be honest, I didn't pay much attention to it.*" **(Source: Personal interview)**

4th February 1970 – Flattened bell-shaped UFO seen over London

At 7.45am, a pale yellow object – "*resembling a flattened bell in the sky*" – was seen close to the skyline over London E10, its top above the tallest building, by a motorcyclist on his way to a garage.

In early February 1970, window cleaners – Gordon Jones and his companion, William – were driving along Parkgate Road, Liverpool, in the evening, when they saw a bright object heading over the City, "*moving like a snake through the sky*". **(Source: *Liverpool Echo*, 7.2.1970)**

9th February 1970 – Birmingham couple sight UFO

At 5.30pm, a married couple living in Stechford, Birmingham – a heavy built-up area (well known to the authors of this book) – sighted:

> "*...a dark grey object, shaped like a three pointed flower petal that had curled up. It then started to revolve around its axis before heading away in an eastern direction.*"

It had been a dry and cold day with scattered cloud and no wind. **(Source: Derek Samson)**

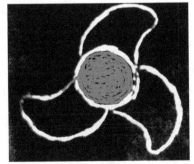

10th February 1970 – UFO encounter on Elm Hill, Warminster

Arthur Shuttlewood:

> "*At 7.20pm, I went for a short stroll up Elm Hill, before setting out for my reporting date. Again the pyramid-carrying UFO manifested, in about the same sky region betwixt downs and Cop Heap. Once more, the '3' and '9'*

aspect struck me. 7.20pm (7 + 2 = 9) on the 10th. It is dangerous and negative, obviously, to think subjectively: it is alien to my job as a qualified news reporter, who always seeks the objective angle of any story, but what does the reader think of the following, which came after much 'concentrated thought' on this three and nine mystery that occurs with strange frequency in the UFO pattern of late? My mind, free from mundane considerations, was simply open to ideas that filter through all minds occasionally – and should be welcomed if not of egotistic volition."

Silver circle, with cross, appears

Arthur:

"First, against a dark backcloth, a silver circle appeared, then a cross lighted up the centre, and from each end of the cross formation the figure '9' flashed with tremendous brilliance. Here in a brief illustrated form is what I saw. But even more vividly, as a sense of drama awoke within me and my startled eyes tried to make my brain understand something even more inexplicable than any of the genuine UFO sightings I have been privileged to witness, the pattern expanded and I became aware of the following: The cross became of the dimensional status of a Union Jack, with the circle filled by eight instead of the former four sections in separation. Then the number '90' began to flicker at the right on the second line down, then at its side. Excitedly, my brain raced and came up with the rather shocking revelation that 9 must be the most significant figure perhaps in the entire Universe, not just on Earth, together with the 3 that the spiritual and scientific factions among us recognise as having importance. Here, then, is the completed pattern of the circle: you will note that it is literally full, chock-a-block, of nines. Add any two numbers together and the answer is always NINE. – For example, 360 and 180 total 540 = 9, or 270 with 225 = 495 = 18 = 9. Do you follow the reckoning? Try any random or deliberate additions and you cannot escape the finality of that nine."

11th February 1970 – Bright lights in the sky over London

Mr Arthur Hayward from Abbey Wood, London, was looking out of his kitchen window, at 7.45am, when he noticed two bright lights, one above the other, due west, low in the sky. About a minute later, they moved off towards the south-west and were gone from sight.

13th February 1970 – Cigar-shaped UFO over London

A bright cigar-shaped object, surrounded by flashing lights, was seen hovering a few hundred feet in the sky above the Tate & Lyle factory, Stratford, London.

At 9.30pm, 6-10 yellowish lights were seen in the southern sky, 30 degrees off the horizon, over Portsmouth, Hampshire, by Mr R. Beaven – a keen astronomer, who could offer no rational explanation for what he saw. (**Source: South-West Unidentified Aerial Phenomena Investigation Group**)

In the same week, Roy Day – a coastguard from Margate – reported having sighted a brilliant circular object in the sky, which was reported to the MOD.

25th February 1970 – Dull orange object over London

Alan Johnson of Highams Park, London E4, happened to look out of his bedroom window, at 6.45am, when he saw a dull orange object, with a thin faint line running through its middle, at an elevation of some 20 degrees off the horizon, in the north-west direction.

"The edges of the object were clear and it appeared solid. After 30 seconds, it diminished in size and disappeared before I could summon my parents."

MARCH 1970

3rd March 1970 – UFO hovers over Alexandra Palace, London

Police Constables M. Cargill, from Wood Green Police Station, London, and D. Tilley, were on foot patrol on the Bounds Green Industrial Estate, during the day, when they noticed an unusual object hovering over Alexandra Palace, described as:

"...a very dark, long, cigar-shaped object, with a yellow glow coming from one end. It had no wings, or tail, and was hovering with its nose pointing to the ground. Eventually, it moved away to the north-west."

(Source: Omar Fowler, 'SIGAP'/Unknown newspaper – 'Policemen see UFO over Wood Green)

4th March 1970 – Red 'ball of light' in the sky over Derbyshire

At 9.30pm, Derbyshire resident – Mr Peter Baker, was looking out of his bedroom window when he saw a red 'ball of light' in the sky. Knowing it was far too large to be an aircraft light, he picked up his camera and took six frames of film at 1/60th shutter speed with the lens set to f8. When the film was developed, there was no sign of the red 'ball', but instead two dots or streaks were present.

The incident was brought to the attention of much respected Bournemouth-based UFO researcher – Leslie Harris.

"A bright star is visible on each slide and the 'UFO' plainly changed its position in relation to the star; in other words, whatever he captured was moving."

9th March 1970 – Ex RAF pilot sights bright orange object over Leicester

Ex-RAF Pilot John Bodein, and his daughter, Sara (9), were on their way back to the family home at Leicester, when they sighted a bright orange star with a long trailing flame, travelling swiftly across the sky, at 7.50pm.

Was this a satellite, burning up in the Earth's atmosphere, as believed by John, or was there another explanation? **(Source: Geoffrey Coxon)**

12th March 1970 – Rotating UFO over Leicester

At 3am, Miss A. McDonald of Colman Road, Leicester, heard a high-pitched whining noise – like a factory siren – which went on for about five minutes. Her curiosity aroused, she went to the window and looked out, seeing:

"...a round white object, surrounded by a white halo, on which were many small lights, slowly descending through the air. The 'halo' appeared to rotate. As it did so, it made the object flash with light. It then stopped, now motionless in the sky.

I shouted my parents. My mother joined me and watched the object as it rose upwards and away – now a flashing 'star' – until out of sight".

After reporting it to the *Leicester Mercury* **(White trail across City sky from 'UFO', 12.3.1970)**, Miss McDonald was to become the subject of considerable ridicule and expressed the opinion she wished she had never bothered to report it, especially after the newspaper journalist had misinterpreted what she had said. **(Source: Isle of Wight UFO Society/Geoffrey Coxon, BUFORA)**

Another witness to the phenomenon was Mrs J. Spiers, who wrote to UFO Investigator – Geoffrey Coxon, confirming she was awoken by the strange noise:

> *"…like a factory siren or aeroplane going berserk. It did not fade away gradually but stopped and was heard again almost immediately in the distance, but only for a moment or two. On enquiring about the incident at work, the next morning, I found out other people had also heard it."*

13th March 1970 – Strange behaviour from UFO over Woking, Surrey

A young couple were sat in their car at Horsell, Woking, Surrey, at 11.05pm, eating a snack. The girl opened the window to throw out a piece of paper when she saw a yellow object, with spiky edges, circling around the top of a tree in a clockwise motion. After it had circled the tree for about ten seconds, it moved closer by gradually descending by increments until it was about 100 feet away. The 'light' then went out, but within seconds another light appeared behind the tree. This completed half a revolution and moved away as the first one had done. When it reached the spot where the first one had vanished, it did likewise. The estimated speed of the object(s) had been 8mph. and was 80 feet from the ground. **(Source: Omar Fowler BUFORA)**

24th March 1970 – Dronfield, Derbyshire

Residents of the Frecheville, Dronfield, area of Derbyshire, telephoned the police after sighting a number of flashing objects moving through the sky. Enquiries made at RAF Finningley revealed they knew all about the sightings, but declined to offer any explanation.

(Source: Dr. David Clarke, 'Sheffield Saucers', 1970-1979, W.W.W)

27th March 1970 – Three black lines, followed by UFO 'fountain', Southampton

At 7.50pm, a resident of Chandler's Ford, near Southampton, Hampshire, saw three pencil black lines rise up to a hundred feet in the clear sky, forming what looked like a 'fountain', about 12 inches high.

> *"From this tiny 'fountain' suddenly appeared a number of solid-looking white 'slabs of light', about 8-10 in number, splayed out around the 'central disturbance'. I immediately thought it was a rocket firework, exploding in the air. To my astonishment, a beautiful green 'ball', solid in composition, suddenly appeared in the centre of the white oblong and left the white 'slabs', descending from right to left at an incredible speed, and vanished from view at a height of some 500 feet. As it did so, it projected in front of it a further succession of solid looking oblong white' slabs of light', which also vanished."* **(Source: UFOLOG)**

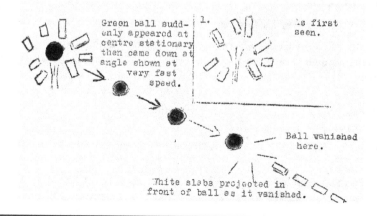

APRIL 1970

11th April 1970 – Pulsing orange UFO over Bournemouth

At 7.30pm, a pulsing, glowing, orange 'disc', with a white band around it, was sighted motionless in the sky over Hurn Airport, Bournemouth, by members of the Owen family, from West Howe. This was followed by the appearance of:

> "...a second cigar-shaped object (much smaller), showing a white 'field' around it, which was seen to approach the first one and attach itself to one end, for a couple of minutes, before veering off across the sky towards the north-west direction, leaving a thin curious streak of light – as if, in some way, still attached."

[The authors saw and captured a similar effect over London, many years later, on photograph.]

A beam of light was then seen to shoot out of the larger UFO and head across the sky, towards the direction of Poole.

Three 'bright lights' over Devon

At 10.47pm, three bright orange lights were seen over the coast of Ottery St. Mary, Devon, (south-east of Dawlish), by local resident Peter Walker, who rushed to collect his camera from inside. By the time he came outside, the lower of the three had gone, followed immediately by the upper two.

(**Source:** *Scan Magazine*, December 1970, Leslie Harris/The South-West Aerial Phenomena Investigation Group)

22nd April 1970 – UFO over Arkansas, USA

Two women driving near Blytheville, Arkansas, saw an object with small white lights, hovering over a field. As it moved away, it made a whistling noise before being lost from view. (**Source:** NICAP)

MAY 1970

1st May 1970 – Eight UFOs sighted over Glastonbury Tor

At 8.30pm, a young Police Officer, and four others, sighted eight objects, stationary in the northern sky over Glastonbury Tor.

They were described as being bright maroon in colour, egg-shaped, showing a halo of light around the surface edges and solid-looking in appearance but hazy. The silent objects were visible for five minutes, before breaking up and disappearing at the same time. It was a warm day, with a moderate wind.

(**Source:** Mr R.M Skinner/*UFOLOG*)

Horsenden Hill

12th May 1970 – Mexican hat-shaped UFO over ancient site

Historic Horsenden Hill, Perivale (from old English *'Fairy vale'*), Middlesex – a meeting place of several prehistoric ancient track- ways, whose route appears to have been marked with the discovery of ancient Sarson stones, some over 3,000 years of age, transported from Wales (as used in the construction of places like Avebury and Stonehenge) – was also the scene of a number of UFO sightings in the late 1960s. They included a mysterious incident, involving the appearance of a UFO and the attendance of two police officers, whose identity and reason for visit still remain shrouded in secrecy.

At 10.50pm, Mr Brian French – then living about a mile away from the hill, noticed a white 'light' moving slowly through the sky above a wooded area on top of the hill. Almost immediately he received a telephone call from friends, Rosina Bishop and Michael Howard, living on the opposite side of the hill, who told him they had seen:

> *"...an object, resembling a Mexican hat with curved ends and a rather high centre, containing an oval, showing a black mark in the middle, about 150-200 yards away."*

Brian went outside to have a look but, by this time, the 'light' had dropped down beyond the hill, out of view.

Rosina and Michael decided to investigate further and made their way, by car, to a vantage point lower down the hill, offering a clear view across open countryside over its north slopes, where they saw the mysterious light circling the hill, at fast speed.

They then drove to the *'Ballot Box'* – a public house, situated at the bottom of the hill, which was in darkness, (closed for the night), and parked up, hoping to see something.

> *"Suddenly, two white lights flashed from the slope, followed by the appearance of two huge red lights moving silently towards us – completely round in shape, with an impression of a dark object between the lights – but it was impossible to distinguish it clearly.*
>
> *As it glided towards us, we became frightened and drove down the road. After stopping a short way down, we looked but, because our view was now restricted, we didn't see it again."*

The couple then drove to Brian French's house, and telephoned Captain Mackay, (BUFORA's Chairman), who arrived at the house 30 minutes later.

After some conversation, the four of them returned to the Hill and had just parked the car in the car park, when a police 'Panda' car, with two officers, drove up and stopped.

In an extraordinary conversation, details of which were recorded by Captain Mackay, we learn of the following:

Brian asked them: *"What's going on up there?"*

Police Officer: *"You've not got the right code word – it's the Official Secrets Act."*

Captain Mackay: *"We were wondering whether –* (interrupted by Police Officer) *– H.G Wells had a word for it. They've done it this time. You will read about it all in the newspapers tomorrow!"*

Michael: *"It can't be that secret if it's all in the papers tomorrow."*

Police Officer: *"This is it. The world's really coming to an end."*

Rosina: *"We saw this strange 'thing' circling the Hill. What is it?"*

Police Officer: *"It's an official secret – can't tell you."*

The police Panda car then left the scene but returned shortly afterwards, accompanied by a 'Black Maria' (vehicle used in escorting prisoners). Both vehicles then made their way to the car park at the top of the hill, where a number of police officers alighted and dispersed around the locality, carrying torches. Now beginning to feel very uneasy, the parties concerned decided to leave the area and return home. Enquiries made the following day with various police stations, failed to obtain any information about the incident.

What did the officers mean by their comments? Why were they called out and who, or what, were they looking for?

25th May 1970 – Yellow 'disc' seen in the sky over Leicestershire

At 7.05pm, on a warm summer's evening, a yellow/orange coloured 'disc' was seen travelling towards the south, over Hinckley, Leicestershire, at an estimated height of 2,000 feet, climbing at an angle on a straight direct course, before being lost from sight over Hollycroft Park. (**Source: Geoffrey Coxon**)

28th May 1970

During the early hours Police Officers in Winooski, Vermont, USA, sighted bright 'discs of light' moving overhead.

29th May 1970 – Square UFO sighted over sea

An unidentified flying object was seen in the sky by coastguards from Berry Head, Brixham, at 2.15 pm, one of whom said:

> "We spotted something which looked like a bright star. Visibility was good and I thought it was about twenty miles away. I looked at it through strong binoculars and it was almost square, with what looked like a trail of wires out of the back. It was there for about three minutes and then it headed off towards the north-east."

This wasn't to be the only time the coastguards at this station were to sight a UFO. (See 28th April, 1967)
(**Source: Lionel Beer, BUFORA**)

At 10.15pm, a bright coloured 'saucer' was seen in the sky over Great Witley, Worcestershire, illuminating the ground and sky with red and orange lights as it passed overhead.

May 1970 – Motorist encounters green 'cigar'

We spoke to Colin Jacobs about what he saw, while delivering supplies of coal to power stations in the Staffordshire area.

> "I was driving along the old A50 road, at 2am, near to the abandoned airfield at Doveridge, when the sky was illuminated by a flash of green light, followed by the appearance of a green cigar-shaped object, which passed a hundred feet above the top of my Ford Transit. I slammed on the brakes, jumped out, and watched with disbelief, as it hovered in the night sky making a crackling noise.

> Out of this 'tube', or 'cigar', now vertically positioned, was ejected a green 'ball of light'. It raced off across the sky and dropped down into a field and disappeared. I don't know what it was I saw. I still think about it. I often used to drive along the same road, but never saw anything like that again. I found it very exhilarating."

Spring 1970 – Were RAF jets scrambled?

David Bryant – a retired Royal Navy helicopter pilot – was stood at a bus stop in Hanging Hill Lane, Hutton, Middlesex, just before dawn, in spring 1970, waiting for a bus to arrive.

> "It was still dark but with a hint of sunrise. Suddenly, three huge globes, scintillating with light, passed overhead at a height of about a thousand feet.

> I shouted out to a group of women waiting alongside me, pointing upwards into the sky. Much to my surprise, some of them became hysterical.

> A few minutes later, two RAF English Electric Lightning jets thundered across the sky, following the same path taken by the UFOs."

David Bryant and wife Linda

It is a matter that still causes him puzzlement, despite the passing of years. Were the aircraft scrambled to intercept the UFOs, or was it a coincidence they were in the locality?

David – who is also a retired teacher, wildlife photographer and rock guitarist – and his charming wife, Linda, who have met many of the US and Russian Astronauts through their 'Space Rocks' business, helped us organise a visit by retired Colonel Charles Halt (former Deputy Base Commander at RAF Bentwaters/Woodbridge) to Woodbridge, Suffolk, in July 2015. Colonel Halt is now a friend and wrote a book with John Hanson, entitled *The Halt Perspective*, published in 2016. David has published three books under *Heathland Books*, which range from ghosts, religious apparitions to evolution, planetary astronomy and the Apollo missions.

Did the Americans go to the Moon? Ask David Bryant!

Left to right: John Burroughs, Jim Penniston, David Bryant and Nick Pope at Rendlesham Forest, Suffolk.

Retired Colonel Charles I. Halt. Former Deputy Base Commander at RAF Bentwaters/Woodbridge, Suffolk.

Early 1970 – 'Flying Saucer' over Reading Atomic Power Station

Brian North – a retired printer, from Reading – wrote to us about something he witnessed with a colleague, during early 1970, while on the way home along the A4.

> "As we approached the Rising Sun *public house*, at 8pm – a regular journey made most days – we saw a semi curved object, with glowing lights, hovering over some trees next to the public house. I stopped the car and we watched, thinking it was a helicopter, until the lights went out, leaving a shadowy outline of where the object had been. This then disappeared.
>
> After getting back into the car, we carried on our journey but, within a few hundred yards, realised we could see what we presumed to be the same object – now hovering over the Atomic Weapons Research Establishment, at Aldermaston.
>
> On reaching the Southcote estate, on the outskirts of Reading, I stopped the car to enable John to get out. To our astonishment, we saw a number of residents standing outside, pointing upwards at a saucer-shaped object, similar to what we had seen over the public house. When I arrived home, a short time later, the UFO was now over houses close to the newly built Junction 11 of the M4 Motorway."

The next morning, while reading the newspaper, Brian discovered a number of people had contacted them after sighting a UFO over Woodcote, Reading.

Threatened by officials to keep quiet!

Brian also brought our attention to a rather chilling incident, involving a friend from work, whose cousin used to farm at Chaddleworth, on the Berkshire Downs.

One summer's evening (in the 1970s), while working the land on his tractor, he heard a roaring noise and saw a large disc-shaped object rising up from over the hill where he worked, before disappearing over the next rise.

The man drove over and discovered a circular mark on the ground and decided to report the matter to the police.

Shortly after this, it is alleged he was visited by 'officials' who interviewed him about what he had seen, but then suggested he may have been drinking, or dreamt it. Somewhat annoyed by the men's scepticism,

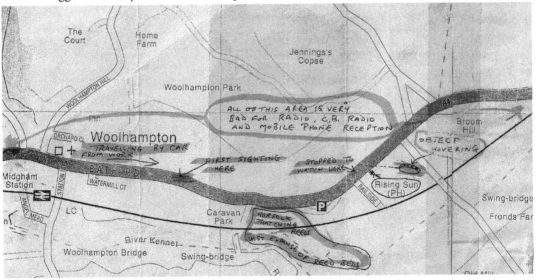

he took them to the scene of the incident and showed them the impressions in the field, at which their attitude changed completely; warning him of the dire consequences of discussing what had taken place with anybody else.

Unfortunately, according to Brian, his friend chose to 'air his views' at a UFO meeting held in the Newbury area, some months later, when he disclosed details of the incident concerned during a heated conversation with someone, who stood up in the audience.

About a week after this, Brian noticed the foreman at the printing press speaking to his friend, who then came over and told him:

"I've got to go home. My wife rang. She's extremely distressed."

The next day, Brian asked him what was going on. He replied:

"My wife received a visit from two smartly dressed men, whom she mistook to be Mormons or Jehovah witnesses. After asking for her husband she told them he was at work, to which one of them replied: 'We know that already. We would like you to relay a message to him that if he valued the wellbeing of his wife and three children, he should desist from his unhealthy interest in UFO meetings and keep his opinions to himself' ".

(Source: *'Cosmos'*, November 1970/Norman Oliver)

JUNE 1970

5th June 1970 – Mysterious 'light' in the sky

Just after midnight, the Emergency Services were inundated with calls from the public, after a bright 'light' (approximately four times the size of a full moon) was observed moving slowly through the skies, as far away as Eire and Northern Ireland.

Twenty people watched a mystery object in the sky above Clydach, Swansea, on the same date, described as looking like *'a round white ball, the size of a dinner plate'* – important enough to bring to the attention of the *Wales Today* TV programme, who told of other reports from Cwmbran and Aberystwyth.

(Source: *Wales Evening Post*, 5.6.1970)

8th June 1970 – UFOs over Yorkshire

A huge 'flash of light' lit up the sky over Clayton, Yorkshire, followed by the appearance of a perfectly circular pale green object, seen at 12.10am, before fading away.

12th June 1970 – Schoolchildren sight UFO over Buckinghamshire

At 8.55am, over thirty pupils at Denbigh School, Bletchley, Buckinghamshire, watched a sparkling orange object moving across the sky. Much to their surprise, the same, or similar, object was seen returning along its original path, at 10.05am.

16th June 1970 – Blinding light over Leicestershire

A letter sent to the *Leicester Mercury* (22.6.70), by Mr F.J. Brooks, tells of a blinding light seen by him and his daughter, at 11.15pm, resembling a 'ball of fire', travelling through the night sky – bright enough to light up the interior of their house. It was also seen moving across the sky over Leicester, Knighton, Oadby, and Sowerby Bridge, followed by a sighting at 12.15am [17th June 1970], over Carnforth on the Lancashire coast, by Mr Edward Hoggarth, who had this to say:

"Through binoculars, it seemed to be cigar-shaped with large spiky shapes protruding from its edge. By 12.30am, all that could be seen was a thin streak of white light moving slowly westwards."

On the same evening, several people in the Reading area reported having problems with television reception, following the appearance of a yellow 'light' seen in the sky, changing colour from yellow, red, to green.

18th June 1970 – Strange light over West Yorkshire

During the late evening, a Sowerby Bridge man – Mr Frank Hartley – sighted a bright stationary light in the sky, over Norland Moor.

"It then began to move to the right slowly, and accelerated upwards at an angle of about 90 degrees off the horizon. As it gained speed it became clearer to see its light now becoming more intense. It appeared to be followed by turbulence in the air; soon it was out of sight."

(Source: *The Illuminer/UFOLOG*, Issue no. 2, July 1970)

19th June 1970 – UFO hovers over Army base, Hampshire

In the early hours of the next morning, a GPO Engineer, at Farnham, sighted a white 'cone of light' flying across the sky in a north-west direction. This was followed by a sighting, at 12.20am, by two WRAC Communications Operators at Aldershot, in Hampshire, who called the police, after seeing a strange yellow 'light' hovering over the Army camp.**(Source: Omar Fowler, BUFORA)**

26th June 1970 – Black 'star' reported over Hertfordshire

A mysterious black 'star' was seen silently flying across the sky over Rickmansworth, Hertfordshire, at 11pm, by David Penney and his wife – then living at Sarratt.

"It looked, at first, like a bright star and then, as it got further away, it stopped and appeared to hang in the sky, going dimmer and higher, now resembling a black shape, wider when it was high. A few minutes later, while we were discussing it, another 'light' appeared."

(Source: *Watford Echo*, 28.6.1970)

27th June 1970 – Orange saucer-shaped UFO seen by motorist

At 1.30am, Mr Gordon McKinnon from Galston, Ayrshire, was in the front passenger seat of a car being driven home.

When two miles away from his destination, he noticed:

"...an orange sparkling 'light', behind trees on the left-hand side, close to a line of electric pylons – the cables stretching over the road ahead."

He presumed it was an electrical fault and the vehicle carried on.

"Then a bright orange saucer-shaped object dropped down from the sky, at an angle of 30 degrees, projecting a beam of light as it did so. It then shot upwards to about 500 feet, some mile and a half away, and began to move in a parallel line to us, before heading away over Galston."

(Source: Personal letter)

29th June 1970 – Glowing object paces family car at Apopka, Orlando

At 9.30pm, a married couple, along with their two sons, were returning home from Apopka, Orlando, by car. The wife sighted a glowing green oval object, with a smaller blue inner ring and convex base, about a thousand feet to their left, about a hundred feet off the ground. She alerted her husband, by which time it was descending at an angle towards their vehicle. The husband, who was driving at 45 miles per hour, increased his speed to 90 miles per hour. The object paced their car for about a mile, but was temporarily lost from view. They reached their home and turned into the driveway leading to the house, when they saw 'it' moving slightly ahead over orange groves. The family dashed from the car; as they did so, the object made a low level sweep of the area and left a trail of 'mist' about 20 feet wide, giving off a pale green light. The curious 'mist' spread out evenly, but did not fall to the ground. The path of the 'mist' left by the UFO was thick on the outside of the turn and thin on the inside. It was thick enough to block out the stars, to begin with.

The family dog, which had been in the car, seemed aright. However, a second dog belonging to the wife's mother ran away howling –just before family and UFO arrived at the house. Apparently the family were not the only ones to sight UFOs around the Apopka area; several other objects hade been reported during the last year, but nothing matching this. (**Source:** *APRO Bulletin/UFOLOG*)

June 1970 – Three lights forming a triangle seen by police

Metropolitan Police Officer – Humphrey Bishop – was driving a Rover 3.5 police car along Lyndhurst Road, Hampstead Heath, accompanied by a PC observer.

"I noticed what I took to be a safety light left on at the end of the jib of a crane.

As we turned into Fitzjohn's Avenue, along Netherhall Gardens, we saw three lights, forming a triangle, low down in the sky.

I stopped the car and watched the lights as they began to move away diagonally from our position. The front one then vanished, followed by the second and third – almost as if they had gone behind something, rather than disappearing in front of one's eyes." (Personal interview)

June 1970 – Passenger train paced by a UFO

John Allen was a regular rail passenger, commuting between Portsmouth and Southampton, in the summer of 1970, and had just left Cosham Railway Station, at 6.30pm, with the train gathering speed, when:

"I saw this very peculiar object travelling parallel to the railway carriage, approximately one hundred and fifty feet away. It was completely cylindrical, with a grey/brown coloured surface – like burnt metal. As the train reached a junction, it changed its course but the object continued on its original course. All of a sudden, it shot upwards into the sky, at fantastic speed, and was gone. I would like to think that what I saw was no Alien machine but rather something representative of a Top Secret technology."

(**Source: Personal interview/Letter sent to Gordon Creighton,** *FSR*)

FIG.1
←——— 20ft. approx. ———→

160ft. approx.

60ft. approx.

Portsmouth   Cosham

FIG.2

Fig. 1   Appearance of the object.
Fig. 2   Position of object relative to the train.

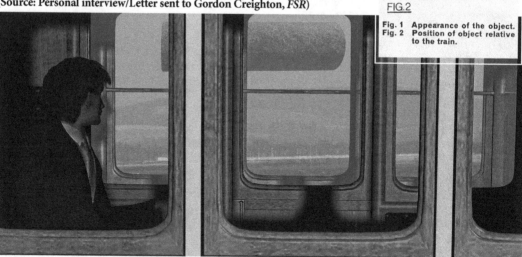

Summer 1970 – Close encounter, followed by medical ailments

Keith Pines was parked off the road, with his girlfriend, one late evening, adjacent to the Royal Ordnance Factory at Burghfield (5 miles south of Aldermaston), near Reading – (a locality that was to attract a number of UFO sightings, over the years).

> *"We both heard a humming noise coming from above the car – then the interior light began to dim. I wound down the window and peered upwards into the sky, shocked to see a huge grey coloured 'saucer' hovering above us, showing a number of white lights around its circumference. Nearby trees started to sway, as if in a strong wind, and then within seconds it had gone, leaving us terrified. A few months after the incident, my doctor diagnosed me with Shingles. He said it was very unusual for a person of my age to contract the disorder. I also had a problem with my thyroid gland, which caused swelling of my eyes – a condition that persisted for many years."*

(Source: Personal interview)

Close encounter – Summer 1970 – Strange 'beings' seen in house

Leslie Harris – the Bournemouth-based UFO Researcher and Editor of an excellent UFO magazine, entitled *'SCAN'*, produced during the 1970s – still ponders as to the true implications of an incident brought to his attention, involving the sighting of a number of small 'beings', by schoolgirl – Merita, in the bedroom of her house at Petersfield, Hampshire, in 1970, when ghostly footsteps, shadowy forms, and a young boy, dressed in a white garment, was occasionally seen and heard around the house.

Merita told Leslie she had always been afraid of the dark and, on the night of the experience, awoke in the early hours needing to go to the bathroom.

> *"Getting out of bed, I reached with my left arm to turn the light switch on and was conscious of a sudden fear – as if something, or someone, was watching me – a feeling that became worse when I realised my arm was paralysed in a vertical position.*
>
> *Glancing through the door, I was petrified to see a group of five or six small 'beings' in the open doorway of my eldest sister's bedroom, each about two feet tall, surrounded by a bright green aura down to their upper legs."*

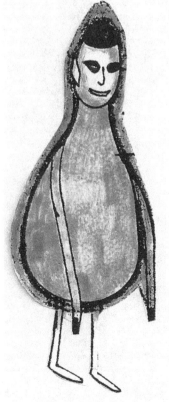

Long head and pointed ears

> *"They had long heads, oval or pear-shaped, with pointed ears close to the sides of their heads. Their eyes were black, teardrop-shaped, reminding me of the early Egyptians, with no visible detail such as pupils. They had short, turned-up noses, normal mouths without teeth. Their bodies were short and fat, with arms and legs long in proportion to the body, long fingers and straight feet, which shuffled forward in a bouncy movement. They were clad in tight-fitting garments."*

Became aware they were being watched!

> *"At some stage they realised I was watching them and began to laugh and point at me, behaving like naughty children.*
>
> *After ten minutes, I could stand it no longer and cried out. My father entered the room. As he flicked the light switch down, they just vanished and I was able to drop my arm down. When I told my parents what had happened, the next morning, my*

father seemed quite interested but my mother was very sceptical, so at nine years of age I tried to forget about it."

It would be so easy, in the cold light of day, to dismiss the experience as being the fanciful imagination of a nine year-old child, or the product of some terrifying dream, rather than accept the possibility that these things, 'funny as they look', actually exist, but Merita (who was judged as being a sensible, honest girl, by Leslie) found the experiences very frightening.

JULY 1970

1st July 1970 – Triangular UFO over Illinois

An Illinois resident – Mr Ralph Kramer, accompanied by his five children (9-15 years of age) – was driving east on Highway 24, near Reas Bridge, north-east of Decatur, when the family saw 15-30 red and green lights moving over nearby treetops in a geometric formation.

"Suddenly the lights stopped and were replaced by three brilliant white searchlights, which came on for a couple of minutes, lighting up a nearby house owned by a Mr G. Davis on the south side of Reas Bridge. When the searchlights ceased, the object moved towards the east, then south. By this time a few minutes had elapsed."

Mr Kramer said the red and green lights spanned a distance of about 20 feet; the white lights 12 feet.

"They were acorn-shaped and in a double layer, alternating red and green lights forming a definite pattern. They appeared to be mounted on a frame rather than a solid body. The lights were suspended like an acorn, with the tip down glowing and translucent.

The three bright searchlights were mounted at the level of the lower row of coloured lights."

Karen (10) told her father the lights reminded her of a Christmas tree.

(Source: Mrs Norma E. Short, *Skylook*)

2nd July 1970 – 'Flying cigar' over Gloucestershire

At 9.58pm, Rita Seeley – a housewife from Cirencester, Gloucestershire – was in her garden, when she saw what looked like a brilliant star emerging out of a dense cloud, travelling south-west to north-east, across the sky.

"As it drew nearer I could see it was cigar-shaped and about two feet long, as viewed from my position. The front half of the object was extremely bright in relation to the remainder – a dull red colour and apparently solid in construction.

Within ten seconds, it had crossed the blue sky and disappeared into cloud."

(Source: Personal interview)

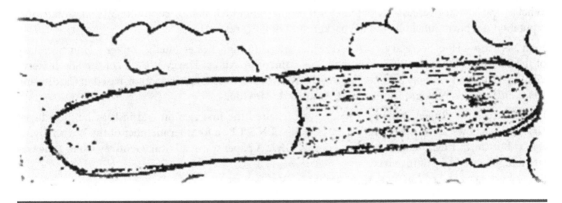

3rd July 1970 – UFO formations over Kent

John Male from Folkestone, Kent, was sat talking to friends in the late evening, when four bright silver objects appeared in the sky, heading towards the south-west, at high speed. A few minutes later another four objects appeared, which then changed into a **T** or **X** shaped formation – now pale orange in colour – before speeding up and glowing silver once again.

The Folkestone Police and MOD also received reports from others living in the Kent area that evening, who described seeing:

> "...*four red and orange globes, flying in formation over the County*".

Another witness was Nicholas Ashman from Cheriton Road, who was looking out to sea from Lower Sandgate Road, when he saw:

> "...*four bright orange objects, flying in a 'cross' or 'diamond' formation, just below cloud cover, at 2,000 feet. They were travelling at high speed, keeping in tight formation as they passed the land. A few minutes later they returned – this time heading up the Channel. There was no noise. It was an eerie experience.*"

Writing to the MOD

We discovered that a Miss J.A. Proctor of 7, Bronte Grove, Newport, Monmouthshire, had written to the MOD on the 21st July 1970, seeking any information on the sighting that had taken place over Kent on that evening, following disclosure of her letter, many years later, but never received a reply.

(**Source:** *Folkestone & Hythe Gazette*, 8.7.1970 – 'Flying oranges'/
London Evening News, 4.7.1970 – 'Channel riddle of lights in the sky'/
Fred O. Gardner/*FSR Case Histories*, Supplement One, October 1970 –
'UFOs over the Strait of Dover', Charles Bowen and Dr. Bernard E. Finch/
UFOLOG, July 1970, Issue 72)

CHANNEL RIDDLE OF LIGHTS IN THE SKY

A MYSTERY in the sky over Kent during the night was today puzzling police, coastguards and Ministry of Defence experts.

Sightings of four glowing objects moving at a fast speed about 1,500 ft. over the English Channel towards the south-west were reported shortly after midnight.

The UFOs were reported to be flying in a cross formation, which later changed to a diamond shape.

Clearest view of the objects was obtained by people on the Lower Sandgate Road at Folkestone, who normally have an unhindered view across the Channel to the French coast.

NO SOUND

Mr. John Male, of St. Martin's Road, New Romney, said the glowing objects changed colour and swept across the sky in front of him at great speed. There was no sound.

Kent police have asked RAF Manston, near Ramsgate, to investigate the sightings, but so far they had not been able to help.

18th July 1970 – UFO Lecture, Kensington Library, London

Kensington Central Library was the venue of 'Practical UFO research'. The proceedings were opened by Lionel Beer – Managing Director of *Space-link*. He then introduced the audience to the voluntary staff and consultants of *Space-link*. They included people we had heard so much about, over the years. What a pity that fate decrees we would never meet them, but their names, commitment and professional reputation, are burnt indelibly into the background of UFO research...

Joan Nelstrop – Hon. Secretary of DIGAP, which meets in Manchester, **Sheila Walker** – Hon. Secretary of the Scottish UFO Research Society, based in Edinburgh, **Albert Davey** F.R.A.S., of the South Herts. UFO Investigation Group, Four members of the Welsh UFO Research Association, based in Cardiff, and *Space-link*'s correspondent from Brussels, **Andrew de Muylder**.

Lionel introduced **Roger Stanway**, F.R.A.S., who chaired the first session and in turn he introduced **Graham F. Knewstub**, C.ENG, M.I.E.R.E., F.B.I.S., A.I.N.S.T.E., a founder member of the British Flying Saucer Bureau, in 1952, and first President of BUFORA. A paper was read from **Geoffrey Doel,** as he was attending the wedding of his niece.

(**Source: Volume 6, No. 4,** *Space-link,* **April 1971**)

SPACELINK STAFF, CONSULTANTS AND GUESTS AFTER ATTENDING THE SYMPOSIUM IN KENSINGTON ON 18th JULY 1970

Edgar Hatvany		Eliane with	David Thompson		Pam Kennedy	Janet Gregory
	Gerry Brown	Andrew de Muylder	Roger Stanway	Joan Nelstrop		Anthony Pace
	Graham Knewstub	Christine Henning		Dagmar Sarkar		
	Norman Hardy	Rev.Norman Cockburn			Charles Elrick	(Photo: Lionel Beer)

28th July 1970 – Bright yellow 'light' over Bedfordshire

At 10.15pm, a bright yellow 'light' – smaller than a rugby ball – was seen in the sky over the Woburn Animal Kingdom, Bedfordshire, by Mr Barry Snoxhall, who was riding home to Bletchley on his moped.

(**Source:** *The Illuminer*)

29th July 1970 – Shield-shaped object over Devon

At 11.30pm, a shield-shaped object was sighted over Exeter, Devon, by two people stood on Dunsford Hill. The object appeared slightly transparent, and stars could be seen through it.

(**Source:** *UFOLOG*)

```
Ref.          55/65
Date          29th July 1970.
Time          2330hrs.
Location      Exeter, Devon.
```

From Dunsford Hill, Exeter, two observers saw a swiftly moving and luminous, bat, or shield-shaped object travelling south-west through the sky, at about 23.30hrs.

Its dimensions and altitude were impossible to even guess at. The object appeared throughout as slightly transparent. A number of stars were visible through its large form.

The Illuminer.

30th July 1970 – UFO over Middlesex

A woman from Hillingdon, Middlesex, was about to get into bed at 1.05am, when she glanced through the window and saw a bright twinkling object in the sky.

> *"I knelt on the floor, to get a better view, and fixed its position between the tops of two trees. After a while, I noticed it had moved – now parallel with a lower clump of trees. It then moved away from its north-east position, towards the east, bobbing up and down in the sky – then straight on for a short distance, before bobbing up and down again. It then 'zoomed' back to where I had first seen it. On the top of the object was a very intense white light, which occasionally gave off a flash of red sparks from underneath. When it did the 'zooming' action, I saw puffs of white vapour ejected from underneath, with what appeared to be tremendous force. As it continued on its course in the peculiar bobbing up and down motion, it was now directly overhead, at which stage I saw another twinkling light appear at the precise spot where I had seen the first, although this one displayed no white light and was pink all over. I became aware it was now getting light at 4.20am and decided to get some sleep, but still awake at 5am, I looked through the window. There was nothing to be seen."*

(Source: Dan Goring, Essex UFO Group)

AUGUST 1970

1st August 1970 – UFOs over Kent

At 7.30pm, Mr Keith Mason and his mother-in-law – Mrs Jean Lucas, were walking across Crockham Hill Common, Westerham, Kent, when they saw, *'two yellow glowing objects, followed by a third, roughly triangular in shape'*, heading towards Croydon, at a height of approximately 2,000 feet. Within thirty seconds, the formation was out of sight. **(Source: John E. Ben)**

10th August 1970 – Unusual object over the sea, Isle of Wight

At 9.30pm, a housewife was walking her two dogs above the cliffs at High Down, near Freshwater, Isle of Wight, when she noticed what looked like a hovercraft travelling a few hundred feet above the sea, at the speed of a helicopter, half a mile away,

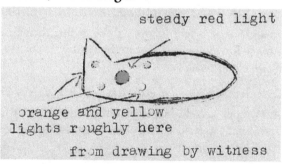

> *"...showing a red light near the back with several orange and yellow flashing lights around it, resembling a rather squat, small, airship without any wings. Had it been at sea level, I would have taken it for a hovercraft. Daylight was fading; the moon, in its first quarter, cast a path of light across the sea, enabling me to keep observation on the object as it continued along its path, towards Portland Bill, where I lost sight of it."*

(Source: letter to Isle of Wight UFO Society)

12th August 1970 – Deep black UFO over Essex

Company Director – William Huntingdon (56), of Coronation Road, Balby, Doncaster, was driving at 60 miles per hour down the A12 towards London, at 10.40pm.

> *"We reached Chelmsford when my oldest son (28), remarked 'what's that up there?'*
>
> *We looked and saw a deep black oval object, showing four brilliant*

lights in the sky. It passed in front of us, going from right to left and flying at about 100 miles per hour, before vanishing in the distance." (**Source: Ron West**)

12th August 1970 – Motorist encounters red glowing object

Richard Jones and his girlfriend – Pauline Routledge – from Rainham, Essex, were driving home just before 11pm, when they heard a heavy electrical noise, or buzzing, above their car. Thinking they were about to break down, they stopped and got out, when they were staggered to see:

> *"...a glowing red object, approximately 20 feet long by 10 feet wide, showing four white lights along its side, hovering a few feet above the ground in front of them".*

Seconds later, it took off towards the direction of Hornchurch and was soon out of sight. The couple reported the incident to the Police and MOD, who admitted they were baffled.

(**Source:** *Brentwood Argus,* **20.8.1970/NUFORO Bulletin**)

14th August 1970 – Cylindrical object falls into a Lancashire river

What lay behind a report made of a cylindrical object, with a flashing light attached to it, seen to drop into the *River Mersey,* at Barrington, Lancashire? Unfortunately we have no further details about this incident, or who made the complaint. (**Source:** *UFOLOG*)

Also in the same month a silver, metallic object, with a *'helmet dome'* on top, was seen moving silently through the sky over the direction of White Lee, Batley, Yorkshire, in August 1970, by Tony Woodhead – an employee, working shifts at a local carpet factory.

19th August 1970 – Oval UFO over Leicestershire

A dark, perfectly oval, object was seen crossing the sky over Hinckley, at about 3pm, by local youths – Ian Truslove and Michael Ford. (**Source:** *UFOLOG/Hinckley Times,* **21.8.1970**)

21st August 1970 – Police Officers sight UFO over London

Andrew Mark Grant (21) was then a Police Officer living in single men's accommodation at Gilmour House, Renfrew Road, London. At 9.45pm, he was crossing the road between the Police Station and his quarters when he saw a green luminous object in the sky.

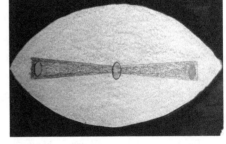

> *"It was showing two red lights at each end, with a blue light in the middle. I could see a silver-grey line in the middle connecting the lights. I called out the Desk Sergeant to come and have a look. We stood there watching it for a few minutes, before it suddenly and silently shot off over the station roof."* (**Source: Ron West**)

22nd August 1970 – Object over Heathrow Airport, London

At 8.20pm a woman writer and journalist, was travelling as a passenger in a car being driven along the M4 Motorway, towards London. The other passenger in the car drew her attention to a large dark circular object (approximately the size of the moon) she could see over or near Heathrow Airport. In a letter to Gordon Creighton, of *Flying Saucer Review,* she said:

> *"It was still light; the sky was clear, except for a few patches of sparse, almost imperceptible cloud. It seemed to sprout a number of plumes of darkish grey mist from the upper side and then halted for about a minute, before sinking again and vanishing from sight." Unfortunately, the witness asked Gordon not to release her name.* (**Source:** *FSR,* **Supp. 5, June 1971**)

26th August 1970 – Orange 'light' over Bedfordshire

Mrs Anne Bollins of Luton, Bedfordshire, was staying with friends. She was awoken at 11.35pm by a bright orange coloured 'light' shining on her face. She looked out of the window facing north and saw:

> *"...a disc-shaped object (about the size of a dinner plate) hurtling towards me, at tremendous speed. I tried to get a look at it, but the 'light' was so bright that it seemed to burn my eyes, so I had to hold my fingers across my face. Suddenly it stopped in mid-air, its light flooding into the bedroom. I jumped out of bed and watched it from behind the dressing table.*
>
> *A few minutes later it shot back from the route it had taken and was gone."* (**Source:** *UFOLOG*)

28th August 1970 – Cigar-shaped UFO over Leicestershire

At 4.18pm, a man was stood outside a local garage in London Road, Hinckley, Leicestershire, with a friend, when they saw:

> *"...a black solid looking cigar-shaped object, just below clouds. As it approached closer we could see it was no aircraft, as first thought. When directly overhead it made a right turn and headed away in the south-west direction, two minutes later. When it turned, two lines of smoke were emitted from the back, of which one of the lines appeared longer than the other."*

The witness believes that the powerful longer line enabled the object to make a right angle turn.

(**Source:** *UFOLOG*, **Issue Number 76**)

31st August 1970 – Red and white lights over Illinois, USA

Robert Paterson of Lynwood Drive, Champaign, Illinois – who was then an assistant Professor of Psychology at the University of Illinois – was out cycling with his wife and child.

> *"We were stopped at the corner of Mattis and Kirby Avenue, facing south, after walking the bikes over the Intersection. We happened to look to out left and see a very bright white 'light', the brightest in the sky. It split into two lights – a red one and white. The red one floated slowly downwards, until it disappeared. The white 'light' continued to stay in the sky; it dimmed after the white one split away from it. The white 'light' then began moving away towards the south-west; two to three minutes later it was out of sight."*

Summer 1970 – UFOs over Birmingham

UFO researcher and author, Michael Freebury – who is actively involved with investigating reports of animal mutilations – told us of some strange events he experienced, during August to November 1970, beginning with an incident that occurred in the summer of 1970.

> *"Myself, and two friends – Ron, Buck and Fred Snelson – were walking back from Walsall to Pheasey estate, Great Barr, at 11pm.*
>
> *As we turned into Barr Lakes Lane, we noticed a bright star-like object slowly moving above us. After a minute or so, the object began moving again and disappeared into a large bank of cloud, but reappeared within seconds. It then accelerated away out of sight."*

The following week, the three men retraced their journey and were approaching Barr Lakes Lane from Skip Lane, when they saw a bright star-like object, no more than tree height, in the sky. To their astonishment, the object dimmed – then brightened, before 'hedge hopping' away from them. During a third visit to the locality, a week later, they began 'sky watching' at a place called Doe Bank Lane playing fields, allowing an unrestricted view across open countryside, towards Birmingham.

> *"We were astonished when a metallic sphere floated down from the sky and hovered about 100 feet above us, as if it was watching us. On another occasion, Ron came around to my house, at 7pm and*

we set off for another couple of hours 'sky watching'. As we began our journey, we noticed a bright star-like object heading for Barr Beacon. We ran virtually all the way to Doe Bank playing fields, half a mile from my house, stopping only a couple of times to monitor its flight direction as it changed colour from diamond blue to dull silver. After arriving at Doe Bank, we had a fantastic view of the object, estimated to be fifty feet in diameter and only six or seven hundred yards from the school. It then began to rotate, changing colour several times, from diamond blue to bright red, to orange/brown – it was awesome."

Michael Freebury

"After about ninety seconds of this spectacular show, we lost sight of it as it moved off behind the school in the direction of Crook Lane and Barr Lakes Lane. Shortly after this sighting, I was walking along Gretton Road, Aldridge, at 7.30pm, when a jet aircraft flew overhead, quite low. I looked up and saw what I thought was the moon, except it was bathed in an eerie suffused light. Stunned, I realised the light was, in fact, two lights illuminating an object hovering a few feet above the roof of the house opposite! The thing began to move. I was completely terrified – so frightened I couldn't shout for help. I was paralysed with fear. The UFO, resembling an 'Adamski' craft, made no sound as it moved to the middle of the road junction, hovering about fifty feet in the air. After about two minutes, or so, the craft appeared to wobble slightly. It then tilted into a position where it was now on end and shot straight up into the sky, before disappearing."

August 1970 – Dr. Joseph Allen Hynek visits the UK

Lionel Beer (left) with Dr. J. Allen Hynek

FLYING SAUCER REVIEW
A FLYING SAUCER SERVICE LIMITED PUBLICATION

Editorial
21 Cecil Court,
Charing Cross Road,
London, W.C.2. England
Subscriptions:
49a Kings Grove,
London, S.E.15.
Telephone:
NEW Cross 0784

6 August 1970

Dear Mr Llewellyn

We would very much like you to join us
in talking to Dr. J. Allen Hynek on
August 28th (see enclosed note).

Will you please let me know as soon as
possible if you can manage to come.

Yours sincerely,

R.H.B. Winder
Director

Please reply to:

R.H.B. Winder,
'Cobbins',
Halfacre Hill,
Chalfont St. Peter,
Buckinghamshire.

FLYING SAUCER REVIEW   *JD Llewellyn*

A FLYING SAUCER SERVICE LIMITED PUBLICATION

Editorial
21 Cecil Court,
Charing Cross Road,
London, W.C.2. England
Subscriptions:
49a Kings Grove,
London, S.E.15.
Telephone:
NEW Cross 0784

Colloquium Correspondence:

R.H.B. Winder
'Cobbins',
Halfacre Hill,
Chalfont St. Peter,
Buckinghamshire.

J. ALLEN HYNEK PRIVATE COLLOQUIUM

28TH AUGUST, 1970

LECTURE THEATRE, KENSINGTON CENTRAL LIBRARY

6 - 10 p.m.

Since the recent termination of his 20 year consultancy
with the Department of the U.S. Air Force responsible for
the investigation of UFO's, Dr. Hynek has continued his
interest in the subject. He will be visiting here in
August and wishes to ascertain our opinions on certain aspects
of the UFO problem, particularly the questions of alternatives
to the postulated extraterrestrial origin of UFO's. We, of
course, would also like to hear his views on many matters.

In order to make the best possible use of this 'short
duration sighting', he has asked us to arrange a discussion
in which you and he can shoot questions and answers back and
forth with the least possible formality.

Directors: C. A. Bowen (Editor)   G. W. Creighton   D. D. Dempster   C. H. Gibbs-Smith   R. H. B. Winder

JD Llewellyn

- 2 -

The Lecture Theatre in the basement of the Kensington Central
Library, just North of Kensington High Street is ideal for
this sort of occasion and the evening of August 28th is the
most convenient time. We do hope that you will be able to
attend.

If you intend, as we hope, to participate in the discussions,
it would help the Chairman if you could, in due course, send
me a piece of paper bearing your name and a brief indication
of the nature of your contribution so that he can call upon
you at the most appropriate stage in the proceedings. This
arrangement does not, of course, preclude spontaneous
contributions on the day, and we hope that our "distinguished
laymen" guests will not hesitate to join in. The only
restriction that we would urge would be the avoidance of time
wastage on matters which are familiar to us all or which could
just as well be discussed without Dr. Hynek. If you
anticipate further private communication with Dr. Hynek you
should add your full address to that piece of paper.

Please let me know as soon as possible if you can attend and
make sure that I have addresses and telephone numbers through
which I can reach you between now and August 28th, even if you
are on holiday.

Although accommodation is limited, you may wish to recommend an
invitation to someone you feel may be unknown to us but could
make a meaningful contribution. If so, will you please write to
me without delay, because it will not be possible to admit anyone
on the day who has not been invited.

There will be light refreshments, by courtesy of the Flying Saucer
Review, during an interval.

Dr. Hynek has particularly asked that there should be no
publication revealing either the existence or the content of these
proceedings. We have, therefore, to insist that your acceptance
of our invitation also means that you will not publish any
reference to this meeting in any form. If, at a later stage, you
persuade Dr. Hynek to agree specifically to some disclosure then the
Flying Saucer Review would not, of course, raise any objection.

Lionel Beer, of *Space-link Books*, was kind enough to supply us with many period photographs of UFO researchers and personalities from the middle to late 20th Century, including his own personal recollections, spiced with an occasional anecdote of the forming of BUFORA – history in the making!

In August of 1970, Dr. Joseph Allen Hynek – the Director of the new Lindheimer Astronomical Research Centre, at Northwestern University, Illinois, travelled to Brighton, England. This was his third time of visiting the UK. Previously, he had been here during 1955 and 1963, to visit the MOD to look at their UFO files, being funded by the American Government. It is said that he did not have any constructive discussions with the MOD, but was casually given a file on the Father Gill (New Guinea) sighting, as the Ministry staff did not know what to make of it.

It is of particular interest to note the contents of a letter sent to John 'Dennis' Llewellyn, by the Editor of *FSR* – Mr R.H.B. Winder, who brings his attention to the fact that Mr Hynek had asked, quote:

> *"... that there should be no publication revealing either the existence, or the content of these proceedings."*

He was to take part in an International Astronomical Congress, held at where a number of talks were given, including one by Dr. Hewish – Director of the Mullard Radio Astronomy Laboratory, at Cambridge – who told the audience:

> *"If unusual radio signals were received from outer space, astronomers would keep quiet about it until it had all been sorted out."*

Other topics of interest were pulsars, which attracted comment by Dr. Hynek, who confirmed that some lasted millions of years and could well be used as navigation beacons by space travellers.

He also spoke of nocturnal lights and strange meteors. Of practical research he said:

> *"I've gone to so many damn meetings, which turn out to be nothing but 'coffee clutches'; we just sit and talk about it and nobody does anything."*

At the end of August 'Flying Saucer Service' laid on a meeting at Kensington Central Library, so that UFO researchers could exchange views informally with Dr. Hynek.

Lionel:

> *"Unfortunately, he was inhibited from letting his 'hair down' by the large audience, and some of the quasi-scientific contributions from the floor. I can't help wondering if the Doctor would have regarded this as just another 'coffee clutch'."*

(Source: Lionel Beer, *Space-link*, Volume 6, Number 4, April 1971 – 'Dr Hynek, in London')

SEPTEMBER 1970

2nd September 1970 – Police Officers sight UFO over Essex

Police Constable Keith Marston (19) of Benfleet, Essex, was out on mobile patrol in his 'panda' car, when he received a radio call to go to Southend, where a strange light had been seen.

> *"We were only seconds away, so responded. When we arrived, we found about a dozen people staring into the night sky. On looking up we saw a very large orange glow, as if something was on fire. Within this glow could be seen a silver-grey object. This was stationary over the estuary. Five minutes later, it moved away towards the Kent coast."* **(Source: Ron West)**

Mr G Hall also sighted something strange on that date.

```
DATE     September 2nd 1970.
TIME     2340hrs.
LOCATION Near Atherstone, Warwickshire.
```

<u>STATEMENT BY MR. GRAHAM HALL OF HIS
SECOND UFO SIGHTING.</u>

" The time was about 11.40pm Wednesday night while I was driving along the Atherstone Bypass on the Leicestershire - Warwickshire border when I noticed straight in front of me a bright silvery coloured light with a dimmer one next to it, very low in the sky.

It was travelling slowly at first then increased speed. As this happened the dimmer light shot away from the bright one and disappeared. The bright light then increased in size and stopped dead to the right of me. It hovered like this for about 4 seconds after which time it stated to decend untill I lost sight of it behind some trees.

I slowed down the speed of my car to about 30mph to see if I could catch sight of it again when suddenly it rose vertically upwards in the sky, this time much bigger and more of an orange colour. It travelled at tremendous speed then disappeared as if a light had been smithed off."

(signed)   G. Hall

15.9.70.

5th September 1970 – Mysterious light seen over grain bins, Illinois, USA

Allen Robinson (20) and his friend Steve (20) of Bushnell, Illinois, sighted a blinding white light the size of a car – hovering 300 feet in the sky over the McDonough FS grain bins, in the south-west of the town, at 9pm. When about two blocks away, the light appeared to dim for a few seconds and then turned bright again, before heading away west, at speed, and out of sight, half a minute later.

7th September 1970 – Cigar-shaped UFO over Southampton

At 11pm, Boscombe businesswoman – Mrs Gilbert, and her son, Barry – were on holiday in Burley, Hampshire, when they were approached by Barry's friend, Terry, who told them he could see a strange 'star' descending rapidly in the sky, towards the direction of Southampton.

Barry:

> *"It moved over a wood at Mill Lawn, heading southwards, then halted in mid-air and approached our position, enabling us to see a cigar-shaped object with a pulsating red light on its front, moving towards Highcliffe."*

(Source: Leslie Harris, SCAN/*Southampton Echo*, 7.9.1970 – 'Cigar with flashing nose'/*Bournemouth Evening Echo*, 14.9.70/*Christchurch Herald*, 18.9.70/Personal interview)

8th September 1970 – UFO display over Wisconsin, USA

At about 8.45pm, Martin Verhoven – a teaching assistant in history at the University of Wisconsin – and his wife, Christine, were motoring north on Highway 14 (also called Park Street) and approaching Highways 12 and 18 (The Beltline), when they noticed a coloured light, high in the sky to the west of them. The object was moving erratically, up and down, sideways, and occasionally stopping in flight.

> *"It moved both fast and slow at the same time – when it moved, it changed colour from orange to red; when halted, it was silver-white in colour. We watched it for 15 minutes, as it headed in the general direction of Lake Monona."* **(Source: UFOLOG)**

12th September 1970 – Red 'lights' seen over Cannock Chase, Staffordshire

At 10pm, several red 'lights' were sighted moving across the sky over Cannock Chase, by a party of girl guides out camping – probably the same UFOs seen over the Staffordshire town of Weston, Staffordshire, at 11.30pm, heading silently eastwards. **(Source: John 'Dennis' Llewellyn)**

15th September 1970 – Flashing 'lights' over London

At 8.30pm, schoolgirl – Brenda Spicer, reported having sighted a semi-circle of flashing lights, descending over Churchill Gardens, London. According to the Isle of Wight UFO Society, there were three witnesses to this incident. **(Source: NICAP/*UFOLOG*)**

20th September 1970 – Four orange 'lights' sighted over Staffordshire

At 8.30pm, four orange 'lights' were sighted flying through the sky over Great Haywood, Stafford, by Mr L. Bates, who was out walking along the A51.

> *"They were visible for about five seconds and were travelling at a terrific speed, heading in a north to south direction and forming a huge 'diamond', before disappearing behind cloud."*

(Source: *The Illuminer*/South West Aerial Phenomena Investigation Group [SWAPIG])

September 1970 – Mr Arthur Shuttlewood

Mr Arthur Shuttlewood gave a talk on 'Flying Saucers' at Bridport, Dorset, to an audience of a hundred people. He said:

> *"I am convinced that these objects in the sky are closely linked with man's destiny and I compare them with biblical descriptions of miraculous sights in the heavens".*

His third book had just been published – *(UFOs – Key to the New Age*, Regency Press)

Paul Devereux

At 8.45pm on the same date, Paul Devereux – then living at Pages Hill, London N.10 – was at home with his wife, Jay, and a friend – David Potts, when Jay had a premonition to look out of the window. As a result of her call to the two men, Paul and David rushed over to separate windows and looked out.

Paul:

> *"I saw a 'light' approaching our position, about a mile away, over the North Circular Road. I felt compelled to somehow attract its attention and remembered I had an Aldis slide projector, borrowed from the school where I was teaching at the time.*

I switched it on and directed a beam of light, projected from the 750 watt bulb, at the object – with no response. I flashed my hand rapidly across the beam. David told me the 'light' had turned red and he could see two small red lights – one on either side of the larger object – one of which was flashing, although I didn't see this owing to the glare given-off by the lamp."

Paul, well-known for his views and books on the 'Earthlight' phenomena, told us:

"There are two kinds of actual UFOs (i.e. something truly seen in the sky and not hallucination, hoax, mirage, or misperception), which between them account for most UFO reports, Earthlights type phenomena and really bizarre and truly unexplained events.

I once saw, as a child in the 1950s, a huge airship hovering over a hilltop, in broad daylight. This was no mental aberration, as I had another witness with me. As far as I am concerned, the two real enemies to interpreting the UFO Phenomenon, in my opinion, are:

(1) Assuming there is one single answer. (2) The ET Hypothesis. The latter has stopped almost all serious debate and 'intellectual' investigation." (**Source: Personal interview**)

September 1970 – Landed UFO, Norfolk

In the same month, Mrs Frances Mason of Meadow Way, Attleborough, Norfolk, was out picking black-berries, at 4.30pm, a couple of hundred yards off the main Attleborough to Norwich Road, (close to MOD property).

"I saw what I thought was a metallic blue car resting on the ground, with a transparent top half, but then realised it was unlike any car I had even seen before. I thought to myself how disappointed my husband would be not to have seen it, as he suffers from Multiple Sclerosis and was sat in his wheelchair near the car, some distance away. Suddenly, it just disappeared in front of my eyes.

I walked back to the car and told my husband and then went back to the scene and made a search of the undergrowth, but found nothing disturbed or marks on the ground."

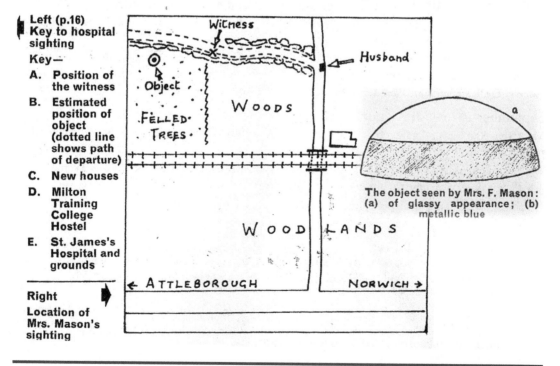

Left (p.16) Key to hospital sighting

Key—

A. Position of the witness

B. Estimated position of object (dotted line shows path of departure)

C. New houses

D. Milton Training College Hostel

E. St. James's Hospital and grounds

Right

Location of Mrs. Mason's sighting

The object seen by Mrs. F. Mason: (a) of glassy appearance; (b) metallic blue

Rather poignantly, she later told UFO Investigator Dennis Tye – from the local UFO Group, at Norfolk – that she *'hoped to live to see the day when someone finds out what this object is'*. Sadly, this was not to be.

September 1970 – 'Silver Ball', over Filey – RAF scrambled?

Rex Burns, in his mid 20's from Filey, Yorkshire, was walking along the cliff top (close to Butlin's holiday camp), with his two young children, at 8am.

> *"It was a strange morning – the early morning sun burning off the mist, rolling along the ground. One of the children threw his kite into the air, which went straight upwards, very oddly, as there*

was hardly any wind. I glanced upwards and saw this huge 'silver ball' hanging low down in the sky, above Filey Bay. I thought to myself, what the hell is that? A few minutes later, it vanished in mid-air." Fifteen minutes later two RAF jet fighters screamed across the sky, heading towards where the object had been. Was it a coincidence, or had they been scrambled?

(Source: Phil Dillon/Rex Burns, David Sankey/Personal interview)

28th September 1970 – UFO landing, Warminster

From records kept at The Dewey Museum, Warminster, left by the late Ken Rogers, we learnt of a spectacular sighting, which took place on the side of a track way, near Lord's Hill, Warminster. It involved Barry Canner, who claimed to have come across a saucer-shaped object, at 9.30pm on 28th September 1970, while out running. Mr Canner (28) described what he saw, following his cross-country run, which had started at 8pm.

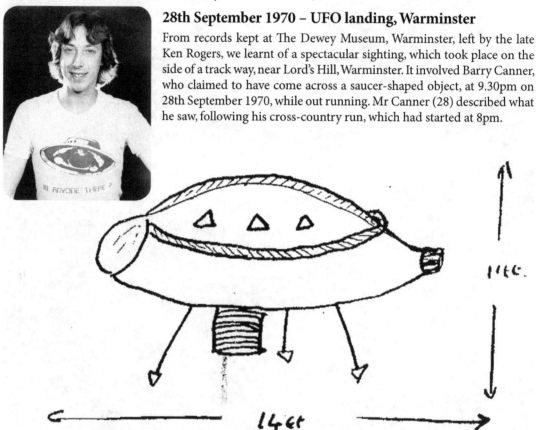

"As I was nearing the car I noticed a weird looking object, some ten yards away, to my left, in a field alongside the lane that had not been there when I had set out earlier. The object gave off a faint pinkish glow – like a watch dial at night; the shape was like a biconvex oval, rising up to a projection at the rear, which looked like an exhaust pipe. At what could have been the forward end was a dome-shaped window, containing three triangular windows, and at one side were three triangular markings, which might have been portholes, giving out a whitish hue.

The structure was supported by three 'legs', some six feet off the ground. Each of these 'legs' tapered from a diameter of about two feet at the top, to three feet at the base, terminating in a triangular foot pad. There was also a cylindrical hatch projecting from underneath, about two feet off the ground. The length was about 12 feet and its diameter 12 feet."

According to Ken Rogers, who visited the location, two days later, two distinct two-inch deep depressions were found in the ground where the object had reportedly stood. Other accounts tell of triangular markings found in the ground where the object had stood.

In the centre of the 'feet marks' were found three pieces of metallic substance, copper or bronze in colour. In addition to this, a number of unusual types of stones were found.

Tony Justice obtained a sample and arranged for it to be analysed, but no-one was able to identity it.

Ken Rogers, in his book, entitled *The Warminster Triangle*, tells the reader:

> *"The feet of the three 'legs' forming a tripod were of equilateral triangle, with sides of one and a half feet. These were seen as two- inch depressions. The area between the pad marks was also of an exact triangle, measured by John Clarke and Francis Pullen, of the Cambridge UFO Society, as being equal distant one to the other, i.e. 9 feet 5 inches in length on the left side of the triangle, the base 10 feet, right-hand side length 10 feet by 8 feet 33 inches. Pieces of a heavy metal-like substance, varying in size, and copper or bronze in colour, were found within the triangle, including a translucent marble with a pearly grey sheen to its surface."*

Chris Strevens, B.Sc., at Bath University, analysed some of the samples and concluded that the substance contained iron and silica.

Somebody else who interviewed Barry Canner was Eileen Buckle – assistant Editor of *Flying Saucer Review*. She was accompanied by *FSR* Editor – Charles Bowen, and *FSR* Consultant – Bryan Winder, B.Sc., C. Eng., M. I. Mech. E., after having been contacted by Arthur Shuttlewood.

Eileen described a meeting with Mr Canner over lunch, at Warminster, who told them he was a cross-country runner and had trained with Mary Rand – an Olympic gold medalist.

Barry also had a number of UFO magazines in his car, which had been given to him by Bob Strong, a couple of months before the meeting, whom he knew previously, as they had both worked in the same line of employment as civilian truck drivers, employed by the Army.

Bob and Barry later returned to the scene and took some photos of the area. The whereabouts of these photos are not known. Barry told Bob about his experience, which was later brought to the attention of Arthur Shuttlewood, and that's how *FSR* learnt of what had transpired.

(Sources: Ken Rogers, The Dewey Museum, Warminster/Eileen Buckle, *FSR*, Supplement Three, February 1971 – '*Was there a landing near Warminster?*'/Page 76, The Warminster Triangle, Ken Rogers, Coates and Parker, Warminster/The Dewey Museum Warminster)

Ken Rogers began his career as a reporter with the *Daily Express*. His curiosity about reports of UFO sightings, brought to his notice by members of the public, led him to join BUFORA. Following a 'wave' of publicity, as well as sightings around the Warminster area, he moved to the town to conduct his own research, and was to himself sight some unusual objects.

In 1970 he joined *BBC Radio News and Current Affairs*, based at the Palace of Westminster, running a teleprinted copy service, which foresaw the televising of Parliament. He then transferred to Broadcasting House, inputting news material for Network and local Radio. He contributed frequently to the columns of the *Warminster Journal* on a variety of local topics. He pondered on the significance between the appearance of UFOs and ley lines, and ancient sites of historic religious interest, such as Stonehenge, Avebury, Silbury Hill, and Glastonbury – as, indeed, we have done since and continue to do so.

29th September 1970 – UFO over Bournemouth

At 7.30pm – a cold and clear evening – Mrs Carter of Calvin Road, Winton, Bournemouth, was at her home address, when her daughter burst into the house and told her, very excitedly, that she and her friend – Carol Elverd, had just witnessed a UFO sighting. Following further conversation, Carol told her mother that they were riding home on their cycles, at 7.30pm, when they heard a loud droning noise. Glancing upwards they saw a huge circular object, moving across the sky, and rushed to the front of the house in order to obtain a closer view.

Carol:

> *"It was silver with orange edges, making an unearthly 'bubbly' tone – then it disappeared behind some trees.*
>
> *When it reappeared, it was orange all over – like a huge fireball. As it sped away, the sound stopped."*

Jane was so impressed by what she had seen that she wrote a letter to the local newspaper. Was this the same object photographed earlier, on the same day?

(Source: Leslie Harris, Cosmic Research Group, Bournemouth)

Close encounter over Norwich

Mr William Woodcock from Oulton, near Aylesham, was exercising his dog, during one early evening in late autumn 1970, when he noticed a steady glowing 'light' moving towards his position. Fear gave way to curiosity. Instead of diving into the nearest ditch, he stood his ground – now aware of a slight vibration emanating from the UFO, which halted in mid-air, a few feet away, about 30 feet off the ground.

> *"I saw this dimly lit spherical object, some 8-9 inches in diameter, with a single opaque, round, window inset into the body.*
>
> *After a few seconds the object made a light turn, until the 'window' was now facing the dog, creating the impression it was studying the animal. Suddenly, it jumped over a hedge and disappeared from view."* **(Source: Dennis Tye, Norwich UFO Group)**

OCTOBER 1970

2nd October 1970 – Silver sphere over Manchester

The United Kingdom was to see an increase of UFO reports during October 1970, beginning with a sighting over Prestwich, Manchester, when a silver sphere was seen by hospital worker – Mr Stephen Rosenfield, and his neighbour. This was later explained away by Manchester Weather Centre as likely to be a meteorological balloon – although they admitted being puzzled why it was travelling against the wind. **(Source: *UFOLOG*)**

4th October 1970 – Metallic object in the sky over Hampshire

Kevin Smale (9) and his family, were driving along the A31, between Ringwood and Cadnam, Hampshire, when they noticed a shiny (almost circular) metallic object directly in front of them in the sky (cloud level 5,000 feet) before being obscured by cloud and lost from view, a couple of minutes later. Enquiries made with the Weather Centre, at Southampton, revealed it was unlikely to have been a weather balloon. **(Source: Leslie Harris/*SCAN* Magazine)**

UFO over Bolton, Lancashire

In 2006 we were contacted by a Bolton man, who told us about 'Squire Foster' from Bolton, Lancashire, whom, it was alleged, according to him, had seen a UFO landing in the nearby Moors and met with the Alien occupants – matters he assured us would be confirmed by various newspaper accounts. We spoke to 'Squire Foster's granddaughter – Pamela Rigby, who had this to say:

> *"I can't say what year it was. It might have been 1969, or 1970. At the time I was living at 101, Egerton Street, Farnworth, with my grandparents, who brought me up. I was aged 8, at the time. Granddad was a very much 'down-to-earth' man, who didn't believe in spirits or UFOs, who thought it was a load of old rubbish, and worked until he was aged 91, as a man's hairdresser at' Squire Fosters'.*
>
> *I remember the excitement generated, late one night, when my grandparents saw a circular object hovering over the house, surrounded by flashing lights. They woke me up to come and have a*

look. When I got there, it had gone. My granddad talked about the incident for many months. I remember my grandmother said it was over the Hawker Siddeley Works, and that a police officer, in Wigan, had also reported seeing it." (**Source: Personal interview**)

5th October 1970 – Strange sighting at Wisconsin, USA

During the early hours of the morning, a nurse's assistant at the Memorial Hospital, received a call at 4am from a patient. She made her way to one of the three bed wards and asked the man who was sat on the edge of the bed what he wanted. He told her that he had seen some monkeys swinging from trees and also sitting on the window ledge.

"I didn't bother looking out of the window and told him to go back to sleep; he had rung the bell off and on for a long time and each time I answered it. The curtains were closed but he could have been looking outside before I came in. I settled the patient back down in bed. As I was doing so, I saw a bright light coming through the sides of the curtains.

I went to the window and opened the drapes and immediately saw a pulsating balloon-like object, about a hundred feet long by over 30 feet in diameter, a diffused yellow-green showing a stream of intense white light protruding from the object. I was shocked and startled, and stood there paralysed for about five minutes."

It then started to move upwards and, as it did so, the colour changed to an orange glow around the outer edge of the object. By this time she had come to her senses and went to fetch another nurse. On their return all that remained was a streak of fading light.

She never gave it another thought, until speaking to a UFO investigator – Mr A.J. Andropolis, of Sturgeon Bay, who told me about the incident at Sutton Farm, near Kelly, Kentucky, and wondered if there was any connection. (**Source:** *APRO Bulletin*/**Kathleen Smith**, *UFOLOG*)

9th October 1970 – Shining 'disc' over Derbyshire

Mr and Mrs Brocklesby of Queens Avenue, Ilkeston, were looking out of the window during the late evening, towards the Trowell direction, when:

"...a white shining 'disc' appeared in the sky, stationary to start with – then it moved horizontally to the left, then to the right and back again, before vanishing."

The MOD, who was informed, suggested they had seen a satellite used for weather and observation purposes!

11th October 1970 – Motorist sights two UFOs

Michigan resident – Roger Jayo, was on his way home from Bay City to Caro, where he played in a band at the weekend.

It was 2.15am when he drove onto the M15, when suddenly two brightly lit flat 'discs' flashed over the top of the car, heading southwards – the radio buzzing with static as they did so.

"It lasted for only five or six seconds, but it seemed like a day. When I saw the first object it appeared to be about 85 feet in diameter and 50 feet off the ground."

Roger contacted the Bay County Sheriff's department and told them what he had seen. They telephoned the radar installation, at Port Austin, who told the officer:

"We can neither deny nor confirm the sighting."

Jayo said the objects were travelling at a speed between 100 and 150 miles per hour, very bright with lights emanating from the centre to the edges of the 'disc', in a greenish blue haze.

Mr C. Williams, of Rochester, and Fred Varner interviewed Mr Jayo and retraced his footsteps, when they were able to identify the location as being the junction of the M15 and Kinney Road. That intersection is crossed from south-west to north-east by high tension power lines and six conductors. The power lines seemed not to have been affected by the incident. (**Source: 'Skylook', Stover, Mo, USA**)

11th -18th October 1970 – Incredible account of UFO activity around a Scottish *BBC* TV mast

Mr Hughes – then living in a cottage at Berthengam, Flintshire (not far from Holywell) – was in the process of returning home and about to enter the back door, when he saw:

> *"...this 'thing' around the BBC TV mast at Afonwen, about five miles away. It was saucer-shaped, red – like a tangerine – and had a tail to it like a piece of string. It was followed by four or five others at intervals of a minute or so. They seemed solid enough – glowing but with no flames – then they shot away and disappeared from sight."*

In an interview conduced by Norman Oliver of BUFORA, Mr Hughes accepted it was difficult to estimate a size of the objects but guessed they were probably about 15 feet in diameter. Due to the position of his house, Mr Hughes was only able to see the top part of the mast and the three objects.

12th October 1970 – Orange-red globular object sighted

During this day, Mrs Dickson (a neighbour) sighted:

> *"...a flattened orange-red globular object, showing a small protrusion moving through the sky from the western direction. It switched or went off before reaching the mast. A few seconds later either this or a similar one reappeared two and a half miles away, westwards of the mast, to the right of Tremeirchion."*

13th October 1970 – Heavy interference on the TV set

On Wednesday (13th) no sightings were reported, although the TV set belonging to Mrs Dickson began to show heavy interference with white dots blotting the picture out completely.

14th October 1970 – UFOs sighted over Colorado, USA

At Cortez, in Colorado, several residents reported having sighted 'Flying Saucers' during the night. One was Dale Kell, who was riding a motorcycle with his girlfriend:

> *"It was shaped like a large jelly, with three lights on it. It rose out of the sagebrush in front of Ute Mountain. It followed us for a short time."*

Dale made his way back home and returned with members of the family. Once again the UFO was sighted. *Radio Station KVSC*, in Cortez, told the listeners that many people had called them about this object, which was described as:

> *"...a large bean-shaped thing with three lights and a bright orange centre."*

15th October -Huge 'Saucer' seen

At 7.45pm on the 15th October 1970, Mr Hughes was astonished to see:

> *"...an object – like a huge saucer on its side – come up from the ground above the hill interposing, move horizontally, then sink from sight below the hill; other objects followed."*

18th October 1970 – Observations made after a visit to the locality

On the 18th October 1970, Mrs Dickson felt strongly that she should get closer to the mast. As it was a very lonely rural location, she asked two neighbours – Mr and Mrs Woodward – to come with her. They parked the car about a mile and a half away from the TV mast on the verge of a narrow, practically unused, country road on high ground known as Sodom.

Shortly after 7pm a UFO appeared, described as:

> "...*red, like the sun; you couldn't look at it from the west heading towards the TV mast. On reaching it, it turned as if to go round – then disappeared. The same thing happened every few minutes, by which time seven or eight of them had been seen. Some of these had 'string like' appendages hanging below them and attached to each string was a red 'ball'. Some UFOs went out and just left the red 'balls', before they disappeared; others 'burst' with a jagged green flash. Some of them made a muffled 'backfire' but not all of them. Very oddly, the sound took considerably longer to reach the assembled party in some cases than in others. We estimated the 'lights' (larger than the mast lights) to be 15-20 feet in diameter. At 8pm, the 'lights' ceased to appear.*"

Another vehicle arrives

At this point the headlight of a vehicle was seen approaching up the hill. Mrs Dickson put her car lights on; as she did so, a van shot around the bend at speed and halted at the next bend, before backing off the road. The three witnesses then made their way to see what was going on, curious as to the arrival of the vehicle on a road which is normally deserted. A man got out of the van, carrying a box, and began scraping a hole in dead leaves to put the box in. He then fiddled with the box and a bulb lit up the top. Then running to the van, he put a large aerial on the platform of his 'pick up' van. He then went inside and he was heard apparently broadcasting in what sounded like nasal Japanese. By now it was 9pm, at which stage they decided to leave. MrsDickson suggested they should tell the police and, on arriving home, this was done.

Shortly afterwards, the police telephoned and asked if she could show them the location. Ten minutes later, a police car then arrived at the house. About halfway into the journey, a message came over the police radio to say that there had been *"a military exercise taking place"* in the general area, but they were ok to continue. They arrived at Sodom at 11pm; the van was still there with the man inside. The police went into the van and questioned him. On their return they told Mrs Dickson he was a 'radio ham' and that his papers were in order. Despite a visit to the location by Norman Oliver, and observations made, nothing further was obtained. (**Source:** *BUFORA Journal,* **Vol. 4, No. 2, Spring 1974**)

19th October 1970 – UFO over Eastern Counties

People living in Norfolk and Suffolk coastal villages, near Lowestoft, sighted:

> "...*a strange luminous effect, racing across the night sky*".

One of the witnesses was Mr R. Chestney, a warden at the Scolt Head Island bird sanctuary, off Brancaster Staithe, near King's Lynn – a shingle dune and saltmarsh island.

> "*A brilliant blue 'ball of light' with white tail, yellowish-white at its tip, appeared over Brancaster Staithe, a few degrees east of North in the sky, for about five seconds, illuminating the cloud ... and then vanished. It reminded me of a stream of molten metal being poured from a furnace.*"

20th October 1970 – Motorist encounters UFO over Isle of Wight

At 7pm, Isle of Wight resident – Rick Barr – was driving from Brading to St. Helens, Sandown, Isle of Wight, over Culver Downs.

As he turned right, towards St. Helens, after passing through Brading, he became aware of a large multi-lit aircraft on his right, about half a mile away between the road and Bembridge Downs.

> "*I stopped the car and got out. It looked enormous as it flew low over swampy terrain, silently hovering, apparently aimlessly, over the River Yar, allowing me to see a ring of seven or more lights, each of them resembling a large, clearly defined, sphere – like a cherry – each interspersed with a turquoise and white light. I then continued on my journey, noticing the object was apparently*

keeping parallel with me. As I neared St. Helens, it cut across, about 30 yards behind me, and descended slowly over distant hedges – now showing four red lights, which seemed to be rotating slowly. I stopped and got out of the car and signalled with a torch to the object – now weaving backwards and forwards in the air – but after receiving no response, set out once again.

After arriving at my destination I alerted a friend, who confirmed he could see the object playing 'hide and seek' through the distant treetops." (**Source: Leonard Cramp, Isle of Wight UFO Society**)

21st October 1970 – Bright 'light' over Essex

At 7.35am, engineer Graham Bober (23) of Tyhurst Crescent, Colchester, was driving home down Hythe Hill, when he saw a strange object in the sky.

"It was stationary but kept disappearing and reappearing in the same position; the cone or triangular-shaped light was lesser illuminated than the oval one at the top. We stopped the car in Hawkins Road and watched it for several minutes, until it finally disappeared. We heard no noise, such as engine – completely silent."

[**Authors: Graham's illustration is similar to what Mr Powell described on the 21st November, the same year**]

A bright star-like 'light', accompanied by an angular shaft of light behind it, was seen five minutes, later at 7.40am, over the Hythe Hill area of Essex, by Mr Philip Beeton of Colchester, and other residents. (**Source: Ron West/*The Illuminer*/SWAPIG**)

October 1970 – Did a 'Vulcan' bomber try and intercept UFO?

Another witness was Mr Richard 'Dick' Arthur Thompson – then employed at a local chemical works, just outside Saxilby, close to RAF Scampton – now immortalised in history as the home of the famous 'Dambusters' Squadron.

Report. 19.10.70.

1859
X

Name. Richard Arthur Thompson. Age 46.
Address. No5 Western Avenue, Saxilby Nr Lincoln.
Occupation. Process Machine Operator, (Chemicals)
Date of sighting. 19. 10. 70.
Time of sighting. 2203 pm. Number of objects. One ONly.
Place of sighting. Approx. One Half Mile East of Saxilby Village.
Weather conditions. Good, scattered cloud, stars could be identified,
strong North-Westerly blowing.
Size of object. About 3½ inches in diameter.
Colour of object. Very brilliant Red, Flashing.
Shape of object. No shape could be discerned, only the flashing light.
Elevation. No more than 100 ft, possible less.
Distance away from observer. Probable 2 Miles possible more, difficult
to judge in the dark with no guide marks.
Direction of object when first observed. Approx. N.N.W.
Duration of observation. About 15 Minutes.
Noise. None was heard. Luminosity. Very brilliant flashing light.
Metallic. Impossible to tell since the shape could not be made out.
I was leaving an afternoon shift, I was about to enter the works car
park when I happened to catch sight of a vivid flashing Red light low in
the sky which was approx N.N.W of my observation point, which was also
about 2 to 2½ Miles from Scampton aerodrome as the crow flies, and is
between ½ to I Mile from Saxilby village.
The light was stationary and very brilliant, so much so one not help but
notice it, I was about to get a telescope from my car for a closer inspection, when I noticed a Vulcan getting up from Scampton and as it approached the area I was observing the light either dimmed considerably or it
moved away I could not be sure, also prior to the arrival of the Vulcan
I could not detect any noise, I thought the crew of the plane had seen
the object and was investigating because they began to circle the area
of observation, this they did about three times, by now the light had
disappeared completely, at no time could I make out any shape other than
the vivid Red flashing light. I decided to set offhome, I had only gone
about 400 yards up the road when I spotted the object again, but before
I could stop the car it had disappeared again, although I looked all
around I did not see the object again. I rang Scampton the next morning
and spoke to the station Commander, but he informed me no one had reported any thing out of the ordinary. I have been unable to find anyone to
verify what I saw as yet. The main things which puzzle me, are; If it
was a plane how could it have remaind stationary?, How was the light so
big and vivid?, and most of all Why did the object disappear when the
Vulcan came on the scene?. I also wonder why it was'nt reported.
It seems strange that I could make out the shape of theVulcan ~~quite~~ Quite
easily, but yet I could not make out any shape beyond the vivid flashing
light of the object. I had no psychological effects beyond being puzzled.

*"I was about to
enter the works
car park, when I
saw a vivid red
flashing light,
quite low in the
sky, approximately
north-north-west of
my position, some
two miles from RAF
Scampton.*

*I stopped and
watched a 'Vulcan'
bomber take-off
from the airfield
and approach the
UFO, which either
dimmed or moved
away prior to
the arrival of the
aircraft. I presumed*
the crew of the aircraft had seen the UFO, as it circled the locality three times before heading back
to base. I decided to make my way home, but had only gone a couple of hundred yards away, when
I saw the 'light' again in the sky. The next morning I rang the airbase and spoke to the Station
Commander and told him what I had seen. He denied any knowledge of UFOs, or of having sent
an aircraft up into the sky. Why did he lie to me? Why did the UFO disappear when the 'Vulcan'
Bomber approached it?"*

(Source: Personal interview)

27th October 1970 – UFOs over Northampton

At 3.30pm, Mr Stanley Lilford of Wootton, Northampton, was at his home address, which overlooks the village green, when he saw a large circular object in a patch of bright sky.

> *"The object was travelling rapidly and silently in a rough south-west to east direction. It was the size of a football and had four pale lights connected by a distinct dark cross-shape. It appeared to be on a definite course and didn't drift, or bob, as one would have expected if it had been a balloon. After about a minute, I saw a sudden puff of blue smoke issue from its edge, followed by its immediate vertical descent and out of sight behind a row of houses."*

(Source: *Chronicle and Echo*/SWAPIG/*The Illuminer*, No. 3, November/December 1970)

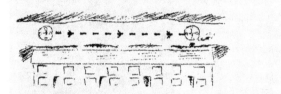

Mr Lilford suggests that from his positio; he may have obse: ved the object's base only.

(Sketches of scene and object taken from Mr Lilford's completed report form)

28th October 1970 – Mysterious 'lights' over Northampton

Northampton resident – Ronald Dartnell, of Far Cotton, was with several other workmen when they saw a shining, circular or spherical, object appear in the sky, heading south-west to east.

> *"This was followed, in quick succession, by two others. The three of them disappeared over the horizon, towards the direction of Hardingstone, as if on a predetermined course."* **(Source: Personal interview)**

NOVEMBER 1970

5th November 1970 – Glowing 'light' in the sky over Swindon, Wiltshire

Carol New was on her way back to Swindon, with a friend from Devizes. They stopped to admire the view from the hill above Wroughton.

> *"We noticed a large, yellow, glowing light hanging in the sky over Swindon. Suddenly, it moved with tremendous speed over Princess Margaret Hospital, hung there for a minute, and then headed towards our position. It made no sound as it passed overhead, and disappeared in the direction of south."* **(Source: *Swindon Evening Advertiser*, 11.11.1970)**

UFO over Birmingham

On the same day, Ron and Michael Freebury went to Doe Bank playing fields for what would turn out to be their final 'sky watch', but saw nothing apart from fireworks, until 9pm, when they noticed a red pulsing object approaching from Barr Beacon.

> *"It was very low and looked as though it was going to fly under the power line cables that crossed the lower part of the Beacon, but then rose, suddenly, over the power lines and approached our position, no more than 20-30ft from the ground, allowing us to see a bell-shaped object, which continued on its course towards Birmingham – totally unlike any of the other UFOs we had seen before."* **(Source: Personal interview)**

9th November 1970 – Fluttering object in sky over Northamptonshire

At 5.15pm, an object resembling an old three-penny bit was sighted fluttering slowly across the sky over the town of Kettering, Northampton, by four workers from the Mobbs Miller factory in Carrington

Street, before heading away towards the direction of Barton Seagrave. The first to see it was Bob Hackett of 127, Reservoir Road, Kettering, who pointed it out to Mrs Bartholomew and colleagues – Susan Urban and Maureen Luck. Mrs Norma Bartholomew of 61, Fuller Street said:

"All four of us definitely saw it. People will say that we are mad, but it was there we are certain."

Mr Geoffrey Parry – Head of Kettering Grammar school, suggested they had seen a weather balloon.

(Source: *Kettering Leader,* **13.11.1970 – 'Mystery object in the sky may have been a balloon'/***UFOLOG***)**

Later, the same evening, Mrs Molly Rooney from Pensby, Cheshire, was walking to choir practice, at 7.15pm, when she saw the *"red glowing light"* drop down from the sky and take up the same position as she had seen, four days previously.

She ran up to two teenagers, who were also watching it.

"Suddenly, to the left of the main light, a red light appeared and began to grow larger. To my right I could make out a pure black shape – like a zeppelin, but smaller. It looked about 3feet long, but may have been bigger; the distance was confusing. After a few seconds, the silence was broken by a whirring sound and the light disappeared up into the night sky in the direction it had come from."

(Source: *Birkenhead News,* **13.11.1970)**

10th November 1970 – Flash of light seen

Just before 5pm, an electrical engineer was carrying out essential maintenance work on overhead cables on the London to Shoeburyness railway track, when, *"suddenly, a huge flash of light lit up the sky".*

Looking upwards, he noticed a peculiar cloud of what looked like smoke rather than vapour, illuminated by the moon, at a height of approximately 10,000 feet, moving across the sky.

(Source: Isle of Wight UFO Society)

13th November 1970 – UFOs over Lincolnshire

At 2am, British Rail signalman – Cecil Hardy (59), was on duty at Kelveston signal box, half a mile east of the small town of Saxilby. Looking out of the window, which faced west, he noticed an orange/lemon, bright (but not brilliant), sphere hovering at a height of about 50 feet off the ground, about half a mile away from the box. Thinking it to be a reflection on the glass, he went to the door and opened it.

"As I did so, another identical object appeared, as if from nowhere, and took up a side-by-side position in the air. I thought it might have been the lights of an aircraft, but then thought this couldn't be as they were as large as footballs and not moving. I stood on top of the steps and watched them. After a short time, they started to move silently; one heading towards the north-east, the other headed towards where I was stood. Its shape and luminosity remained unchanged, although it moved very leisurely through the air. I thought to myself, I must contact the next signal box down the track and let him know what is happening. All of a sudden, both of them vanished from sight. The whole episode was over in a few minutes."

(Source: Richard Thompson)

Report 14 November 1970.

1838

Name. Cecil E. Hardy (MR) Age 57. Address No.9 Lincoln Road. Saxilby.

Occupation. B.R. Signal man. Date of sighting 13 November 1970. Time of sighting approx 2 A.M.

Period of Observation approx 3 minutes. Place of Sighting. Kesteven Signal Box appeox ½ mile S.E of Saxilby.

Number of objects. First one - then two. Direction first observed 2° N of W. Weather Conditions. Excellent, cloudless sky, stars easily recognisable, Moon high in the sky, clear observable conditions. Shape of Objects Spherical.

Colour. Whitish - Orange to Whitish - Lemon. Size. Described as big as a football. Luminosity. Bright but not glaring or brilliant. Elevation, appear estimate 50 ft. Distance at least ½ mile possibly more. Movement. Hovering or stationary. Sound. None could be detected. Psychological Effects. None, except bewilderment and being unable to find a logical answer relating to earthly concepts.

Mr Hardy was working a 12 hour night shift duty at the Kesteven Signal Box which lays appox ½ mile S.E of Saxilby Village.

At about 2 A.M on the morning of the 13th of November 1970, Something attracted his attention, upon looking out of the windows on the Westerly side of the signal box, he observed a round sphere, which was illuminated with a whitish - Orange to a Whitish - Lemon coloured light, which was bright but not glaring. The object was at a low altitude of about 50ft as far as Mr Hardy could estimate. After a few seconds watching and not detecting any movment he thought it possibly was a reflection on the windows from a signal situated a short distance from the box, he had to reject this idea, because it was then that another identical object came into focus, seeming to appear as from nowhere, the two objects now appeared to be side by side, hovering or just stationary. Mr Hardy's next thought was that of an air craft. but once again this did not fit, because of the size of the lights. described as being as big as footballs, also the fact that they stayed in the same place all the time, some thing air craft cannot do, and also although he strained and listened there was no noise or engine sounds what so ever. His next logical deduction was satellites, but he reasoned this could not be, because the objects were so low, he resolved to him self then that he just could not find an answer as to what he was observing. His next move was to go out side of the signal box for a better view, and he continued observing from the top of the steps which are necessary to gain access to the box and also provide an excellent observation post. Mr Hardy estimated the objects to be at less ½ mile away possibly more. By this time the objects had started to move, one going toward the N.E. the other advanced towards the observer, upon moving he noted that the objects neither changed shape or luminosity, and their motivation was more of a leisurley floating movment than a forward drive. After watching the objects perform for about a minute or so, Mr Hardy contemplated ringing another signal box which is down line at Saxilby, to see if any thing could been seen from there; and also to verify what he was actually observing him self. Before Mr Hardy had time to move or decide whether to ring, both objects, to his amazement just disappeared in an instant, one second they were observable, the next - nothing remained to indicate any thing had been there at all. He describes their disappear- ance likened to an electric power switch being put into the off position. He watched and looked around for some considerable time but saw nothing else or any thing to satisfy his mind as to what he had observed. He was left rather bewildered and swears that what he had been watching was not;· air craft, balloons, clouds, planets, stars, reflections or any known phenomena he had ever seen in his life before. The whole sighting took about 3 minutes from begining to end.

R.A. Thompson.   C.E. Hardy

In mid-November 1970, a resident of Barking, Essex, told of watching a white 'light' low in the sky over the Manor Park area, at 9.30am, when:

> "...what looked like a huge 'rocket' appeared over Canning Town, motionless in the sky, throwing out a cascade of white lights for, maybe, 30 seconds, before moving away, leaving the solitary light in the centre, which hung in the sky for about a minute, before it, too, flew off."

(**Source:** *Barking and Dagenham Express*, **13.11.1970**)

14th November 1970 – Spinning object in the sky over Northampton

Just before dawn on the same day, eight year-old Robert Lewis – a patient at the Northampton ear nose and throat hospital, whose ward window faces south – got out of bed to watch:

> "...an object that appeared to be spinning in the sky; it came from the left (east) and then went down, then up, down again, and then up. It zigzagged for a while and disappeared towards the south." (**Source:** *Northants. Chronicle and Echo/UFOLOG*)

On the same day, Mr Desmond Ward of Bulwell, Nottinghamshire, sighted a bright glowing violet coloured cylindrical object hovering over Bulwell Golf Course, before it shot up into the sky. Another resident sighted a bluish light, moving over Bulwell Common, and stop, before moving away again.

(**Source:** SWAPIG/*The Illuminer*, **No. 3, November/December 1970**)

15th November 1970 – Strange 'red line' seen in the sky

At 5.10pm, a strange 'red line' was seen in the sky, west of Burgess Hill, by a couple walking along Mill Road.

> "For a while it was stationary, and then it seemed to roll over and eject a second object that showed a red light, which soon faded away from sight, leaving the first one to move away at fantastic speed – soon gone over the horizon." (**Source:** *Mid-Sussex Times*, **November, 1970/UFOLOG**)

16th November 1970 – UFO over Lincolnshire

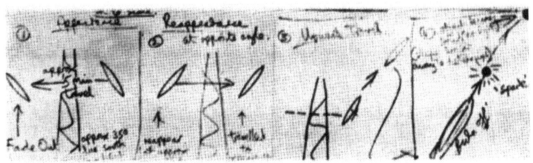

Sketches by Allan McGregor, reproduced from the Immingham News

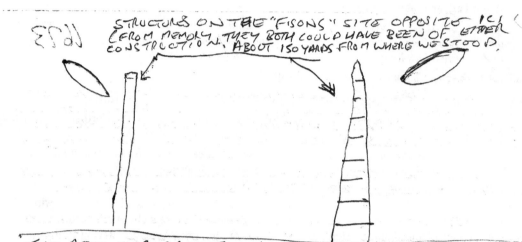

STRUCTURES ON THE "FISONS" SITE OPPOSITE ICI (FROM MEMORY). THEY BOTH COULD HAVE BEEN OF EITHER CONSTRUCTION. ABOUT 150 YARDS FROM WHERE WE STOOD.

THE ABOVE REPRSENTS THE SAME OBJECT AS IT CHANGED POSITIONS. MY FEELING WAS THAT WE WERE LOOKING AT A LARGE OBJECT MANY MILES AWAY RATHER THAN A SMALLER BODY NEARER TO US BUT THIS IS ONLY MY FEELING. CERTAINLY THE DISC PASSED BEHIND THE TWO STRUCTURES.

IN CLOSING I WOULD JUST LIKE TO SAY THAT MY INITIAL RESPONSE ONCE THE INCIDENT ENDED WAS ONE OF HUGE DISAPOINTMENT. I WAS CONVINCED THAT SOME THING OF ENORMOUS CONSEQUENC WAS OCCURING, AND THAT GOOD OR BAD SOME MAJOR EVENT WAS AND WAS ABOUT TO HAPPEN. OF COURSE WE/I SPOKE TO MANY PEOPLE ABOUT THIS. THE RESULT BEING SOME GOOD HUMOURD RIBBING FOR SEVERAL TEDIOUS MONTHS. IN THE DAYS FOLLOWING THE SIGHTING I REMEMBER BEING AMAZED THAT THERE WAS NO CONFIRMATION OF WHAT WE HAD SEEN FROM LOCAL PEOPLE OR THE NEWS MEDIA. THE DISC MUST HAVE BEEN POTENTIALY VISIBLE TO TENS OF THOUSAND OF PEOPLE.

HOPE THIS HELPS AND IF I CAN ADD OR CLARIFY ANYTHING THEN PLEASE DON'T HESITATE.

Yours Mal. Dunnell.   13.3.2002.

TO CLARIFY ONE OTHER POINT ALAN AND I WERE WORKING ON THE ICI SITE AS CONTRACTORS, NOT FOR ICI ITSELF.

We spoke to Malcolm Dunwell from Immingham, Lincolnshire, who was working as a fitter's mate, carrying out some work at the ICI factory, during the firm's shutdown, on this date.

"At 4.30pm, I was helping Mr Allan McGregor to install a blind into the flue gas supply of the furnace, when we noticed an elliptical golden-shaped light, tilted 30-40 degrees along its axis, hovering in the sky close to the neighbouring Fison's factory, about 150 yards away from us. Allan went off to try and find other witnesses, leaving me to carry on watching the UFO as it slowly moved over from one side of the structure to the other, before shooting off upwards into the sky at an incredible speed – like a 'shooting star', in reverse."

Allan McGregor (left) and Malcolm Dunwell: "It moved so slowly that nothing I know of could have copied it."

(Source: Personal interview/originally published by *FSR*/*Immingham News*, 20.11.1970)

20th November 1970 – Domed UFO seen

Melvyn Batty and his young son, Paul, were walking through the town, at 11am, when they saw a domed silver object, travelling across the sky.

"A few days later I was talking to my daughter, completely unaware of what we had sighted. Imagine my surprise when she told me about having seen a strange luminous 'globe', stationary in the sky at the same time as our sighting."

(Source: Personal interview)

21st November 1970 – UFO over London … Police seen to take photographs

Student Philip Morris (20) of Rosebank Close, London, was driving home at 2.30am, after having been to a party.

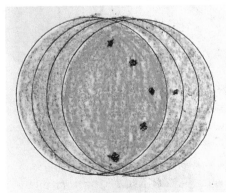

As he neared the *Cambridge Arms* public house, Edmonton N18, he noticed a mauve 'circle of light', with an orange centre, in the sky at an angle of 30 degrees elevation.

"I stopped the car and got out; it was like looking down a tunnel.

Inside were six black circles. At this point a police car pulled up, ordering me to move on. I pointed the light out to them, but they insisted I move on. As I left, I peered through the rear view mirror and saw one of the officers taking photographs of the UFO."

Dome-shaped Scunthorpe UFO

From the Scunthorpe *Evening Telegraph* of November 25, 1970, comes the following account—

"Busman Melvyn Batty . . . (30), who lives at 56, Teale-street, Scunthorpe, said that he was walking from his home to shops in Frodingham-road last Friday morning when Paul (his son, aged 3) pointed to the sky and asked 'What's that?'

" 'I asked him if he meant the sun,' said Mr. Batty. 'Then I saw something silver in the sky. I thought it might have been a jet plane but then I noticed that it had no wings. It was domed shaped and was going across the sky faster than any ordinary aeroplane without leaving a trail. It was a perfectly clear sky and I'm sure I was not mistaken.'

"The object he saw, appeared from the direction of Doncaster in the west and he watched it disappear into the east.

"Mr. Batty said that he did not think too much about what he had seen until Sunday when his daughter, Julie (7) told him that she had been at school when she had seen a round ball in the sky.

"He asked when she had seen it and Julie said that it was on the Friday. Mr. Batty said that Julie had told him it looked like a round ball and it moved around and around in the sky before flying away.

"Mr. Batty said that he would have mentioned the sighting earlier but he did not really expect people to believe him.

"Neither RAF Manby nor RAF Scampton report having seen anything unusual at that time.

"In June, however, an unidentified object that looked like the moon but smaller and moving across the sky was sighted by a number of people.

"And last year, Scunthorpe police received four calls in the space of half-an-hour from people claiming to have seen an oval object about the size of the moon."

Police Officers interviewed

Ron West, who investigated this incident, tracked down the police officers. One of them – Police Constable Alan J.D. Rea (28), had this to say:

> *"At 2.30am on the 21st November 1970, my partner and I were directed to the Cambridge Arms, Edmonton, after receiving a 999 call from a member of the public, reporting an unusual incident in the sky. When we reached the public house, we had to move two or three cars that had stopped to have a look. We then stopped to take photographs of the object, which consisted of four circles – orange in the middle with bands of bronze around the edges, with eight circles within the orange light. My partner took a whole reel of film. About five minutes later the light vanished.*
>
> *We went back to Edmonton Police Station, where the film was handed to the duty officer. We filled out a report on what had taken place and were told to forget about it. To the day (1971), I cannot come up with a rational explanation as to what it was we saw."*

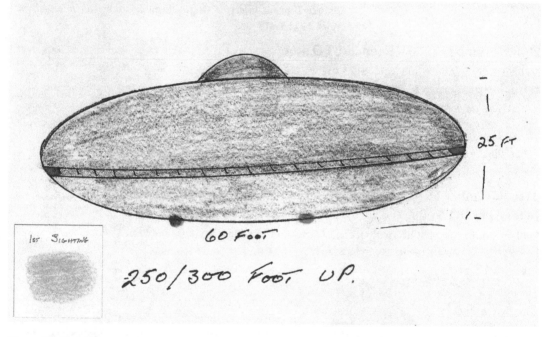

Douglas Lockhart UFO sighting

Douglas Lockhart (aged 32) – a freelance journalist, living in Downs Park Road, Clapton – sighted an object with a yellow/orange nucleus and black oval outline, surrounded by a corona of red light, passing through the sky. We contacted Douglas, now living in Hobart, Tasmania.

> *"My memory of what happened, at 11.30pm on the 21st November 1970, is still pretty clear, thirty-six years after the event and for good reason – it seared itself into my memory. My partner at that time, Maureen Boyle, noticed a 'bright light' in the night sky through our bay window. At first I dismissed it as an aircraft heading towards, or from, Heathrow Airport. When she mentioned it for the third time, I went to the window and saw this rather odd 'light' stationary in the sky, unusually bright, high up, and descending. Intrigued, we went to the front door and continued our observations, realising the sparkling object was growing in size and getting nearer."*

What happened next is difficult to explain

"What happened next is difficult to explain. From being high up – no more than a bright blob in the sky – the object was suddenly very low down, very bright, and apparently coming up the street at just above rooftop level. I reasoned it had to be a helicopter but, when it grew in size, I knew I was wrong. What we were observing was not merely odd in appearance and behaviour – it was also totally silent and unnerving. Just how unnerving this object would become we could not have guessed, changing from brilliant white to that of a large inky-black outlined oval nucleus of yellow/ orange, with a jagged corona of blood-red that fanned out like a giant cardboard cut-out, the central object (about the size of a single-decker bus) moving at a snail's pace – its effect so profound that I can still feel it today. It was as if a hole opened up in the sky, and we were watching something pass by on the other side of the hole. Oblivious to the coldness of the November evening and aware we were watching something extraordinary, I articulated the word 'stop' in my mind, believing it was departing."

Object stopped!

"The object stopped! Astonished, I told Maureen to go and get the chap from upstairs – a psycho-therapist, I think. She left and, during the next few seconds, things got out of control. Whatever it was seemed to backtrack. Something inside me made contact with 'it'.

I was overcome with fear and panic, knowing that something alien had probed me and I couldn't

handle it. As if in response, the object stopped and moved away. I watched it move off. As it did so, Maureen and the neighbour, Bryan Haddon, arrived just in time to see it gather speed in a zigzag motion."

Douglas contacted the MOD and briefly explained what he had witnessed and was questioned by someone over the telephone, who asked him a number of questions from what appeared to be a prepared questionnaire.

A few weeks later he received a letter from the MOD, confirming there had been no aircraft, either civilian or Military, flying over the locality at the time in question.

After being interviewed on *Thames Today* TV programme, by Eamon Andrews, Mr Lockhart was contacted by various representatives of UFO groups, eager to hear what he had seen.

A visit from three men

One evening the door bell rang and, when Douglas answered, he was confronted by three men, the tallest of whom turned out to be a retired RAF Officer by the name of Prevost; the other a Sergeant in the Army, the third a Naval man.

After a brief discussion about the incident, Douglas was asked to 'replay' the events of the evening concerned, during which time white stickers were placed on windows, in order to calculate the exact angle that the object was first observed. Measurements were also taken from the street, from which it was deduced the object had been at a height of between one and three thousand feet.

"About a week later, Mr Prevost turned up on his own and, during a long and fascinating conversation, admitted to having an interest in the UFO subject, stretching back to World War Two.

He spoke of having been buzzed by 'Foo fighters' – small 'discs', about a foot in diameter, that sometimes circled their aircraft during missions. On one occasion, while delivering paratroopers to a drop point, one of these small 'discs' had appeared inside the aircraft and frightened the life out of them. He then told me something extraordinary.

Apart from three others, who had seen a bright object pass over our area on a trajectory which coincided with our sighting, a RAF plane spotter – a woman at a nearby RAF Station had, on the afternoon prior to our sighting, seen part of a large metal coloured 'disc' hanging out of a cloud, close to where our UFO was seen."

TV Programme about incident cancelled

Not long after this, Douglas hatched the idea of a television programme called, '*Taking the question mark out of UFOs*', with the *Today* programme. They seemed interested and asked Douglas to contact Mr Prevost, as they wanted him on the programme.

Initially, Mr Prevost agreed, but a week later spoke to Douglas and told him, '*I've been put on the mat and can't appear*'. Why, he told Douglas, he couldn't appear on the TV is not known, as this would have allowed him an excellent opportunity to highlight not only the UFO cause on television, but to present details of a genuine multi-witness sighting.

Mr Alastair Prevost

Mr Alastair Prevost was a retired RAF Squadron leader, living at 4, Western Avenue, RAF Henlow, Bedfordshire. He had written various letters to *Flying Saucer Review*, expressing an interest in corresponding with other people on the subject and described himself as a Pilot Officer. We learnt that a Mr & Mrs Knapp, who were visiting friends in Hackney on that evening, also saw an unusual flashing 'red light', at 7.20pm, accompanied by four distinct 'white lights'. Another witness was

SAUCER IS BACK

By GEORGE FALLOWS

THOSE flying saucers are back again. Three sightings were reported yesterday — along with a thing that went bump in the night.

Defence Ministry experts are investigating one saucer report, from writer Douglas Lockhart and his wife, who live in Hackney.

The couple say they saw a "pulsating" flying object over Hackney on Saturday night. It was yellow, black and red.

Student Philip Morris claims he saw a similar object over Hyde Park an hour earlier. It was changing from white to red.

Taxi driver Stanley Simmonds and his wife spotted something in the sky from their home at Clapton, yesterday morning. It was silver.

The thing that went bump in the night was just a piece of stone which two schoolboys say came out of the sky at Walthamstow.

DAILY MIRROR
23 November 1970

FLYING SAUCER OVER HACKNEY?

Ministry investigates claim

YESTERDAY the Ministry of Defence was investigating a reported sighting of an unidentified flying object over Hackney. Mr. Douglas Lockhart, a 32-years-old freelance journalist, of 97 Downs Park-road, Clapton, told the *Gazette*: "It was seen by myself and two others at 11.35 Saturday night . . . it glided across an almost clear sky at a height of not more than three thousand feet."

He claimed that the object— "clearly visible and seemingly large"—had a yellow-orange nucleus, a black oval outline, was surrounded by a corona of red light which looked like flame and was totally silent.

The other people who saw it, he said, were Maureen Boyle, a secretary, and Mr. Brian Haddon, who live at the same address.

"Maureen saw it out of the window and told me. I did not think it was a normal aircraft and we went out into the street," he said. "When our strange visitor stopped, changed direction, and headed back towards us, Maureen ran back into the house for another witness.

"When Mr. Haddon, who lives upstairs, arrived, the glowing visitor, now only an orange ball of light, slowly zig-zagged its way off . . . and finally disappeared."

Mr. Lockhart immediately reported the matter to the Ministry of Defence.

The street was deserted at the time and unfortunately we could find no other witnesses," he said. "But if anyone else in the Hackney area saw the object I have described, they they should telephone the Ministry."

It is not the first time Mr. Lockhart has had such an experience. Ten years ago, he said, he saw *three* orange triangles flying in formation over the town of Coatbridge in Lanarkshire, Scotland. "According to the papers next morning, hundreds of people had witnessed the same thing and it was suggested seriously by many reporters that the objects had been UFO's."

Saturday's object was clearer, he asserted.

Said a spokesman at Hackney police station: "Nobody reported an UFO to us."

Mrs E. Oxford, who told of seeing an unusual *"bright orange light"* hovering above Millfields. Further observations revealed a *"bright orange oblong object, with a small brilliant red light at the rear"*. It appears the same object may have been seen later over Matlock, Derbyshire, at 8pm, described as showing two white lights with a red light underneath.

(Sources: *Hackney Gazette*, 21.11.1970 – 'Flying Saucer over Hackney'/*Daily Mirror*, 23.11.1970 – 'Saucer is back'/*Flying Saucer Review*, Supplement 3, February 1971, Squadron Leader Alastair Prevost – 'Hackey Flurry of UFOs')

November 1970 – UFO over Chingford

David Powell (19), of Marmion Avenue, was approaching the house at about 9.30pm, when he saw:

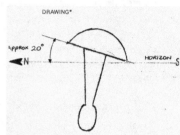

> *"...what looked like a parachute – then I realised it couldn't be, as it was just over the nearby rooftops and heading silently and slowly in a north and south direction."*

24th November 1970 – UFO over North Walsham

At 6.45am, Olaf Davey was cycling along the North Walsham to Wroxham main road, near Tunstead, to catch the train to work, at Wroxham Station, when he noticed a brightly-lit object in the cloud, resembling:

> *"...an upside-down plate, with various holes dotted around its base, which dropped down and took up a hovering position a few hundred feet above the road, making a noise like a dynamo. After a few minutes, the 'craft' tipped at an angle and went straight upwards into the sky, before coming to a halt and slowly moved into cloud cover."*

> *UFOLOG gives the date as the 25th November and makes no reference to any 'upside-down plate', although his versions of events (according to them) makes reference to a mysterious light that dropped out of the sky and that enquiries, made later, revealed others had seen it. Mr Davy, who it is said had only one eye, later told people that he had not, prior to this sighting, believed in 'Flying Saucers' before. Bearing in mind the integrity of Peter Johnson, who interviewed him, there is no reason to doubt that is what he saw.* (**Source: Peter Johnson/UFOLOG**)

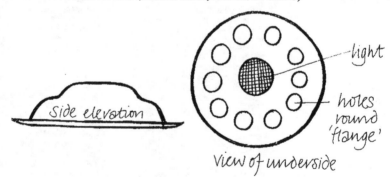

24th November 1970 – UFO over Illinois, USA

Mr Sam Alli was on his way home from the Miller Lumber Company, Centralia, where he was employed in the sales department. It was a cloudy night, with no stars visible.

At 4.45pm, he wound down the car window and saw a round fuzzy object in the sky. As it approached closer, he saw:

> *"...a perfectly round object, moving at the speed of a jet aircraft. Suddenly, it stopped in mid-air as I turned into my driveway. I watched it for about five minutes – then went in."*

There was a knock on the door; it was his neighbour – Mr Larry Patterson. He asked Sam if he had seen anything peculiar on his way home. Larry told him, while stopping to pick up his daughter from nursery school, that he had sighted a round object in the sky, which was moving in rapid spurts of movement. He stopped the car in Gragg Street to have a closer look, and then made his way to Sam's house to tell him.

(Source: 'Skylook')

25th November 1970 – Silver cigar-shaped UFO seen over Cornwall

Staff and pupils at Tolgus County Secondary School, Redruth, Cornwall, sighted a '*silver cigar-shaped object, with short stubby wings*', moving backwards and forwards in the sky. Apparently, the same object was seen over the Culdrose area by other people, some of whom contacted the RAF and Police to report the matter.

28th November 1970 – 'Flying Saucer' over London

Richard Harris (20) of Theobalds Way, London, was walking home from his girlfriend's house, at 11.20pm.

> "*I noticed a 'light' in the sky, orange in colour, dropping down at terrific speed. Suddenly it stopped dead, about 300 yards off the ground, and hovered there silently. As the 'light' began to dim, I was able to make out a silver-grey saucer-shaped object, displaying red, green, and blue lights within the glow. It was roughly 50-60 feet across and 25 feet high. I was astonished when 5-6 minutes later, it vanished from sight.*"

Richard claimed that his watch stopped during the time of the incident, and was later interviewed by Ron West.

30th November 1970 – Orange 'light' seen over Dorset

In Dorset, at 6pm, an orange 'light' was seen moving eastward in the sky, at over a hundred miles per hour, by local resident – Phyllis Wallace from 34, Grove Road, Wimborne, who was with her son – Gordon (15) and friend Garry Tilley – possibly the same UFO sighted by Anthony Watson and his daughter from New Milton, Hampshire, who spoke of seeing an object resembling a street lamp, stationary in the sky over Wimborne, before it headed away eastwards in a series of peculiar stop and start movements.

(**Source:** Leslie Harris/*FSR Case Histories*, Supplement 5, June 1971)

DECEMBER 1970

1st December 1970 – Brilliant flashes light up the sky

At 6.20pm, a number of mysterious brilliant flashes lit up the night sky over Whitwick, Leicestershire, according to Philip Bradley and his sister, Elaine, occurring at four second intervals over a period of several minutes. At the time of the sighting, there was low scattered cloud, at a height of 2,500 feet, with high scattered cloud at 4,000 feet. Other witnesses included Mrs Patricia Lowe, of Whitwick.

(**Source:** Isle of Wight UFO Society/Geoffrey Coxon, BUFORA)

6th December 1970 – Motorist encounters UFO over Warwickshire

Eric Harrison and Frank Newbold from Coventry, Warwickshire, were on their way to Northampton, travelling along the A45, when they noticed a 'bright light' over the car factory to their right.

Eric:

> *"As we passed the factory, we were surprised to see the 'light' above our car, apparently keeping pace with us. After a couple of minutes, it moved back to its original position over the factory, before once again, appearing in front of our car. The next thing that happened is that it shot upwards into the sky, in a blur of speed, and was lost from view. You could just about see it as a tiny dot in the night sky. We continued on our journey, very excited by what had happened. To our astonishment it appeared again once more, hovering over the factory, before passing overhead and dropping down behind some trees on our left – still visible, a few feet off the ground. As we approached Dunchurch Island, near the M45, we were understandably agitated when the 'light' appeared in front of the car, illuminating trees at the side of the road. I decided to stop the car. A couple of minutes later, whatever it was shot upwards into the sky, at an angle, and disappeared – never to be seen again."*

(**Source:** Personal interview/*Didcot Advertiser*, 10.12.1970)

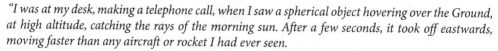

Many miles away at Billingham, Teesside, Helen Baum (18), was visiting friends at Hepburn, when she and her boyfriend – Alan Brown, saw *"a four-sided shape, with three brilliant lights and a larger orange light in its centre"*, hovering over the town, the same evening?

8th December 1970 – UFO hovers over football ground

The Molineux Football Ground – home of the famous *'Wolverhampton Wanderers'* – proved to be the source of a different kind of interest on this date, according to Brian Banks of Windmill Lane, Whitewick – then working a short distance away from the Stadium

> *"I was at my desk, making a telephone call, when I saw a spherical object hovering over the Ground, at high altitude, catching the rays of the morning sun. After a few seconds, it took off eastwards, moving faster than any aircraft or rocket I had ever seen.*
>
> *Why it chose that location, and what it was doing, I have no idea."* (**Source:** Personal interview/UFOLOG)

8th December 1970 – Landed UFO seen by motorist in Berkshire

At 1.30pm the same day, a motorist was driving his Morris van near Brightwalton, Berkshire, up a hill on an unnamed road, when he was shocked to see through the car windscreen, a disc-shaped object with a surface resembling aluminium on the ground, some distance away.

> "It was about half a mile away. I estimated it to be 15-20 feet in diameter. I could see what looked like portholes around the surface, and some sort of telescopic device on each side. There seemed to be some sort of door in it towards the bottom. It took off five seconds later – like a rocket, upwards into the sky, making a high-pitched whistle – leaving a black vapour trail, and was soon out of sight.
>
> I reported it to the Wantage Police."

The witness, who declined to be named, said he had returned to the scene of the incident later, with a friend, and that they found a number of small holes in the ground. Frustratingly, the location is not identified. The incident was also reported to Mr Bennett, of the BUFORA organisation.

Tadpole shaped UFO seen

Mrs Joy Rowe was another resident of the same town to sight something strange – this time at 9pm, one evening in 1970.

> "1 saw a tadpole-shaped 'thing'. It came whizzing across the sky and stopped dead over the house, before moving onwards.
>
> A short time later, while still trying to settle my nerves, my two daughters – who had been out exercising their horse, over Penn Common – ran into the house, very frightened. After calming them down, I was shocked to discover they had seen what they referred to as a 'flying tadpole', with windows, or portholes along its side, flying over the Common. This meant they must have seen it lower than me, as I can't remember seeing any detail on it."

(**Source: Personal interview/***Express & Star,* **date not known**)

12th December 1970 – Strange 'light' in the sky over Coventry

At 7.25am, Mr C. Carnell of Holbrook, Coventry, was going through the gates of the Standard factory, when he saw a strange light in the sky.

> "There was an aeroplane leaving a vapour trail, but this other 'light' was too low for an aircraft and much too fast to be one." (**Source: *SYNTONIC,* Jan/Feb. 1972**)

14th December 1970 – Not UFOs this time over an Atomic Power Station!

A spate of mysterious 'glowing lights' were seen in the sky over Wantage, Berkshire. Through binoculars, 'five globes of light' were seen in the sky over Harwell Nuclear Power Station, Didcot, attracting the attention of local newspapers. Local Parish Councillor – Mrs Gwyneth Wall – decided to conduct her own investigation, suspecting this to be the work of hoaxers, after having seen for herself a strange 'yellow light' passing over the Atomic Energy Authority housing estate, where she lived at the time:

> "I discovered a group of employees from a firm of Architects, in Wantage, had been responsible by inflating plastic cleaning bags, attaching them to metal frameworks, and igniting cotton wool soaked in methylated spirits, before launching them into the air."

...an explanation we accepted as valid, after having spoken to some of the youths concerned.

(**Source: *Evening Advertiser,* 18.12.1970 – 'More UFOs, Mystery lights buzz Harwell A-Plant'/Personal interviews**)

Sometimes of course, explanations can be found for strange objects seen moving about in the sky. A couple of years ago this was seen over Alvechurch Worcestershire. Further scrutiny revealed it to be a large fish-shaped balloon which we presume had come adrift from its moorings!

CHAPTER 2 – 1971

INFORMATION – OBTAINED FROM ORIGINAL SOURCES

JANUARY

1st January 1971 – Cigar-shaped UFO sighted over Wales

2nd January 1971 – Fluttering UFO over Shropshire

8th January 1971 – 'Bowl' shaped UFO over Scotland

10th January –Blood red UFO over Cheshire

12th January 1971 – Spinning UFO over Essex

21st January 1971 – Close encounter with UFO over Maryland, USA

22nd January 1971 – Three orange 'globes of light' sighted over Devon

28th January 1971 – Two 'bright lights' over Kent

FEBRUARY

2nd February 1971- Orange UFO over Aldershot

17th February 1971 – UFOs over Northamptonshire

18th February 1971 – Police Officers sight UFOs while on patrol

22nd February 1971 – UFO over London

23rd February 1971 – Ex-Police officer sights UFO over the Midlands

24th February 1971 – Coventry Police Officers sight UFOs

MARCH

2nd March 1971 – UFOs over Dorking

12th March 1971 –spinning UFO sighted

13th March 1971 – Yellow 'blob' over Surrey

15th March 1971 – UFO showing three lights seen over Dorking, Surrey

23rd March 1971 – 'Turnip' shaped UFO over Surrey

25th March 1971 – 'Flying Cross' frightens girls, Greater Manchester

26th March 1971 – 'Diamond' UFO over Coventry

27th March 1971 – UFO over Dorking, Surrey

28th March 1971 – Blue-green 'light' seen over Ford Works, Dagenham

APRIL

Early April 1971 – London Gliding Club pilot sights UFO

April 1971 – Motorist encounters strange 'figures', Cornwall

MAY

2nd May 1971 – UFO over Croydon

6th May 1971 – UFO landing, followed by crop marks found and a strange rash

10th May 1971 – 'Flying Saucer' over County Durham

14th May 1971 – Report of landed UFO?

22nd May 1971 – UFO display, Surrey

25th May 1971 – UFO over Leicestershire

25th May 1971 –Strange lights over Surrey

26th May 1971 – Triangular UFO over Manchester

31st May 1971 – UFO over Lancashire

JUNE

June 1971 – Spinning UFO – Did RAF jets respond?

15th June 1971 – Three star-like objects seen over Dorset

28th June 1971 – Strange 'light' over Essex

Triangular UFO over Loch Ness

JULY

9th July 1971 – UFO over Bournemouth, Early 1970s UFO over Leicester

15th July 1971 – UFO photographed over Poole

17th July 1971 – UFO over Hull

22nd July 1971 – UFO over Clacton seafront, Essex

23rd July 1971 – Fan-shaped UFO seen

25th July 1971 – 'Flying Cones' and 'Triangle' reported in the sky

29th July 1971 – Followed by a UFO

30th July 1971 – UFO over Leamington Spa

31st July 1971 – 'Spinning top' UFO seen over Dorset

July 1971 – RAF chase UFO over Warminster

1971 – UFOs tracked on Radar

1971 – RAF tracked 35 UFOs on radar – warned to keep quiet

AUGUST

1st August 1971 – Orange 'light' over Hereford

4th August 1971 – Object, showing three circles, seen over Stafford

8th August 1971 – 'Falling star' over Leicester

12th August 1971 – UFO over Worcestershire

15th August 1971 – UFOs over Lancashire

15th August 1971 – UFO over Tynemouth

16th August 1971 – Police Officer sights UFO over Staffordshire

16th August 1971 – Five sided object seen in the sky … Two RAF Jet fighters respond

16th August 1971 – Five-sided object seen in the sky over Leicester

16th August 1971 – Bright orange 'ball' seen over London

16th August 1971 – Cigar-shaped UFO

16th August 1971 – 'Golf ball' UFO, with five sides, seen

17th August 1971 – Flashing lights over Small Heath, Birmingham

18th August 1971 – Spectacular UFO sighting Newcastle

18th August 1971 – 'Things' in the sky over Gloucestershire

19th August 1971 – Red 'star' over Lincoln

20th August 1971 – Yellow 'light' over Northfield

24th August 1971 – Vertical shaped UFO over Staffordshire

25th August 1971 – UFO display, Bedfordshire

26th August 1971 – Bright golden light over Lincolnshire

27th August 1971 – UFO landing, Kent, UFO landing Norfolk

28th August 1971 – 'Flying Saucer' over Colchester Essex

28th August 1971 – Yellow globe reported over Solihull, West Midlands

30th August 1971 – Orange light phenomena …did this cause a power cut?

31st August 1971 – UFO seen to take off over Rutland

SEPTEMBER

1st September 1971 – UFO sightings over the West Midlands

2nd September 1971 – 'L'-shaped UFO seen in the sky over Staffordshire

3rd September 1971 – Strange UFO over Leicester

5thSeptember 1971 – Square-shaped formation and saucer-shaped objects reported

7th September 1971 – Phenomena explained

8th September 1971 – Strange 'light' in the sky over Colwyn Bay

8th September 1971 – 'Flying Saucer' sighted over Clee Hill Radar Station, Shropshire (Grid reference 3528)

10th September 1971 – UFO over Romford, Essex

7th-14th September 1971 – Reports of a 'T'-bag ghost sighted!

15th September 1971 – UFO over South west London

24th-25th September 1971 – Sightings of a 'Monster' in Berkshire

27th September 1971 – Claim of UFO, with occupants, seen at RAF Base

28th September 1971 – Cigar-shaped object over Banbury

30th September 1971 – 'Creature' seen outside the family home

Winter 1971 – 'Flying Saucer' lands in a field near Honiton, Devon

Winter 1971 – Landed UFO leaves three scorch marks in the grass

OCTOBER

1st October 1971 – Cigar-shaped haze, with three lights in it, over Essex

10th October 1971 – Seen over Oxfordshire

11th October 1971 – Police sight cigar-shaped UFO

18th October 1971 – Strange 'light' and then ear-piercing noise over Banbury

19th October 1971 – UFO display over the M3 Motorway

20th October 1971 – UFO landing, Northampton

23rd October 1971 – UFO over Portsmouth

October 1971 – UFO over Bolton

21st October 1971 – Yellow pulsing 'light' over Banbury

26th October 1971 – Banbury again!

27th October 1971 – UFO over Banbury

27th October 1971 – Curious Phenomenon sighted over Oxfordshire

30th October 1971 – UFO flies around a bus

October 1971 – UFO over Bolton

NOVEMBER

2nd November 1971 – UFO over Loch Ness, Scotland

2nd November 1971 – Delphos 'ring', Kansas

10th November 1971 – Red objects over Suffolk

13th November 1971 – UFOs over Stockfield-on-Tyne

16th November 1971 – Schoolboys sight UFO over Stourbridge, West Midlands

21st November 1971 – 'Flying Saucer' over Worcestershire

21st November 1971 – UFO display, Derbyshire

DECEMBER

4th December 1971 – Silver 'disc' sighted over Banbury, Oxfordshire

7th December 1971 – UFO over Derbyshire

11th December 1971 – Orange 'disc' over Stoke-on-Trent

12th December 1971 – Elliptical object over Lowestoft

18th December 1971 – Silver UFOs over Oxfordshire

19th December 1971 – UFO over Kent

23rd December 1971 – UFO over Hampshire

25th December 1971 – Flaming objects over St. Albans, Hertfordshire

31st December 1971 – UFO encounter, Lincolnshire

JANUARY 1971

1st January 1971 – Cigar-shaped UFO sighted over Wales

A cigar-shaped object was seen flying through the sky over Hafodrynys, by Newport mini bus driver – Mrs Pamela Morrison, who attempted to give chase but lost it at Griffithstown.

(**Source:** *UFOLOG, Issue 82, May 1971/South Wales Argus*)

2nd January 1971 – Fluttering UFO over Shropshire

At 4.15pm, farm worker Gerald Redman from Corfton, Bridgnorth, sighted

> *"... a bright orange-red object, with a black smoke trail, seen fluttering from side-to-side, falling through the sky, reminding me of a lighted newspaper. It stopped burning just before it struck the ground."*

Farmer Ken Edwards also witnessed the incident and corroborated what Gerald had seen. His son, Colin, went out, the next day, to have a look around, but found nothing untoward. Enquiries made at RAF Shawbury, Cosford, and Tern Hill, could find no explanation for what was seen.

(**Source:** *Bridgnorth Journal, 8.1.1971*)

8th January 1971 – 'Bowl' shaped UFO over Scotland

At 3am, Dumfries housewife – Elizabeth Bunn, who suffers from insomnia, got out of bed and was walking around the room, when she glanced out of the bedroom window and saw what appeared to be a particularly bright star high in the northern sky.

> *"I stood looking at the 'star' and then realised it was approaching Dumfries, apparently at great speed, 'pushing aside' the clouds as it sped through the air – like the bow wave of a boat."*

As the object reached what appeared to be a predetermined location in the sky, at a distance and height which Elizabeth was unable to estimate, she saw an object:

> *".... resembling, a pure white bowl. It was surmounted by a very bright light. It remained stationary for a spell and then began to move slowly to and fro, for ten minutes – then it took off and, in a matter of seconds, disappeared from view."* A Ministry of Defence spokesman at Ayr said, in response to the sighting:
>
> We have had no 'flying saucers' in the Dumfriesshire area, this morning; any reports we get usually come from the police." (**Source:** *Dumfries and Galloway Standard, 9.1.1971*)

Mrs Marie Wilcox (38), of Orby, Skegness – a radio assembly worker by trade – was travelling to work at 8.30am, near Burgh-le-Marsh, Lincolnshire, when she and her companion – Mrs E. Galyer, saw a round to oval, silver-white light, moving across the sky westwards, emitting sparks of alternate silver and red. They kept it in sight for two to three minutes – then it was gone. (**Source** *UFOLOG*)

10th January 1971 – Blood-red UFO over Cheshire

At 6pm, a sharply defined blood-red object was seen over Winsford Industrial Estate by local men – Roy Everall (28), and his friend Bryan Bishop – moving at an approximate height of 20,000 feet. Suddenly, the object dropped down to about 8,000 feet and settled over Bostock woods, for ten minutes, until rising to the same height in a second of movement. (**Source Mr G. Clegg, BUFORA**)

12th January 1971 -Spinning UFO over Essex

During the afternoon, *"a round, bright object, spinning on its axis"*, was seen by Karen Tomlinson and Jeanette L. Carpenter (9) and other schoolchildren, while out playing at Yardley Primary School, North Chingford, before disappearing into cloud, several minutes later. Another witness was Jasmin Brown

(**Source:** *Chingford Guardian, 15.1.1971/UFOLOG*)

21st January 1971 – Close encounter with UFO over Maryland, USA

Between 7.30pm and 8pm, Mr Elvis Arnold (20), and his wife Sharon and her sister Lynn Holding (16), were driving north on Oldfield Point Road, about three miles south of Elkton, Maryland. Mr Arnold sighted a 'light' in the sky and joked *"There's a flying saucer"*. They were stunned when the object moved to the left of them and appeared to halt over trees. Mr Arnold instructed his wife to stop the car; as she did so the object veered away in the direction of Elkton, heading westwards over Route 40. The family decided to give chase and then saw another object in the northern sky, which met up with the first one over a farmer's field.

After a minute or two the second one flew away towards Elkton and was out of sight. The first UFO came back towards the car, crossed over the road just ahead of them, and halted over a farmer's field 60 yards away. The couple switched off the lights and engine, and Mr Arnold got out, by which time it was at 70 degrees to the horizontal, allowing him to see:

> *"…something the size of a Piper Cub – dull in colour, grey not shiny, shaped like an aircraft. It had a fuselage and slight swept-back wings placed in normal airplane position, except it had no tail assembly. At the front end was a very large and very bright white searchlight where the nose of an airplane would be. On the underneath was a circle or cluster of lights, the outer one being plain white, with flashing red lights in the middle. The latter blinked constantly and increased the pulsing as the object moved or picked up speed. I heard a sound like the hum of a muffled generator. When it changed direction it merely pivoted rather than banking as an aircraft would do."*

The entire sighting lasted between 15-20 minutes. Shortly afterwards it flew off towards the direction of Elkton, circled the area before heading south-east, and disappeared from sight. (**Source:** *APRO Bulletin*)

21st January 1971 – UFO sighted over Essex

22nd January 1971 – Three orange 'globes of light' sighted over Devon

During the late evening, David Jeffrey was one of three employees of the Devon General Bus Company, who were towing a bus from Budleigh to Exmouth, when:

> *"We all sighted three orange 'balls of light', moving in a straight line across the sky. There was a lot of smoke around them and they disappeared after a few seconds."*

(**Source:** *Western Morning News*)

28th January 1971 – Two bright lights over Kent

At 6.30pm, Mr A. Abell of St .Mary Cray sighted *"two steady bright lights"*, low on the horizon over Sidcup, Kent, drifting westwards. (**Source:** *Orpington & Kentish Times*, **12.2.1971**)

FEBRUARY 1971

2nd February 1971 – Orange UFO over Aldershot

Mrs and Mrs A. Thurston (then aged 62) of Kingsway, Aldershot, Hampshire, had turned into Ayling Hill, from Church Lane West, at 6.30pm, when Mrs Thurston saw:

> *"...a round, orange coloured object in the sky, perfectly still, not quite as big as the full moon, some 30 degrees altitude. After a few minutes it began to descend slowly. By that time our observation was impaired by the houses."*

(**Source: Mr Toft, BUFORA/***Aldershot News*)

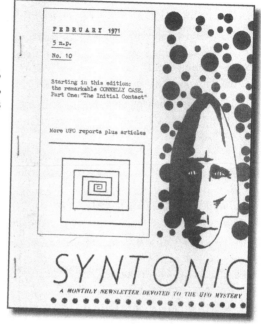

17th February 1971 – UFOs over Northamptonshire

An unnamed motorist went into Wolverton Police Station, just before midnight, and reported having seen a landed UFO in a field, described as *"a large, round object, surrounded by red lights, with an amber flashing light on top"*, which moved off across fields beside the Grafton Regis to Old Stratford road, Northamptonshire, a few minutes earlier. The police, who thought the witness was a genuine man, sent a police car from Towcester Police Station to the location, but after finding no trace of the UFO, wrote the following report: *'Orbited A5 area in Apollo 15 – found nothing. Smooth re- entry'.*

(**Source: Isle of Wight UFO Society/***Buckinghamshire Standard*, **19.2.1971**)

18th February 1971 – Police Officers sight UFOs while on patrol

At 7.20pm, a fiery object was seen rushing across the sky in Leicestershire and Warwickshire, described as looking like an oblong, green flare. At Rugby, two separate sightings told of:

> *"...a silvery egg-shaped object, surrounded by a green haze, ejecting a short jet of flame from its rear, before disappearing over roof- tops."*

Was this the same phenomenon, witnessed by two Police Officers whilst driving between Stratford and Alcester Road, at 7.30pm, described initially as a white object, changing in colour to blue, then red, as it sunk lower in the sky before disappearing over the direction of Bidford-on-Avon?

At 7.30pm Mrs O Hodgson of Combe Lodge , West Alvington sighted a '"Flaming glow, which merged into green leaving a long vapour trail heading towards the direction of Thurleston ,then lost as it merged into clouds over the sea.

At 8.30 pm, the same officers were directed to a report of *"a round, blue/pink, flying object"*, seen to land in a field at the rear of the *Griffin Inn* Public House, a mile outside Studley, by a motorist travelling along the B4099. A search by the officers failed to find anything of significance.

Mr Howard G. Miles, of the British Astronomical Society, confirmed he had received many sightings of the object as it sped downwards from Blackpool to Kent, and concluded it had crossed the central regions of England, and then passed over the Bristol Channel, before possibly falling into the Irish Sea.

(Source: John 'Dennis' Llewellyn/Derek Samson, NICAP GB.)

22nd February 1971 – UFO over London

At 4am, several strange noises were reported in the sky over Thamesmead, south of London, by a number of people – including Mrs Jackie Fillery of Lensbury Way, who heard a buzzing sound, which went on for over an hour. At 5.10 am, she arose to feed the baby. Looking through the window, she saw a red glow over the flats, opposite, surrounding what looked like:

> "…a dark-grey bowler hat in the sky, with a flattened top; it then tilted from side-to-side and slowly descended behind the flat, opposite. Ten seconds later, the red glow faded away. It was a frightening experience."

Another man living in Pegwell St, Plumstead awoke at 4am after being disturbed by a strange continuous hum high in pitch towards the east.

> "This lasted for about 20minutes…Five minutes later it came back, the noise reminded me of the 'Thunderbird 2 as shown in the Gerry Anderson's TV series. Strangely no body else in the family was awoken."

Enquiries made with the police, at Erith, revealed nobody else had reported having sighted a UFO to them, although Mr and Mrs R. Wilton, from Plumstead, heard what sounded like *"a squadron of aircraft droning across the sky to the north-east, between 4 and 5am"*

Was there any connection with the presence of the nearby Lesnes Abbey Woods, Plumstead Common, and Bostall Woods – the scene of other alleged UFO encounters, over the years?

(Source: Mark Stenhoff & David Oakley, Society for the Investigation and Research into UFOs, No. 3, 'February flap in south-east London'/*Kentish Independent Newspaper*, 25. 2.1971/4.3.1971)

Grace Wilton

At 7pm, Mr Frederick Munns – a retired newsagent living in Sidcup Road, in New Eltham, was sat in his chair facing south-west, when he saw a small orange 'light' on the horizon over the Crystal Palace direction, some 8 miles away.

> "It then increased in size – now appearing as a lozenge-shape, with two very bright orange glows or plumes beneath it. I wondered if it was an aircraft on fire. I called my wife and sister-in-law to come and have a look."

Mrs Munns described seeing a bright horizontal 'bar' of orange light; Mrs Moseley saw the object's vague outline, but with two orange glows. It then became narrower, a couple of minutes later, as if turning, and then appear to come straight towards them, before once more becoming broader – and lost, as it went behind cloud. It then emerged and shot off rapidly in a western direction, straight down the Sidcup Bypass.

Interestingly, Mr Munns, who served in the Observer Corps during the Second World War, recalled seeing a similar object back in the spring of 1946, from Wrotham Hill, in Kent. The object was a few miles away in the sky, over Otford. By the time the car he was in pulled up, the object had gone.

Frederick Munns

23rd February 1971 – Ex-Police Officer sights UFO over the Midlands

At 6.20am, ex-Police Officer Clarence Gilbert of Coundon, Coventry, was looking out of his window, when he saw a 'brilliant light' travelling north to south, which halted in mid-air, for a short time, before continuing its journey across the sky.

24th February 1971 – Coventry Police Officers sight UFOs

Police Constables Graham Edwards, John Crutchlow, and Brian Hewitt, were on patrol at 6.15am, the following day (24th February 1971), in the Lythalls Lane area of Coventry, when they sighted three single 'bright lights' heading westwards, towards the direction of Birmingham.

Brian, now a retired Chief Inspector, (known to John Hanson) had this to say:

> *"It is still very vivid in my memory. The lights appeared in an 'L'-shaped formation, very clean and sharply defined, as they passed overhead at an incredible speed. I haven't a clue what they could have been. I don't believe in 'flying saucers', or anything like that.*
>
> *I can only say what we saw. When I contacted Air Traffic Control, at Birmingham Airport, they informed me the first plane to land had been at 7am. According to their Radar Logs, no aircraft had been plotted in the same locality where we saw the UFOs."*

The officers were not the only ones to see the objects. A night worker, in Coventry, watched them pass overhead.

Four objects over Clent Hill

At 8.50pm, the same day, four orange and red objects were seen in the sky over Clent Hills, Worcestershire, by housewife – Janet Haywood – who described seeing them as:

> *"... flying in an erratic manner for over two hours, often merging into each other, occasionally forming an orange 'cross' in the sky."*

(Source: Personal interview/*Evening Tribune*, 24.2.1971, 26/2/1971/Mr G. Coxon)

MARCH 1971

2nd March 1971 – UFOs over Dorking

Dorking resident – Mr C. Lecluse (59) of Lusteds Close, Goodwyns, was sat in front of his fire, at 7.50pm, when he noticed:

> *"...a blue-green light, the shape of a large carrot, surrounded by a glowing aura; inside was a large blood-red 'ball' which twisted and turned, shooting off sparks, at a terrific rate."*

He called his wife and they watched the object – apparently burning, or on fire – as it headed across the sky, westwards. Suddenly, it vanished from sight before dropping down over the horizon.

(Source: *UFOLOG/BUFORA/SIGAP*)

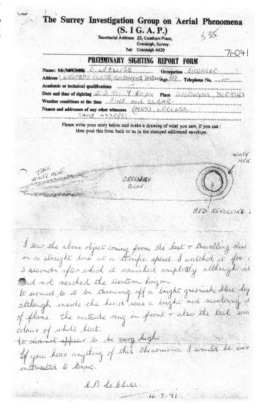

12th March 1971 –spinning UFO sighted

The *Hereford Times* (12.3.1971) reported that they had been contacted by Ronald Sterry, of Little Woodend Farm, at Linton, Herefordshire. He was driving into his farmyard, just before 8pm, when he saw

> "... *a thing coming across the horizon, not very high off the ground. It seemed to be spinning and was giving off a dull greenish-yellow light; it looked as if it was going to land.*
>
> *I switched off the car engine but couldn't hear anything. I've seen falling stars and things before, but it wasn't one of those.*
>
> *I wish someone else could have been here to see it.*" (**Source: Mrs J. B. Delair**)

12th March 1971 – Orange 'cone' seen over the Birmingham area

At 10.45pm, an orange 'cone' was seen in the sky over Great Barr, Birmingham, by local resident – Julie Evans, who told of watching it slowly moving downwards, towards the north-north-east direction, before appearing to disintegrate in the sky. (**Source:** *UFOSIS/Birmingham Mail,* **13.3.1971**)

13th March 1971 – Yellow 'blob' over Surrey

The activity continued over Dorking, with a report from Miss R. Cousins of Norbury Park, Dorking, Surrey, happened to look out of her bathroom window, at 7am, and saw:

> "...*a large square 'blob' of yellow light, hanging in the sky. Its outline was blurred, and the light was brighter in a beam towards the centre. I called my friend, but before she could come up to have a look it had gone.*" (**Source: Dorking Investigators**)

15th March 1971 – UFO showing three lights seen over Dorking, Surrey

A number of people living in the Dorking area contacted the authorities, after sighting *"a slightly curved object, showing three white lights"* in the sky.

The first report came from motorist Judith Anne Grunsell (34) of Broad Lane, Newdigate, Surrey, and her companion. At 7.50pm, she was driving her Volkswagen 1200 at 30-40 miles per hour, along the Dorking bypass from Reigate Road, heading towards Leatherhead, on a dry, clear evening, with very little traffic about, when they saw:

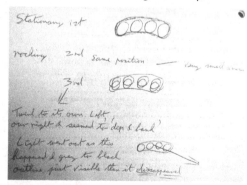

> "...*three lights in a slight 'banana curve' in the sky, as we passed Pippbrook Garage. As we approached the Friends Provident Building Society, they appeared to quiver – then extinguished, leaving a faint grey shape, which disappeared from sight. I have always been sceptical about 'flying saucers' and UFOs, but seeing them left a weird uncanny*

from drawing by witness.

from Dorking Investigators of UFO's

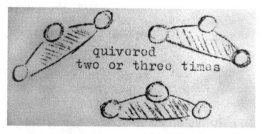

quivered two or three times

feeling that it was no aircraft. It did not become smaller as a plane would do when moving away into the distance. Between the lights was a dark grey mass."

The passenger said:

"It was about 250 feet up in the sky, hovering – a banana shape with four very close together lights, large as car headlights, not quite joined up. It stayed there quivering, for some time. A couple of minutes later, it banked away towards the direction of Dorking North Station. The lights then extinguished, leaving a black silhouette in the sky – then it just vanished from view."

Dome-shaped UFO over St. Martin's Church, Dorking

At about the same time, a brilliantly lit dome-shaped object, illuminating the ground below, was seen over St. Martin's Church, Dorking, by Gillian Mary Cheesman (27), who was visiting St. Paul's School.

Initially, she thought it to be a weather balloon – an explanation soon rejected, after it was seen to move over the Council Estate of St. Paul's, heading eastwards.

"The lights then went out, allowing me to see two small red lights on the top of the object."

Triangular UFO sighted at Dorking

At 10.10pm, a motorist and his family were driving through Buckland, between Reigate and Dorking, on the A 25, when they noticed a 'bright light' in the sky. The man stopped, a short distance further along the road, and heard a noise like an aircraft but much quieter. As it passed overhead, they saw what looked like *"a 'Vulcan' Bomber in shape, showing a light at each corner of the 'triangle'."* Seconds later it disappeared, leaving two lights on the 'tail section', which also went out, leaving the daughter very distressed.

(Source: *UFOLOG*, Isle of Wight UFO Society, Kath Smith)

23rd March 1971- 'Turnip' shaped UFO over Surrey

The activity continued with a report of *"a whiter than white 'turnip' shaped coloured object"*, seen motionless in the sky over Dorking, at 7.20am, by Mr Patrick O'Brian and Fred Staunton. After a minute, the object – showing what looked like a snub nosed exhaust pipe from its base – headed off towards the direction of Gatwick. According to Mr Staunton:

"It was unlike anything I had ever seen before in my 53 years of life on this planet."

(Source: Dorking Investigation of UFOs, Mr F.A. Woodcock/*UFOLOG/BUFORA Journal*, Volume 3, No. 5, Winter 1971/2)

25th March 1971 – 'Flying Cross' frightens girls in Greater Manchester

A luminous cross-shaped object, with sparks ejecting from it, suddenly appeared in the sky over Windmill Lane, Denton, in front of two girls who were out exercising their ponies, causing the animals to rear in fright. According to one of the girls:

"The first time it seemed a long way off. It then it disappeared for a second, but reappeared about a hundred feet up in the sky, and began to follow us towards the road. There was a loud bang and it disappeared for good." **(Source: *Denton Reporter*)**

26th March 1971 – 'Diamond' UFO over Coventry

At 2am, Joyce and Michael Piff from Coundon, Coventry, were awoken from sleep by a brilliant flash of blue light. Wondering what was going on, they rushed to the window in time to see the spectacular sight of between 30-50 yellow diamond-shaped objects, rushing across the sky. This was followed by two further flashes of blue light, as they dropped below the horizon.

Peter Jones (18) of Richard Road, Leytonstone was outside his house, at 9.45pm, when he heard a screeching noise. He looked up and saw:

"...a four-sided object flying along through the air, changing colour from red to white as it did so. I estimated it was 800 feet up, and moving at 120 miles per hour, heading westwards. It suddenly speeded up and was gone."

Another witness was Robert Chandler of St. Mary's Road, London E10.

(Source: Bob Tibbitts, CUFORG/*Syntonic*, May 1971, No. 12/BUFORA)

27th March 1971 – UFO over Dorking, Surrey

A mysterious object was seen circling the sky at 9.40pm, over Dorking, Surrey, by Janet Coskery (14) of Vincent Road, Dorking. Janet was with Peter and Brian Jenkins, Graham Christian, Andrew Jordan and Robert le Fuerre, crossing Coldharbour Lane, at the time, when the strange flashing light was seen heading in a SSW to NNE direction.

"It appeared to have taken off from Old Bury Hill Lake. We telephoned the police and then told our parents." **(Source: BUFORA)**

28th March 1971 – Blue-green 'light' seen over Ford Works, Dagenham

At 10pm, James Farr (52) of Marleigh Avenue, Rainham, Essex, was out walking with his wife past the Ford Works, in Dagenham, when they sighted:

"...a blue-green 'light', motionless in the sky, at a height of about 10,000 feet. We kept it under observation for ten minutes, and then it moved at fantastic speed towards the north direction and stopped in mid-air again. My wife became frightened, so we went back into the house."

APRIL 1970

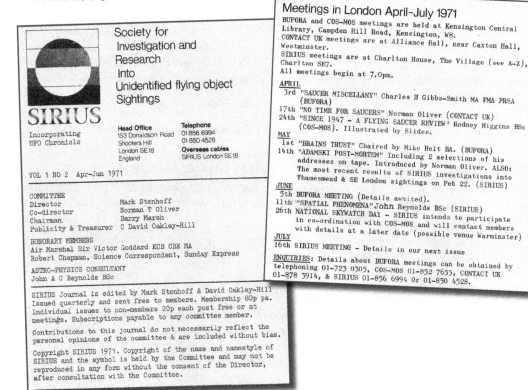

Society for
Investigation and
Research
Into
Unidentified flying object
Sightings

SIRIUS

Incorporating
UFO Chronicle

Head Office
153 Donaldson Road
Shooters Hill
London SE 18
England

Telephone
01 856 6994
01 850 4528

Overseas cables
SIRIUS London SE18

VOL 1 NO 2 Apr-Jun 1971

COMMITTEE
Director   Mark Stenhoff
Co-director   Norman T Oliver
Chairman   Barry Marsh
Publicity & Treasurer C David Oakley-Hill

HONORARY MEMBERS
Air Marshal Sir Victor Goddard KCB CBE MA
Robert Chapman, Science Correspondent, Sunday Express

ASTRO-PHYSICS CONSULTANT
John A C Reynolds BSc

SIRIUS Journal is edited by Mark Stenhoff & David Oakley-Hill
Issued quarterly and sent free to members. Membership 80p pa.
Individual issues to non-members 20p each post free or at
meetings. Subscriptions payable to any committee member.

Contributions to this journal do not necessarily reflect the
personal opinions of the committee & are included without bias.

Copyright SIRIUS 1971. Copyright of the name and namestyle of
SIRIUS and the symbol is held by the Committee and may not be
reproduced in any form without the consent of the Director,
after consultation with the Committee.

Meetings in London April-July 1971

BUFORA and COS-MOS meetings are held at Kensington Central
Library, Campden Hill Road, Kensington, W8.
CONTACT UK meetings are at Alliance Hall, near Caxton Hall,
Westminster.
SIRIUS meetings are at Charlton House, The Village (see A-Z),
Charlton SE7.
All meetings begin at 7.0pm.

APRIL
3rd "SAUCER MISCELLANY" Charles H Gibbs-Smith MA FMA FRSA
   (BUFORA)
17th "NO TIME FOR SAUCERS" Norman Oliver (CONTACT UK)
24th "SINCE 1947 - A FLYING SAUCER REVIEW" Rodney Higgins BSc
   (COS-MOS). Illustrated by Slides.

MAY
1st "BRAINS TRUST" Chaired by Mike Holt BA. (BUFORA)
14th "ADAMSKI POST-MORTEM" Including 2 selections of his
   addresses on tape. Introduced by Norman Oliver. ALSO:
   The most recent results of SIRIUS investigations into
   Thamesmead & SE London sightings on Feb 22. (SIRIUS)

JUNE
5th BUFORA MEETING (Details awaited).
11th "SPATIAL PHENOMENA" John Reynolds BSc (SIRIUS)
26th NATIONAL SKYWATCH DAY - SIRIUS intends to participate
   in co-ordination with COS-MOS and will contact members
   with details at a later date (possible venue Warminster)

JULY
16th SIRIUS MEETING - Details in our next issue

ENQUIRIES: Details about BUFORA meetings can be obtained by
telephoning 01-723 0305, COS-MOS 01-852 7653, CONTACT UK
01-878 3914, & SIRIUS 01-856 6994 Or 01-850 4528.

Early April 1971 – London Gliding Club pilot sights UFO

At 9.40pm, a greenish-blue illuminated object, estimated to be five times the size of any star, was seen heading eastwards, over Totternhoe, by Lesley Seymour – an experienced pilot with the London Gliding Club. According to Mr Seymour, the object was:

"...flying at a height of some 20,000 feet; it then halted in mid-air, showing a white diffused light on its underside. This extinguished and it recommenced its journey across the sky, but stopped once again when overhead, for a few seconds – then the light went off again and it accelerated away at speed. I estimated it to be moving at a speed of 25,000 miles per hour. It was about 40 feet in diameter and in sight for 20 seconds. It was like nothing I had ever seen before in my life and I know of nothing that can accelerate to that phenomenal speed."

(Source: *UFOLOG/Albert Davey, F.R.A.S., SHUFOIG Journal/BUFORA Journal*, Vol. 3, No. 5, winter 1971/2)

April 1971 – Motorist encounters strange 'figures', Cornwall

A Midlands woman – Judy Cadman – was driving home across Bodmin Moor, Cornwall, one early morning, with her boyfriend.

"We suddenly noticed, in the glare of the headlights, two very odd looking characters walking towards us, on the opposite side of the road. The first was dressed in what looked like a dark-green garment, covering him from head to toe, with slits where the eyes would be. The second was dressed in a similar manner but the garment was red, rather than green. After driving past, my boyfriend, (who had been asleep), awoke and asked me if I had just seen those queer looking people. To this day I don't know who, or what, it was that we saw, but I don't believe they were wearing fancy dress."

(Source: **Tony Bagley/Judy Cadman/Personal interview**)

MAY 1971

2nd May 1971 – UFO over Croydon

Mr Abdul Khan (then aged 35) was stood in his front porch at Addiscombe Grove, East Croydon, at 10pm, when he heard a whirring noise similar to a helicopter, but was puzzled by the intermittent bursts of noise rather than one continuous sound. He looked straight up and saw:

"...a dark brown ellipse shaped object, hovering between two houses on the other side of the road. After 20 seconds the sound ceased, and the object vanished from view without moving. I've no idea what it was. I can only tell you what I saw." (**Source Dan Goring**)

6th May 1971 – UFO landing, followed by crop marks found and a strange rash

Val Newman from Leigh Lane, Wimborne, Dorset, was sat talking to her mother, at 9.30pm, when they heard what sounded like the drum of a washing machine, speeding up and starting. Puzzled as to where the noise was coming from, they looked around but were unable to identify the source.

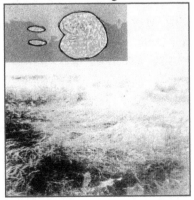

"About ten minutes later it started again, seeming to come from the back of the house. We went around checking all the electrical appliances, but found nothing untoward. I looked out of the window but couldn't see anything. I asked my husband if he had heard any strange noises. He replied in the negative and made some jocular remarks about 'little green men'.

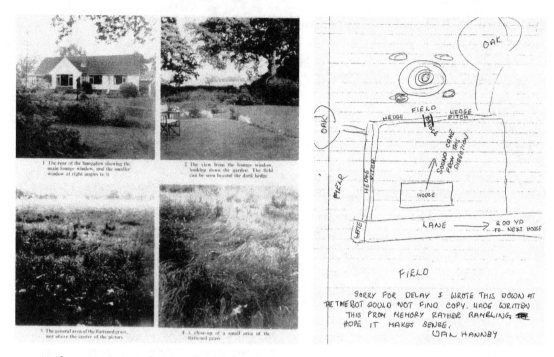

1 The rear of the bungalow showing the main lounge window, and the smaller window at right angles to it

2 The view from the lounge window, looking down the garden. The field can be seen beyond the dark hedge

3 The general area of the flattened grass, just above the centre of the picture

4 A close-up of a small area of the flattened grass

SORRY FOR DELAY I WROTE THIS DOWN AT THE TIME BOT COULD NOT FIND COPY. HADE WRITTEN THIS FROM MEMORY RATHER RAMBLING, HOPE IT MAKES SENSE.

VAL HANNBY

At about 10pm, I tried to put the dog, 'Sam', out. He refused, which was out of character. I tried pulling him, but he wouldn't go outside the back door."

The following morning, Val's mother (who was in the back garden), shouted out urgently for her daughter to 'come and have a look'. Val made her way to the end of the garden and saw, with her own eyes, an area of flattened grass in the adjacent field, forming a heart shape, with two smaller egg-shaped areas flattened close by, measuring 17 feet in length by 13 feet wide. The 'egg' shapes were 5 feet long and 2 feet wide at their widest point, 6 feet apart, and approximately 60 feet from the main heart-shaped area.

We spoke to Val and asked her if she had noticed anything unusual *after* the event.

"My mother complained of a rash appearing on her hands and wrists, which the doctors were unable to diagnose, although one of them suggested it may have been an allergic reaction to the washing powder – which was unlikely, as we had been using the same product for many years.

(Source: Personal interview/Leslie Harris/Val Newman, 1971)

10th May 1971 – 'Flying Saucer' over County Durham

At 8.15pm, Miss L. Linton of Dunston, in County Durham, happened to look out of the window and see a 'bright light' hovering above Dunston Power Station.

"It reminded me of the contrast between a pane of glass and a beautiful diamond – that's the only way I can explain it. The light hovered in a diagonal aspect for some minutes, and I could see smoky-grey spots appearing under the light. These gave the appearance of moving in a circle. Above the 'light' was an impression of a grey, round, dome; this was visible in the same way when the dark part of the moon is half lit. My mother, who had been watching it, exclaimed, 'It's going round!' (or spinning). As the light grew smaller, it straightened into a horizontal position and, in a few seconds, was just a small dot in the distance. A fighter aircraft – possibly a 'Lightning' Jet – swept into view from the north-west, just as the dot disappeared."

Miss Linton was sufficiently curious as to go to the local library, and then wrote to the Tyneside-based UFO organisation – *ORBIT* – but, after discovering they had ceased publication, then contacted *Flying Saucer Review* and wrote a letter to them about what she had seen.

(Source: *FSR Case Histories,* **Supplement 6, August 1971**)

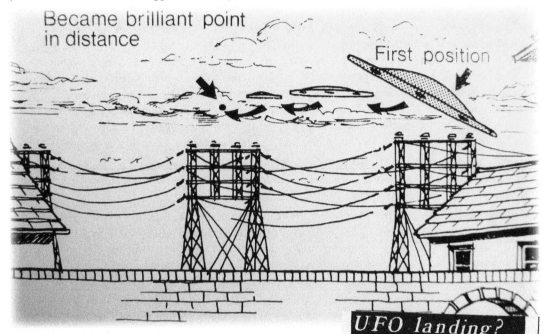

14th May 1971 – report of landed UFO?

22nd May 1971 – UFO display, Surrey

At 11pm, William Barnes, of Dorking, was walking home from Dorking fair, when he sighted two white 'lights' in the sky. He watched them for about 30 seconds, until they disappeared behind cloud. About a minute later, another object appeared in the north-east part of the sky, south of where the first two had been seen.

> "Over the next five to six minutes I saw up to six of these objects at once, cloud sometimes blocking my view completely, and though they intermittently hovered or moved slowly northwards, they did not change their altitude. On two occasions, two of the objects made a curious 'fusing' movement, meeting and seeming to join for a few seconds in the middle, before returning to their positions. Twice, one of them projected a beam of light across the sky. At this stage two friends came up and we watched together. At one stage there were a total of seven bright objects, seen stretching across the sky in a straight line, moving in and out of cloud."

(Source: Dorking Investigation of UFOs)

UFO landing?

I have just come home from a six-day holiday in which I popped across to Affpuddle in Dorset. This is about a mile south of the Bere Regis-Dorchester main road, and was the site of a reputed landing. The evidence was:

a) A light seen for three nights running- on the ground – in the middle of the night.
b) Radiation within a precise area.
c) Loss of grass
d) Area found to have been subject to heat.

The Bristol 'Contact' group investigated the landing site with great care and much thoroughness, but would not give away its exact location. I am pretty certain I know where it is, and was most interested in what I saw, a full half circle of what looked like a vehicle track, only with this difference: the heather was not growing over the 6" x 8" wide track, a good 130' or so round the half circle.

– REV H.D.L. THOMAS

25th May 1971 – UFO over Leicestershire

"…Just talking about it makes the hairs on the back of my neck feel as if they are standing on end"

…was how Eunice Rose described her feelings, when talking to us about what she witnessed, over thirty years ago, while driving home to Hinckley, Leicestershire, along the A.30, at 10.45pm.

"It had stopped raining and I was about half-a-mile away from the Belcher's Bar Junction when I noticed a large glowing light through the windscreen of my A.35 car that I took to be the headlights of an oncoming lorry. After nothing happened, I continued on my journey and turned right at the junction, heading along the A.447, towards Hinckley. At this point I noticed the radio began to fade and the headlights were dimming, with the engine running very roughly. The car came to a halt just past the junction to Nailstone Grange. I looked out of the window and saw a saucer-shaped light to my left, moving over nearby fields, about 20 yards away – strong enough to illuminate the interior of the car. After whatever 'it' was had moved out of sight, I started up the car and drove home."

The following day, Eunice contacted the couple whom she had been visiting. Imagine her surprise to discover that their son, Terry (aged 10), had reported seeing what he took to be the lights of a car arriving at the house, *but no car ever arrived.*

She then contacted the *Leicester Mercury* to report the matter. After publication of the incident, a day later, she received a letter from Stephen Freary (13), who told her that while travelling along Coventry Road, Hinckley, with his father, at 10.45pm on 25th May, he had seen *"an orange 'light', surrounded by a halo"*, moving across the sky, towards the direction of the Electricity Board building.

At 11.30pm, Ripley, Woking, Surrey man – Mr Roy Frederick Burt (18) was driving home on his scooter, after his shift at a petrol Station at Cobham. After leaving the woods at Wisley, and entering open road near the Ockham turning, he noticed two separate flashing lights of different colours in the sky over Ripley Village. They were low and appeared stationary. As he entered the village he saw they were moving and, in fact, further away than he first thought. He continued along the A3 and last saw them as they headed away, towards East Horsley. **(Source: Personal interview/BUFORA)**

25th May 1971 – Strange lights over Surrey

26th May 1971 – Triangular UFO over Manchester

At 9.25pm, student Miss Leslie Bridgwater (18) from Mornington Crescent, Fallowfield, Manchester, sighted a sharply defined grey- black diamond-shaped object, at a height of about 3,000 feet in the south-west part of the sky. She believed it was moving at a speed of 100 miles per hour, at an angle of 45 degrees elevation, and was 60 feet in width. As the object passed overhead, she was able to obtain a very good view of it. **(Source: *BUFORA Report*, 71020)**

Insert image 88

31st May 1971 – UFO over Lancashire

Six people living in Harwood, Bolton, Lancashire, watched an object, described as resembling, *"a lump of meat on a plate"*, hovering in the sky, and contacted the police. One of the witnesses was Christine Campbell of Hazelwood Avenue. She confirmed the UFO had appeared a few minutes after midnight over Winter Hill, hovering high above the TV mast, glowing amber and making a buzzing noise.

(Source: *Bolton Evening News,* 31.5.1971 – 'Meat on a plate')

Later that same day, Mrs Shirley Ogden (54) of Armiger Way, Witham, Essex, was looking out of her bedroom window, at 12.55am, when she noticed a bright object, fairly high in the western sky, *"resembling a strip of light, with a dome on top"*, and called her husband. The couple then watched it for ten minutes.

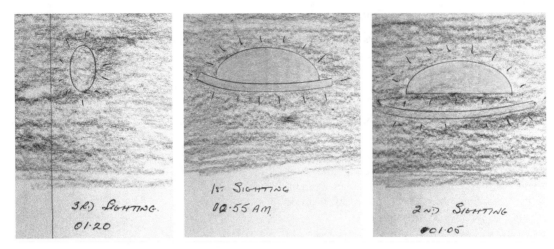

"3RD SIGHTING. 01·20"   "1ST SIGHTING 12·55 AM"   "2ND SIGHTING 01·05"

"Suddenly the 'dome' seemed to disappear, leaving the strip – now flattened out in the middle – to become cigar-shaped. It then rotated into a vertical position, apparently pulsating. After a further ten minutes, it disappeared slowly from the bottom, upwards, but reappeared to the right of where it had been originally, lower in the sky, close to the horizon, and disappeared at 1.20am."

(Source: Trevor Whittaker, BUFORA, Halifax)

JUNE 1971

June 1971 – Spinning UFO – Did RAF jets respond?

At 1.30pm on an undated day in June 1971, a spinning object was seen heading across the sky over Mablethorpe, Lincolnshire, by at least forty people, including Blackpool resident – Carole McGeechan, who said:

"It was spinning upright. A couple of minutes later, two RAF Jets appeared and headed towards where the UFO had been, about 500 feet off the ground, allowing me to judge the UFO had been twice the size of the aircraft." **(Source: Personal interview)**

4th June 1971 – UFO over Warminster

Mr Peter Hogben – serving with the Worcester Regiment at Battlesbury Barracks – was leaning out of the window, getting some fresh air, at 11.15pm.

Peter Hogben

Arthur Shuttlewood

"I saw a cigar-shaped object, hovering over the nearby copse at Cradle Hill, showing what looked like three portholes along its side and a huge red light at one end. On the other end was what appeared to be a curious mark, or gap – like a horizontal striation; suddenly it vanished in front of my eyes. I telephoned Arthur Shutlewood and ex-plained what I had seen. Although we kept observations until 4am, nothing more was seen."

15th June 1971 – Three star-like objects seen over Dorset

At 1am, a resident of Poole, in Dorset, got out of bed, unable to sleep, and glanced through the window, when he saw a cluster of strange 'stars' in the sky, low on the horizon, giving out a very bright light over the Purbeck Hills, consisting of:

"...one star to the right (apparently made up of two) – one on top of each other – with a third, single one, to the left. The 'two' pulsated from bright light to dim, while the third went through a process of nearly fading out then reappearing with a blinding light, which reflected against the bedroom wall."

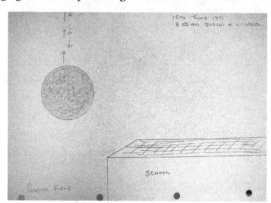

At 6pm on this day, Mr D. Barker, with his wife and four children from Mersey Road, Sale, Cheshire, was travelling along Glebelands Road, looking for a caravan site. Lillian and David shouted about seeing an orange fuzzy object in the sky, heading towards the north-west direction.

It started to drop in an arc of 60 degrees and disappeared behind some trees nearby, apparently landing in a meadow.

A search of the site revealed nothing. Could there have been a connection with a nearby Power Station?

(Source: BUFORA)

16th June 1971 – 'Globe of light'

At 8.50am, Beverley Daney (14) of Ashingdon Road, Rochford, Essex, was walking up the school path, when she saw a red/orange 'globe of light' dropping from the sky.

"I thought it was going to hit Ash-ingdon Road. Suddenly, it stopped in mid-air and shot straight up into the sky and was gone." **(Source: Ron West/Isle of Wight UFO Society)**

Dear Ken,
As I have not heard from you for a couple of weeks I thought that you may be ill, or that the martians have carried you off? Anyway I thought you might like to know about what I saw when Two friends and myself came to Wa rminster on the 26th June, 1971 Well we stayed at Starr Hill until 2.30 am in the morning,and during that time we saw a bright red star,which I at first thought was Mars until,It suddenly moved to our right,then went straight up in the sky and remained stationary ,during this time I took four photographs including One Time exposure,Hope they come out this time.Also we saw a strange Black Cloud saucer shape hanging over Starr Hill although It was probaly just an o rdinary cloud it did look strange especially when the rest of th sky was clear during this period.The last thing of interest that we saw was a ghost or at least thats what a chap from a group known as UFONIC. told us it was later that night.Cant really described what we saw properly,it was like a green misty thing over in the field in front of us about 75yards away from us and it kept moving around,another thing we noticed was that to see it you had to kind of look out of the corner of your eye at it because if you looked straight at it you couldnt see it properly for some reason.I hope this also shows up on our photos After that we went to Cradle Hill to see if you were there and to see if anything had been seen,but apparently nothing had, so at 5am we left for home.Have drawn a rough sketch to give you idea of what we saw if you can understand it.Hope to hear from you soon,
Steve

P.S. Have now seen article in fsr. I see what you mean about my drawing,but I still strongly disagree with mr.J.Ben as to the object being below the hill,also for the frist time I had to age with Mr Simpson when I saw him 26th June as he agrees that it was def abve the hill, as he has gone into it deeply and discov ered that the drawings by T.Collins in FSR are out and dont correspond,suggest you ask him to explain next time you see him think you will find it interesting.

P.S. Also forgot to tell you
we heard footsteps and
my friend said he heard
a breathing noise although
I must admit I did't hear this
Steve

26th June 1971 – Visit to Cradle Hill, Warminster

28th June 1971 – Strange 'lights' over Essex

At 10.20pm, Allen Stockel – then living at Ongar, in Essex – happened to look out of the rear window of his house, when he saw a strange, large, star-shaped 'light' in the sky. He called his mother and father, who then accompanied him outside, where they were joined by their next door neighbour – Mr Trundel. They watched the 'light', which was west of due south, about a mile away, 200 feet high in the air, and about 20 degrees off the horizon.

Allen went to his bedroom, upstairs, and collected a pair of binoculars and camera from his mother.

Suddenly, the 'light' began to increase in size

and brilliance, before moving right in a westwards direction, silently, across the sky.

> *Through binoculars, it was still in the same configuration; but now there was a red flashing light. Behind these was what appeared to be a fuzzy shape, but nothing positive – as if they were searchlights, or landing lights of some sort. Just before I lost sight of it, due to the eaves of the roof, it changed course, upwards, and shot away – its light extinguished – the whole thing over in five minutes."*

The photographs were later developed, but showed nothing of interest.

(Source: *FSR Case Histories,* Supplement 6, August 1971)

Triangular UFO over Loch Ness

Although we do not know the exact date in June 971, we came across a report that may or may not have anything to do with the above sighting, but it is of interest. Mr Frank Searle came to the Ness in 1969, and ultimately wrote a book, *Nessie: Seven Years in Search of the Monster* (Coronet Books, 1976)**,** in which he relates a sighting by Mr and Mrs Leonard Ellicott from Middleton Moor, County Durham, at 9.15pm, who were there on holiday. It appears that Frank was also present, although details about what exactly the Ellicott's saw is 'sketchy'.

Frank:

> *"We saw a large triangular object in the sky to the north-west. It was definitely a solid object and was reflecting the light of the setting sun. It looked like a huge kite. We took it to be a meteorological balloon, to start with, as it was moving with the light westerly wind. It hovered for a short while over the hills above Abriachan Village – then moved down the Loch, some two miles to the SSW. This caused us to take much more notice. To our great surprise, it moved back the way it had come – heading north-west. As the sun sank lower, it changed from silver to pink.*
>
> *The next morning Leonard went to Inverness Police Station and was surprised to hear that they had no other reports of the object."*

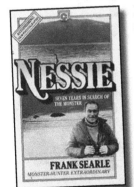

Explanation offered – likely to have been a radiosonde balloon, released from Stornoway at 6.15pm.

(Source: BUFORA)

*Malcolm Robinson

Our esteemed colleague – Malcolm Robinson – has written extensively about the Monsters of Loch Ness and those who have researched it over the years. (See *The Monsters of Loch Ness, The History and the Mystery* available on Amazon)

Malcolm:

> *"I remember that glorious summer's day in 1982 when I conducted an interview with 'Nessie' researcher, Frank Searle. What I really wanted to know that day was the time when Frank took a 'cracker' of a photograph of a UFO which swooped down over Loch Ness, near Foyers, and screamed away into the morning sky. Frank refused point blank to discuss that picture with me and said that he would terminate the interview if I continued to bring it up, strange or what! Some weeks after I had visited Frank, I wrote to him asking again if he could tell me what happened on the day that a UFO swooped down across his site. In his letter back to me (the days before email, eh!) he had this to say: 'Hello, nice to hear from you. But as for UFOs, well I'm interested in all unusual subjects but you must realise that I get 25,000 visitors a year for my Loch Ness Project. I answer about 2,200 letters every*

year on the same subject. There's no way that I will get involved with UFOs. I'd get bogged down. At the moment I am without a girl Friday. It's taking me all my time to keep up with the mail, talk with visitors, etc. And I am out in my boat from 5am till 10am. So I just don't have time to discuss other subjects you see. Even when I find a new girl Friday, it won't be on. Sorry, but that's how it is.

All the best,

Frank Searle'."

Malcolm:

"Thankfully, I have kept the newspaper clipping (Daily Record, Monday, December 2nd, 1974) which shows Frank's UFO photograph. Here in part is what Frank had to say to the Daily Record about what happened."

Frank:

"I was halfway across Loch Ness in my boat, when suddenly I saw this 'thing' coming from the direction of the new hydro-electric station at Foyers. It was travelling about the speed of a jet and at around 2,000 feet, when suddenly it shot away westwards over Meall Faurvounie. It was only in my viewfinder for a few seconds."

Frank sent his UFO photograph to a Dr. Fred Backman who, according to this newspaper report, was a scientist at Evanston, near Chicago. Mr Backman said,

"Mr Searle's photographs are good and sharp. But on the other hand it is very easy to make a sharp picture which isn't real. I don't doubt his word but it is impossible to say anything positive because there is no background but blank sky."

Malcolm:

"... and that's all we know. The American UFO researchers (as far as I can tell) never submitted any further information about this photograph, or if they did I never came across it. I've checked the internet, but alas didn't come up with anything, so I guess the only person who knows what really happened that day, is the man himself, Frank Searle, and sadly he is no longer with us."

Malcom Robinson on the lookout!

Loch Ness UFO sighting

Malcolm:

"It wasn't until a good few years later (around 1982 or thereabouts) that I saw my next UFO. By now my research group – Strange Phenomena Investigations (founded in 1979) – was just three years old and not only were we researching accounts relating to UFO incidents, but we were also involved with ghost and poltergeist events as well. Then, of course, there was my deep interest in one of Scotland's most cherished mysteries (or tourist attractions!) – The Loch Ness Monster.

It was 1982. I was up at Loch Ness with my wife, Rose, who at this point in time was now well accustomed to my investigative travelling work. I termed this a 'working holiday', whilst she preferred just to call it a holiday. For me this was yet another great opportunity to meet and interview people who lived and worked along the loch side in regards to their own observations of 'Nessie'. It had been quite a tiring day and having completed my interviews it was time to retire back to our base, which was the camping and caravan site at Invermoriston on the shores of the loch. After a quick wash and change, my wife and I went out for a stroll down by the loch side where we happened to come upon a party of tourists, who were all sharing a camp fire on the shores of the loch. We asked if we could join them and with a resounding 'by all means', sat down."

Dome-shaped light appears

"I remember there were an American couple there and also some English tourists as well; we soon struck up a conversation, which needless to say centred around 'Nessie', herself. Before we knew it, it was around 11.50pm. I remember the night so well; it was a lovely cool evening with a fantastic dark sky, peppered with the multitude of heavenly stars in every direction. Someone threw some logs back onto the camp fire and the discussion continued. Listening to what was being said I gazed across the loch and looked at the dark silhouette of the hills on the opposite side of the loch. The conversation was interrupted by an American woman, who was facing me (I had my back to the loch) who shouted out, 'What the hell is that?'! I looked at her surprised face and followed her pointed finger in the direction which pointed to the silhouetted hills on the other side of the loch. I watched what I can only describe as a half circle or a 'dome-shaped light', which was moving up and down behind the hill at the opposite side of the loch. This was a bright white light which was pulsating. By now everyone in the party was aghast at this strange spectacle. Now I knew that at this particular spot there were not any houses or roads in which, perhaps, one could surmise that if it was a car heading up an incline, then perhaps the car headlights may reflect of low lying cloud. This I knew was not the case. Firstly, because there were no roads at this spot and secondly, the sky was devoid of any cloud for this effect to have been accomplished. The object continued to bob up and down behind the hill, when all of a sudden it completely stopped above the hill – then, with a tremendous burst of speed, vanished off into the heavens and was gone in seconds. Silence prevailed, everyone knew that we had witnessed something spectacular and out of the ordinary. I've since learned that there have been a number of UFO sightings at Loch Ness over the years. In point of fact, a year or so before this UFO sighting I was again up at Loch Ness, interviewing witnesses and also a chap called Frank Searle."

Frank Searle:

"Frank had left his home in England and travelled up to Loch Ness to devote a good part of his life by trying to 'prove' the 'monster's' existence. All he did, however, was to create suspicion when numerous photographs that he claimed he took of 'Nessie' in clear sharp focus, were the subject of much scrutiny and debate. Some even went so far as to say that the 'creature' captured in Frank's photographs closely resembled the image of a dinosaur which could be found on a postcard for sale in a souvenir shop in Inverness. One of my main questions to Frank that day was in regards to his remarkable daylight photograph of a UFO, as it swooped over Loch Ness, and was published in the Scottish Daily Record newspaper. However, I soon learned that Frank was none too keen to speak about that photograph and quickly said that if I didn't stick to the 'Nessie' questions, he would terminate the interview! Well, needless to say, I didn't continue with the UFO question. I had travelled many miles to see him and I wasn't going to throw the baby out with the bathwater at the final hurdle, although admittedly, when I completed my interview with him, I 'did' ask him about this photograph, but he still wouldn't tell me. Frank mysteriously left Loch Ness in suspicious circumstances. A model 'Nessie' was found under a boulder at his campsite, although admittedly that could have been left by anyone. Frank (I later found out) went back to England and died peacefully in 2005."

˙Malcolm Robinson. Founder, Strange Phenomena Investigations (SPI)

He is an established speaker, presenter, scriptwriter and author of the following books: *UFO Case Files of Scotland* (Volume 1) *Amazing Real Life Alien Encounters* (ISBN: 10 1907 712 6023) *UFO Case Files of Scotland* (Volume 2) *The Sightings* (ISBN: 10 1907 126120) *Paranormal Case Files of Great Britain* (Volume 1) (ISBN: 10 1907 126066) *The Monsters of Loch Ness (The History and the Mystery)* (ISBN: 978-1-326-72942-4) *Paranormal Case Files of Great Britain* (Volume 2) (ISBN: 978-1326-874-223)

[All available from www.amazon.co.uk or www.barnesandnoble.com or www.lulu.com]

Malcolm is assistant editor of *Outer Limits Magazine*. Malcolm was the first Scottish person to speak on UFOs in the following countries – The United States of America: (Laughlin, Nevada) France: (Strasbourg) Holland: (Utrech) and Ireland. He is one of only a handful of people on this planet to have gone down into the murky depths of Loch Ness in a submarine.

JULY 1971

2nd July 1971 – UFO over North Somercotes

Geoffrey Kane (19) – a laboratory control supervisor from 44, Wetherby Crescent, Lincoln – was out night fishing at North Somercotes. At some stage he fell asleep. When he awoke at 2.30am, he looked out towards the south-west, wondering what the weather was like, when he saw what appeared to be a bright star moving in the sky, but then realised it was spheroid in shape, heading south-east – until lost behind cloud, 7-8 seconds later.

After leaving work on July the first, Mr Kane journed along to Somercotes with the intentions of an all night fishing expedition, being on his own and possibly feeling some-what tired through lack of activity, he fell asleep, when he finally awoke he began to look around the sky for weather signes, it was then that Mr Kane's attention was attracted to what appeared to resemble a very bright star in a Southwesterly direction.
The star like object was a spheriod shape, and on perception gave the impression of being stationary a' after about a second or so it began to move away at a constant v a South-East direction untill it disappeared behind some cloud; although Mr Kane continued to observe the area around this particular cloud he could not find any trace of the star like object again, the sighting lasted between 7 to 8 seconds, at no time during or after the observation period was any sound detected at all; Mr Kane further states it was impossible to tell whether the object was metallic or not and niether did it pulsate, also the elevation was far to high to estimate with any accuracy.
When asked about any psychological effects, Mr Kane said that in no way was he aware of any.
The object did not have any extra-ordinary characteristics.
Unfortuneately there was no other witnesses.

Signed... G. Kane.....   Signed...R.H......

9th July 1971 – UFO over Bournemouth

A glowing magenta coloured 'ball' was seen hovering over the sea off Lyme Bay, west of Lyme Regis, at 12.30am, by a number of people, who later contacted the *Bridport News*, describing it as resembling a *"... ball of fire, as large as the moon, which became cone-shaped and decreased in size, before shooting upwards with a roaring noise"*, and disappearing from view. It was claimed of the six people that saw it, one was a physicist, who later calculated it moved at a speed 15 times faster than an Apollo rocket.

Enquiries were made with the Coastguard, Police, and other Authorities, but failed to identity the object.

Early 1970s – UFO over Leicester

In 2009, we contacted Julie Mayer (wife of BBC Radio presenter, Tony Wadsworth) after having spoken to her about what she witnessed, while waiting for a bus near Leicester University, with her sister, in the early 1970s.

"It was the movement of the object between two tall buildings that caught our attention. It seemed to glide down and stop in the sky. Although it happened over 30 years ago, I can remember it very well indeed. I suggested my sister go and fetch somebody else to witness the sighting. She thought it might be better to hang on, as we didn't know how long the UFO was going to be there. Suddenly, it shot upwards into the sky and vanished from sight."

Julie Mayer

15th July 1971 – UFO photographed over Poole

At 10.30pm, Poole resident – Brian George, was preparing for bed when he noticed a large 'ball of light' moving slowly across the night sky, heading in a south-east to west direction. Brian grabbed hold of his Polaroid Swinger 2 camera and took a photograph, using the flashbulb in his excitement. By the time the photo had developed, the object had gone. The incident was brought to the attention of Leslie Harris – a UFO researcher from the Bournemouth area – who forwarded a copy to us. This was not the only occasion that Mr George was to experience UFO activity. He and his family were to tell Leslie of other sightings of strange objects seen during this period, some of which we will outline in due course. As for the photo, it certainly appears to be genuine.

(**Source: As above/***FSR Case Histories,* **No. 7, October 1971**)

17th July 1971 – UFO over Hull

Two blue and white disc-shaped objects were seen heading in a north to south direction, at speed, over Hull, by ex-RAF serviceman James Sturdy, and his brother – Michael. To their amazement, they were followed by four more identical objects,

> "...one of which was orange in colour. This object veered away from the others in a right-hand movement and then moved back to the 'formation'. About a minute later, two more 'discs' arrived in the sky – one blue and white; the other, orange – flying silently, one behind the other, across the sky."

(**Source: BUFORA, Halifax Branch**)

22nd July 1971 – UFO over Clacton seafront, Essex

Housewife Betty Stott (49) of Munnings Road, Colchester, Essex, was walking along the seafront, at Clacton, with her son

Photograph (a)

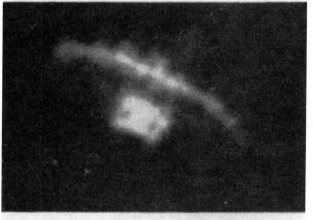

Photograph (b)

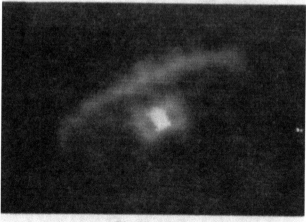

Photograph (c)

(16) and daughter (18), at 10.45am, when she was stunned to see a most peculiar glowing orange object flying overhead.

> *"It was shaped like a shallow ball and its glow dimmed and brightened. It moved away towards the direction of Frinton-on-Sea, near Walton-on-the-Naze, weaving across the sky as it did so. Ten minutes later, it was gone from view behind the coastline."*

(Source: Ron West)

23rd July 1971 – Fan-shaped UFO seen

At 7.15pm, a large fan-shaped object with a tail was seen slowly crossing the sky, by many people living in the Southern Counties of the UK – later explained away as an exploding meteorite.

As a result of a newspaper article about UFOs, Susan Cook, of *The Sun* readers department, wrote to BUFORA in London, forwarding on a report from Upperton Road West, Plaistow, London, reader – Antony Tansley, about a UFO sighted by him and Stephen Hosmer, Martin Littlefield and Shirley Smith, at 10.15pm on the same evening.

A bright object was seen in the sky by the assembled party, over the Canning Town area. They presumed, from its size, that this was no star. A pair of binoculars was obtained and, on looking through them, a saucer-shaped object was seen. At this point it moved to the south-west direction, stopped, and reversed its course. Within seconds, it shot away at immense velocity and was gone from view at 10.22pm.

(Source: UFOSIS)

23rd July 1971 – UFO over London

Antony Tansley, Stephen Hosmer, Martin Littlefield, and Shirley Smith (ages not given) from Upperton Road West, Plaistow,

London, E.13, sighted something unusual at 10.15pm. The first person to see it was Antony, who said:

> *"I thought it was a very bright star, until it began to move. I asked my friend to go and fetch a pair of binoculars.*
>
> *At this point two people came out from next door and began to watch the strange 'light'. They then went back in.*
>
> *I looked through binoculars and saw what resembled a 'flying saucer'. It then moved towards the south-west, stopped, and reversed. Its luminosity faded and it shot off, at terrific speed, and I lost sight of it."*

(Source: Lionel Beer/Letter from *The Sun*)

25th July 1971 – 'Flying Cones' and 'Triangle' reported in the sky

An object – described as looking like a *'cone'*, *'spinning top'* and *'inside-out umbrella, with white lights on its top'* – was seen to move across the sky in a display of behaviour typical of these objects. The same, if

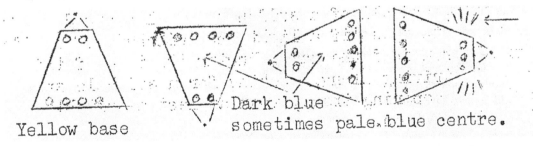

not similar, object – *"showing a dark blue body, with red lights at the end, making a loud roaring noise"* – was seen moving across the sky, between 11.40pm and 2.30am, over the Leicester area, by at least eight separate witnesses. During the period between late July to mid-August 1971, Derek Samson, of NICAP UK, interviewed a number of witnesses, one of whom told of watching a 'triangular' object hover, glide, roll, and turn upside-down, as it manoeuvred across the sky. (**Source: NICAP GB, Derek Samson**)

29th July 1971 – Followed by a UFO

Mr and Mrs Douglas Dains – field investigators for APRO – were returning from a camping trip to Old Forge, New York, on what had been a stormy evening. The couple sighted a 'bright light' in the sky, at 10.25pm, south-west of their position near east Hamilton – unusual, bearing in mind low cloud cover and light rain,they stopped to watch it again. Mr Dains shone a flashlight at it several times and then it reappeared. When lightning lit up the sky, it was clear the light was behind cloud cover. It then dropped down lower in the sky and following another flash of lightning, Mrs Dains saw *"a dark ovoid object, showing a bright orange light in its centre".*

They decided to leave at this stage, as Mrs Dains was becoming upset. The couple stopped another car and showed the driver the object, which continued to follow their vehicle at a height of 1,000 feet and 500 yards away, until they reached Sherburne, New York. They later discovered there had been a power blackout in Waterville, and wondered if there was any connection with heavy static noticed on the car radio during the sighting which lasted 30 minutes. (**Source: *APRO Bulletin*, Tucson, Arizona**)

30th July 1971 – UFO over Leamington Spa

Paul Mancini, from Leamington Spa, was one of a number of people who saw something very odd on the morning of this day.

> *"I was walking down the Queensway, when I noticed a curious object in the sky. I managed to obtain a pair of binoculars and saw something that looked like an egg, with a black line around it and blue light on top, constantly changing colour, moving towards the direction of the Ford Foundry, before being lost from view."*

(**Source: *Leamington Spa Morning News*, 31.7.1971 – 'Officials at Elmdon Airport, Birmingham, reported seeing the same UFO hovering over the Airport'**)

It appears that this may well have been seen by Tony Hall (14) of Wyndley Lane, Sutton Coldfield, Warwickshire. He saw an unusual white object in the sky for about an hour, until midday, when it vanished from sight.

31st July 1971 – 'Spinning top' UFO seen over Dorset

Mr Lance Druce of Poole, Dorset, who was to experience a number of UFO sightings over the years, told of another incident which took place at 11pm on this date, involving his mother and sister, Jenny, who later contacted Bournemouth-based UFO researcher – Leslie Harris, who is to be congratulated for his thorough investigation into some very interesting cases, over the years.

On this occasion the couple told of having watched a large object, described as:

> *"...like an old-fashioned child's spinning top, at an elevation of 75 degrees in the sky. It moved from the right and appeared to lose altitude – then stopped, apart from a slight vertical oscillation. Another smaller UFO seemed to emerge from the larger one, consisting of five red-orange lights, which might have been carried by a solid object. This 'light' then moved away and was out of sight in 10-15 minutes. The large object remained in the sky and, after a time, we decided to retire for the night".* (**Source: As above/Personal interview with Mr Druce**)

July 1971 – RAF chase UFO over Warminster

Whilst we have decided not to include any sightings from around the Warminster area, as they will have been published in the *Haunted Skies* Wiltshire book, in 2017, such reports are classified as Top Secret by the authorities and are unlikely to be *ever* released into the public domain.

An example of this RAF response was given by Mrs Crystal Hogben, who was on Starr Hill, Warminster, accompanied by Mr Arthur Shuttlewood.

> "We saw about six pink/red lights move up from the horizon, towards Warminster, and cross the sky overhead in a great arc. They seemed to be propelled by mechanical action, involving small geometric movements, equally spaced between each other – almost looking like they were dancing. A RAF Jet then appeared and, to our astonishment, began to chase one of the 'lights', which had become separated from the rest, before it doubled back to its companions and moved away, at high speed, leaving the jet way behind." (**Source: Personal interview**)

1971 – UFOs tracked on radar

We spoke to Crichton E. Miller – navigator, inventor, and author of a number of books, including *The Golden Thread of Time* – in October 2006, about his employment as a radar operator, at RAF North Luffenham, during the 'Cold War', covering most of England – responsible for military aircraft moving in and out of various bases in the Midlands and East Anglia regions.

> "Most people had no idea how busy the skies were, even in those days, when the sophisticated radars often picked up flocks of birds, clouds, squalls, and even cars on the road at lower levels. Some time in 1971, I was on night watch and operating a height finder, when I noted and reported a contact, climbing at speed, which was normal for an aircraft at that time. I checked with the main radar and saw that it was travelling at great speed, from east to west, not in the vicinity of airways, or in close proximity to aircraft under our control. Significantly, the contact was not signalling a radio beacon transponder, known today as RBT. The ground based ATC radar system consists of a primary surveillance radar (PSR) and secondary surveillance radar (SSR). The PSR locates and tracks aircraft within the control area by transmitting a beam of energy, which is reflected from the aircraft and returned to the PSR antenna. The SSR transmits interrogation signals to the airborne radio beacon transponder. Data received from the PSR and SSR are used in conjunction to develop the total air traffic situation display on the controller's radar scope. This enables the controller to identify transponder equipped aircraft in addition to determining the range and direction of all aircraft within the control area. We estimated the speed to be in the region of Mach. 3 and the contact disappeared off the height finder at over 30,000 feet. It was reported to RAF Neatishead. We were later told it was probably a weather balloon."

Crichton has no fixed views as to the origin of this UFO. For all he knows, what was tracked could be representative of a covert technology which would not have had a transponder fitted; neither does he believe it was an Alien spacecraft, although he has considered, within the vastness of the Galaxy, there may well be other life forms.

1971 – RAF tracked 35 UFOs on radar – warned to keep quiet

Wing Commander Turner, who was awarded an MBE in 1983, was guest speaker in October 2007, at the *Close Encounters* conference in Pontefract, West Yorkshire, organised by Philip Mantle, of *UFO Data* magazine, who said: *"His testimony is remarkable."*

In summer of 1971, RAF Air Traffic Control officer Alan Turner was the duty military supervisor at RAF Sopley, which was a joint military/civil air traffic control radar unit. He said:

> *"I saw a series of radar blips, one at a time, travelling south-east, at regular six or seven-mile*

Wing Commander Turner, seen far right of group

*One of 10 speakers at the two-day conference on October 25th and 26th, joining people such as Rosalind Reynolds, who claims to have been abducted by Aliens in September 1983, and Kevin Goodman – an expert on UFOs at Warminster.

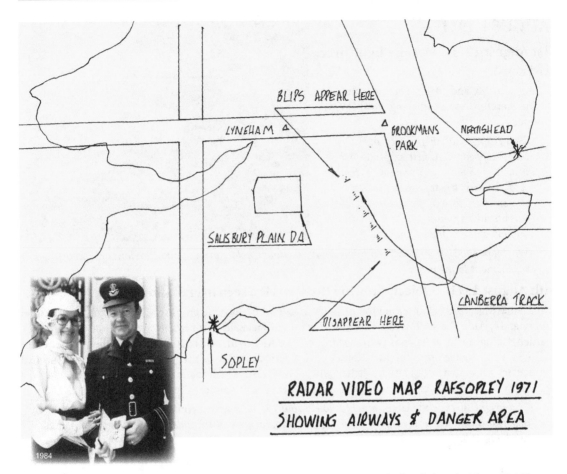

intervals, climbing fast for about 40 miles, before disappearing. I calculated their height at 3,000 feet, climbing to 'in excess of 60,000 feet' – the instrument wouldn't read any higher. I knew I was not watching military aircraft. The only craft with that rate of climb were supersonic 'Lightnings', but they wouldn't have held such perfect formation. They're also noisy."

The phenomenon was also witnessed by four civil and six military controllers. Afterwards, everyone had to write a report. Wing Commander Turner says six military radars in southern England picked up the craft, as did operators at Heathrow. He also instructed a 'Canberra' aircraft, returning from Germany, to turn around and investigate.

"There was something about a quarter-mile away from him which, to quote him, was 'climbing like the clappers', but he didn't see anything really, nor did his crew."

Wing Commander Turner plotted the course of the UFOs. They travelled from near Marlborough, in Wiltshire, to near Alton, Hampshire, before disappearing. He said, a few days later, that they were interviewed by two anonymous men and told not to talk about the incident. He kept quiet until 11 years ago.

Was it UFOs?

"They were unidentified, they were flying, and they were objects. I've got to keep an open mind. It's arrogant to believe that we're the only ones in this universe."

AUGUST 1971

1st August 1971 – Orange 'light' over Hereford

At 1.30am, Mr and Mrs J. Palmer from The Oval, Hereford, were driving near Withington.

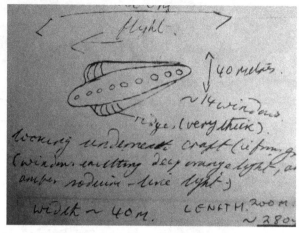

> *"Something shot in front of our car and disappeared. At first we presumed it was a Shooting Star, but a few seconds later it reappeared low in the sky, swaying to and fro in the air. It was just like a round orange light with another smaller one behind it.*

> *We stopped the car and watched it for about two hours, before driving into Hereford and reporting the incident to the police."*

4th August 1971 – Object, showing three circles, seen over Stafford

Mr Henry Macefield (who served for 22 years in the RAF), his wife and son – Michael (12), were then living at 14, Aldershaw Close, Parkside, Stafford. Mr Macefield and his son were sitting in their back garden, facing north, at 9.30pm (which is just off the A34 road, east of Redhill roundabout junction of the A34, with the feeder to the M6 Motorway at Creswell viaduct). They were 'plane spotting' and had binoculars with them. A faint high-pitched whine was heard, which made the father look up and see in a gap between the clouds, estimated to be at 30,000 feet or more, almost directly overhead,

> *"...a bright silver-white 'cone', moving slowly south-west. It had a circular base – the apex being uppermost, slanted in the direction of flight. The outer part of the object gave the appearance of revolving at high speed, while the inner part seemed fixed."*

Michael confirmed the sighting, but said he could see *"a line of three circles delineated in the bottom of the object."* (**Source: Wilfred Daniels**)

7th August 1971 – UFO display over North Bradley, Wiltshire

Henry James Thomas (21), student, of Chester Avenue, Luton, Bedfordshire, Michael Roy Hunt (21) of Wyneham Road, North Dulwich, along with his mother and Sandra Ann Hawkins of Church Lane, North Bradley, near Trowbridge, Wiltshire, sighted an orange object in the sky, at 10.10pm – an incident they deemed important enough to bring to the attention of BUFORA investigator, Lionel Beer.

> *"At 10.15pm, a white luminous object appeared in the sky, moving in an erratic manner. This was followed by at least another 5-6 objects. At one stage we saw three objects mark out the points of an isosceles triangle. This was followed by a tiny light seen to speed across the sky delineated by the triangular formation. At 10.45pm, we saw an orange light, clearly visible in front of the cloud bank. On occasions rays of orange light, resembling antennae, seemed to emanate from this light source.*

> *By 11.50pm, the activity had died out."* (**Source: BUFORA**)

8th August 1971 – 'Falling star' over Leicester

Leicester woman – Nora Gawthrope, was called to the window by her 10 year-old daughter, at 9.30pm.

> *"I saw what looked like a 'falling star' – spherical, with sharp edges, glowing bright orange. It descended slowly in a vertical movement, leaving a smoke or a vapour trail, before disappearing behind houses. The sky was obscured by heavy clouds at the time."* (**Source: UFOSIS**)

Bedfordshireshire UFO Society

BEDFORDSHIRE U.F.O. SOCIETY

MOBILE LABORATORY OPERATIONAL PROGRAMME - WARMINSTER 1971

As the result of an extensive two year research and development programme members of the Bedfordshire U.F.O. Society have succeeded in producing what is thought to be the world's first electronic observation system aimed directly at the U.F.O. problem. Constructed entirely from private funds by members of the Society, the BUFOS mobile laboratory is a high sensitivity data gathering system able to carry out continuous monitoring and recording of variations in most of the atmospheric and geophysical parameters.

The purpose of the project is to attempt to study by direct physical means, disturbances created in the earth environment by the passage of postulated extra-terrestrial spacecraft and to indicate thereby whether or not such space vehicles actually exist.

There is clearly much common ground between this project and the study of U.F.O. sightings and indeed was originally initiated from this viewpoint, although quickly became detached from it as a result of the unobjective nature of U.F.O. data. It is in fact possible to view the project as a logical extension of conventional 'Ufology' - putting the observer at the event when it happens instead of interviewing witnesses in retrospect.

As part of our 1971 operational programme the Society is co-operating with Dr. John Cleary-Baker of the British U.F.O. Research Association in his "Project Warminster". This Wiltshire town has long been considered the most likely location for the completed mobile laboratory, and in fact the original specification was drawn up in 1968 by Society members at the Carey household, in Corton nearby. Quite apart from this historical connection, the remoteness of the location from heavy industry promises a low background interference level and exceptional visibility. It was indeed fortunate that the projected "first operational run" coincided both in time and place with Dr. Cleary-Baker's admirable enterprise, and it is to be hoped that this happy coincidence will be to the considerable advantage of both organisations.

The experiment will begin with the arrival of the mobile laboratory at the Society's site near Warminster in May 1971. Commencing operation forthwith, research targets for Summer 1971 are as follows:-

(1) To assess the feasibility of U.F.O. studies by direct instrumented means, under operational conditions in an area of supposed high U.F.O. activity.
(2) To continue development and proving of the privately constructed BUFOS instrumentation system, leading to a thorough appraisal of the practicability of such systems.
(3) To enhance the value of any visual sightings made by Dr. Cleary-Baker's team through time-correlated instrument records of environmental parameters.
(4) To study lesser known atmospheric phenomena, particularly the variation of electric field intensity with meteorological conditions, over a substantial period.

It is intended to submit the results of these programmes for publication in the relevant quarters when appropriate; this may include some U.F.O. journals.

Visitors to the project will be welcome, but by appointment only please, and any communications regarding this project should be addressed to:-

MR. DAVID R. J. VIEWING,
LAMBS COTTAGE,
SOULDROP, BEDS.
TEL. SHARNBROOK 548

97

12th August 1971 – UFO over Worcestershire

At 11pm, an enormous UFO was sighted hovering over a field at Himbleton, Droitwich, Worcestershire, by a troop of girl guides, from the 1st Netherton Group, Dudley, West Midlands, under the supervision of Guide Leader – Mrs Olwyn Granger, and Divisional Commissionaire – Miss L. Hare, and guider – Mrs Betty McGowan.

We contacted Mrs Granger, in 2008.

Olwyn Granger

"It was a long time ago, but some memories never fade. There were about 30 of us camping, near Droitwich, on 12th August 1971. The girls had gone to bed. We heard a very loud noise and thought that it was an aircraft about to crash – then this object – approximately 30 to 40 feet long, flashing, with little red and green lights – came over the trees lining the side of the field and hovered 50 yards away, for about an hour. We decided not to approach whatever it was, as we felt scared, and heard the sound of a jet aircraft flying around the camp, above. The UFO then rose upwards and disappeared over nearby trees. This was the last we saw of it. When the plane flew away, so did the object."

The U.F.O.-spotters

Evening Mail Reporter

A PARTY of Girl Guides are compiling a special report on the latest sighting of an unidentified flying object in the Midlands.

Guide leader Mrs. Olwyn Grainger, of the 1st Netherton Group, says she spotted the U.F.O. at Droitwich with Miss Lottie Hare, the Dudley divisional commissioner, and Mrs. Betty McGowan, another senior member of the Guides.

They were sitting around a camp fire when they say they heard a "terrifying noise" over their heads.

Mrs. Grainger said they saw an "enormous object" about 40ft. long which they thought was going to crash into the tents.

"It went into the next field about 50 yards away and stayed hovering harmlessly for about an hour," she added.

"It had red and green lights and was cigar shaped. There was no sign of any wings.

"We were too terrified to go and make a close inspection. It was quite a frightening experience."

She said they would compile a report on the sighting for one of the U.F.O. societies.

● Photographs of a U.F.O. taken by Staffordshire police officers are now being studied by R.A.F. experts.

1971.

BIRMINGHAM EVENING MAIL 24-8-71

Olwyn Granger, who still takes Girl Guides camping to the same location, was kind enough to show us the location of the incident, in early 2008. It is a matter which still baffles her to this present day.

Olwyn Granger as a child

Prepared but for U.F.Os ?

IT'S not just the Scout and Guide movements who are familiar with the revered motto "Be prepared." It is surely one of the most well-known saying in the land.

Yet a group of Dudley Guides at camp near Droitwich last week were taken completely by surprise as they were preparing to go to bed.

Mrs. Olwyn Grainger and Miss Lottie Hare, the Divisional Commissioner for Dudley, were two of the people in charge of the camp at Himbleton Manor.

Mrs. Grainger telephoned the Herald this week to tell us of a quite astonishing incident.

ASLEEP

Most of the camp was asleep at about 11 p.m. yesterday week but Mrs. Grainger, who is in charge of the 1st Netherton Guides, and Miss Hare were among a group of senior guiders who were having a last cuppa around the camp fire.

Mrs. Grainger said: "There was a terrific roar and we saw what looked to be like an aeroplane out of control coming towards us.

"It swerved over us and stopped in a meadow about 50 yards away."

She added that four guiders and two young guides watched the "U.F.O." hovering silently for about an hour before it moved off.

The object was above a meadow about 50 yards away and at rooftop height.

Mrs. Grainger described it as disc-shaped and illuminated.

This incident coincides with a spate of U.F.Os reported in the M'dlands last week, and Mrs Grainger commented, "We weren't all imagining it."

Birmingham U.F.O. Investigation Group

Alan K. Crowe,
511, Warwick Rd.,
Birmingham,11.
Tel : 021-706-1917.

Mrs O. Grainger,
166, Bridgnorth Rd.,
Wombourne,
Worcs.

August 25th,1971.

Dear Mrs Grainger,

We were very interested to read of your sighting of an unidentified flying object in Himbleton, recently. As you will see from the above heading our group collect and investigate U.F.O. reports in this area. I am also an area investigator for the British Unidentified Flying Object Research Association, a nationwide organisation with similar aims.

We would very much like the opportunity to speak to you personally and have your own account of the incident for our records. I wonder if it would be convenient for us to call on you this coming weekend, perhaps on Sunday afternoon ? I know that this is very short notice but, as you will appreciate, it is important to get details of a sighting as soon after the event as possible. You will probably not have time to reply by post and so, if Sunday would be convenient for you, perhaps you would be kind enough to telephone me at the above number to confirm this, reverse charges of course. If this date is not convenient I will wait to hear from you by post.

Incidentally, I have spoken to Mrs Mills, the County Guides Commissioner, and she told me that it would be quite in order for me to get in touch with you direct.

I look forward to a favourable reply either by telephone or post and thank you in advance for your interest.

yours sincerely,

Alan K. Crowe.

"After contacting the police, I received a flood of people, eager to interview me from various UFO organisations and the local radio and TV Stations. Later, two men – who told me they were from the MOD – visited me at my home, in possession of the newspaper cutting, and in no uncertain words, after spending 20 minutes chatting with me, remarked 'You've said enough. You should have said it was definitely a plane', in a threatening tone."

Enquiries made with the RAF revealed no knowledge of any aircraft having been flown over the locality, at the time.

Is it possible that the whining noise heard was not, in fact, any RAF jet but the UFO?

(Sources: Personal interviews/John 'Dennis' Llewellyn, Stratford-upon-Avon UFO Group/*Times Today*, 24. 8.1971 – 'Guider tells of silent airborne machine'/*Birmingham Evening Mail*, 24. 8.1971 – 'The UFO spotters')

15th August 1971 – UFOs over Lancashire

David Stretch – then a clerical officer with the National Coal Board, at Lowton, Lancashire – was at his home address, at 10.30pm, when he looked through the open window and saw:

> "...four unidentified flying objects moving across the sky, in pairs; I shouted for my wife to come and have a look and we watched as they drifted across the sky, apparently just above the houses, but probably several hundred feet off the ground. They looked like old-fashioned dumb-bells – gold in colour. I managed to take some photographs while my wife alerted the neighbours, who came rushing out. They were as surprised as we were. We watched them as they headed over Winter Hill (the site of a number of other UFO reports over the years) towards Bolton. When I had the films processed, I was disappointed to discover that although the

26th January, 2004.

Mr. J. Hanson,
31 Red Lion Street,
ALVECHURCH.
Worcestershire.
B48 7LG.

Dear Mr. Hanson,

Re: UFO Phenomenon.

Thank you for your recent letter, which was re-directed from our previous address in Bolton.

We were please to note your interest in the above matter and resultant investigation. Your letter brought back the memories of that night when our 'happening' took place.

It was early evening and we were in the middle of our evening meal, The table was next to the dinning room window and I just happened to look out to the garden and the houses at the rear of our house. The skies were very clear and I was looking at the sky just above the roof-line of the rear houses. Suddenly, without sound two objects came into sight. They appeared to be drifting along just above the houses , but were probably several hundred feet above the ground. They were identical in appearance, size and colour They literally looked like old-fashioned dumb-bells, gold in colour.

My wife and I were flabbergasted, so much so, I grabbed a camera, to record the event and called out our next door neighbours to witness everything. They too were amazed at what they saw. Unfortunately, whilst the developed photographs appeared clear and normal the 'objects' were missing. Very puzzling and even more, disappointing.

However, I hope the above will be helpful in your project.

Yours sincerely,

D. H. Stretch.

pictures had come out, there was no sign of any UFOs on them. I have to admit, prior to that, I didn't believe in the existence of UFOs, until we saw those glowing silent objects. I contacted the Bolton Evening News, the following morning, who published my sighting on the 16th August 1971."

(**Source: Personal interview**)

Further investigations revealed a number of people, living in the Hull area of the United Kingdom, had reported seeing 'flying saucers' during 11pm-4am.

(**Source:** *Hull Daily Mail,* **16.8.1971 – 'Claims today that a 'flying saucer' hovered over North Hull, for at least five hours, last night and early this morning, was made by a number of people today'**)

A housewife told the *Hull Daily Mail* that she watched a round, saucer-shaped, object through a pair of binoculars borrowed from a neighbour. Mrs Florence Leech, of North Hull Estate, reported that her eldest daughter, Catherine, had sighted a UFO while returning home with her boyfriend, on his motorcycle, along Sutton Road.

> "When they came in they said I would not believe them, but I borrowed binoculars and got a good look at it. It was round, with bright flashing lights on it. It seemed to have legs hanging down and they had lights on them too. It really 'put the wind up us'. I thought the 'little green men' were coming for me. It was in the sky from 11pm to 4am, when I got up for a drink. When we looked at it, it seemed to be moving slowly to the right. This morning, it had moved to the other side of the house." (**Source:** *Hull Daily Mail*/**Personal interview**)

15th August 1971 – UFO over Tynemouth

At 11pm, Mr Geoffrey O' Brady-Jones – a resident of Tynemouth, in Northumberland – was walking home, when he was approached by a friend – Mr Wolfgang Von Metz (grandson of World War One Field Marshall Von Metz), who directed his attention to a 'cigar' or 'saucer' shaped object in the south-east direction of the night sky. The two

men decided to conduct an observation of the movements of the object, with a tripod mounted telescope, preparing a written 'log', calculated from plotting an imaginary line drawn from the top of the West Tower of Tynemouth Castle, using the fingers of an outstretched arm in line with the eye – crude but very effective.

Mr O' Brady-Jones:

"We measured the motion of the object across the sky by noting points on the ground directly underneath it, later converting them to degrees of motion in the horizontal plane by using a theodolite. We knew it wasn't Mars, as we could clearly see the planet – very prominent in the night sky. Apart from that, the object we were looking at occasionally spun and pulsed with light. At about 2am, we decided to return home, as it was now becoming very cold. On Monday morning I contacted the Police, who came around to see me and inspected my notes and equipment. The Superintendent in charge of the Police Station advised me to contact the Ministry of Defence – which I did, but was told that no department exists to deal with such matters."

In conversation with Mr O' Brady-Jones he told us, in his opinion,

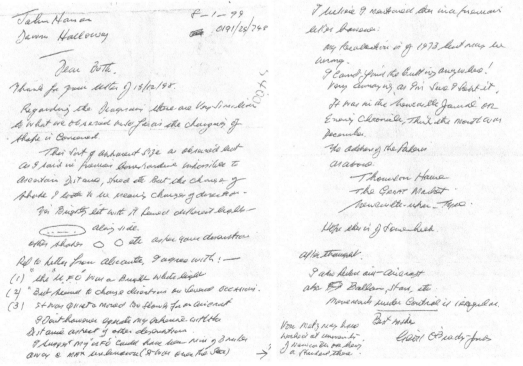

"It had been under control. It moved erratically and showed different colours. What we saw was unique and never to be repeated, over a span of thirty years. I can't accept the explanation given that what we saw was Mars, or Venus."

(Source: Personal interview/*FSR Case Histories*, Supplement 8, December 1971/*Sunday Express*, 22.8.1971)

The two men were not the only ones to sight something odd in the sky that evening. At 12.45am, Mr R.W. Hopkins from Broad Lane, Coventry, was surprised to see a saucer-shaped object, with what appeared to be portholes along its side and a red tail light moving across the night sky, heading in a north-west direction.

Five minutes later, another identical object appeared. This time, Mr Hopkins was able to view the object through a pair of binoculars and see, quite clearly, the 'portholes' along its side. Within minutes, it had gone out of sight. (**Source: letter to Bob Tibbitts, CUFORG**)

16th August 1971 – Police officers sight UFO over Staffordshire

Mr Joseph Wilcox – a shopkeeper, living on the Walsall Road, Aldridge (to the North of Birmingham) – noticed a huge, glowing object, much larger than a Jumbo Jet at 2.30am moving towards the direction of Birmingham Airport, at a height of between 700-800ft. Concerned, he telephoned the police, who told him they would send some officers to have a look.

Police Officers attend scene … twelve photographs taken

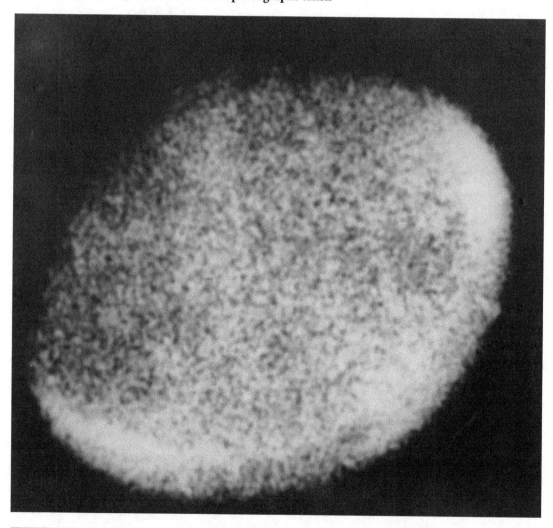

Stunned top cop filmed UFO craft

"IT'S the strangest thing I've seen in 30 years as a policeman."

Les Leek, now a chief inspector at Walsall Police, is not the sort of man to dream up little green men.

But what Les saw and photographed one August night in 1971 remains the best 'unsolved' UFO case ever in the West Midlands.

Les and three disbelieving colleagues were called to an Aldridge petrol station at 2.20am. They found a stunned crowd staring skywards.

There in the inky darkness hovered an oval craft, shining silently thousands of feet above.

Les dashed for the 35mm camera stowed in his patrol car, and fired off a reel of pictures.

The ship stayed perfectly still for an hour, then moved off slowly towards West Bromwich.

"It was like a very big bright egg," Les remembers.

"I don't think I believe in aliens, but I'm certain it was not man-made."

Four photos came out, and were immediately passed on to the Ministry of Defence.

"Only one was ever released," says Les. "Which is strange, because the others showed the craft much more clearly."

Les will probably never know what he saw. Was it something the Government could not explain — or some-

ABOVE: Chief Insp Les Leek. RIGHT: That light in the sky

thing they chose to suppress? "Experts told us it must have been Venus, but since when does Venus show up on Birmingham Air Traffic Control?" says Les.

"If that was Venus, I'll eat my hat."

SUNDAY MERCURY
-Birmingham-

We spoke to one now retired) Chief Inspector 'Les' Leek – who remembered the events vividly.

"It was one of the strangest things I had ever seen in thirty years of service. At the time I was a Police Constable, seconded to the Traffic Department. After being instructed to attend at the scene, together with two other officers, I arrived at the site of a Petrol Station, situated on the Aldridge Road.

The first thing I noticed was a crowd of people, many of whom were pointing upwards into the darkness. I looked up and was amazed to see an egg-shaped object, hovering silently, thousands of feet above me. I ran for the camera (Minolta TR1 X35mm), which was used by us for recording traffic offenders, and took a number of photo-graphs using 200 ASA Film.

What on earth are they?

Trevor Alston examines the flying saucer controversy

FLYING SAUCERS are back! Since police-constable Les Leek, of Aldridge, photographed a strange, unidentified flying object in the sky over Staffordshire this week, evidence has been coming in from people over a wide area who claim they too saw a UFO in the sky.

Once again, people are asking: "What are they?"

Between Stoke-on-Trent and Ashdown, a party returning from holiday on Sunday night saw a yellow, star-like object moving up and down in the sky.

Someone else spotted a bright light, flaming rhythmically, moving at about 500 feet near Stoke-on-Trent shortly afterwards.

An amateur astronomer near Telford spotted an oval object through his telescope, travelling fast, pulsating bright red.

Other people reported a reddish-orange, star-like object with a silver and gold tail, and a UFO was reported from as far away as Liverpool and Matlock, and notifed to air traffic control in Manchester.

Convinced

And Police-constable Leek, who took several photographs of the UFO, has described how he and four other officers kept watch on it for over two hours, after seeing it move slowly up in the sky at a 45-degree angle, then hover at about 1,000 feet. At one stage it was directly overhead, glowing bright yellow.

The policemen are convinced it was not a plane or balloon. But if it was not—what on earth was it?

Many dedicated UFO investigators in this country are convinced that these strange objects are the product of more highly advanced beings than ourselves, who are keeping the earth under close surveillance.

Not unnaturally, the Ministry of Defence has other, far more mundane explanations. A Ministry spokesman said the Government had a special department where experts looked into reported UFO sightings, because of their possible defence implications.

"But the vast majority turn out to have quite ordinary explanations, and we are satisfied that there is no evidence that they represent an air defence threat to the UK," he said.

Out of 1,497 sightings reported to the Ministry between January, 1959, and December 31, 1970, the experts discovered that 538 were caused by aircraft, 322 by satellites and other space debris, 119 by balloons, 110 by meteorites and natural phenomena, 115 by other "miscellaneous" causes.

Only 139 remained unexplained, usually because insufficient information had been given to the Ministry, he said.

Some sightings were hoaxes, some caused by the reflection of towns' lights from clouds, then there were kites, lights on tall buildings, people whose cameras had faulty lenses and a large number of people who mistook Mars, Venus or Sirius for undentified objects.

There are other possible explanations for UFOs.

Mr. Anthony Pace, the joint author of a report on about 100 UFOs which were sighted over the Potteries and Staffordshire in 1967, said some sightings could be due to a mysterious electrical phenomenon called "ball lightning."

Subsequently, we were interviewed not by the police but by civilian representatives of some UFO organisation – possibly the MOD – who seized four of the photographs, but allowed us to keep one of them – which I thought was rather strange, as the photographs taken by them showed a number of peculiar irregular horizontal and vertical lines across the surface of the UFO, which I understood was the result of a 9x magnification."

P.C. Lynn Hopkins:

"'Les' and I were on night duty at Aldridge Police Station, having our refreshment break, when, as a result of a telephone call made to the front office, we decided to respond. It is several years since I left Aldridge and I don't remember the road and street name, but I do remember heading towards Walsall. We went over the bridge and turned first left in the general direction of Barr Beacon. Somewhere along this road, we first saw the UFO as a bright white 'light'. I don't remember its shape. I got the impression that it was not very high... by that I mean that it was not as high as an aircraft would be. It was a quiet night and I couldn't hear any noise coming from it.

The 'light' was moving slowly and we began to follow it in the traffic car. It didn't go in one particular direction but seemed to change directions on several occasions, although there were times when it was stationary. At this time Staffordshire traffic cars were issued with cameras and, during one of the stationary movements of the UFO, 'Les' took several photographs of it. After about thirty minutes, we found that we were following 'this thing' along the Walsall Road, Aldridge, but had to call off the pursuit in Lichfield Road, Walsall, after being instructed by the Police Control Room, at Stafford. Some time after this, 'Les' and I were interviewed by an American, who was a UFO Researcher. He asked me about

Les Leek

the size of the 'light' I saw and a number of other questions. Several years later, whilst working in Stafford, I spoke to the person who developed the film that was sent by 'Les'. He told me the film was blank! Whatever it was that we saw was certainly no aircraft. It was quiet and moved too slowly. If it was a Meteorological balloon, where did it get its bright white light source from?"

Les Leek, – UFO tracked on radar

"I believe that enquiries made at Birmingham Airport showed the UFO had been tracked on radar. I knew that what we had seen could never have been Mars, or a planet, because it was moving rather than being stationary in the sky."

On 7th September, an interview with the officers was screened by BBC TV, *Midlands Today* programme, who showed four photographs from the twelve taken. Details of the incident were featured in the *Birmingham Post* (17th August 1971), when the newspaper outlined an opinion, expressed by Birmingham Airport, that dust in the atmosphere could make stars appear very large and bright as a possible answer.

Birmingham Observatory suggested it was Mars

There was also a comment from Birmingham Observatory, who pointed out that Mars was visible in the object's reported position – very bright and low on the southern horizon – and that they had received approximately forty 'flying saucer' calls from members of the public.

Chief Constable

The Chief Constable of Staffordshire – Mr A. Rees – was quoted as allegedly saying:

"The camera can't lie and you don't know whose experimenting with what these days."

It was obviously of paramount importance to obtain a copy of this photograph, so we contacted the

Photographic Department, at Staffordshire Police Headquarters, where a conversation took place with a civilian employee who had been responsible for processing the original film, after taking it from the possession of P.C. Leek.

> *"Please don't disclose my name. I can tell you that the official explanation was never accepted by this department. I am sorry that I can't help you with a copy of the photograph. Believe it or not, we had a number of copies of them just lying about for many years after the incident. I suggest that you contact the Staffordshire Police Headquarters. Perhaps they can help."*

Staffordshire Police HQ

We wrote to Staffordshire Police and were told in a letter that the photographs and negatives had been disposed of. We also contacted *News Team International Limited*, after discovering they had used a photograph about the event, some years later, in the *Sunday Mercury*, showing Mr Leek pointing to a photograph of the UFO.

We discovered the *Stoke-on-Trent Evening Sentinel* had, themselves, also covered the story in their front page edition of 8th February 1977, which included a copy of the UFO photograph, loaned to them by Staffordshire Police Headquarters, together with a quote from a police spokesman, who said:

> *"It is a complete mystery ... one that remains unsolved. The object was spotted hovering over a garage and no one has since been able to explain what it was."*

We found it rather odd that the police would allow the photograph to be used, understanding their reluctance to allow anybody access to the photographs shortly after the event had taken place – an attitude highlighted by a story printed in *The Sun* (18th August, 1971), in which it was alleged that a security ban had been ordered on the photographs by the then Chief Constable of Staffordshire, Mr Arthur Rees.

(**Source:** *Daily Express*, 18.8.1971 – 'Police silent over Flying Saucer', Dr. J. Allen Hynek interviews Officers ...

Explanation – It was Mars!)

We ascertained that the 'American' who had interviewed the two police officers was Dr. J. Allen Hynek, who was visiting the United Kingdom to present a paper on UFOs at the University of Cambridge. He concluded, after visiting the scene for himself, with Julian Hennessey, that the altitude and azimuth of the object coincided with the position of Mars – at its brightest since 1924 – a similar opinion also expressed by the Assistant Chief Constable of Staffordshire Constabulary, in a letter dated 28th September 1971.

> *"Dear Sir,*
> *I refer to your letter of the 4th September 1971, addressed to my officers at Aldridge Police Station, who were witnesses to the supposed unidentified foreign object on the night of the 14th/15th August. For your information I can inform you that the incident has been investigated by representatives of the National Investigation Committee on aerial phenomena, who are satisfied that the object was, in fact, the planet Mars. A similar conclusion was reached by the duty watch officer, at Jodrell Bank.*
> *Signed, Assistant Chief Constable'*

Or even street lights!

Worse was to come. Dr. Hynek suggested that the other photographs were nearby street lights, taken inadvertently, backed up by examination of the original twelve negatives kept on file at the police station. His findings, later published in *Flying Saucer Review* (February 1972, Supplement No. 9), were received with great concern by the officers involved – who rejected the explanation that what they had seen was Mars, pointing out that there had been no street lamps within forty feet of the viewfinder and the object, according to Les Leek, quote:

> *"It was not Mars. Had it been, it would have remained stationary in the sky. This object eventually moved eastwards at speed, turning an orange colour, before disappearing."*

Police Sergeant asked to discontinue his investigation

One man who chose not to accept the verdict was Michael Davis – a Police Sergeant, stationed in the Midlands, and keenly interested in the UFO subject to such a degree that he told us of one occasion when he was visited by members of a Government Department, who suggested he discontinue his research.

> *"Dr. Hynek was not permitted to view the complete file on the incident. If he had, there would have been ample evidence to indicate the object seen was not Mars, Venus, nor a planet, and that the accounts given by the officers hardly corroborate the concluded findings."*

We decided to write to the MOD, hoping they might be able to give us more information. In return, we received a letter from Kerry Philpott, in April 1998:

> *"With regard to your question about an alleged sighting in the West Midlands, in 1971, as explained previously, the MOD has a well established review programme to release files into the public domain, after 30 years, in accordance with the terms of the Public Records Act of 1958 and 1967."*

We wrote to the MOD in 2011, asking if we could have viewed this file, and were told:

> *"In the light of the Government's commitment to greater openness, the Under-Secretary of State for Defence has asked for some files due for release to the public, over the next few years, be considered for earlier release and the files covering the 1971 period are part of this batch. I am afraid it is too soon to say when a decision might be made, particularly since factors such as personal privacy must first be addressed. I shall write to you again when this issue has been resolved. I hope this explains the position."*

(**Sources: As above**/*Daily Express,* **19.8.1971**/Birmingham UFO Group/*Birmingham Post,* **17.8.1971, 19.8.1971**)

We still await the release of these files, 46 years later!

16th August 1971 – Five-sided object seen in the sky over Leicester

Mrs Peggy Metcalf of Oadby, near Leicester, was in her garden at 6.30am when she saw what she thought was a helicopter in the sky.

> *"It had no rotor blades and was completely silent. It moved at a fairly low speed and had a wide 'V'-shaped vapour trail. The surface resembled silver cooking foil and the object slipper-shaped. It went from north to south and was out of view in five minutes."* (**Source: UFOSIS**)

16th August 1971 – Saucer-shaped object sighted in the sky over Shropshire

Charles Edward Royle (then aged 68) and his wife, Margaret (69)- a qualified teacher of 44 years experience – of 23, Sundial Road, Offerton, Stockport, Cheshire, contacted BUFORA in 1978, wanting to tell what they witnessed – at 2.30pm.

The couple was on a caravan holiday at Hamperley Farm, Marshbrook, Church Stretton, Shropshire.

Charles:

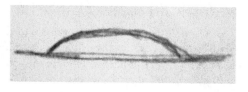

"It was a gorgeous summer's day; we were the only ones on the campsite. My wife brought my attention to something she could see in the sky. I looked up ands saw a white circular object – like a plate, with a dome – hovering there soundlessly, at some height, silhouetted against the perfect blue sky. We watched it for a short time – then it streaked away southwards, at a staggering speed, 15 minutes later."

The couple learnt that others – including a police officer – had also sighted it. Later that day, they went to the farm to pick up some milk, and were told by the farmer's wife that there had been a report of a strange object over Hereford. (**Source: Bryan M. Hartley, BUFORA, Lancashire**)

16th August 1971 – Bright orange 'ball' seen over London

Robert Browning then (28) from Will Crooks Garden, Eltham, London, was mowing the lawn, at 7.45pm, when he saw:

"...a bright red-orange 'ball of light' in the sky, at a height of roughly 2,000 feet, towards the direction of Eltham, some 2 miles away. He thought some one had fired a flare into the sky, but discarded this as an explanation as it was completely stationary. He wondered if it could have been a balloon, catching the sun.

I noticed that my next door neighbours were also watching it. I then alerted my wife as to what was happening. When I looked back, it was in the throes of disappearing towards the east."

Terrific noise heard

Mr David Belton then (26) of New Eltham, London, was another witness. He was asked what he had seen.

"I was in the bedroom when I heard this terrific noise, like scaffolding poles being rolled on concrete. I dashed to the bedroom window and looked out to see a very bright red-orange object in the sky. I thought there was an explosion and that something had shot into the sky. I ran down to the front garden, where next door's two little girls [Elaine Bell (11), and Jackie Spry (11)] were also watching the bright orange object. We watched it for 30 seconds – then it disappeared from sight."

(**Source:** *Kentish Times*, **19.8.1971/Investigator David Oakley-Hill, BUFORA**)

16th August 1971 – Bright orange object over Kent

Civil servant – Mrs Ricky Richardson then (35) of Westwood Lane, Welling, Kent, and her husband, were just completing dinner at 8.15pm. It was a heavy and overcast day.

"This large, bright orange, circular object came into sight wobbling on a zigzag course through the sky. It left a short trail of black smoke coming out of the centre, which appeared to be pulsating. I grabbed the binoculars; it looked like the sun, with flaming ragged edges. The first thing we thought was that it could have been a plane on fire. It seemed to become elongated as it headed away south-west, and disappeared from view." (**Source: BUFORA**)

16th August 1971 – Cigar-shaped UFO

Eltham, London family – James Earl (15), his sister – Jesse (13), father – John (43) and mother – Valerie (39), from Balcaskie Road, were on their way home in a train, after having been out for the day to

Llwyngwril, Merionethshire, on the Welsh coast, at 8.40pm, when they saw a dull flame yellow coloured

cigar-shaped object, motionless in the sky just above the mountains and coastline. (Grid reference SH 589098, sheet 116)

16th August 1971 – 'Golf ball' UFO, with five sides, seen

The *Peterborough Evening Telegraph* (17.8.1971) reported that a number of people had telephoned RAF Wittering and the police, after a 'gold and orange light' had been seen east of Stamford, at a height of about 5,000 feet, just before midnight.

We spoke to Paul Hodgeson, one of the witnesses:

> *"Whatever I saw through the telescope, just before midnight, was no star or aircraft; it looked like a huge golf ball, with five sides, or sections. It must have been important enough for the RAF to 'scramble' two 'Harrier' jets that came to have a look at it."*

The arrival of a RAF Jet, presumably endorsing the likelihood that the UFO had been plotted on radar, as opposed to a visual sighting, was an event which was to be brought to our attention, on many occasions, during our research into the UFO subject. However, one should appreciate, in the majority of such cases, by the time the pilots arrived, the UFO had gone.

According to the *Birmingham Post,* in their edition of the 19th August 1971, they stated that the Staffordshire Police were still convinced the object seen by their officers, over Streetly, was a UFO and showed a copy of the photo that was taken, despite the suggestions made by some astronomers who still believed Mars was the answer.

17th August 1971 – 'Flashing lights' over Small Heath, Birmingham

At 12.45am, four flashing lights, positioned to the left and below of a larger object, were seen over Small Heath – a suburb to the south of Birmingham. During the same day, a Mr D.H. Cooper of Long Street, Dordon, Staffordshire, wrote to the *Tamworth Herald,* after he witnessed:

> *"...an egg-shaped object in the centre of a dark cloud, stationary for ten minutes. It then started moving and climbed upwards, leaving a brilliant white and red glow rather than any vapour trail."*

9.20pm. Mrs P. Emery (then aged 24)of Bradley Lakes, Rugeley, Staffordshire, wrote to Tony Pace – head of BUFORA Investigations – about what she witnessed.

> *"I went to fetch the washing in and noted a bright 'star' in the sky. I didn't take much notice and carried on un-pegging the clothes. The 'star' started to flash red – like the light on a police car, but of course red – as if it was revolving. It moved to the right. I ran to the door and shouted my husband to come out. We watched it come to a rest again, still flashing, and it just faded away a couple of minutes later."*

Mrs Emery then telephoned the police at Rugeley to report the incident.

9.31pm. Henry Gordon Curry (18), living in Tower Gardens, Tottenham, London – a keen amateur astronomer – was looking north, towards the direction of the constellation of Ursa Major, when a 'bright light' came into view from the east.

> *"I thought it might have been an aircraft, but it had no navigation lights. I shouted for my mother to come and have a look.*
>
> *We saw it disappear above, not over the horizon."* (**Source: BUFORA**)

9.45pm. Miss Caroline Balston (23) – a secretary by employment – of Lissended Gardens, Kentish Town, London, was out walking on Hampstead Heath, London, with a friend, when they saw:

> *"...a large 'light' – far too big to be an aircraft – gliding silently across the sky; it was going too slow to be a Shooting Star, in my opinion. By 10pm, it was out of sight."* (**Source: BUFORA**)

10pm. John L. Khan (16) – a resident of Northumberland Place, London – was looking out of his bedroom window.

> *"I saw, near Welbourne Grove, two white 'lights', both the same size, on top of the other – larger than aircraft lights – vertical in the sky.. Suddenly, they stopped and began to rotate about their own axis for just a few seconds. They then moved back along their original path, until out of sight 20 seconds later."* **(Source: East Anglian UFO & Paranormal Research Association)**

18th August 1971 – 'Things' in the sky over Gloucestershire

On the evening, a couple from Cirencester, Gloucestershire – Duncan Edwards (19), and his girlfriend, Judith Wills (16) – were parked up outside the town, when they saw an orange 'light' appear in the sky.

Judith:

> *"This was joined by a second 'thing' and the two of them hovered together. They were definitely not airplanes; if someone had told me about 'flying saucers' before, I would not have believed them. I was terribly frightened."*

Duncan:

> *"They made a terrible noise. I went like a block of ice."* **(Source: The Sun, 20.8.1971)**

18th August 1971 – Spectacular UFO sighting, Newcastle

Frances Hilda Ashley (47) of Eleanor Crescent, Westlands, Newcastle, was inside her house, at 10.10pm, when she saw what she first took to be the planet Mars – then realised this could not be the case.

> *"It was moving, bright orange-yellow in colour. I went outside and saw it was actually one large 'body' with a smaller one on each side, i.e. three separate objects. Another object then appeared moving towards the houses; this one was making a humming noise that appeared to emanate from the side, as this vast object passed overhead at a length I estimated to be 200 metres long by 40 meters wide, and about 60 feet away from me.*
>
> *I saw it had 12-14 windows on the outer surface. It was so close and low that the interior was visible to me; the windows were dome-like in nature. The soft light inside became much brighter as it spilled out of the windows and bathed the vessel in light. Then without banking or making any discernible noise, it lifted suddenly higher in the sky.*
>
> *Near the front end could be made out two silvery-grey pod-like structures; these were corrugated in nature with prominent ribs. On either side were two dark parallel metallic lines, close to the lights. It was a beautiful and graceful object; it appeared to possess a quality of intense power that defies description."*

Mrs Ashley originally wrote a letter to Lionel Beer, who passed it on to Roger Stanway – head of BUFORA Investigations, on the 6th September.

19th August 1971 – Red 'star' over Lincoln

At 9.40pm, electrician Brian Stow, from Lincoln, was parked by the side of the road in Broxholme Lane (just off the Saxilby to Lincoln road) after running out of fuel, waiting for a friend to bring a spare petrol can.

While watching the sky, he noticed a bright-red object, stationary in the west of the sky, about the size a half-crown, held out at arm's length, hovering silently in the clear night sky, for a few minutes. It then suddenly vanished from sight. **(Source: Richard Thompson)**

Brian Stow

The photo on the left is marked with an 'X' where Mr Stow was at the time of the UFO sighting.

The photo on the right is marked with an 'X' showing where the UFO (aparently hovering over a factory) was seen.

©1971 Richard Tompson

20th August 1971 – Yellow 'light' over Northfield

A mysterious bright yellow 'light' was seen moving slowly over Northfield, Birmingham, at 10.45pm disturbing many dogs, who set up a frenzied barking as the object silently flew overhead.
(**Source: UFOSIS, Birmingham**)

24th August 1971 – Vertical shaped UFO over Staffordshire

Between 6am and 6.30am, a vertical cigar-shaped object, with two extending 'arms' top and bottom, was seen hovering in the sky over Brownhills, in Staffordshire.

"After about four minutes it started to descend, with 'arms' taking up a folding position.

When approximately 50 feet from the ground, its 'arms' folded – like a 'penknife' – leaving a vertical, cigar-shaped object, which rose upwards at about 100 miles per hour and headed northwards."

At 11.20pm, the same day, Susan Evans of Heath Hayes, Cannock, Staffordshire, sighted a yellow object in the sky that dipped up and down for 30 seconds of observation, before heading away towards the Aldridge area. She reported this to Tony Pace of BUFORA. (**Source: John 'Dennis' Llewellyn**)

25th August 1971 – UFO display, Bedfordshire

At 9pm, a mysterious boat-shaped object, flashing red and green lights, was seen in the sky for over three hours, at Cardington, Bedfordshire, by at least 50 residents from the nearby Grove Caravan Park.

One of the first people to see it was TV Engineer – Chris Robinson, aged 20, (who was to develop psychic powers of precognition, later in his life). He thought it was an aircraft, to start with, until it began to,

"... move at very fast speed across the sky, right to left and up and down. By this time, there was quite a crowd gathered."

The incident was brought to the attention of the local newspaper – the *Evening Post* (no longer in publication), who sent Keith Dobney – a photographer – to the scene. He arrived there at 11.30pm.

"I first thought it to be a star, but it was bigger than the other stars and moving. I took a picture, using a one minute exposure, which

Chris Robinson

showed it as having moved. It was not something you could recognise and some considerable distance away." (Lightened slightly with filter)

A time exposure photograph showing the unidentified flying object

FRIGHTENED children ran to their mothers saying: "Don't let the spacemen get us," when a mysterious boat-shaped object appeared in the sky north of Caddington last night.

The object, which had green and red flashing lights, was observed for over three hours by a group of 80 people at The Grove caravan site.

TV engineer 20-year-old Christopher Robinson, who lives on the caravan site, was the first person to spot the object.

"I saw it just after 9pm and thought it was an aeroplane, but then I noticed it was going too fast for a plane and, it cut across the

'Mummy, mummy, d let the spacemen s

flight paths, which no plane would ever have done.

"Then it started moving left and right and up and down.

"A lot of people came out to watch it and at one stage it looked so near that the kids started running around and shouting with fear. In fact, some of the adults were frightened as well."

Mr Robinson said the object's lights changed from very bright red to very bright green.

"I know people like Patrick Moore will say it was just an optical phenomenon," he said, "but you don't get 80 people watching an optical illusion. I know there was something there and it will be watching again tonight."

Mr Alan Millins, who also lives on

The Grove caravan site, watched the object for over an hour through a high-powered telescope. "I was doubtful at first, but it soon changed my mind.

"The object looked like a small new moon and occasional flashes of light came from it. It was bobbing about all over the place and must have been pretty large because it was over an inch across on the telescope.

"It disappeared at about 1am and nobody has a clue what it was."

Evening Post photographer Keith Dobney got to the caravan site at 11.30pm.

Long way away

"My first impression was that it was a star, but it was bigger than the other stars in the sky and it was moving.

"I took a picture on a one minute exposure which shows that it moved. It was a long way away and it was not something you could recognise, but there was something there moving around the sky."

A spokesman at Luton Airport said they had no reports of an unidentified flying object last night.

Mr Tony Northwood, chairman of Bedfordshire UFO Society, said the sighting sounded "pretty incredible" and the society would investigate it.

Story: DICK DAWSON
Pictures: KEITH DOBNEY Christa

People on the caravan site watching the UFO last night

Another witness was resident – Mr Alan Millins. He was dubious, at first, but when viewed through high-powered binoculars, soon changed his mind when he saw what looked like a new small moon, with occasional 'flashes of light' coming from it, bobbing about all over the sky.

Over the years we were to meet many people who developed new-found abilities, such as precognition, an increase in their extrasensory perceptions and changes of behaviour and lifestyle, following the sighting of a UFO, while others seemed apparently 'unaffected', apart from a passing curiosity to identify the nature of what it was they had seen. Perhaps factors such as distance, length of time involved, and the witness's susceptibility, based on predetermined beliefs, should be taken into consideration – although we speculated that these changes in behaviour are influenced by the rays of

SKY WATCH:
Bill Dillon, a witness to the Ramridge encounter and a sketch of the mysterious object (above). Right, The Luton News report of Chris Robinson's 1971 experience and below the Luton News report of the 1962 Ivinghoe Road incident

'Mummy, mummy, don't let the spacemen get us'

ANOTHER amazing Luton encounter involved the now famous dream detective Chris Robinson.

Chris has gone on to become a well-known psychic who has appeared on TV and successfully helped police with investigations.

But 35 years ago this month he was a 20-year-old TV engineer and yet to make his mark in the world.

As reported in The Luton News' now defunct sister paper the Evening Post on August 26, 1971, Chris was the first person among a group of 60 people to spot a boat shaped object with green and red flashing lights over Caddington. "I saw it just after 9pm and thought it was an aeroplane, but then I realised it was going too fast for a plane and cut across the flight paths, which no plane would ever have done," he said.

"Then it started moving left and right and up and down. A lot of people came out to watch it and at one stage it looked so near that the kids started running around and shouting with fear. In fact, some of the adults were frightened as well."

Chris said the object's lights changed from bright red to bright green and he defended what everyone had seen against the possible response of sceptics.

"I know people like Patrick Moore will say it was just an optical phenemonon," he said. "But you don't get 60 people watching an optical illusion. I know there was something there."

Chris, who still lives in the area and has travelled all over the world as the dream detective, spoke to The Luton News again after reading our original Ramridge UFO story and said he was still convinced by what he saw in the 1970s and has learnt about the subject since.

"There is so much evidence, nobody is ever going to convince me that there's nothing out there," he said.

unseen 'paranormal' energy given-off by the objects as they hover in the sky. Perhaps there is a more sinister purpose behind the display of these objects in the atmosphere than we can possibly believe?

Whilst we could not directly attribute Chris's development of his new-found abilities to glimpse future events (which had not yet happened) to that initial UFO appearance, all those years ago, we should bear the possibility in mind. When we spoke to Chris, in 2006, we learnt that the police had regretfully dispensed with his sought-after services, after being instructed to do so by a very senior Cabinet politician, (name withheld), who deemed this psychic source of information went against Christian beliefs, rather than any lack of confidence in Chris Robinson's work. The public will never know the results of Chris Robinson's service to the Security Agencies in this country, for obvious reasons, but is there not something rather unique, and a little frightening, about being able to peer into future events which haven't yet happened, and ultimately change fate, or was it preordained this was going to happen anyway?

(Source: *Evening Post*, 26.8.1971/**Personal interview**)

26th August 1971 – Bright golden 'light' over Lincolnshire

At 9.15pm, Mrs Edith Carr from Moor Lane, Potter Hanworth, was in her kitchen when she noticed a bright golden 'light', stationary in the sky towards the south-west.

"Every now and then the 'light' would go out was replaced by a short yellow 'tail'. By 10.30pm, it began to move away and was soon out of view." (**Source: Richard Thompson**)

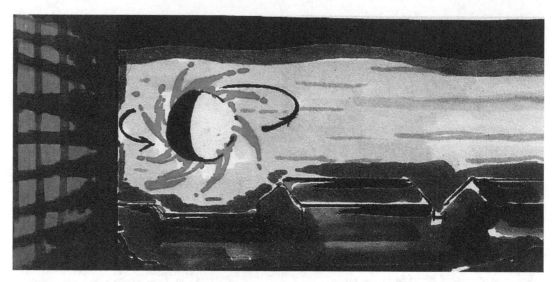

27th August 1971 – UFO landing, Kent

Mr Gary Harrison of Broadway, Gillingham, Kent – a freelance draughtsman by occupation – was driving to work, at 8.45am, when something shone in his eye as he approached the turning for West Malling.

> *"I looked to my right and could see that whatever it was appeared to be hovering over trees in a nearby field. Thinking it might be a helicopter, I got out of my car for a better look. By this time the sun had come off it and I was able to make out an oblong-shaped object, with rounded ends. It had a silver metallic finish, with a black rim around the bottom. I estimated it to be about 50 feet long.*
>
> *It was completely stationary when I first saw it – then it started to slowly drop down behind the trees and I lost sight of it."*

Mr Harrison reported it to the police, who told him they had not received any other reports – although a spokesman for the Force added, rather surprisingly:

> *"Whatever these things are, they are no laughing matter. I saw one myself in Malaya."*

(Source: *Kentish Post*, 31.8.1971)

UFO landing, Norfolk

Mr Peter Arthur, from New Hainford, was on his way home, at 9.15pm, when he noticed:

> *"...a bright orange, saucer-shaped object, with five flashing lights around its base, descending over a nearby field, about a quarter of a mile away from the house. I watched it for about fifteen minutes as it moved about, illuminating the ground below, until losing sight of it as it descended behind the trees. During this time, I was acutely aware of an eerie silence which developed while the object was airborne – a sensation that left an indelible mark on my memory.*
>
> *I arrived home; I telephoned the Evening News to report the incident. While I was doing this, my mother shouted out that she had just seen a bright orange object shoot up into the sky from behind trees at the bottom of our garden, some four hundred yards away."*

Ivan W. Bunn

As a result of newspaper publicity, Ivan W. Bunn, from Lowestoft – keenly interested in all aspects of inexplicable UFO/paranormal events occurring in the Norfolk area – contacted Mr Arthur and arranged to visit the locality. Unfortunately, as Mr Arthur was going to be away on business, Ivan – accompanied by his colleague, Keith Williamson – decided to have a look themselves on the 12th September, knowing, as time went by, the chances of finding anything on the ground would decrease.

Ivan:

> *"From examination of the report given to the newspaper, the only possible location appeared to be a small wooded area, about three quarters of a mile away from the house of the witness. We made our way through the wood – no easy task, due to the denseness of the undergrowth and marshy ground underfoot – and came across a small clearing with slightly flattened long reed grass.*
>
> *A short distance away, we came across another small clearing with similar effects, followed by our entrance into a third clearing, where the long grass was found to have been definitely flattened and laying in the same north/south direction, forming part of a 'trail' of 25 yards in length. The leaves of the surrounding bushes were covered in what appeared to be a grey coloured dust. This effect was localised and not found outside the clearings.*
>
> *In order to confirm this was the same place as described by Mr Arthur, we sent him a map drawn of the area, asking him to mark the movements of the UFO and where he had seen it descending, without informing him of the visits to the locality. When the map was returned to us, we discovered the parts penned in by Mr Arthur matched up exactly with ours."*

Another witness to these events who was subsequently traced, a couple of months later, was Mrs Moore of Motum Road, Norwich, who told of sighting a brilliant object descending slowly through the sky and disappearing behind some trees, before rising upwards, flashing with red light, at the same time and date.

At 9.45pm, two straight *"sausage-shaped objects"* were seen moving slowly below scattered cloud, heading south-west – each one the apparent same distance behind the other, over Andover, in Hampshire, according to Kevin Gentleman, Alison Taylor, Edward Clapcoll and Janet Harris. The objects, which were seen to pulse, were lost from view a few minutes later. (**Source: Andover Ufologists**)

28th August 1971 – 'Flying Saucer' over Colchester, Essex

Janet Bond (31), of Baden Powell Drive, Colchester, Essex, was having a late evening with the neighbours. Around 1am, her husband drew her attention to something in the sky.

> *"I looked out and saw an orange coloured conical, or saucer-shaped, object with a fuzzy outline. We spent the next two hours watching as it revolved around the sky, making a faint buzzing sound, during which time it actually split into two; the top separated but remained attached. White beams of light shone upwards from the lowest part. A few minutes later, it merged into one part again.*
>
> *It finally disappeared from view by shooting upwards into the sky."*

UFOs over Banbury

At 4.50pm, while on their way home from school, situated on the opposite side of the Ruscote housing estate, Banbury, three schoolboys – Tony Pettinger (11), Ian Sales (11) and Colin Wood (10) – sighted a cigar-shaped object in the north of the sky, at an elevation of approximately 15 degrees. This was accompanied by four or five other smaller objects. They were last seen heading eastwards. (**Source: BUFORA**)

'Yellow globe' reported over Solihull, West Midlands

During the same late evening, residents living in the small village of Hampton Lucy, near Solihull, West Midlands, contacted the police after sighting a mysterious 'yellow globe' hovering in the sky. (**Source: UFOSIS, Margaret Westwood**)

29th August 1971 – 'Orange globe' over West Midlands

A bright 'orange globe' was seen motionless in the sky over Tudor Grange Park, Solihull, before vanishing from view minutes later. (**Source: UFOSIS**)

30th August 1971 – Orange 'light' phenomena – did this cause a power cut?

Mrs Margaret Bores of Bignolds Close, Claydon, Banbury, sighted:

"...something definite and unusual, like nothing I had ever seen before – a white 'light', which gradually blossomed into a cluster of orange 'blobs' across the horizon. This happened on successive nights, from dusk until the early hours of the morning."

Her daughter also told of a power cut to the domestic supply, lasting over four hours, during the same time, and that the engineer was unable to diagnose the problem. Was it connected with the appearance of the UFO?

Another witness to this phenomenon was Mr Trebilcock, who decided to investigate further after seeing some 'lights' in the field, which he took to be a combine harvester at work. As he approached the 'lights', now strung along the length of the low horizon, he was surprised to see them dim in brightness every time a car passed along the road.

We learnt of power cuts of four hours duration, which had occurred the previous week – the source of which was never identified – accompanied by loud whining noises coming from overhead, and the appearance of peculiar 'bright lights' that took up positions over some of the houses on the estate, which were seen by Geoffrey Smith – a reporter for the *Banbury Guardian*. This was later explained away as being stubble being burnt in the fields and the noise made by combine harvesters at work in the fields.

Banbury resident – Steven Palmer, told us:

"I remember the year and month very well. I had just taken possession of a blue Hillman Hunter car, registration number CUD 471K. My mother was upstairs, cleaning the bedroom sill, when she shouted out to the next door neighbour, 'Sam', that she could see what looked like a ship's capstan in the sky. The two of them watched it for about a minute, until it sped away at high speed."

Steve also spoke of an incident that was brought to his attention, involving a family friend – Joyce Oxlade – who was driving her car along an unclassified road, between Doddington and Milton, when a 'bright light' shot past, causing the engine to cut out.

(**Source: Mr R.L. Seaman, Andover Ufologists/***Coventry Evening Telegraph*, **2.9.1971/***The Banbury Guardian*, **2.9.1971 – 'UFO over Banbury'/** The *Southern Evening Echo*, **1.9.1971 – 'Villagers alarmed by mystery lights')**

Over Southampton

At 6.10pm, a UFO was seen in the almost cloudless sky over Southampton for over ten minutes, by a local resident, who later contacted Andover UFO researcher – Mr R.L .Seaman.

"At first, this thing appeared to be a halo and I thought it must be a curious formation of white cloud, and that it was such a perfect circle. As I watched, it narrowed into an eclipse and, to my amazement, it tilted to the right and I saw what seemed to be two bright 'points of light' on the lower right edge. A moment or two later, it reappeared from the lower right edge of the cloud and sped into the remote distance, until it was lost from view as a pinhead of light. The direction was somewhat to the right of the sun, at the time."

Over London

At Eltham, south-east London (Grid reference 5417), Mr Bennett was in his back garden, exercising the dog 9.15pm, when he saw, at an angle of 15 degrees up in the sky, towards the direction of Lee Green, two large bright stationary 'lights'. He described them as:

"...like car headlamps, close together, the outer halos of light overlapping the dog, a Labrador, which ran inside, clearly agitated – its hair on end."

He called for his wife and daughters to come and have a look, by which time the objects had been stationary for 15 minutes.

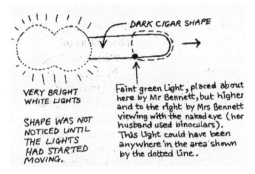

"A kind of shutter came over the 'lights' and they started to glide towards the right (north-west) – much slower than an airplane – making a low whirring noise, like a child's humming top but of a deeper pitch. As the 'lights' moved, we saw a dark cigar-shaped object to the right, which remained equidistant. Through binoculars we saw a faint green light near the right end. It took about 45 seconds to travel across the sky, where we lost sight of it due to our observation being blocked out by a church."

(Source: *Gemini*, Volume 1, number 1, January to March 1972, Mark Stenhoff)

Over Warwickshire

Schoolboy Simon Day was looking out of his bedroom window, at 10.40pm, at Solihull, Warwickshire, when he saw:

"...a shape that was in a rough curve, almost as bright as the moon and the same colour – yellow-white. I called my brother, Crispin, and we watched it for about five minutes, before it scattered and went into little pieces – tiny little objects. My parents also saw it before it went over the moon in a rainbow shape, and disappeared from sight."

The following day, the brothers were talking to their friend – Mark Brown – who told them he had also seen the UFO, which he described as:

"...pure white, with a green light flashing under it about every ten seconds; it was completely still, so I didn't think it was a plane.

I watched if for about forty minutes, before it disappeared."

(Source: Malcolm Drew and Alan Crowe, Birmingham UFO Investigation Group)

Mr John 'Dennis' Llewellyn

In 2003, we took the opportunity to visit John 'Dennis' Llewellyn – a UFO Investigator for BUFORA – and his wife, Ruby, then living in Stratford-upon-Avon, Warwickshire, after learning of their interest in a number of UFO sightings which had taken place in Warwickshire and Oxfordshire, going back to the 1950s. John outlined a 'wave' of approximately 100 sightings reported around the Midlands and Oxfordshire, between August and September 1971, when all manner of peculiar things were seen and brought to his attention. They included clusters of orange/red 'lights', and pulsating noises heard

Ruby Llewellyn holding a photo of her husband, John

in the sky – many of which attracted the interest of the local newspapers – as can be seen from headlines, such as 'More UFO reports at Banbury'/'Mystery object at Bretch Hill'/'Police report fireball over Banbury'/'The witnesses of the inexplicable'/'Are they coming ?'/'UFO pattern repeated'/'On the track of Banbury UFOs'/'Monster in the park'/'Police see mystery light' – just a few of the banner grabbing headlines brought to our attention – now long forgotten.

31st August 1971 – UFO seen to take off over Rutland

At 9.30pm, a motorist and his girlfriend were driving past a field near Uppingham (Grid reference 4829), when they saw what looked like a large spinning top land, and then take off. (**Source: South Lincolnshire UFO Study Group**)

August 1971 – Report of a UFO over Harwell Laboratories, Berkshire

Barbara Snow (24) of Manor Road, North Woolston, Southampton, was on her way home, accompanied by her father, William Edward Purser (55), and her mother, Ivy Doreen Purser (62) – and passing Harwell Laboratories, Didcot Berkshire, at 7.30pm.

Barbara noticed:

> "...a silver, circular object, hovering in the sky about 400 yards away, over the fields. We stopped the car and got out; an eerie silence fell about the place. The road that we had been travelling on – the busy Newbury to Oxford road – suddenly changed – no traffic was seen, no birds singing – nothing. It was like being in a vacuum; time stood still. I watched the 'craft' for about ten minutes. I made no attempt to get closer, as it was on MOD land – then, without any prior indication, after ten minutes, it shot upwards at tremendous speed. I was awestruck and knew I would never forget what I witnessed on that evening." (**Source: Martin Keatman, BUFORA**)

SEPTEMBER 1971

1st September 1971 – UFO sightings over the West Midlands

Two UFOs were sighted over Weston Coyney, Staffordshire, by local resident – John Hancock, who described them as being: "*...cylindrical- shaped objects, showing a row of coloured lights*".

Another witness, Bucknall schoolboy – William Boyd, reported having seen:

> "*...a red, triangular, object heading across the sky towards Stoke*".

Other witnesses were Simon Day (13), and his brother Crispin (12), from Solihull near Birmingham. They told of seeing a strange bright object in the sky, at 10.40pm, which they first took to be the moon but then saw it was:

> "*...a rough curve – almost as bright as the moon. We watched it for five minutes, until it scattered into little pieces, each one the same colour as the large one.*"

The boys called their parents to come and have a look.

At 10.15pm, a pulsating bright orange object was observed moving through the sky over The Nook, in Cornwall. The witness was Sheila Aucott (27) – a State Registered Nurse. This was also seen by Enid McGowan (50) of Kings Lane, South Croxton, Leicestershire, and Rita H. Middleton (55) of Salisbury Avenue, Croft, in Leicestershire – also at 10.15pm. (**Source: Malcolm Drew, Alan Crow, UFOSIS, Birmingham**)

2nd September 1971 –'L'-shaped UFO seen in the sky over Staffordshire

An 'L'-shaped UFO was seen in the sky over Aldridge and Great Barr, Birmingham, constantly changing colour and flight, by crowds of people who stopped to gaze upwards – seen to change into a 'cigar' before vanishing.

Lynette James (17) from Cardington Avenue, Great Barr, was one of a number of people who telephoned the police.

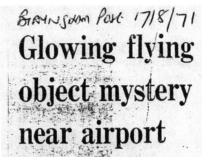

"I saw this strange 'L-shaped object, mostly green with red at the ends, in the sky. It then changed into a flat, long object, which became white in the middle and glowed even redder at the ends. Its next shape was into a flat sort of shape.

I telephoned the police, because children in the street were getting really scared."

A police spokesman, later consulted over the incidents, confirmed officers *"had attended, because children in the area were becoming frightened"*.

Other sightings for that evening included a glowing orange 'ball' seen over Kingswinford, for at least ten minutes, before accelerating away at terrific speed towards the north-east, a pulsating 'star' seen over Penn Common, and four unusual lights over Wolverhampton, seen by at least 30 people.

(Source: Birmingham UFO Investigation Group/*Daily Express*, 4.9.1971 – 'Flying Cigar' Mystery/*Birmingham Evening Mail*, 3.9.1971)

3rd September 1971 – Strange UFO over Leicester

At 9.30pm, Mr Edward Remington (69) – ex-member of the mercantile marine – saw:

"...an object in the sky, moving in a north-west to south-east direction, at fast speed. It resembled a Chinese lantern, illuminated brilliantly from within – like a spherical balloon, encased in light girder work. This radiated in spokes from a central spindle at the top of the sphere."

(Source: *BUFORA Journal*, Volume 3, Summer 1972)

5th September 1971 – Square-shaped formation and saucer-shaped objects reported

Gwyneth Thouard from Wordsley, Kingswinford, sighted a shapeless object of bright red, green and yellow colours, moving high across the sky, while accompanied by her husband, for over 2 hours.

"It was vey high in the sky. While we were watching, an aircraft flew past the object."

(Source: *Birmingham Evening Mail*, 7.9.1971 – 'UFO report over town')

At 4,30pm, Mr Harold Hiley (63) – a local government officer from Vegal Crescent, Ovenden, Halifax, in Yorkshire – was at Barden Tower, Wharfedale, Skipton, with his wife – Ivy, watching a single seat light aircraft descending towards Yeadon Airport.

He was surprised to see a UFO, about 6-7,000 feet above the plane, described as *"a hazy, metallic, inverted 'saucer' or 'cone',"* which was following a parallel course and speed. He said:

Birmingham Post 17/8/71

Glowing flying object mystery near airport

Birmingham Post Reporter

It was large, it glowed and several people saw it — but no-one can explain the flying object which was seen over South-east Birmingham early yesterday.

Air traffic control at Birmingham Airport said there was no aircraft in the area, meteorological officers said they thought it very unlikely that it belonged to them, and the RAF wondered why no one had bothered to report it.

The mystery began when Mr. Joseph Willcox, a shop-keeper, spotted the object from outside his home in Walsall Road, Aldridge, at about 2.30 a.m.

"It was low in the sky in the direction of Birmingham Airport. I could not see the shape because of the light from it," he said.

Seen by police

"It was definitely not an aircraft. I would think it was about 700 to 800ft. up, and bigger than a Jumbo jet. My wife and I watched it for about an hour and a half. I'm not a crank. It was something I can't explain at all."

Aldridge police were told, and four policemen saw the object. Finally it disappeared, heading west, about two hours after the first sighting.

A spokesman at Birmingham Airport said: "In my experience, these reports usually turn out to have a natural explanation.

"Dust in the atmosphere can make stars appears very large and bright. I've seen the effect and it's quite impressive." he said.

No signals

The object was reported to Jodrell Bank radio telescope observatory in Cheshire, but it did not pick up any signals.

The RAF was not impressed by the report. "We are not interested in flying saucers, but we are interested in these reports from a defence point of view. This is the first I've heard of it and its a bit late now," said a spokesman.

A spokesman at Edgbaston Observatory, Birmingham, said last night that Mars was visible in the object's reported position.

"The planet is almost in its closest position to the earth. It is very bright and low on the southern horizon all night. We have had about 40 calls in the past few from people they had saucer," he sa

"After five seconds, the plane moved into a very thick bank of cloud and out of view. The UFO stopped and hovered for a few seconds and then reversed its course, moving at high speed".

(Source: G.N.P. Stephenson, Surrey – BUFORA)

This was followed by a report, on the same evening, of two UFOs *"forming a square of rotating lights",* seen moving over Worcester.

(Source: *The Birmingham Evening Mail*, 7.9.1971 – 'UFO report over town')

5th September 1971 – UFO over Wharfedale, Yorkshire

7th September 1971 – Phenomena explained

The *Weekly News* (9.9.1971), of North Wales, also told of being contacted by Llanfairfechan residents, who had seen a UFO during the evening of the 7th September 1971. They included Mr and Mrs E.C. Williams, and Llandudno teacher – Mr J.C. Griffiths.

Mr Williams said he had seen:

"...an oval-shaped white light, rather like the beam of a car headlamp in foggy weather, moving in a north-west direction over the Irish Sea. It was partially obscured by haze; we watched it for 20-30 minutes, as it slowly moved away."

He rejected the explanation put to him that it might have been a reflection of a light on a cloud, and said:

"It was an oval light and never varied in shape".

Other witnesses include several schoolboys on a beach.

The *Daily Mail* told its readers that hundreds of people, from Scotland to Cornwall, had reported having sighted a 'bright light' travelling westwards; sometimes hovering, other times moving at speed, during the evening of the 7th September 1971.

According to Ivor Beston, at Manchester:

"It was round, with a kind of cotton wool rim. I saw it move behind a cloud, but it was so bright it shone right through – then it moved off at high speed."

Over Guildford, Surrey, it was described as a 'white ball'. Over Weybridge, it had sprouted flame. At Tavistock, in Devon, it appeared as yellow-white, while at Bude, in Cornwall, it was sighted as a blue blob. The MOD suggested it was a noctilucent cloud, a vapour cloud still reflecting sunlight, while officials at Glasgow Weather Centre explained it away as being a fluorescent chemical cloud, at a height of 50 miles, ejected by a meteorological research rocket launched from South Uist in the Hebrides.

Mr Arthur Tomlinson, of DIGAP, said:

"The MOD is idiots; you would find no cloud so widely reported, and moving at different speeds. I checked with the RAF Farnborough and they said the sightings had nothing to do with rockets, clouds, or Russian satellites."

Omar Fowler of SIGAP

Thanks to Omar Fowler – then the investigations co-coordinator for SIGAP (Surrey Investigation Group on Aerial Phenomena) – a post he also held with BUFORA, we were to learn that the UFO was, in fact, a barium thermite cloud, fired by *'Petrel'*- a rocket launched from South Uist, as part of an experiment, and photographed over Glasgow by BUFORA member – Duncan Hogg.

London Air Traffic Control Centre

Joe McGonagle writes in the *Magonia* website (2011) about the role of NICAP researcher – Julian Hennessey, who was to badger the MOD for answers, over the years. We had the pleasure of meeting

Julian, some years ago, and would like to tell the reader about a remarkable visit made, unofficially, to the London Air Traffic Control Centre, on the 8th September 1971.

Joe:

"Hennessey told me, in a telephone conversation, that he obtained a list of internal military telephone numbers from somewhere, and called the London Air Traffic Control Centre (military) (LATCC). Because he knew the telephone number, they assumed that he was authorised to have access to the records, and set up an appointment for him to view them on 8th September 1971, which he attended. Hennessey said that he was nervous they would discover that he wasn't authorised to see the records and that LATCC had allocated a female officer to assist him! He copied a few documents related to cases that he was investigating and left, breathing a sigh of relief. Hennessey wrote to the LATCC on 20th September, requesting access to their UFO records again. LATCC replied, on the 25th October 1971, directing Hennessey to request access via S4f (Air).On 22nd December, the MOD wrote to him, mentioning:

'I know of your visit to the LATCC (military) on 8th September, but I must confess that I am at a loss to know how on that visit you managed to see UFO reports received on 26/27th October 1971 – No doubt you will be aware that on the 25th November the Parliamentary Under-Secretary of State Defence for the Royal Air Force wrote to Mr Julian Ridsdale MP, who had taken a question on your behalf, advising him that UFO records remained closed to public scrutiny until they become available under the rules laid down'."

8th September 1971 – Strange 'light' in the sky over Colwyn Bay

At 9.30pm, Mr E. Jackson of Colwyn Bay, and his fiancé, reported having sighted an oval, white light – the size of the full moon in the sky – described as resembling a bright bulb, as seen through frosted glass, at an elevation of about 35 degrees off the north-western horizon. The couple kept the object under observation for ten minutes, by which time it had moved about 10 degrees and was lower in the sky, approximately 25 degrees off the horizon. (**Source: Mrs E. Jackson**)

8th September 1971 – 'Flying Saucer' sighted over Clee Hill Radar Station, Shropshire (Grid reference 3528)

At 11.40pm, a couple driving near Clee Village, in Shropshire, sighted

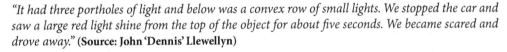

"... a cone-shaped object with a flat top, metallic silver in colour, hovering in the sky in a low valley to the right of the road, about 500 feet off the ground, near to Clee Hill Radar Station".

A similar object was reported three weeks previously, over the same area, at midday, by an unnamed witness, who said:

"It had three portholes of light and below was a convex row of small lights. We stopped the car and saw a large red light shine from the top of the object for about five seconds. We became scared and drove away." (**Source: John 'Dennis' Llewellyn**)

10th September 1971 – UFO over Romford, Essex

Nicholas Andrew Spring (27) of Beambridge Road, Basildon, Essex, was walking down Clockhouse Lane, Collier Row, Romford, at 7.30pm, when he sighted:

"...a long, thin, reddish-orange object in the sky above the school building, shaped like a cigar with a small green 'ball of light' moving around it horizontally. The object was making a high-pitched sound – like 'blowing into bottle'. I watched it for 10-15 seconds, before it disappeared behind the school building." (**Source: Ron West**)

7th-14th September 1971 – Reports of a 'T'-bag ghost sighted!

Following reports of 'apparitions' and UFOs, seen by a number of people using Palmers Rough Park, off Jacey Road, Shirley, Solihull (adjacent to Robin Hood Cemetery, South Birmingham), local NICAP UFO Investigator – Derek Samson, decided to visit the scene for himself, after learning that his two sons – Christopher and Julian – had also witnessed what was to become known locally as 'The 'T'-bag ghost'.

Derek:

> "I contacted the Solihull Times newspaper and told them about the investigation. They suggested I meet up with their reporter in the park and wait for something to happen. Unfortunately, nothing untoward happened. As far as sightings were concerned, they always took place during the night of the full moon and involved the appearance of what was believed to be the ghost of a little girl. The majority of these sightings took place between 8pm- midnight, and lasted for a period of one week – between the 7th and 14th September 1971. Christopher and Julian told me they had seen what appeared to be something looking like a sack of flour, oblong in shape, which was seen to fall over a bench before gliding underneath it and disappearing. Rather oddly, I remember that several years ago, a similar incident was reposed in another park, approximately one mile away (Hobs Moat), when a number of children sighted a white sack-like shape being dragged along the ground."

We asked Julian Samson, in 2007, for his recollection of the incidents.

> "I was 12 years of age and often visited Palmers Rough Park with my brother, Christopher, and remember talk going around about a glowing square-shaped object seen by some of the kids in the wood, always to the right of the children's swing area, that became labelled as 'the T-bag ghost', believed to be connected with the crash-landing of a World War Two Bomber in the vicinity.
>
> One night I was in the play area, talking to some boys, as dusk began to fall, when I noticed two boys enter the wood by climbing over a shallow ditch that runs around its perimeter. A few minutes later they came rushing out, screaming, dropped down into the ditch and scrambled away, followed by this amazing 'thing', resembling a square plate, showing dimly lit windows, slightly on edge, moving slowly a few feet above the ground. I watched it head off towards the route taken by the boys and disappear into the darkness.
>
> I never saw those boys again and presumed they must have been really frightened."

As a result of publicity given to the incident in the *Solihull News* (2005), we were contacted by Dorothy Gilbert, from Shirley, who told us about an incident involving her son, Steven, who had arrived home in a very frightened state, some time in the autumn of 1971.

We spoke to Steven, who said:

> "It's something I have never forgotten and still forms the subject of occasional conversation in the family, although the exact date escapes me. I was in the park, one evening, accompanied by Steven Broadhurst, Carl Edgington, Mark Harrison, and Trevor Betley who had gone for a walk in the wood with his girlfriend. All of a sudden, Trevor and his girlfriend came rushing out of the woods, screaming, stumbling over the ditch, followed by a luminous shape which stopped in mid-air and slowly drifted back into the woods. We stood there, undecided what to do, and shocked by what we had just witnessed. Imagine our fear when whatever it was came back out of the wood and moved over to the nearby bench, appearing to sit down. My impression of this 'luminous mass' was that it resembled a small girl in shape, with long white hair, although I didn't see any legs or facial features. Steven Broadhurst pointed at this 'luminous mass' and urged his dog, 'Tim', to confront it. 'Tim' rushed over towards it, stopped, came running back, and urinated all over Steven's leg. This may sound funny, but it certainly wasn't at the time. The dog was terrified. We stood shouting at it, but were far too frightened to go up to it. Slowly, it moved back into the wood. Oddly, this was not the"

only time I saw these manifestations. Where it came from and who it was I cannot say, but there were rumours it was the ghost of a young girl, murdered in Cut Throat Wood, many years ago."

Tracey Carling

Tracey Carling contacted us after having read the newspaper article, sent by us, appealing for any witnesses to come forward.

"I was living with my parents in Olton Road, Shirley – the old Police house, which backs onto the park.

One morning I woke up early, during the summer of 1993. When I looked out of the bedroom window, I was stunned to see what looked like a white 'glowing lady', standing in our garden. She had a thin face, long hair, wearing a dress with long flowing arms.

I shouted for my mum to come quickly and have a look. When I looked back at the 'figure', I was horrified to see her looking up at me and waving with her right hand, before walking towards the three trees at the bottom of our garden – where she disappeared from view."

Carl Edgington

In October 2005 we met up with Carl Edgington, who had no difficulty in remembering what he considered to be the most unusual event he had ever witnessed in his life, who was in the park when the Press turned up. He confirmed that nothing untoward happened, apart from someone attempting to play a practical joke by hiding under a sheet – a ruse which was quickly detected.

"The actual sightings of the 'ghost' went on for over a week, during early September 1971. I remember seeing a girl called Marie, move from behind one of the trees, followed by the definite figure of a small girl, wearing a cloudy white dress with pleats in it, who promptly vanished. A couple of nights later, I saw the 'girl' floating just above ground level, heading across the park, disappear, and then reappear on the other side of the brook. To my amazement I saw two men on bikes ride over 'it' – the form, ghost, whatever you want to call it. One of them was Mark Harrison, who was on home leave from the Royal Marines. On another occasion, I was with some other boys when we saw 'it' move out of the woods and sit down on the bench. I went towards it and it rose up and began to move towards us. Steve Broadhurst urged his dog to confront it. The dog went forward, stopped, came back, and urinated on his leg, very frightened – as we all were by then. I have no idea where the name 'T-bag ghost' came from. As far as I am concerned, I believe it to be the ghost of a young girl, who was murdered by hanging, just after the end of the Second World War, but it's only what I've heard." (**Source: Personal interviews**)

15th September 1971 – UFO over South west London

Gerald and Terrence Moran from Lessingham Avenue, Tooting, South West London, happened to look out of the window, at 10pm, on what was a clear night, and saw an object moving slowly and silently in a west to east direction.

A minute later it was out of sight.

16th September 1971 – Sightings of a 'Monster' in Berkshire

Our curiosity was well and truly aroused after learning of a strange 'being' – nicknamed locally as 'The Stockham Monster' – which was seen walking around the Park housing estate, at Wantage, by a member of the public, who had reported it to the police on the 16th September 1971.

This was followed by another sighting in Denchworth Road, Grove, Wantage, at 5.30am on 25th September 1971, by a local woman – Linda Milne – who sighted 'it' making its way into woods near the old Wantage canal – matters eventually brought to the attention of *BBC Radio Oxford*, who interviewed a number of witnesses, including two schoolboys who described being chased by the 'creature' and of throwing stones at it.

We met up with Richard Colborne, in January 2007, after learning that he had initially investigated the incident concerned along with Michael J Prewett and Keith Palmer.

Dawn Holloway with Richard Colborne

He told us that he had himself interviewed Martin Halstead, Michael Nichols (14), Steven Ellis (16), Linda Milne (18), and Nicky Lawrence (14), who was local teenagers at the time. As a result of this and access to his original BUFORA report made in 1971, we then spoke to a number of those witnesses ourselves, who described the 'being' as:

> *"...eight feet tall with broad shoulders, featureless head, glowing red eyes, about 12 inches apart, two small horns on the head, a very deep protruding back, thick arms, with a covering of greyish/ white hair or fur, and the ability to run through dense undergrowth without making noise, and jumping large obstacles" (reminding us of a strange 'leaping man', seen at RAF Alconbury).*

The old Grove Airfield

Our enquiries revealed that the majority of the sightings appeared to have occurred on wasteland, close to the local youth club, 'Garrisons' – a brick built building, situated on the old Grove Airfield (demolished in 1993), one mile north-west of Wantage, during the period between the 14th/16th September 1971 and November, by which time the reports appeared to have died out.

At first glance, it could have been all too easy to dismiss the sightings as either products of fertile imaginations, or localised hysteria, triggered by reports of UFOs seen around the Banbury area, or even somebody playing a hoax by dressing up in fancy dress.

We decided to contact the parties involved, after being unable to obtain the current whereabouts of the original reports submitted to BUFORA, and Richard had never kept copies or a tape-recording made at the time.

Dawn Embling

We first spoke to Dawn Embling (sister of Martin Halstead), who told us Martin had passed away nine years ago, at quite an early age, but she still remembered the 'wave' of curiosity and fear which had pervaded the locality, after she heard about it from her brother, Les, and some of the others to whom we spoke, and rejected the suggestion made that the culprit was a local man, who had been to Africa recently, and for reasons best known to himself had decided to frighten the local residents by hiding in the undergrowth, wearing an African headdress!

Another not dissimilar suggestion was also made by Chief Inspector Norman Goodley – Head of the

local Police, who thought it may have been someone playing a prank. Two of his officers, Police Sergeant Gutterdidge and a PC had visited the area on the 24th of September after being called out. A search made with a spotlight on the Police car failed to identify anything or anyone that could have been responsible. Other explanations offered were a local goat, standing on its back legs!

Nicky Lawrence

Nicky Lawrence was asked if he had any knowledge of the suggestion of someone allegedly wearing an African headdress, who could have been the person responsible. He confirmed there was a rumour going around at the time to that effect, although what he saw near the canal,

> "...was much bigger than a man – more like a horse, or animal standing up on its back legs in the air. Maybe it was a ram, or a deer. We all thought we saw things then. If you want to go and have a look, go down to 39 Stockham Park. My aunt used to live there. The fence goes onto the field. You've got one field, and then there's a line of trees by the canal. There were one or two sightings by the water tower as well. I also heard that somebody was supposed to have been abducted by Aliens, who stopped their car near where the old banger track was, by the Faringdon turn-off. They also reported having missing time – 2 hours, I think."

Nicky told us that the building had been demolished, some years ago. The land was then built on and acquired by Metal Box – a food packing research company now, (2007), Worldwide Business Solutions, Grove Business Centre, and Grove Technology Park.

Our research was to show that a number of employees working at the Metal Box establishment, in the 1980s, had reported having seen a ghostly figure, wearing flying gear and oxygen mask. Other employees told of a presence sensed towards the rear of the works, where the old wartime chapel and officers mess were located.

Page 12

A

WANTAGE HERALD

ONE OF THE NORTH BERKS HERALD SERIES OF NEWSPAPERS

THURSDAY, SEPTEMBER 30, 1971

Play field empty after stories of 'monster'

A field on the edge of the Stockham Park Housing Estate, at Wantage, normally used as a play area by children, has been deserted since the weekend following reports that a "monster" had been seen on the land.

Parents say their children are now afraid to go into the field, uncultivated and occupied only by an old water tower.

the estate are worried about the "monster." Some children are frightened to play out after school and many parents have experienced difficulty with children at bedtime.

Searched wood

One mother said : "My 13-year-old son arrived home crying and in a distressed state saying he had seen the 'monster'. This is completely out of character. I find it hard to believe there is such a thing roaming around, but at the same time I cannot in any way discover my boy."

Herald reporter Alan Cousins accompanied by photographer Ron Walker searched the woods near the old Wantage canal soon after Saturday's reported sighting of the "monster."

Cousins writes: "The perimeter of the wood where the monster was said to be seen moving quickly is covered by thick bramble.

"It would be impossible for anything to move at speed without leaving some traces.

"It is almost certain that a hairy or furry object or animal would have its coat torn by the brambles. Walker himself experienced this with a wool jumper he was wearing at the time we investigated.

"We also searched the field but again no trace of anything which might substantiate the 'monster' sighting was found."

Hairy object

Later the same day an 18-year-old girl also claimed seeing "a large hairy object" entering some woods near the old Wantage canal between the Stockham Park Estate and Grove.

Linda Milne, of East Challow, said : "I am not the type of person to imagine things. The object was very tall and had broad shoulders. It seemed to move very quickly through the woods. Don't ask me what it was — all I know is I was very frightened."

But though no further sightings have been reported since the weekend many parents on

Police searched the field and surrounding area on Friday night after receiving a telephone call from one of the estate residents saying children had been "terrified" by seeing a creature described as being eight feet tall, off white in colour with a furry skin and large eyes one foot apart, horns and a pointed beard.

Two boys told police they had been chased by the "monster," and one of them 14-year-old Michael Nicholls, of Vicarage Hill, East Challow, drew a sketch for the officers.

But although Police Sgt. Jack Gutteridge and P.C. Tony Ennew using searchlights and the headlights of cars combed the field for traces of the creature, the search proved negative.

On Saturday, however, Mr Herbert Halstead, of Stockham Park, Wantage, said he had been startled by something he saw on a grass bank in nearby Denchworth road when he was driving to work at 5.30 a.m.

"The headlights of my car picked out a big white head which appeared to have two large eyes," he said. "As I drove nearer to it the head appeared to move back and then disappeared. I'm certain it wasn't a cow or other animal, but I didn't stop to find out."

We spoke to another witness – Steven Ellis. Unfortunately, he was unable to remember the events that had taken place because of a injury, following an accident at work, but provided us with details of other witnesses.

Linda Milne

Linda Milne – now Linda Wilkins, living in Sterling, Scotland – also contacted us after the newspaper appeal was brought to her attention, and had this to say after confirming no knowledge of ever being interviewed by *Radio Oxford* with regard to the matter:

> *"It remains vivid in my memory. There was a group of us walking home, one dark, cold, night. My future brother-in-law, Mickey, was with us when he asked could we hear what sounded like footsteps coming from behind. I thought, at first, he was trying to scare us, as he was quite a prankster – but he insisted, so we stood still and listened. I heard this 'thump, thump' noise and looked out across the field and saw, in the near distance, what looked like the outline of a person (rather than any tree swaying) walking along the ground, although this was no person ... (he or she was about 8ft. tall, and covered in hair, with long arms reaching to the ground). We were really frightened and ran home. When I told my parents, they thought we were joking. We contacted the newspaper and told them what had taken place."*

We asked Linda whether she had ever thought the persons could have been someone on stilts, or a prankster wearing an African headdress. She rejected both ideas as being a possible explanation and remains still as perplexed now, as she did all those years ago, as to exactly who, or what, it was that she and others saw.

16th September 1971 – Bell-shaped UFO over Clacton-on-Sea, Essex

At about 6.30pm, Allen Tyrrell of Mantilla Road, Tooting, was returning from having attended a demonstration in Hyde Park, London, and was accompanied by Paul Turner, walking down Oxford Street, when they saw a dark, narrow, cigar-shaped object in the sky. Suddenly after 10-15 minutes of observation, it vanished in front of their eyes.

Doris O'Conner – (then aged 65) of 19, Bentley Avenue, Jaywick, Clacton on Sea, Essex – was out on the seafront with her husband, at 9.30pm, walking the two dogs, when:

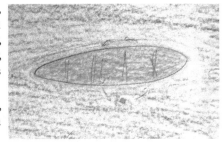

> *"We saw a bell-shaped object just above the sea, which appeared to be spinning, moving very fast, heading from sout-east to north- west. Within 10-15 seconds it was out of sight."*

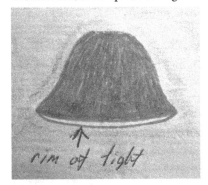

rim of light

17th September 1971 – UFO lecture by John 'Dennis' Llewellyn

20th September 1971 – Mysterious 'lights' above RAF Radar Station

During the evening a red and white coloured 'light' was seen, motionless in the sky above the *River Weaver*, near the RAF Hack Green Radar tracking station, by Christopher Gwyne Walker and Stuart Farr of Nantwich, Cheshire.

"It was joined by a second red 'light'. Both began to flash, followed by the arrival of a third 'light' – white in colour. The 'lights' – then positioned horizontally in the sky – changed to a triangle of red flashing lights, before, once again, changing to one single red flashing light. A few minutes later, they had all gone." **(Source: NICAP)**

27th September 197 – Claim of UFO, with occupants, seen at RAF Base

Another strange incident, involving a 'humanoid' seen at an airbase, was *alleged* to have happened during the late evening of 27th September 1971, when four USAF security guards at RAF Croughton (formerly RAF Brackley) witnessed *'a strange, hairy, 'creature', with large red eyes'*, near the guardhouse – apparently jumping, or bobbing up and down. It was then seen to hop across a hedge, near the Base, and then take-off in a silvery disc-shaped object, before disappearing out of sight.

According to the source involved, the matter was hushed up. Unfortunately, we were unable to corroborate any of this *'alleged incident'*, but wondered if there was any connection with the other incidents brought to our notice, over the years, involving an entity which was seen to leap distances that a human being would have great difficulties in emulating.

Triangular UFO sighted

Harry Brookes – (then aged 60) of Churchill Road, Altringham, Cheshire – was in his garden at 6pm, when he saw a triangular object moving through the sky, heading in a SSW to NNE direction, which then

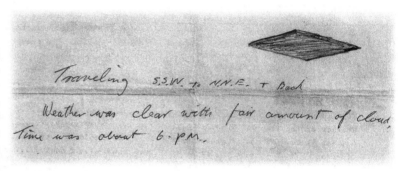

Traveling S.S.W. to N.N.E. + back
Weather was clear with fair amount of cloud.
Time was about 6.pm.

came to a halt over the Shell-BP Petrochemical Plant, at Carrington, for a short time, before accelerating away out of sight.

Weird 'being' seen by lorry driver at Banbury

Lorry driver Leonard Delman was driving to the new Bodicote Flyover, Banbury, on the late evening of 27th September 1971, when he saw what he took to be a man in a white suit, directly in front of him on the road. Len desperately applied his brakes and came to a halt. Jumping out of the cab, he ran to the back of the lorry, but couldn't see anything untoward. On returning to the cab, he said:

"I was shocked to see this 'spaceman' about 7-8 feet tall, with big staring eyes, 8-12 inches apart, extending around the sides of his head. He had this pack on his back, with two pipes coming from it to his head. The pipes looked like horns. I jumped back into the lorry and sounded the horn, about eight times. The 'man' then jumped up into the air, a good three feet, ran across the road, and leaped over the hedge."

At this point, according to Mr Delman, two other Lorries arrived. Their drivers got out and stood watching with Mr Delman, as a disc-shaped object took off from the field. The matter was reported to the police and attracted a comment by Inspector Raymond Sayers, of the Coventry City Police, who confirmed that police officers and members of the public had reported seeing UFOs, the previous evening, although the exact nature of what was seen was never disclosed.

(Source: Richard Colborne, SIGAP/John 'Dennis' Llewellyn)

Banbury
Oxon

Dear Mr Hanson,

I have just read your letter in the Banbury Guardian about the UFO's of 1971. I don't know if this is any good to you.

I was 18 and a pupil nurse at the Horton General Hospital. I worked on 'B'ward' at the time. A nurse and myself had just washed a patient and were making her bed. Another nurse came up and asked if we saw the lights the night before. We said no and asked what had happened (thinking it was an accident).

She told us " a flying saucer was seen and landed in a field by Bodicote bridge (the flyover) and a man in silver was seen running across the field". She also said the police were there as someone thought "he" was an escaped prisoner.

Over the years I have heard this story several times in various ways, including the spaceship was a cigar shape, and even the 'silver man' had stepped over the bridge! (Which must have made him at least 100 feet tall or more!) I know some of us nurses being young and away from home were quite scared, especially as the nurses' home was more or less in the same direction, though some way did joke about being whisked away and seeing stars. (I'm sorry to waffle on). Yours sincerely Mrs Maya Bowler

30th September 1971 – Creature seen outside the family home

At 2am on the 30th September 1971, Mr Ron Foreman of West Malling, Kent, following a strange noise heard at the family cottage, accompanied by the lights dimming, went outside to find:

> "…a creature standing there; it was about 7 feet tall, in a silvery suit and glass helmet. It glided away over a fence, but later returned with a second entity, surrounded by a haze of light. I then reported it to the police."

Although we checked with the local library, the police and the local newspaper (including an appeal from us), we were unable to find out any further details relating to what was, after all, an incredible experience and well worth further investigation. We believe that the reference number 3/6/7, forming part of the report, relates to an investigation made by BUFORA. However, they were also unable to assist us further, as they had no details of this matter on file.

Winter 1971 – 'Flying Saucer' lands in a field near Honiton, Devon

The winter of 1971 was also the scene for another UFO sighting, this time near Hembury Fort – an Ancient site, situated off the A373, a few miles from Honiton – when a motorist, travelling home, heard a crackling noise, accompanied by a loss of power.

> "After getting out of the car, I looked under the bonnet, at which point I heard a loud 'swishing' noise coming from a nearby field, but was unable to identify where it was coming from, owing to the height of the hedge, and presumed it was a helicopter. I was amazed to see a glowing saucer-shaped object shoot across the sky and come to a halt, hovering a few feet off the ground, approximately 80 feet from where I was stood. It then began to perform a very curious manoeuvre, as though

quartering the ground in a rough pattern of a square. After about ten minutes, the 'saucer' – making a loud humming and 'swishing' noise – took off and, within ten seconds, was just a mere speck moving upwards into the night sky."

OCTOBER 1971

1st October 1971 – Cigar-shaped haze, with three lights in it, over Essex

Bernard Young – (then aged 32), a psychiatric nurse, of Oakley Road, Great Clacton, Essex – was driving along St. John's Road, Clacton-on-Sea, at midnight, when he saw a bright shining 'light' in the distance.

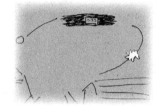

"As it approached closer, I stopped the car. I was stunned to see a cigar-shaped object, which was shrouded in haze. As it drifted past me, I was lucky to get a good luck at the centre of the haze – a gunmetal object, showing three distinct portholes along its side. As it went past, it became very hazy again and was soon lost in the far distance."

(Source: East Anglia UFO Phenomenon Research Association/BUFORA)

10th October 1971 – Seen over Oxfordshire

11th October 1971 – Police sight cigar-shaped UFO

At 4.30am, Police Constables Ray Parker and Brian Giles were on duty in a crime car in the Walthamstow area, when they saw a long cigar-shaped object flashing through the night sky, giving off a blinding light. Seconds later, it disappeared over rooftops. PC Parker rejected explanations later put to him that they had seen an aircraft, or Shooting Star, pointing out that it was flying at about a quarter of the height of an aircraft.

At 10pm, James Edwin Cureton – (then aged 14) of Farm Road, Kendray, Barnsley – was exercising the family dog. He saw a blue 'Flying Saucer' coloured object, moving at speed through the sky, going towards the north-east at a height he estimated to be 4,000 feet. Within a few seconds, it was out of sight. He discussed it with his father, later, and was shown the cover of *Flying Saucer Review*, Volume 16, Number 5, September/October 1970, and agreed that it was identical to what he had seen.

(Source: *Daily Mail*, date not known/BUFORA)

18th October 1971 – Strange 'light' and then ear piercing noise over Banbury

At Middleton Cheyney, near Banbury, with rain pouring down, a man was awoken by a powerful 'light' being shone into the bedroom, at 2.15am. On looking out of the window he saw a 'light', fairly close to the house, towards the eastern direction, near to a junction of overhead electricity, casting a shadow over most of the lawn – bright enough to see worms. The light then extinguished. The husband awoke his wife and they looked out to see it a little towards the north direction. Once again it went out. This was followed by an ear-splitting, pulsating, whining noise – unbearable, even with their hands pressed firmly over the ears. This noise continued for several minutes – so disturbing that it was not possible to judge the time accurately. After several minutes it stopped, but then carried on – now a single note, accompanied by the intense light now to the east, at an elevation of about 35 degrees.

(Source: David Oakley-Hill and Richard Colborne)

19th October 1971 – UFO display over the M3 Motorway

At about 10.15pm, Lance Druce and his brother-in-laws – Roy and Brian George were travelling in their removal van along the M3, between the Reading intersection and Winchester, when they noticed numerous 'red lights' in the sky.

Lance:

> "Some of them were round; others oblong, some moving, others not. Some were close to the ground. There were about 200 'lights'. We stopped, but were immediately told to move on by a police car that pulled up behind us [it is not said whether the police saw them as well].
>
> We stopped again, while on the Winchester bypass, and Brian went into a field but come running back, very alarmed. After he had gained his breath I asked him what was the matter, and he replied 'Come and see for yourself'.
>
> I went into the field and saw, about 40 yards away, a brilliant white object, shaped like a letter 'M', with a black area in each of the arches. The object was about 10ft. high, 7-8ft. wide, and 2ft. off the ground. It was moving slowly and silently to the right, over a rising inclines. Frightened, we ran back to the van and drove away."

20th October 1971 – UFO landing, Northampton

Just after 7pm on 20th October 1971, Mrs Eileen Muir – a resident of caravan 72 on the Woodlands caravan site, Weldon, Northampton – was the first to see a bright white 'light', while walking through Weldon, on her way home.

> "I watched in terror as what looked like an upturned mushroom-shaped object, surrounded by white mist, landed at the back of my home, making a shrill high-pitched whistle as it did so. It seemed to stand on three pointed legs and had a glowing red and green middle. I ran to my neighbour's house and we went to call the police."

Another witness was Mrs Carmen Gray – then living at number 57, who was to provide an almost identical account to that given by Mrs Muir, describing it as having a bright glimmering light on top, surrounded by a green glow. By the time police arrived, there was nothing to be seen.

(**Source: Local UFO Group/***Northampton Evening Telegraph,* **21.10.1971**)

21st October 1971 – Yellow pulsing 'light' over Banbury

At 11.50pm (approximate date), a retired RAF Pilot – Mr Ruck Keene of Foxholes, Farnborough – watched a yellow-white 'light' pulsating in the night sky, over Banbury. Fifteen minutes later it disappeared from view, followed by a report of a circular 'craft', showing many lights, seen by a Miss A. Flowers, who was driving through the Banbury area, later the next evening.

(**Source:** *Banbury Guardian,* **21.10.1971/Ken Rogers**)

23rd October 1971 – UFO over Portsmouth

At 3.30pm, a silver 'cigar' was seen hovering, some 30-40 feet above the floodlights, during a football match at Fratton Park, Portsmouth, by Ian Glasby, accompanied by his grandfather, at the time.

> "The thing was huge. It looked like an inverted saucer, silver in colour, as it just hovered in the sky, catching the sun's rays, creating an impression it was spinning. We sat there, dumbfounded, watching it only 5-15 yards above the floodlights. It then began to move around in an erratic manner, reminding me of an insect being drawn to a flower – then it rapidly decreased in size and moved away.
>
> A few minutes later, we were even more astonished when a similar object appeared in the same place. Thirty seconds later, it disappeared from sight."

We spoke to Mr Glasby, over 33 years later, who still remembers the event with great clarity and remains puzzled why only he and two others (apart from his grandfather) saw this UFO out of a crowd of 14,000 spectators. (**Source: Nicholas Maloret, WATSUP**)

26th October 1971 – UFO sighted by *ATV* film crew

7.30am, UFO over Banbury

Banbury resident – Mrs Balbirnie, was putting some food out for the cats, when she noticed:

"...an orange, stationary, object in the sky towards the west. After a few minutes it left, heading eastwards, showing a 'fishtail', or delta-shaped, image. Within several seconds, it passed overhead – the 'tail' remaining attached to the object." (**Source: Richard Colborne, BUFORA**)

8.10am – UFO over Oxfordshire

Mr C.H. Walls and his wife from Hailey, Oxfordshire, sighted a strange object in the sky. With the unaided eye it looked like a vapour trail. Through binoculars, two objects could be seen – shaped like oxygen cylinders – one yellow; the other, orange. The yellow one, which appeared nearer, was brighter than the sun.

11.50am – UFO sighted over Enstone, Oxfordshire

The incident: A small, bright orange 'ball of light', apparently spinning around its axis – emitting, at times, a thick dense trail of vapour or smoke – was seen by several people, heading in a west to east direction across a clear blue sky, in a manner of movement familiar to UFO behaviour. On several occasions it stopped and started in mid-flight, for up to 30 seconds, before continuing on its journey.

The location:

Farmer Jordan's field, Radford Bridge, Enstone, Oxfordshire (Grid reference 398234, OS Sheet 145)

The main runway of a disused airfield lies about one and three quarter miles north of the location. Upper Heyford lies 7 miles to the east, and the town of Banbury eleven miles to the north-east.

The witnesses:

Six members of an *ATV* film crew were standing on a northern facing slope of a field, situated about one quarter of a mile north-east of the A34 road, which links Stratford-upon Avon and Oxford. The witnesses (1) Lionel Hampden – Interviewer (2) Sidney Kilby – Director (3) Noel Smart – Cameraman (4) Christine Fewlass – Production Assistant (5) Charlie Lynch – Lighting Electrician, and (6) Alan (?) – Sound. They were standing about 50 feet below the top of the hill, at a height of approximately 400 feet above sea level.

We are eternally grateful for being able to examine for ourselves a comprehensive report into the matter, put together by Roger, Julian, J.A. Hennessey, on behalf of Dr. Allen J. Hynek, and Charles Bowen – Editor of *Flying Saucer Review*, London.

We came across a copy of this 41 page report, catalogued by the late Ron West.

TAPE TRANSCIPT – Lionel Hampden's account (extract):

"On Tuesday October 26th, at approximately seven minutes to 12 (noon), and if I were to veer away from that time I would go closer to 12 o'clock than before seven minutes to, we were on Jordan's Farm on a stubble field, filming a flock of sheep and the shepherd. We were facing roughly east, filming this, when it was noticed, over our left shoulders, an orange object in the sky that appeared to be a revolving object. There was, perhaps, a little black that gave the impression of a revolving object. We noticed it and not much attention paid to it, and the filming progressed – then it drew all our attention and the film unit stopped filming."

Noel Smart – Taped interview (extract):

"We were in Oxfordshire, in this field, and we had started some of the shots and were set up on the top of this ridge – the place we were filming from. We were waiting, actually, as this military plane had been over a couple of times – two or three times, back and forth – and she seemed to be doing circuits and bumps around the area. It had no markings on it at all – a sort of matt black and brown camouflage."

Enstone, overlooking fields over which UFO was seen.

"We were watching this, a couple of times. It was disturbing us, as it was making a noise and getting in a camera shot. We started to shoot again and, all of a sudden, we noticed 'this thing', high in the sky. It was a clear day – absolutely perfectly clear, no clouds at all – and 'this thing' appeared to be hovering and someone said, as a joke, that it was a UFO! We all laughed and joked and started to watch it …it was definitely hovering at a hell of a height. It was bright silver and it either changed to a bright fluorescent or luminous type of orange as it travelled. It wasn't one colour all of the time. As she seemed to go off, she was spinning and hovering in one position. She seemed to be losing height and then gaining height; it was either doing that or going away from us and coming back. There was definitely movement, apart from this spherical movement – then, all of a sudden, she went flying off, about south-east, leaving a normal sort of vapour trail you see from an aircraft. After seconds, the vapour trail widened out and the object stopped again, very suddenly, and the speed she had gone from one point to another was absolutely unbelievable.

When she was first hovering, the first time we saw her, I grabbed my camera; it was on a tripod. I knew roughly what the exposure was – the nearest I could find while my assistant was getting the correct reading.

I was flat out on the 120mm zoom. The exposure was more or less correct. I followed it, rather than let it go out of the frame.

I followed it as best as I could to try and see as much as I could about it.

We got the film of the thick vapour trail and it then hovered again. When she hovered I got another close-up of her while she was hovering, and then she was there for the second time again … and off she went again. She did this about three times. She was obviously going away from us, south-east as I said, and it got to the point where I could not see it anymore. It could have been anything on the horizon. During the episode of observation, I got various shots close-up. I also had a shot of it coming into frame, as I had guessed roughly where it was going to come through my frame, and then going out of it to try and get a relationship of the speed that it was travelling at. As it was going away from us it was obviously shifting at a hell of a speed – nothing I have seen before. I have filmed jets before, and high speed aircraft, and this was unbelievable speed."

The taped transcript continues for some length and involves a number of questions put to Noel, and his answers. Rather than replicate the whole text, it may be more expedient to include the relevant points as follows:

Noel mentions that after the object had left the Production Assistant – Christine Fewlass, she noticed a very dark vapour trail.

"It was dispersing as a normal vapour trial, but it seemed a dark colour – a dark green. It was just visible and a lot of people didn't see it."

The film was not cut or edited

Charlie Lynch - Taped interview (full extract):

"Noel or Chris noticed it first and I had a look myself and it, to me, actually didn't look like a plane at all, because it was revolving round itself – then, all of a sudden, it seemed to stop and hang in the air, and then shoot away at terrific speed. I've never seen anything like it. It then stopped again and then shot off again, and the vapour was coming out of the back. It wasn't a jet as I saw a jet half an hour later, climbing high and traveling steadily, whereas the object I saw was revolving and seemed orange coloured to me. The speed it shot off at was quite out of this world. The object was drawn to my attention and to my way of thinking it was revolving and stationary for about 10-15 seconds. I saw it for about 30-60 seconds before the camera stared filming it. Later, after it disappeared, we looked back and saw a big trail – a sort of greenish colour; this lasted for several minutes.

If you have a ball and you paint it two colours, dark blue and white and you turn it around you will see the different colours all the time. The object in the sky was going around and there were two different colours; black and orange, then orange and black, sometimes black all the time. This is how it appeared to me. I am convinced it could not have been a plane."

At 12 noon – Orange sphere sighted over Cherwell Heights, Banbury

Mrs Blaise Smith tells of hearing a roaring, crackling, noise outside her house. When she went to have a look outside, she saw a sharply-defined orange sphere, leaving a trail of vapour behind it.

"I saw it stop twice during its trajectory, and leave a puff of vapour when doing so. When the vapour stopped, the noise stopped. When the vapour restarted, there was an audible explosion and a puff. I saw no flames when the trail stopped."

12 noon – 26th October 1971 – Orange sphere sighted over Ruscote Estate, Banbury

David Chatt – (then aged 16) of Ruscote Estate, Banbury – sighted an orange sphere with a sharp outline, leaving a thick white vapour trial, about 3-4 times wider than an aircraft's trail. The object was as wide as its trail.

"On looking back on the trail, I could see a double bend in the trail where the object had evidently turned sharply to its right (south), travelled a short distance, and then turned to its left (east), taking up a course parallel with the other one. The sphere passed directly over me, at which stage the trail ceased. A 'puff' or 'blob' was left at the termination, but the sphere continued. The object decelerated as it moved away from the end of the trail, but I can't be sure if it stopped completely. The vapour trail resumed with another 'puff'."

The above sequence was repeated again, after the object had moved further toward the east, and when the object accelerated away for the second time.

David:

"I ran into the house to get my binoculars. However, when I went back out again it had gone. I did notice that the end of the trail did not terminate with a 'puff' as before, but tapered and faded out."

12 noon – 26th October 1971 – Orange sphere sighted over Evenley Hall, Oxfordshire

Trevor Twynham (16) was accompanied by three older men, when they saw a sharply-defined aircraft of unconventional design leaving a trail of white vapour and, on one occasion, a flame. It was first seen in the north-west and last seen in the north-east.

"It travelled east at 45 degrees elevation, leaving a white trail. When it was above Evenley Hall [43 degrees east of magnetic North] but beyond the hall, the vapour stopped and the object continued a short distance – then a flame came out to the rear of the object.

The flame was twice the size of the object. The smoke started coming our again and then it vanished. I saw no wings, or cockpit, and it was silent."

12.10pm – 26th October 1971 – Over Towcester, Northamptonshire

Mr and Mrs Peachey of Jenkinson Road, Towcester, Northamptonshire, had this to say:

"We sighted a white rocket-shaped object, with a pointed nose cone, which was offset to one side. It had a blue diagonal stripe across it. It made a noise like distance thunder – a strange sound, unlike anything we had ever heard before. There was a noticeable gap between the end of the missile and the start of the vapour trail. It went over our heads and, during this time, it stopped twice. It was visible for about one and a half minutes and finally disappeared from sight, upwards into the sky."

12.15pm – Rocket-shaped object seen at Milton Keynes

Simon Douglas Pearce – (then aged 16) of Elm Drive, in Milton Keynes – was stood by the gate of a field behind Shrub Spinney, Hayes Road, Deanshanger, with two friends – Stephen Worrall and Martin Nichols.

> "We saw a rocket-shaped object, moving fast in the sky towards us, from the direction of Deanshanger. It was spilling out white vapour, in equal lengths, with a reddish-orange flame. It went behind trees at the spinney, and we lost sight of it."

3.40pm – UFO over Upminster, Essex

Schoolboy Paul Thacker of Canterbury Grove, Cranham, Upminster, Essex, was sat in the classroom at Gaynes School, Upminster, in Essex.

> "I was looking out of the window overlooking the sports field, when I saw a cylindrical object, about 40-50 feet in height, some 200 feet in width, showing no lights or illumination, flying across the field at 40-50 miles per hour.
>
> My first thought was a low flying aircraft, or balloon – then I realised it had no form of propulsion. It was flying 200 feet horizontally of the ground. I lost sight of it when it reached a wooded area.
>
> I looked around and saw another boy – David Cook – sat behind me; his eyes were transfixed on the view in front of the window that I had seen the object through. I asked him what he had seen. He described in detail exactly what I had seen."

Over Middlesex on the same day

During the same day, an unidentified flying object was seen hovering over Northwood Golf Course, West Middlesex, at an estimated height of 1,000 feet, described as:

> "...constructed of glass-like material, gleaming like aluminum foil, with ten 'windows' or facets, each about a hundred feet in width. The 'windows' were inset at an angle to the vertical. The whole lower section of the gigantic craft was seen to be revolving, giving off flashes of light as each came into view. After a few minutes it shot upwards into the sky, at colossal speed, in the space of a second." (**Source: BUFORA Report, 1182**)

5.40pm – Pine cone shape UFO sighted over Halifax, Yorkshire

Dorothy Denton – (then aged 35) of Noreton Drive, Noreton Tower, Halifax, Yorkshire – was called by her son, Simon (6), and daughter, Fiona (8), to come and have a look at a strange silver object in the sky.

> "It wasn't moving, so we went into the garden to get a better look. My son said, 'It's completely silent'. The shape was similar to a rocket – round at one end, the other end tailing off. After a few minutes, it faded away and vanished from sight."

The incident was reported to the *Halifax Courier*.

5.50pm – 'Flying Saucer' over Pershore, Worcestershire

Two unusual 'lights' were seen in the sky by a number of people. Five minutes later, a group of boys – Timmy Philips, Tony Cripps, Nicholas Taton and Melvyn Bettle – were out playing on the local Drakes Broughton football pitch, near Pershore, Worcestershire, when they saw three trails of smoke appear in the sky over the Malvern Hills. The lower of the three trails were larger and longer than the other two, and motionless in the air; the middle one was bright yellow in colour and moving towards Malvern Hills – apparently spinning.

Timmy Philips:

> *"Suddenly, the top one – the smallest of the three – seemed to move from where it was and appear again with a thick vapour trail behind it. This happened twice, and then on the right of the local junior school appeared a black object, hovering over the building. As if from nowhere, another black object appeared, identical to the one we were watching. It then headed off towards Peopleton. We ran across the fields, hoping to catch up with it as it grew larger and clearer. We stopped and saw it change direction, heading towards Pinvin – now horseshoe in shape – then it vanished. A second or two later, we saw it change from black to yellow. Its flashing seemed to speed up as it went off across the sky. I looked at my watch. It was 6.20pm."*

While making their way home, they saw a 'fiery red ball' in the sky and decided to telephone the Royal Radar Establishment at Pershore, from a call box, to ask them if any of their aircraft were flying. After being told that this was not the case, they explained what had taken place. The 'official' seemed interested and took their names. Just before the boys reached home, they saw another red object in the sky flashing on and off, towards the north-east, out of which something dropped over nearby trees.

Rushing into the house they alerted their parents, who came running outside – in time to see the 'red ball' passing over the Royal Radar Establishment Airbase, before disappearing out of sight.

(Source: Keith Palmer)

7.50pm – UFO over Banbury

Mr and Mrs Alfred Burton (51), A.M.I. Mech. E., licensee of the *George & Dragon* public house, were driving from Shutford, Banbury, when they noticed a 'flashing red light' on the left-hand side of the car.

Mr Burton:

> *"I realised this was something unusual and stopped the car. My wife and I watched this completely silent 'machine', approximately 50 yards in diameter, ascending through the sky, at a height of about 500 feet. In a flash, it had gone."*

Further information revealed that they estimated the object to be 9-12 feet in length, and had yellow 'window frame lights'.

The 'lights' were more than half way around with bright orange- red 'quickly flashing lights', three to four times per second.

The object was stationary for two minutes. It moved away slowly and was seen from inside the car for half a minute – then outside.

It was a dry, dark night – warm, with no wind – and was reported to the *Banbury Guardian*. Elevation 50-100 degrees, Location 5 Ways (OS Map Reference SP390402). Round Hill was in the background.

BUFORA investigators Richard Colborne and David Oakley-Hill interviewed the couple, in February of the next year, when they discovered that the couple was interviewed by the *BBC* on the 2nd February 1972, for the programme *Man Alive*, aired on the same date.

Not surprisingly the BBC interview with the couple was not included, although they had been invited to take part. Instead, the audience and viewers were offered much less credible evidence, presumably in support of the UFO subject. Nothing changes there!

Quoting from the BUFORA file – Mr Burton told the BUFORA investigators that, during an interview, a document was lost – which was supposed to have been loaned by the MOD. As a result of this, it was claimed that Miss Cherry Farrow, the producer, was sacked and the bias of the subject matter was shifted against (serious Ufologists) BUFORA. Representatives of the *BBC* present were David S. Filton, Jeremy

James, Sue Burgess, Maurice Everett, Cherry Farrow, Martin Peterson and John Pewson. [Not sure what the relevance of this is. Presumably, they were there when the programme was aired(?)]

Another reports for this date included a sightings of *"a white delta-shaped object"*, seen in the sky over Stonehill.

9.40pm – Police officers sight UFO

Banbury Police Officers – PC Perry Jackson, accompanied by Cadet, William Byron – sighted an orange colour UFO, moving across a moonlit, star-filled sky, near the water tower at Bretch Hill, Banbury, for three seconds, before it moved downwards to the ground at a 45 degree angle. We spoke to PC Perry (now retired) about the incident. He was unable to offer any further information about the matter, other than it was still inexplicable and that he remained sceptical about UFOs in general. Sadly, we learnt Bill later died in a road traffic accident, while on duty as a motorcycle officer.

(Source: Personal interview)

27th October 1971

The *Birmingham Evening Mail* put their readers minds at rest with a short article, headed 'UFOs evaporate' – explaining away the hundreds of calls from the public about UFOs being seen as caused by clear air from an anticyclone, according to the Edgbaston Observatory!

A visit to Upper Heyford Airbase

Roger Stanway, his wife, and Julian Hennessey, made an appointment to see Colonel 'Skip' Burns, at Upper Heyford Airbase, to discuss the views of the Base personnel on the 16mm film taken – not forgetting the xplanation offered by the MOD that it was an example of fuel being dumped into the upper atmosphere by an aircraft. The meeting took place in December 1971.

Roger:

> *"Colonel Burns, and several of his fellow senior officers, gathered in a briefing room and the film was shown to them about four times, along with still images. The officers were visibly impressed with the film. During discussion, Colonel Burns considered there was nothing to indicate that the subject was anything other than a high flying jet leaving an intermittent vapour trail, as it entered and reentered the troposphere again. Although we repeated the comments of the eyewitnesses, it was clear that the absence of any fixed frame of reference in the view finder for most of the film did not assist in establishing whether or not the jet plane was performing abnormally in the sense that its sudden apparent stops and dramatic accelerations were quite unlike any existing ability of a jet in similar conditions."*

Statement … There was no dumping of fuel!

> *"It was abundantly clear that Colonel Burns and his officers were well-acquainted with the UFO phenomenon. One of them even recanted his own UFO sighting, some years ago, in the United States.*
>
> *We left the base with little doubt in our own minds that the pilots to whom we had been talking took the subject of UFOs seriously. There was no attempt by them to dismiss the phenomenon as mere misidentifications, although in this specific film case Colonel Burns felt that the object was probably a plane, leaving a vapour trail. He confirmed that none of his planes had been dumping fuel on the morning in question, as such a course of action is only adopted in cases of emergency and there was none that morning!"*

The *Daily Telegraph* – 'TV crew film mystery flying object' – published the story about this incident, which, by the way, was shown to Midlands TV viewers on the 'Today' programme.

Statement from MOD … there was dumping of fuel!

Julian Hennessey wrote to the Officer in Charge, at West Drayton, asking him about this matter, and received a reply back on the 7th January 1972 from the Ministry of Defence S4 (Air). Mr A.N. Davis, D.S.O., D.F.C., replied:

"I confirm that our records show that a military aircraft did dump fuel over Oxfordshire, at about midday on 26th October 1971. There is no record of the exact location of the aircraft when the fuel was dumped."

Julian Hennessey (well-known for his dogged determina-tion) then contacted Mr Julian Ridsdale MP – presumably expressing concern about the validity of this statement, bearing in mind his previous visit to the airbase and meeting with Colonel Burns.

On the 7th February 1972, he received a copy of a letter sent to the honorable gentleman, by MOD spokesman – Antony Lambton, in which he once again confirmed (part extract)

"…that the aircraft was a F-111, based at Upper Heyford. Of course the fact that an aircraft dumped fuel in the area does not prove that that was the event recorded on film. The observation was certainly consistent with an aircraft emitting a condensation trail or dumping fuel."

This incident has, of course, over the years, attracted a lot of publicity – probably for the reason that it was filmed. The film is available on YouTube and on the Internet. Most people (including many UFO enthusiasts) appear to accept the official explanation given by the MOD that this was a plane dumping fuel, although no aircraft has been identified or the name of the crew.

Chairman of BUFORA – Roger Stanway …. BUFORA rejects explanation by MOD of aircraft dumping fuel!

We agree with Roger H. Stanway – then Chairman of BUFORA – that it is highly unlikely this was the explanation. In fact, we would refute this as an explanation, taking into consideration the overwhelming amount of evidence offering the opposite. We concur with Roger, who says:

"Readers of this report should bear in mind that the event described was one of scores of similar reports which emanated from the residents of Oxfordshire and neighbouring counties during the autumn of 1971 and the spring of 1972, and which were energetically investigated by a number of people – in particular, Mr Richard Colborne devoted a considerable amount of his spare time and energy in an attempt to record all the relevant information, especially with a view to obtaining corroborative evidence from reliable independent witnesses. Acknowledgement must also be made of the encouragement and valuable assistance provided to the writer, Mr Julian Hennessey, during the course of the investigations."

Incredibly, after nearly half a century later, we are no further forward in being able to identify the origin and agenda, if any, of the appearance of these mysterious flying objects that have most certainly plagued the history of mankind, going back many thousands of years. It is pretty obvious that while the subject is still denigrated by the media and authority in general as being the domain of crackpots and having little substance at all, one cannot deny the fact and figures of something which should cause concern instead of the opposite.

27th October 1971- Curious phenomenon sighted over Oxfordshire

At 8.10am, Mr C.H. Walls and his wife from Hailey, Oxfordshire, saw:

> "...what looked like a vapour trail; through binoculars two objects were seen, shaped like oxygen cylinders – one yellow and one orange; the yellow one nearest was brighter than the sun."

30th October 1971 – UFO flies around a bus

Bus conductor Mr Patrick Devine of Green Lane, Ilkeston, Nottinghamshire, was aboard the bus being driven along the Ilkeston Road, at 10.30pm, when a noise like a siren was heard. This was followed by an object – the size of a steering wheel, with sparks around it – being seen to fly around the bus, twice, before heading away. Other motorists apparently saw it, but the police denied any other reports.

A member of Raleigh's security staff reported that, at about the same time, a klaxon on a propane tank, near Ilkeston Road, went off. This may well explain the noise but not the object.

(Source: *BUFORA Journal*, Volume 3, Summer 1972)

October 1971 – UFO over Bolton

Gordon Peake, then in his late seventies (2012) – a retired Royal Navy diver, who had 'diced with death' many times over, while engaged in underwater mine clearance, during the Second World War – described an unnerving incident that took place near Mosley Common, Bolton, Lancashire, in September/October 1971.

> "I decided to pay a visit to the Yew Tree public house, Mosley Common, accompanied by my son, Graham – a regular journey I had been making since my own father took me there, in 1947. After parking the car next to the pub, Graham left to book a game of dominoes, while I let 'Whisky' (the dog) out of the car, who ambled over to the nearby playing field as dusk was falling.
>
> At this point, I noticed a peculiar 'mass of light' travelling approximately fifteen feet above the ground, moving from side to side, over the derelict site of the old Mosley Common pit, reminding me of the effect you would get if you dropped a plate into a bucket of water.
>
> I shouted for Graham to come and have a look, as he was just about to enter the pub. He rushed over and agreed he could also see it but then disappeared back into the pub, eager to sort out the game of dominoes. I watched it drop over the railway embankment and move toward a small hamlet of pit houses, called 'The City', wondering if it had come from Barton Airfield.
>
> Suddenly, I realised 'Whisky' was petrified, so I picked him up and walked past the embankment bridge, expecting to see the familiar sight of horses in the field. Instead, I noticed a huge circle of misty steam rising upwards, about twenty feet in diameter – as if something had landed. The locality where this incident occurred is now a private burial ground, some two miles away from Madams Wood – most of which has now been built on. I suppose if somebody had told me a story like this, I would have laughed at them ... but I know what I saw. It really frightened me. I would have preferred to have defused live mines on the seabed any day than see what I did."

(Source: Personal interview)

NOVEMBER 1971

2nd November 1971 – UFO over Loch Ness, Scotland

Winifred Elizabeth Cary – (then aged 67) of Strone, Drumnadrochit, Inverness-Shire, Scotland – was standing behind her house, at 8.50pm, overlooking Loch Ness, which was 250 feet below her.

"I saw a brilliantly lit, light orange coloured object, with an outer edge of dark red light, travelling in a south-west direction over the Loch. It appeared to be following the line of the Loch and was moving silently at a height of some 2,000 feet and a couple of hundred miles per hour. I watched it for a few seconds, until it disappeared behind a hill on my right next to where I was standing. I called my husband to come out and see it; by the time he came out of the garage, it had gone from sight." (**Source: Ron West archives/Stuart Campbell**)

2nd November 1971 – Delphos 'ring', Kansas

On the 2nd November 1971, 16 year-old Ron Johnson was out walking his dog and tending to the family sheep.

Suddenly, a metallic with brilliantly-lit multicoloured lights, mushroom in shape, UFO appeared just ahead of him in the night sky.

After recovering from his initial shock, Johnson ran to get his parents. Together, the family watched the craft ascend and disappear into the night sky.

Afterwards, the Johnson family discovered something even weirder – a glowing 'ring' on the ground below where the UFO had been hovering. When that year's snow finally melted – the glowing material was still there. The Johnsons sent a sample to a laboratory.

The technicians found that the sample contained organic fibres. The fibres were related to an order of organisms somewhere between fungi and bacteria, called Actinomycetales. Some species of Actinomycetales become fluorescent under energy stimulation. This suggests that the stimulant could very well have been the energy of the hovering object.

Dr .J. Allen Hynek – chairman of the Department of Physics and Astronomy at Northwestern University, confirmed that a mysterious white substance and other physical traces were found at the site of an alleged UFO landing near Delphos, Kansas.

> *"Tests carried out at four separate laboratories from the 'ring' differed markedly for the surrounding soil. It had abnormally high calcium content (up to ten times the earth around it), would not absorb water as normal soil does, and plants refused to grow in it." He was unable to offer any analysis for the white fibrous substance.* (**Source: *News Indianapolis,* 13.9.1972 – 'Follow up'**)

Early winter 1971-marks found in the grass

In early winter 1971, Mount Pleasant resident – Ronnie Thomas – described an incident, which happened one night, when aged 11. Unable to sleep, he looked out of his bedroom window, at 2am, towards the newly built High School, called Woodford Lodge, Winsford, in Cheshire.

> *"I saw a 'bright light' in the one of the playing fields to the right of the school. I sneaked out of the house and made my way over to the field. Suddenly, there was this big 'whoosh' of air. I thought I was dreaming, until I saw this big disc-like object. I ran and hid behind a wall by the school. To my amazement, I saw three circular scorch marks on the grass and there was a smell – like burning sulphur. I ran back home to bed, trembling, and went to sleep."* (**Source: *The Guardian series,* 8.1.2003/**

10th November 1971 – Red objects over Suffolk

Mr William McCann – advertising manager for *Essex County Newspapers* – was with his wife and four children at the family home in Capel St. Mary, Suffolk, when, just after darkness, his son – Stephen (12), brought his father's attention to a bright red object he had seen through his telescope slowly cross over the top of the house. A second object then shot away from it and disappeared behind cloud. Apparently this was not the first time red lights had been seen moving about in the sky over the same locality.

(**Source: Peter Johnson/*Colchester Evening Gazette***)

11th December 1971 – Golden 'globe' over Staffordshire

At 7.20am, Mr Lovatt of Smallthorne, Stoke-on-Trent, was waiting at the bus stop in Hanley, close to the *Green Star* public house.

> *"I saw a glowing orange 'disc' below cloud cover, which appeared to be slowly following the main road to Hanley.*
>
> *I reached the Sneyd Arms; it stopped in mid-air, for a couple of minutes, before changing direction and shooting away towards Milton. The object was 40-50 feet across and emitted what looked like some kind of exhaust – not like a jet exhaust, but sparks behind the disc."*

13th November 1971 – UFOs over Stocksfield-on-Tyne

On the evening, Mr P. Bolam from Stocksfield-on-Tyne was washing his car, when he noticed:

> *"...a star-like object, moving across the sky in a north to south direction. I continued watching, sensing something unusual, not wanting to get my binoculars in case the object had disappeared in my absence. I was able to see that it covered the length of the*

A GOOD REASON FOR WORLD
GOVERNMENT SUPPRESSION OF
UFO INFORMATION ?

RAIDERS FROM MARS STRIKE PANIC AGAIN

A RADIO dramatisation of H. G. Wells's "War of the Worlds" story of invaders from Mars, which panicked thousands throughout America in 1938, again caused widespread alarm on Sunday night.

The programme, originally devised by Orson Welles, included "news bulletins" reporting invaders from space landing in New Jersey.

At one point, a man described as "the Secretary of the Interior" announced solemnly: "Citizens of the nation. I shall not try to conceal the gravity of the situation that confronts the country."

Despite a five-minute explanation of the drama immediately before it began, scores of nervous listeners who thought the invasion was real telephoned the police and the radio station in Buffalo, New York, which broadcast the play.

horizon – some 15-20 miles in about a minute. I then lost sight of it. Another 'star' then appeared at the same point in the sky as where I had seen the first object. It, too, followed the same route as before I lost sight of it. I carried on with washing the car, when, to my surprise, about 20 minutes later, I saw a third object once again – this time following a different path across the sky." (**Source: BUFORA**)

16th November 1971 – Schoolboys sight UFO over Stourbridge, West Midlands

Stephen Young (then aged 10) of Vicarage Road, Amblecote, and Bryan Nichols (then aged10) of Queens Crescent – both pupils at Beauty Bank Primary School, in Stourbridge – told of sighting a spinning object,

> "...looking like glass, showing a red and blue light, hovering above Corbett Hospital during the early evening, before it flew away towards the Brierley Hill area ten minutes later."

A second sighting took place, the same evening, involving the headmaster's son – Stuart Horne (16), who was outside his home, in South Road, when he saw an object through a gap in the clouds, moving north-east, leaving a vapour trail of light.

(**Source:** *Stourbridge County Express*, 19.11.1971 – 'UFO over Hospital shone like glass')

19th November 1971 – UFO sighted over UK

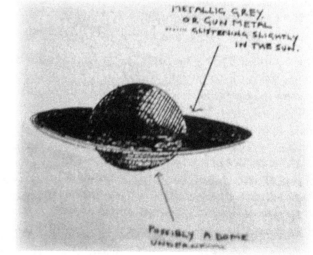

21st November 1971 – 'Flying Saucer' over Worcestershire

At 5.40am, Dorothy Keyte from Woodward Road, Pershore, Worcestershire, was disturbed by her dog barking.

> "I opened the door, wondering what was going on and gazed into the sky. I saw a saucer-shaped object, heading towards the south-west direction.
>
> Within ten minutes, all that could be seen were three stars in the distance."

(**Source: Personal interview**)

17th November 1971 – Red object over St. Austell

At 6.45pm, student nurse – Mr Rupert Ernest Whalley (then 19 years of age) of Polpey Lane, Par, Cornwall, noticed a bright red flashing 'light' travelling across St. Austell Bay,

> "...moving in a stopping and starting manoeuvre across the sky, in an east to west direction. I watched it for about ten minutes, until the flashes of light became weaker and then stopped."

UFO display – Derbyshire

Later that day, Gavin Wilshaw from Hilton, Derbyshire, was driving from Derby to Hilton, along the Derby to Uttoxeter Road, with his wife, at 5.45pm. As they neared Burnaston, Gavin's wife pointed out a bright white 'light', moving slowly northwards at an estimated height of 2,000 feet, performing a number of slow gyrations in the sky,

> "...like someone waving a torch in the sky. The 'light' was flashing irregularly, dimming dull-white and then very bright; ten minutes later we passed through Etwall, by which time it had began to look red at its lowest illumination. I pulled off the main road and got out of the car to observe closer. It was still hovering and rotating. To my surprise, a similar object appeared from the south, over Rolleston-on-Dove, at the same elevation as the other, approximately 40 degrees in the sky.
>
> The second 'light' – a definite red colour – flashed irregularly from dull red to bright-red, the other object being completely still in the sky. I started the car and continued on our journey, arriving home a short time later, where I made my way into the back garden and watched the two 'lights' – now close together in the north of the sky. The first 'light' then moved slowly westwards, while the second one moved eastwards." (**Source: Personal interview**)

DECEMBER 1971

4th December 1971 – Silver 'disc' sighted over Banbury, Oxfordshire

A silver-grey 'disc' shaped object *"with a slightly higher top half"*, about 90 feet in length, was sighted over Margaret Close, Banbury, at 1pm, by Mr Peter George Spackman (then aged 24), and his wife, who were sat on a river bank having a cup of tea, when the object was seen moving in an out of cloud cover, heading eastwards, at an estimated height of 1,000feet. (**Source: BUFORA**)

7th December 1971 – UFO over Derbyshire

Mr Paul Bannister of the High Street, Alton, in Derbyshire, was shocked to see an object with two huge flashing lights, hovering in the sky above St. George's Church, Alton, at 10.25pm.

> "It shot off in a zigzag manner over the village. I reported this to the police; they told me that someone in Denstone had reported seeing a similar object." (**Source SIGAP**)

8th December 1971 – Wilfred Daniels writes to Frank Marshall

11th December 1971 – Orange 'disc' over Stoke-on-Trent

Mr Lovatt of Nellan Crescent, Smallthorne, Stoke-on-Trent, Staffordshire, was stood at the bus stop outside the *Green Star* public house, at 7.20am, when he saw:

"...an orange 'disc', apparently following the main road to Hanley. It was below cloud level and a few hundred feet off the ground. It travelled slowly until it reached the Sneyd Arms, when it then stopped in flight, hovering momentarily, before changing direction and shooting away towards Milton. It was about 40-50 feet across and had what looked like some kind of exhaust (not like a jet) with sparks behind it."

Coincidently, at 7.45am, the same day, John Brown – (then aged 31) of Clynes Way, Meir, Stoke-on-Trent – was walking to work down Dividy Road, Bentilee, when, as he approached the *Thurston* public house, he noticed:

"...a very bright 'light' over the housetops, moving up Dividy Road from the Hanley direction. I thought it was some kind of flare, but as it passed directly overhead I saw it was a 'ball' or 'globe' moving fast, with sparks shooting out of it, heading in a south-east direction – soon out of sight."

(Source: BUFORA)

12th December 1971 – Elliptical object over Lowestoft

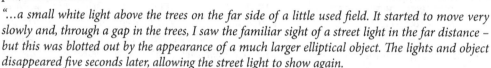

Richard Haxell – (then aged 18) of Fleet Dyke Drive, Lowestoft – had occasion to look out of the window on what was a slightly foggy evening, at 9.42pm, when he saw:

"...a small white light above the trees on the far side of a little used field. It started to move very slowly and, through a gap in the trees, I saw the familiar sight of a street light in the far distance – but this was blotted out by the appearance of a much larger elliptical object. The lights and object disappeared five seconds later, allowing the street light to show again.

I looked at my watch; it was 10pm." **(Source: UFOLOG, Isle of Wight UFO Society)**

16th December 1971 – Pulsating UFO over Essex rooftops

At midnight, Doreen Alice Steer – (then aged 41) of Drysdale Avenue, Chingford, Essex – went to the window to see if there was anybody about, as she wanted to let the dog outside.

"I noticed a very bright yellow 'star', just above the rooftops on the nearby crossroads. I first thought it was the North Star, but it was in completely the wrong position. It seemed more like a firework that had passed its peak, with bits; instead of exploding it fell away and hung underneath the object, which pulsated. I called my husband to come and have a look. It then moved parallel to the road and headed away silently at the speed of a light aircraft. Through binoculars, it could be seen to be hovering in the sky again.

Suddenly the object changed to white in colour and, after a few minutes observation, went vertically upwards into the sky and was gone."

BUFORA investigator – Ken Phillips, visited the witnesses and went to the nearby King George V Reservoir, where it was claimed by another witness that a UFO was seen to emerge near to where Doreen and her husband saw the star-like object.

Ken:

"Yet another report from the Waltham Forest district. This one is like so many others of the LITS (lights in the sky) and probably of no importance."

(Source: BUFORA)

[Authors: What an odd comment. Whilst such sightings were prolific around the Essex area, surely that is a rather derogatory statement, taking into consideration that nobody has been able to explain to anybody's satisfaction what these 'things' are and where they come from, never mind their agendas – if, indeed, they have one.]

18th December 1971 – Silver UFOs over Oxfordshire

Retired Naval Officer David Towers (then aged 61), and his wife, from 60, Seymour Street, Greatworth, near Banbury, Oxfordshire, arrived home at 3.10pm, after a morning out. He was putting the cat out, when his wife shouted out for him to come outside as there was something in the sky.

David:

> *"When I reached her, I looked up in amazement to see a bright silver, oblong object, moving in a south-west direction, about a mile away – far too slow to be an aircraft … maybe a few miles an hour, that's how slow it was. It looked like it was 1,500 feet long and about 5-10,000 feet high. Next to it was another object. We watched it (them) for a good ten minutes before it was out of sight."*

19th December 1971 – UFO over Kent

Mr Malcolm Pay of Rochester, Kent, watched a 'bright light' moving across the sky, at about 4.30pm. At one stage it stopped dead for eight minutes, before carrying on its journey. (**Source: SIGAP**)

23rd December 1971 – UFO over Hampshire

Brenda Wicking – (then aged 32) of Dulverton Mansions, Grays Inn Road, London – wrote to BUFORA about what she witnessed at 4.10pm.

> *"My son – Mitch (8) and I had just sat down in the dining carriage of a train going south, from London to Exeter, and we had just pulled out of Andover Station, when we saw a very bright yellow narrow object in the sky, for a few minutes. It was slightly curved, and tilted towards the ground. A few minutes later it went out – not fading, but like three switches being turned off in succession."*

23rd December 1971 – UFO over Staffordshire

Miss Susan Mills (13), and her father – Arthur, from Young Avenue, Holmcroft, Stafford, contacted Tony Pace to report what they had seen, at 5.30pm, over Staffordshire.

25th December 1971 – Flaming objects over St. Albans, Hertfordshire

At 10.45pm, Jean and Ronald Munden of Commons Lane, Kimpton, St. Albans, and their three children – Susan, Mary and Steven, were returning home. As they got out of the car they saw a fiery object in the sky, moving over from the direction of St. Albans, at a height of only a few hundred feet, and about three times the size of a football. As it passed overhead, they saw flames coming from it. A piece broke away and fell towards the ground – the glow changing to smoke as it dropped. The object reached the fields beyond the wood yard. A second 'fiery object' appeared, following a few hundred yards behind the path of the first one, until it, too, disappeared from sight. Ten minutes later, another larger object appeared in the sky and disappeared in the direction of Hitchin.

The next day the family searched the fields for any sign of the piece that had fallen away, but found nothing.

(**Source:** *BUFORA Bulletin* – **Nigel Stephenson**)

Susan Mills with father, Arthur

5   Dashool ⚹TREE   IV

This is the COLOUR I seen when it was coming from the north to south over Holmcroft ahead in the sky and after it passed the school it went out of site and I did not see it again and there was no sound from it at all and notights to say it was a aeroplane but my Father seen the object a fournight ago and it was the same colour. it 8.30PM.

29th December 1971 – Strange light seen

Bryan Bishop of Cedar Grove Winsford, in Cheshire – a senior lathe operator (aged 19) – had just come out of the house when he sighted a white object moving through the sky, with the 'Pegasus' constellation behind it As it neared the 'Taurus' constellation, it inexplicable vanished from view.

31st December 1971 – UFO encounter, Lincolnshire

On 31st December 1971, Edith Carr from Potter Hanworth, in Lincolnshire, found herself involved in *another* strange experience, when she sighted a second bright 'ball of light' hovering silently, a few feet off the ground, near some trees at the bottom of her garden, at 9pm.

> "*It appeared to be metallic in composition, with a flashing yellow 'light' that disappeared occasionally, as it revolved on itself, replaced by a golden 'tail' – in view for a few seconds – then the yellow 'light' would pick up again. After about thirty minutes it rose a few feet in the air, at which point I decided to go back into the house and watch it from a safe distance, through the bedroom window. By 10.30pm, it had gained height. At 11pm, it could no longer be seen.*"

This incident was investigated by Saxilby UFO Researcher – Richard Thompson, who confirmed to us that he had interviewed Mrs. Carr and a lodger, who was staying at the house, whose account was identical to hers, and that both of the witnesses described the visual effect as,

> "*. . . like bars of solid material passing in front of a brilliantly lit window, or porthole*".

(Source: Dick Thompson)

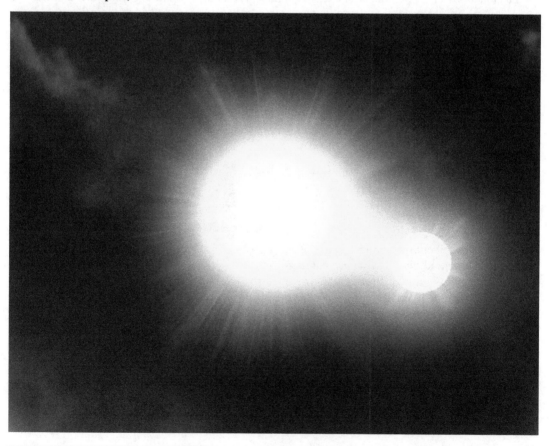

CHAPTER 3 – 1972

THE ACTIVITY CONTINUES – 'SAUCER' AND 'TRIANGULAR'-SHAPED CRAFT REPORTED

JANUARY

3rd January 1972 – Orange flashes wake up couple

11th January 1972 – Strange object over Braintree, Essex

12th January 1972 – UFO display over Rickmansworth

UFO with 'metal beams' paces motorist at Illinois

13th January 1972 – Disc-shaped UFO over Southern County

19th January 1972 – UFO sighted … strange marks found on the skin

20th January 1972 – 'Flying Saucer' over West Midlands

21st January 1972 – UFO over Andover, Hampshire

22nd January 1972 – Saucer-shaped UFO over Essex

23rd January 1972 – UFO seen to change shape over Colchester

January 1972 – Landed UFO. Close Encounter, South Yorkshire … entities seen!

FEBRUARY

4th February 1972 – Finned object over Surrey

6th February 1972 – Two black 'triangle' UFOs seen over Grays, Essex

11th February 1972 – Fireball over Nottinghamshire …?

12th February 1972 – Yellow 'light' over London

February 1972 – Square-shaped UFO sighted over Leicestershire

17th February 1972 – Motorist sights strange lights

February 1972 – Kensington Library, London – UFO talk

MARCH

3rd March 1972 – Two orange objects over Essex

5th March 1972 – 'Flying Saucer' over Sussex

14th March 1972 – Cigar-shaped UFO over London

17th February 1972 – Motorist sights strange lights

19th March 1972 – UFO sighted over Colchester

24th March 1972 – Cigar-shaped UFO sighted by schoolboy

APRIL

8th April 1972 – Kensington Library, London

13th April 1972 – Three cigar shapes over Yorkshire

24th April 1972 – UFO and its occupant, seen over Manchester

March 1972 – Close encounter with a 'Flying Saucer', Staffordshire

Early 1970s – UFO fleet over Reading … interference with motor vehicle

Spring 1972 – Mystery 'light' over Essex

Spring 1972 – 'Circle of lights' seen in the sky over Worcestershire

MAY

6th May 1972 – Kensington Library, London – UFO lecture

15th May 1972 – UFO, in the shape of an umbrella, seen over Leicestershire

16th May 1972 – Diamond-shaped UFO over Lincoln – Five 'lights' seen over Scotland

JUNE

8th June 1972 – UFO over Hartlepool

12th June 1972 – Police Officer sights UFO

13th June 1972 – 'Flying Saucer' seen over London Park

19th June 1972 – Orange UFO over US Air base

28th June 1972 – UFO seen … reported to RAF Lyneham

29th June 1972 – UFO over Coventry, Warwickshire

JULY

6th July 1972 – Triangular UFO sighted over Clacton-on-Sea, Essex

July 1972 – Silvery object over Brighton

22nd July 1972 – UFO zigzags across the sky

25th July 1972 – Police Officer reports sighting a UFO

28th July 1972 – Craters found in soybean fields

July 1972 – UFO over Norfolk

AUGUST

3rd August 1972 – UFO over Hampshire

6th August 1972 – UFO over Liverpool

7th August 1972 – UFO over Bat

9th August 1972 – RAF jet fighter and UFO activity over Warminster

10th August 1972 – Bizarre falls of straw over airports

13th August 1972 – Mysterious object over Gatwick Airport, London

14th August 1972 – UFO interference with motor vehicle, Wisconsin

16th August 1972 – UFO over London

16th August 1972 – UFO lands at Alaska

18th August 1972 – 'Red light' over Hampshire
19th August 1972 – UFO lands in Swamp
22nd August 1972 – Bright Orange UFO sighted over Iowa
22nd August – UFOs over Kansas
22nd August 1972 – Motorist chased by UFO
23rd August –UFO over Iowa
28th August 1972 – Perfect silver 'ball' over the sea
August 1972 – Mysterious object over Gatwick Airport, London
Summer 1972 – UFO over Suffolk
Summer 1972 – Wedge-shaped UFO seen over London, with occupant!
Summer 1972 – Police sight tube-shaped objects over Kent

SEPTEMBER

3rd September 1972 – Yellow 'globe' over Essex
13th September 1972 – UFO lands in field
14th September 1972 – UFO over Wales
16th September 1972 – Triangular-shaped UFOs over Essex
Winter 1972 – Landed UFO, Buckinghamshire

OCTOBER

3rd October 1972 – Cigar-shaped object seen over Lincolnshire

4th October 1972 – Eight 'lights' over Cheshire
8th October 1972 – UFO over Lancashire
11th October 1972 – Police Officers sight UFO over London
20th October 1972 – Six rectangular objects seen in the sky over Surrey
22nd October 1972 – UFO over Lincoln

NOVEMBER

3rd November 1972 – UFO over Cheshire
1972 – Dr. J. Allen Hynek – *The UFO Experience: A Scientific Inquiry*
5th November 1972 – Close encounter, Gloucestershire … occupants seen
11th November 1972- UFO photographed over Arizona

DECEMBER

Winter 1972 – Sighting of 'craft', with occupants, over Sussex
5th December 1972 – UFO over Kent
9th December 1972 – UFO over Warwickshire
11th December 1972 – Rectangular object sighted
14th December 1972 – UFO over Yorkshire
15th December 1972 – Three UFOs seen over Essex
19th December 1972 – Strange object sighted by householder

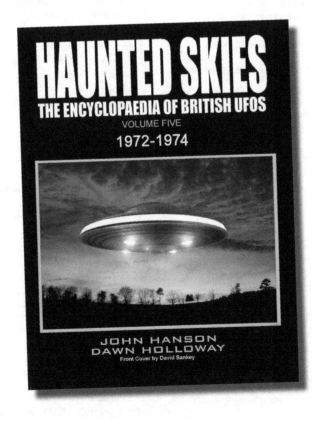

JANUARY 1972

3rd January 1972 – Orange flashes wake up couple

At 1am, Mr Philip Edwards of Upper Park Road, Brightlingsea, Essex, was awoken by an extraordinary 'rushing' noise.

Thinking it was an aircraft about to crash, he ran to the window. When he looked out with his wife, they saw:

> *"...a great light between us and the river, accompanied by a series of orange flashes from lights in the sky. The next morning I spoke to my sons – Richard and Charles – who told me they had also been awoken and had seen the lights."*

Enquiries with the Police and the Army revealed no knowledge of anything that might have explained the incident away. (**Source:** *Colchester Evening Gazette*/BUFORA *Journal,* **Volume 3, No. 7,** Summer 1972)

11th January 1972 – Strange object over Braintree, Essex

Elaine Freeborn (15) of Ellen Way, Great Notley, Braintree, Essex, had just arrived home on the school bus, at 5pm, and was in the act of crossing the road, but looked first to see if there was any traffic. She was surprised to see an object in a gap between the trees.

> *"I watched it move behind the trees and could see it shining through them. It crossed over the road and moved behind buildings.*
>
> It then carried on over the rooftops and I lost sight of it."

(**Source: Ron West**)

12th January 1972 – UFO display over Rickmansworth

At 10.15am, four workmen on Woodcock Hill, Rickmansworth (four miles from Watford), sighted a 'silver disc', motionless in the perfect clear sky, at an angle of 60 degrees. A short time later, five more of these objects were seen moving at height in different directions. These objects were observed for a total of two and a half hours. Enquiries were made with London Meteorological Office, who pointed out that it was nothing to do with them, as they do not release balloons in batches. One of the witnesses contacted the MOD and spoke to an official there, who seemed very interested in what he had seen, and asked him:

> *"...if he had told any others about the sighting and were there any installations, or bodies of water, in the vicinity?"*

Enquiries made revealed that a power line passed over the vicinity, and that the adjacent valley from Rickmansworth to Denham, and beyond, contained a number of deep lakes, formed from gravel workings. This valley was the scene of at least a dozen UFO reports over the last ten years. On the same day, a woman resident of Chalfont St. Peter sighted a number of tubular objects.

January 1972 – UFO with 'metal beams' paces motorist at Illinois

Miss Donna Wilkins of Breese, Clinton County, Illinois – a senior at the school – was out driving in a rural area with her boyfriend, when they saw lights travelling in odd patterns across the sky.

> *"They were moving real funny, back and forth. Suddenly, a lighted object appeared right next to us. We were both frightened and began to drive faster. We had only driven about a fifth of a mile, when the object began to hover over the car; it was twice the size of the car and triangular. Its underside appeared to be constructed of 'metal beams'. It stayed with us, despite driving at 85 miles per hour. As we drove into Bartelso, it disappeared behind a tree line – that's the last time I want to see one."*

(**Source:** *Data-Net,* **Volume 7,** July 1972)

13th January 1972 – Disc-shaped UFO over Southern County

The following day, another sighting took place over the Watford/Rickmansworth areas, involving 'disc' or 'star-shaped' objects seen in the sky.

(Source: South-west Hertfordshire UFO Investigation Group [SHUFOIG])

19th January 1972 – UFO sighted … strange marks found on the skin

A flickering red 'light' was seen in the sky over Corsham, at 2.30pm, by housewife – Mrs Dorothy Greenhalgh – to whom we spoke, over 33 years later.

> "I was reading to my daughter, aged 4 at the time, when I became aware of a red flickering 'light' just outside the range of my peripheral vision, but decided to finish the story before looking upwards into the sky through the window when I saw a huge bright red 'light' – about six times the size of an aircraft – just hanging there, at a height I took to be several thousand feet.
>
> I directed my daughter's attention towards the object and we watched, for a short while, before it flew away.
>
> The next day, my daughter complained of some red marks on her stomach. I looked and saw three, in a triangular shape. I was shocked when I saw it, because I had noticed similar marks on my stomach which hadn't been there prior to the appearance of the UFO. What did defy explanation was the fact that Cyril also discovered an identical triangular inflammation on his stomach. How could this be, as he was working some miles away? Within days the marks faded."

(Source: Ken Rogers)

Exactly why people became afflicted with these medical conditions seems beyond comprehension. However, if you consider those occasions when, as a result of UFO interaction, domestic electrical appliances in the house are rendered inoperative and cars are brought to a halt, is it no wonder people find themselves unable to explain – never mind come to terms with the nature of puzzling medical conditions following an encounter with a UFO?

20th January 1972 – 'Flying Saucer' over West Midlands

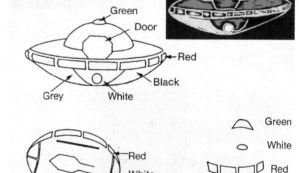

At 4.30pm, a saucer-shaped object was seen wobbling, a few hundred feet off the ground, over a block of flats close to Carters Lane Baptist Church, Halesowen, West Midlands, by three schoolboys on their way home. We traced two of the boys, who asked that their personal details be kept confidential fearing ridicule.

(Source: UFOSIS)

South Shields

At about 10.30pm, the same day, Jim Todd – an electrician from John Readhead's shipyard, South Shields – was at work, with three other workmen, when crane driver – Jack Short – alerted them to something strange in the sky. The men looked up to see:

> "…five roundish objects, high up, flying in a cross formation, heading eastwards over the sea; two were red, the others orange, yellow and blue. They were visible for two to three minutes."

(Source: Isle of Wight UFO Society)

21st January 1972 – UFO over Andover, Hampshire

At 1.40am, Special Police Constable George Edward Harris (53) from 6, Jasper's Green, Panfield, near Great Dunmow, Essex, and his wife and son, sighted a circular object in the sky.

> "It had a green glow around its outer edges. Through binoculars an inner ring of evenly spaced white lights could be seen. It was stationary, at first, but after about four minutes it dropped vertically to take up a new position nearer the horizon, when it changed into an ellipse. The object changed position, once more – this time ascending until it reached an elevation of about 40 degrees, slightly higher than when first seen. At 1.52am it became smaller, before finally disappearing from sight."

(Source: BUFORA Journal, Volume 3, No. 10, Spring 1973)

22nd January 1972 – Saucer-shaped UFO over Essex

Amanda Clancy (16) of Harwich Road, Clacton, Essex, was walking along London Road, at 4.50pm, with two friends – Deborah Pellow and June Bolitho.

> "We saw an orange saucer-shaped object in the sky; it just came out of nowhere. We watched it for ten minutes, and then it vanished in front of our eyes." **(Source: Ron West)**

23rd January 1972 – UFO seen to change shape over Colchester

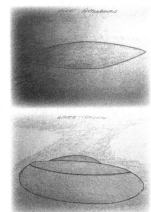

At 11.15am, Ernest Drover (56) of Penicuik, Straight Road, Boxted, Colchester, was driving along the A12 from Marks Tey to Colchester, with four other people in the car, when they noticed something moving out of a cloud. He stopped the car and they watched:

> "...a silver saucer-shaped object, which came to a halt in the sky and apparently tilt towards us. It then turned and became a cigar shape, turned again and now looked like a child's spinning top. It was visible for a few minutes before heading away." **(Source: Ron West)**

January 1972 – Close Encounter, South Yorkshire ... entity seen!

Mr Anthony Cureton was out walking the family dog with his two children – Jacqueline, and son, Tony – some 150 yards away from their house at Kendray, Barnsley, in South Yorkshire, at 7pm, when they saw a strange torpedo-shaped 'craft' with what appeared to have two or three levels to it, full of dark lights, with a halo around, which descended vertically through the sky. The object, then about 700 feet above them, landed on the other side of a 6 feet high concrete wall (forming the boundary line to a large complex of football fields). According to the two children:

> "...a 'pointed' face then popped up above the wall, showing pointed ears and large red eyes."

Frightened, the children ran away and told their father, who was trailing a short distance behind them.

On looking back, there was no sign of the 'craft' and its 'occupant'. Mrs Cureton confirmed that the children had arrived home in a very frightened state, and refused to go out in the dark for some time afterwards. Jacqueline, who was apparently the worst affected by the experience, could remember little about what had taken place, whereas Tony (who was older) had no problem remembering, with clarity, what he had witnessed.

Mr Cureton:

> "I remember Tony mentioning this event, from time to time, and didn't attach much importance to it; besides, one UFO had been actually reported to have landed in the school playing fields, some years previously – around 1958, or 1959."

Attempts to obtain further details of the incident, which allegedly took place in 1958, were unsuccessful. **(Source: Dan Goring – Editor of *Earth-link***

FEBRUARY 1972

4th February 1972 – Finned object over Surrey

At 1.25pm, Neil Hards (9) and his friend – Jacinth, were walking towards the schoolroom at Great Ormond Street Hospital annex, Kingston-on-Thames, Surrey, when they heard a noise above them. They looked upwards into the sky, but seeing nothing continued on their journey. After the noise was heard again they stopped, and looking upwards saw what Neil described as:

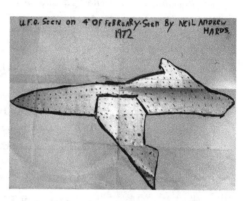

> "...a silver coloured object, with 'scree' all over it. It made noise like rough sandpaper, and kept stopping and starting."

The object then took up a hovering position in the air, during which time it rocked from side to side.

> "I could see a fin on the side of the object; when it rocked I saw one on the other side. It had an underneath which was concave, and a red coloured 'bump' on the top, showing a thin gold coloured line running across it from front to back."

The object – which was seen for 2-3 minutes – eventually disappeared behind trees, leaving the children very frightened by what had taken place.

(Source: Ken Phillips, *BUFORA Journal*, Volume 3, No. 10, Spring 1973)

6th February 1972 – Two black 'triangle' UFOs seen over Grays, Essex

Gardner John Fouch of Rosedale Avenue, Grays, Essex, was returning from a night out, at 11.45pm, when he saw:

> "...two very black (darker than the night sky) triangular-shaped objects in the sky, moving as if in formation; they stooped for about a minute and then carried on, stopped, and abruptly disappeared from view."

11th February 1972 – Fireball over Nottinghamshire ...?

At 1.30am, Mr William Dowman – a labourer by occupation – (then 59 years of age), from Harby, Nottinghamshire, was in the process of going back to bed, after having visited the bathroom, when the bedroom lit up with intense light. Thinking it was a car he went to the window and saw with amazement:

> "...a large spherical 'ball' – as big as the full moon – crossing the skyline; it had a pale green outer rim, with a yellow centre like the sun. As it passed by, it swept the countryside with light. In 2-3 seconds, it had gone from view, heading in a north-west to south-east direction."

Is it possible, from the description given, that Mr Dolman saw a fireball meteor, rather than a UFO? If this was the case, how many of us are given the rare opportunity to see such a brilliant example at first-hand? **(Source: Richard Thompson)**

Square-shaped UFO sighted over Leicestershire

Later that same day, as darkness fell, two Loughborough schoolboys – Halit Akkan (11) and Warren Green (13) – residents of the St. Matthew's estate, Leicester – noticed an apparently square object in the sky, showing a central flashing red light and a light in each of its four corners. It was seen to hover before sinking in the light of powerful beams, towards a field. **(Source: *Leicester Mercury*)**

12th February 1972 – Yellow 'light' over London

Brian Knight (27) from Grove Hill, South Woodford, London – a gardener by occupation – happened to be in his front garden around midnight, when he saw:

> "...*a yellow light come zooming in from over the Estuary. I ran around to the back of the house and saw it apparently hovering in the air – then it moved towards the west, at great speed, towards Leytonstone, East London.* **(Source: Ron West)**

During the middle of February 1972 scores of people telephoned the police, reporting that they had sighted a brightly lit object moving through the sky over the Liverpool, Cheshire, and Wales area. Some accounts included a white 'light' with a 'tail' that changed to a dazzling green flare.

Residents in Rhyl, Prestatyn, Wrexham, Mostyn, Broughton and Birkenhead, also contacted the police – some of whom had been patrolling the M6, between Birmingham and Preston, when mysterious 'lights' were seen crossing the sky.

17th February 1972 – Motorist sights strange 'lights'

Mrs Michelle Ryan and her husband were driving along Birkenhead Road, towards Moreton, at 8pm.

> "*It was dark. There were no street lights, due to a power cut, when my husband told me there was a lorry right on top of our back window. I looked round and saw no lorry, but two dull off-white 'discs of light' in each corner of the rear window; it was as if someone was peering into the car. My husband slowed down, and then accelerated; the next thing they had gone.*"

(Source: *Liverpool Echo*, 18/21.2.1972)

Kensington Library, London – UFO talk

People were invited to a lecture, held at Kensington Central Library on 4th March 1972, at 7pm, by Charles H. Gibbs-Smith, M.A, F.M.A, F.R.S.A, member of Executive Committee of the history group of the Royal Aeronautical Society, and author of many Science Museum books and articles of Aviation History – *UFOs and Documentation.*

MARCH 1972

3rd March 1972 – Two orange objects over Essex

At 8.30pm, Joan Londors (32) of Uplads Road, Romford, Essex, felt restless and had an urge to go out into the garden.

> "*I stood watching the night sky till 9.25pm, and decided to go back inside. I was in the act of doing just this when I heard what sounded like the rushing of air. Two orange oval 'lights' appeared, one above the other – almost as if there was one, and its reflection – moving like a saucer, skimming*

across water. I turned away and went indoors. I felt very excited over the next seven days, being on a 'bit of a high' after seeing this." (**Source: Ron West**)

5th March 1972 – 'Flying Saucer' over Sussex

Mr Francis Chard from Crawley, in Sussex, was walking home from East Crawley Railway Station, a few minutes before 9pm.

"As I walked along Haslett Avenue, forming part of the A.264 trunk road, I noticed an unidentified object hovering directly over an electrical transformer, carrying high voltage power into the town. It was 'mushroom' looking in shape, sharply etched against a background of yellow glowing light, about four feet in width. From the left and right-hand corner of the domed top were two red and blue in colour spotlights, shining downwards. It then started to move, completing an arc in the sky of about 180 degrees, passing behind my position, before shooting off towards the south-west."

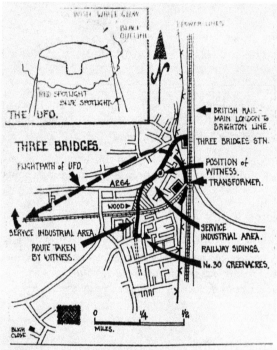

Flightpath of UFO over Three Bridges and Crawley. Inset: How the object appeared to witness. Cover drawing: UFO and transformer towers as seen over the fence from Haslett Avenue

Francis rushed home and told the rest of his family, who watched the unidentified flying object – now looking like a bright yellow 'star' hovering over a field, some two miles away – before fading from view at 9.30pm.

In conversation with his mother, he learnt from her that the picture on the television screen had been replaced by what she described as *"interference, resembling tweed cloth"*, which she had never seen before – caused, one presumes, by the presence of the UFO. This abnormal picture, as seen on the screen of a TV, was to be brought to our notice on other occasions during reports of UFO activity.

On the 19th March, the television set began to show heavy interference, at 8.40pm, similar to before. Francis ran outside and was astonished to see what looked like an identical UFO in the sky, but at a much higher altitude. He telephoned the police, who sent an officer to the house, who agreed he could see the object – which was later explained away in the local newspapers as being the planet Venus!

(**Source: Personal interview/H. Watkins,** *Flying Saucer Review*)

6th March 1972 – Three red 'blobs' seen by Essex schoolgirls

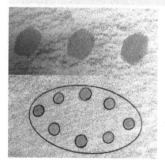

Sharon Wicks (14) of Priory Avenue, Chelmsford, had been out dancing with her friend – Teresa Lyons, of Brindwood Road, Chingford. At 7.30pm, the two girls noticed a "red 'blob' in the sky" but they carried on walking. All of a sudden, the red 'blob' split into two – then split again, making three 'blobs'. Two of them shot away into the sky, leaving the original one behind. Five minutes later, this too flew off in the same direction. (**Source: Ron West**)

14th March 1972 – Cigar-shaped UFO over London

At 7.50pm, Mrs Lyons of Bridge End, Walthamstow, London, was putting her baby down for the night when she saw, through the window,

> *"...an orange, oval or cigar-shaped object surrounded by a hazy glow, standing vertically in the sky".*

About a minute later, it vanished from view. (**Source: Ken Phillips, BUFORA Report, No. 1226**)

Mid-March 1972 – Hovering 'red light' over Lancashire

Mr Leslie Morris of Beechfield Road, Swinton, in Lancashire, was walking home with his daughter – Marlene. They noticed a strange 'red light' in the sky.

Leslie:

> *"It looked to be the size of a tennis ball, and appeared to be about 500 feet up in the sky. It hovered for several minutes, then turned and vanished."*

Upon his arrival home, Leslie telephoned Manchester Airport about the incident but was told there had been no air traffic for at least a quarter of an hour before the sighting. (**Source: *Eccles Journal***)

They did not appear to be the only witnesses. Whilst we cannot say it was the same object, The *Manchester News,* in their edition published around the same time period, told of a sighting by schoolgirls – Ellen Chapman and Fiona Cannon, who reported having seen four 'red lights' in the sky, one of which was continually flashing and apparently leading the others across the sky. (**Source: *Manchester Evening News***)

19th March 1972 – UFO sighted over Colchester

Janet Buttery (52) of 37, Dedham Meade, Dedham, Colchester – a sales assistant at *Woolworths* – was out walking with her nephew, Neil Buttery, and sister, Nicola Buttery, at 8pm, when they noticed a very bright object heading across the sky over the *Ford* Motor Works.

> *"It stopped in the sky. Neil ran indoors and fetched his binoculars. We both looked at the object in turn. It was a silver-grey metallic 'disc' with a ring of green lights around the middle that seemed to be rotating anticlockwise. There were two red lights. Suddenly, a beam of yellow light projected down from he base of the UFO, which lasted for a couple of minutes – then, ten minutes later, it went out and the 'Saucer' headed away, eastwards, soon lost in the distance."*

24th March 1972 – Cigar-shaped UFO sighted by schoolboy

Schoolboy Gavin Hudson from Overchurch Middle School, Moreton Road, Upton, Wirral, reported having sighted:

> *"...a large, silvery unpainted cigar-shaped object, heading from the south-west towards the north-west".*

By the time he alerted the teachers and other pupils, it had gone from sight.

(**Source: Martin Jones/*Merseyside Bulletin*, Spring 1972**)

APRIL 1972

8th April 1972 – Kensington Library, London

People were invited to a lecture, held at Kensington Central Library, at 7pm – 'UFOs, COMMUNICATIONS and SEMANTICS' – by Mr C. Maxwell Cade, MIEE, MIERE, FRAS, FRAeS, Consultant to *Flying Saucer Review*, Psychical Researcher, Inventor, and author of many important scientific papers and books.

Mr Cade was to discuss *"Who is trying to communicate with whom and to what extent is the message garbled?"*

13th April 1972 – Three cigar shapes over Yorkshire

Hilary Dawn Marson (38) of Foston Lane, Beefield, Driffield, Yorkshire, was sat at the breakfast bar, at 8am, looking out of the window towards the north-east.

> *"About two miles away I saw what appeared to be three cigar shapes, joined together in a white, black, white, formation – heading in a westerly direction through the sky. There was bright sunshine and people out, crop spraying, but I know what I saw."*

15th April 1972 – Mystery object over Yorkshire

What appears to have been a 'repeat performance': Driffield, East Yorkshire housewife – Mrs Hilary Marson (28) – was in the front room of her house when she saw what she took to be a small aircraft, heading towards her house. As it came closer, she realised her mistake.

> *"It had what appeared to be wings of a shiny material, a dark coloured body, with two triangular windows on top, and something rotating underneath. When it was about 200 yards away, it halted in mid-air for about a minute. It then moved away, backwards, at about 5 miles per hour, and headed away in a curve, before disappearing behind a wood. My children also saw it through binoculars."* (**Source: BUFORA**)

24th April 1972 – UFO and its occupant, seen over Manchester

At 2am, Manchester woman, Mrs Taylor – who was suffering from insomnia – happened to look out of the window, opposite a tall factory chimney, when she saw a glowing, yellow-white 'ball-shaped' object, out of which emerged a 'figure', wearing boots, described as

> *". . . similar in appearance to an astronaut, landing on the moon".*

After two hours, the object eventually disappeared from view.

(**Source: Roy Dutton, Joan Nelstrop and Peter Rogerson**)

1972 – Close encounter with a 'Flying Saucer', Staffordshire

Karen Hills was then living in Castle Drive, Great Barr. She told of being awoken in the early hours of the morning by a whirring noise outside. On going to the curtains to have a look outside, she saw:

> *"...a huge 'machine', its base surrounded by light. Inside a clear dome on top, I could see bright lit machinery. I rubbed my eyes several times to make sure I wasn't dreaming, but it was still there. I was very frightened and awoke my sister by shaking her, but she wouldn't listen and told me to shut up. I went to have a look and it was still there, although it had moved slightly. I went back to bed and lay awake, feeling very scared."*

In 2011, we traced Karen (now 50) and spoke to her at some length about her sighting. She had this to say:

> *"I can remember being in my bedroom. I used to share a bedroom with my sister and heard a strange noise outside. I looked out of the window and saw this real 'bright light', this circular thing – a bit like a cup and saucer – whirring away. It was absolutely huge. I tried to wake up my sister and couldn't. I wondered if I'd had a dream, but it seemed so real. I remember seeing it later in the distance between the houses. I did have a very odd dream, involving a massive UFO which was calling the people. I remember going up this ramp thing into the UFO. Inside the UFO there was this seating all the way around."*

Karen Hills

Having talked to Karen, it was obvious that she was a very genuine, intelligent woman, who remained curious about the sighting and the strange dream that both she and her sister experienced. We are well aware of the implications of what this strange version of events might mean, to some people, but Karen was aged seven or eight, at the time; hence, her limited recollection of what took place. One thing is assured; she is not the only one to sight something like this. What they are and where they come from is the ultimate question, but whether they exist is not in contention as far as we are concerned.

(Source: Irene Bott, Staffordshire UFO Group)

Early 1970s – UFO fleet over Reading … interference with motor vehicle

During the early 1970s, Kate Saunders was a front seat passenger in a car being driven home by her boyfriend, from a nightclub in Bracknell, at midnight, when the car spluttered and came to a halt.

> *"I sat in the car and looked across the road, and saw a dark 'disc' shaped object ascend from behind some trees. After a little while the car started and we drove home. I was quite scared, by this time, and although my boyfriend hadn't seen it, he seemed pretty concerned. We pulled up outside his house and, as we got out, we saw a large 'craft' moving silently overhead that had a searchlight underneath it, panning left and right as it moved forward.*
>
> *We ran into his house and his dad came out with a camera, hoping to get a few shots. After a while I decided to go home and asked him to take me, but because he was shaken up he asked his sister to come with us. It was a clear, cold, night and as we drove to my house, we were watching the sky and could see more of these 'craft' overhead – no sound, complete silence. I ran in and went up to my room. I didn't try to wake my parents, as they were strict about what time I should be home. I sat looking out of my window until dawn and saw dozens of 'craft' in the sky, travelling towards the Newbury area. We never told anyone, but some years ago I was talking to my brother and he said he was watching the same thing on the same night. It was reported in the local newspaper, but was explained away as being the Armed Forces on a joint operation. I really thought that it was an invasion of some sort and was unable to sleep properly for many weeks after the sighting.*
>
> *At a later date, his dad had the film developed and was told that the film had been overexposed."*

Spring 1972 – 'Circle of lights' seen in the sky over Worcestershire

In spring of 1972 (it may have been a little later) local farmer – Trevor Edmunds, from Gorcott Hill, just outside Redditch,

Worcestershire (dwarfed now by a giant telecommunications tower) – was out walking, late one evening, contemplating the loss of four acres of his land, due to construction of the new dual carriageway, when he noticed a 'circle of lights' hovering silently in the sky.

> *"I gazed at them with great curiosity. They were far too big to have been any aircraft. They then started to curl in and out of each other before moving left, towards the direction of Studley."*

Spring 1972 – Mystery 'light' over Essex

Paul Ronald Stock (22) of East Park Close, Chadwell Heath, Essex, was walking home from his girlfriend's house, at 11pm, near the junction of Chadwell Heath and Lee Avenue. As he crossed the car park, he saw an aircraft high up in the sky. He then completely forgot about the airplane after he saw a 'light' coming from behind a tall building, about 100 yards away. Puzzled, he halted and looked up, seeing:

> *"…a semicircular object rising up towards me. I ran to the exit, frightened. By now, the light was 60 feet above me. As I ran, I saw an amazing sight – the whole car park was lit up; light and particles on the*

ground were reflecting that light. The object, or 'light', continued on its journey, now speeding away – the whole episode over in ten seconds." Paul made his way home, much shaken by the experience, and told his parents what had taken place. He kept quiet for some years, but in 1975 his father mentioned it to Bob Easton – area investigator for BUFORA, and Paul was interviewed about it.

MAY 1972

6th May 1972 – Kensington Library, London – UFO lecture

People were invited to a lecture, held at Kensington Central Library on 6th May 1972, at 7pm, by Roger Stanway – a solicitor and amateur astronomer of some repute, being a director of the Newchapel Observatory and co-author of the *Flying Saucer Report*, internationally acclaimed as a blueprint for efficient investigation – *Investigations of Landing Cases*.

On a personal note, we have had the pleasure of talking to Roger Stanway, who withdrew completely from any research and investigation of the UFO subject many years ago.

In 2011, Roger reiterated his belief that UFOs are examples of something demonic in origin rather than extraterrestrial, which appears to be more likely from the nature of evidence accrued over the years, although one cannot rule out that if we can send probes to other part of the universe, is it possible that we have also intercepted theirs? We wished him well and thanked him for allowing us permission to refer to some of the sightings that he and Tony Pace investigated during the 1970s.

15th May 1972 – UFO, in the shape of an umbrella, seen over Leicestershire

At 9.55pm, retired Nurse Florence Freeston from Cherry Avenue, Kirby Muxloe, Leicestershire, contacted the police after sighting an object, resembling:

> *"...a car's headlight, in the shape of an umbrella, with something attached to it. It looked like a burning parachute, and remained stationary until covered by clouds. It was positioned next to the moon in the sky."* (**Source:** *Leicester Mercury*, 16.5.1972)

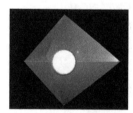

16th May 1972 – Diamond-shaped UFO over Lincoln

The following evening Michael, and his father, from Ermine Street, Lincoln – both keen amateur astronomers – were outside in the garden, at 8.15pm. Michael noticed something strange, low in the sky, moving over nearby rooftops. His first reaction was to think it might have been Venus, but then he realised the colour and position was all wrong. On looking at the object through the telescope, he was surprised to see:

> *"...a diamond shape, with a red 'ball of light' in the centre, showing a variety of colours in a sequence I had never seen before, with a red glow surrounding the outer 'diamond', with a fainter red inside. The best way to describe what we saw is for you to imagine three circles, one inside of each other – the outer yellow, the inner green, with a golden-red centre. As it moved slowly through the sky it pulsated, before being lost from view as it disappeared behind some houses."*

(**Source: Richard Thompson**)

Five 'lights' seen over Scotland

A group of five yellowish-white lights were seen flying over Nairnshire, heading on a north-west to south-east course, at 9.30pm, by Dr. and Mrs Finlay – then living at Brackla, in May 1972. The couple told of seeing them,

"...apparently descending from the direction of Ben Nevis, quickly followed by a group of six similar objects and then a single 'light'. Ten minutes later, the display was over".

(Source: *The Nairnshire Telegraph*, May 1972)

JUNE 1972

1972 – Mysterious 'Thing' seen over West Sussex

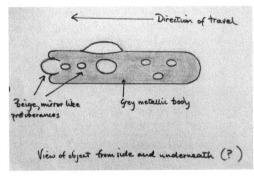

Mr Stephen Van-Linden (26), and his companion, were strawberry picking at a deserted farm located between Bognor and Littlehampton. At about 3pm they noticed a strange craft in the sky, at a height they estimated to be 1,000 feet, making a whining noise – but unlike the noise one would associate with a jet turbine. The couple hid behind nearby trees, fearing for their safety, where they came across two just as fearful girls and a boy, who had also seen it from their vantage point, several hundred yards away on the other side of the field. We do not know the location of the farm. The object, whatever it was, made three circles of the area before flying away. It was described as being the size of a twin-engine civil airliner. **(Source: Peter Spink, EUFOSG)**

8th June 1972 – UFO over Hartlepool

At 10.30pm, a mysterious object – described as resembling *"a flying electric light bulb"* – was seen by residents of Wingate, Hartlepool. They included James Anderson, who was driving through Wingate with his wife, Rita, when the car in front of him skidded to a halt.

"The people jumped out and looked up into the sky. I saw a brilliant light in the sky – like an electric light bulb. It was making a terrific noise. It seemed to fly along for a few seconds before stopping, and then it shot straight upwards at speed."

Another witness included Mr Richard Roberts, who was driving home with his two sons from the *Fir Tree Inn*, who said:

"...something came from the west, towards the east coast. I thought it was a rocket, at first. It seemed to hover for a few seconds and then climbed vertically, making one hell of a rumbling noise as it did so. It was like a brilliant spinning light, with a centre and a sort of flare around it."

(Source: *Northern Daily Mail*, 9.6.1972/Personal interview)

12th June 1972 – Police Officer sights UFO

David Harris – a Police Officer with the South Wales Constabulary – was off duty, at 11.45pm, when he saw what he believed to be an aircraft in trouble, flying low over Llangeinor Mountain.

"The object was about the size of a bus in length. I waited for the explosion. There was nothing – just silence. I drove to the police station and telephoned Air Traffic Control, at Rhoose Airport. They confirmed no aircraft were in the vicinity. I then reported the matter to the police control room, at Bridgend."

As a result of submitting a report, David received considerable ridicule from his colleagues and some very offensive remarks made by senior officers, who suggested he was lying. **(Source: Personal interview)**

1970s – UFO display over Chippenham, Wiltshire

Retired Police Officer Frank Brace told of two separate sightings of UFOs, whilst working in the Wiltshire Police in the 1970s.

"The first was as a result of a call from the public of a mysterious object seen over Monkton Park, in Chippenham.

Following retirement I met an officer (known to me), who reminded me of a UFO seen by us, while investigating an accident which had taken place on the bridge in Chippenham. All I can now recall is lots of strange, fast moving objects, flashing across the sky – much faster than even this new 6,000km thing that they are trying to develop now. I watched the ISS again this week and at 17,164 miles per hour, it was very slow by comparison. The objects we saw were much lower before disappearing into infinity. Very odd!

The notes that I made at the time are not available to me now.

The other time I was on plain clothes observation with a female officer in a car sales showroom forecourt, south of Devizes, when it appeared low in the sky and hovered towards us and then disappeared. It was a low light situation, so not a clear sighting. Both locations are close to military ranges, but they were unexplainable and nothing that I have seen since can explain them further, except to say that this one could have been a P.1127 in the early days, but I am not sure."

13th June 1972 – Flying Saucer' seen over London Park

Miss Shirley Devereux, and her parents, of Danebury Avenue, Roehampton, London, sighted a 'cluster of light' landing in Richmond Park, at l0pm. Miss Devereux later said:

"It hovered above the park, 30 feet above the ground, and then moved across the park but stopped near the Priory. Between then and 12.15am, we saw a number of other 'lights' converging on the same spot where the previous one had come down; they were so bright you could see them clearly with the naked eye. The 'lights' were a brilliant orange and seemed to go dull. Just before they landed, I saw a distinct saucer-shaped object behind them."

According to Gordon Creighton, Editor of *Flying Saucer Review*, this was not the only occasion when things had been seen to land in the park. Apparently, another resident in the area – Mrs Joan Kinneir – had observed a flaming object descending into the park, some years previously.

(Source: *Barnes and Mortlake Herald*/Gordon Creighton)

19th June 1972 – Orange UFO over US Airbase

Airmen Gary Corley and Randolph Wogoman from George Air Force Base, in San Bernardino, reported having sighted an orange object, estimated to be over 300 feet in diameter, which dropped down behind a building south-west of their security patrol area at the base, at 1am. They reported it to the Air Police, Victorville Sherriff's office and Adelanto Police department.

A search was later conducted but nothing was found. **(Source: *Data-Net*, Volume 7, July 1972)**

28th June 1972 – UFO seen … reported to RAF Lyneham

On the afternoon, a UFO was seen flying over the Penhill area of Swindon, Wiltshire, and was reported to RAF Lyneham, who confirmed they had received a number of UFO sightings. One of the witnesses was a local woman – Wendy Eales.

"It was about 12.30pm when my sister, Lesley, came in and grabbed binoculars. It was white, with a ring around it, and spinning very fast. It didn't frighten me. I was fascinated."

A shining silver 'globe' was seen in the sky over Scarborough, during the same afternoon, by residents of Princess Street, before it moved away towards the north-east. One of the witnesses was Mr R. Sewell, who said:

"I don't know what the hell it was; it was a round, silvery thing, with a point on top. It's hard to say how high it was, but certainly higher than the low cloud."

Other reports of a similar object seen on the same day came in from Coventry and Norfolk, but the sightings were later explained away by RAF Lyneham as a weather balloon – which appears highly unlikely, bearing in mind the nature of the sightings concerned.

(**Source:** *Evening Advertiser*, 29.6.1972/*Scarborough Evening News*, 29.6.1972)

29th June 1972 – UFO over Coventry, Warwickshire

At 11.30pm a red, green and silver object was sighted over Coventry by Leamington woman – Katherine Laws, who called the police. They attended and confirmed that they had the object under observation, which appeared to have *"a fan-shaped tail"*.

This was yet another sighting later brought to the attention of local UFO Investigator – Bob Tibbitts, who was to discover that on occasion, rational answers could be found!

(**Source:** *SYNTONIC*, July/August 1972/*Coventry Evening Telegraph*, 3.6.1972)

JULY 1972

6th July 1972 – Triangular UFO sighted over Clacton-on-Sea, Essex

Doris O'Connell (65) of 19, Bentley Avenue, Jaywick, Clacton-on-Sea, who was to find herself witnessing at least three examples of UFO activity over the Essex area, was outside 'sky watching' with her husband, and two friends, at 12.30am, when they saw:

> *"...a huge red 'triangle', travelling in a south-north direction, which had a small triangle in the middle."*

Authors: Doris would have passed away by now. Without her courage in coming forward, like so many others, we wouldn't have any books – so well done, Doris, and people like Ron West and his colleagues, who painstakingly catalogued what feels like thousands of sightings from around that area, showing just how prolific UFO activity was. This is important UFO history and we take great pleasure in showing the public the 'real truths' about what exactly took place, now so many years ago. (Apparently lots of people saw this UFO and the local newspapers reported on it.)

July 1972 – Silvery object over Brighton

As the sun began to set, a silvery object was seen flying across the sky over the coast off Brighton, by a woman and her daughter – out exercising the family dog.

A few days later, the same couple was astonished to see a 'repeat performance', when a large 'red light' appeared moving from the east, at 10pm, which they thought was a satellite but dismissed this as a likely explanation when it stopped in mid-air, for a few minutes, before rising upwards into cloud cover.

They watched, hoping for another glimpse of the 'visitor' and were rewarded, a short time later, when it appeared once again, close to its original location – now projecting bright rays of light – before disappearing once more into cloud. To their amazement it reappeared, slowly descending in a peculiar *"rocking motion, 'like a leaf falling through the sky' – then it stopped and shot upwards, never to be seen again"*. (**Source: Leslie Harris, Bournemouth UFO Group**)

Over Essex ... domed object, showing portholes

In the summer of this year, two young girls (aged 9) – Nicola Frostick and Michelle Tiffin of Orchard Road, Malden, Essex – were walking across a field, at 9pm, when they sighted what they initially believed to be some sort of new electricity pylon, until they realised this was not the case.

In an interview, later conducted with UFO Investigator Andrew

Collins (four years later), with mother Valerie Frostick (who claims to be psychic), Nicola described seeing:

> *"...a silver-orange dome like object, showing a number of portholes along the edge which showed clear light; its bottom portion was covered by trees and it appeared transparent. There was a ghostly glow around the edges. We became frightened and ran away."*

Michelle was also consulted but declined to be interviewed, claiming that she could not remember anything about the sighting.

(Sources: As above/*Flying Saucer Review,*** Volume 22, No. 4, 1976 – 'British reports old and new', Jenny Randles/ Andrew Collins)**

22nd July 1972 – UFO zigzags across the sky

A bright orange object, about the size of a volley-ball, was seen zigzagging across the sky, at a height of approximately 800 feet, by police and members of the public living in Shawano, Waupaca, Outagamie, and Brown County, Wisconsin. **(Source: Milwaukee Journal, 30.7.1972)**

25th July 1972 – Police Officer reports sighting a UFO

Police Constable Brian Nichols, of North Walsham, was on duty, at 9.15pm, when he noticed a strange 'light' hovering in the sky above the village of Happisburgh. Thinking it was a flare fired at sea he radioed the Police Force control room and asked them to contact the coastguard, who confirmed they had no knowledge of any ship in distress near Eccles-on-Sea. The officer got out of the police car.

> *"As it approached closer, I could see the outline of an object behind the flickering light – transparent in nature, reminding me of a polythene bag with a candle burning in one corner, totally silent. It then disappeared from view over the direction of Stalham, at a speed I estimated to be a hundred miles per hour – which ruled out any chance of it being a plastic bag, as there was no wind."*

(Source: Ivan W. Bunn/Personal interview)

UFO over Norfolk

In summer of the same year, Lilian Nettleship of Bradwell, Norfolk, was walking through Gorleston, near Great Yarmouth, with her small son, at around noon, when she saw:

> *"...a large, dark grey, 'U'-shaped object crossing the sky, east to west, before it partially disappeared through some light cloud.*
>
> *It looked like three metal cans, stuck together, with a matt metallic finish. I ran over to the other side of the road to follow it, but it went too fast for me. I drew other people's attention to it before it went out of view".* **(Source: Ivan W. Bunn)**

28th July 1972 – Craters found in soybean fields

After an absence in UFO sightings, the subject was back in the news after mysterious depressions, ringed with silvery dust, were discovered on several Iowa farms. The craters, located in soybean fields, are described as the same width and depth, about 50 miles apart. Spokesman for APRO (Aerial Phenomena Research Organisation) said:

> *"The craters were definitely caused by spaceships from intelligent beings from another world, who took off for outer space again after viewing Iowans and the rest of the world as little animals running around, and they figured there was nothing to gain by staying."*

(Source: Argus Leader, 28.7.1972, 'Silver dusts are of this world')

AUGUST 1972

3rd August 1972 – UFO over Hampshire

On 3rd August 1972, a mysterious red, glowing 'light' was seen hovering over the New Forest, Farmington, Hampshire, at 11.35pm, by Sir John and Lady Chichester living at Battramsley Lodge, Boldre, before suddenly dropping downwards, at terrific speed, behind a line of trees. A short time later, a similar object appeared in the sky to the north and circled the area, once, before it, too, disappeared.

Sir John:

"The 'light' was scarlet in colour and pulsating regularly as it wandered about the sky."

Lady Chichester:

"Through a pair of binoculars it looked like a circular object, with red flames projecting from a mass of holes on its outer surface. We then reported it to the Southern Evening Echo newspaper. I've no idea what it was, although I did wonder if it could have been an experiment carried out at *Porton Down."

Sir John tried to ring Hurn Airport, but received no reply. He then contacted the police at Lyndhurst, who sent out two officers, but by the time they arrived there was nothing to be seen.

(Source: Personal interview/*New Milton Advertiser*, 19.8.1972)

6th August 1972 – UFO over Liverpool

At 8.45pm, Liverpool residents – Victor Stevens, and his wife – were sat watching the sunset when they noticed a bright object, stationary in the sky, at extreme height.

Victor:

"We watched it through binoculars. After about three minutes, it veered rapidly towards the westerly direction, and then it halted in flight for a couple of minutes. During its movement we saw what looked like a condensation trail – like that made by a jet aircraft. There appeared to be red flames issuing from its rear. At 8.57pm, it sped rapidly out of sight, towards the west. We also saw a jet aircraft in the sky at the same time, but this was an easily recognizable object."

(Source: *Merseyside UFO Bulletin*)

7th August 1972 – UFO over Bath

Mrs Barbara 'Babs' Honey was then living at Upper Milford Farm, Bath, with her husband.

"During the early hours of the 7th August 1972, we were awoken by a 'bright light' shining into the bedroom. We looked out of the window and saw what looked like a gold 'eyeball', with 'lashes' of light, slowly flying through the sky, making this weird 'beating' noise – like a heart, beating. My husband, who was very sceptical of such matters, was astonished. Thirty minutes later, it was lost from view as it entered a bank of cloud."

Source: **Personal interviews/*Bath Weekly Chronicle*, 10.8.1972 – 'Eyeball in the sky')**

9th August 1972 – RAF jet fighter and UFO activity over Warminster

From the *'sky watchers'* log, kept by Cleve Stevens, to whom we spoke – then a regular visitor to the Warminster area, during the 1970s period – we learnt of a sighting which took place at 11.10am, *"in broad daylight"*, according to John Lewis – a hairdresser by profession.

"I was watching a jet fighter 'loop the loop' high in the sky, and was about to fetch a pair of binoculars to obtain a closer look, when, all of a sudden, this object – looking like a gigantic frozen snowball, dwarfing the size of the aircraft – appeared from the direction of Norridge Wood, near Cley Hill.

It shot past, and then stopped in mid-air over the Downs to the North. From out of this enormous object emerged two smaller 'white things' that spun out to either side of the 'ball', resembling solid white clouds. They dropped downwards in a perfect white triangle. I rushed inside and grabbed the binoculars but, when I dashed outside, the two white fleecy, cloud-like 'things' had gone. The larger object then faded away and out of sight."

10th August 1972 – Bizarre falls of straw over airports

Mr W. Jelly – an employee at London Airport – was out shooting pigeons, south of the airport, when he saw what looked like a whirlwind pass through the sky in a west to east direction, during a period of ten minutes, between 12.30-12.40pm.

Very oddly, a large quantity of loose straw was raised from the airport's perimeter and reached an altitude of four miles up into the sky. On the same date, the *Daily Mirror* claimed there had been a fall out of straw at Heathrow and that pilots had encountered these layers of straw suspended at high altitude.

(Source: Arnold West) [On the 14th August it was reported straw fell over Heston, Cambridgeshire.]

13th August 1972 – Mysterious object over Gatwick Airport, London

At 3pm, an off-duty officer at Gatwick Airport noticed an object, resembling a Zeppelin, heading across the sky in a north-east to south-west direction, with its rear end enveloped in blue smoke. A minute later the smoke cleared and revealed nothing further to be seen.

14th August 1972 – UFO interference with motor vehicle, Wisconsin

Mr Greg Faltersack (18) – restaurant manager, who had applied to join the USAF – of Lilac Drive, Sussex, Wisconsin, was driving home along the Waukesha County Trunk road between Highways F and 164, at about 2.15am, in his '1963 Plymouth', when the car suffered a complete electrical failure – the engine cut out and the radiator boiled.

"I slammed on the brakes and then saw a large orange circular object in the sky, hovering over treetops. It looked about 20-30 feet in diameter. About 10 seconds later it made a 'beeping' noise and rose out of sight. I was able to restart the car but the lights, horn, and radio, would not work. When I arrived home I told my sister – Mrs Lenore Hildebrandt – and we went back to the scene, but could find nothing. I then reported it to the Sheriff's Department. Deputies Thomas Audley and Jeri Kraus attended the scene and found tyre marks but nothing else."

Police Sergeant Charles Hughlett, of the Sheriffs office, said

"He was pretty shook up; he certainly saw something."

(Source: *Milwaukee Journal*, 21.8.1972/*The News American*, Baltimore, 30.8.1972)

16th August 1972 – UFO over London

During the early hours of this morning, a policeman on patrol sighted a white 'light' hovering in the sky over Acton, London. He reported it to Hounslow and officers took a closer look through binoculars, when they saw:

"...an object, showing black spots on it, over the London City Centre – also corroborated by night workers from Acton and Chiswick. The sighting was later confirmed by Scotland Yard, although they would not give any names of the officers. **(Source: *Acton Gazette*, 17.8.1972)**

16th August 1972 – UFO lands at Alaska

St Michael, Alaska Eskimo scout – Sgt. John Cheemuk – and his wife, sighted:

"...an object in the shape of a football, flying slower than an aircraft. It had a cockpit, a large window, and red lights at its front and rear. It took off, five minutes later".

The following day, another UFO sighting took place north-west of St. Michael, involving 20 residents of Stebbins, including Eskimo scout Sgt. Pius, and Gabriel Bighead. A report was sent to the National Guard's first scout battalion headquarters in Nome, following which Army advisor – Captain Tom Williams, flew to the area.

Captain Williams:

> "The spot where the object landed showed a hole three feet in diameter, and two inches deep. There was burned grass on the bottom of the hole. I felt an eerie feeling. I took photographs and samples."

(Source: *Post Intelligencer*, Seattle, Washington, 27.8.1972 – 'Landing and ground depression')

18th August 1972 – 'Red light' over Hampshire

Sir John Chichester of Battramsley Lodge, Boldre was in the process of drawing the curtains at 11.35pm, when he saw a strange red pulsating 'light', moving across the sky. He called his wife and daughter, and they watched as the *"light danced across the sky"*.

Sir John telephoned Hurn Airport, but could not get a reply. He then called the police at Lyndhurst, who sent a police car out to have a look, but by that time nothing could be seen.

(Source: Personal interview/*New Milton Advertiser*, 19.8.1972)

19th August 1972 – UFO lands in swamp

Mountainside Drive, Andover, New Jersey … Children – Anthony (8), Joseph DeCarlo (10), and John Lovett (12), were camping outside, when they sighted:

> "…a large white 'light' – shaped like an egg – spinning slowly, making a humming noise, fly over the street skimming telephone poles and treetops, before landing in a wooded swamp across the street about 30 feet away."

Mrs Patricia DeCarlo called the State Police, at Newton. They told her:

> "Swamps sometimes produce bright gasses; we take it as a natural phenomenon."

Enquiries made by the family revealed that the swamp water had been waist high on Saturday, but after the UFO was seen it only came up to the ankles. Whether there was a connection can only be speculation.

(Source: *Daily Advance*, (Dover, N.J.), 21.8.1972 – 'Was it a saucer in the swamp?')

Over Kansas

At 11.20pm, Larry Smith of 221, North Cherry Street, McPherson, Kansas, was with five other Western Railway employees, working nights, when they saw three 'red lights forming a triangular-shaped object in the sky, north of the town.

> "They moved south to a point near the old US-81 Bypass and then turned around, moving northwards along the old US-81 – until out of sight."

(Source: *Daily Sentinel*, 23.8.1972 – 'Several residents report UFO')

22nd August 1972 – Bright orange UFO sighted over Iowa

On the same date – this time at Dubuque, Iowa, USA, Brian Downey (19), and Kathy Atkins (18), were out driving near Flora Park on the crest of a hill, at 5am, when they saw a bright orange object appear in the sky, westwards, about five miles away.

Brian – a Loras College Psychology major, who lived at 818, Kane Street, said:

> "It was flat-bottomed, with a hump on top, and passed from view in ten seconds. We wouldn't have reported it, except we read about a similar UFO sighted by a Waukesha, Wisconsin man, at 2.30am."

Officials at Dubuque Municipal Airport, Cedar Rapid Flights Centre, and Chicago Air Traffic Control, were unable to explain away the sightings. A spokesman for Offcut Air Force Base, near Omaha, Nebraska, said:

> *"The Air Force had discontinued its 'Bluebook' listing UFO witnesses."*

(**Source:** *Telegraph Herald,* **Dubuque, Iowa, 24.8.1972 – 'Chased by UFO')**

22nd August - UFOs over Kansas

At 9pm, Mrs Patty Herman Russell (23) was eastbound on the 1-70, about 25 miles west of Salina, when she saw:

> *"...a UFO; it was big – I couldn't see the shape. It came up from behind a hill, lit. It was taking off or something. It lit up the whole highway. It was very bright white, rimmed, with red light directly to my right or south, and took off over me, heading northwards, fast. About 15-20 minutes later, a second one moved overhead from the south direction when 10 miles from Salina – out of sight in seconds."*

(**Source:** *Salina Journal,* **Kansas, 23.8.1972 – '3 UFOs rise from behind hill')**

22nd August 1972 – Motorist chased by a UFO

John Burgess (then aged 32) – a pie fitter for Newall Engineering, Market Deeping – was driving home from Spalding.

> *"I saw a 'red light' coming across the fields towards me. I thought it was an aircraft. I'm one of those people who believed 'flying saucers' were codswallop. I soon changed my mind. The 'light' approached closer and I could see it was no aircraft ... a vast 'globe', 20 feet across – now some 200 yards away. I slammed the accelerator pedal down and drove at 75 miles per hour, but could not shake it off. It kept pace with me; the faster I went, so it did the same."*

John pulled up outside his house at 17, Halfleet Grove, Market Deeping, frightened to get out of the car.

> *"The 'light' was now circling the village above me. When I saw it shoot away towards Stamford, I got out shaking. I reported it to the police later."* (**Source:** *Evening Telegraph,* **Peterborough, 23.8.1972)**

23rd August – UFO over Iowa

Mrs Lester Avery and her brother – Clarence Wernimont, of 2976 Central Avenue, Asbury, Iowa – were on Bahl Farm when they saw:

> *"...a bright object, showing red, blue and green lights, stationary in the sky, making a humming noise. It then dimmed, brightened, and moved slowly northwards, heading towards the airport. Suddenly, it vanished from sight."* (**Source:** *Salina Journal,* **Kansas, 23.8.1972)**

28th August 1972 – Perfect 'silver ball' over the sea

Doris O'Connell (65) of 19, Bentley Avenue, Jaywick, Clacton-on-Sea, contacted BUFORA after she and her husband saw a perfect silver 'ball of light' hovering silently above the sea where she lived, at 3.30am.

Summer 1972 – UFO over Suffolk

We spoke to Paul Tricker, living in the Ipswich area of Suffolk, after discovering that a UFO had been sighted over the town, in summer 1972, by a number of people – including Paul (then aged 18).

> *"Until that night I was a non-believer, a legacy of my father's influence, who firmly believed people who saw such things were as the result of an over-imaginative mind. It was a crystal clear evening – no clouds, the time 10 pm – when I noticed a 'bright light', not arching and unlike a shooting star, heading towards me. It then stopped in mid-air, hovering over the nearby Whitehouse estate,*

close to Bamford village. I tried to fathom out what it was. It then began to pulse large coloured lights – unlike any aircraft, which often flew from and to RAF Woodbridge and Bentwaters. I was unable to discern any structure because of its brightness. Suddenly, it performed a series of instant accelerations and stops, doing virtually 180 degree turns in the air, zigzagging across the sky. I took careful note of the way in which the lights seemed to be connected to its speed. When it was hovering, I saw a white light; when moving, the coloured lights came on. When stopped, the white light came on and the coloured lights ceased. It then rushed upwards into the sky, at a colossal speed, and disappeared."

Paul pondered whether the speed of the object could reach light speed and beyond, which would be impossible to calculate, but if these UFOs were capable of such speed, were they from the future, past, or a different Dimension? **(Source: Personal interview)**

Summer 1972 – Wedge-shaped UFO seen over London, with occupant!

In summer of the same year David Jones, and a friend from Balham, London, were looking out of the first floor window of their flat, at midnight, when they spotted a single 'light', low, above the terrace house roofs, some distance away. The 'light' was seen to divide into two – then rapidly into three, as it approached their position, at a fast speed. They were clearly able to see:

"...a wedge-shaped 'craft', flying so low we could plainly see a man in high collared, black or navy-blue uniform, looking back at us, from inside some type of cabin. The 'craft' passed over the roof, emitting a sound similar to air displacement, and then turned around and shot away into the night." **(Source: UFO Reports/Albert Rosales)**

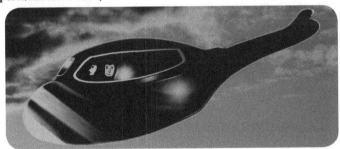

Seen – Barnhurst, London 1978 – was there a connection?

Summer 1972 – Police sight tube-shaped objects over Kent

In the summer of the same year, Police Constable Keith George was on patrol with another colleague, travelling along the A26, near Mereworth, Maidstone, heading towards Tonbridge, Kent, at 2.20pm, when they sighted:

"...two objects, at what appeared to be high altitude, flying in a diagonal formation. They were tube-shaped, but flying 'sideways'. They were moving slowly but then stopped and reversed, at enormous speed, for a short while (10 seconds) – then continued forward as before, and accelerated fast forward out of sight.

This was reported over Force radio and we were instructed to go to Tonbridge Police Station and then took a phone call from a RAF officer, after which we were sent forms to fill in. We never heard another word about it and took a great deal of 'stick' from other officers. I can give the name of my colleague, but as I no longer know his whereabouts, feel it is unfair to name him without his permission. We never sought publicity over this – the opposite, in fact. I did think it would be mentioned in the latest list of MOD sightings and cannot understand why it has not been."

(Source: www.uk-ufo.co.uk)

SEPTEMBER 1972

13th September 1972 – UFO lands in field

At Burlington, Colorado, farmer's wife – Geraldine Ludwig, was out with her husband, Ronald, and daughter, Tamie (12), in the family car, during the evening, when they saw:

> "...a dim 'light' in the sky – then a strange glowing object – which, at first, we thought might have been a reflection of our car headlights on the telephone lines. It veered over the top of us – as big as a house. The object then landed in a field but took off again, lighting up the area with what looked like rays of light coming from it."

Mrs Ludwig contacted the police and spoke to Kit Carson Sheriff – George Hubbard, who sent deputies out there and even arranged for a light aircraft to fly over the field to see if any impression had been left – none were noticed.

Sheriff Hubbard:

> "I don't really think we are going to find any 'little green men', but the responsible people who reported this were scared to hell. I know them personally and they defiantly saw something."

(Source: *The Indianapolis Star,* **Indianapolis, Indiana, 15.9.1972/***Rocky Mountain News,* **Denver, Colorado, 16.9.1972)**

14th September 1972 – UFO over Wales

Police were called by villagers on a housing estate, at Croespenmaen, Crumlin, Monmouthshire, who reported having sighted a bright orange object in the sky on the 14th September 1972 (some accounts give the 15th), moving towards the direction of the Brecon Beacons, changing rapidly in colour and size. It was first spotted by plumber – Robert Philips, on his way home from Oakdale, who described it as:

> "...looking like an inverted soup bowl, with dark rings underneath – apparently spinning. When an aircraft approached it disappeared, but reappeared. On the third occasion, it went for good".

One of the police officers called to the scene was Police Sergeant Clive Williams.

> "I saw an orange-red circle in the sky, which seemed to turn over to a cone-shape – its colour changing from red, to white and green, before moving away".

(Source: *The Western Mail,* **16.9.1972 – 'Soup bowl in the sky – villagers in a spin')**

16th September 1972 – Triangular-shaped UFOs over Essex

Danny Harle (15), and Colin Hastings (18) from Hainault, in Essex, were on their way to Kingswood Youth Club, at about 8pm., when they saw three 'clouds', motionless in the sky above them, glowing with brilliant light, accompanied by a deep electric hum.

As the sound grew louder, one of the 'clouds' changed into a small triangular shape and rushed away across the sky, leaving an incandescent trail. The second 'cloud' then vibrated from side to side, at an estimated height of approximately 400 feet, while the third suddenly shrunk into a tiny pinpoint of light before increasing in size – now cigar-shaped. This tilted and appeared to move closer towards the frightened youths, who ran to the youth club. When they looked back, there was just the vibrating 'cloud', which began to dart about in the sky – 'as if lost'. It then turned triangular and vanished in the same direction as the other.

After contacting the police, at Barkingside, they were told a police officer had reported seeing UFOs in the same area, the previous evening (15.9.1972), and details of the incident had been forwarded to Air Traffic Control at West Drayton. The police later offered the explanation that their officers had seen a ship's searchlight on the Thames!

(Sources: Essex UFO Group/*Ilford Pictorial and Guardian,* **20.9.1972/***Redbridge Guardian,* **22.9.1972/***Independent Weekly*)

Winter 1972 – Landed UFO, Buckinghamshire

Ernest Scott, from High Wycombe, holder of a pilot's licence, was to find himself witnessing another example of UFO activity – this time just after midnight. He was travelling towards Marlow on the A4155, between Henley-on-Thames, in winter 1972 – a journey that normally takes between 35-45 minutes. As he approached a bend at the end of a long, straight, part of the road, he noticed some lights by the verge of the dual carriageway ahead of him. When he drew nearer, he was astonished to see a strange object in the bushes by the side of the road.

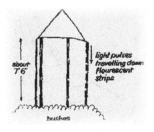

> "It was the size of a telephone kiosk with a conical top, with four fluorescent strip lights, pulsing with light, that moved slowly from top to bottom, attached to the outside of the object – which I thought would have been hexagonal if you could have looked down from the top."

Mr Scott decided to stop, but his mind went blank as he approached it.

The next thing he remembers was driving through Marlow, some miles further. Looking at his wristwatch, he realised it was about one and a half hours later than when he last looked. An examination of a map of the area shows us the site of a Roman villa on the outskirts of Medmenham and a nearby Hill Fort.

(Source: John Makin, serving Police Officer/Nicholas Maloret, WATSUP)

OCTOBER 1972

3rd October 1972 – Cigar-shaped object seen over Lincolnshire

A Boston, Lincolnshire, newsagent – Thomas Trinder – and his son, Alan, were opening up the shop at 4.30am, when they saw:

> "...a glowing orange and green cigar-shaped object, with what looked like tiny flames projecting from each side, floating slowly across the sky close to the crescent moon".

When they looked out again, at 6.30am, it had gone. **(Source: *UFOLOG*)**

4th October 1972 – Eight lights over Cheshire

Mr Bryan Bishop – an amateur astronomer and keen meteor observer – was on the night shift at Winsford, in Cheshire, when he was privy to sighting UFOs again, this time a series of eight lights forming a diamond shape in the sky, at 10.25pm.

> "When I fist saw them there were only five – then, as it moved, I saw eight objects or one object carrying eight lights. They were visible for four minutes, heading east to south-west, and disappeared into the distance." **(Source: Gordon Clegg)**

8th October 1972 – UFO over Lancashire

Five days later, ex-legionnaire John Byrne – then working as a security guard for Ferranti's Cairo Mill, Oldham – had just 'clocked in' to the security point, at 11.55pm, next to the cycle shed, near the car park, when he heard what sounded like a swarm of bees moving through the air. In a tape-recorded interview, held with UFO investigators – Gordon Clegg and Ron Drabble – Mr Byrne had this to say:

> "I looked upwards over my right shoulder, and was amazed to see a large, slightly oval-shaped object, descending vertically towards the car park, directly overhead. It was black at the back and lit up at the front, with a blue/white fluorescent light shining through a bulge or 'window', covering approximately one third of the base of the object. I thought the object was going to descend on top of me. I tried to move but couldn't. My fear then changed to terror. My right arm was devoid of any feeling. The hairs on the back of my neck felt as though they were standing on end."

The object then moved downwards until its base was almost level with the top of the mill tower (90 feet),

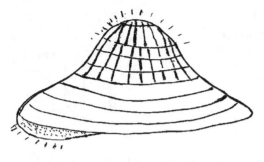

and halted in mid-air, blocking out Mr Byrne's view of the sky. Although John didn't see anybody in the 'craft', he felt as though he was being watched. Suddenly, the object flipped over onto its edge with its underside facing the mill wall, showing a dome, about one third as high as the object itself, illuminated by blue/white light and an upper surface of blue metallic sheen. However, this could have been caused by a reflection of the white light from the dome. Less than half a minute later, without warning, the UFO then shot straight up, nose first, into the sky, at terrific speed. Almost immediately, Mr Byrne found he was able to move and ran back towards the checkpoint at the main gate, where he found the factory cat cowering in a corner – a position it remained in for two days, refusing food and drink.

(Source: Richard P. Colborne, National Investigations co-coordinator, BUFORA/Issue 1, *The Investigator*, February 1973)

11th October 1972 – Police Officers sight UFO over London

Police Constable Denis Giles (31) and PC Parker reported having sighted a cigar-shaped object flying through the sky, over London, at 4.30am.

Denis:

"We were patrolling the Walthamstow district and driving up a steep hill, allowing us to look directly into the sky, when we saw a cigar shaped object with a 'blunt nose', showing brilliant white light on the tail. We stopped the car, transfixed. It took six seconds to fly from one side of the field of our vision to the other. As it headed away, the white light went off and a brilliant red light came on – then it disappeared from sight."

A spokesman for the MOD said:

"We have a number of reports about this object, but we don't know what it was; nothing was flying. We are investigating."

(Source: UFOLOG)

Police Constable Denis Giles holds a sketch of the UFO he and another policeman saw while on patrol

20th October 1972 – Six rectangular objects seen in the sky over Surrey

At 6.45pm, Mr John Hedger of Oxford Road, Wallington, Surrey, sighted:

"...six bright lights in the sky. They made up a formation that was roughly rectangular and were individually recognizable as 'discs'. They were white in colour and stayed in the same position for about three minutes, until cloud obscured them from sight."

During the same year, Mr Clive West – then the owner of Ceres Hotel, Bude, in Cornwall – was driving home with his family, along the A303, across Salisbury Plain, when they saw what they took to be a star in the sky. They soon realised this was not the case when further observation revealed the presence of two red lights, which were circling it.

"It was about 500 yards from the road and at an altitude of about 400 feet. As it dropped lower, it lit up the whole area with its brilliance. The two red lights remained on opposite sides of the UFO. When the object 'touched down', they left and departed skywards."

Mr West – previously employed as a reporter and photographer for the news media – made an appeal in the newspaper.

Subsequently, he was contacted by another family from Salisbury, who had also seen the same UFO.

(**Source: Terry Cox**)

22nd October 1972 – UFO over Lincoln

Also at 6 45pm, two days later, Harold Rollins – a retired railway worker, living in Queen Elizabeth Road, Lincoln, with his wife – happened to look out of the window, when he saw a strange luminous object slowly descending in the sky. Harry shouted for his wife to come and have a look. The couple then stood watching as the object slowly settled in the air, between two houses opposite, 30-40 feet away, allowing them to describe fully what they saw, later, to Richard Thompson – the Lincoln-based UFO investigator.

"It was a 'round ball', about 30 feet in diameter, bright red in colour with a mauve tint. Projecting outwards were streaks of golden coloured light – a bit like the rays of the sun against a backcloth of pale mauve.

We watched in amazement as it slowly began to move away, eastwards, before losing sight of it."

(**Source: Richard Thompson**)

NOVEMBER 1972

3rd November 1972 – UFO over Cheshire

Damon Munday (10), and brothers – Dale (10), Waine (13), and Anthony (16) – from Verdin Comprehensive School, Winsford, Cheshire, were walking to their home in Pulford Road, at 5pm, as dusk fell, when

"... a glowing bright cigar-shaped object was seen hovering in the sky, above the school", which was seen to move towards the right and then slowly disappear – as if going behind something in the sky. Upon their arrival home, the boys told neighbour – Mrs Mary Roberts, what they had seen.

Suddenly, the object reappeared in the sky, once more, over the school.

Mrs Roberts fetched Mrs Barbara Munday to show her, from which the following description was taken:

"It was a bright cigar-shaped 'light', with tapering ends, at an elevation of about 20 degrees in the sky, giving off a yellowish-white light, as brilliant as a full moon. Along its length were six dark portions, or specks – like portholes. It then began to increase in size, until twice its original length, before decreasing in size like a 'ball of light', before vanishing inexplicably from view, a few minutes later." (**Source: BUFORA/*The Investigator,* Issue 1, Bob Skinner**)

1972 – Dr. J. Allen Hynek –*The UFO experience: A Scientific Inquiry*

In 1972, Dr. J. Allen Hynek published his classic book – *The UFO Experience: A Scientific Inquiry* – a scientific study presenting his categories for grouping UFO sightings, from which was coined the phrase, 'Close Encounters'.

In 1973, he started the Center for UFO Studies and served as its Scientific Director, until his death in 1986.

Close Encounters of the Third Kind describes confrontations between humans and alleged 'Aliens' from landed unidentified vehicles. Statistics drawn from over 800 UFO entity sightings received during this period, left him pondering why these 'creatures' should resemble humans so closely, and he theorized whether they could be mechanical robots, whose environment is very similar to ours on Earth.

J. Allen Hynek during a visit to Wiltshire

5th November 1972 – Close Encounter, Gloucestershire – occupants seen

Incidents involving UFOs and their 'alien' occupants will always be treated with suspicion, despite determined efforts made by the witness to convince their fellow peers that what she or he experienced occurred as a result of an incursion into our physical plain of existence, rather than anything subjective in nature. Over the years, we were to come across a number of accounts involving the appearance of humanoid figures, seen close to their 'vessel', often apparently observed to be carrying out some form of examination of the ground. Their resemblance to people of Scandinavian descent has led to them being labelled 'Nordics' – a description now familiar to the reader.

John Hickman, of Tewkesbury, sights large 'bubble' between houses opposite

John Hickman from Tewkesbury, in Gloucestershire, born on the 23rd April 1946 at Droitwich – an employee of the Water Board (then living at 12 Station Lane, Tewkesbury) – described what he witnessed on 5th November 1972.

"I was putting the children to bed, at 5.30pm, after having taken them to bonfire celebrations, held on waste ground (formerly the old railway yard at the rear of his garden, in Rope Walk, Tewkesbury), when I glanced through the bedroom window and noticed a patch of green coloured 'mist' in the air to my right, approximately 30 feet off the ground, some 60 feet where I was stood, in Cotswold Gardens, and first presumed it was smoke or the residue of a firework – as the bonfire was still burning, with people gathered around it. A patch of 'green mist' then appeared between the two houses, situated at the end of the garden, and slowly changed into what looked like a large 'bubble', about 20 feet in diameter, surrounded by a blue/green luminous glow. Inside the bubble was what I can only describe as a painted white light."

Two 'figures' seen inside 'craft'

As this light cleared, I was confronted by the amazing sight of two 'figures', which became clearer as the 'mist' subsided. They appeared to be sat down in front of a type of hooped headrest. I watched, daring to breathe, fearing what might happen if they realised they were being observed. They appeared to resemble males in build, rather than females, and were identically dressed, wearing a black garment looking like leather, or plastic, covered in little whorls of patterns over it. Behind their heads were what I took to be pointed collars. I can't be sure whether these collars were part of the seat's headrest, or their apparel. The one nearest me seemed much older than his companion. He had thick, long, bulky, wavy hair above his shoulder line, with a pronounced wrinkled skin – like elephant hide. His partner looked very similar but his hair was receding, creating an impression he was younger.

I struggled to get a grip on myself, knowing this was no dream. I quietly opened the window, which was beginning to steam up, wondering if the whole thing was some kind of reflection … it was still there. I closed the windows and continued to watch them for about ten minutes, then shouted to my

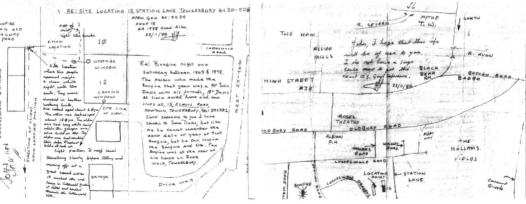

wife to come upstairs and have a look. While waiting for my wife to arrive, I saw the elder of the two 'figures' slowly turn his head, raise his arm, and point towards me – as if realising they were being watched. His companion also turned, both of them now looking straight at me. I felt my blood run cold when this happened.

Within a split second, the 'bubble' changed colour to a green glow and accelerated away, gaining speed, heading towards the Cotswolds."

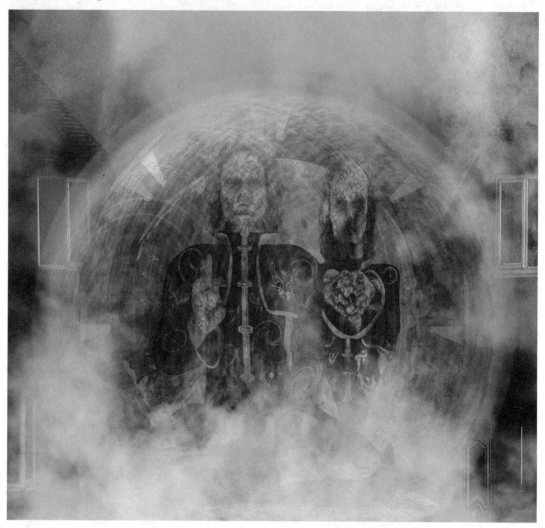

John has never budged from what he saw, all those years ago, and was later inspired to write a number of poems, later published, one of which refers to this particular incident.

A flash of light across the sky, the soft blue green mist attracts the eye. Then in a flash, less than the blinking of an eye, the light has disappeared in the distant sky. Are these the visitors from other worlds, sometimes seen but never heard? Described in detail when they are seen, but concrete proof there's never been. So do you believe what people say, or await the proof the scientific way?'

(Source: Personal interviews)

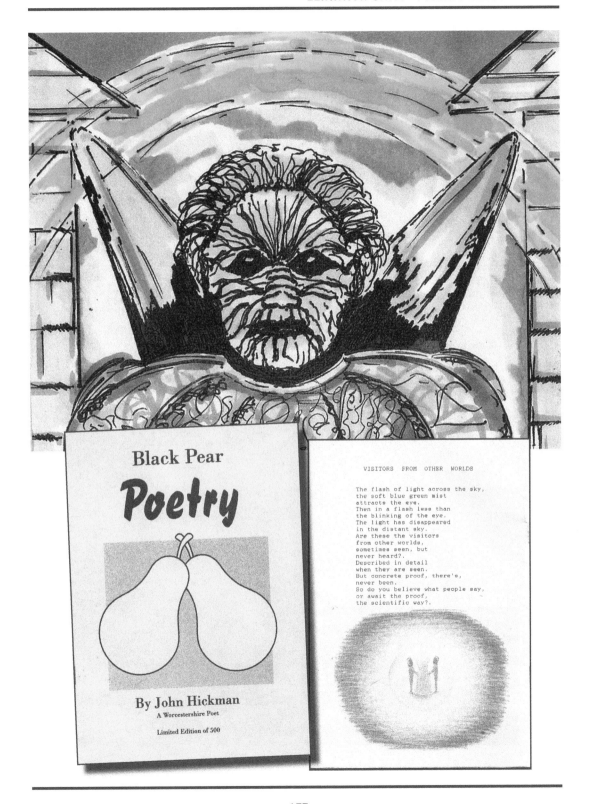

Black Pear

Poetry

By John Hickman

A Worcestershire Poet

Limited Edition of 500

VISITORS FROM OTHER WORLDS

The flash of light across the sky,
the soft blue green mist
attracts the eye.
Then in a flash less than
the blinking of the eye.
The light has disappeared
in the distant sky.
Are these the visitors
from other worlds,
sometimes seen, but
never heard?.
Described in detail
when they are seen.
But concrete proof, there's,
never been.
So do you believe what people say,
or await the proof,
the scientific way?.

QUEST INTERNATIONAL

SIGHTING REPORT FORM

QUEST INTERNATIONAL IS AN ORGANISATION WHICH SEEKS THE ANSWER TO ONE OF THE MOST ELUSIVE MYSTERIES OF OUR TIME... THE INVESTIGATIVE BUREAU HAS RESEARCHED THOUSANDS OF REPORTS PERTAINING TO THE UFO PHENOMENON OVER THE YEARS, AND OUR INVESTIGATORS WHO ARE EXPERIENCED IN THIS FIELD WILL VISIT AND TALK WITH YOU SHOULD A NEED ARISE.

ANY INFORMATION GIVEN TO THE ORGANISATION WILL BE STRICTLY CONFIDENTIAL. WE WELCOME YOUR COOPERATION AND SHOULD YOU REQUIRE FURTHER INFORMATION REGARDING QUEST INTERNATIONAL OR UFO MAGAZINE, PLEASE WRITE TO:

THE SECRETARY P.O. BOX 2, GRASSINGTON, SKIPTON, NORTH YORKSHIRE, BD23 5AU

FULL NAME: (MR MRS MISS MS) JOHN HICKMAN

ADDRESS: HUNTERS LODGE,

OLD ROAD NORTH, KEMPSEY, WORCS WR5 3SZ

AGE: 49 OCCUPATION: S/E WATER CONSULTANT.

TEL (HOME): 01905-820729 TEL (WORK):

QUALIFICATIONS (IF ANY): C&G CRAFT AND C&G ADV PLUMBING / NEBBS + WATER RELATED QUALIFICATIONS

APPROX YEAR.

SIGHTING DETAILS

DATE: 1972 DAY: SATURDAY TIME: 19:30 to 20:00 AM/PM
NOV 5TH ? BONFIRE NIGHT

PLEASE GIVE EXACT LOCATION OF SIGHTING I.E., TOWN, COUNTY, AND A GENERAL DESCRIPTION OF AREA (OPEN LAND, BUILT-UP AREA, POPULATED, MAP REFERENCE (IF POSSIBLE), TOWN, VILLAGE, ETC):
THROUGH BEDROOM WINDOW OF 12 STATION LANE, TEWKESBURY GLOS. THE OBJECT APPEARED BETWEEN MY HOUSE AND THE PROPERTY AT THE REAR. (COTTESWOLD GARDENS

DID ANYONE ELSE OBSERVE THE PHENOMENON? IF YES, PLEASE GIVE DETAILS. INFORMATION SUBMITTED SHALL BE DEALT WITH IN THE STRICTEST CONFIDENCE: I DO NOT KNOW.

1: .... 2: ....

3: .... 4: ....

HOW LARGE DID THE OBJECT APPEAR IN/ON THE GROUND, COMPARED WITH THE FOLLOWING OBJECTS HELD AT ARMS LENGTH? (REMEMBER, A GARDEN PEA HELD AT ARMS LENGTH WOULD COVER THE FULL FACE OF THE MOON):

PIN HEAD (STAR) ☐   MATCH HEAD ☐ (PLANET)   PEA ☐ (MOON)

ONE PENCE ☐   FIVE PENCE ☐   TEN PENCE ☐

OTHER PLEASE STATE: APPROX 8' DIA IN THE WHITE LIGHT AREA BUT APPROX 15' OVERALL ACROSS THE SURROUND. LIGHT.

IF YOU HAVE EVER SEEN A SIMILAR OBJECT BEFORE, OR EXPERIENCED THIS PHENOMENON IN THE PAST, PLEASE GIVE BRIEF DETAILS:
NO.

DID THE OUTLINE OR ANY PART OF THE OBJECT APPEAR: SHARP ☐ FUZZY ☑ TRANSPARENT ☑

STRUCTURED ☐ DETACHED ☐ IF YES, PLEASE GIVE DETAILS: Very difficult to explain but something looked solid (as in image inside of light with a dark outer light covering the main structure in its interior

DID YOU OBSERVE ANY FIGURES OR MOVEMENT ON/IN PHENOMENA? YES ☑ NO ☐ IF YES, PLEASE DESCRIBE YOUR EXPERIENCE:
I watched the movement of two people inside the light bubble. They observed the fire work display and the one pointed his finger at me and both turned and looked at me.

DID ANY ANIMAL DISTURBANCE OCCUR, IF YES, PLEASE STATE: NO.

HAVE YOU OR ANY OTHER WITNESS TO THE EVENT SUFFERED PHYSICAL, PSYCHOLOGICAL EFFECTS, PRIOR TO, DURING, OR AFTER YOUR EXPERIENCE/OBSERVATION? IF YES, PLEASE STATE:
NO.

HAVE YOU ANY OBJECTION TO YOUR NAME OR OCCUPATION BEING PUBLISHED IN CONNECTION WITH YOUR SIGHTING/ EXPERIENCE? YES ☐ NO ☑ (but not my home address)

SIGNED (WITNESS): J Hickman   DATE: 16 / 11 / 95

INVESTIGATOR: _____   DATE: / /

IF YOU WOULD LIKE FURTHER DETAILS OF HOW TO OBTAIN MORE INFORMATION ABOUT THE UFO PHENOMENON, PLEASE TICK THIS BOX: ☐

PLEASE RETURN THIS FORM TO:
J HANSON, 3, REDDITCH Rd
ALVECHURCH
B48 7RS

THE DIRECTOR OF INVESTIGATIONS,
QUEST INTERNATIONAL,
P.O. BOX 2,
GRASSINGTON, NEAR SKIPTON,
NORTH YORKSHIRE, BD23 5AU

24 HOUR UFO HOT LINE
(01756)
752216

SUMMARY OF EVENTS

PLEASE DESCRIBE IN YOUR OWN WORDS THE CIRCUMSTANCES OF YOUR SIGHTING/EXPERIENCE, (USE ANOTHER SHEET OF PAPER IF NECESSARY):

WE HAD RETURNED FROM THE BONFIRE EARLY AND PUT THE CHILDREN TO BED. THE BONFIRE WAS HELD ON THE OLD RAILWAY YARD. I WAS LOOKING OUT OF THE BEDROOM WINDOW AT THE FIRE WORKS WHEN A GREEN COLOURED MIST APPEARED TO MY RIGHT. AT THE TIME IT LOOKED LIKE SMOKE. THE GREEN MIST DRIFTED ACROSS BETWEEN THE BUILDINGS AND SUDDENLY STOPPED. WITHIN A FRACTION OF A SECOND WHAT LOOKED LIKE A LARGE BUBBLE APPEARED. THE OUTER CASING OF THE BUBBLE GAVE OFF A BLUE/GREEN GLOW. WITHIN THE BUBBLE WAS A WHITE LIGHT. LOOKING INTO THE BUBBLE I COULD SEE TWO PEOPLE. THE TWO PEOPLE WERE SAT ON CHAIRS INFRONT OF WHICH APPEARED TO BE

WEATHER AND LIGHT CONDITIONS AT TIME OF SIGHTING (TICK APPROPRIATE BOX):

THIN CLOUD ☐	HEAVY CLOUD ☐	CLEAR ☐	MIST ☐	DRY ☐	HEAVY RAIN ☐
DRIZZLE ☐	SNOW/ICE ☐	WARM ☐	COLD ☐	CALM ☐	WINDY ☐
DARKNESS ☑	DAYLIGHT ☐	DAWN ☐	DUSK ☐	MOON ☐	STARS ☐

WAS THE OBJECT/PHENOMENA SEEN IN THE VICINITY OF ANY OF THE FOLLOWING?:

CIVIL AIRFIELD ☐	MILITARY AIRFIELD ESTABLISHMENT ☐
POWER LINE ☐	RADIO OR TELEVISION MAST ☐
STREET LIGHTS ☐	RESERVOIR/RIVER/CANAL/WATER ☐
MOOR/FARMLAND ☐	ANCIENT MONUMENT SITE ☐

AIR ROUTE ☐
QUARRY/MINE ☐
WOODLAND ☐
URBAN AREA ☑

PLEASE TRY TO DRAW WHAT YOU OBSERVED TO THE BEST OF YOUR ABILITY:

A CONTROL PANEL. AFTER A FEW SECONDS THEY (THE TWO IN THE BUBBLE) TURNED THEIR HEADS TO THEIR RIGHT AND APPEARED TO BE LOOKING AT THE FIRE WORK DISPLAY. I CAN ONLY DESCRIBE THE TWO PEOPLE AS MALE. THE ONE LOOKED VERY OLD SAY 15# TO 24# YEARS. THE OTHER ONE LOOKED BETWEEN 6# & 7# YEARS OLD. THE OLDER LOOKING ONE HAD LONG GREY WAVY HAIR AND HAD GREY SKIN THAT LOOKED LIKE ELEPHANT HIDE. THE YOUNGER ONE WAS SLIGHTLY BALDING ALTHOUGH HE TOO HAD GREY SKIN. HE LOOKED A LOT YOUNGER THAN THE OTHER. BOTH OF THEM WORE IDENTICAL CLOTHES THAT LOOKED LIKE A TYPE OF BLACK PLASTIC WITH A PATTERN. THE COLLERS WERE RIGID AND POINTED. BECAUSE OF THE POSITION THEY WERE SAT LOOKING TO THEIR RIGHT I COULD SEE CLEARLY THE BACK OF THE SEAT ON WHICH THEY WERE SITTING IT WAS SHAPPED THUS.

← ? HEAD REST

← BACK OF SEAT.

I COULD NOT BELIEVE WHAT I WAS SEEING, SO I QUIETLY OPENED THE WINDOW AND TOOK A GOOD LOOK OUTSIDE TO SEE IF IT WAS SOME KIND OF REFLECTION. BECAUSE OF THE POSITION OF THE BUBBLE THERE WAS NO WAY THIS WAS A REFLECTION. I QUIETLY CLOSED THE WINDOW AND CONTINUED WATCHING FOR A FEW MORE MINUTES, THE WINDOWS KEPT ON STEAMING UP AND I KEPT CLEANING THEM DOWN WITH MY HAND

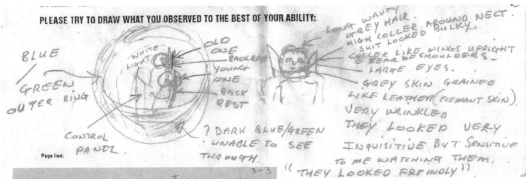

PLEASE TRY TO DRAW WHAT YOU OBSERVED TO THE BEST OF YOUR ABILITY:

BLUE / GREEN OUTER RING

OLD ONE BACK

YOUNG ONE BACK REST

CONTROL PANEL

? DARK BLUE/GREEN
• UNABLE TO SEE THROUGH

3-3

LONG WAVEY GREY HAIR. AROUND NECT. HIGH COLLER BULKY. SUIT LOOKED COLLER LIKE WINGS UPRIGHT @ REAR OF SHOULDERS.
— LARGE EYES.
— GREY SKIN GRAINED LIKE LEATHER (ELEPHANT SKIN).
VERY WRINKLED
THEY LOOKED VERY INQUISITIVE BUT SENSITIVE TO ME WATCHING THEM.
" THEY LOOKED FREINDLY "

Page two:

TO ENABLE A BETTER VIEW. I HAD BEEN WATCHING FOR ABOUT 15 MINUTES WHEN I SHOUTED TO THE WIFE TO COME UPSTAIRS AND LOOK. BECAUSE THE WIFE DID NOT COME UPSTAIRS AFTER A FEW MINUTE I RAN DOWN THE STAIRS AND TOLD HER WHAT I COULD SEE FROM THE BEDROOM WINDOW AND THAT I WANTED HER TO CONFIRM WHAT I WAS SEEING. I RAN BACK UPSTAIRS TO THE WINDOW AND WAS LOOKING AT THE TWO PEOPLE IN THE BUBBLE, WHEN THE OLDER ONE OF THE TWO WHO WAS SITTING IN THE FAR SEAT, SLOWLY TURNED IS HEAD AT WHICH TIME I COULD SEE HIS FULL FACE HE RAISED HIS ARM AND POINTED HIS INDEX FINGER STRAIGHT AT ME. AT THE SAME TIME THE OTHER PERSON TURNED AROUND AND LOOKED AT ME. SEVERAL STRANGE FEELINGS CAME OVER ME AND I CONTINUED TO WATCH THE BUBBLE, WITHIN A SPLIT SECOND THE BUBBLE CHANGED COLOUR TO A GREEN GLOW, IT THEN STARTED TO MOVE BETWEEN THE HOUSES. I RAN DOWN TO THE LANDING TO LOOK THROUGH THE WINDOW AND SAW THE GREEN LIGHT ACCELRATE AT AN ANGLE OF ABOUT 30° AND SUDDENLY CHANGE DIRECTION EASTWARDS TOWARDS THE COTTESWOLDS. IT VERY QUICKLY DISAPPEARED AND THE WIFE COULD NOT CONFIRM THAT SHE COULD SEE THE GREEN LIGHT FROM THE LANDING.

Winter 1972 – Sighting of 'craft', with occupants, over Sussex

Someone else who maintained he saw the occupants of an 'Alien' craft, during Winter 1972, was Howard Johnson – a Councillor from Spalding, in Lincolnshire – then living in Beacon Road, Crowborough, Sussex who we spoke to in 2005.

"At 11.30am, I happened to look through the bathroom window – then fitted with clear glass, not frosted, as the style is now – when I noticed a saucer-shaped object heading towards my direction, low down in the sky, about 75 yards away from the house, solid looking, rather than anything substantive. It then came to an abrupt halt, allowing me to see a transparent dome on top, with a bank of flickering multi-coloured lights underneath. I watched with disbelief, deliberately forcing myself to look away, expecting that when I returned my gaze it would have gone, but this didn't happen. Unbelievably, I could see three 'figures' standing inside the dome. Two looked like the entities now referred to as 'Greys', although I was unaware of such terminology then. The third occupant looked more human in appearance and was taller than his two companions but completely bald, and wearing a silver coloured uniform, apparently manipulating something out of my view. All of a sudden, they seemed to realise they were being watched. The 'craft' slowly moved away – until lost from view, over Tunbridge Wells. I shouted out to the rest of the family, who dashed outside, but unfortunately, by this time, there was nothing to be seen."

The incident still haunts Howard, despite the passing of years, who feels unprepared to accept what he witnessed was irrefutable evidence of any 'Alien' life-force, but remains mystified as to the reason for the appearance of this 'craft', and its never to be forgotten occupants. He was shown the illustration of the 'craft' seen at Bexleyheath, in 1955, by Margaret Fry, and confirmed it *identical t*o what he saw on that date. **(Source: Personal interview)**

11th November 1972 – UFO display, Warwickshire

Clusters of mysterious 'lights' were seen darting about in the sky by Rita Tallis – a resident of Ullenhall Lane (just off the A435 Birmingham to Redditch Road) at 6pm on 11th November 1972.

Rita:

> *"I telephoned a friend of mine, Susan Harris, living a short distance away, and asked her son, Keith (aged 15) to cycle over to my house and take a look for himself. After Keith arrived, I stood in the garden, accompanied by my husband, Gordon, and other family members, watching these strange multi-coloured 'lights' darting about in the sky over the Danzey Green area of Warwickshire, at which stage we decided to call the police."*

Two police officers arrived, a short time later, one of whom was P.C. William Hunt. Unfortunately, by this time, the 'lights' were no longer to be seen. P.C. Hunt advised the family to contact them again, should the 'lights' reappear. Oddly, no sooner had the officers departed when the 'lights' reappeared in the sky.

Rita's husband telephoned the police again, who told him they were already aware – as the officers were now, themselves, actually witnessing a number of mysterious 'red lights' rotating in the sky, over Henley-in-Arden.

In a conversation which took place between him and Rita Tallis, following the officer's return to their house, he told her:

> *"It was like a lighthouse. One of the objects projected a beam, like a searchlight, shining downwards onto the ground. The 'lights' then moved towards Birmingham, leaving a solitary 'white light' behind. Within a short time this too rose upwards, at a sharp angle, and headed away following the same direction as the previous objects."*

Enquiries made at Elmdon Airport, Birmingham, revealed nothing untoward had shown on radar. We also spoke to Keith Harris, who recalled seeing the multi-coloured light forms 'cavorting' about in the sky – totally unlike anything he had ever seen before in his life.

11th November 1972 – UFO photographed over Arizona

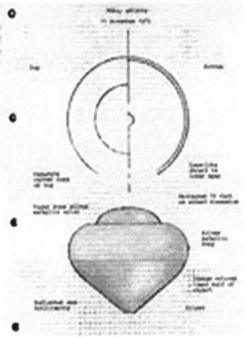

Could there have been any connection with what was not only seen but photographed by Mesa Arizona resident Mr Lee Elders at 1.35am with his 35mm Asahi Pentax SLR camera?

Lee was called outside by Shawn Cheves (10) who had with a number of other young friends seen a bright shining disc in the sky which they described as resembling an

> *". . . upside down bell or fat silver ice cream cone."*

They weren't the only ones reporter Skip Brandt and four of his friends were in the press box at the stadium at Tempe Arizona State University when they saw in the south east direction of the sky at about 40degrees elevation a bright silvery stationary object.

Apparently thousands of spectators saw it- but nobody took a photo of it (apart from Mr Elders)

(Source: Cece Stevens & Colonel Wendelle C Stevens)

Barnt Green

Another similar display of strange 'lights' in the sky took place on the other side of the Warwickshire border, over Barnt Green, Worcestershire – a small village, just outside Birmingham (approximately 20 minutes away from the scene of the previous encounter), according to William Matthews – an elderly resident, living in the village, some time during early winter 1972.

"I was in the back garden, pointing out the various constellations to my wife, when we noticed a cluster of 'stars' moving across the sky. Suddenly, to our surprise, they broke-up into fragments, or particles of light, which split into separate directions, moving backwards and forwards in the sky – unlike any ' Shooting Stars' I have ever seen. The next night, we were astounded to see nine or ten of these 'stars' moving about in the sky, in what was now becoming a familiar pattern of behaviour. On the third night running, we counted seventeen 'stars' (!) involved in a display lasting for about forty-five minutes.

I contacted the police at Rubery, near Birmingham, to report what we had seen. I was surprised to learn from the police officer that many other reports of similar objects had been brought to their attention.

The officer suggested I contact RAF Brize Norton, in Gloucestershire. I telephoned the airbase and spoke to the duty officer, who took a note of what I said, and told me, 'We are very interested in these things'." **(Source: Personal interview)**

13th November 1972

At 10.21am, an object, described as either disc-like or sphere, wobbling slightly and flashing occasionally, was seen heading north-west to south-east, by Mrs Margaret Buxton, who was hanging out the washing at Brown Edge, Staffordshire. **(Source: Mr D. James, BUFORA)**

14th November 1972

An intense yellow light, with a smaller red light on top – *'like a cherry on a cake'*, was seen over Cold Ash Hill road, Newbury, Berkshire, at 10.10pm, by John Drawbridge – then Secretary of the South West Aerial Phenomenon Society, who attempted to 'give chase' to the object heading away at a speed, estimated to be over 100 miles per hour. **(Source: Trevor Whittaker, BUFORA)**

Towards the end of the month, a similar three-day period of UFO sightings was reported over Faversham, in Kent, when more than thirty shipyard workers watched as an object zigzagged across the sky, changing shape from circular to cigar, which discharged a number of red lights. Details of this incident were reported to RAF Manston, who promised to forward a report to the MOD.
(Source: *Faversham Times*, 30.11.1972)

16th November 1972 – Three objects over Essex

Shirley Trower of Jarvis Road, south Benfleet, Essex, was outside the house, at 4.20pm, when she saw a red and white flashing light in the sky, which she took to be a firework moving around in circles, over Canvey Island.

"It began to drift towards the oil refinery, where it halted. I fetched a telescope and looked through it and called my husband and children. We saw an orange 'blob' which was then joined by another two. A few minutes later, they vanished from sight."

(Source: Ron West, Essex UFO Society)

DECEMBER 1972

5th December 1972 – UFO over Kent

An object – described as resembling a beautiful flashing diamond in the sky – was seen over Oare, Kent, at 9.45pm, by Joan Patching and her husband, while exercising the family dog.

Joan:

> *"We were on our way back to the village, after walking 'Simba', our dog, when I noticed a beautiful blue coloured object, pulsing with light, over some nearby elm trees. I pointed it out to my husband, remarking what a beautiful star it was, although I had never seen a star in that position in the sky before, and wondered if it was a new planet. We kept our eye on it as we walked home, when all of a sudden, it began to move towards us, making a faint whining noise, attracting a comment by my husband, who wondered if it might have been a helicopter. To our surprise, it shot up into the sky at terrific speed, and was gone in seconds, proving this was no helicopter."*

(**Source:** Personal interview)

9th December 1972 – UFO over Warwickshire

On the late afternoon of 9th December 1972, Brian and Olive Langford from Dumblepits Lane, Ullenhall (just outside Birmingham), noticed two 'bright lights' moving across the sky, which they believed, initially, to be an aircraft on its way to Birmingham (Elmdon) Airport, until they saw:

> *"...an object, resembling a lampshade in appearance, displaying three lights, passing overhead and drop down over the Beoley area, where we lost sight of it."* (**Source:** Personal interview)

11th December 1972 – Rectangular object sighted

Two days later, Mrs Rouffignac was driving along an unnumbered road, which runs past Chobham Common, near Chobman Clump, between the villages of Longcross and Burowhill, when she sighted an object in the sky to the east, described as, *"rectangular, with what looked like a rudder part on the end"*, visible for about fifteen seconds as she turned right onto the B383 road, heading north-west.

(**Source:** *BUFORA Report,* **Number SS20**)

14th December 1972 – UFO over Yorkshire

Mrs Lorna Butterfield of Eastwood Avenue, Illingworth, Halifax, caught sight of a bright object through the window of her home, at 4.40pm on 14th December 1972. At first she thought it was a star, but then realised it was heading slowly in a south-east direction.

It then changed from a single point of light to three lights forming a triangle, with the top light and bottom left silver-gold in colour, while the bottom right was a definite blue in colour. The object then moved away and reverted to a single point of light in the sky and was eventually lost from view.

(**Source:** Trevor Whittaker, BUFORA)

15th December 1972 – Three UFOs seen over Essex

At 6.15pm, Mr Thomas William Norris (then aged 48) – a resident from Curling Tye, Basildon, in Essex – was stood outside his house, looking up into a perfectly clear sky, when he saw:

> *"...three large, extremely bright orange objects, looking like a cross between an arrowhead and*

boomerang, with defined leading edges, showing blurred red trailing ones, suspended in the sky at an angle of 80 degrees off the horizon.

Ten seconds later, they moved quickly away in a 'V'-shaped formation."

(Source: BUFORA, Richard Colborne, Edward J. Woods)

19th December 1972 – Strange object sighted by householder

Hanford, Stoke on Trent man – Michael William Stanway (then 30), married with two daughters – was on the way home, after working a night shift, at 6am.

It was pitch black, at the time, and he entered the house by the front door and, as was his customary habit before retiring, went outside to the greenhouse to switch the heater down. The time was now 6.15am.

As he opened the back door, he saw:

"...a glowing 'ball' – very bright – just sitting on the lawn; it was white in the centre, then very pale blue to bright red. It was about two inches across. There was a clear division from where it changed colour. The yellow outer edge of the 'ball' was not misty but feathered on the outside. A second later, it lifted off the ground and made its way in curve from south to north direction, and I soon lost sight of it."

Michael placed the dog's ball onto the spot to remind him where it had happened. The weather was dry (neither frosty nor raining), and he retired to bed.

A LANDING IN MINIATURE

The following is the account of an unusual event which occurred on the morning of Tuesday, 19th December, 1972 in Stoke-on-Trent, Staffs. Certain features encountered in this case show strong similarities with some of the commonly recorded characteristics of other UFO sightings. In spite of the short duration of the event (a few seconds) the small size of the UFO reported makes this case doubly intriguing.

Left

Mr. Stanway holding a 3in. cardboard disc just above the depression in his lawn and showing the size and position of the glowing object.

Below Left

Drawing of glowing object and triangular depression, both half scale, centre of object white, shading to blue, with red and outer yellow band.

Below

Close up of triangular burnt depression. The compass measures 1⅛in. in diameter.

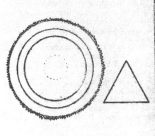

At midday he got up and had a look in daylight at the lawn. He was surprised to see a small triangular, apparent burn mark (it was difficult to ascertain that this was caused by burning) 3-4 inches away from where the object had been sighted. The depression was shallow, about an eighth of an inch in depth. Moss had already begun to grow inside the depression, but not grass.

Anthony Pace, from BUFORA, interviewed Mr. Stanway, in February 1973, and took control samples from the area concerned, although we are not aware of any results.

Tony Pace – former director of Investigations, BUFORA

CHAPTER 4 – 1973

FEW OF THESE FILES WILL BE FOUND AT THE PUBLIC RECORDS OFFICE LONDON – STILL CLASSIFIED!

JANUARY

2nd January 1973 – UFOs over East Yorkshire

21st January 1973 – UFOs over Essex

23rd January 1973 – Mystery flashes over Wales

24th January 1973 – Flaming 'ball of fire' sighted over Kent

FEBRUARY

1st February 1973 – Green UFO sighted over Somerset

5th February 1973 – Glowing 'ball of light', Hertfordshire

6th February 1973 – Object lands in a field in Kent

th February 1973 – Bright yellow sphere over Hertfordshire

11th February 1973 – Coastguard sights UFO

12th February1973 – Triangular UFO over South Wales

1973 – Motorist encounters UFOs over Warwickshire

16th February 1973 – Staffordshire motorist sights cigar-shaped UFO

17th February 1973 – Coastguard's second UFO sighting

21st February 1973 – Motorist followed by a UFO in the United States

22nd February 1973 – UFOs over Portsmouth

24th February 1973 – UFO over Colchester

MARCH

March 1973 – Cornish schoolchildren sight cigar-shaped UFO

22nd March 1973 – Orange sphere seen by motorist

31st March 1973 – Portsmouth Hospital staff sight silver cigar-shaped UFO

1973 – UFO seen hovering over a factory at Cheltenham, Gloucestershire

APRIL

8th April 1973 – Hovering UFO

15th April 1973 – Couple sight UFO over Lincolnshire

MAY

2nd May 1973 – RAF pilots sight UFO

May/June 1973 – Soldiers sight oval UFO hovering above ground

Summer 1973 – Close encounter in Wales

Summer 1973 – UFO over Birmingham, UK

JUNE

1st June 1973 – Cheshire man tells of a number of UFO sightings

21st June 1973 – Close encounter with hooded monk at Surrey

24th June 1973 – 'Orange mass' sweeps the sky with searchlights over West Virginia

JULY

3rd July 1973 – Disc-shaped UFO seen by youth over Jarrow

7th July 1973 – Oval object over Leicestershire

8th July 1973 – Timothy Good's mother sights three UFOs over North Cornwall

9th July 1973 – Flickering UFO seen over Leicestershire

26th July 1973 – Four glowing cigar-shaped objects seen by Kent workers

AUGUST

August 1973 – Strange 'beings' sighted in Scotland … missing time encountered

8th August 1973 – Close encounter in Northampton, and missing time

Early 1970s – Close encounters at RAF Alconbury … creature sighted

SEPTEMBER

September 1973 – UFO over Wales; witnesses experience sunburn

Autumn 1973 – UFO over Hythe, in Kent

September 1973 – Close encounter, Northamptonshire

September 1973 – Phantom helicopter, Derbyshire

20th September – Astronauts' sighting from Sky Lab 3

29th September 1973 – Police officer sights UFO over Union City area

OCTOBER

1st October 1973 – Firemen witness UFO display

3rd October 1973 – Close encounter with UFO by truck driver, Missouri

5th October 1973 – Humanoids seen on Canadian farm

11th October 1973 – Close encounter at Mississippi, with three creatures

16th October 1973 – Allegation of Alien abduction in Somerset

17th October 1973 – Strange 'being' photographed at Alabama

18th October 1973 – US helicopter encounters dome-shaped UFO

NOVEMBER

November 1973 – Mushroom-shaped object seen over Lincolnshire

12th November 1973 – Unusual 'light' seen over Lincolnshire

18th November – UFO sighted over Quebec, Canada

24th November 1973 – UFO over Kent

30th November 1973 – UFO, with occupants, seen over Nuneaton

DECEMBER

December 1973 – Red pulsating 'ball' seen over Essex

10th December 1973 – Triangular UFO seen over Essex

1973 – UFO over Orpington, Kent

JANUARY 1973

2nd January 1973 – UFOs over East Yorkshire

Jonathon Hill (aged 14) of Lime Tree Avenue, Sutton, near Hull, was sat in the back of the family car, travelling towards a new estate, at 2.35pm. His mother was driving and chatting to her mother in the front passenger's seat, when he saw, out of the back window:

> *"...what I thought were two kites, high in the sky, above Sutton Hospital, near Hull, East Yorkshire. At a second glance I saw that they weren't, in fact, kites but two disc-shaped objects, standing out clearly against the overcast sky. I estimated roughly that the objects were about 500 feet above me. Both objects were about 15-20 feet in diameter, translucent, showing six darker spoke-like areas with dark or black outer rims. The lower and nearer object was floating lazily in a clockwise direction around its companion, which was completely stationary. There was a light wind blowing, but it seemed somehow 'locked tight' in the air around it. I watched the objects for about half a minute, until they were out of sight."*

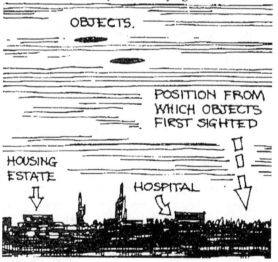 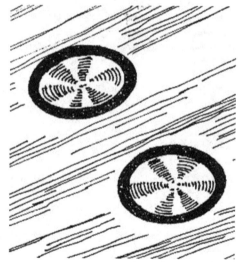

The next day, Jonathon told his father – a teacher by occupation – what he had seen. He suggested that it was more likely that his son had seen two seagulls or even a reflection in the car windscreen! (**Source:** *FSR Supplement,* **15th June 1973**)

21st January 1973 – UFOs over Essex

David Gregory – a Radio One disc jockey, 'standing-in' for Tony Blackburn – brought the listeners' attention to reports of UFOs seen, following a number of telephone calls made to the BBC Radio Station, by members of the public. They included not only David's sighting, but a housewife from Barking, in

Essex, who told of seeing, *"a red ball, with wings"*, (attracting, inevitably, some good humoured scepticism), which landed in her garden and then took-off.

BBC – Gagging order, warned me to keep quiet

In 2011 we spoke to David Gregory, who is still involved with the media. He remembered, with great clarity, the sighting which was brought to his attention by his mother. Interestingly, he told us that following the broadcast, he was warned by the BBC to discontinue any further discussion on the subject on air … *"effectively gagging me to keep quiet"*.

DJ David Gregory (right)

23rd January 1973 – Mystery flashes over Wales

Mysterious green and blue flashes were sighted in the sky over Llandrillo, Merionethshire, accompanied by an explosion at 8pm which shook buildings over a 60 miles radius. This was witnessed by hundreds of people that contacted the authorities.

24th January 1973 – Flaming 'ball of fire' sighted over Kent

At 7.15pm a number of motorists, travelling along the Deal to Dover road, in Kent, reported having sighted an amber object, described as

> *"…a flaming 'ball of fire' flying across the sky, before landing in a nearby field. It then took off and was last seen heading out to sea – like a rocket – over St. Margaret's bay."*

28th/29th January 1973 – UFO over Cheshire

A domed semicircular object was sighted by seven people, hovering over a pond near Winsford, in Cheshire.

The following day a multicoloured light was seen by two people in the sky above Woodford Lane, in Winsford.

FEBRUARY 1973

1st February 1973 – Green UFO sighted over Somerset

A green half-moon or crescent-shaped object was sighted moving silently through the sky over Minehead, North Somerset, by four people. (**Source: not verified**)

5th February 1973 – Glowing 'ball of light', Hertfordshire

At 3am, motorists driving along the A.414 Hemel Hempstead to St. Albans road were astounded by the appearance of a large, yellow, glowing 'ball of light', seen hovering 20-30 feet above the junction, a few hundred yards away. (**Source:** *Evening Echo,* **Hemel Hempstead, 12.2.1973**)

6th February 1973 – Object lands in a field in Kent

Barry Watts reported having sighted a fiery 'ball' or 'globe' appear to land in a field near the *Swingate Inn* on the Dover to Deal road, in Kent. Searches of the locality, made later, revealed no traces of whatever it had been. (**Source: UFOSIS**)

9th February 1973 – Bright yellow sphere over Hertfordshire

At 3am *"a bright yellow sphere of light"* was sighted, hovering 20-30 feet above the road, between Hemel Hempstead and St. Albans, Hertfordshire, causing a vehicle engine to stop. When the 'sphere' rose, the engine restarted. (**Source:** *Flying Saucer Review,* **Vol. 19, No. 2**)

11th February 1973 – Coastguard sights UFO

On this date, Carl Whitley – a reporter for the *Bournemouth Evening Echo* – was on duty as an auxiliary coastguard, at Hengistbury Head, when he sighted *"a luminous 'tube' of light, moving through the sky."*

(Source: Leslie Harris)

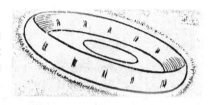

12th February 1973 – Triangular UFO over South Wales

A triangular object, resembling an arrowhead, was seen moving northwards over Newport, South Wales, by two schoolboys, at 11.15pm – possibly connected with later reports of UFOs, described as *"clusters of multi-coloured lights"*, seen over the *Exe Estuary*, in Devon. (**Source: *Weston Morning News*, 19.12.1973**)

1973 – Motorist encounters UFOs over Warwickshire

Nancy and Bill Wilson

Nancy and Bill Wilson – an elderly couple from Baxterley, Warwickshire – described a frightening experience, during early 1973, whilst driving through the village of Baddesley Ensor, towards their home, accompanied by another couple.

Bill – an ex-Japanese 'Prisoner of War', holder of the 'Burma Star', survivor of the infamous Japanese Railway, who, in his own words, had 'brushed with death' many times over, told us what happened:

> *"As we neared the top of Dordon Hill, we saw an object – as big as the full moon – hovering, motionless, over the A5. The car then began to falter and came to a halt. We sat there in the darkness, wondering what to do. Suddenly, the car was bathed in a beam of bright light, projected outwards from the object. To our horror, the 'ball of light' began to move towards us. Just as we thought it was about to strike us, it split into two separate luminous fragments of light and raced across the sky, returned, and merged into one, before heading towards the direction of Middleton."*

(Source: Personal interview)

16th February 1973 – Staffordshire motorist sights cigar-shaped UFO

At 5am, Mr John Spencer from Baddesley Ensor, Tamworth, Staffordshire, was travelling to work along the A5, towards Tamworth, having just passed the village of Dordon on his right. As he drove past the entrance to Birch Coppice Colliery, opposite, he happened to bend down to throw away a finished cigarette through the window, when he noticed something strange in the sky to his right, at 5.05am. The brightly-lit object then approached his position, apparently on a collision course with his vehicle, causing Mr Spencer to fear that this was, indeed, going to take place.

> *"I reduced my speed to about 20 miles per hour and watched, with astonishment, as a cigar-shaped object passed overhead at*

FLYING SAUCER REVIEW

CASE HISTORIES

TWENTY-FOUR PENCE   SUPPLEMENT 14   APRIL 1973

UFO OVER THE A5

A recent report from the Midlands
See page 6

treetop height, about 20 yards away, at an angle of some 150 feet in diameter, trailing a 'cone of flame', pinkish/yellow on the outside, white in its centre, about 12 feet away from the UFO – rather than being discharged directly from an exhaust, as one may have expected if it had been an aircraft."

Sadly, we were unable to speak directly with John (who was then a Dunlop worker in Birmingham), as we learnt that he had died in the early 1990s, although his wife told us that,

"...after having had the courage to report the incident, he was subjected to such a degree of ridicule, he regretted having brought the matter to the attention of the Newspaper in the first place."

(Source: *Tamworth Herald*, 28.2.1973/*FSR Supplement*, 14.4.1973 – 'Low Pass UFO over the A5')

17th February 1973 – Coastguard's second UFO sighting

An object – looking like *"a big 'wheel', with dome, and apparent portholes along its side"* – was seen hovering over the sea off Hengistbury Head, Dorset, by coastguard – Mr Carl Whitley – who found himself, once again, sighting something out of the ordinary. On this occasion, Mr Whitley chose not to report the incident to the newspaper he worked for, fearing he may be discredited.

21st February 1973 – Motorist followed by a UFO in the United States

Basketball coach – Reggie Bone, and five occupants of the car, were travelling near the town of Piedmont, Missouri, during the late evening, when they saw a mysterious flying object in the sky, projecting a shaft of light downwards. The object then began to follow the vehicle from US 60 to Route 40, near Brushy Creek, before Reggie decided to pull off onto the hard shoulder. Although darkness had restricted their views, they were able to say that it had,

"...four lights, emanating from what appeared to be portholes, three to four feet apart, showing red, green, amber and white lights." Ten minutes later, the object silently lifted up into the night sky and disappeared over a nearby hill.

'Project Identification' launched

Over the ensuing weeks, many people reported having sighted UFOs which were eventually brought to the attention of Dr. Harley Rutledge, who launched an investigation that became known as *Project Identification*. [Initially expected to run for three weeks, it lasted eight months] This involved the assistance of Dr. James Sage, of the industrial and technical department, Professor Milton Ueleke, and Dr. Sidney E. Hodges, from the SMU Physics Department, along with a number of SMU students.

The group, sponsored by the *St. Louis Globe Democrat*, set up observation posts, using a variety of scientific equipment that included spectrum analyzers, reflector telescopes, Infrared film, and Geiger counters, in their scientific quest to determine the origin of the mysterious flying objects that were to plague the Ozark region of the State of Missouri over the next two weeks. Following the operation, the findings were handed to the *Globe*, who publicly announced on the 16th June 1973,

"...that the UFOs (many of them 'balls of orange light', moving at speeds of over 1,200 miles per hour reported in the Piedmont area, were not only REAL but they varied in intensity and at times appeared to exhibit 'almost intelligent control' as that sailed across the skies".

A list of notable effects were recorded which included the same characteristics of behaviour that can be seen, time and time again, in the pages of this book.

On the 16th November 1973, the *St. Louis Globe* once again published the findings of the enquiry, informing the readers that a total of 70 UFO encounters had been logged with the startling claim that these objects were powered by a form of ion or electrometric energy not as yet harnessed by man.

Dr. Rutledge was asked if there had been any positive hard evidence to substantiate the reality of such UFOs. He replied:

"What would constitute proof, a landing or a handshake"?

(Source: *The Ohio Sky Watcher,* Volume 1, No. 1, November 1974/UFOs – 'The Scientific search for truth', Gilbert J. Ziemba, Editor of The *Unidentified Magazine*|)

22nd February 1973 – UFOs over Portsmouth

At 6.50am, John Enderby from Copnor, Portsmouth, Hampshire, was getting ready for his newspaper round, when he heard a noise like a loud refrigerator. On going to investigate further, he saw:

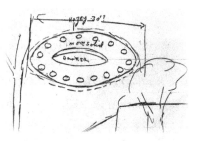

> *"...an orange disc-shaped object, about 30 feet in diameter showing yellow and black lights around it base. There were about ten of these working their way around the base of the object, flashing on and off in continuous sequence (not rotating). The object was hovering about 50-150 feet away over the garden of the house. I wasn't in the least bit frightened and rushed back into the house to tell my sister. It was in view for a total of 25 seconds and my sister saw it as well. As it moved away it took on a cigar shape, showing a rounded dome on top and a smaller one underneath. It disappeared like a dot on a TV screen when you switch the set off."*

(Source: **Richard Nash/***BUFORA Journal,* **Volume 3, No. 10, Spring 1973**)

At 7.55am on the same date, Portsmouth resident – Mrs Stimpson – was waiting for a bus in Goldsmith Avenue, when she sighted a glowing, flickering, flame red object -*"like the glow of a Magicoal fire"*. It came from behind trees in Milton Park, moving very slowly across the sky, and then climbed to a point roughly about 2,000 feet in the sky, making a gentle descent – until lost from view.

(Source: **Nicholas Maloret, WATSUP**)

24th February 1973 -UFO over Colchester

Colchester resident – Elsie Long, went to put the dog out, at 7am, when she saw:

> *"...a bright light in the sky, shaped like a cigarette. It was stationary for about five minutes – then its 'tail' faded and it moved away slowly. It seemed to be spinning when the sun caught it. I told my husband; he just laughed."*

At 9.45pm on the same date, Garry Gill (27) of Park Avenue, Dover, was driving into Dover along Green Lane, on the Buckland estate, accompanied by two friends.

> *"We saw this bright object in the sky over the St. Radigund's Abbey area; it was orange/pink in colour. We set off after it, and had it in view in about 15 minutes. At one stage I believe we were about 200 yards away from the object. It hovered over thorn bushes, about three quarters of a mile away from the Abbey, and about 100 yards off the ground. Suddenly, it began to fade and took on a red colour; within 15 minutes it had disappeared."*

(Source: *Dover Express and East Kent News,* **22.3.1973**)

Another witness was Mr G. Ennew of The Avenue, Wivenhoe, who had this to say:

> *"I was not surprised when I read of Mrs Long's sighting of a UFO, around 7am. I was in Marks Tey on the same morning.*
>
> *The object I saw was in the east, and I couldn't keep my eyes off it. It was the most beautiful golden colour, which I kept sight of for all of 15 minutes. When I first saw it, it seemed like a massive saucer, flat on its back – then it appeared to come upright, the sun's reflection making it appear cigarette shape. I know one thing, I'm not laughing."*

(Source: *Colchester Evening Gazette,* **26.2.1973/27.2.1973**)

MARCH 1973

March 1973 – Cornish schoolchildren sight cigar-shaped UFO

A cigar-shaped object was seen by pupils and staff arriving at Treleigh Comprehensive School, Redruth, Cornwall, moving silently across the sky – quite possibly the same object seen hovering over Carn Brea (an ancient Iron Age site), by motorists travelling between Redruth and Camborne.
(**Source: Personal interview**)

22nd March 1973 – Orange sphere seen by motorist

Mr C. Mark – a butcher by trade – and his wife, from Keyingham, Yorkshire, were driving from Hull to their home address, at 2.40am, when they saw a bright orange sphere pass silently in front of them, at an angle of 45 degrees. Seconds later, it vanished from sight – like a light going out. (**Source: Mr N. Beharrell**)

24th March 1973

Greengrocer Alan Blades (17), of Hawes, was driving over the bleak and lonely Buttertubs Pass, connecting Wensleydale with Swaledale, during the early hours. As he approached the downhill run to Hawes, from the Moorland pass – famous for its limestone formations, which resemble butter tubs – he noticed a red glowing, oval-shaped, object just above his car, and between it and the 2,000 feet summit of Stags Fell.

> *"At first I thought the car lights were shining on something, but when I stopped and switched them off, it was still there. I did not dare switch the engine off, in case it would not start again. At first it was upright, but then seemed to slope to one side and move slowly away. As I watched, it seemed that the underneath was spinning. By this time I was scared stiff and set off for home. As I approached the first houses, at Simonside, it had been keeping pace with me, but then accelerated to the south-east."*

When Alan arrived home he was, according to his father – Joe,

> *"...in a terrible state, and as white as a sheet and in tears"*

This was not the only occasion when UFOs were seen in the locality. Bizarrely, Alan's brother – Bob, and his wife – Elsie, were driving into Swaledale, a couple of months previously, when they saw a similar object some distance away. (**Source: *Northern Echo*, 26.3.1973**)

31st March 1973 – Portsmouth Hospital staff sight silver cigar-shaped UFO

At 7am, Mrs Ludford and Mrs Windsor – nurses employed at St. James Hospital, Milton, Portsmouth, were leaving the hospital near to the Warren Avenue gate entrance, following the end of their night shift. They noticed an object that appeared cigar-shaped and was shiny silver in colour (although they think it may have been a 'disc', sideways on, and completely featureless) hovering in the sky above hospital buildings to the east. Mrs Windsor alerted a porter and a patient to their sighting. The group then watched the object, which was motionless, at an angle of some 60 degrees, with an apparent length of 1-2 feet, hanging in the air at an estimated height of about 10-15 feet above the building, and about 150 feet away from them. Mrs Ludford told UFO researcher – Nick Maloret:

> *"Emanating from the object was an intense white light which hurt the eyes when looked at directly. Around the area of illumination, which was roughly circular, was a dark-grey indistinct ring, although this may have been cause by the intensity of the light."*

Mrs Windsor agreed on the shape of the object, but described seeing:

> *"...a dark-grey smoke-like area, completely surrounding the UFO. It was roughly circular and had around its perimeter a scalloped effect, which I found beautiful."*

Within a few minutes it began to slowly move eastwards, travelling approximately fifty feet above the ground, and was then seen to cross Furze Lane and head out to sea.

A further witness to this phenomenon on the same date and time was Elizabeth Thomas – a midwife sister from Fareham, in Hampshire. She was looking out of her bedroom window, when she saw:

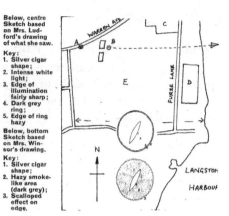

Below, centre
Sketch based on Mrs. Ludford's drawing of what she saw.
Key:
1. Silver cigar shape;
2. Intense white light;
3. Edge of illumination fairly sharp;
4. Dark grey ring;
5. Edge of ring hazy

Below, bottom
Sketch based on Mrs. Winsor's drawing.
Key:
1. Silver cigar shape;
2. Hazy smoke-like area (dark grey);
3. Scalloped effect on edge.

> *"...two bright silver 'rods' hanging vertically in the sky, at an elevation of 45 degrees to the east, towards the direction of Portsdown Hill. Both objects were 'cloud-like' with a fuzzy outline, and remained stationary for about two minutes, before slowly descending.*
>
> *As they came lower their shape distorted, becoming indistinct and finally disappearing."*

(Source: WATSUP [The Wessex Association for the Study of Unexplained Phenomena], Peter A. Hill and Nicholas Maloret)

Ivan T. Sanderson

In one of his last interviews (*Psychic Observer,* February/March 1973) Ivan T. Sanderson said:

> *"It's been known to authorities for forty years now, that they do not come to us through our space time. They don't come from another planet. They come through from another set of dimensions, not another dimension, or a forth dimension, but they come from another whole universe, or whole bunch of universes which are interlocked with ours either in time or space. That's why we can't catch one, because they are not really here ......The intelligences behind certain types of them can make them just the way you, being a New Yorker, might expect in our technological age, such a thing to be. Whereas for a primitive tribesman, somewhere down in the Gran Chaco, they will make it look a thing probably quite different, more like something he would know about...they don't really come from anywhere".*

1973 – UFO seen hovering over a factory at Cheltenham, Gloucestershire

We contacted Jenny Scanlon, from Cheltenham, after learning of what she sighted over the town, when aged 11, walking to school near the Bafford Industrial Estate, at Moorend (well-known to the author, John Hanson, who served his apprenticeship as a trainee Chef, at the Moorend Park Hotel, during the early 1960s).

Jenny:

> *"I was with a group of friends when we saw this jet-black object, with a flat bottom and semicircular dome, above what I believe was the plastics factory. We watched as it silently rose upwards into the sky, before disappearing out of sight behind some buildings. We were scared stiff."*

(Source: *Cheltenham Independent,* 28.9.1995)

APRIL 1973

8th April 1973 – Hovering UFO

Mr Glanmor Bebb (52), and his wife – June, of Maes-yr-Haf, reported having watched a saucer-shaped object hovering over an empty factory, towards the direction of the Brecon Beacons, during the early evening of this date. After about ten minutes the object flashed across the horizon, faster than the eye could follow.

Mrs Bebb said later:

> "It was hovering 300 yards away. I did not know what it was, but it definitely was not an aircraft, light, or a star."

The couple reported the incident to Blackwood Police.

(**Source:** *Western Mail,* **10.4.1973/***South Wales Argus,* **10.4.1973**)

15th April 1973 – Couple sight UFO over Lincolnshire

A couple from Lincoln were motoring from Lincoln to Caister, on a day out, and decided to stop for a picnic lunch, at 4pm, in the gateway of a field overlooking the A46, from Caister to Nettleton, on the Kirton in Lindsey ridge – 400 feet in height above the Brigg valley. While they were enjoying their meal, they noticed a silver cigar-shaped 'light' in the sky, about 10-15 miles away, with a flashing red light on its top left-hand side.

> "It then changed to pink, then deeper pink and bright red – like an electric fire element – before advancing forward, where it stopped and hovered in the sky, glowing at one end with a light silver or grey colour sheen. After four minutes, it suddenly vanished." (**Source: Richard Thompson**)

2nd May 1973 – RAF pilots sight UFO

Jeremy Lane

We spoke to ex-RAF Pilot – Jeremy Lane, who had served with 85 Squadron, flying 'Canberras', from West Raynham, having logged a total of 1,400 hours flying time, with two tours in Germany. He was on a night-time sortie from RAF Leuchars, together with other aircraft, on 2nd May 1973, flying north, to test the northern Radar Defences.

After reaching an altitude of about 38,000 feet, they noticed a strange sight ahead and above, completely stationary in the sky, resembling a Concorde aircraft in shape, with lights flashing around its perimeter, orientated in a North-South direction.

> "I reported the sighting to the Radar Controller, who confirmed nothing was showing on Radar, but he had received other reports from earlier aircraft of a similar object. All of the crew on my flight deck could clearly see the vehicle. As we continued North, I climbed the aircraft with a view to being some 10,000 feet higher on the southbound leg, which would give us an idea of whether
> the vehicle was close, or far away, and its apparent size, depending on how close it was to us. As we came south, the vehicle was still there. I again contacted the Radar operator, who confirmed fighters had been scrambled to intercept, although the Radar had still not picked it up. The lights were still flashing and the orientation of the vehicle was still North-South, but the apparent size of the vehicle remained as it had been, suggesting it was at very high altitude. It was an incredibly clear night and from 46,000+ feet, we could see well into Northern Europe. At some point, as we approached the 'vehicle' from underneath, it became brilliant light and accelerated to the south at an incredible speed; within one to two seconds it had disappeared from view, travelling 500 to 800 miles."

When they landed back at base, all the crews independently drew what they had seen. A report was submitted to Group Operations, as they understood there was no official channel for submitting reports of such nature, and that was the last they heard.

On a subsequent visit to RAF Kinloss, on 25th June in the same year, Jeremy was discussing the incident with a friend of his – then flying 'Nimrods' – when he was told, *"this was a frequent visitor and often sighted by the pilots".*

MAY 1973

18th May 1973 – seen over Colchester Essex

May/June 1973 – Soldiers sight oval UFO hovering above ground

Lance Corporal Mike Perrin, and his colleague – Trooper Carvell, from Catterick Army Camp, were taking part in a regular exercise on Bellerby Moor, at 11pm – a lonely and desolate spot on the edge of the Yorkshire Moors – when the radio fitted to their Landrover failed, followed by the headlights fading and then extinguishing completely. After attempting to remedy the problem they decided to wait, hoping the fault would correct itself, when Mike noticed something approaching in the sky, silently, about half a mile away.

In an interview conducted with Barry King, he told him:

Barry King

"It stopped at a distance of, maybe, 100 metres, hovering some ten feet above the ground. It was shaped like a rugby ball with a row of small, circular, windows around its middle section. Through these windows shone white lights, which seemed to flash. There was also some form of vapour issuing from the lowest part of the object, together with a slight buzzing sound emanating from it. After it left, the radio and lights came back on".

After arriving back at their base, they reported the matter to their Superior Officer, and were promptly arrested and charged with being drunk and leaving war department property unattended!

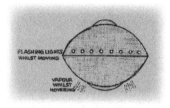

On the following afternoon, the two men decided to revisit the scene of the encounter and discovered a burnt circle of grass, with a diameter of 30 feet, on the other side of some woods. Mr Perrin notified his Commanding Officer of the situation and suggested the MOD be informed. He was told it was of no interest to them, although he believes the incident was later secretly investigated. When he asked if he could check with nearby Radar and military installations for any information on the UFO he and his partner had seen, they were refused permission to do so.

Summer 1973 – Close encounter in Wales

In summer of 1973, Jill (known personally to the authors) – a resident of Redditch, was on a family camping holiday in Broad Haven, Pembrokeshire.

"After arriving at the council-run site, we pitched our tents at the top of the field backing onto woodland, noting that, apart from ourselves, there were only two other tents near the main entrance.

After retiring to bed, I was suddenly awoken by a loud droning/humming noise coming from above our tent. Puzzled, I tried to reason what it could be as it was unlike any aircraft, or helicopter, I had ever heard before. Wide awake by now, I sat up, feeling rather concerned as it was beginning to increase in vibration, although the canvas on the tent remained perfectly still, without showing any signs of increased pressure as one might have expected.

The only way I can describe what I was hearing is that it sounded like the 'whoosh, whoosh' of some sort of blade. I tried to wake up my husband, but for some reason I couldn't get him to wake up. I tried whispering to my daughter, who was sleeping in a separate compartment – there was no response. I could now feel the sweat breaking out on my forehead and tried to move my legs to get up, but it was as if they were paralysed. All I could do was lie quiet and hope this dreadful noise would stop. Suddenly, to my relief, it stopped.... all was quiet, apart from my husband's snoring. Eventually I fell asleep."

The next morning, feeling quite exhausted by what had happened and frightened by the experience, Jill told her daughter and husband what she had heard. They laughed at her, suggesting she must have been dreaming. Jill began to get very upset with their attitude, until they unzipped the tent and went outside, where she saw her son emerging from his tent. He asked her, *"Mum, did you hear the UFO overhead in the night?"* – following which her husband apologised to her, unable to understand why he had slept through it all.

> *"To this day, I still cannot answer why I just didn't get up and go outside to see what it was, although at the time my legs felt paralysed. Why didn't I go outside after the noise had ceased?"*

Little did they know that in four years time, the Broad Haven area was to be the subject of worldwide interest!

Summer 1973 – UFO over Birmingham, UK

Tony Caldicott – an ex member of the Birmingham Group, UFOSIS, in the 1970s – was fishing by the side of the canal, at Parsons Hill, Kings Norton, Birmingham, during Summer 1973.

> *"It was a clear day. I was occupied with fishing, when a small boat – a cruiser – came towards me, heading towards Birmingham.*
>
> *The man piloting it moored by the side of the canal and got out. He came over to me and said, 'Have you ever seen anything like that before?' I looked up and saw this object in the sky, quite low. I was flabbergasted to see what looked like an 'Adamski type UFO' – silver, with three 'globes' set into its underside – just hovering silently in the sky. Suddenly, it flew away and was soon lost from sight."*

(Source: Personal interview)

JUNE 1973

1st June 1973 – Cheshire man tells of a number of UFO sightings

The *Birkenhead News*, of the 1st June 1973, carried an article about hairdresser – Douglas Fletcher of Pemberton Road, Arrowe Park, who claimed a series of UFO sightings, accompanied by his girlfriend, Dianna Smethurst – formerly of York Avenue, West Kirby, (now living in Wallasay). Douglas described that on the first occasion, he and Dianna had been parked on Hoylake promenade, Wirral Cheshire, one evening, when:

> *"...lights above the water appeared. There was a red light at the rear, with a white light in the front. They were moving along the Dee, at a terrific speed, and flashing alternately at irregular intervals. The next night we returned to the same spot – this time taking binoculars and a telescope. We saw a huge yellow shape – the size of a bus – showing a yellow light some 200 yards above it. This was moving about three miles away, across a stretch of beach on the Dee Estuary. On the third occasion we sighted a similar set of lights, which zigzagged their way towards us."*

The couple told the newspaper that they had contacted the Police, the Royal Navy, and the RAF about what they had seen.

A spokesman for West Drayton, London, had this to say:

> *"There are various explanations for some UFOs, such as weird effect of cloud reflections along*

coastline, or even flares at sea, but I would like to stress that all reports of UFOs are meticulously followed up and filed for future reference."

21st June 1973 – Close encounter with hooded monk at Surrey

At 6.20pm, the figure of a hooded monk was seen by three girls, standing close to the entrance gate leading into Coulsdon Common, Surrey. This 'manifestation' was followed by an incident involving a small 'craft' seen hovering over the same locality, a few hours later, which rose up into the air and pursued the girls along the road, before 'flipping over in flight' and disappearing.

A disc-shaped object, with a bright yellow centre, was seen crossing the sky over Jarrow Town centre, at 9.45pm – then lost from view as it went behind cloud above Jarrow Centre School.

(Source: *Shields Gazette*, 4.7.1973/Margaret Fry, Welsh Federation of Ufologists)

24th June 1973 – 'Orange mass' sweeps the sky with searchlights over West Virginia

Another UFO incident that captured our attention took place, we believe, in the same year. Unfortunately, we were unable to identity the date. Attempts in 2017 to trace details of this sighting through the participants on the internet failed. It happened at 10.30pm, in the summer of 1973, and involved Mr James V. Coste (a banker from Hinton, West Virginia, and President of Hinton Television Cable Company) his wife, and a Mrs Oliver Porterfield and her husband – the principal at a local school. They were returning

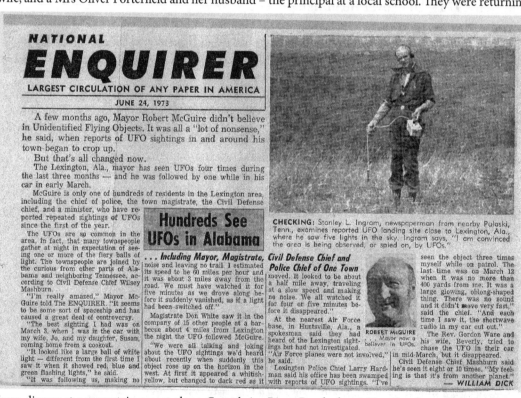

from dinner at a mountain resort along Greenbrier River Road, about 13 miles from Hinton, when a blinding light lit up the sky. Puzzled, they stopped the car. James – a former radio/radar engineer for the US Marine Air Corps in World War Two – said:

"We saw an object showing four giant searchlights, pointing upwards and moving in a circle."

His wife said:

> "It looked to me as if the thing was searching the earth for a place to land, as it lit up the ground for several hundred feet in every direction."

Mrs Porterfield:

> "I was just a little frightened. I couldn't believe my eyes, but there it was."

The group moved about hoping to get a better look at the object, which was described as a round 'orange mass', with shafts of light sweeping downwards from the bottom. After observing it for approximately 15 minutes, the object then flew quickly away.

JULY 1973

8th July 1973 – Timothy Good's mother sights three UFOs over North Cornwall

UFO researcher Timothy Good received a telephone call from his mother – then living in Porthcothan Bay, North Cornwall – who told her son about something strange she and another witness had sighted, the previous evening, at 10.05pm.

Following further conversation, Tim was able to obtain the following account from his mother:

> "I went to draw the curtains; there was a lovely sky of banded colours and some clouds. To my utter amazement I saw three stationary objects in the sky over the sea. One was a perfectly symmetrical 'disc', apparently reflecting the last of the evening sky, on each side of which was an extremely black object, roughly like a cigar in shape, but of indefinite outline (like a black, furry caterpillar); that on the right being larger than the one on the left. After a few minutes the 'disc' entered or went behind the object on the left and the two sped off at fantastic speed, followed by the departure of the third object, moments later."

Daytime photograph by Mrs Good, showing the view from the window, with a drawing of the object superimposed in the position it was seen

Following the matter being brought to his attention Tim wrote to RAF St. Mawgan, explaining what had taken place, wondering if his *mother* had seen an example of some rare *type of* temperature inversion, and asking them if any anomalous ground or airborne radar returns had been brought to their notice. He received a letter in reply, signed by the Flight Lt. on behalf of the Commanding Officer at the base:

> "Our check of the various operational and radar records revealed nothing out of the ordinary during the period in question. However, our senior Meteorological officer states that the duty officer on the evening of Saturday, July 7th, did observe bright mock suns and halo phenomena, which as you will know are produced by refraction of light through ice crystals which are present in cirrus clouds. The alert observer noted in the daily register the following technical remarks: 'Two bright mock suns, partial 22 degrees halo, part parhelic circle from both mock suns, upper circumzenithal arc

of contact to 22 degrees halo; further mock suns to left of primary and 120 degrees from it on parhelic circle.'

The senior Meteorological officer was unable to comment on the 'flight path comments' or the alleged disappearance into the distance at a phenomenal speed. It is however in little doubt that what your mother saw was the vivid mock suns. It is hoped that this information will be of some assistance to you in dispelling your mother's apprehension."

According to Tim, his mother was highly dissatisfied with the explanation proffered – an explanation, by the way, which was later quaffed when Tim established that the duty officer had witnessed the appearance of the mock suns, one to two hours previous to his mother's sighting.

(**Source:** *FSR*, **Volume 21, No. 2, 1975, Timothy Good – 'Strange Phenomenon at Porthcothan Bay')**

9th July 1973 – Flickering UFO seen over Leicestershire

An oval object, with flickering lights and slightly raised middle section, showing a bank of red lights, was seen crossing the sky over Weston Park, Leicestershire. (**Source:** *Leicester Mercury* **9.7.1973**)

3rd July 1973 – Disc-shaped UFO seen by youth over Jarrow

Trainee dental mechanic – Michael Hallowell (16) – (now a successful author of books relating to the UFO subject and widely respected) was with four friends, outside his home in Beverley Court, Jarrow at 9.45pm, when he saw:

"...a disc-shaped object with a bright yellow centre, white rim and long blue tail, travelling at a height of approximately 600 feet over Jarrow town centre. It then disappeared behind a cloud over Jarrow Central School. It looked like a fried egg. Another friend of mine came around to tell me he had also seen it pass over."

Michael contacted the weather centre, at Newcastle, who told him it was not a natural phenomenon.

Coastguards at North Shields, said:

"We are damned if we know what it was."

RAF Acklington was also contacted, and the duty officer took a description from Mike of what he had seen.

The police suggested it might have been something natural, such as a meteor burning up.

In April 2012 we spoke to Mike, who has provided us with assistance over the years:

"I must confess that having read the account in the Gazette, I've become somewhat disturbed, for virtually every fact stated by the reporter is contrary to recollections of my colleagues, and I.

It is almost as if two separate sightings are being described. The weird thing is that the presence of a fourth person had completely obliterated itself from our memories, until I read it in the clipping you sent.

I have been able to contact her, and she states that the day after the event she could remember nothing about it, other than the fact that 'something had happened'.

She is very reluctant to give a statement, or talk about it, and has specifically asked that her name be kept confidential. Since reading the clipping, I've had two episodes which seem like 'flashbacks' that bear some correlation to the Gazette account, but not to my original memory of the event. I'm baffled." (**Source:** *Shields Gazette,* **4.7.1973**)

7th July 1973 – Oval object over Leicestershire

An oval-shaped object, with white flickering lights and a raised central section, showing red lights, was seen hovering in the sky over the Western Park estate, Leicestershire, by eleven year-old Jackie Wilson and Ian Crawford. The boys thought the object was going to land, but it suddenly shot upwards into the sky and disappeared from sight. (**Source: Geoffrey Coxon**)

26th July 1973 – Four glowing cigar-shaped objects seen by Kent workers

Factory worker – Mr M. Barker, was taking a tea break with a number of other men, at 3am, looking up into the night sky, hoping to catch a glimpse of the American Skylab satellite as it passed over Westwood, in Kent. They were surprised to see

> *"...four glowing orange 'cigars', which appeared in the sky, one behind the other", moving slowly towards the direction of Cliftonville – seconds later, gone from view.*

Mr Barker contacted RAF Manston, but they were unable to offer any explanation for what the men had seen and promised to forward the report on to the MOD.

About a fortnight later the MOD sent Mr Barker a letter, explaining the objects may have been

> *"...a sun shadow, cloud formations, reflections, or possibly, space junk",*

neither of which was accepted by Mr Barker as being an explanation for what he and the others had seen. (**Source:** *Kentish Times,* **29.7.1973**)

AUGUST 1973

August 1973 – Strange 'beings' sighted in Scotland ...missing time encountered

Margaret and Christine had just left Lochore Country Park, Fife, Scotland, at 9pm, in August 1973, following a visit, and were travelling in the rear of the vehicle as it pulled up to a junction where the green ended and a housing estate began. A car drew up quietly behind them, at which point the radio went dead and the car engine cut out. As if drawn by a magnet, Christine and Margaret looked to their left, across an area of open ground, and saw, heading towards them:

> *"...two veritable 'giants', moving in a rather mechanical manner – like machines rather than living beings – wearing one-piece silver suits, emphasizing their overlarge heads."*

Christine cannot be sure how long it took the entities to cover the space that separated them, but she does have a vivid memory of the strange 'beings' getting closer and closer to the car, and the car simply refusing to start. When the two 'beings' were almost up to the window, within yards of where Christine sat frozen and unable to move, she experienced a choking sensation and, it seems, passed out. What happened next is a mystery.

When Christine came to, she saw the backs of the two 'giants' as they returned in the direction they had come from. Moments later, after they disappeared from view, a 'cone of light' spread around the trees at the edge of the field – as if marking the path of an object heading skywards. At this precise moment the car engine roared into life, as did the radio.

The driver of the vehicle behind them rushed up and shouted, *"What the bloody hell was that?"*

When Christine arrived home, she noticed a considerable time lapse. **Source: Ron Halliday, UFO Scotland)**

8th August 1973 – Close encounter, Northampton ... missing time

In December 2006, we spoke to Diane and Peter Shepherd from St. James, Northampton – Head of the Northamptonshire UFO Forum – about what they witnessed during the late evening of the 8th August 1973.

Peter:

> "We were just leaving a friend's house, at 3am, when we saw this saucer-shaped object – the size of a football pitch – resting on the ground in a nearby field. I was stunned and climbed onto the roof of the car to get a closer look. It was dark-grey in colour, showing a perfectly smooth exterior, with seven rectangular amber coloured windows, or lights, facing us.
>
> It was beautiful to behold, and was as solid and real as the car I was standing on. The object was accompanied by a number of red spheres, which hovered over nearby trees and the road. I decided to approach closer, so got into the car and drove a few hundred yards towards the object, believing I would be in a good position to see more of the object as it passed overhead. Suddenly, one of the red spheres appeared in front of us. The

Diane Shepherd

> next thing I remember was driving down the road, about 300 yards away, with the dawn now coming up. When we looked at our watches, we realised we couldn't account for forty minutes of lost time."

During conversation with the couple, interjected by Diane's irrepressible bubbly laugh and sense of humour, we were told they had received a visit from the *BBC*, who interviewed them for a documentary, *but suggested the incident had not happened!*

Sadly, Diane – an authority on the UFO subject – was to later pass away from cancer. Her bubbly laughter and wicked sense of humour is sadly missed.

12th August 1973 – UFO seen over Colchester, Essex

Early 1970s – Close encounters at RAF Alconbury ... creature sighted

Marc Uptergrove contacted us by email, from Los Angeles, in 2005, enquiring whether we had any knowledge of strange happenings, which included *ghostly children's voices and the appearance of a bizarre 'leaping man', apparently witnessed by a number of servicemen at RAF Alconbury, Huntingdonshire* – a curiosity triggered by conversations held with his father, Wesley, who served at the airbase in the early 1970s. We knew of no such incidents, other than previous UFO sightings that had taken place at Sawtrey and Godmanchester, and spoke to Wesley, who had this to say:

> "On the third day of duty, at RAF Alconbury, I was instructed to take over the night G shift for a member of the security patrol who had gone sick. This involved keeping watch over the airbase from a 25 feet concrete tower – one of six, that lined the inside of a corridor encircling the perimeter of the airbase. After being transported to the site, I climbed up the ladder and settled down for the night. As night descended I stood there, unable to even see the next tower due to the dark and foggy conditions. I became aware of an area of clearing that stretched out from the fence bordering a dense forest, which I found, for some strange reason, very unsettling although I cannot identify why I felt like this."

Children's voices heard

> "At about 6am, I was sat on the floor inside the tower, reading a book by flashlight, when suddenly I heard the unmistakable sound of happy children's voices, rising and falling – as if borne on the

wind, rather than a fixed source. Puzzled, I went out onto the 'cat walk' and peered into the darkness, feeling perplexed rather than frightened. All of a sudden, the voices stopped. I was about to re-enter the tower when, in that split second, the voices were all around me so close and so loud – as if I was in a school playground. With my heart racing, I made my way down the ladder to the ground. The voices were just as loud. I felt surrounded ... then they began to fade away, leaving me amazed by what I regarded as a privileged experience."

Visit to the local Library

Wesley paid a visit to the local Library in an attempt to discover the folklore of the area, hoping to find a clue as to what had happened, and was surprised to learn that a number of children had been killed in a train accident that had occurred close to the airbase, some years previously, and wonders if the two are connected. It would appear that the incident to which he refers took place near to Abbots Ripton, when three trains – including the 'Flying Scotsman' – collided as a result of signal failure, (caused by ice), on 21st January 1876, causing the death of thirteen people, seven of them children, as shown in a sketch on the front page of the *Illustrated News*, (29th January 1876).

RAF Alconbury

Ghostly stories were rife at airbase

Enquiries made put us in touch with Roger, (another ex-Serviceman, previously at the airbase), who confirmed ghostly stories were rife, although he had never personally spoken to anybody who had experienced something for themselves, first-hand, and took them with a 'pinch of salt' – a situation which was to change when a close friend of his witnessed something or someone so frightening, that he refused to discuss the incident with Roger, telling him:

> *"We were carrying out some routine work to an F-5 aircraft, parked on the runway – a job that should have been completed in an hour. When he failed to make the telephone call, requesting a lift back from the hangar, a search went out to find him. They found him sitting in the aircraft, as white as a sheet, with the canopy closed. Although I asked him, many times, what it was that he had seen, he declined saying that it had frightened him so much he refused to go anywhere near that location again."*

We discovered, from another source, that the man had seen a terrifying hairy humanoid, which had walked past the aircraft.

Bomb went off killing a number of people in Second World War

Roger wondered if the talk of ghosts seen near the hangar, close to the F-5 flight line, could have been connected with an accident taking place during the Second World War, when a number of people were killed after a 500 pound bomb being loaded onto an aircraft had exploded for no apparent reason.

Children's voices and encounters with a strange creature

We received a number of emails from Dennis Prisbrey, who was stationed at RAF Alconbury between 1973 and 1975. He told us of rumours, widespread at the time, about some of the airmen having sighted a 'creature' near the north side of the airfield, but attributed it to tall stories. Like Mr Uptergrove, he was involved in a variety of security tasks; they included tower guard, and monitoring an alarm panel covering the main bomb storage area.

Dennis:

> *"The SAS (Special Ammunition Storage area) was a high security nuclear bomb storage facility, surrounded by a double row of wire fences with concertina wire coils on top, dating back to the 1950s. Around the perimeter were a number of small elevated guard towers, spaced at intervals, manned by a single guard.*
>
> *In late 1974, a new alarm system was installed, involving the use of motion detectors that would eliminate the need to post guards to these towers. Unfortunately, due to problems and their frequent activation, with no visible cause, it was decided to 'man up' two of the three towers. A friend of mine, Sergeant Baker, Airman First Class, who was working at the airbase before I arrived, told me in conversation, one day, that he had heard the voices of children whilst working one of the towers, and it was believed these children's voices were the ghosts of children killed in a railway accident near to the base, at the turn of the century.*
>
> *I also heard about an incident involving two mechanics, who were working on an aircraft parked on the north side of the base, one of whom was so frightened by the appearance of a 'strange hairy creature' that he jumped into the cockpit of the aircraft and refused to get out for some time. I took such stories at face value, purely because I never encountered this 'leaping man', or spoke to any of the witnesses. My attitude was to change, following a conversation with my two regular partners – Sergeants Randi Lee and Jackson – after learning of their involvement in an incident, which happened prior to my arrival at the airbase. One night, while on patrol with their two dogs, they saw some movement near the towers and called the main gate to check if any workmen were still on*

site. When told not, they asked for a truck response team to assist with searching the area. As they approached a tower, they came face-to-face with a hairy 'figure'. The dogs stopped in their tracks, absolutely terrified, frantically trying to get away. One of the handlers urged the dog to attack the intruder, but was bitten by his own animal – that's how frightened the dogs were. The truck arrived just in time to see the creature, whatever it was, climbing over the security fence, where it was last seen entering North Woods."

What Wesley witnessed

Another witness to this event was Wesley Uptergrove who found himself in a terrifying situation according to his son, Marc, who described what his father saw.

"He was the NCOIC of a group of three men and their dogs, charged with guarding bunkers underneath which were stored, I believe, nuclear warheads within a large, fenced area. One foggy night, my father received a radio call that there was an intruder within the perimeter and shots had been fired. He tore out in his truck and sped towards the location of the shooting. Seeing a figure in the fog, he pulled over thinking it was one of his guards. He rolled down his window and was screamed at full in the face by what can only be described as a man-like, bipedal 'creature'. My father nearly wet himself in fear. In an instant the thing ran off at incredible speed and my father drove after it.

Within moments it had sped past another of the guards, who also fired upon it; he missed due to the fact he was practically dragged backwards by his guard dogs that were yelping and straining to flee in the opposite direction.

The third guard and his dogs were running towards the scene when they turned the corner of a bunker, only to be intercepted by the 'creature' running at full speed. As his dogs wailed, the thing hit the taut leashes and pulled them away from his grasp, lacerating a good deal of skin from the unfortunate man's forearm in the process. My father and these men witnessed this 'creature' make fantastic, running bounds across the grounds before leaping over two tall, well-spaced barbed wire fences in a single bound. It disappeared into the surrounding woods.

My father's description of the 'creature' is little vague, but in his defence he only saw it briefly and, as he puts it, the whole situation was fast, confusing, and difficult to process. It was hairy, approximately 5 feet 9 inches in height, and had intelligent, human-like eyes, a flat nose and large ears. The teeth were large but not fanged. The lower face was rounded in a way that suggested the look of a walrus. The face was narrow around the eyes, but the head flared out again at the top. It had very muscular, frog-like thighs with what appeared to be reversed articulated legs like a horse. Incredibly, he and his fellow airmen also witnessed a floating apparition on the very same night they encountered the weird 'man'."

We visited the area in 2006, and saw for ourselves the remains of the towers (now demolished), marked by heaps of rubble along the perimeter of the airbase – still under the control of armed USAF guards.

Our visit to the area … reports of monk like 'figures' seen walking through walls

We then made our way to Monks Wood, approximately a couple of miles away, which lies adjacent to where the watch towers were, next to Bevel's Wood (no doubt connected with Sir Robert Beville, Lord of the Manor of Chesterton), and spent time talking to the security guard at the Centre for Ecology and Hydrology (CEH) – the UK's centre of excellence for integrated research in terrestrial and freshwater ecosystems, situated in Monks Wood. We were surprised to hear from him that:

"...a number of employees had seen monk like 'figures', walking through the corridors. On one occasion, much to the shock of the employee, the figure vanished through a wall."

Old maps examined

We examined old maps, hoping to find clues as to the reasons why these manifestations had occurred, and found a tumulus to the west of Monks Wood but nothing in the adjacent woodland, opposite to where the control towers had been situated, apart from discovering the wooded area, now known as Park Farm (closest to the airfield), was called Long Coppice. Monks Wood had been known as Boulton Hinich Wood, prior to RAF Alconbury being constructed, but we were unable to identify the source of where the name had originated from. Research conducted into the surrounding area revealed some interesting information, when we discovered ghostly children's voices had also been reported at Hinchingbrooke House, Huntingdon, built around an 11th Century Nunnery – a building after the reformation given to Thomas Cromwell, as a reward for overseeing the dissolution of the monasteries, which later became the home of the Earl of Sandwich, i.e. formerly the home of the 9th Earl of Sandwich, whom it was said, according to local myths (and the internet) had demolished *'the west wing of the house, because he thought it was inhabited by a werewolf, in 1947'*; other stories tell of him having *'heard a werewolf'*.

We contacted Huntingdon Archives, in 2009, and asked them if they would examine personal papers (once in the possession of the 9th Earl) if there was any information in support of this extraordinary statement. They told us, in a guide published in 1970, by Philip Dickinson, that:

> *"...during the Second World War, the house had become too large to maintain and the family moved out for the duration of the war, when it was used by families from London and elsewhere as a recuperative home. After the war, the Earl set about a programme of general restorative work on the house to make it habitable again with the architect Marshall Sissonto and it was as part of this process that the wing was demolished."*

Ghostly black dog seen at aerodrome

In 1832, two stone coffins were found containing the remains of two nuns, during repairs carried out to the house by architect – Edward Blore. Was there any connection with modern-day sightings of ghostly nuns seen at Nun's Bridge over Alconbury Brook, reputed to be haunted by one of the nuns who lived at the old convent? One of its students was none other than Oliver Cromwell), not to mention the rumoured secret tunnels supposedly connecting the house to the local train station.

It is alleged that 2005 builders renovating the house refused to work during the night, after apparent sightings of 'the monk'. We also learnt, from a retired USAF Colonel who had been stationed at RAF Alconbury, of sightings of a *ghostly black dog* seen on the aerodrome, which rumour had it belonged to the Old Duke's house, before the runway was built. Apparently the animal had to be shot before the Duke's body could be removed after he died, and that the Officers' mess was haunted.

SEPTEMBER 1973

September 1973 – UFO over Wales ... witnesses experience sunburn

During the same month, a luminous cloud – approximately 100 feet in width, by 200 feet in length – was seen slowly drifting through the sky over Pensarn, Abergele, at 2am, by two young men out walking. The cloud was seen to stop in mid-flight over the local Police Station and then moved back towards the beach. A few minutes later, a huge, black, oval object was sighted flying along the coastline from the direction of Rhyl, accompanied by two other identical objects – no more than 500 feet off the ground. As these gigantic objects passed over Pensarn Railway Station, the 'lead one' halted in mid-air, allowing the others to merge into it, showering the darkness with dull green, blue and red colours. The two youths were to complain, later, of: *'...having sustained sunburn to their faces and hands'* – symptoms also experienced by a third youth, who had been asleep at the time. According to Margaret Fry, who brought this matter to our attention, she discovered a similar incident had taken place years previously.

Autumn 1973 – UFO over Hythe, in Kent

Steven Dadd from Hythe, in Kent (now in his late 50s), contacted us in September 2010.

"Sometime in the autumn of 1973/1974, I was on my way home from school, at about 5pm, when a large 'ball'/light bulb shaped object descended through the sky and hovered approximately 60 feet above my head. I was terrified and unable to move through fear; suddenly, it shot away into the sky and was gone. When I arrived home my parents saw the distressed state I was in and when I told them what I had experienced they just laughed at me in disbelief. I'm not sure exactly when this happened, but within a week or two I saw on the front page of the Hythe/Dover Adscene newspaper a photograph of the same UFO I had seen, taken over Dover Docks, and remember the derogatory opinions expressed by the editor at the time. Unfortunately, I haven't got a copy of the paper but I'm sure it is in the library somewhere."

September 1973 – Close Encounter, Northamptonshire

A resident of Bedford of Italian descent (23), who was employed as an engineer, had been to a dance held at Northampton, approximately 23 miles from his home. As he drove (alone) along theA428, at 2am, just passing the small church in Little Houghton – the first village on the road from Northampton to Bedford – he slowed down on seeing what he took to be the headlights of an approaching car.

"Suddenly, I was blinded by this 'light' heading straight for me. The next thing I knew was finding myself walking along the Bromham Bridge road, about two miles out of Bedford; my coat and shoes were wet – as though I had been walking through long grass. I felt very refreshed and wide awake – as if I had rested well. I made my way to a friend's house and asked him to drive me slowly back along the Northampton road, as I could remember where I had left the car. Near a turn-off from the main road, signposted to the village of Olney, we found the car locked up in the middle of a ploughed field. (The keys had been in my pocket.) The gate was shut and there were no tracks seen in the soil near to the car. A farmer later towed the vehicle out of the field. There were no marks or scratches found on the car."

According to the researcher Miss E.C. Hargreaves, whom the witness had confided in, he decided not to tell his parents what had actually happened, but told of having stayed with his friend after the dance. He did not, in fact, tell Miss Hargreaves what had taken place until 12 months later, feeling that he just wanted to block out the incident from his mind. Understandably, this was a matter that caused him much concern and led to outbursts of moodiness and confusion – not forgetting the fear, as he tried to come to terms with something completely out of the normal. What had happened along that quiet stretch of country road that evening, and where had that missing 5 hours of time gone? Even if he had subconsciously driven the car without any specific memory of having done so, why were there no wheel marks or traces of the car having been driven along the ploughed field? One senses that there was an awful lot of information tied in with this incident that we shall never know about, particularly bearing in mind we do not know the identity of the person concerned and that this matter took place now nearly 40 years ago. What a pity we were unable to track down Miss E. Hargreaves, who was living in Copper Cottage, Ravensden, Bedford, who knew the identity of the man.

(Source: As above, Letter to *FSR*, Volume 22, No. 1, 1976)

September 1973 – Phantom helicopter, Derbyshire

In the early hours, a woman living in the small village of Harpur Hill, which lies south-east of the town of Buxton, in the county of Derbyshire, contacted the police after having sighted an object, which she described as resembling a helicopter, rising out of part of the excavated site at the nearby Hillhead quarry. Another witness to this event was Simon Crowe – a security guard at the quarry.

He told of having sighted the same 'helicopter' earlier in the night, at 10pm, and 12pm. Although he could not positively identify it as a helicopter, he confirmed that it had hovered and made a sound similar to rotor blades.

> *"The first time I saw it (the craft) was hovering about 50 feet from the ground, and shined what appeared to be spotlights onto the quarry floor – as if searching for something. When I approached it in my Landrover, it flew towards the part of the quarry designated as Mines Research. On the second occasion, it rose out of the quarry with its lights on and disappeared in the direction I had seen it take previously."*

20th September – Astronauts' sighting from Sky Lab 3

At approximately 4.45pm, astronauts – Alan Bean, Owen Garriott and Jack Lousma – sighted what they described as a red 'satellite', which they photographed while aboard *Sky Lab 3*.

Of course, they were not the only astronauts to see something highly unusual while on their missions. While we should be careful about forming any interpretation of what these things are, and where they come from, it should be of no surprise that anomalous objects have been seen in the vacuum of space. It is alleged that Buzz Aldrin has disclosed he and other astronauts saw a UFO which paced them for a time during their journey to the moon. This information was kept secret by NASA for all of these years.

> *"There was something out there, close enough to be observed, and what could it be? Now, obviously, the three of us weren't going to blurt out, 'Hey, Houston, we've got something moving alongside of us and we don't know what it is', you know?"*

According to present information, it has been alleged that the object seen from *Sky Lab 3* was similar to what the three astronauts of *Apollo 11* saw. There have been a number of images (both still and moving) of the astronauts on the moon and other NASA missions which seem to show UFOs, and, as we know, Astronaut Gordon Cooper was open about seeing 'unknowns' on numerous occasions. According to a taped interview by J.L. Ferrando, Major Cooper said:

> *"For many years I have lived with a secret, in a secrecy imposed on all specialists in astronautics. I can now reveal that every day, in the USA, our radar instruments capture objects of form and composition unknown to us. And there are thousands of witness reports and a quantity of documents to prove this, but nobody wants to make them public."*

29th September 1973 – Police officer sights UFO over Union City area

Sherriff Nathan Cunningham

Sheriff Nathan Cunningham of Obion County, in an interview conducted by *The Enquirer* newspaper, Nathan told them of his first sighting, which took place on the 29th September 1973.

> *"Just before 9pm, about 18 miles from Union City, someone pointed out a shining object in the sky that was no star.*
>
> *I watched it from the ground, then from a high fire tower with binoculars. It had a central white light and smaller coloured lights. I then saw a second identical object come from the north and hovered over the first. They seemed to be stationary – then moved out of sight to the west. I drove two and half miles to my son's house to discuss it with him. He had just been on the phone to a woman who had seen mysterious lights and had already received other reports. Suddenly a UFO buzzed over his house, about 1,000 feet high, moving at about 100 miles per hour. It seemed to be about 40 feet long, with a glowing white light in the centre and other lights around it. It made a noise – like the hum of an electric motor. We just watched in amazement."*

His son – Deputy Sherriff Danny Cunningham (22), said:

> "*It certainly didn't look anything like an airplane or helicopter.*"

30th September 1973 – Orange 'light' over Union City

At about 9pm, Union City dentist – Fred Hansen (35), was in his yard when he saw:

> "*…a strange orange 'light', zigzagging across the sky moving much faster than any aircraft. I have seen satellites; this didn't behave like one of those.*"

OCTOBER 1973

1st October 1973 – Firemen witness UFO display

Five firemen on the night shift, in Union City, told of two strange objects they witnessed while on night shift, between 9pm and midnight.

Fireman Douglas McGowan (28):

> "*We saw two objects towards the east of the fire station, like no aircraft I had even seen. They were 'V'-shaped and had large white lights and red, blue, and green lights close together.*"

Fireman Gregory Lane (20) described their movement as:

> "*…back and forth across the sky for some four hours, before heading away northwards at high speed*".

Other foremen included David Bobo (26), James Randy King (31), and Rudy J. Skoda (45).

According to the *The Enquirer* journalist, who was interviewing the sheriff in his office at the Union City Court, a resident contacted the police, claiming she had seen a UFO drop down into a bean field near her house. They all rushed out to the site, about 2 miles away, and spoke to Mrs Kay Moore (27), who told them excitedly, that she and her guests – Mr and Mrs Gerry Taylor – had seen two white 'lights' sink towards the ground and vanish into the earth.

> "*They left a bluish glow above the soil – then the strange haze disappeared. The whole thing was so eerie and frightening.*" The police searched the area with floodlights and a tractor, but found nothing. The incidents were reported by the sheriff to the US Naval Station at Millington, 100 miles away from Union City.

(Source: *The Cincinnati Post*/*The Enquirer* – 'UFOs buzz Tennessee town, Stewart Dickson)

3rd October 1973 – Close encounter with UFO by truck driver, Missouri

Between 6.15am and 6.30am, truck driver Eddie Webb (45) of Greenville, Missouri, was driving his tractor trailer rig on Interstate 55, just south of the Jackson exit at Wedekind Park.

> "*I saw a bright turnip-shaped object approaching towards the rear of the truck, behind me, covering both lanes of the road.*
>
> *It appeared to have threes sections, the top and bottom ones being made of what looked like glittering aluminium and spinning.*
>
> *The centre section consisted of glittering red and yellow lights.*"

Eddie awoke his wife, who was in the car next to him, but she did not see anything out of the rear view mirror of the cab.

Eddie then stuck his head out, to look behind, and was blinded by a flash of light, which felt like a huge 'ball of fire' striking him in the face and eyes. His glasses fell off and he could not see, but fortunately managed to bring the truck to a stop.

Mrs Webb said:

> *"My husband screamed 'I'm burned, I can't see'. One of the lenses fell out of the plastic frame, which was warped. I then took over and drove him to the Southeast Missouri Hospital."*

Police Investigate

Sgt. Ed Wright, of the Highway Patrol, took Webb's glasses to a Dr. Harley Rutledge – head of the Southwest Missouri State University physics department – to be analysed. Rutledge, who had been working on UFO sightings in Piedmont, examined the spectacles under a microscope and concluded that:

> *"It appeared they were heated internally; the plastic got hot and the mould came to the surface. The heat warped the plastic, causing the lens to fall out."*

Tests were carried out to duplicate the damage, including a highway flare being passed back and forwards over the glasses, which produced similar results, after other truck drivers reported seeing a flare on the highway. Temporarily blinded, Mr Webb's vision began to return and there was no lasting damage. Asked by the press what had taken place, Mr Webb said:

> *"I just don't know what it was. People want me to say it was a 'flying saucer', but I can't say that – I just don't know. I always thought that people who saw these things were crazy. Now everyone thinks I am cracking up but, by God, I saw something and it blinded me."*

When he was interviewed by a staff writer from the *Southeast Missourian*, at his home, Mr Webb wore sunglasses and seemed exhausted and shaken by his experience. His forehead appeared slightly red, as if he had received mild sunburn, and he complained frequently of pain, which went deep inside his forehead and his eyes. He still flinched at bright lights.

(Source: Norman Oliver, *BUFORA Journal*, Volume 4, No. 2, Spring 1974 – 'UFO Fireball temporarily blinds truck driver')

Evening Courier, Thursday, September 13, 1973

Investigating those U.F.O. reports

SKY MYSTERIES EXPLAINED

CASE HISTORIES

5th October 1973 – Humanoids seen on Canadian farm

It is of interest to mention that a 'wave' of UFO sightings also took place in October 1973, time centered on the Canadian province of Quebec. They included reports of UFO landings, when humanoids were seen, disturbances to vehicles, and complaints of irradiation from some witnesses concerned. It was alleged that in the majority of the humanoid incidents, the entities appeared to be engaged in reconnaissance.

John Keel tells of an interesting incident, involving the appearance of an initial unusual 'light', seen apparently scanning the area on the night of the 5th October 1973, which was believed, by the farmer and his wife, at Chambly, Quebec, to be the police looking for cattle thieves, after cattle had been reported missing.

Thick smoke seen ascending onto field

The following morning, the normality of everyday life around the farm was interrupted by the arrival of a thick smoke seen ascending from a field – which was unusual, as it had been raining for a short time and the field had not been ploughed for a number of years.

UFO and small people seen

At 11.35am, a round yellowish object, resembling a cupola, some 75 feet in diameter, was seen from a distance of about a third of a mile away in a field. Although this was very odd, it was presumed by the occupant's at the farm to be boy scouts, camping – especially after five small people were seen who were approximately 4 feet tall, their legs hidden by the tall grass. What looked like a small bulldozer emerged from the 'tent' and made its way to a small spring, about 200 feet away from the 'tent'.

Strange visitor seen

According to the witnesses, the 'boy scouts', who were wearing what looked like some sort of yellow helmet on their heads, were continually busy, moving backwards and forwards between the 'tent' and the 'bulldozer'. When a cursory check was made of 'them', about 25 minutes later, there was no sign of the objects or the 'boy scouts'.

Large circle of burnt grass discovered

Enquiries made, following this incident, revealed that a neighbour had seen a large object take off from that field and head towards the nearby Rougemont Mountains. Shortly after midday, the daughter of the farmer returned home from work. On hearing what had happened, she went out to have a look and discovered a large circle of burnt and crushed grass, 55 feet in diameter, with paths 6ins across, leading to another smaller circle, 12 feet in diameter, close to a nearby spring.

The girl returned home but later felt very sick, developing a bad headache, nausea, and symptoms of suspected irradiation.

The incident was later reported to Philippe Blaquiere and Wido Hoville, members of the UFO Quebec group, who visited the location on the 4th November 1973. The men took some colour photographs of the circles and paths,which were still visible. They also noted the presence of two high voltage power lines to the west, and found a cyclical axis (a fold of rock layers that slope upward on both sides of a common low point. Synclines form when rocks are compressed by plate-tectonic forces. They can be as small as the side of a cliff or as large as an entire valley).

9th October 1973 – BBC on UFO subject

BBC open their door to the UFO researchers

THOSE mysterious UFOs — allegedly seen around Huddersfield recently — are to be featured on television on Saturday.

The North of England's leading researchers into unidentified flying objects reports will talk about their work on BBC2's "Open Door" programme, broadcast late on Saturday evening.

And among them will be the Yorkshire branch secretary of the British UFO Research Association, Halifax optician Mr Trevor Whitaker, who has been conducting investigations into the wave of reported sightings in Huddersfield's night skies.

"We will be appearing as members of the Northern UFO Network, which is a communications network of a dozen research groups covering the area from Cleveland to the Wirral," said Mr Whitaker.

"Our aim will be to show people that there are groups in existence which deal with the subject in a scientific manner, and to appeal to people who think they have seen UFOs to get in touch with us."

Appearing with him in the ten-minute programme slot they have been allocated will be the national chairman of BUFORA and representatives from the Manchester UFO Research Association, the Wirral UFO Society and the "Northern UFO News" magazine.

Mr Whitaker added that there had been another alleged UFO sighting in the Huddersfield area this week — the ninth in just over a fortnight.

A Batley man, who said he was an experienced sky observer and had always dismissed UFO reports, claimed to have seen a strange object early on Monday morning.

At first he took it to be a bolide or slow-moving meteor, but as it proceeded to do two banking turns he concluded that it could only be "some sort of vehicle."

Charles Hickson (left) and Calvin Parker

11th October 1973 – Close encounter at Mississippi, with three creatures

During the evening, shipyard co-workers – 42 year-old ˙Charles Hickson and 19 year-old Calvin Parker – told the Jackson County, Mississippi sheriff's office that they were fishing off a pier on the west bank of the *Pascagoula River*, in Mississippi, when they heard a whirring/whizzing sound, and saw two flashing blue lights, and an oval object 30-40 feet across and 8-10 feet high. Parker and Hickson claimed that they were *"conscious but paralyzed"*, while three creatures took them aboard the object and subjected them to an examination before releasing them.

Dr. Allen Hynek – chairman of the Northwestern University, Astronomy Department, said:

"There is no question in my mind that these men have had a terrifying experience. Their emotions and very strong feelings of terror are impossible to fake under hypnosis."

Sherriff Fred Diamond, of Pascagoula, confirmed that twelve other local people had reported seeing UFOs at that time. (**Sources: Numerous:** *The Sun*, **16.10.1973** – 'Aiens dragged us into UFO say terrified fishermen')

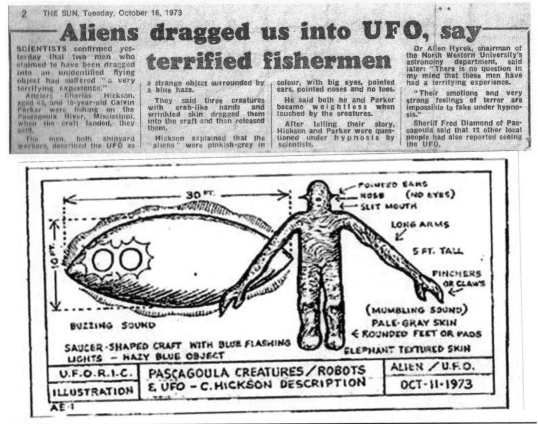

˙Charles Hickson – the chief claimant in the Pascagoula, Mississippi, UFO abduction case, died of a heart attack on 9th September 2011, at the age of eighty. Until his death he maintained the truth of his Alien encounter.

Charles Hickson

16th October 1973 – Allegation of alien abduction in Somerset

Italian born Mrs Gabriella Versilli was driving along the B3187 road to Wellington (A.38), and had just passed the turn-off on her right, to Langford Budville (some 6 miles from Taunton), when she glimpsed a very bright light in the fields ahead and to the right of her. At first she took no notice of it, although she was sure there were no buildings in that locality. All of a sudden, the car's headlights began to flicker and dim and then went out, accompanied by the engine spluttering and finally cutting out – the car then coming to a stop at the side of the road. Gabriella tried to start the engine, without success.

Half-moon shaped UFO seen – then humming noise and hand on her body!

Glancing around her, she noticed a half-moon, or hemispherical shape – flat on the top, with a rounded top, still at ground level – illuminating the grass with its dazzling light. Getting out of the car she opened the bonnet, hoping she may be able to sort out the problem, when she became aware of a humming sound – not unlike a generator, apparently emanating from all around her. She put the bonnet down and was about to open the driver's door, when she felt:

"…a strong hand, fall on my left shoulder, pushing my body down a few inches".

Metallic robot seen

Turning around, she was confronted by the sight of a tall, dark coloured, metallic robot!

She described the 'robot' as:

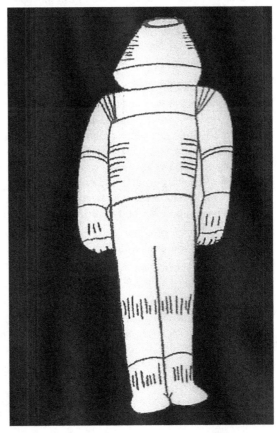

"…tall, over 6 feet – perhaps 6 feet, 6 inches, and seemed to be composed of some sort of shiny dark blue metal. Each time it moved, it made a knocking sound. On its head was a small oblong box device, with a glass panel on the front, containing a small velvet coloured light, which flashed not on and off but across the panel lengthwise, about a flash per second; the head, or helmet, had no human features – just vents, or openings, on the side. Similar vents were seen on the side of the body. It had glove like coverings on its hands, with a chain mail type thing – like on suits of armour – on its palms. The 'robot' had big boots with thick soles, and walked with a stiff movement of the legs, with arms at its side, and then I passed out."

She then became aware of standing in the field next to the 'robot', in front of a large object, in half rounded moonlight, its light having subsided, allowing her to see what was clearly some sort of machine – silver-grey in colour – not unlike aluminium in appearance, supported by thick legs, about two and a half feet high by two feet across. (Two were seen, there may have been more.)

Size of the UFO

The size of the object was estimated to be 20 feet by 40 feet and had large oblong windows around the middle, from which emanated a yellow light; *she then passed out for the second time.* When she gained consciousness, she found herself lying on top of a sheet of smooth rubbery substance on a grey table, about four feet wide by six feet long, bordered on the sides by a three inch in diameter shiny smooth tubular rail terminating in a flat end at the side of her head, in the middle of an icy cold circular room, covered by a light blue blanket. Her clothes had been removed; her wrists and legs were secured against the table by what looked like rubber bands. The floor was completely covered in three feet square sections of what she presumed was black rubber matting – like the sort used in cars, with the 'pimples' uppermost. On the walls could be seen a collection of wire coils – bits of metal. Over to her right was a grey console, with red, yellow, blue and green controls.

Three human looking men appear

Above her head could be seen two transparent tubes, plastic like in appearance, pointing down towards her head, the upper parts being fixed to the curved ceiling.

> *"Then three human looking men came into view, all about the same height – 5 feet 6 inches to 5 feet 8 inches – fair haired and slim. All wore similar garments – a skull cap, ending just above the eyes, tied behind the head, facial masks from the top of the nose to the chin, light blue tunics, with a grey metallic edging, long gloves reaching to the elbows with the normal complement of fingers that we possess on their 'hands', with a long apron going down to their ankles with thick sole boots on their feet. Two moved over to the left-hand side of the table and occasionally nodded their heads. They didn't appear to breathe at all, and at no time did I ever see their eyes blink."*

Retrieving specimens for study

The 'examiner' explained, after he had seen her looking at the 'robot' (still in the room), that he was *"a trained retrieval device to perform manual work outside the ship and bring specimens in for study"*. Three red, green, and probably white, six inch boxes, or cubes, were placed on the rail of the table – one near her feet, the other by her stomach, the last next to her head – which began to glow, one by one. The blanket was then removed. The 'examiner' took several small grey instruments from the far end of the table and obtained a small nail paring from her right index finger, whilst a small plastic bottle with tubes and wires was used to take a blood sample from her right arm. A miniature round device, held in the palm of his hand, was passed over her body, glowing brighter and dimmer as he did so.

> *"He also used a thin pencil-like instrument for probing and a large black rubber suction object which had a row of glowing lights, used mainly around the groin area, causing me discomfort."*

At this stage a black blanket was placed over her, as she was shivering from the cold. The cubes were then removed and placed on the floor, followed by all three men leaving the room.

> *"I lay there for several minutes, looking around, unable to move. My throat was painfully sore and I felt sick. The 'robot' stood immobile by the wall, its light flashing. One of the men then re-entered the room, walked over to the far end of the table next to the cubes, and lifted the blanket, staring, without any visible emotion. I tried to struggle but could only move my head. The man then placed a small pin-like device to my thigh, which made me feel numb and semi-paralysed – then he raped me."*

Afterwards, he produced a small blue cloth of sponge-like material to wipe her body, and left the room, after pulling the blanket down. The flashing light on the 'robot' had stopped.

The three men come back into the room

The three men came back into the room. One removed the pin from her thigh, whilst the other two lifted up the blanket, folded it, and placed it on the floor near the console. The bands were removed from her wrists. She then blacked out for a third and last time. Her next recollection was finding herself next to the car. Shaken, dazed and nauseated, she started up the car and drove away. She arrived home at 2.30am in a very distressed state and went to bed. The next morning, she told her husband what had occurred. After much discussion, they decided to try and forget the whole incident and say nothing to anyone, for perfectly understandable reasons. One cannot even imagine the level of ridicule and embarrassment a complaint of this kind would have attracted if the matter had been brought to the attention of the media.

Mysterious telephone calls

If things were not bad enough, worse was to come (if that's possible), when shortly before Christmas 1973, the family began to receive a number of peculiar telephone calls and anonymous postmarked letters – all addressed to Gabriella, all in the same ink and handwriting, just a few lines only, written on ordinary notepad paper – instructing to *forget what happened to her in October*, signed *'a friend'*. Unfortunately, each of these (up to 25 separate letters up to April1976) was burnt.

Visit from the 'Men in Black'

According to Barry King, right up to the time of the investigation made by him and Andrew Collins into the matter (first brought to his attention on the 12th October 1977), the couple received a number of visits from two sinister men – described as looking like father and son – both wearing thick black spectacles, who usually appeared in a black 'diplomat-style car' which had darkened windows, often seen cruising slowly around the area.

> *"The younger was about 25, tall and slim build, and he had short dark hair with a beatnik beard. He nearly always wore a roll neck sweater, black jacket, jeans and moccasins. The older was about 50, tubby, balding, and about five feet, six inches tall. He wore a brown overcoat, navy trousers, and boots. They never identified themselves or answered any questions put to them by us."*

The appearance of these two men and their unwarranted intrusion into the home of Mr and Mrs Versilli may seem difficult to understand, especially after the husband threatened them with the police – to which they replied:

> *"It would be very unwise, as there would be unpleasant repercussions."*

The sole topic of conversation, held with the husband and wife during these numerous visits, appears to have consisted of repeated warnings from the two men that they should forget about the matter for the sake of the couple's health, welfare and sanity – a threat the couple obviously took seriously.

According to Barry, the strange visitors – who would now be referred to in today's UFO climate as the 'Men in Black' – continued to keep in contact with the family right up to when he and Andrew Collins became involved, advising the couple they would be discontinuing their visits because the matter was in the hands of the investigators, and was being officially recorded – which doesn't appear to make sense, but of course, nothing about the UFO phenomena rarely does!

Since 1974, Gabriella was to be the subject of various examinations by several doctors and psychiatrists, who suggested she was hallucinating. We tried to find out the current whereabouts of Gabriella, who had been given various pseudonyms by other authors, over the years, but were unable to find her in person and believe she has either emigrated or changed her name.

(**Source: Barry King/Andrew Collins,** *UFOIN report/New BUFORA Journal***, April 2003, Issue number 8**)

17th October 1973 – Strange 'being' photographed at Alabama

Falkville, Alabama police chief Jeff Greenhaw received a phone call from an excited lady, during the evening, who said she had witnessed a *"spaceship"* land in an open field not far the town. Greenhaw responded, taking along his Polaroid camera, bearing in mind it was claimed that he received similar reports of UFOs being reported around the area.

He arrived at the location given at about 10pm, and after a cursory look around, he found no trace of any spaceship. As Greenhaw continued his search of the area, he was taken aback by the sight of an alien-like creature standing just off the side of the road.

The 'being' appeared to be wrapped in aluminium foil as it began to walk toward Greenhaw.

> *"It looked like his head and neck were kind of made together ... he was real bright, something like rubbing mercury on nickel, but just as smooth as glass – different angles give different lighting. I don't believe it was aluminium foil."*

Police chief Jeff Greenhaw displaying one of the photographs taken of the 'being'.

The tinfoil alien's movements were very mechanical like. An antenna was attached to his head. Though in shock, he managed to snap off four pictures of the odd looking Alien.

When he flicked on his headlights the alien was obviously frightened, as it began to make its escape. Greenhaw immediately took off in his truck in pursuit, but because of the rough terrain of the field, he was only able to manage 35 miles per hour.

The robotic movements of the alien were now in high gear, as it raced across the open field. Greenhaw could not keep up, and the 'being' escaped into the night.

"He was running faster than any human I ever saw." he stated.

Although Greenhaw was exhilarated by the strange encounter, he would soon regret the whole affair. He was mocked and ridiculed by many of the town folk, and he received threatening phone calls. A string of bad luck began to affect his life also. Whether related to his report or not, his house burned down and his wife left him. Approximately a month after the incident, the town council fired him. Greenhaw would eventually regain some semblance of a normal life, but he would always regret the night he met the mysterious 'figure'.

MUFON examined the photos

Greenhow later allowed MUFON to examine the negatives of the photos and they found them to be completely legitimate.

Not only did they find no sign of tampering, they found what appeared to be UFO-like objects on the negatives, which did not show up on the photos. However, Greenhow's life took a swift nosedive after the report of this encounter went public. Locals from the area all claimed that it was nothing more than a hoax by a bored police officer. The police force also took this view and fired him from his position immediately. His wife tired of all the ridicule, leading to divorce, and his family home burned down. Police chief Jeff Greenhaw had no reason to lie about this matter – he was well-known as a serious man and an excellent officer. He has always stood by his initial report on the incident.

(Sources: **Unknown newspaper – 'UFO Creature Breaks up Police Chief's marriage'**)

18th October 1973

At midnight, six brilliant white 'lights' were seen floating downwards through the sky over Luton, in Bedfordshire. They were then seen to drop to the approximate height of an aircraft approaching from the London area and change into a 'V'-shaped formation – now orange in colour and apparently rotating or pulsing – before disappearing over rooftops. (**Source: Mr J. Cowley, BUFORA**)

18th October 1973 – US helicopter encounters dome-shaped UFO

On this date, a four-man crew of an Army Reserve helicopter was flying ten miles east of Mansfield Air Force Base, Ohio, around

11pm, when they *"encountered a near mid-air collision with an unidentified flying object"*, according to the official report, signed and submitted by the crew after the incident. A full explanation for this terrifying UFO close encounter has never been offered and, to this day, the helicopter-UFO incident remains one of the most credible – and terrifying – in the history of the subject.

The commander of the helicopter Major Larry Coyne (35) and his crew – Staff Sergeant John Healy, First Lieutenant Arrigo Jezzi (at the controls) and Specialist Robert Yanasek – thought, at first, that the light on the horizon was a radio tower beacon.

Captain Lawrence Coyne

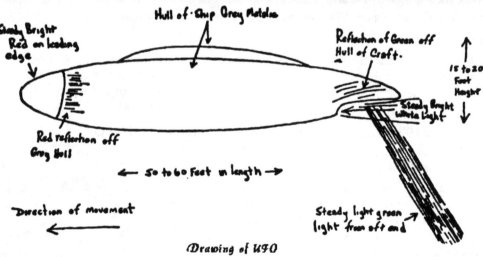

Hull of Ship Grey Metalee

Steady Bright Red on leading edge

Reflection of Green off Hull of Craft.

15 to 20 Foot Height

Steady Bright White Light

Red reflection off Gray Hull

← 50 to 60 Feet in length →

Direction of movement ←

Steady light green light from aft end

Drawing of UFO

"*We were flying along at about 2,500 feet, when the crew chief on the helicopter observed a red light on the east horizon. He then informed me that the light was closing on the helicopter, and that it was coming at us on a collision course. I looked to the right and observed that the object became bigger and the light became brighter, and I began to descend the helicopter toward the ground, to*

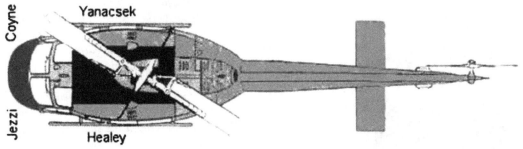

Positions of the crew members during the encounter.

get out of the collision course path. We were descending and this object was like a missile locked onto the helicopter – only it came at us on a perpendicular angle, to hit us almost broadside. It looked like we were going to collide with it and we braced for impact, and then I heard the crewmen in the back say, 'Look up!' and I observed this craft stopped directly in front of us — stopped — it was hovering, right over the helicopter!"

Further research into this incident by Jennie Zeidman can be found in Volume 22 of *Flying Saucer Review*, number 4, and Volume 23, of *Flying Saucer Review*, number 4, 1977)and reveals further eyewitness testimony – not from the crew but from a family on the ground. In addition, the exact location of the incident was about a mile and a half away to the west and the helicopter at lowest altitude and closest approach of the object was about 700 feet high, not 400 feet above the terrain as initially believed.

The witnesses – a mother and four children – were returning from their rural home, following a visit to the grandmother in Mansfield. As they drove south, they observed a single steady 'red light' – brighter than a normal aircraft port wing light – which was flying south, *"like a jet, at medium altitude"*.

31st October 1973 – Halloween mystery

Ronald Stone described a very odd experience which happened to him and his colleague, while driving between Countesthorpe and Foston, on the evening of the 31st October 1973.

"Just south of Leicester we narrowly missed hitting a fallen tree in the road, which gave us quite a shock, and decided to stop for something to eat and drink. After travelling some miles, we saw a sign for 'The village', on the main road. Despite it being a main road, it was a small metal sign, about 8-10 inches wide by 20 inches long, attached to an old unlit lamp post painted a dark colour blue with faded red lettering, pointing down an unlit lane. We turned right and came to a junction, where we noticed two 'figures' walking towards us. Peter, my colleague, wound his window down, in order to speak to them. As they grew closer, we saw they were identically dressed in black long cloaks, with a loose hood framing a long neck, showing small bald white heads, with black trousers and shiny black shoes. I shouted in alarm and drove away quickly, feeling frightened. It got

Ronald Stone

stranger. We drove down the road for a couple of hundred yards, and turned into a well-lit pub car park. It was a most charming pub, devoid of customers, glowing polished brass and a real burning log fire. I looked at my watch. It was 9.30pm. The barman asked us what we wanted. 'Two pints of Bass', I replied. He poured the drinks and asked us for two shillings. I was taken aback because, even in 1973, the cost of a pint of beer hadn't been a shilling (5 pence) for a long time. Although we had metric money, we did have a few coins of the old silver coinage on us and scraped the shillings together and paid him. After drinking our beer, without any sign of other customers, we hastily left, some minutes later, and found our way back through the village to Northampton, where I arrived home at 11pm, after dropping off Peter."

Ron Stone and Peter returned to the locality in daylight, a few weeks after the event, hoping to locate the public house, but found no trace of the building or the street sign. He still seeks the answer to what happened, over thirty-five years later. Who were the strange 'figures'? Were they dressed up for Halloween? Why could they never find the missing pub? Were they, in some way, catapulted back in time, or was there some other rational explanation? (**Source: Personal interview**)

NOVEMBER 1973

November 1973 – Mushroom-shaped object seen over Lincolnshire

Marjory Cammack from Gainsborough, Lincolnshire – employed as a care assistant at a local nursing home – was carrying out checks on the residents, at 6am, when she saw a large mushroom-shaped object hovering in the sky, flashing orange, red and yellow lights, underneath which could be seen smoke, or mist, billowing out of the base. (**Source: Richard Thompson**)

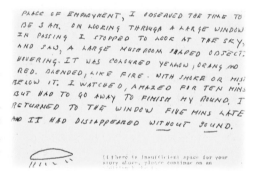

12th November 1973 – Unusual 'light' seen over Lincolnshire

At about 10.30pm on 12th November 1973, Mr John Spalding of Lincoln Road, Washingborough, sighted an unusual 'light' heading towards the direction of Lincoln, across the southern sky.

"It then stopped in the sky and was still there when I went to bed, at midnight. It was much too high to be a plane; I thought it was a satellite until it stopped dead. People may think I am barmy, but I know what I saw. The only explanation for the object is that it came from an outside intelligence."

This was not the first time John has seen something strange in the sky. In 1959, when aged 14, he and his mother were in Portland Street, Lincoln, when they sighted a grey, cylindrical object, heading across the sky. (**Source: South Lincolnshire UFO Study Group/*Lincolnshire Echo*, 14.11.1973**)

18th November – UFO sighted over Quebec, Canada

Another incident important enough to include, which excited our interest, apparently paralleling that of English citizen John Day, took place during the evening of the 18th November 1973, involving four young women, aged between 14 and 24, who were travelling to Montreal. Near Sorel-Tracy in southern Quebec, they noticed a luminous 'ball' – about the size of a water melon – hovering over a pylon, about a quarter of a mile ahead of their position. As the car passed this point, the object – which was described as being white in colour with a slightly yellowish tinge, surrounded by a thin halo, alternately dimming and shining – started to move, from right to left, before flying over the *Saint Lawrence River*. Within a short time, they realised that the object was now following them.

> "It seemed to move closer when we were passing through uninhabited districts and recede when driving through populated areas. Sometimes it was ahead of us; other times, it was behind. Its height constantly changed from 30 feet, to the height of low clouds. Before arriving at Contrecoeur a red and grey car overtook ours, at great speed. At that moment, the UFO ascended high in the sky. After leaving Contrecoeur the object stood still at poles height, far in front of us."

While still discussing the events and recovering from what had been a frightening experience, they saw the UFO fly towards the river and hover over a field. At that time they were in a line of cars, separated by approximately 6 feet and travelling at about 60 miles per hour. One of the women later said:

> "We were forced to slow down, due to the cars in front having to pass a pink 'cloud' lying down on the road, light red in colour, similar to and about the same length of four cars, joined together – the width of the road and the height of a car. We had no idea what was causing this 'cloud' to appear and were astonished by what was happening and forgot about the UFO – which was hovering over a field, to our left. Everything seemed very quiet and silent; our car was functioning well, and we have not felt any physical indisposition or psychological effect, neither at that moment nor since. In the 'cloud' we had to slow down to 20 miles per hour, but when we were clear I accelerated to 40 miles per hour, but had to reduce my speed again when we saw a car that had overtaken us – now in the ditch, with its headlights on, aimed at the road."

Small 'man' seen

Incredibly the story gets even more spectacular, when we learn of the following:

> "Just before we left the 'cloud', at 6pm, we saw the appearance of a small 'man', standing exactly on the white line of the road. I had to make a sudden manoeuvre, and stopped the car to avoid hitting him. This 'little man' seemed unconcerned with the passage of the vehicles and appeared to be sweeping or cleaning the road, even if the apparatus he was using seemed very unusual for that kind of job moving it back and forth exactly on the white line in the road. 'He' was wearing clothes that were dark green in colour, or black, and was only seen from the side. His head was covered in a peaked cap that hid his face. His legs were very short, as was his outer garment. He was about five feet tall."

She drove past, feeling angry that she might have hit the man and also tells of seeing another car stopped by the side of the road, a little farther up, with two or three persons, in dark clothing, stood next to it. On their return journey, at 8pm, she says the pink 'cloud' was still there but there was no sign of the car that had been in the ditch, and arrived home at 9.15pm.

One might think that this was the end of the story … not so.

Police sight oval UFO

• At **9.15pm,** a police officer of the Provincial Quebec Police sighted an oval object, above the parish of Saint Gerard-Majella.

• At **10.15pm,** two white parallel bars, resembling beads or globes, joined together, were seen to cross the sky in six seconds, heading in a south-east direction.

• Five minutes later, at **10.20pm,** a luminous 'ball' was seen, stationary in the sky over Sorel, some 20 degrees above the horizon. Its colour was seen to change from vivid blue to green, then to red. Fifteen minutes later, it had gone from sight.

• **At 10.30pm,** a luminous object, resembling an upside-down pear, with red and green lights on both sides, was seen motionless in the sky over the Boulevard industrial area, Joliette, estimated to be 100 feet above ground level. It then headed away slowly, southwards, before being joined by two other similar objects.

• **At 10.46pm** an object, described as looking like a truck's headlight revolving in a clockwise direction, was seen in the sky over Longueuil, on the south-eastern edge of Montréal. Seven minutes later, it moved away towards the Jacques-Cartier Bridge.

• **At 11pm,** numerous luminous spheres were seen performing an aerial display over Saint Thomas, Joliette and Berthierville (three 'globes' were seen) until the early hours of the next morning.

This was just the start of a heavy period of UFO activity – until now, long forgotten. It seems absurd that people still fight to convince us that the majority of UFO sightings can be explained away. The evidence is overwhelming in its implications and disturbing in nature.

(**Source: As above/***The UFO Register,* **Volume 7, Parts 1 and 2, Contact International, UK**)

Royal Canadian Air Force officer sights UFO

In the same month an ex-Royal Canadian Air Force officer, who had just left the force after serving five years – then living on a farm, a couple of miles from Greenwood Air Force Base, Nova Scotia – was looking out of the window, at 8pm, on what was a cold, clear, crisp night, with no moon and lots of starlight, when he noticed a 'bright light' above the horizon, but at first paid no attention.

"At first I thought it was landing lights from an aircraft coming in for a landing at the Greenwood base. After a minute or two, curiosity got the better of me and I grabbed my coat and went outside. I saw a white 'light' illuminating the horse coral from above; the horse was prancing around and acting skittish – then the 'light' began to slowly drift towards me. I immediately yelled out to my friend, Paul, to come outside. As the 'light' came closer, I could make out a circular, saucer-shaped object, about 40 feet in diameter, with a single white light coming from its centre.

By the time my friend, Paul, came outside, the object was still moving slowly towards me. There was no sound, except for a slight whistling noise – the kind of noise you might expect if a large object was passing through the air. It came to a complete stop when it was directly above us, bathing us both in light – bright enough to read a book.

The UFO was no more than 100 feet above our heads by this time. We were both totally in awe. Seconds later, a military tracker (CP-121) aircraft came roaring over the rooftop of our farmhouse from behind us. It seemed they were on a collision course. In a blink of an eye, the UFO made an abrupt 90 degrees evasive move, travelling 80 feet to the North. Even above the noise of the aircraft, we could both hear the whooshing sound of the object when it moved. The tracker aircraft made a steep bank to align itself with the UFO again, and put on full throttle to its engines, hell bent to intercept this hovering object. Within a matter of five seconds, the UFO had made three quick jolting movements, before I saw its lights disappear over the North Mountain, about 6 to 7 miles away. The tracker aircraft immediately throttled down its engines and returned towards the Greenwood Air Force Base."

After collecting his thoughts and realising what he had just witnessed, the man called a close friend (still stationed at the airbase), and asked him to contact Greenwood Control Tower and find out what was going on. To his amazement, he was told there had been no aircraft in the air at that time.

(**Source: UFOINFO.WWW, 2012**)

John Keel and his views

Dear Norman,

.... We are in the midst of a great wave here. It started last year and is continuing unabated but is receiving very little publicity. The innumerable sightings around Piedmont, Missouri this spring, and around Manchester, Georgia in August/September, have gained national attention, however if previous patterns are repeated, and if the flap continues, UFOs may become a momentary sensation again sometime next spring. In recent weeks there have been many sightings in the Catskill Mountains (where I spend most of my time these days) but I have not seen anything myself here. As you know from Dr. Schwarz's FSR articles on the " Woodstock UFO Festival " of 1966, this area had quite a wave during the 1966-67 peak ....

.... If a new publicity wave materialises I expect it will be quite different from those of the past. The anti-Air Force/anti-Government propaganda of the Keyhoe era will probably be absent. There will be greater emphasis on the psychological and philosophical aspects, and a number of sociologists and folklorists will surface with articles and books which will offer new perspectives and new approaches. A whole new storm will brew between the physical scientists and the behavioural scientists. The reality of UFOs as extraterrestrial vehicles will not only be seriously challenged, but a new set of explanations will be offered. As usual, these explanations will deeply offend the ET believers. The controversy will become more diffuse and certainly more complicated.

Since 1967 I have reluctantly supported Dr. Doel's first possibility (BJ, Vol. 3, No. 11, p. 29) " That in fact saucers don't exist, and we have been duped these many years." And I have been trying to determine exactly how this hoax has been accomplished and, more importantly, why? I do feel that the Fort/Sanderson viewpoint is the correct one, that all paranormal manifestions are interrelated, and that the core of this thing is the manipulation of human beings through what was known in other ages as magic and "enchantment." Space and Time being distorted, hallucinatory allegorical events are staged to cover up the real meaning and activities of the manipulative force. This is not a " Keel Theory " but is thousands of years old and a basic tenet of all theological concepts. Fort and Sanderson (and Keel and Vallee) attempted to simplify this, never claiming originality. Yet people like Alan Sharp are still grumbling about the " Keel Theories!"

I could cite hundreds of relatively obscure books which deal with the ufological problems in surprising ways (*e.g.* Bentham's THE THEORY OF FICTIONS, 1832) but it is my experience that hardcore ETists are not only poorly read but seem to choose to remain that way. The works of the great thinkers and observers of the paranormal of the past remain remote and even incomprehensible to the armchair ufologists. A scholarly friend of mine once remarked. " Never try to argue with a Marxist or a Hindu. They think they have the answer for everything." We might add ufologists to the list. They presuppose the intervention of extraterrestrials in all events, past and present .... just as Von Daniken finds evidence of the gods in every lump of carved stone.

No " Dark Force " turned me away from the ETH. Careful in-depth investigations into hundreds of UFO cases and bizarre events forced me to reject any belief and accept the available facts. The USAF and the RAF apparently underwent the same process in the 1943-55 period.

In one of his last interviews (PSYCHIC OBSERVER, February-March 1973, pp 150-55) Ivan Sanderson said, " It's been known to authorities for forty years now that they do not come to us through our space-time. They don't come from another planet. They come through from another set of dimensions, not another dimension or a fourth dimension, but they come from another whole universe, or whole bunch of universes which are interlocked with ours either in space or time. That's why we can't catch one, because they are not really here .... The intelligences behind certain types of them can make them just the way you, being a New Yorker, might expect in our technological age such a thing to be. Whereas for a primitive tribesman somewhere down in the Grand Cheaco they'll make it look a thing probably quite different, more like something he would know about .... They don't really *come* from anywhere."

john a. keel,
New York, USA.

We have nothing but praise for Mr Keel's views. Dr. Hynek himself suggested that UFO manifestations appeared to owe their origin to something more in keeping with the paranormal than the visitations of some extraterrestrial species. Apart from that, one is minded to ask what interest an advanced civilization would have in us. While UFOs have been with us down the ages, they have apparently made no direct effort to contact us as a race, if only to explain their presence on this planet. We have always felt that 'they' exist alongside us, going about their everyday business, *seemingly* having no interest in the affairs of man. One thing is assured, they won't go away and will continue to be seen in our skies, irrespective of whether we believe in them or not. When we set out to discover if there was any truth to UFO phenomena, many years ago, we never considered how prolific sightings had been. If we had found only a little evidence to support the existence of such phenomena, we would not we writing these books (especially bearing in mind that we are constantly being told by those in authority that they do not exist!)

24th November 1973 – UFO over Kent

Kent resident – Peter Hildebrand, and his friend – John, were fishing on the beach at Grain, in Kent, at around midnight.

Peter's friend brought his companion's attention to what he thought was a fishing boat out at sea, about a mile away, showing a very bright light. They put it to the back of their minds and continued fishing, but noticed, a short time later, that the light was approaching their position. Minutes later, it was now in line with the beach and about the height of a nearby army lookout tower.

Peter:

> "It then turned and came towards us. When it was about 60 yards away, we looked at it and were amazed. I have never seen anything like it before. We ran to the bank and lay down while continuing to keep our eyes on the object, which had stopped directly above John's Tilley lamp. There was no sound from it – not even a downdraught. It resembled a dirty, silvery-grey, giant clay pigeon, with a dome on top, and had oval windows showing a bright light. It hovered above the Tilley lamp for about five minutes, before moving away slowly, at walking speed, along the beach, towards Sheerness, and then became lost from view."

There have been many sightings of mysterious glowing white lights and orange spheres reported all along the coast of the *Thames Estuary* and *River Crouch* during the 1970 and 1980s. Groups of strange glowing lights 'flying in formation' were also seen.

Does the secret military testing area of Foulness hold the key to some of the strange objects seen over the *Thames Estuary* and local areas?

(Source: Southend-on-Sea UFO Group/*BUFORA Journal*/March/April 1978/Mr J. Castle/Mr Larry Dale)

30th November 1973 – UFO, with occupants, seen over Nuneaton

At 6.45pm, Nuneaton resident – Michael Currie (16), reported sighting an unusual 'craft' hovering silently above his house, estimated to be 20-25 feet long, pointed at both ends, with five large oval windows along its length, brightly-lit from the inside, showing no sign of any external lights, propulsion, flight or control surfaces.

> "Inside the craft were three occupants, one facing me at the back edge of the first window, apparently looking at the wall between the first and second windows, a second on the far side in the same position with his back to me, while a third walked past the front window towards the front of the object, allowing me to see their top halves. They were wearing grey coloured clothing, had shoulder length gold/blond hair, and were human in appearance."

The 'craft' moved very slowly, at apparent walking pace – then flew over the neighbour's house, at a height of about 40 feet off the ground, and disappeared (**Source: www.ufowatch.com/sightings/display**)

DECEMBER 1973

10th December 1973 – Triangular UFO seen over Essex

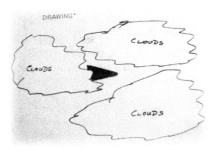

William Anderson (then aged 87) of 16, Trafalgar Road, Clacton-on-Sea – an ex first mate in the Merchant Navy, who had served during the Second World War – was out shopping with his wife. William was stood outside waiting for his wife at 1.50pm, and looked up into the sky, when he saw:

> "...in the middle of three white clouds, drifting over the town, a dark object; it looked like half saucer. Five seconds later it was covered by cloud."

December 1973 – Red pulsating 'ball' seen over Essex

A few days before Christmas, a mysterious array of lights was seen in the sky over Abridge, Essex, one late evening, by resident – Caroline Ebborn:

> "I saw a red pulsating 'ball' next to the moon, which began to rise upwards into the sky, changing shape to a diamond with bright yellow lights at each end and neon red lines at the rear. It reminded me of a jet on take-off. After a while, a pale green fluorescent light appeared."

Caroline was not the only one to see the UFO. Two other Epping residents also described seeing *"a similar object"* later, the same evening. (**Source:** *West Essex Gazette*, 4.1.1974)

1973 – UFO over Orpington, Kent

During 1973, Graham Brooke and his then girlfriend – Julie Taylor, had been to a party held at Orpington Hospital, but left early at 8.15pm. They were walking towards Sidcup, along the Orpington Road, as darkness fell, when they saw something moving through the sky, above the road.

> *"It stopped in front of us, at an angle of about 50-60 degrees. It's hard to say how big it was, because there was nothing nearby to compare it with – it could have been small and close, or huge but further away.*
>
> *I would say it may have been 300 yards away and was as big as a football pitch. It was a 'flying saucer'. It had a round panel underneath, which turned slowly, and about seven illuminated panels that gave off a glow, rather than a beam. It stopped in front of us as we stopped walking, and just stayed there for a few seconds. It must have seen us. It then altered its direction by turning left and away, over some trees. We ran across the road and stood on a small brick wall, but it disappeared over the trees.*
>
> *We were flabbergasted and really excited; we couldn't wait to tell someone – anyone – so we flagged a car down and two guys stopped. We told them and asked for a ride to Sidcup. They didn't believe us and made fun of us, but when we asked them the time – it was now 11.10pm. We only left the nurses' quarters at 8.15pm, which seemed like less than half an hour ago. We were as shocked about the time as we were the sighting."*

Update 1972

24th June 1972 – Rocket-shaped UFO seen over Berkshire

Alan Shepherd from Hartland Road, Reading, Berkshire, whose multi-witness sightings are reproduced below, (thanks to the late Essex-based UFO researcher – Ron West), told of another sighting which took place in mid-summer 1972, when aged 40. This one took place at 9pm.

> *"My wife and I spotted this rocket-like object in the sky, about 200 feet high, heading silently in an east to west direction, before turning sharply to the south. There were flames shooting out of the back; no wings or tail fins were seen. I estimated it was about 60 feet long. We stood rooted to the spot; my hair was standing on end. It was so low we could see it clearly. A few seconds later it made a sharp turn left and headed away, at approximately 35 miles per hour."*

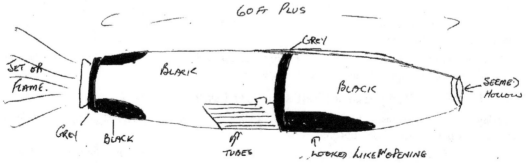

Update 1973

6th August 1973 – 'Flying Saucer' over Reading

Alan Shepherd of Hartland Road, Reading, Berkshire, and his son, David, were walking through their local park, at 8.50pm.

Tracing of witness's sketch.

> *"Suddenly, a dark grey saucer-shaped object, showing a row of white lights around its centre with what appeared to be some kind of door on top, appeared in the sky in front of us, about 150 feet away, hovering 5-6 feet above a stream. We stopped and stared at it for a couple of minutes. The stillness was eerie.*
>
> *We could see people walking about; a couple had just walked by. Suddenly it vanished, and the next thing we became aware of was the couple walking away from us."*

(Source: Ron West)

Its fair to say that while we found the reports very interesting and judged genuine by Ron we would have liked to have seen details of the family in order to not only confirm that authenticity of what was claimed but also to obtain additional details, especially bearing in mind that the above sighting occurred in John Rabson Park which was the venue for a spectacular sighting in 1969 covered in *Haunted Skies* Volume 2 Revised.

11th October 1973 – Police vehicle attacked by a UFO!

Twenty-four hours after the claims made by Charles Hickson and Calvin Parker was a report from Louisiana, 150 miles away, by a Sheriff's deputy, who claimed that after seeing five strange objects in the sky, his car was *"attacked by an orange-red object"*.

The sighting was apparently confirmed by a number of other people. Deputy Sherriff Michael Moor said:

> *"One of our deputies was scared pretty badly."*

At Slidell, on Lake Pontchartrain, Louisiana, Lloyd Mercer told police he also witnessed a glowing red object, about 15 feet in diameter, in the sky.

(Sources: Unidentified newspaper articles, 15.10.1973 – 'US Cops attacked in new UFO flap.'/ 'Aliens dragged us into UFO say terrified fishermen', 16.10.1973)

Sketch showing the incident at Pascagoula in 1973

CHAPTER 5 – 1974

ONE OF THE 'BEATLES', JOHN LENNON, SIGHT UFO OVER MANHATTEN, USA

JANUARY

3rd January 1974 – UFO over Lowestoft

6th January 1974 – Golden UFO seen over Norfolk

11th January 1974 – Harrowing sighting for Derbyshire Police Officers

23rd January 1974 – Motorist encounters rectangular object

23rd January 1974 – Explosion over the Berwyn Mountains, Wales

FEBRUARY

February 1974 – Chris Evers – UFO over Kingston-upon-Hull

19th February 1974 – Minnesota police officer chases UFO

MARCH

1st March 1974 – UFO and creature seen

2nd March 1974 – Strange 'stars' over Lincoln

10th March 1974 – Strange lights sighted over Reading

20th March 1974 – Landed UFO … shots fired!

23rd March 1974 – UFO photographed

31st March 1974 – Strange 'star' seen over Lincolnshire

Spring 1974 – Egg-shaped UFO seen over Bournemouth, Dorset

APRIL

8th April 1974 – UFO hovers over motorist

April 1974 – Motorist encounters UFO over Maidenhead

30th April 1974 – Landed UFO at New York, USA

MAY

May 1974 – Strange Encounter at Farnborough, Hampshire

7th May 1974 – UFO landing, occupants seen

11th May 1974 – Close Encounter, Bedfordshire

28th May 1974 – UFO over Worcester

28th May 1974 – Landed UFO

Summer 1974 – UFO over Combe Martin, Devon

JUNE

6th June 1974 – 'Spinning top' UFO over New England, USA

7th June 1974 – Two brilliant 'lights' seen moving over Worcester

12th June 1974 – UFO display

Mid-June 1974 – UFO display over Birmingham

14th June 1974 – Pulsing object hovers over trees at New Hampshire, USA

20th June 1974 – UFO display, Bournemouth

21st June 1974 – Metallic object reported in the sky over Lincolnshire

22nd June 1974 – Strange 'lights' over Devon

22nd June 1974 – Strange 'lights' over Fort McCoy, Wisconsin, USA

29th June 1974 – UFO over North Carolina

JULY

6th July 1974 – UFO over London

10th July 1974-Strange being seen at Warminster

12th/13th July 1974 – Reservoir emptied at Banbury!

18th July 1974 – Beeping noises heard over Gloucestershire

22nd July 1974 – UFO over Lexington

July 1974 – Three UFOs sighted over Hampshire

31st July 1974 – Three 'lights' seen over Watford – did the RAF respond?

AUGUST

Curious phenomena over London

1st August 1974 – Orange object sighted over Carolina

2nd August 1974 – Two UFOs over Idaho, USA

8th August 1974 – Saucer-shaped UFO seen over East Sussex

10th August 1974 – Close encounter, Dagenham

12th August 1974 – Red sphere over Leicestershire

12th August 1974 – Mississippi motorist Chased by a UFO

14th August 1974 – UFO over Cheltenham, Gloucestershire

20th August 1974 – UFOs over Surrey

20th August 1974- UFOs over Surrey

20th August 1974 – Light display over New York

23rd August 1974 – John Lennon and May Pang sight UFO

August 1974 – UFO over Hertfordshire

1974 – Giant UFO over Hampshire

SEPTEMBER

19th September 1974 – Three dark red 'lights' sighted over Washington

24th September 1974 – UFO over Dorset

29th September 1974 – UFO over Portsmouth

JANUARY 1974

3rd January 1974 – UFO over Lowestoft

Schoolboys playing on Beccles Common, near Lowestoft, ran home in fright after a *"cigar-shaped object passed overhead"*, accompanied by a loud noise (from which the boys were to develop headaches), before dropping below the horizon.

6th January 1974 – Golden UFO seen over Norfolk

On this day, a family was visiting Ashby Church (four miles north-east of Aldeby) when they noticed:

> *"...a golden metallic object, motionless in the clear blue sky, towards the south-east – which vanished from sight, a few minutes later".*

To their astonishment, ten minutes later, a dark grey 'cigar' appeared from behind cloud in the south-west, heading slowly towards the south-east, before disappearing and reappearing in a different part of the sky.

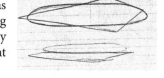

At 8.30pm, the same day, John Guthrie from Bordon, in Hampshire, was driving home along the A3, towards Hindhead, with his mother, along a stretch of new dual carriageway, still under construction, when they noticed a 'bright light' in the western part of the sky, at an estimated height of between 2-300 feet, some 400 yards to their right. He said:

> *"I wound down my window and reduced speed, in order to observe this rather strange object, which was long, diamond in shape, brightly-lit all around on top. I knew from its shape and the absence of any navigation lights it was no aircraft. By the time I stopped the car and got out, it had gone."*

(Source: Ivan W. Bunn, 'The Lantern' Series/Frank Marshall, BUFORA)

11th January 1974 – Harrowing sighting for Derbyshire police officers

Walter Buswell – a retired police officer from the Derbyshire Constabulary – spoke of an experience which was 'to scar him mentally for life'.

> *"I was on night duty, at 11.42pm on 17th January 1974, in the front passenger seat of a police car being driven along the A50 trunk road, near Mayfield Golf Course – a fine dry night with good visibility – when I noticed a number of unusual lights, low down in the sky, and brought it to the attention of the driver – 'Mo', PC Maurice Barsley, who suggested they were probably the Northern Lights. Suddenly, without any explanation, or further discussion, Maurice stopped the police car in the middle of the road, got out, and walked to the side of the road, where he stood listening intently. I shouted out to him 'What's the matter?'*

Maurice replied,

> I don't know, Walter … that noise'. I listened carefully, but couldn't hear anything, somewhat puzzled by my partner's out-of-character behaviour. I wound down the window of the car and immediately heard what sounded like the noise of a loud engine coming from the left, together with a noise similar to a child's spinning top and a high-powered flame gun. I looked around the bleak landscape, hoping to identify the source of these three strange sounds – unlike anything I had ever heard before in my life."

Walter picked up the radio telephone and contacted the force control room, after explaining what was happening. They advised him to observe and report back.

> "I got out of the police car and stood in front of the vehicle – the noise still quite loud and continuous. A man on a motor scooter rode past us, stopped, got off his machine and ran over to us in a very agitated manner, saying, 'I hope you don't think I'm barmy, but I have been followed by this bright light'. Unsure of how to deal with the situation, I advised him to seek shelter with us and updated Force control room. We decided to move from our present position on the hill to flat ground, so as to obtain an uninterrupted view of the open countryside, taking the frightened witness with us. The first thing l noticed was a bright light, low down in the sky, that suddenly vanished but reappeared a couple of minutes later, now to the left of its original position, before reappearing at another location.

> A bright light appeared in the sky to our right – far brighter than the one previously seen – accompanied by an increase in volume.

> A brilliant thin beam of light then either shot upwards from the ground into the sky, or the other way around. It happened so quickly, illuminating the landscape in the near distance – then extinguished. This was followed by a red 'light', which shot off across the sky. Darkness then returned."

Mystery helicopters

Was there any connection with what was seen by the officers and a spate of what became referred to as the appearance of 'mystery helicopters' seen around Cheshire and Derbyshire during this period? In the *Derbyshire Times*, dated 18th January 1974, it was reported that police were baffled by the same mystery helicopter, as it had been seen in the Macclesfield area, where they had kept it under constant observation before it disappeared towards the High Peak region.

The Macclesfield Police Force contacted the Derbyshire Police and alerted them to the elusive helicopter, which was sighted by patrol men heading over Mam Tor in the Vale of Edale. The police set off in pursuit, but lost sight of it when it changed its heading and disappeared in the direction of Sheffield. There was another report, at the same time, that the helicopter had made a landing close to Jodrell Bank radio telescope in the small village of Goostrey. A total of seven police forces were involved in attempting to identify this mysterious helicopter by January 1974, and although many more sightings were made of this mysterious night flying helicopter, no civilian or army helicopters were found to be responsible to this day. (**Source: Personal interviews**)

Over the United States – three UFOs sighted by family

In the same month we learn of a sighting by Frank Pilon, his wife, and ten year-old daughter. They were driving to the town of Washington, in New Jersey, and passing through Spruce Run, near to a large power station, when they saw three objects in the sky approaching their position and thought, initially, they were aircraft. Believing that the objects were on a collision course, the family pulled up. The three objects were then seen to simultaneously break formation while making a 45 degree turn – seconds later, they were out of sight.

"As the lead object passed overhead its glow intensified, shooting upwards at a high rate of speed; one light changed from a definite white to a blurred glow, remaining visible in this position for about five seconds. Again, simultaneously, one went north, the other west and the last to the east. They were completely silent." (**Source: [NICAP]** *The UFO Investigator*, **December 1974**)

23rd January 1974 – Motorist encounters rectangular object

Mr Trevor Duell was heading home, southwards, towards Liphook, along the Guildford bypass, at 8.10pm As he began the journey towards the summit of the hill, with Guildford Cathedral on the left of the A3 he saw some lights in the distance, which he thought might be connected with the construction of the new bridge. After realising this could not be the case, as the lights were now hovering about 200 feet above the bridge, he stopped the car and got out, finding he was almost directly under the lights – now visible as two beams of light, projecting downwards from a rectangular shape in the semi-darkness. At this point several other cars pulled up. The drivers stood or sat watching the completely silent object, estimated to be 20 feet long by 10feet wide, illuminated by red and green navigation lights, showing no sign of any tail or wings. Ten minutes later, the 'craft' turned slightly and headed away northwards, towards the direction of Guildford. The following night, a similar UFO was seen over Farnham.

(**Source: Omar Fowler, SIGAP/PRA**)

23rd January 1974 – Explosion over the Berwyn Mountains, Wales

At 8.38pm, a huge explosion shattered the peace of the night sky around the villages of Bala, Llandrillo, and Llandderfel, situated next to the Berwyn Mountains. Little did anyone suspect, in their wildest dreams, then, that this incident was to lead to huge media curiosity – still current, despite the passing of many years.

It has been the subject of hundreds of newspaper articles published, and extensive coverage by both radio and TV documentaries.

Explanations offered

Typically in matters like this – where due to a lack of substantive evidence to confirm exactly as to what the cause of this was – rumours quickly spread like wildfire, dependant on individual belief systems, which are often, in the main, dictated by personal financial gain rather than applying the rule of common sense based on the available evidence. These range from rational to the bizarre and have, and still do, include:

1. – An alleged landing of an Alien craft, followed by the recovery of small Alien bodies covertly extracted from the scene by the military.
2. – Top secret aircraft that crashed.
3. – Earthlights.
4. – Misidentification of natural phenomenon.

It was never our intention to write this matter up in any length, taking into consideration the numerous and varied accounts published over the years, by people such as Andy Roberts – *UFO Down; The Berwyn Mountain UFO Crash,* Margaret Fry of the Welsh Federation of Independent Ufologists (who has conducted her own research through investigation into this matter, which was published in her book *Link to the Stars,* 2009), and fellow UFO researcher Scott Felton, whose burning determination to uncover the truth behind this and other incidents does them credit. However, we felt the incident warranted the presentation of what actually happened, rather than depending on other sources which should be treated as dubious to say the least. In addition, we remain perplexed as to why (even more so in the second decade of the 21st Century, when one might have logically thought the press would have treated the matter with some concern) the National Newspapers continually (especially on-line) denigrate reports from members of the public, who simply want an answer for what they have seen.

Tony Dodd – claims of crash landing and alien bodies recovered!

UFO could have been a flare ~~UFO's~~

AN UNIDENTIFIED flying object seen heading out to sea by several High Salvington residents on Thursday afternoon was most likely a flare dropped by an aircraft to test wind velocity, Worthing police told the Gazette.

Miss Diane Medwell, of Woodland Avenue, High Salvington, and her mother saw it over their house apparently heading out to sea over the Goring Ferring area.

'It was like a red flare, or burning, and after a time black wavy smoke came out of the back,' she said.

They saw it for about four minutes continuously before it disappeared. Mr P. Webb, of Hayling Rise, High Salvington, also saw the UFO, and was one of several people who reported it to the police.

WEDNESDAY 23 JAN 1974

Tony Dodd

One of the sources behind the suggestion of a recovered UFO was retired Police Sergeant Tony Dodd – then head of UFO investigations for Quest International. He told of being contacted by a high ranking military officer ......

> *"He told me that the military had been put on standby alert, three days before a UFO would be landing on a lonely mountain range in North Wales. On the 19th they proceeded to the border town of Chester. At 8.13pm on the 20th they were told to proceed to Llangollen North Wales, where they split into four groups. At 11.36pm they made their way to the Berwyn area and decamped in a car park of the above and to the side of the B4391, which cuts through to the top of the mountain before making its way to the village of Llangynog. Soldiers then arrived from the mountainside carrying oblong boxes, which were loaded onto the officer's vehicles.*
>
> *The informant told me he was ordered to take the boxes to Porton Down, Wiltshire.*

When they arrived the boxes were then opened in front of staff there, who were astonished to see what appeared to be two dead alien bodies; they were 5-6 feet tall and thin, and looked almost like skeletons covered with skin."

It was brought to Tony's attention that the incident had not happened until the 24th January.1974. He suggested the possibility that a second UFO had gone to the assistance of the first one, which had crash-landed on the Berwyn Mountains.

This was not the only time we were to hear of what we believe to be a wild story without any substance.

Terry Hooper – similar story told

According to Bristol-based UFO researcher "Terry Hooper-Scharf, in 1990, an Army Air Pay Corps officer of Flight Lieutenant rank contacted him by telephone, and told him that he and a colleague – who were then members of an operational Unit (unnamed but still in existence today) – were instructed by their Commanding Officer to take part in an I.O. (In and out job), in 1974.

Andy Roberts

The man admitted he was part of an army unit that travelled up past Birmingham, and arrived at Llangollen on the 20th January 1974. (If this was true it would corroborate what was told to Tony Dodd, with regard to his suggestion that the military were expecting this 'object' to land). According to this man (whose identity was not disclosed, surely degrading the reliability of his information), he was part of a troop of soldiers that escorted a number of oblong boxes to Porton Down, Wiltshire, and he and the others were warned that if they opened the boxes they would be arrested, and if they resisted arrest they would be shot! The man also claimed that ...

> *". . . a pilot friend of his had flown Army men to Berwyn Mountain with containers in three army helicopters to the mountains, which they filled with wreckage and flew to Porton Down!"*

Silver fragments claimed to have been from the UFO

The informant then sent Terry four silver fragments from the RAF man, that was claimed to have been taken covertly from the debris, which was taken to Porton Down, near Salisbury, Wiltshire – a place that, to the layman, is sinisterly synonymous with germ warfare. Now known as Defence Science and Technology

"Terry Hooper-Scharf is editor/publisher of a number of books and comics that can be found on *Lulu. com* under the *Black Tower* imprint, formed in 1984. Over the years he has also helped promote creators, written articles as a comic media journalist, and interviewed creators from the UK, USA, Australia, New Zealand and Europe. He is a UK Police Forces wildlife consultant on exotic species and has interviewed witnesses, written reports, and dealt with local/national BBC and Independent TV and Radio as an expert guest.

Laboratory, an Executive Agency of the Ministry of Defence (MOD), Terry gave the samples to two separate parties, who promised they would analyse them – but these were never returned.

The fourth, some 2 inches x 2 inches, he sent to UFO researcher – Margaret Ellen Fry. This arrived at her house on the 23rd January 1997.

Margaret:

> *"I gave this fragment to Roy Winch – a family friend – who was knowledgeable with aircraft components, both in the UK and the USA. He told me that it was not aluminium, lithium steel, iron and wasn't magnetic. The silver fragment was slightly pitted and scratched and was light as a feather, yet impossible to bend, flatten or scratch. When we first had the fragment we noticed it showed complicated patterns of circles and, at one time, four three-dimensional florets – which have now faded."*

Margaret later gave us the samples contained in the matchbox.

Terry Hooper – metal from the Bristol Bus Company

Terry:

> *I know exactly what and where the fragments of metal I had come from. I even obtained other samples. It was sheet alloy used by the then Bristol First Bus Company in their Winterstoke Road depot, Bristol.*
>
> *I explained this is full detail to Margaret Fry and ascertained the impressions in the metal were*

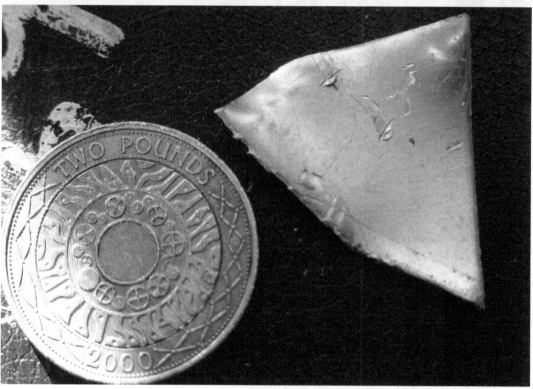

achieved by using a hammer, while the alloy was on a concrete surface – traces of concrete are in the scratches. The 'florets' that later disappeared were NOT present in any sample. My book contains photos of the fragments, which DO NOT show any such 'florets'."

Nick Reiter

We confirmed this was the case and that it was aluminium alloy, after examination by US scientist Nick Reiter – a well respected member of the scientific community and a privilege to know. Sadly, he passed away at an early age. Our condolences to his family.

"I have the photographs to prove it. I do not agree with any conclusions reached by Margaret Fry, who told me that I had been 'duped' and the facts I provided had been 'fed' to me my government agencies. I deny any accusation of being a government agent, or acting as an agent provocateur. This case was part of an Anomalous Observational Phenomena Bureau investigation and not down to some naive 'Ufologist' but one active since 1974. Every aspect was looked into, investigated and meticulously reported on, based on evidence not fantasy. The MOD statement is spot on. There never was any crashed 'UFO'/'flying saucer'/'extraterrestrial craft' as described. No Army special forces were involved in 'UFO retrieval' and the accounts seemingly accepted show an absolute lack of any knowledge as to what would happen and procedures if any Alien craft fell to Earth."

23rd January 1974 – The Event

At 8.38pm on 23rd January 1974, a ten mile stretch of the Berwyn Mountain range, between the B4391 Bala to Llangynog road, that included the villages of Llandderfel, Llandrillo and Cynwyd, were shaken by a strong earth tremor – its epicentre being some 5,000 metres below the town of Bala. As a result of this tremor many people came out of their houses, curious as to the cause of the loud 'explosive 'noise. Some saw 'beams of light' over the ridge of Cefn Pen-Llety, which rises steeply above Llandrillo towards the peak of Cader Bronwen Mountain, and thinking it might have been the result of an aircraft, striking the ground, telephoned the police – who set up a major incident log, instructing police officers to make their way to Llandrillo to conduct a search and rescue, where they were joined by a three-man team from RAF Valley Search and Rescue.

Police Officers conduct search

The officers arrived in the yard at Garthiaen Farm, situated below the lower pastures of Cader Bronwen, at 9.10pm, and spoke to Huw Lloyd – the teenage son of the occupants. Huw agreed to drive the officers along the farm tracks above Llandrillo in his Land Rover.

A few minutes into the journey, they found their passage partly blocked by a car belonging to local men, out 'lamping' – (shining a large powerful beam of light along the field, to disturb rabbits and hares, before setting dogs onto them) – an action which illuminated the area, seen by some of the villages from below. Whether those 'beams of light' were the ones seen by the residents, or associated with the object later sighted by Nurse Evans, can only be conjecture.

Despite a drive around by the party concerned, who chose to stay inside the vehicle rather than conducting any search on foot – which would have been impractical at that time of night, understanding the terrain of Cader Bronwen – nothing was seen out of the ordinary, apart from a brief white glow in the terrain to the south.

District Nurse Pat Evans sights UFO

Another witness to the mysterious sound and tremor felt was District Nurse – Pat Evans, from Llandderfel, who, thinking that it might have been caused by an aircraft, crashing, contacted the police at Colwyn Bay, to offer medical assistance, just before 9.30pm. Due to the telephone lines 'being heavy with traffic', she was told to *"go and have a look"*. Despite knowing officers were searching land above Llandrillo and a major log being opened, Mrs Evans was not given any specific location. [It is reported that the bright 'ball of fire' observed over a large area was at 9.58pm – almost one hour and twenty minutes after the explosion.]

Mrs Evans decided to make her way up to a vantage point on the B4391 road, which leads up and over the Berwyn Mountain range (some 15 minutes travel time from her home) accompanied by her teenage daughters – Diane and Tina – both of whom possessed basic first aid training.

Pat Evans

Diane Evans

Tina Evans

Moon sized object sighted on the side of the hill

When they arrived at the road summit, the mother and two daughters were astonished to sight:

> "...a massive full moon sized object, glowing and pulsating on the dark hillside. We didn't see it land or take off. We saw some vehicle lights in the distance and small torch-like twinkling lights around the object itself, which we took to be rescuers lights. We judged the object was about a mile away and impossible to get to easily on foot, so we decided to return home. However, we did hear that something loud had taken off about ten minutes after leaving the scene."

After watching it for a few minutes they drove along the road, turned around, and continued to observe it for a little longer.

It is now believed that the vehicle lights seen were the police conducting their search of Cader Bronwen (approximately four miles away from their position), who would not have seen the UFO because of undulations of land which would have hidden it from them. Unknown to the women, the same object *was seen by several other witnesses* – one of whom told of observing it initially at 8.40pm, and then later watching it slowly descend onto Cader Bronwen by 9.25pm.

The next day, after an unsuccessful search was made of Cader Bronwen by police and the RAF team (despite no aircraft having been reported missing) – this search being officially completed just after 2pm in the afternoon of the 24th – contrary to popular belief, there is no evidence of them having conducted any search of Cader Berwyn.

Huw Lloyd

Huw Lloyd, who guided the police up to Cader Bronwen on the 23rd January, claimed the RAF team (only) was spotted searching Cader Berwyn later in the afternoon. This probably resulted in gossip circulating locally. Pat Evans and her daughters was the subject of humour directed against them of having encountered 'Dynion bach qwrydd' ('little green men').

Scott Felton – The price of courage

"Pat Evans regrets ever having reported this matter and was effectively hounded out of her home by disrespectful UFO enthusiasts. These days she spends much of her retirement abroad – small wonder that people who treat others like this are incapable themselves of analysing evidence and testimony and presenting it correctly. She got hardly a moment's peace and in so harassing this woman, UFO enthusiasts themselves have probably done as much harm to this event's case as the debunkers. Fortunately, Mrs Evans is well but equally unhappy about being misrepresented by virtually everyone with whom she has spoken about the event, apart from North Wales based UFO researcher – Margaret Fry. Nor would she knowingly give any information to anyone, directly or indirectly, which would be used to debunk her claim of what both she and her two daughters saw."

Egg shaped.
Defused no light.
Well defined.
More pointy than real.

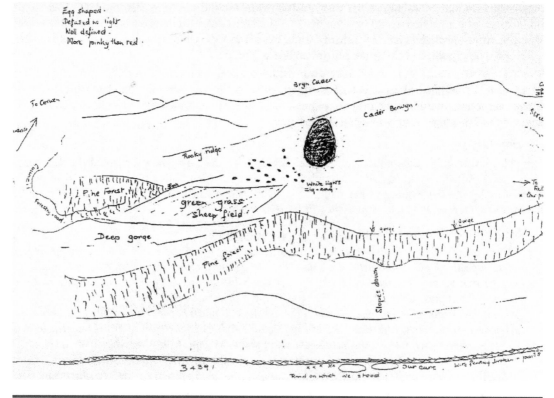

Margaret Fry

No UFO crash

"To this day, there are some who persist in claiming three witnesses saw a poacher's lamp, rather than an Alien craft – which is inaccurate, as the poachers had left the mountain range completely 45 minutes before that particular witness observation, and testimonial prove that police officers <u>did not</u> conduct a foot search and thus their torches were mistakenly seen, and – most important of all – it omits the fact that the UFO and the poachers/police were actually on two totally different mountains, several miles apart. Another debunker deliberately omitted records of the distance travelled by Mrs Evans and the distance concerned, which showed several miles difference; the idea being that a search had been carried out by the Emergency services on Cader Berwyn when, in fact, it was Cader Bronwen, some four miles away from where the UFO was seen – not forgetting that the poachers were not even on the range after 9.30pm when reports of activity on Cader Bronwen (above Llandrillo) began to come in – the authorities carried out a search of that location (the wrong location). Without Mrs Evans, and her daughters' eye-witness accounts, there would be no Berwyn Mountain case at all. Contrary, there is too much of the rubbish bandied about in books and reports and on the Internet."

Scott Felton at the location of the incident

This week's TV

DOCUMENTARY
BRITAIN'S
CLOSEST
ENCOUNTERS
FIVE Wednesday

The sightings were like those in movies such as Close Encounters Of The Third Kind

NEW

My close encounter

One man shares his amazing story of the day an alien spaceship visited his street

In the middle of the night, Adrian Roberts awoke to a scene that could have been in alien movie Close Encounters Of The Third Kind. He saw bizarre lights in the sky and felt the earth shake!

Adrian was one of dozens who were stunned by what they saw on 23 January 1974 in the Berwyn Mountains, Wales. The alien sightings have never been explained.

"The whole house rattled," recalls Adrian, 54. "I went out into the street and couldn't believe what I saw."

Adrian's remarkable tale is told in the first of a four-part series, profiling Britain's strangest extra-terrestrial experiences.

Other eyewitnesses saw a bright light, arching across the sky and a red circle, hovering on the hillside, surrounded by flashing lights.

Locals were convinced it was otherworldly. Now, as the government opens its X Files – top-secret Ministry

Adrian was shocked by what he saw

of Defence reports – there may be answers.

Dozens of theories were put forward at the time, including a crashed airplane or meteorite shower. But despite searches by the police and armed forces, no explanation could be found.

This silence led to many conspiracy theories and rumours of dead aliens being found and governmental cover-ups!

"It was kept quiet," says Adrian. "There are things we should know about that have been covered up. What are they hiding?"

● Words by Anne Richardson

Behind the scenes on Boyzone's comeback tour ➤ **23**

I REFER to a letter from Andy Roberts from Caerwys (*Leader*, February 11) headlined 'Believers in UFO crash are limited in their research'.

From 1979 onwards when my daughter and her husband ran a pub in Llansannan, locals gave me accounts of the night of the Berwyn incident on January 1, 1974.

I was the first ufologist who decided to investigate this and did so for years with a friend Alan Hilton who was my car driver, and periodically with Wales Fellowship of Independent Ufologists members.

1. Scott Felton became a valuable colleague some seven years ago. At no time have either of us said a UFO crashed in the Berwyn Mountain. We research, and continue to research, for this but to date we have no evidence of a satellite or UFO crashing on the night of the January 23, 1974 on or near Cader Berwyn or Cader Bronwen mountain ranges.

2. What did happen was that local witnesses saw a UFO hover in the air quite a while, which then came down in a controlled way to sit on a mountain ridge of the Cader Berwyn range. The witnesses were farming families from the Llandderfel mountain opposite.

The UFO sat there quite a while before going down on to Cefn Coch opposite Cader Berwyn. It was there quite a while when the Evans family then saw it. In all it was on the ground one hour and 45 minutes before it flew up where

Questions over thoroughness of investigation

villagers in Llandernog saw it pass over. An unusual event, and one with a lot of questions yet to be answered, but one can hardly call that a crash.

3. In Scott's thorough research he camped one night with poachers lanterns used in 1974 on a Berwyn mountain side. He and a friend who travelled from Bolton, Lancashire, to assist him were able to ascertain these lights were impossible to be seen from the Cader Bronwen mountain tops because of the intervening high mountain peaks four miles in between.

4. Andy Roberts, Jenny Randles and the four man geological team did not check this or consult local farmers in the Llandrillo and more especially the Cader Berwyn areas, so how thoroughly did they investigate?

Both Scott and I over the years have had these farmers tell us how angry they feel that outsiders in television documentaries have the nerve to expound on what the locals did not see, without bothering to ask them what they witnessed.

**Margaret Fry
Co-founder of the WFIU 1993,
Founder member in 1967 of
Contact International UK,
The Broadway, Abergele.**

The Sun

Friday, 13 May 2011

Sunemployment

Log in to comment

Search
powered by Google

The RosWelsh incident

Weird ... UFO mystery

Believers in UFO crash are limited in their research

2274

YOUR piece about the alleged Berwyn Mountain UFO crash (*Leader*, February 8) was interesting in that it demonstrated the research limitations of those who believe in the physical reality of a UFO crash.

Scott Felton rails against me for my theory that one of the lights seen that night was that of a poacher's lamp.

I did hold this theory for many years, based on documented evidence about the times and location of the poachers on the hillside, the type of lamp they were using and what Nurse Pat Evans saw.

But good research never stagnates and when, two years ago, I came across further information about the poachers and their whereabouts at the relevant time, I altered my theory to fit the facts.

In my book about the Berwyn events, *UFO Down* (CFZ, 2010) which Scott clearly chose not to read for fear of being exposed to documentary evidence, I detail all the relevant theories and twists and turns of this most unusual event.

There is no evidence – but much wishful thinking – to suggest an 'alien' spaceship crashed on the Berwyn Mountains on January 23, 1974.

But the huge light Pat Evans and her daughters observed for 15 minutes remains unexplained and as such the mystery of the Berwyns continues.

**Andy Roberts,
Caerwys.**

■ An artist's impression of the UFO crash.

Saturday, June 28, 2008 *Sun* 23

SPACE ODDITY

Riddle of molten lump off 'crashed spaceship'

Heavy metal . . . Russ with the UFO debris

Out of this world . . . melted blob found in Wales

By ALASTAIR TAYLOR

ALIEN hunter Russ Kellett yesterday revealed a lump of mystery metal which he says was recovered from a crashed UFO 34 years ago.

The shiny one-and-a-half inch melted blob was found near Llandrillo in Berwyn Mountains, Wales, after reports of a spaceship plunging to earth.

Russ says it is similar to melted aluminium, yet heavier.

Police logs described a "terrific explosion" shaking houses on January 23, 1974, and locals said hundreds of cops and military personnel ordered everyone off the mountain.

It has been claimed that alien spacemen were whisked off to a secret military installation — all hushed up by the Government.

Former building worker Russ said: "That and this piece of metal from the spaceship proves in my mind the existence of aliens.

"The metal was picked up by someone who was on the mountain at the time. They have since died and it was passed to me about a year ago.

"I passed it to a jeweller who showed it to an expert but they have no idea what it is."

Russ 45, of Filey, North Yorks, has amassed more than 30 years of data about flying saucers — but only unveiled the shiny metal after reading recent UFO reports in The Sun.

We told of three sightings in five days earlier this month — in Shropshire, near Cardiff and over the Brecon Beacons.

Russ, who started studying UFOs after being surrounded by inexplicable lights while on a motorbike in 1988, said: "None of these incidents surprise me.

"It is only a matter of time before we get conclusive proof."

a.taylor@the-sun.co.uk

Army spot UFOs over Shropshire

Sunspot . . . page 1 story   LLand of llegend — P34&35

One UFO specialist, Russ Kellett, who has spent the past 23 years investigating such incidents after his own "close encounter" believes he has uncovered evidence that the MoD could have been searching for crashed alien craft on that night.

For the first time Russ has shared, with The Sun, a document from the Maritime and Coastguard Agency (MCA) which suggests a military operation - codenamed Photoflash - was under way.

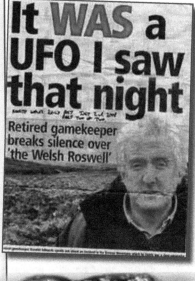

It WAS a UFO I saw that night

Retired gamekeeper breaks silence over 'the Welsh Roswell'

Space debris ... Russ Kellett with mystery fragment

Russ said: "The Photoflash operation was used to light up the coast so they could see submerged UFO craft in the sea.

"I believe there were three separate craft that were flushed out of the ocean that night, military craft were involved and there was an engagement.

"I spoke to a fisherman who saw one come out near Puffin Island. His colleagues at the time told him to say nothing about it because it was considered bad luck. He never spoke about it for years."

Russ adds that he had correspondence with a group of men who told him they were moved on by military personnel on the roadside at Llandrillo, where one of the craft came down.

He said: "They said they saw aliens getting out of the craft helping two of their own who were injured. They were then loaded on to a flat-bed truck and taken away."

Alas, 47-year-old Russ's "eyewitnesses" are now all dead, he says.

However, he still has a piece of strange-looking metal recovered by witnesses after the incident.

One theory about the event was that a meteor shower coincided with an earthquake, the epicentre of which was at Bala Lake.

A year ago, files released showed the MoD officially backed the meteor theory.

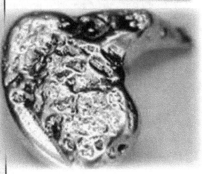

Comment from the authors

The validity of the witnesses, especially Pat Evans, has never been in issue. Sadly, for having the courage to just report what she and her two daughters had seen, she was herself the target of inane comments made to her by sceptical locals. Unfortunately, the media has, and will, chose to continue to portray this incident as a mystery of epic proportions, when common sense and rationality suggest otherwise.

Scott Felton would be the first one to point out that while he would consider any theory to explain the origin of this incident, built on the accumulated evidence obtained by himself and Margaret Fry, he will not condone any conclusions arrived by the presentation of inaccurate statements, for obvious reasons.

> "There is no evidence to support a UFO crash. This was invented, sadly, by UFO enthusiasts who tried to link noises from an earth tremor that same night with an impacting UFO. There was a seismic event that evening and a coincidental meteor shower. Debunkers have used these natural events to try and explain away what people saw. It is also the case that locals have been looked upon as rustic and ignorant and by definition, must be wrong about their observations. Whether or not there was a UFO about that night is to me not important. I am more concerned about the lengths certain persons have gone to, to cover up and debunk the event. Something must be frightening these people for such extreme measures to be enacted. I myself have persistently had Wikipedia entries (2009) countering the debunking versions removed.

Army in attendance

A woman living in Caernarfon told Margaret Fry that she was returning home from work, at 3am, on the Caernarfon to Bangor road between the villages of Bethel and Pentir, a few weeks into 1974, when she was stopped by a military policeman. She said:

> "He told me I had to stay there. About 20 minutes later, three Army Lorries arrived and drove into the nearby electric power station. Two contained armed troops. In the centre of the third lorry could be seen stone oblong boxes, at which point I was motioned away by the soldiers. I was then escorted back to my home. About a month later I received a visit from a member of the military, who asked me a number of questions including my affiliation to the Communist party."

Mike Saville – enormous dark orange UFO seen

Mike Saville contacted Margaret Fry, in 1996, and told her:

> "In January 1974, I was living with my young family on a steep hill outside Llandderfel in one of three houses Garn-Goch, Cae Pant, and Tyn-y-Fron, which were situated opposite the Cader mountain range, some 5 miles across to Cader Berwyn.
>
> On the 23rd January 1974, we felt the terrible earthquake and ran out carrying the children down to Cae Pant Farm, where our neighbours – Arthur and Dyliss Prichard – were stood outside. We then all saw this enormous dark orange object, moving silently and slowly down the mountain, some three miles away from them. This then slowly settled down onto the mountainside, just below the plateau – it was so big we thought the world was coming to an end. After watching it for between 30-35 minutes, it suddenly went downwards and disappeared from view."

Margaret discovered that other people had seen a similar object, which corroborates what Mike told her. She is sure that this was the same object seen by Pat Evans, but at a greater distance away.

Margaret:

> "Mike Saville and his neighbours did not see or hear any military vehicles, because of the position of their houses on a steep concealed mountain slope opposite the Berwyn Mountain range. Mike told me that it had a definite shape; it was a UFO.
>
> We were very angry when the press passed it off as a meteor; there was no explosion, or crash – it just blanked out. They covered the whole thing up. We stood outside for a while and then everyone came into my house and stayed for hours after."

Firefly Productions produce televised documentary on incident

An example of the way in which the media constantly offer entertainment, rather than presenting the evidence, was a televised documentary produced from interviews with several non-primary witnesses, made by *Firefly Productions* on 2nd July 2008. Unfortunately, the programme contained many inaccuracies – both testimonial and material evidence was not broadcast – and, in our view, failed to offer a balanced account of what had taken place.

Scott Felton:

> "Firefly Productions and Channel 5 programme failed to deliver a fair and balanced production, despite having promised me differently. I am very disappointed with their coverage of this event, and am surprised they had the opportunity to finally put the record straight, knowing that not one single newspaper article or other documentary has ever managed to convey the true information known at the time. In fact, this is probably the worst and most prejudiced programme ever to be shown, giving large amounts of air time to those opposed to the event and absolutely none to those for the event. With hindsight, I now believe that this particular documentary, and the series as a

whole, was commissioned with the deliberate intention of debunking Britain's best known UFO event in the light of the release of hitherto classified files and public interest in a spate of UK UFO sightings earlier in 2008. Several other UFO investigators involved in other cases were asked to take part and it seems the purpose was to learn the extent of their evidence with no intention of whatsoever using it. This would be of no value to a TV company, so I believe it will have been passed on to persons or agencies unknown."

Media lies- We declined to be involved

This was the same company that contacted us and Margaret Fry for information relating to various investigations carried out by us, including a spectacular incident in July 1955 involving Margaret Fry when she and her companion witnessed the extraordinary landing of a UFO at Bexleyheath, in Kent – details of which can be found in Revised Volume 1 of *Haunted Skies*. After emailing them copies of our 'write up', which included corroboratory evidence from other witnesses, they inexplicably changed their mind about using the material.

Firefly Productions … 'Zygmund Adamski'

Another case we discussed with *Firefly Productions* was the Zygmund Adamski incident, reinvestigated by us and Doncaster-based UFO researcher, David Sankey. Despite it being patently obvious to all and sundry, there was no connection between this man's death and UFO activity. *Firefly Productions* advised us that they were still going to publish the article linking Mr Adamski's death with reported UFO activity, (rather than including any of our article, which would have shown nothing of the kind) because they said:

"…it would help the viewing figures".

How offensive it was to link this man's death with claims of Alien abduction, when it was nothing of the sort! Should we really be surprised?

As time has gone on, more and more lurid accounts have appeared in the press – which include published images of three-eyed Aliens and weird spaceships that have nothing to do with the actual reality of what took place.

One of the offenders was the Wrexham *Leader*. What is the matter with these people? They call themselves investigative reporters but cannot be bothered to write the truth……..as our colleague on the Nationals remarked to us:

"Editors don't want the truth but just entertainment".

Sadly, nowadays (2017), it's fake news which dominates the internet, and on-line newspapers, with their never-ending stories of inaccuracy and sensationalism – necessary ingredients to sell papers!

2010 – Release of MOD documents on the incident

In 2010, The National Archives released a number of declassified MOD 'UFO' documents. They included a file referring to what has become known as the "Berwyn Mountains incident".

In a letter, dated 14th February 1974, it outlined five separate reports of *"unusual objects seen in the sky"*, in different areas of the UK, on the night of 23rd January 1974.

According to the letter, these were all in the South of England and all described a 'bright light' falling to earth. It suggests that these may have been a "bolide" – a meteor disintegrating during its passage through the atmosphere.

Another document is an extract from the meteorological logbook of the *SS Tokyo Bay*, travelling from Port Kelang (Malaysia) towards Southampton. This report describes *"five bodies, spectacularly incandescent … traversing the sky"*. The ship's captain – M. Lees, attributes the observation to a satellite disintegrating, having re-entered the Earth's atmosphere, and an attached MOD memorandum suggests this was

"...probably the decay of the Soviet Communications relay satellite, Moluiya 2-8's rocket body".

Another declassified letter, later released to the Public Records Office, tells us:

"With regard to the events of the evening of January 23 in the Berwyn Mountains; we did receive a number of reports of an unusual object seen in the sky just before 10pm on the evening in question ... Later on, personnel of the Royal Air Force mountain rescue team participated in a search of the area where the object was thought to have come down, but as you probably know nothing was found."

The Leader, 11th March 2011

Margaret wrote a letter to the Wrexham *Leader* newspaper, wishing to put the record straight, after reading an article published on the 11th February 2011 sent in by UFO enthusiast and author – Andy Roberts (who is personally known to us).

13th May 2011 *The Sun* newspaper – 'The Ros Welsh Incident'

On the 13th May 2011 *The Sun* newspaper published an article, entitled 'The Ros Welsh Incident' and showed an artist's illustration of a saucer-shaped object, hovering above the village of Llandrillo, accompanied by a story from Yorkshire-based UFO researcher – Russ Kellett. Russ claimed that following his acquisition of a document released by the Maritime and Coastguard agency, codenamed 'Photoflash', it was evidence of a military operation to light up the coast in order to see submerged UFO craft in the sea, and that the MOD had been looking for crashed alien craft on that night.

They tell, we understand, of an altercation that took place in the Irish Sea when military vessels clashed with UFOs and that, as a result of this action, one of the objects later crash-landed on Cader Berwyn.

"I believe there were three separate craft that were flushed out of the ocean that night. Military craft were involved and there was an engagement. I spoke to a fisherman who saw one come out near Puffin Island. His colleagues at the time told him to say nothing about it because it was considered bad luck. He never spoke about it for years."

Russ said he was in possession of correspondence with a group of men, who told him they were moved on by military personnel on the roadside at Llandrillo, where one of the craft had come down.

"They saw the aliens getting out of the craft, helping two of their own who were injured. They were then loaded onto a flatbed truck and taken away."

He also said that the eyewitnesses are all dead, and that he was in possession of a strange piece of metal recovered after the earthquake.

Wild stories of Royal Navy engaging UFOs – then pursued by RAF!

Are we seriously expected to believe that UFOs were constantly seen for three weeks before in the sea off Puffin Island under the continental shelf in the Irish Sea, which led to the arrival of Royal Navy ships which fired torpedoes into the sea? (Presumably to disrupt or destroy the objects)

UFOs fired on Royal Navy Ship!

In addition to this rather bizarre story, to say the least, the informant claimed there was a NASA recovery vessel also present and that its communications were rendered inoperative (presumably by the force fields of the UFO)

"One of the vessels fired upon the UFOs. The smaller of the 'craft' went up into the sky, leaving the larger one which retaliated and 'zapped' one of the navy vessels with a beam, injuring some of the seaman; worse, it was said some were killed. It then flew off towards the direction of North Wales,

pursued by RAF fighter planes from Anglesey, flew over Bangor and continued on its flight towards Capel Curig in the Snowdonia range of mountains, where a RAF Jet finally intercepted and shot at it. The object, now damaged, zigzagged across the sky before crashing in the Berwyn Mountain. Aliens with big eyes and large heads, wearing grey jump suits, being led to vehicles which they entered by themselves, before being driven down a forest road. Not forgetting they claimed the UFO had lifted itself onto a military transporter."

Scott Felton

"The documentation relates to an incident where an alleged military exercise was buzzed by two unidentified submerged objects; one flew off, the other was involved in a 'shoot out'. In the course of this, the UFO was hit by gunfire from a vessel and seemingly disabled to a point where it could not fly straight up into space or re-submerge. It had no choice but to run. What alerted me to the possible fake nature of the document were contradictory references to the location of the event. Puffin Island in the Irish Sea was mentioned and the continental shelf. Any 'O' level standard student of geography, geology and ocean science, would have known that Puffin Island is a lump of limestone about 500 yards off the island of Anglesey. The entrance to the straits from the east is a vast shallow area of sandbanks, most of which is exposed at low tide. In fact, it is so shallow that there is an ancient route over the low tide sands from Abergwyngregyn to Anglesey – still usable today. This means it is totally impossible for any warships to negotiate."

Scott Felton – not the slightest scrap of evidence

Scott Felton – an authority of the events that took place in Berwyn – conducted a thorough investigation into this matter and believes there is not the slightest scrap of evidence to prove this military intervention took place, and believes it is likely this is yet another example of disinformation deliberately put out to confuse the issue, which we wholeheartedly concur with.

The information supplied as to the recovery and transport of the bodies, in apparent total defiance of any public health issues – never mind the unknown 'biological' dangers posed to the population, and army personnel involved with the removal – stretches the bounds of imagination. Surely if any alien bodies had been found, this would have attracted a high level of security and involved specialists, whose objective was to ensure that these alien bodies were not a source of contamination to us humans!

It seems unbelievable that these bodies would have been placed into containers and loaded onto the back of lorries in caskets, and that escorting soldiers had opened the boxes and peered in while on their way back to *Porton Down. We accept that undoubtedly there are contingency plans drawn up by the authorities to deal with the recovery of 'alien objects' which could – if it hasn't already happened – include extraterrestrial entities, whether dead or alive.

It did not happen

However, one thing is patently obvious; *if this had happened*, the personnel involved would have adhered to scrupulous guidelines laid down to ensure that the artifacts would have been sealed in airtight and bacterial free containers, to safeguard any danger to the human agency involved. This would have been of paramount importance.

---

*It is one of the United Kingdom's most sensitive and secretive government facilities for military research, including CBRN defence. The Dstl site (Defence Science and Technology Laboratory) occupies 7,000 acres (28 km). It is also home to the Health Protection Agency's Centre for Emergency Preparedness and Response as well as a small science park which includes companies such as Tetricus Bioscience and Ploughshare Innovations. Porton Down was originally opened in 1916 as the Royal Engineers Experimental Station as a site for testing chemical weapons. The laboratory's remit was to conduct research and development regarding chemical weapons agents such as chlorine, phosgene and mustard gas by the British armed forces in the First World War.

The recovered items would have then been transported under massive security, possibly with a cover story to explain their presence on the roads. Commons sense dictates that the likelihood 'they' were moved by army vehicles and driven down the motorway, sounds more in keeping with an episode of *Dr. Who*, but of course this is what the newspapers adore. They enjoy nothing else than a 'flying saucer' yarn, dished out with lashings of covert operations and aliens who may have conquered the vastness of space with their far more advanced technology, only to crash-land on Earth! As for the suggestion that the UFO was shot down by the RAF, after being incapacitated by a ship fired torpedo, and the barrage of naval artillery, there is no substantive evidence to indicate this took place at all.

We managed to interview one of the main witnesses and see no point in writing what is clearly the figment of wild imagination rather than fact, entertaining as that story is.

FEBRUARY 1974

February 1974 – Chris Evers – UFO over Kingston-upon-Hull

In February, 1974, a new council housing estate in Kingston-upon-Hull, called Bransholme, was under construction; the nearest shops to the estate being four small prefabricated premises, halfway down Wawne Road (approximately a 20-minute walk, or about a mile from the local village shop in Sutton-on-Hull).

To accommodate the absence of supermarkets in the vicinity, Hull City Council began construction on a large shopping precinct on the site of the former RAF Sutton camp, later opened by Hughie Green – former presenter of *Opportunity Knocks* – whom, it is believed, had his own experience of UFOs. Local schoolboy Chris Evers and a few friends, aged 11 to 14 or so years-old, were playing 'war games', one early evening in February. 1974. The night was cold and crisp, with a wonderful clear sky showing an array of stars directly above and all around.

Chris, who was hiding on a large mound of mud, which the constructors had bulldozed together, was looking up at the stars when he noticed a 'light' that appeared to be moving across the sky, travelling in a strange leapfrogging style as it did so.

> "The light would blink on, and then it would appear to blink directly behind itself in this formation – 1....3....2....4.... It continued to move in this erratic style for approximately two minutes. I jumped up and shouted to my friends 'Look up in the sky ... a UFO!'
>
> The 'lights' simply vanished in the clear sky, directly above where I was standing – never to be seen again."

This raised Chris's interest and he read as much about the subject as he could. Books by Arthur Shuttlewood and Major Donald Keyhoe were standard fare. A keen sportsman, Chris later went on to set up the Hull UFO Society (HUFOS), in the mid-1990s, and worked with Quest International as an investigator for Tony Dodd.

Chris recently set up the successful on-line *Outer Limits Magazine*, working alongside Malcolm Robinson. He is also now a successful wedding photographer (in 2017). In addition to this, Chris was responsible for forming the Hull-based American football club – *The 'Liberators'* – during the mid 1980s. In 1991, he left and formed the *Hull Pirates* Youth American football club, which in 1992 came third nationally. He was also club chairman of the *Hull Hornets*, from 2005-2007.

45 years later! 1st Outer Limits UFO Conference, Hull 2017

Chris Evers

David Young

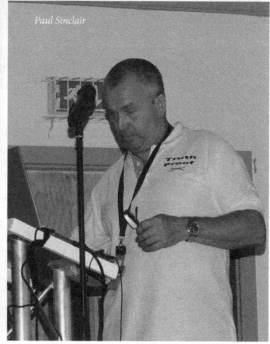

Paul Sinclair

Kelli Hollis (left) with friend Sacha Christie at the Hull Conference

On the 9th September 2017, Chris proudly produced the first *Outer Limits* UFO Conference, held at the *Freedom Centre,* Hull, UK, which Dawn and I attended, and thoroughly enjoyed every part of – not forgetting the honour of being presented with an award, by Chris, for our commitment to the UFO cause.

We met some of our good friends, such as Christine and Philip Mantle, Paul Sinclair, Sacha, and her friend – former soap star *Kelli Hollis, who played Ali in the long running TV series *Emmerdale* ... What a pleasure that was! and also met the two **'Brians' (senior and junior) from C.E.IV – an alternative Rock Band, formed in the winter of 1983 – the title chosen from the later Dr. J. Allen Hynek's category of UFO case reports.

---

*Kelli Hollis is a British actress, best known for playing Tina Crabtree in the three *Channel 4* related films shop owner Yvonne Karib in *Channel 4's* popular comedy drama, *Shameless,* and Ali Spencer in *ITV* soap opera, *Emmerdale.*

Hollis played Melanie Say in *Emmerdale* in 2002, portraying Yvonne Karib in *Shameless* for six years, starting in 2004. She also played the character of Tina Crabtree in two television dramas, *Tina Goes Shopping* (1999), *Tina Takes a Break* (2001), *Mischief Night* (2006) and a cinema-released feature film called *Mischief Night,* all three of which were directed by Penny Woolcock.

**They are the founder members of the band. Both take part in writing music/lyrics, recordings and artwork, for CDs, etc. Brian (Jnr.) also looks after the website and all the technical stuff that Brian (Senior) hasn't a clue about! During rehearsals and live performances, a keyboard technician completes the band. They all enjoy producing music and working together, but it's the common interest in Ufology that really bonds C.E.IV (Website http://ceiv.co.uk/)

Philip Mantle (centre) with the two 'Brians' (senior and junior) from rock band C.E.IV

Kelli with Dawn Holloway

Philip with John Wickham BUFORA Chairman

Malcolm Robinson (left) and Alien Bill

Tony Buckingham and Alison, East Anglia UFO Society

19th February 1974 – Minnesota police officer chases UFO

Shortly after midnight, Rochester, Minnesota police officer Jim Preiss (who had served in the Air Force for four years) was cruising along Highway 52, when:

> *"In front of me, about a thousand feet away, was a mysterious object with jets of fire coming out from underneath. I stopped the car for a closer look and estimated it was hovering some 100 feet off the ground. It then started to move, so I decided to follow it.*
>
> *I drove after it for a mile and then pulled up after Jim Kuhlman (27) in his parked truck, who was also watching it. Kuhlman told me it had passed over him."*

Jim Kuhlman (right) tells policeman Jim Preiss that the UFO had a square base with a dome on top

Preiss then gave chase with Kuhlman following behind in his truck. During the chase the police radio dispatcher reported that the station were receiving quite a few phone calls from people, saying that they had seen something strange moving across the sky.

Jim later recalled:

> *"I almost pinched myself to make sure it was happening. As it passed over my head, I could clearly see that it had a square base with a dome on top. The UFO was about the size of three tow trucks and was travelling at 20 miles per hour.*
>
> *The strangest thing of all was that it had five rows of what appeared to be afterburners – like those on a jet plane. Six jets of very bright orange flame were spewing out of each row. When it passed over me it made no noise at all. Just then, a police car screeched to a halt next to me; it was Officer Preiss. I asked him 'Did you see that? I'm going crazy'."*

Assistant Police Chief James Ryan said:

> *"I have no doubts that what my officer saw was a UFO. We had many calls that night from citizens who described seeing the same strange object that Officer Preiss was chasing."*

MARCH 1974

1st March 1974 – UFO and creature seen

At Vesta, Virginia, six people sighted a red coloured UFO – about the size of a saloon car rising from the ground – to about 300 feet, making shrill, penetrating sounds as it did so, which frightened nearby farm animals.

Incredibly, this was followed by the appearance of *"a tall, heavyset creature, seen on the ground."*

The witnesses ran to fetch their shotguns, but by the time they returned to the scene all that was left were patches of charred ground, which extended several hundred yards across the hillside. Broken tree limbs, fence posts, bushes, twigs, and other vegetation, were found charred and blackened in a random manner. **(Source: George Fawcett)**

2nd March 1974 – Strange 'stars' over Lincoln

At 8.10pm, Thomas Albert Bradley from Ermine East, Lincoln – an amateur astronomer – was outside his home address, checking the night sky, when he noticed a 'double star' in the direction of the north-east. After watching it for ten minutes, he looked at it through binoculars and noticed:

> *"...the right hand 'star' pulsed once, then slowly moved downwards and away towards the horizon, but abruptly and without slowing down, turned right, heading now towards the east. My impression was that they were very high up on the edge of space. I had them under observation for ten minutes."*

(Source: Richard Thompson)

10th March 1974 – Strange 'lights' sighted over Reading

Reading, Berkshire, resident – Alan Shepherd, was to be involved in another sighting of something very odd. At 10pm he and his three sons were in the back garden, looking up into the clear starlit night sky.

> *"A large bright white 'light' caught our attention, heading in a north-east to south-east direction. It stopped in flight and changed direction, heading westwards for a short distance – then stopped again for a couple of minutes. Then a second similar 'light' appeared, heading towards the first one from the west. It came level with the first one and it, too, stopped in flight. We kept them under observation for 20 minutes and then went in when we came out. Ten minutes later they were gone."*

(Source: Ron West)

13th March 1974 – 'Flying Saucer' over school

At 6.30pm Alan was out walking with his wife, three children, and two friends of their children. As they approached the local school, close to where they lived, they were stunned to see:

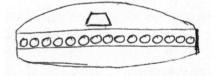

> *"...a glowing yellow-orange object, shaped like two saucers, about 30 feet off the ground. It was approximately 15 feet in height and 30 feet wide. Around it were red and blue flashing lights in an anticlockwise motion. A beam of orange light shone down from underneath it, lighting up a section of the school grounds. The object was accompanied by a slight humming noise and a smell like rotten eggs. A few minutes later it shot upwards into the sky and was out of sight."*

The incident was reported to the police. **(Source: Ron West)**

20th March 1974 – Landed UFO ... shots fired

George also tells us that on the 20th March 1974, fifty people lined the shore of a frozen lake at Boshkung, Ontario, to watch six snow mobiles approach a landed UFO, at 10pm. One of the men fired shots at the UFO, which made a distinctive clunk as it hit it. The UFO then ascended and disappeared at speed.

23rd March 1974 – UFO photographed over Argentina

Photographs of strange objects seen in the sky, often referred to as 'Flying Saucers', wherever seen in the world, are always worth mentioning. Thanks to Wendelle Stevens and August Roberts we know that, at 7.30pm, Mr Cesar Elorda – an employee of Y.P.F (Dance studio) based in Comodoro Rivadavia – was 16 kilometres out from Caleta Olivia, driving along a coastal highway running along the shoreline of Golfo San Jorge, when he noticed a strange circular aircraft approaching from the ocean to the east, about 200 metres from land, travelling silently in a westerly direction at no great speed.

"It continued its course and passed over the highway over the top of me, like no airplane I had ever seen before.

I stopped the car and got out with my camera – a Voigtlander Bessamatic – and obtained one colour photo of the object, which was dull, dark grey, circular-lens shaped with a flat bottom and raised dome on top. The sun at this time was already below the horizon, although the sky was still quite bright." (**Source: Sr. Guillermo Carlos Roncoroni/***UFO Photographs,* **Volume 1**)

31st March 1974 – Strange 'star' seen over Lincolnshire

At 2.20am, Laboratory assistant – Mr Ashlyn Brown from Bracebridge, Lincoln, was out fishing at a lake by the side of North Scarle on a clear, cloudless, but cold night, when he saw what he first took to be a shooting star – blue and white in colour with a glow around it, at an angle of 45 degrees off the horizon – but felt this was unlikely, as it headed along a steady and level course through the sky, heading south to the North, and out of sight 20-30 seconds later. (**Source: Richard Thompson**)

Spring 1974 – Egg-shaped UFO seen over Bournemouth, Dorset

Teenagers Angela Johnson and Lorraine Terry were out playing near Ibbertson Way, Bournemouth, one evening, when the sky lit up with a brilliant flash, followed by the appearance of *"a dark orange egg-shaped object"*, moving slowly through the sky, heading north-east.

The girls ran home and alerted their parents, who rushed out of the house in time to see *"an oval object, showing a shadow effect across it in the design of a cross"*. (**Source: Leslie Harris, 'Scan', Bournemouth**)

APRIL 1974

April 1974 – Motorist encounters UFO over Maidenhead

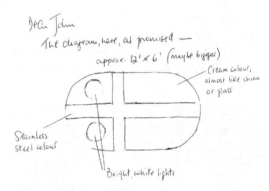

Dear John
The diagram, here, as promised —
approx. 12' x 6' (maybe bigger)
Cream colour, almost like china or glass
Stainless steel colour
Bright white lights

In April 1974, Yvonne Sanders was a driving a *Volkswagen* 'Beetle' car, about 40 miles per hour, near Hawthorn Hill, located between Maidenhead and Ascot, at 11.45pm, when she noticed a red and green 'light' in the sky, some distance apart.

> *"My car was then surrounded by light. Looking upwards, I saw an elliptical 'craft, hovering above my car about 15 feet above me; it was cream coloured and divided by a crucifix-shaped, stainless steel cross, with a round white light in each small quarter; no other markings, no rivets, the body was very smooth, no wings or appendages. In the time it took me to look away in shock, and return my gaze, it had gone. At the time I was persuaded into thinking that the object concerned was some sort of Ministry of Defence aircraft that was being tested, but that was over 30 years ago, and I have yet to see anything resembling what I saw."*

8th April 1974 – UFO hovers over motorist

At Olympia, Washington State, a cone-shaped object, showing coloured lights around it, making a high-pitched whine, was reported hovering over a car with two girls inside, for a period of several minutes, before heading away at tremendous speed. (**Source: George Fawcett**)

30th April 1974 – Landed UFO at New York, USA

At approximately 10pm (give or take 30minutes), Mrs Ruth Currie, her daughter, and another employee of the Nash nursing home in Altamont, New York, sighted something very strange in the night sky. It started when Mrs Currie's daughter told her mother about a 'bright light' seen by her, several hundred feet from the house. The two women decided to go out and have a look at the source of the illumination, which was now in the road. They noticed that dogs in the locality had began to bark, clearly agitated. They saw:

> *"...an oval 'craft', with windows around the top. From those windows emanated a brilliant golden glow, with an undefined shape moving around inside."*

Mrs Currie sent her daughter to summon a Mrs Curtis, who came immediately and confirmed the sighting. Mr Curtis was summoned and, as he arrived, he saw the object rising upwards before heading away into the night – then lost from view.

Large burned area found the next day

The next morning they went to the scene in daylight and found a large burned area, about 60 feet in diameter. (**Source: Mr Jahn, NICAP**)

MAY 1974

May 1974 – Strange Encounter at Farnborough, Hampshire

Wally Churn

Mr Wally Churn – a self-employed carpenter from Cove, in Farnborough – was cycling to work, at 7.50am. As he crossed the road, intending to call into the paper shop adjacent to a shopping centre, known as the Queensway – (part of his regular habit) – a man spoke to him. Wally ignored him, as it was 8.10am, and he was already late for work. The man spoke again, saying: *"I am Freka Alfreka"*, or something like that, and he held out his hand. He said: *"I am from the saucer people, do you understand?"*

Wally Churn's impression of the man he met

Mr Churn took his hand, walked two or three paces, stopped, and turned around – the man had vanished.

Churn went into the shop and collected his paper, remarking on the strange man, and later brought the matter to the attention of Mr Omar Fowler – an investigator for BUFORA/Surrey Investigation Group on Aerial Phenomena, in December 1975.

In an interview with Omar, he described the man as:

"…having a round, smooth face, almost without a chin, small hands like a woman, cold to touch – his eyes, green in colour, had no pupils. He was wearing grey clothes, with a trilby, and was about six feet tall and looked in his early thirties."

Mr Churn complained of suffering 'pins and needles' in his right hand and forearm by the time he arrived at work, followed by the appearance of a red spot on his right thumb, which lasted for a fortnight.

Another witness

Incredibly, this was not the only time we were to hear of a strange person seen in Farnborough. Mrs Cheryl Chuter, from Aldershot, told us of her own frightening experience in the same year.

"I was working for a company in North Camp and on the way to deposit the day's takings into a bank at Farnborough. I noticed a man, wearing ordinary clothes and a hat, walking towards me. As he came closer, I felt an apprehension creep over me; my first thoughts were that he was going to steal the money. As he passed, I looked into his face and saw that his eyes were like no other eyes I had ever seen. They were like deep black pools, devoid of any colour, and he had no pupils – just deep black holes where his eyes should have been. By the time I pulled myself together and turned around, all I saw was him fading away. The following week I read in the local paper – The Star – that a man had reported seeing a UFO land in a school field while out exercising the family dog. I am fairly sure it was the same day, although I cannot be sure of the exact date."

7th May 1974 – UFO landing, occupants seen

At 9pm, a nurse at a Veteran's Hospital at Coatesville, Pennsylvania, heard a swishing sound at 9pm. On looking out she saw, nearby, tree branches shaking violently as a circular UFO, showing four silver 'gears,' landed on the hospital roof about 150 feet away. The nurse said:

"I saw three creatures with large heads, grayish skin, and long arms with claw like hands emerge, who made 'squeaky' sounds." (**Source: George Fawcett**)

Incidents like this seem too incredible to believe, especially when contrasted with the events that took place in the UK and the lack of detail. However, these are not one-off instances of UFOs being seen to land, and then the appearance of what we perceive to be the occupants of these alien vessels, who no doubt view us in the same light. Where they come from and what their agenda is, if any, can only be speculation.

11th May 1974 – Close Encounter, Bedfordshire

A close encounter of chilling proportions took place at 8.45pm, involving Dagenham-based BUFORA investigator – Barry King, and Chingford investigator – Ian Vinten, who were driving back from Leighton Buzzard, in Bedfordshire. As they approached Chingford, they decided to make a detour and visit Barn Hill, off Sewardstone Road, where there had been previous reports of UFOs seen in the area. The two men pulled off at the side of the road and left the engine running of Ian's Ford Anglia, while they stood at the wire fence, casting their eyes over the ridge opposite – some 400 yards away, with a copse of trees to their left – noticing two grey vans parked along the road, but thought nothing of it at the time.

Barry:

> "Ian shouted out something. I couldn't hear what he was saying, because of the noise of the car engine. I asked him to repeat it. He shouted out, 'there's someone over there', and pointed towards the ridge."

Barry saw nothing, to begin with, but after further scrutiny, saw someone standing near the trees – not moving. They fetched their binoculars and trained them on the figure.

Barry:

> "A feeling of unease spread over me when I saw a tall 'figure', dressed in a full-length gown, with long blonde/white hair. What scared me was 'its' completely featureless face.
>
> 'It' stood there, not moving, facing us. I lowered my binoculars and reached for a cigarette; my hands were shaking. Ian shouted 'It's gone', and looked around for any sign of the 'figure'. We then saw it a little further along the ridge. Suddenly, out of the corner of my eye, I saw strange white featureless 'blobs' darting about at terrific speeds, close to a hedgerow, approximately 200 yards away; in an instant they had gone."

The two men tried to fathom out what on earth the two 'white blobs' had been and what their presence meant to the weird 'figure' they had seen previously. Above the treetops appeared a small 'red light', which rose slightly upwards and became two 'red lights' with a white light in the centre – *part of something* – that began to head towards the two men, whose attention was on this object – the strange 'figure' being momentarily forgotten.

Barry:

> "A distinct outline could now be seen. It was spherical in the centre, with cone shaped sides – like a tennis ball with an ice-cream cone on either side. It displayed large, round lights – the red ones flashing in unison. The white one stayed on, with a small blue light circling the centre clockwise. There was a strange pinging noise – two-tone, like a ship's sonar – and it continued its flight towards us. A combination of fear and amazement swept over me. Ian ran to his car and picked up his camera, and managed to take several shots of the UFO as it passed overhead."

Incongruously the traffic continued to flow past, as if ignoring the passage

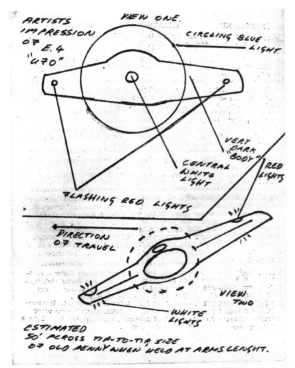

ARTISTS IMPRESSION OF E.4 "U70"

VIEW ONE.

CIRCLING BLUE LIGHT

VERY DARK "BODY"

CENTRAL WHITE LIGHT

RED LIGHTS

FLASHING RED LIGHTS

DIRECTION OF TRAVEL

VIEW TWO

WHITE LIGHTS

ESTIMATED 50' ACROSS TIP-TO-TIP SIZE OF OLD PENNY WHEN HELD AT ARMS LENGTH.

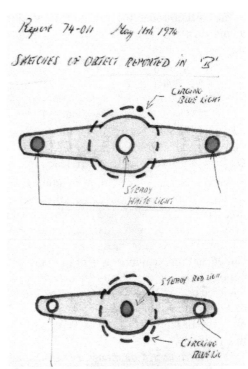

Report 74-011 May 11th 1974

SKETCHES OF OBJECT REPORTED IN 'B'

CIRCLING BLUE LIGHT

STEADY WHITE LIGHT

STEADY RED LIGHT

CIRCLING BLUE LIT

of the object through the air. The two men looked around for any potential witnesses and noticed two young girls, talking nearby. When asked if they could see the UFO, they took one look at it and ran off.

Barry:

> "We noticed a guy standing at the front gate of his house, intently watching the object. All of a sudden I had this really weird sensation, as if I was actually inside the object – then I was back on the road, looking up at it – then all went quiet … no sounds, no traffic. The next thing I was aware of was seeing the object heading west, over Enfield, before being lost from view."

Now very subdued, the two men returned home. Barry reported, not surprisingly, that he had slept badly that night, and believes there may well have been some *missing time* as the TV programme *Match of the Day* was just starting when he arrived home.

Following consultation with Ken Phillips – National Investigations Co-ordinator for BUFORA – enquiries were made at the scene with another man, whose identity was not disclosed. He later denied ever having been involved, clearly concerned about any adverse publicity. Examination of the locality revealed extensive treetop damage, with burnt branches lying on the ground. Following this discovery, a comprehensive report was submitted to the MOD and to Professor J. Allen Hynek, of CUFOS (in the United States). The film was sent to Omar Fowler – then head of SIGAP (Surrey Investigation Group on Aerial Phenomena). Unfortunately, while being removed from the camera, the film jammed and was rendered useless. Worse, Ian went to the Press against the wishes of Barry, as a result of which the whole matter was sensationalised out of all context. The story does not end here; another frightening incident was to occur on the 10th August 1974.

Barry:

> "I was contacted by many newspapers, asking for an interview – but declined. Ken suggested I contact Ian and see how he was reacting to all the public interest. When I telephoned his house, a stranger answered and told me nobody of that name lived there. I was astounded and went around to the house and spoke personally to the occupier, who invited me in. I was shocked to see the décor and wallpaper were different. I telephoned Ken and explained what had happened. He promised to make some enquiries. A few days later he advised me that Ian had abruptly left and gone to live in the West Country. I have never heard from him since."

(Source: Barry King/Credit: Dave Sankey, BUFORA & Mark Rodeghier, CUFOS)

28th May 1974 – UFO over Worcester

At 11pm, Mrs Margaret Webb – member of a Worcestershire-based UFO group, called 'Sky Scan' – was in the back garden of her home in Cromer Road, Worcester.

> "I was looking up into the clear night sky, noting the various constellations, when I noticed what looked like a mass of stars, grouped in a triangular shape with a bright centre, hazy at the edges, crossing the night sky – unlike anything I've ever seen in the night sky before."

(Source: Personal interview)

28th May 1974 – Landed UFO

At Albuquerque, New Mexico, two housewives reported to the police that they had come across a UFO, about 50-75 feet in diameter, which had landed on a nearby hill. The object remained on the ground for about an hour, during which time the women chose, through fear, not to approach it any closer. It then took off, rotating around its central axis, and disappeared into the distant sky. It is reported that grayish material was found at the landing site by the investigators. **(Source: George Fawcett)**

Summer 1974 – UFO over Combe Martin, Devon

John Keen – an ex-resident of Combe Martin (a seaside village of much character and charm) – spoke about what he and his brother saw when young boys, playing on the football pitch during summer 1974.

"It was broad daylight, when we saw this shining silver cigar-shaped object, hovering silently 30 feet above the ground. It had five circular shapes or portholes around it, with a dome or fin on its blunt end, with a wire or rope hanging from it trailing sparks. It then moved away, and we watched it following the contours of the countryside. When we told our parents they laughed at us, but I know what we saw and will never forget it despite it being over 40 years ago."

JUNE 1974

6th June 1974 – 'Spinning top' UFO over New Hampshire, USA

Mrs Vivienne Stevens of Locust Street, South Hampton, New Hampshire, was driving home after attending a PTA meeting with her son – Richard, daughter – Barbara, and niece – Helen Mispilkin, along Route 150, at 9.30pm, when they noticed a red 'beacon' light in the sky ahead of them. At first they thought it was a light on a tower or at a construction site.

The 'light' then increased in size but was soon lost behind trees.

Red dome-shaped object seen

A short time later they approached an open area, where they were astonished to see a large, red, illuminated dome-shape, hovering over the clearing. They described this as having a bright white rectangular opening, with something like blades spinning around inside. White, blue, and yellow sparks spewed out at the opposite sides around the base of the dome. At this stage they became frightened and drove away.

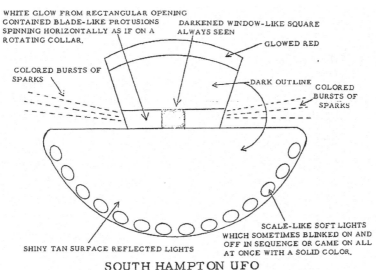

SOUTH HAMPTON UFO

Object follows vehicle

They were horrified to see the object was now following their car; when approximately 100 yards away, the object passed directly in front of them – now flying ahead of the car. It stopped and hovered with a bobbing, fluttering motion, now 120 feet high and about 400 feet away.

Mrs Steven's niece stopped the car to obtain a closer look. Suddenly, a band of soft glowing coloured lights – *"like a string of beads"* – flickered on and off. After watching the lights for several minutes, all the lights then would go on and off, showing one solid colour – first red, then blue and green. The UFO was described as looking like a child's spinning top, with its point truncated and having a round pointed base.

Begins to descend to the ground

At this stage it began to make very jerky actions and descend towards the ground. Now very frightened, the family fled.

When they arrived home in Locust Street, Mrs Stevens told her older son – Todd (17), about the incident. Although she wanted to telephone the police he advised her not to do so because, by the time they arrived, he felt the object would have left.

Todd then left with his girlfriend and went to the scene, but there was no sign of the UFO

Upon his return he noticed a red 'beacon' light in the sky. Immediately he drove home and came back with the family, where they observed the strange phenomena for the second time. At this point, Mrs Stevens went and fetched Mr and Mrs Frank Cynewski back to the location – but, by the time they arrived, it had gone. The sighting was later reported to Pease Air Force Base, at 9.30pm on the 6th June 1974. The matter was later referred to NICAP, who assigned Mr John Oswald to investigate the occurrence.

(**Source:** *UFO Investigator*, **August 1974, NICAP**)

7th June 1974 – Two brilliant 'lights' seen moving over Worcester

Two brilliant lights, a few minutes apart, were seen heading across the sky over Worcester, by a number of people, including a local councillor. (**Source:** *Evening News, Worcester,* **7.6.1974**)

10th June 1974

An object – resembling *"a yellow torpedo"* – was seen over Derby, by a number of people.

(**Source:** *Derby Evening Telegraph*, **10.6.1974 – 'Yellow torpedo seen as UFO season opens'**)

12th June 1974 – UFO display

Four large and small UFOs were seen 'bobbing up and down in the sky' over Grantham, North Carolina. One of the objects halted over a nearby house, 300 feet away, making a whirring noise. 'Windows' could be seen and rows of lights about 15 feet wide. Twenty minutes later they all moved away and out of sight.

13th June 1974 – UFO over Essex

An *"orange glowing, oval object – a mere 100 feet off the ground"* was seen over Hornchurch, by two men, who called the police.

By the time they arrived, it had gone. The MOD were contacted but declined to give any statement.

(**Source:** *Herts Advertiser and St. Albans Times*, **13.6.1974**)

A *"rusty red revolving ball of light"* was sighted rushing through the sky over Halifax, Yorkshire, on the 14th June 1974, for a few minutes, travelling at a speed of about 100 miles per hour and at an estimated height of 2,000 feet. (**Source:** *Evening Courier*, **Halifax**)

Mid-June 1974 – UFO display over Birmingham

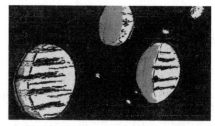

In mid-June 1974, a number of residents living in Wentworth Drive, Harborne, contacted the police after sighting a number of mysterious glowing objects, darting about in the sky over the nearby Harborne golf course. We spoke to retired police officers – Margaret and Geoffrey Westwood – who were responsible for the running of the Birmingham UFO group – **UFOSIS,** and living in Wentworth Drive, at the time.

Margaret:

> "I can confirm that a
> report was submitted
> to the MOD about
> the incidents, which
> were brought to our
> attention by some of
> the residents – one
> of whom described a
> frightening experience
> when one of the objects
> swooped down over her
> head while near the golf
> course.

Margaret and Geoffrey Westwood of UFOSIS

> I saw some of these
> objects for myself,
> flashing across the sky.
> They looked like 'globes of light' constantly changing colour, leaving red trails behind them. When
> I looked through binoculars I could see a number of bars of horizontal light, moving downwards
> over the face of the UFO – like the sort of effect you get when frames of interference roll down
> over the face of a TV screen; it reminded me of the film taken, in 1974, of the UFOs over New
> Zealand that attracted such huge publicity at the time."

One evening Margaret, on her return home, was told by the babysitter that she had seen a vivid lime
green coloured 'light' shoot over the house. The following morning, she discovered the top of a young
eucalyptus (transplanted 12 months previously) was blackened – as if burnt.

> "At the base of the tree I found a fragment of material, about two inches in size, that I hadn't seen
> there before. When later analyzed, it was found to be rich in aluminum with large traces of silicon
> and smaller amounts of iron. I don't know whether it was connected, but the leaves on the tree grew
> very elongated. The tree itself grew to a height of 16 feet, over 12 months – an abnormal growth
> rate."

We discovered that MOD officials had written to several people living in Bourneville Park estate,
confirming that their reports *"...are being examined to see if there are any defence implications"*.

Margaret told the *Birmingham Evening Mail*, at the time:

> "One of the sightings was very frightening; it seemed to hover right overhead and then drop suddenly.
> More than a dozen people living near their home in Wentworth Way had seen the unidentified
> objects. Among them were a doctor and electrical engineer. Initially the lights travelled in a south
> to north direction but, following a spell of inactivity during cloudy weather, had changed to an
> east-west direction."

(Source: Personal interview/*Birmingham Evening Mail***, 8.7.1974 – 'Flying Saucer probe in City')**

Although we cannot be 100 per cent sure, we realised that this incident formed part of an investigation
by Peter Guy. – (then living in Olton) – who was a member of the Birmingham group, UFOSIS. It appears
(contrary to our previous belief) that the UFO incident took place in Harborne, rather than Olton, which
is likely to be the case.

The piece of black matter in my hand felt curiously light and alien. UFO researcher Peter Guy told me it was found on the lawn of a house in Birmingham, shortly after a mysterious, pulsating light had been seen hovering above trees at the bottom of the garden.

"There were several pieces scattered over the lawn. We had the material analysed at a university and it was found to have a rather peculiar make-up," said Peter.

"There was nothing in it that couldn't be explained by normal chemistry, it was just peculiar. It was extremely rich in aluminim with a large amount of silicone and smaller amounts of iron. I can see no earthly reason for that."

I looked at the black lump with a genuine sense of awe. Could it really be connected with the strange, pulsating light which amazed several witnesses in Birmingham — and was that light a UFO? If so, where did it come from? Who controlled it?

Peter Guy would also like to know the answers to these and many other questions that arise from the unexplained sightings of lights and objects in the sky.

He is a member of the British Unidentified Flying Object Research Association and a dedicated investigator for the Birmingham - based UFO Studies Information Service.

DIRTY

Mention flying saucers to Peter and he frowns. "That's a dirty word to us." Even the object seen over Olton about two years ago and drawn by Peter from the evidence of eye - witnesses, is described unemotionally as an alleged unidentified flying object, although it has all the characteristics of the traditional "saucer" — high dome, with small round windows and a base like an up - turned saucer.

Talk of invaders from other planets will provoke a similar reaction. "We are extremely wary if anyone reports a contact. The last thing we want to hear of is little green men.

"We have got contact cases, of course. One is under serious investigation at the moment. A professional psychiatrist has offered to interview the witness under hypnosis."

Peter, who lives in Chelmscote Road, Olton, has never seen a UFO. At least, his unbiased and scientific mind will not allow him to accept his own sightings as positive evidence.

Most sightings, he will tell you, can be put down as natural phemomena — aircraft and other lights in the sky, meteorites and metal from man - made satellites re - entering the earth's atmosphere.

But his studies and investigations — "I once taced a UFO from North Yorkshire to the Thames estuary" — have brought him to the conclusion that some UFO's could be manufactured craft, possibly the product of extra - terrestial intelligence.

Peter has scientific and technical know - how which helps him in his research into UFO's. He works for a major oil company and is reading for Open University degrees in mathematics and geology.

He has designed a spectroscope to be fitted to the cameras of UFO spotters and is optimistic that some day the researchers will receive official recognition for their work.

FUTURE

"We hope it will produce at some time in the future, once and for all, a solution to the problem. I want to know what these craft are, and how they are powered. And I want to know something about the technology that produces them."

So far, official recognition has not been forthcoming. "We write to the Ministry of Defence and get absolutely no reaction. All we get is a steroetyped letter, 'Dear Sirs, this matter is being attended to ...' and that's the last you hear. If you write again, you're sent exactly the same letter. We find it very frustrating."

Peter Guy with his spectroscope designed for UFO spotters, and his drawing of the Olton UFO. "Flying saucer's a dirty word to us."

14th June 1974 – Pulsing object hovers over trees at New Hampshire, USA

Mrs Barbara La Porta had just finished work at 12.30am, and was leaving the employees car park at Nashua, New Hampshire, when she noticed an unusual illumination near some pine trees ahead of her. She stopped the car to get a better view.

Suddenly, she saw an object hovering over the pine trees, estimated to be 50 feet wide, showing red pulsing lights. She got back into the car and left the parking lot and headed home. As she did so, she occasionally caught glimpses of the strange phenomenon.

"Several times it would stop and move sideways, before heading out northwards".

Barbara had an impression that other motorists may have seen it, as the traffic seemed to be moving considerably slower. [Later checks with the police revealed they had not received any other reports.]

On her return home drive, after picking up the babysitter, she sighted the same phenomenon and reported the matter to the Federal Aviation, who told her they had not received any other reports from the public or tracked anything on radar. That organisation gave her the number for NICAP investigator – Ray Fowler. Incredibly, Barbara – now accompanied by her babysitter and a Mr Larry Roberts – went back out to the locality, where (for what appears to be a brief time) they saw a 'circle of lights' and heard some unusual high-pitched tones, before it finally left for good.

(**Source:** *UFO Investigator*, **August 1974, NICAP**)

20th June 1974 – UFO display, Bournemouth

In 2010 Paul Usher contacted David Sankey, seeking any further information or knowledge of a UFO sighted by himself, at 11pm on 20th June 1974 (approximate date) over the Bournemouth area.

"I saw what appeared to be an orange coloured torpedo-shaped object with a central flashing light, pulsing on and off, twice a second, following a random course across the sky. I got the impression that the light was also rotating around the whole object, which was spinning like a drill. The central light could change colour, from white or red/orange – then very bright.

The object was moving in a zigzag manner, or 'castle' formation. Sometimes it would travel along for about 10-20 seconds in this odd fashion, then suddenly disappear – then reappeared instantly in another part of the sky, and so on; direction could change and was impossible to predict. Its altitude must have been very high, some 80 to 180 miles (as a rough guess) and, as such, its speed must have been quite fast. However, it sometimes came to a full stop!

Paul still seeks an answer for what he regards as being one of the most baffling things he has ever seen and cannot understand how anything would behave in such a manner, nor instantly appear in other parts of the sky – sometimes at considerable distance away, then reappear in any part of the sky, zigzagging around, doing 90 degree turns for probably half an hour. Incredibly, Paul saw the same 'display' for four nights in a row.

On the 21st June 1974, amateur astronomer – Philip Wheeler, and three friends, sighted UFOs over the town. (**Source:** *Bournemouth Times*, **Poole, 21.6.1974**)

21st June 1974 – Metallic object reported in the sky over Lincolnshire

Mr Brendan Taylor was in Brumby Wood Lane, Scunthorpe, at 11pm, when he and his female companion sighted *"a yellowish-white metallic object"* crossing the sky, heading eastwards.

(**Source: Personal interview/Richard Thompson/***Scunthorpe Evening Telegraph***, 28.6.1974**)

22nd June 1974 – Strange 'lights' over Devon

Strange red, pink, green and blue, 'lights' were seen on two separate occasions by people living in Exeter, Devon. Through binoculars, a solid shape could be made out. (**Source:** *Express & Echo*, **Exeter**)

22nd June 1974 – Strange 'lights' over Fort McCoy, Wisconsin, USA

Several reservists on guard duty reported seeing several 'lights' in the distance, moving quickly across the sky. As the objects moved closer, their movement became more erratic and they grew brighter. Suddenly all disappeared – apart from one which streaked away to a point within one mile of the guards, before inexplicably vanishing. (**Source: NICAP**)

Busy month

June and July 1974 were very busy months with literally hundreds of sightings of UFOs reported in the local British newspapers, but very rarely in the Nationals … why? The reader is invited to conduct their own research into these incidents through personal contact with the local library, or newspaper archives, as time and space prevents us from obtaining this information.

29th June 1974 – UFO over North Carolina

A businessman was out fishing on Rogue Inlet, Washington, North Carolina, at 9.30pm, when:

> "I saw a cone-shaped object, shaped like a three-quarter moon, green in colour, hovering in the sky. When a plane flew near it, the UFO ascended at high speed, with an orange jet like flame."

JULY 1974

2nd July 1974 – *Northern Echo*, Darlington

'…yellow-orange thing with black markings; flat and dome shaped on top, disc-shaped underneath.'

6th July 1974 – UFO over London

A brilliant pulsating 'light', judged to be one third of the moon in size, was seen motionless in the sky over London, in broad daylight, before then commencing to fly in a series of triangular movements.

(**Source:** *Aquarius Viewpoint,* London, 1974)

6th July 1974 – *Solihull News*'

A bright white light seen over the borough and reported to Birmingham Airport.'

Nick Gilman (36) of Burnt Ash Road, Lee, London – a local Government Emergency Control Officer – was on Cradle Hill, Warminster, at 11.30pm, accompanied by his girlfriend and a friend in the back of the car, facing the locked cross bar gate at the end of the track.

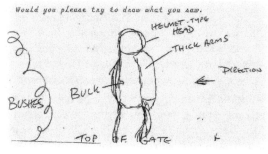

> "By midnight all was quiet; we were all dozing in the car. I awoke a couple of minutes before 1am, and flashed the headlights of the car on and off a couple of times, when a 'figure' passed from right to left behind the gate illuminated by the lights. It was tall, about 7 feet in height, and moved in a

> 'bouncy gait' – like a moon walker. I flashed again and it had gone. I awoke my companions and we searched the area, but found no trace of the 'being'."

Some four years later, the *BBC* made a documentary on Warminster. Residents in the town were interviewed and several told of having seen a mysterious 'figure' lurking about in the back garden, often in a 'bouncy' movement – was there a connection? This was not the only time that we were to hear of mysterious 'figures' seen around the Cradle Hill area. Undoubtedly, though, some were hoaxes. The reader is advised to obtain our book on Wiltshire, containing a full overview of Warminster and other parts of Wiltshire, including letters from Arthur Shuttlewood – which have not, up to now, been published before.

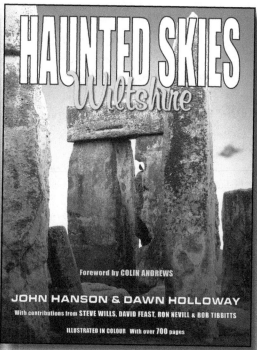

12th/13th July 1974 – Reservoir emptied at Banbury

An object – resembling a white golf ball – was sighted in the sky over Walthamstow, accompanied by reports of UFOs sighted over Staffordshire and Gloucestershire. The *Evening Echo* newspaper, at Basildon, also carried a double column about UFOs being sighted, along with three shots of the UFO. It was said that the negatives had been sent to the MOD, who made no comment.

(**Source:** *Evening Echo,* **Basildon/***Stafford Newsletter,* **12.7.1974**)

Also on the same day was the sighting of an object over Warrington, described as *"... pearly, brilliant, and absolutely controlled – unlike anything seen before."* (**Source:** ***Warrington Guardian,* 12.7.1974**)

The Forest Guardian – 'Mysterious object in Banbury reservoir' – (Approximate date: 12th July 1974) – told of the reservoir being emptied at Banbury, after it was claimed divers carrying out essential work had discovered a *'metallic object'* on the bottom. Despite it being drained of its millions of gallons of water, nothing was found. We were unable to obtain any further information, about this intriguing matter.

The following day, two bright red objects were reported over Gloucester before merging into one – described as

> *... huge as a block of flats, making no noise, were seen. Five minutes later, the two lights merged and took off at fantastic speed".* (**Source:** *The Gloucester Citizen,* **13.7.1974**)

18th July 1974 – Beeping noises heard over Gloucestershire

High-pitched electronic noises were heard after a vaguely circular 'light' was seen shining through the clouds, causing strange beeping noises on the domestic television sets at Cheltenham, Gloucestershire, along with bright red 'stars' seen over Stroud.

(**Source:** *Gloucestershire Echo* – 'They're back after months of comparative silence')

22nd July 1974 – UFO over Lexington

At Lexington, Missouri, nine people reported having sighted a circular UFO in the sky, at 12.15am.

> "It had something like a church steeple on its top, flashed blue lights, and gave off what looked like vapour trails when it manoeuvred."

July 1974 – Three UFOs sighted over Hampshire

Mr H. Page of Albert Road, Peel Common, Fareham, Hampshire, was weeding the front garden, in July 1974, at 4.30pm, when he saw:

> "...what looked like three large 'dinner plates in size' bright orange objects, motionless and low down in the sky set at each distance from each other, forming a triangle. After five minutes they moved away towards the direction of Gosport. I contacted the Portsmouth Evening News and told them about it. After they published the sighting, lots of people contacted them reporting having also seen it go over." (**Source: Nicholas Maloret, WATSUP**)

Further reports of UFO activity for this period included *"a rugby ball shaped object, topped with brilliant white with grey dots"* seen over Middlesbrough, sparking off numerous calls to the police. (**Source:** *Teesside Evening Gazette*)

On the 23rd July 1974, the *Torquay Herald Express* told its readers about *'six UFOs forming a crescent shape, sighted over the town, which broke into a perfect half-moon formation before joining up again'*.

A *'silver cone-shaped UFO'* was seen over Kidsgrove, in Staffordshire, on the 26th July 1974, by a number of people – who contacted the police. (**Source:** *Evening Sentinel,* **Stoke on Trent, 26.8.1974**)

The *Newcastle Evening Chronicle* – 'UFO claim after Wizards forecast', in their published edition of the 27th July 1974, told its readers of reports of *'bright white flickering lights'*, which may have been either satellites or meteors crossing the night sky, by Bensham couple – Marylyn and Joseph Edgar.

31st July 1974 – Three 'lights' seen over Watford – did the RAF respond?

According to the *Southern Echo* (31st July 1974), four people – including a coastguard – sighted an object in the sky, describing it as: *"...like looking through a slot in a furnace"*, visible for fifteen minutes, at 2am.

(**Source:** *Aquarius Viewpoint,* **Number 29, September 1974 – Peter Merriot**)

Another sighting for the same day told of a tiny 'point of light', seen in the sky over Watford, which was soon joined by a second and then a third 'light', which was observed to circle a tree. Another three 'lights' then appeared in the sky; this time they flared into brilliant light. Soon after a fourth appeared, but did not – according to the witness – 'flare up' like its predecessors.

> "Suddenly they all disappeared from sight, followed by the arrival of a small Jet aircraft, making its way to where the objects had been. After the aircraft had gone, two 'lights' returned. Shortly afterwards, they were gone for good."

AUGUST 1974

1st August 1974 – Orange object sighted over Carolina

An orange object – brighter than the full moon – was seen over Albemarle, North Carolina, hovering above treetops for 15 minutes before rushing away.

Curious phenomena over London

On 2nd August 1974, the *East London Advertiser* carried the start of a number of articles, including the sighting of *"curious pink 'balls of light' seen carefully avoiding buildings as they slowly floated through the air, sometimes just above the road"*, by people from Catford and Downham, during the early part of the month.

2nd August 1974 – Two UFOs over Idaho, USA

At Boise, Idaho, a young man was driving up a mountain road, just before midnight, when he saw:

> *"...two objects in the sky, showing shiny metal tops. They appeared to be moving slowly."*

The man stopped the truck and, as he did so, the objects ceased all movement – at which point he became frightened and drove away. **(Source: NICAP)**

On the same date – this time at Calvert, Texas – a newspaper editor and his wife were out in their car when they heard some strange metallic noises, followed by the appearance of a deep red UFO in the sky above them that roared and pulsated, while chasing their car for several miles down Route 979. As it approached closer, the car began to shake all over – as if falling apart.

5th August 1974 – *South Wales Evening Post* – 'Bright white objects moving at speed'

7th August 1974 – *Havering Romford Express* – 'More witnesses come forward'

8th August 1974 – Saucer-shaped UFO seen over East Sussex'

At 9.40pm, a bright saucer-shaped object was seen moving slowly across the sky, by East Sussex resident Peggy Mason – author of *Tales of Two Worlds* – who had this to say, at the time:

> *"The sky was not yet dark, still remains of sunset. I saw this enormous light and went into the garden to watch it, hoping it could tune in to me. After about ten minutes it expanded and dimmed out, leaving a 'point of light' that slowly travelled northwards from the direction of Ashdown Forest. I had the strong sensation that it wanted me to see it."*

(Source: *Aquarius Viewpoint*, Number 29, September 1974)

10th August 1974 – Close encounter, Dagenham

Barry King, still curious as to what he and his colleague had seen previously, in May 1974, was sat at his bedroom window on the late evening of 10th August 1974 – a warm and stuffy night – watching out for any sign of the Perseids meteor shower, visible from mid- July each year, with the bulk of its activity falling between the 8th and 14th August, when his attention was drawn to a small 'red light' seen moving from right to left. As it drew level with his position, it bounced up and down a few times in the air, then carried on to Barry's left, before stopping in mid-air and reversing its direction, where it once again began to retrace its original journey, occasionally bouncing up and down.

> *"I flashed a large heavy duty torch at it. To my surprise, it responded with a bounce in the air. I flashed twice; it bounced twice. I flashed three times; it did it three times. This went on for a few minutes and then it disappeared, so I recommenced my observation for any sign of the meteor shower. Suddenly, I heard a noise from the garden below and shone the torch, thinking it was a cat. The beam caught a 'figure', standing near the shed. I froze with fear, realising this was the same 'figure' we had seen at Barn Hill back in May. Oh My God! I thought. It's moving towards me. I dived away from the window and crouched down next to the wall, at the bottom of my bed, terrified. After some time had elapsed, I gingerly went over to the window and plucked up the courage to look out – there was nothing to be seen; relief flooded through me. I got into bed and felt relief."*

The next morning, Barry went out into the garden and examined the ground – there was nothing to be seen. Within a few weeks of the event, he became afflicted with a strange rash on his hands and face – a medical condition the doctor was unable to diagnose. Fortunately, with the application of ointment and bandages, the condition cleared up.

12th August 1974 – Red sphere over Leicestershire

A red sphere was seen over the Leicestershire area, at 1.30am, described as:

> "...*moving low down in the sky, clearing the tops of houses, before changing to a yellow colour, lighting up the whole street with its illumination, then changing course and heading out of sight*".

12th August 1974 – Mississippi motorist Chased by a UFO

An Air Force officer and his wife were out motoring in Laurel, Mississippi, when an oval object bathed the car in blue light and pursued them along the road for some distance.

On the same date – this time at Sanbornton, New Hampshire – police officers in four communities reported that they had been approached by an elliptical, domed, UFO, 30-50 feet in diameter, which had come within a few hundred feet of their vehicles on the Interstate Highway 1-93.

13th August 1974

14th August 1974 – UFO over Cheltenham, Gloucestershire

Brian Savory from Cheltenham, Gloucestershire, was observing Jupiter through a pair of l6x magnification binoculars, at 1.55am – a clear night, with a little haze in the distance – accompanied by his father.

> "I was turning to look at Sirius, when I noticed bright red and green lights over Leckhampton Hill, moving towards us. As the lights came closer, overhead I could see a distinctive crescent shape, with a domed top, and a riot of multicoloured lights swirling around the object. It then began to swing to and fro – like the pendulum of a clock – rose slightly, and then descended."

(Source: Personal interview)

15th August 1974 – UFO display over Bedfordshire?

At about 7pm, Dunstable man Leslie Moulster – an instrument fitter (47) – was driving along a minor road, between Stanbridge and Billington, in Bedfordshire, on what was a sunny evening with a light breeze and scattered cloud. He noticed a vapour trail that crossed the sky in front of him in the north-south direction, with an aircraft at its northern end which disappeared into Cirrostratus cloud near the horizon. He presumed, possessing quite knowledge of aircraft, that this was a Boeing 747 on a transpolar route, although he was curious about the vapour trail, which was unusually wide and spread out. [Authors: A common sight in this day and age, when a clear sky can cloud over with the remains of vapour trails.] He turned right onto the A4146 at the Billington junction, about half a mile from the Bedfordshire/Buckinghamshire border, heading north-west, towards Leighton Buzzard, and now directly under the trail.

> "I noticed a silvery object in size – no bigger than a pinhead – flying parallel with the trail, heading northwards, which I took to be another aircraft, and wondered why it too wasn't leaving any vapour trail. I passed through the village of Billington and then noticed, in the eastern direction, a clear disc-shaped object similar to the first but a dull reddish-brown. Within seconds they collided, with a vivid flash that temporarily blinded me and obscured everything in the vicinity. Then they commenced an aerial ballet, circling one another far too tightly to be conventional aircraft.
>
> A few minutes later the brown object disappeared from sight, leaving the silvery one to carry on its course – until lost in the horizon, northwards." (Source: Ken Phillips)

Newcastle Journal 13.8.74

Lights in sky shock couple

THE bright lights were too much for Sylvia and Brian Charlton — the young couple were left shaking in the street as the illuminations flashed across the midnight sky.

For the lights were bright orange and became brilliant as they grew bigger and changed shape over Kenton, Newcastle.

But Sylvia, aged 22, and husband Brian, aged 27, of Bradwell Road, Kenton, didn't have to worry about being branded as "nutty" UFO spotters — for other people around the city saw the mystery lights on Sunday night.

People in Longbenton and other areas of Tyneside telephoned The Journal to tell of frightening lights.

Sylvia said yesterday: "We were disturbed by the lights in the sky as we were watching the television with the curtains open.

"They were not clouds and we always keep an open mind on things like this— we think it was a flying saucer.

"We both went outside to check we weren't seeing things because of the television. There was a man walking his dog and he said he had seen something. We were shaky but not frightened."

Newcastle Airport said they had no flights between 11 p.m. and 4 a.m. The lights were spotted around midnight.

The "sighting" comes after a number of recent UFO reports in the area, and after a prediction by mind-reader Kreskin that Tynesiders would spot unidentified flying objects by the end of this year.

19th August 1974 – *Enfield Weekly Herald* – 'Two humanoid figures seen floating above ground'

20th August 1974 – UFOs over Surrey

At 9.45pm, Mrs Mills – a housewife from Camberley, in Surrey, and a former member of the Royal Observer Corps – sighted a UFO moving through the air over a local youth club, at an estimated height of 100 feet off the ground.

The following evening (21st August 1974) she was stood in her back garden, taking in the air at 9.45pm, when she saw:

> "*...a bright 'beam of light' approaching the house – so close I thought a light aircraft was about to crash-land, so I ducked behind the side of the house. After nothing happened, I peered around into the garden and saw the amazing sight of a 'ball of light', about ten feet in diameter, accompanied by a number of smaller red lights darting about just above the ground where I had been standing.*
>
> *I decided to pluck up my courage and confront the object, now making a humming noise. Suddenly it moved a few feet upwards and crossed over into my next door neighbour's garden, where it was joined by the arrival of four similar objects – all of them bobbing up and down before moving away, out of sight.* (**Source: Peter Paget, *Fountain Journal*, No. 8, 1977**)

20th August 1974 – Light display over New York

The area around Albany, New York, was also the subject of UFO activity, after dozens of people contacted the police and authorities, reporting having sighted mysterious 'lights' in the sky between 8pm and midnight. State troopers – Michael Morgan and Warren Johnson – attended. When they arrived they saw a bright red object, flashing on and off – like a strobe light – some 500 feet up in the sky.

> "*The object was joined by two similar lights; for a time they began to disappear and reappear. After about 90 minutes, they vanished from sight.*" (**Source: *UFO Investigator*, November 1974, NICAP**)

23rd August 1974 – John Winston Lennon and May Fung Yee Pang sight UFO

The intriguing sentence above can be found on the bottom right of the back cover of John Lennon's album – *Walls and Bridges* – released in 1974. The July 1996 issue of the British UFO Magazine *Alien Encounters* (issue 9, page 53) tells May Fung Yee Pang's story in quotes, about a sighting she and ˙John Lennon had in the 1970's from their 434, East 52nd Penthouse 1928 Art Deco building.

˙John Winston Ono Lennon, MBE (born John Winston Lennon; 9 October 1940 – 8 December 1980) was an English singer, songwriter, and activist who co-founded the Beatles, the most commercially successful and musically influential band in the history of popular music. He and fellow member – Paul McCartney, formed a much-celebrated songwriting partnership.

Born and raised in Liverpool, Lennon became involved in the 'Skiffle' craze as a teenager; his first band, *the Quarrymen,* was named the *Silver Beatles,* and finally evolved into the *Beatles* in 1960. When the group disbanded in 1970, Lennon embarked on a sporadic solo career that produced albums including *John Lennon/Plastic Ono Band* and *Imagine,* and songs such as *Give Peace a Chance, Working Class Hero,* and *Imagine.* After he married Yoko Ono in 1969, he added 'Ono' as one of his middle names. Lennon disengaged himself from the music business in 1975 to raise his infant son, Sean, but re-emerged with Ono in 1980 with the new album *Double Fantasy.* He was shot to death in front of his Manhattan apartment, three weeks after its release.

Lennon revealed a rebellious nature and acerbic wit in his music, writing, and drawings, on film and in interviews. Controversial through his political and peace activism, he moved from London to Manhattan in 1971, where his criticism of the Vietnam War resulted in a lengthy attempt by the Nixon administration to deport him. Some of his songs were adopted as anthems by the anti-war movement and the larger counterculture.

By 2012 (thirty-two years after his death), Lennon's solo album sales in the United States had exceeded 14 million units. He is responsible for 25 number-one singles on the US Hot 100 chart as a writer, co-writer, or performer. In 2002, Lennon was voted eighth in a BBC poll of the 100 Greatest Britons and in 2008; *Rolling Stone* ranked him the fifth-greatest singer of all time. In 1987, he was posthumously inducted into the Songwriters Hall of Fame. Lennon was twice inducted into the Rock and Roll Hall of Fame – first in 1988, as a member of the Beatles, and again in 1994 as a solo artist.

"We had just ordered up some pizzas and since it was such a warm evening, we decided to step out on the terrace", recalled Pang. *"There were no windows directly facing us from across the street, so John just stepped outside with nothing on, in order to catch a cool breeze that was coming in right off the East River. I remember I was just inside the bedroom getting dressed when John started shouting for me to come out on the terrace. I yelled back that I would be right there but he kept screaming for me to join him in that instant. As I walked out onto the terrace, my eye caught this large, circular object coming towards us. It was shaped like a flattened cone and on top was a large, brilliant red light, not pulsating as on any of the aircraft we'd see heading for a landing at Newark Airport. When it came a little closer we could make out a row or circle of white lights that ran around the entire rim of the craft – these were also*

flashing on and off. There were so many of these lights that it was dazzling to the mind. It was, I estimate, about the size of a Lear jet and it was so close that if we had something to throw at it, we probably would have hit it quite easily. We often had helicopters flying above us but this was as silent as the night and about seventeen storeys above street level. It then went down the river turned right at the United Nations and then left down the river. The light was so brilliant coming from the craft that no additional details could be seen. We did take a couple of pictures but they turned out overexposed. We even called the police – that's how excited we were, and they told us to keep calm, that others had seen it too. During what was left of the evening, John kept saying, 'I can't believe it... I can't believe it... I've seen a flying saucer!"

Interview with John Lennon

In the November 1974 issue of what was then known as Andy Warhol's magazine, an interview was conducted with John Lennon, by Dr. Winston O'Boogie, (one of Lennon's better-known aliases) from documents stored at the Library and Archives of the Rock and Roll Hall of Fame and Museum in Cleveland, Ohio.

John Lennon outlines the circumstances which led to the UFO sighting, and denies being under the influence of drink. He says he was lying naked on his bed, when he had an urge to go over to the window. He turned his head and saw, hovering over the next building, no more than a hundred feet away,

> *"...this thing, with ordinary electric light bulbs flashing on and off round the bottom and a one non-blinking red light on top".*

He tried to rationalize what he was seeing, wondering if it was a balloon or aircraft but then rejected this pointing out that the object was flying very slow, about 30 miles per hour, below most rooftops. He shouted for his 'friend' to come and have a look; she came running out and bore witness.

Photographs taken handed over to Bob Gruen

Bob Gruen

May took some photographs with the camera; apparently the Polaroid was broken [which was later given to Bob Gruen to process. He told them the photos were blank – as if they had been through the radar at customs]. A short time later the object headed away. Bob was also asked to report the matter to the *Daily News* and the Police, who confirmed that others had reported seeing the object in the sky.

The picture that accompanied the piece, by Bob Gruen, is one of the most iconic images in rock and roll history – John Lennon standing on the roof of his building, wearing a sleeveless white 'NEW YORK CITY' shirt, on the 29th August 1974. It has been reproduced countless times, and is certainly the most famous image Gruen – even with his illustrious history as an elite rock photographer – ever took. This appearance in *Interview* was probably the first time anyone in the world at large ever saw that picture.

[John Hanson – I had the pleasure of seeing the Beatles perform, in London, resplendent in my Beatles jacket as a young man. I could hardly hear, due to the screaming of their adoring fans. What an exciting experience, never to be forgotten – still vivid in my memory.]

Conversation between Uri Geller and John Lennon … Aliens seen

May Pang, in her book *Loving John* said:

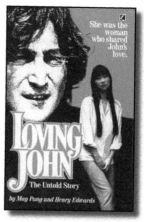

> *"The large, circular object was coming towards us. It was shaped like a flattened cone and on top was a large, brilliant red light. When it came a little closer we could make out a row or circle of white lights that ran around the entire rim of the craft."*

It is said May Pang later claimed that Lennon had seen other UFOs before this night, and that he felt he might have been abducted by extraterrestrials while still a child living in Woolton village, Merseyside. ['Mendips', 251 Menlove Avenue, Woolton, with his Aunt Mimi, from 1946 onwards]

Initially we weren't sure what to make of this, but have considered an association after hearing what John Lennon told Uri Geller – which came about after talking to Philip Mantle about the above sighting in 2017 – when we were surprised to learn of a matter that we had not heard before, involving an interview between Uri Geller and John Lennon, who told of a mysterious encounter with 'aliens'. Uri Geller has astonished and confounded the world of psychics, magicians and cynical reporters, who thought they had seen and heard it all. Mysteriously bending spoons, making broken clocks and watches tick once more, reading minds, and including millions of newspaper readers in experiments, has kept his name at the forefront of the paranormal. On top of his numerous TV appearances, tours and his busy schedule of psychic experiments and seminars abroad, he has recently produced his own monthly magazine, *Uri Geller's Encounters*, which features the paranormal.

Graham Birdsall (left) and Philip Mantle

John Lennon talks to Uri Geller

The two men were sitting at a table in Manhattan in the mid 1970s, when the UFO subject was brought up by John. Uri told him that he also believed in UFOs and had photographed them.

Uri:

> *"I've kept this story to myself for many, many, years and never told it to anyone. When John Lennon told me of this event, it was so bizarre and weird and so ahead of its time that no-one would have believed it, but today people are telling how they have been taken into UFOs and probed by aliens from outer space. I always think if 90% of these stories are made-up fantasies and dreams, and if 10% is real that is enough for something being true out there and really happening. John never asked me to keep his story a secret, so I thought it would be interesting to tell it in my first magazine. It basically blew my mind because I was already then a believer in extraterrestrials visiting our planet. There was a minute that I questioned John's integrity – maybe him being under the influence of LSD or drugs – but he wasn't."*

Bright light seen under the bedroom door

"One night he was lying in his bed in the Dakota building where he lived in New York, and suddenly noticed an extremely bright light pouring in from around the edges of the bedroom door. It was so powerful; he thought it was someone aiming a searchlight through his apartment. He got up, crossed to the door and flung it open; the next thing he could remember was four, thin-looking 'figures' who came over to him. Two of them held his hands and the other two gently pushed his legs and he was gently guided into a tunnel of light where he was shown all of his life, just like watching a movie."

John told Uri it was the most outstandingly beautiful thing he'd ever seen.

Strange 'globe of metal' handed over

Uri:

"John recalled something being given to him. That was all he remembered, but when he opened his hand there was this odd-looking, not quite egg-shaped, ball of metal – very smooth and very heavy, about an inch or so wide. I was astounded. I said it sounded like an alien encounter and he seemed to agree and said that he couldn't think of another explanation himself. He was very serious about the incident but also funny about it. Then he put his hand in his pocket, pulled out the object the aliens had given him and gave it to me. When I touched it I felt a deep sadness – I don't know why – it was like loneliness. Maybe it was a premonition about his murder, but anyway, that was John's alien story and it happened in the middle of New York. He gave the object to me and I didn't want to accept it. I said, 'Isn't this precious to you, because I think you should have it?' I have had this since the day he gave it to me. I really cherish it."

Sadly as we all know fate was to decree that John was murdered in December 1980. Rest in Peace.....

O ✱ ✱ ✱ **3**

John Lennon shot dead

BY PATRICK DOYLE, ROBERT LANE and HUGH BRACKEN

Former Beatle John Lennon, the 40-year-old lead singer of the most popular rock group in history, was shot to death last night as he stepped from a limousine outside his home in the Dakota, an exclusive apartment building on Central Park West and 72d St.

Police arrested a suspect, "described as a local screwball," minutes after the shooting and charged him with Lennon's murder. The "smirking" suspect, identified as Mark David Chapman, 25, of Hawaii, was seen in the vicinity of the Dakota for several hours before the shooting and reportedly had hounded Lennon for an autograph several times in the last three or four days.

Lennon and his Japanese-born wife, Yoko Ono, were returning to their apartment from a recording session when the shots rang out.

LENNON WAS TAKEN TO ROOSEVELT Hospital in a police radio car and was pronounced dead on arrival in the emergency room.

"We tried to save him," said Dr. Stephen Lynn, director of emergency services, "We opened his chest and massaged his heart, but he was virtually dead when they brought him in." Lennon's body was then taken to the Bellevue Hospital morgue for an autopsy.

Police said Lennon was shot several times at close range inside the large iron gate on the W. 72d St. side of the building and was bleeding profusely when he was placed in the radio car.

Lynn said Lennon was brought into the emergency room a few minutes before 11 p.m. and was pronounced dead at 11:07 p.m. "Extensive resuscitation efforts were made, and despite

See **LENNON** Page 19

GENE KAPPOCK DAILY NEWS

John Lennon—shot to death outside West Side apartment house.

Lennon's grief-stricken widow, Yoko Ono, leaves hospital last night.

The Beatles—the rest is music history

John Lennon (second right) and fellow Beatles Ringo Starr, George Harrison and Paul McCartney (l. to r.) made a big hit with Ed Sullivan—and American TV audiences—when they appeared on his show in 1964.

By WILLIAM CARLTON

"Close your eyes, have no fear the monster's gone.
He's on the run and your daddy's here, beautiful, beautiful, beautiful, beautiful boy. .. Before you cross the street take my hand. Life is what happens to you while you're busy making other plans."
"Beautiful Boy" by John Lennon

John Lennon wrote those words in a song for his son in his latest album, the first album the ex-Beatle had made in five years, an album that ended his self-imposed exile from the rock-music world. It was a world that Lennon, his songwriting partner Paul McCartney, George Harrison and Ringo Starr so completely dominated from the time they had their first hit in 1963 until their bitter breakup in 1970 and the release of their last album, "Get Back."

The Beatles were the biggest thing ever to hit the postwar world. Bigger than Elvis, bigger than Kennedy, "bigger than Jesus," as Lennon once boasted. It was not an empty boast.

From humble beginnings in a blue-collar section of Liverpool, Lennon and his schoolmate Paul McCartney went on to become the most successful songwriters in history, certified by the Guiness Book of Records. They formed a partnership in their early teens and agreed to put both names on whatever songs either of them had written.

THEY STARTED OUT imitating late '50s rockers, such as Buddy Holly and Elvis Presley, and wrote songs for their own band, called at various times the Quarryman and the Silver Beatles. Lennon played rhythm guitar and sang, while Paul played bass. Another schoolmate, George Harrison, added his talented lead guitar, and Ringo Starr later was recruited on drums, the Beatles were born, and nothing ever in music was the same again.

Their meteoric career is legendary: their scuffling days at dives in Germany and Liverpool, their swelling success that brought them to the atten-

See **FAME** Page 19

A part of cop's past lies dead

THAT SUMMER IN BREEZY POINT, when he was 18 and out of Madison High in Brooklyn, there was the Beatles on the radio at the beach and on the jukebox in the Sugar Bowl and Kennedys. He was young and he let his hair grow and there were girls and it was the important part of life.

Last year, Tony Palma even went to see "Beatlemania."

And now, last night, a 34-year-old man, he sat in a patrol car at 82d St. and Columbus Ave. and the call came over the radio: "Man shot, 1 West 72d St."

Palma and his partner, Herb Frauenberger, rushed through the Manhattan streets to an address: they knew as one of the most famous living places in the country, the Dakota apartments.

A car was there ahead of them, and as Palma got out he saw the officers had a man up against the building and were handcuffing him.

JIMMY BRESLIN

"Where's the guy shot?" Palma said.
"In the back," one of the cops said.

Palma went through the gates into the Dakota courtyard and up into the office. A guy in a red shirt and jeans was on his face on the floor. He rolled the guy over. Blood was coming out of the mouth and covering the face. The chest was wet with blood.

Palma took the arms and Frauenberger took the legs. They carried the guy out to the street. Somebody told them to put the body in another patrol car.

JIM MORAN'S PATROL CAR was waiting. Moran is from the South Bronx, from Williams Ave., and he was brought up on Tony Bennett records in the jukeboxes. When he became a cop in 1964, he was put on patrol guarding the Beatles at their hotel. Girls screamed and pushed and Moran laughed. Once, it was all fun.

Now responding to the call, "Man shot, 1 West 72d," Jim Moran, a 45-year-old policeman, pulled up in front of the Dakota and Tony Palma put this guy with blood all over him in the back seat.

As Moran started driving away, he heard people in the street shouting, "That's John Lennon."

Moran was driving with Bill Gamble. As they went through the streets to Roosevelt Hospital, Moran looked in

See **COP** Page 19

Daily News, Tuesday, December 9, 1980.

DAILY Mirror

SPECIAL ISSUE

JOHN LENNON shot dead in New York Dec 8 1980

DEATH OF A HERO

August 1974 – UFO over Hertfordshire

Mrs S. Eaton, of London, was driving her open-topped sports car to meet some friends for a drink in Hatfield, Herfordshire, one warm evening in August 1974, and was travelling along the A1000 road through Brookmans Park, when she noticed an object in the sky towards the north-east.

> *"I slowed down to about five miles per hour, so as to get a better look, and saw a long craft, 2-300 yards in length, travelling at a height of about 3-4,000 feet in the sky. I pulled the car over onto the side of the road, to obtain a closer look – bearing in mind dusk was falling.*
>
> *This was no aircraft; it had no wings and was tremendous in size. There were no visible protrusions on the upper and lower surface of the object, but along its length were a number of lights in a line – not bright but bright enough to be seen. The body of the vessel was darker in colour but not black – possibly a matt or satin finish, which didn't reflect the light.*
>
> *It was making this deep humming noise, accompanied by a whirring sound. It was stationary in the sky at this point positioned very close to Brookmans Park aerial – a TV and aircraft flight beacon. After about five minutes it moved away, its course taking it almost directly overhead. I continued on my journey. My emotions were mixed, feeling both thrilled and terrified."* (**Source: Dan Goring, Earth-link, Winter 1979/1980**)

Autumn 1974 – Giant UFO over Hampshire

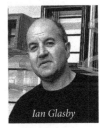
Ian Glasby

At 8pm, Ian Glasby from Cosham, Portsmouth, was with two other youths watching the night sky, in late autumn 1974, with a pair of binoculars, when they noticed a bright stationary light in the sky towards the south-east, flashing green and red lights, which they first thought was a helicopter.

On looking at the 'lights' through binoculars, they were staggered to see a gigantic object – *"the size of a battleship"*. According to Ian:

> *"It had a rectangular body surmounted by a raised dome, with a number of protrusions along its length. Midway along the base of the structure was a single row of oval portholes, out of which spilled green, red, and white lights into the sky. At both end of the UFO were what looked look antennae. The surface was covered with what looked like grey coloured squares and rectangles,*

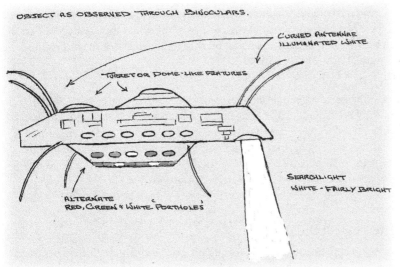

> *almost metallic in appearance. There was a beam of white light projecting downwards, towards the horizon. We ran around to the local newspaper office, but found they were shut.*
>
> *When we looked back into the sky, it had gone – although we actually saw it again in the same place, two nights running."*
>
> (**Source: Nicholas Maloret, WATSUP**)

SEPTEMBER 1974

19th September 1974 – Three dark red lights sighted over Washington

A family from Olympia, Washington, USA, sighted three dark red lights near their home, during the evening, forming a triangular pattern, moving up and down in a curious bobbing motion. They were visible for 15 minutes, before disappearing from view behind timber. (**Source: NICAP**)

24th September 1974 – UFO over Dorset

At 12.10am, ex-RAF Michael John Byatt from Bridport, in Dorset – an experienced gliding instructor, then employed as a TV engineer – was returning from Maiden Newton, with a companion, and heading towards home in his Bedford motor van. As he turned left at the crossroads on top of Eggardon Hill – an ancient hill fort, with its commanding views over Eggardon Downs, reputed to be haunted by ghostly baying hounds and roman soldiers:

> "We both became cold. I turned the heater up to full, but it made no difference. The engine began to lose power and the electrics dimmed, but did not go completely. Had we not been travelling downhill, we would have stopped.
>
> An object appeared to our right, at a fairly high altitude, approximately 300-600 feet above us (at the same time as the vehicle lost power) before disappearing vertically from view. Whether it disappeared before we left I cannot say, as I was frightened and beat a hasty retreat.
>
> On looking back at the hill we could see it at the top – rather like a parachute flare, only not quite as bright."

Mr Byatt still seeks an answer for what he saw, following an interview conducted in 1974 (over 30 years later), and is adamant that what he saw was no aircraft – as suggested to him, following publicity in the local newspapers, after the event.

He told us it looked like a circular neon tube, moving backwards and forwards, in the sky.

(**Source: Frank Marshall, BUFORA/Personal interview/*Bridport News*, 27.9.1974/*Dorset Evening Echo*, 25.9.1974**)

29th September 1974 – UFO over Portsmouth

At 12.30am, Mr and Mrs Oliver were driving westwards along Romsey Road, in an Austin A60 Cambridge car, near Hursley, in Hampshire. They had just reached the crest of a hill, when they noticed a flashing light in front of them – which they took to be an aircraft, but on reaching the base of the hill realised the light was stationary and they were almost underneath it.

Mr Oliver later told Nick Maloret:

> "It was clearly visible and made up of a circular arrangement of 'V'-shaped white lights, flashing on and off rapidly, as it hovered over open fields about a hundred feet away from the road. I slowed down to about 5 miles per hour, and watched it through the side window; my wife kept her eye on it by looking through the windscreen. A car in front had stopped; the occupants were already outside watching the object, which was under cloud level. We eventually lost sight of it as our view was obscured by trees bordering the side of the road." (**Source: Nick Maloret, WATSUP**)

OCTOBER 1974

4th October 1974 – White 'ring' in the sky

Steven Furk – a TV engineer by occupation – was out fishing off Portland Bill, with his friend – Mr Hartley, just after midnight, when their attention was drawn *to a luminous white ring*, slightly blurred at the edges, stationary in the sky – out of which projected a beam of light arcing over towards the horizon. After twenty-five minutes, it disappeared from sight. (**Source: Frank Marshall, BUFORA**)

15th October 1974 – UFO photographed over Vancouver

According to the *Vancouver Sun* newspaper of 26th October 1974, David Knutsen (11), of Surrey, had kept the biggest secret of his life locked inside his Kodak Instamatic camera.

At the time, David – a pupil at Old Yale Road elementary school – was talking to a friend in the St. Helens apartment complex, when he noticed two RCMP officers stood in the building lot, pointing in the sky towards the east. David, picked up his camera, looked out, and was in time to take a colour photograph of the object, estimated to be only 400 feet away at is nearest point – which was *"going round and round in a circle, up and down, and then took off super fast"*.

David Knutsen's through-the-window UFO photograph

David's father – Harold, instructed his son not to develop the film until the other 19 pictures were taken. When processed, it showed a circular – almost black, with a sharp but narrow blue glow – around its exterior.

Enquiries made with RCMP Sgt. Arnold McPherson, revealed no knowledge of any UFO reports made to them, or the identity of the two officers seen. Air Traffic Control were also contacted; they, likewise, stated no reports of UFOs had been made to them for that day.

(Source: Mrs O. Beaton Vancouver/*Flying Saucer Review*, Volume 20, Number 4, 1974)

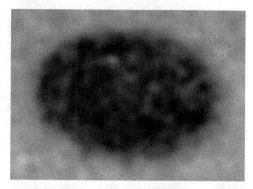

17th October 1974 – Strange phenomena over Sussex

Amateur astronomer Dave Stringer from Clapham, Worthing, Sussex, was out walking with his wife, at 6pm, when they saw an enormous 'bright light' hovering in the western sky above their position, before veering off at incredible speed. Apparently they were not the only ones to see it; two other Worthing residents also reported having sighted:

"…*objects – like pink clouds – moving in formation, two abreast, from south to north-east, at 6pm*".

Another witness told of seeing what looked like "*oval pinkish objects – like candy-floss in the sky*".

Mr Stringer stated that research into these and other events indicated a connection with Devil's Dyke, near Brighton, as many of these objects were seen hovering over this local landmark.

23rd October 1974 – UFO photographed over Bournemouth

We spoke to Bournemouth-based UFO researcher Leslie Harris, about his investigations into a number of UFO sightings, some bordering more on the paranormal rather than UFO, many of which were published in his *Scan* magazine – often accompanied by artwork provided by John Ledner.

On this occasion, we discussed a photograph taken by Bournemouth man – Greg Merchant, of a UFO seen during the evening of the 23rd October 1974, which was to be the subject of considerable media attention. It was featured on the *BBC News*, TV and Radio, and was reported in the *Bournemouth Evening Echo* (23.10.1974).

We contacted Greg, who told us:

"*I was in the bedroom and looking out of the window when, suddenly, I noticed a bright blue-green 'light', moving across the sky.*

I grabbed my Polaroid camera, which had a few exposures left, and ran downstairs and into the garden. The object was moving across the sky, quite fast, in a straight line from west to north-east. The stars were bright and there was a moon quite low down.

The object did not hover. By the time I got there, it was moving fast. I leaned right back, quickly followed it in the viewfinder, and took the photograph when it was almost overhead – brighter than the moon. When I took the photo, I didn't realise it, but there was a flash in the camera. When I took the camera away from my eyes, the object had gone from view. There was absolutely no sound from the object. This I couldn't understand. I had seen aircraft – in fact lots of them, as we are on the flight path to Hurn Airport."

Greg then went into the front room where his parents were, and 'peeled the film', waving the photograph in front of the fire for exactly 30 seconds – then peeled the two parts of the film away. He watched, with baited breath, as it appeared. Excited, he showed his father, who thought he "*was mucking about*".

The next morning Greg's father tackled him again about the photograph, but Greg assured him it was genuine. This was followed by the threat of *"a thick ear"* by Greg's father, after his son had told him that he was going over to the Airport to show them the photo.

Instead, his father took the photo himself and was told the radar had been switched off that night.

SCAN Newsletter

NO. 3

1

<u>GENUINE "FLYING SAUCER" SIGHTING.</u>
AT KINSON, BOURNEMOUTH - - - - PHOTOGRAPH TO BACK IT UP.

This report was on the B.B.C.news, T.V. and Radio on 23rd October, and reported in the Bournemouth Evening Echo of the same day, as front cover news.

The following, is a copy of the news transcript by Mike Buckle, reporter from the "WESSEX PRESS AGENCY" Bournemouth.

Sincere thanks to Wessex for their kind help and co-operation.
Ed.

. . . . . .

When 21 year old Greg Marchant saw a strange moving light in the sky, he did a double take . . . . for it was as big as a double decker bus and moving fast.

Then he grabbed his camera - a Poloroid. And the result is an amazing picture of an Unidentified Flying Object.

Greg was in the bedroom of his home, "I was looking out of the window, when I suddenly saw this greeny-blue light moving across the sky, and it was moving quite fast !
He said.

His camera had a couple of exposures left on the film and he ran downstairs and out into the back garden to get a picture.

"I only had time for one photograph, and the strange thing was there was no sound, just the traffic noise outside on the road."

"I've never believed in UFOs before . . . . . . but I do not. I never want to see anything like it again."

An enlargement of the object Greg Marchant saw through the viewfinder of his £7 camera. He claims the object was rotating slowly.

The house is under the flight path into nearby Bournemouth Hurn Airport, but a check revealed that no aircraft were flying at the time. Airport staff and radar operators were we mystified as Greg.

Said airport director, Mr. Harry Longhurst . . . . . . "It's like nothing I've seen before. I can't explain it".

Added Greg . . . It scared me - it's just fantastic".

Above Credit to
Mike Buckle - "WESSEX"

It's NO HOAX . . . . . SCAN.

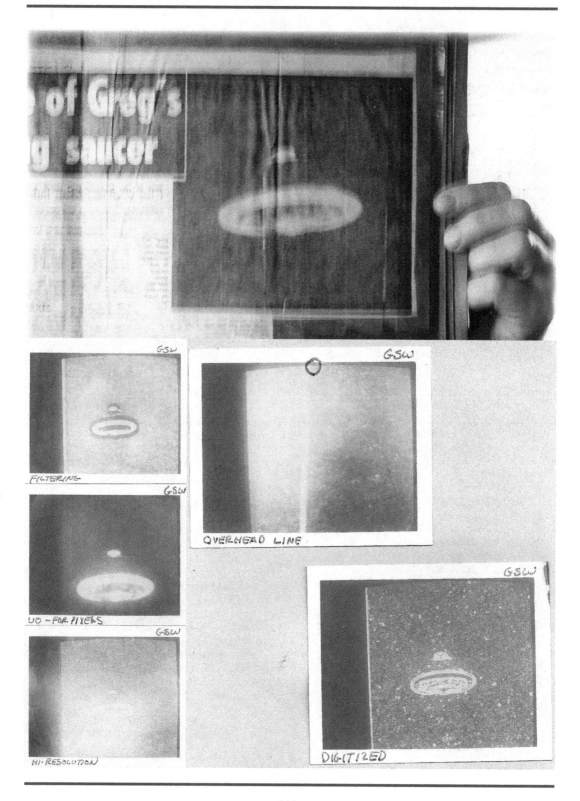

FILTERING

GSW

OVERHEAD LINE

GSW

UO - FOR PIXELS

HI-RESOLUTION

DIGITIZED

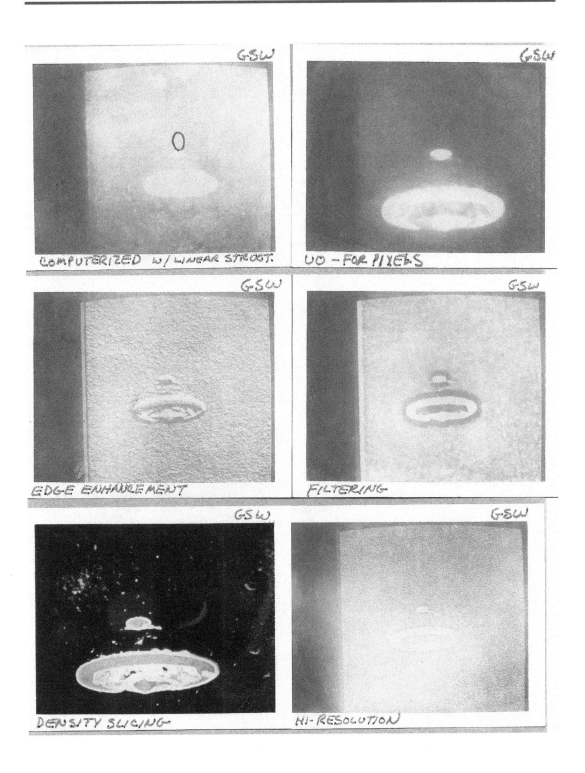

COMPUTERIZED W/ LINEAR STRUCT.

UO - FOR PIXELS

EDGE ENHANCEMENT

FILTERING

DENSITY SLICING

HI-RESOLUTION

496

"CIVILIAN AERIAL PHENOMENA RESEARCH ORGANIZATION"
GROUND SAUCER WATCH · 13238 N. 7th DRIVE · PHOENIX, ARIZONA · 85029

October 1974 UFO Photograph -
Computer Photographic Evaluation (critique)

A lone black & white Polaroid   enlargement photo of a purported UO (unidentified
object) was forwarded to GSW for analysis. The photograph was taken in the
nocturnal mode and reveals a "typical" saucer-shaped image near a clothesline.
The balance of the photograph is void of any foreground/background data. It appears
that a flash attachment was utilized for the exposure due to the unbalance of light
on the image's surface.

All major modes of computer enhancement were utilized during the evaluation including;
computerized filtering, color contouring (density slicing), edge enhancement and
digitizing for distance calculations. The following information was discerned during
the interpretation:

1. The UO image is being affected by the use of the flash attachment. The
    image is reflecting light from the flash at multiple points around the
    periphery of the "object".

2. The UO is extremely close to the camera. Edge analysis of both the UO and the
    clothesline reveal that they are both within a similar film plane. There is no
    evidence that the UO is being affected by atmospherics.

3. There is no other photographic data in the picture.

4. There appears to be a linear structure above the UO used for supportive purposes.

5. The UO is extremely small in size, based on the pixel (picture cell) distortion
    testing and the cursory camera data supplied, therefore, the effective distance
    of a normal flash attachment and the size of camera lens.

6. The photograph, which gives the effect of an object-in-the-distance, can be
    manufactured very easily. The camera is simply placed low to the ground to
    give the illusion of distance from the camera/witness.

7. If the 'object' were truly distant the flash would have no direct affect on the
    picture and at least some distortion would be discernible.

8. There is no evidence of obvious markings, portholes or protrusions on the 'object'.

CONCLUSIONS:

Based on the photographic evidence, i.e., the lack of distortion on edge features,
the technical limitations of a Polaroid camera, the proximity of the UO, etc,
it can be concluded that the photograph represents a crude attempt to simulate a
UFO experience. There is no photographic evidence to support an extraordinary
flying object.

Fred Adrian   William H. Spaulding
GSW PHOTOGRAPHIC CONSULTANT   Director

NOTE: Permission is granted to publish. Provide credit for GSW, INC

27th October 1974 – UFOs over Georgia, USA

At 7pm, a 24 year-old college student was travelling towards Atlanta, via Interstate 85. Her husband was driving. When the car was 15 miles south of Atlanta, she noticed a light source low down in the north-west sky, which was bobbing up and down. They first took it to be an aircraft from the nearby Atlanta airport. It moved up and down about seven times before moving away, at tremendous speed, on a horizontal plane to the north-east. It then made a 45 degrees turn and vanished from sight.

(**Source:** *UFO Investigator*, NICAP, January 1975)

27th October 1974 – Close Encounter, Aveley, Essex

Over the years we were to hear of numerous occasions involving reports of strange 'globes of light' seen by motorists whilst driving along lonely country roads. Many of the reports involved an initial sighting of a 'globe of yellow or white light' – approximately the size of a rugby/football – which would often fly alongside the vehicle, sometimes for many miles, before inexplicably shooting up into the sky. Without doubt the following incident is one of the most interesting ones that we were to come across, over the years, because it involves those all too familiar traits of

John Day

behaviour that form the background of cases like this. Undoubtedly it changed the lives of the participants for ever – not necessarily for the better.

This well-documented case involving a close encounter between a UFO and motorist John Day and his family followed by a number of mysterious incidents bordering on the paranormal, was not in fact brought to the attention of Andrew Collins until August 1977. He conducted a very professional investigation assisted by fellow researcher – Barry King, and later wrote an extensive article in *Flying Saucer Review*, published in 1978, although he named them as the Avis family.

On the 27th October 1974, John Day (then aged 32) and Elaine Day (then aged 28), accompanied by their three children – Karen (11) Kevin (10) and Stuart (7) – went to Elaine's parents house in Harold Hill, Essex. John and Elaine's father went to the school to collect Elaine's sister – Anne – from school, following a trip to Belgium. Unfortunately, she was four hours late getting to the school and did not arrive there until 9pm. After Anne had been taken home, the family set out from Harold Hill at about 9.50pm, anticipating that they would be home within 20 minutes.

John drove along Hacton Lane (a mile away from Hornchurch) in his white Vauxhall Victor car, on what was a beautiful clear night, mild and dry, with little traffic about. Karen and Stuart were asleep on the back of the car; Kevin was awake in the back, looking out of the window. Suddenly, Kevin brought his father's attention to a 'light' he could see above a line of terraced houses to their left. John and Elaine glanced around and saw:

The Route taken by the Day family

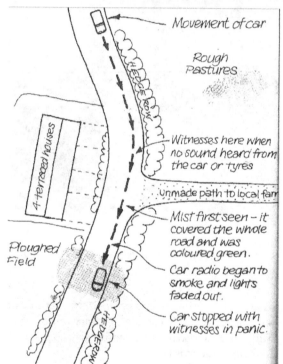

Movement of car

Rough Pastures

Witnesses here when no sound heard from the car or tyres

Unmade path to local farm

Mist first seen – it covered the whole road and was coloured green.

Car radio began to smoke and lights faded out.

Car stopped with witnesses in panic.

HEDGEROW

4 Terraced houses

Ploughed Field

HEDGEROW

"...an oval shaped 'light', bluish iridescent, resembling a large star, about 30 degrees off the horizon, approximately 500 yards away; it seemed to be travelling in a similar direction to our car, in a series of stopping and starting movements. We thought it was a helicopter's light and continued to watch as it moved behind a small wood."

Within seconds of seeing the 'light', they passed the end of houses on their left-hand side and lost sight of it, due to their vision being momentarily obstructed by a small wood. When they looked again it was still there, travelling in the same direction but a little slower than before; they noted the time 10.10pm. Throughout, Karen and Stuart remained asleep.

John again remarked on the absence of traffic on the road. At this point they were now driving through the darkness of the open countryside. This enabled them to obtain a good view of the 'light', which was still about the same distance away – some 500 yards. They continued along the road and turned 90 degrees left and drove along Park Farm Road, with the *White Hart* public house on their right-hand side – which was the scene of activity outside. John drove steadfastly on heading east, towards Aveley, commenting once again at the lack of traffic to his wife. About half a mile east, along Park Farm Road, the 'light' – which appeared to have changed course to south-easterly – was now observed heading towards the road, at an angle of 50 degrees.

John:

> *"It picked up speed and passed in front of us at a high angle. I slowed the car down and craned my neck upwards to see it, before it was obscured by bushes on the right-hand side of the road. As the car went down a dip, we thought this was the end of it and our initial excitement began to fade."*

After the 'dip', the road bends to the right and continues along Aveley Road. They drove on for about a

mile, passing gravel pits on their left and the road to Upminster. As they began to negotiate a right-hand turn (with a block of four terraced houses to their right), they had a terrible feeling that something was wrong – as the sound of the engine and tyres on the road receded into the background, with just the radio still playing.

John:

"In front of us, some 30 yards away, covering the whole road, was this 'green mist' or foggy /gas bank, about 9 feet high, bordered on the left by bushes – its right-hand part curved to the ground behind a thin line of trees along the verge of the road. Its top was flat; the bottom was touching the ground. The car radio began to crackle and smoke. I pulled the wires out of the back of it and disconnected the appliance – then the lights on the car failed and everything went black.

As darkness settled, the 'fog' – unlike any fog I had ever seen – engulfed us. The windows were up; Kevin was standing on the floor behind the other two children, who were still asleep. It was light inside the fog and very cold – dead silent. I could feel a tingling sensation; things seemed hazy, then there was a jolt – like the car going over a *humpback bridge – and seconds later, the 'mist' or 'fog' was gone. The oddest thing was that I felt I was alone in the car.

My next recollection was being aware of driving along the side of White Post Wood, exactly half a mile away!"

['The bridge marks the boundary between London and the Essex boundary of Greys Thurrock – this was the location of *another remarkable close encounter.*]

Elaine's recollection began about half a mile further up, near to Running Water Wood, at which stage the car was now behaving normally and the coldness had gone.

Missing time

On reaching home, John rewired the radio and carried the two children – Karen and Stuart (still asleep) – up to bed, but was surprised to discover the time was now 1am – which seemed impossible as they expected to have arrived home at 10.20pm, and meant there were three hours of time they were unable to account for.

The next day Elaine telephoned her mother and told her about the incident, but didn't mention about the 'missing time'. Both John and Elaine felt tired, but all three children went to school as normal. In conversation about the matter, the couple decided they should try and forget about it.

The car started breaking down after the incident and suffered a broken crankshaft, which required a replacement engine and clutch renewal. In early 1975 they scrapped the car.

Suffered inexplicable breakdown

Shortly after the incident, John – a talented carpenter and joiner – suffered an inexplicable nervous breakdown, sometime before Christmas of 1974, forcing him to give up employment until September 1975, when he found a job working with mentally handicapped people – something he had wanted to do for years, feeling much more confident of himself, and then went on to University where he obtained a degree in art.

Change in character and lifestyle

We were not surprised to hear that, after the event, John was to develop a new-found interest in art, craft, and writing poetry. Such changes in behaviour appear common, following UFO close encounters like that described by John and Elaine. In addition the couple were to complain of physical interruptions to power supply and electrical devices within the family household, together with sightings of 'shapes' and strange noises heard.

Vegetarians

Similarly Elaine, now much more self-confident, decided to take up a college course in September 1975 – something she had intended to do for years. Kevin, who had been awake during the UFO encounter (the first one to sight the mysterious 'light') suddenly began to improve his reading ability and was soon way

MYSTERY OF A CLOSE ENCOUNTER WITH MEN IN A GREEN MIST

by JOHN CLARE

JOHN DAY is convinced his family has had a close encounter with creatures from another planet after driving through a green mist.

He says the strange beings were 7ft tall, pink-eyed and communicated by telepathy. His amazing story emerged under hypnosis after John, a 33-year-old student and his wife Sue had nightmares about their experience.

He says: "I had never really believed in UFOs before this happened. Now I'm convinced aliens are here and only show themselves when they want to."

The couple's close encounter happened on a moonlight night as they drove to their Essex home.

They had been visiting Sue's parents in Harold Hill and the journey home normally takes 30 minutes.

But after driving through the mist, John and Sue arrived to find three hours had mysteriously passed.

The clock on their mantelpiece showed it was 12.45 a.m. —yet they had set out at 9.20 p.m. the previous evening.

Then the couple began to have the same bizarre dream that they were on an operating table being examined by aliens.

ZOOMED

The dreams became so vivid the couple were afraid to go to bed. Finally John contacted a group which researches UFOs, in the hope of finding out what really happened that night.

He was taken to one of Britain's leading hypnotists, dentist Leonard Wilder.

Under hypnosis John recalled how a white light followed and finally zoomed across in front of his car on a lonely road.

Then a beam of light transported the couple and their car aboard an alien spacecraft parked in a nearby field. John, a father of three, told me:

I went on a spaceship and met the 7ft aliens

ful woman walked in. She looked just like an earth woman.

She had bright gold hair, and all around her there was a grey mist. She really was beautiful. She walked towards me, and I took one step towards her. Then suddenly she vanished.

Soon after the visit was over, and the next I knew I was driving down the road again.

The beings k e p t telling me they were friendly and I enjoyed it immensely.

Sue, a 39-year-old nursery nurse, refused to be hypnotised because she did not want to relive the experience.

But she told me: "When I lay on the operating table they painted me with

a mauve liquid. Then they washed it off.

"They prodded me all over with a pen-like object, and didn't spare my blushes. Then I screamed.

"One of the tall beings came over and put his hand on my forehead. Then I went out like a light.

VANISH

"Later they took me on a tour around the ship. They showed me a screen and said, 'That is Earth.' They pointed out England on it. Then we seemed to zoom in, and they showed me where I lived.

"I told the beings I didn't want to go back. I asked if I could stay on the craft, and they agreed.

"I saw John climb into

the car, and it started to vanish. As it disappeared, I said I had changed my mind, and wanted to go back. Then I found myself sitting in the car.

Hypnotist Mr Wilder said: "I have no doubt that Mr Day is telling the truth.

"I say this because when I first hypnotised him I conditioned him to tell only the truth.

Mr Barry King, member of the UFO Investigators Network, said: "We've made exhaustive inquiries and are convinced this couple had a close encounter.

"Certain aspects of it are similar to other abductions, like the design and furnishing of the rooms. We can find no reason to doubt its authenticity."

THE ALIEN: John's sketch

STAR TREK: John at the spot where he says he met the aliens

ahead of his reading age, whereas previously, he had been backward in his reading at school. Additionally, John, Elaine, Kevin and Karen gave up eating meat and could not even stand the smell of it. They sampled fish, but the taste made them ill and began eating health foods to some extent, avoiding foods with preservatives and additives, becoming teetotal, and giving up cigarettes.

Couple followed by mysterious blacked out vehicles – allegation of police harassment!

Shortly after the encounter, John and Elaine became aware that they were being followed on a number of occasions (individually) by three cars, a small red 'sports' car, a blue 'Jaguar', and a large white car (Ford Executive?); the number plates were the British new-style, white at the front and yellow at the rear. All of them had darkened windows.

John:

> "I was being stopped at least five times a week by the police, while driving the car, and given a ticket to produce my driving documents. When I did produce at the police station, the officer there was very curious as to why, on occasion, the officers details had not been included on the HORT/1 slip; this took place in December 1974. This harassment lasted well into the summer of 1975."

One is bound to ask why and who sanctioned this action against Mr Day and for what purpose. In addition to this the couple began to have strange recurring dreams, involving being 'operated on' by small ugly 'beings', resembling gnomes. [Authors: Not the only time we were to hear of this – In 2006, a retired police officer from Northamptonshire told us about a UFO sighted by him over nearby lakes. After reporting it only to the MOD and asking that his name be kept confidential, he was the subject of a number of stop checks by the police and was to discover his medical records had been tampered with.]

Hypnotic regressions

John and Elaine also took part in three hypnotic regressions – which took place on 25th September 1977, the 2nd October and 16th October 1977. During those sessions, conducted by Dr. Leonard Wilder – a qualified hypnotherapist and dentist by profession – John described meeting,

> "...tall hooded 'beings' with pink eyes, wearing one piece suits, and tables made out of a peculiar substance (not wood or metal) and a thick metal honeycombed bar – 30 inches long by ten inches wide – which was moved over my body, causing a vibrating sensation. There was also a small 'being' present, clothed in 'fur, but not fur'."

> "He touched my left shoulder and I passed out. When I regained consciousness I found myself lying on a table, two and a half feet wide a few feet off the ground. The surface of the table was soft and covered with small grey bubbles. Eighteen inches above my head was a 'scan' type of apparatus – rectangular shaped, 30-36 inches in length, about 3 inches in width, approximately one inch thick with an underside of honeycombed design, supported by two circular rods, one on each side of me."

> "The device took about one minute to pass over my body, creating a warm, tingling sensation on the area being apparently scanned.

> I was aware of three tall entities to my right, and two small ugly looking ones to the left, referred to as 'examiners'. They were four feet tall, no apparent neck, with large slanted triangular eyes, light brown nose or beak, a slither for the mouth, pointed, slanted back ears, large hairy hands, four digits on each with claws or long nails. This 'being' walked awkwardly, making an occasional guttural chirp."

John asked the tall entities if he could get up. "*Sit there for a while*", he was told. He started to realise that the words were not spoken but received telepathically. Shortly afterwards, he was allowed to get up. The 'examiners' then left the room, at which point he became aware that he was dressed in a one-piece garment, similar to what the tall entities were wearing.

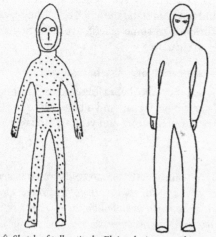

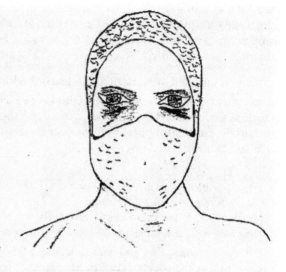

Left: Sketch of tall entity by Elaine during second interview: note 'nose' and also belt, which was worn by 'leader' only.
Right: John's sketch of tall entity. Nose and belt are omitted, although John says he believes that at least one entity was wearing one.

© John day.

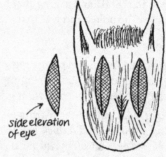

side elevation of eye

eyes black and convexed.

brown fur-like covering on face

Early impression by John of an 'examiner'

B.

narrow, pointed eyes, shaped like winged glasses

pointed ears

beak, or nose

hunched shoulders

white coat or gown

pen-like instrument

wire

Sketch based on an early attempt by Elaine to draw one of the small entities, or 'examiners'

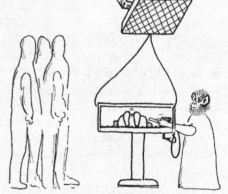

Sketch based on John's impression of himself on the examining table, while the 'three' watch 'examiner' at work

"The room was oval shaped, perhaps 20 feet in length, by 12 feet in width, and about 7-8 feet high, very smooth – like being inside a bubble – the only furniture being the table and two overhead lights."

John described the taller entities to be 6 feet, 6 inches tall, except the 'leader', who seemed to be a few inches taller. They all appeared to be wearing a one-piece suit made of material resembling Lurex or synthetic felt that even covered their hands and feet.

"They had two eyes (slightly larger than ours), with pink irises and creamy eyeballs. No nose or mouth was seen and I speculated whether they were wearing masks. I saw what appeared to be only three fingers on each hand and their skin looked very pale – almost transparent. They reminded me of a 'bendy toy' or 'blow up doll' when they moved, as they seemed devoid of joints in their arms or legs – yet walked gracefully but with no long strides."

During his entire onboard encounter, the tallest entity was the only 'being' that John had direct contact with. John asked these 'beings' what they did when they went outside their ship, and was told they used a visor – which was shown to him.

We felt that this was one of the most detailed accounts we had ever come across, involving considerable conversation between the parties known as the 'Watchers', who told John they had formerly inhabited the planet long ago. All manner of topics were discussed, including the 'Aliens' form of communication. They were also given a 'guided tour' of the layout of the 'craft' and shown maps, charts and instrumentation. Sadly the couple split up many years later, as they both entered separate lives. Sue became a pagan witch and midwife, who served with the Allies in Iraq during the first Gulf War. John now lives in a rural part of Scotland.

Andrew Collins was to tell of *"strange happenings inside the house"*, which he himself witnessed. He said:

Andrew Collins

"I find it intriguing that in European occultism, egregoris (Greek for 'Watchers') was the name given to the 'balls' of etheric light that watched over the affairs of mankind. Perhaps John might have been closer to the truth than he could ever have imagined.

The family are very credible, and what is important is that they have always attempted to analyze what happened from grounded perspective, suggesting even that the whole thing had been an astral experience after they all entered the 'green mist'. In my opinion, the whole incident happened instantaneously for the family and car, but outside usual space-time for the rest of the world, leaving them with a three hour time loss. I am sure I could eventually work out that something like this is possible on a quantum level, using Einstein's theory of special relativity. It seemed the more we talked together on the subject the more information would be released.

As Elaine put it, 'It's like if you hit the right note, the floodgates will open.'"

Strange phenomena reported at the family home

"Myself, and Barry King would camp round at the Day's home every Friday night to see whether any paranormal phenomena might occur, and sometimes it did. Another night John, Barry, and I, sat up chatting until the early hours, so as not to disturb his wife – Sue, who was asleep. John remained with Barry, and I, as we settled down for the night. John and Barry were in sleeping bags on the floor and I was on the sofa. I slept, and was then awoken around seven o'clock that morning by the sound of the door handle moving behind my head, at which I craned my neck to see, in the dawn light, the door opening – just feet away. I thought that John or Barry had gone to the toilet upstairs, and were returning to the room."

Tall 'figure' appears

"A tall silhouetted 'figure' stood momentarily in the doorway before moving quickly out of sight – as if walking away. It was at that moment that I glanced onto the floor and saw that both John and Barry were clearly present and both fast asleep. I became slightly anxious, but assumed that the person had to be Sue, the only other adult in the house, despite no sound of anyone going up the stairs. It could not have gone anywhere else, as it had stood in the house's tiny reception area, which leads only onto the stairs. It was then, very suddenly and unexpectedly, that I was engulfed by an extremely pungent smell – like rotten eggs – which stifled me, and then instantly I fell back to sleep and woke up around 10 o'clock. The whole thing eventually came back to me, and I recounted what had happened. Sue assured me she had not come down at all, which made sense as the 'figure' was, in my opinion, male. Moreover, Sue was quite sure there was

definitely no one in the house, and an intruder can be ruled out as the doors to the outside were locked. The strangest aspect was the pungent smell, which we know is associated very strongly with UFO entity cases. The person/entity was unquestionably physical and not etheric.

John:

"There has been a great deal written about the case, over the years, much of it without any communication with myself and family and much of it incorrect. 'The Watchers', as they have become known, have a great sense of humour. They are like children when it comes to new experiences; they need to feel. They have always been here and always will be. They have progressed from the physical being and, in doing so, have lost so much. The desire for perfection only leads to despair and it is that that drives them. They fear humans, for they know that they are so insignificant in the scheme of things and yet so very rare and very fragile."

We wish John, Sue, and his family, all the best with their new life.

(Source: Andrew Collins, UFOIN/The Aveley abduction, *Flying Saucer Review*, Volume 23, No. 6, April 1978/ Personal interviews with John Day)

NOVEMBER 1974

Uri Geller under scrutiny

The respected Journal – *Nature*, Volume 251, of the 18th October 1974, published a paper by Drs. R Targ and Hal Puthoff of the Stanford Research Institute, California, on experiments carried out regarding the powers claimed by Uri Geller.

On the previous day the *New Scientist* was published showing on its front cover a photo of Mr Geller, followed by an article inside by its technology Policy Editor – Dr. Joseph Hanlon, who stated that every one of Uri Geller's feats were nothing more than simple stage magic, trickery, cheating or hoaxing! He mentioned that while Hal Puthoff was sceptical of some of Uri's metal bending, he mentioned an occasion when, while driving with Uri as a passenger, during a conversation about 'Flying Saucers', Uri said he would give an example of his powers from 'them', and promptly stopped the car without touching anything. The *New Scientist* set up a research panel,

Saturday 11 March 2017 ··· telegraph.co.uk Irish Republic €2.30 No.50,326 £2.00

Is your bed big enough? Should you ever lie in? Do you take naps? REBOOT YOUR SLEEP

The 20-question test that will guarantee a good night *Saturday*

The Daily Telegraph

NATIONAL NEWSPAPER OF THE YEAR

Calcutta crunch
England & Scotland clash in The Big One
Sport

Spring break
50 ultimate long weekends
Inside

Lisa Armstrong
The new designer label we can afford
News Review & Features

Dan Stevens
On Beauty, Beast – and being adopted
Magazine

Letters	23
Obituaries	31
Business	33
Weather	38

Tories 'no longer low-tax party'

May suffers Budget poll blow as almost half of the public say they are less likely to vote Conservative

By Gordon Rayner POLITICAL EDITOR

THE Conservatives are no longer seen as a party of low taxation following Philip Hammond's tax raid on the self-employed, a new poll for *The Daily Telegraph* shows.

Just one in four voters now regards the Tories as a low-tax party, while almost half of those polled say they trust the Conservatives less as a result of Mr Hammond's Budget. More than half of

voters – 55 per cent – say Theresa May should have honoured the party's manifesto pledge not to raise taxes.

Figures on voting intentions are equally worrying for the Prime Minister, with almost half of those questioned saying they are less likely to vote Tory because of the Budget, including one in seven Conservative voters.

The Prime Minister and her Chancellor have faced a rebellion from their own MPs following their decision to increase National Insurance contributions for self-employed people.

Lord Lamont of Lerwick, the former chancellor, today advises Mr Hammond to adopt "Thatcher radicalism" by giving workers incentives to fund their own welfare if he is to avoid future tax rises.

Lord Lamont urges Mr Hammond to scrap the NI increase, saying the policy "goes against the entire grain of Conservative policy since 1979".

Writing in today's *Telegraph*, he argues wholesale reform, not "bureaucratic tidiness" is the only way to tackle the "unsustainable" rise of the cost of welfare.

Mr Hammond must first survive a plot to oust him which has been concocted by hardline Brexiteers.

A former minister said Mr Hammond's opponents were "hunting as a pack" and using the row as an excuse to try to force him out, because they do not trust him to pursue a hard Brexit.

The extent to which the Budget has damaged trust in the Conservative

brand is detailed in a ComRes poll of 1,035 adults carried out yesterday.

Asked whether they agreed that "the Conservative Party is no longer a low-tax party", 49.5 per cent of voters agreed, with just 26 per cent disagreeing. On the question of whether the Budget made them trust the Conservatives less, 47 per cent said it did, while 40 per cent said they trusted Mrs May less as a result.

Fewer than half of those questioned – 44 per cent – thought Mr Hammond should carry on as Chancellor, with *Continued on Page 5*

MATT

"Everything is disposable these days. I remember when a Budget would last nearly 18 hours"

Charles Moore Page 21
Norman Lamont and
Editorial Comment Page 15

May poised to fire Brexit starting gun next week

By Steven Swinford DEPUTY POLITICAL EDITOR

THE Prime Minister may formally trigger Brexit as early as Tuesday after European leaders said they were making preparations for an announcement.

Ministers are increasingly confident that Theresa May's Article 50 Bill could clear both the Commons and the Lords on Monday.

The swift passage of the legislation would clear the way for Mrs May to trigger Brexit negotiations in the Commons the following day.

Ministers are privately pressing Mrs May to "get on with Brexit" and trigger Article 50 "as soon as possible", *The Daily Telegraph* understands.

The announcement would help Mrs May move the debate away from Philip Hammond's Budget.

Downing Street has said that Article 50 will be triggered by the end of the month but refused to commit to a date.

Donald Tusk, the head of the European Council, said that EU leaders were prepared to respond within 48 hours of Mrs May triggering Brexit.

Angela Merkel, the German chancellor, confirmed that if Mrs May invoked Article 50 next week, an "extraordinary meeting" of the remaining 27 members of the EU would be held on April 6.

The Government has suffered defeat in the House of Lords on two amendments to the Article 50 Bill. One of them guaranteed the rights of EU citizens living in the UK, while the other said that Parliament should be given a "meaningful vote" on the final deal.

The Government will oppose both amendments in the Commons on Monday, and could face a rebellion by up to 20 Tory MPs.

However, Tory whips are increasingly confident that they can win over many of the rebels by giving assurances on the timetable of the deal.

The legislation will then pass to the Lords, where Labour sources indicated that the party's peers are prepared to give way gradually.

Uri Geller, the illusionist and spoonbender, claims that MI5 arranged for him to visit Britain to examine his telepathic abilities, with David Dimbleby's talk show used as cover

MI5, Dimbleby and Uri Geller's secret mission to Britain

By Hannah Furness

MI5 arranged for Uri Geller to come to the UK by using David Dimbleby's talk show as a smokescreen so they could see his psychic powers for themselves, the illusionist has claimed.

Mr Geller and MI5 and MI6 knew he had been tested by the CIA to determine his telepathic abilities in the Seventies, and hoped to explore his poten-

tial in person. In an interview with *The Daily Telegraph*, he claims he was invited to appear on the *David Dimbleby Talk Show* in 1975 as cover for his trip. Involved CIA documents have already shown the Americans believed he really did have psychic powers.

Mr Geller, who lived in Britain for 35 years, also disclosed how he told Theresa May she would be Prime Minister after she visited him in 2015, making the pre-

diction while touching a spoon once owned by Sir Winston Churchill.

Earlier this year, an extraordinary series of declassified US documents revealed how Mr Geller was tested by the CIA over eight days in 1973, with his handlers concluding: "We consider that he has demonstrated his paranormal perceptual ability in a convincing and unambiguous manner."

Speaking in full about the episode

for the first time, Mr Geller says: "Part of me is certainly glad that the world knows the truth about that secret part of my life. The declassified documents released by the CIA in January are only the tip of the iceberg, really. As for any current involvement, I cannot confirm and I will not deny it. Whatever I say now could endanger my life."

Interview: Page 25

---

which included Dr. Bernard Dixon (editor), Dr. Hanlon, Dr. Christopher Evans, and magician – David Berglas, inviting Uri to attend. Uri declined what appears to be an inquisition, saying that he had received a threat of assassination.

Press conference in London

In the early days of November 1974, a long playing record of Uri Geller's compositions was launched at a press conference at the Savoy Hotel, London,

attended by many newspapers, magazines, journals, and TV, who had read a detailed report of the proceedings published in the *Psychic News* on 9th November 1974. Dr Andrija Puharich stated in his book – *Uri* (W.H. Allen and Co. Ltd., London) that Uri has claimed that he obtained his powers from UFO entities whatever and whoever they may be.

Two scientists that believed Uri was genuine were ˙Professor John Taylor, of London University's Kings College, and Professor John Hasted, who had organised experiments conducted in strict scientific conditions to evaluate the powers of Uri.

Dr. Hasted:

> "Its time to stand up and be counted. Uri Geller can soften metal. Metal does not normally behave in that way. I do not know the cause, but believe the final result could change science."

Professor Taylor:

> "I was at first highly sceptical of the Geller bending metal feats, but changed my view after finding many children with similar psychic abilities. The problem is how to convince my scientific colleagues. The New Scientist article was not a scientific one and, while fair to a point, went too far. I have seen Uri bend objects and that insufficient pressure was used by him to bend them by mechanical means. Articles were also twisted at a distance. Investigations showed that molecular changes in the metal were involved. What causes this is not easy, but I have speculated that the power comes from the brain."

Professor Taylor told of a Geiger counter that registered an alarming count when Uri was near it, 500 times above radiation danger level. A battery placed over the Geiger counter produced a similar result.

(Source: Charles Bowen – *Flying Saucer Review* (extract), Volume 20, No. 4, 1974)

We telephoned John Taylor's house, hoping to learn if this was in fact the case. His wife declined to let us speak to him, but told us:

> "The Professor has finished with all of that, many years ago, but if you obtain a copy of his book Science and the Supernatural *it will give you some information relating to a scientist's view of the supernatural."*

˙Professor John Taylor had allegedly witnessed for himself a number of manifestations which had taken place at Winchester housewife – Joyce Bowles home address, in 1976. John Taylor appeared at a BUFORA Conference on the 10th/11th May 1975, which included an appearance by Leonard Cramp.

24th November 1974 – Three UFOs over Rossendale Valley, Lancashire

LANCASHIRE ROUND-UP

Jenny Randles

Our contributor is Secretary of the Northern UFO Network, an association of UFO investigation groups in Northern Britain. She is also Research Co-Ordinator of BUFORA (British UFO Research Association).

THE Rossendale Valley area of Lancashire was the scene of intense activity during the month of November, 1974, and work on the sightings was done by the Rossendale Astronomical Society, who have a strong UFO contingent. One of the best documented cases came from Haslingden, a small town between Bury and Burnley; the event took place on November 24.

At approximately 4.10 p.m. on a cold, grey day, at least three sets of independent witnesses claim to have observed the passage of between one and three cigar-shaped objects.' Mr. Daniels and his wife were crossing the street towards their home when three such objects of a sharp golden-bronze colour swept across the sky in a long arc from SSE to NNW. They estimated that there was about a ½-mile separation between the first two and a little further between these and the last one. The overall length was given as 50–80 feet, but the latter object was at least one and a half times as big as this. They also noted a faint humming noise and got the impression that a fuzzy region across the middle of the objects represented lights.

About a mile away, a housewife, Mrs. Tate, had just stepped outside for a moment when her attention was caught by two small objects like bullets with a flat and rounded end. She heard no sound but noted they were moving against a strong prevailing wind. After a few moments they joined together and the junction was marked by a fuzzy region. It continued on its previous path, moving in and out of cloud, and she insists it was glowing a golden colour and not reflecting light. She went indoors for a few seconds and telephoned one of the Astronomical Society members, Tim Evans, who rushed to the scene. He did not see anything, though Mrs. Tate could still see the object moving away in the distance over the hills. It was growing quite murky however and she said the object was frequently passing through cloud layers. Mr. Evans could attest to the fact that Mrs. Tate was obviously excited and was viewing something unusual to her. Also her dog was barking and generally disturbed during the incident and calmed down soon after Mr. Evans arrived and the object went out of sight.

Subsequently, two teenagers had a frightening experience on the night of January 14 at Moor Side. They were walking home along a dark lane after stabling their horses at a nearby farm when they saw a brightly-lit object hovering over the cottages. It was like an inverted saucer with a steady green light and a flashing red one and seemed to swoop down on them. One of the girls shone a powerful light on to it and it appeared to react, rocking to and fro in a gentle motion. At this they ran from the scene as fast as they could. MUFORA was able to investigate this, and other cases, within hours of their occurrence. It was very apparent that these normally stable girls were in a state of fright. The next morning one of them refused to walk along the lane alone — even in broad daylight.

Not only children reported these things, as evidenced by a report from a well respected glider pilot and his fiancee who saw a low-level object at Lees with red, orange and blue lights on January 10. Reports died away from the third week in January, and from the latest information reaching NUFON from BYUIG the scene of activity seemed then to have transferred to Merseyside.

The Moorside object

Unknown to both sets of witnesses, Joyce Thorne, a young housewife, was also seeing the object from another part of the town. Her description of one object closely follows that of the others except that she saw a row of lights across the middle of the craft. It is quite possible that further witnesses will be found since those so far have all come independently. The region is not densely populated, consisting of much open land surrounded by hills, but it is a growing centre of overspill housing.

From the above reports we can perhaps piece together the procession. It would appear that the first two cigars passed over close together and were only seen by the Daniels. Mrs. Tate being further south on the supposed course saw two other small objects merge and proceed to the NNW where the other witnesses saw them only as one, larger object. The duration of observation was generally agreed as between five and ten minutes and the height, judging from cloud levels, must have been about

3,000 feet. Checks were made with local radar, and it was learned that no aircraft were in the vicinity (aircraft normally pass on a NE course, or alternatively SW, at a height of about 10,000 feet).

During the early weeks of 1975, the Manchester UFO Research Association were involved with a number of reports from the moorland regions to the north and east of Oldham.

On Sunday, January 5th, two young children who had been playing at Upermill described to the police a disc-shaped object with a flickering yellow rim and a flashing red light which they saw shooting across the moors and making a humming sound. MUFORA were able to trace a group of eleven older boys who were playing nearby and who also saw it.

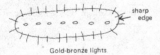

Gold-bronze lights

The Rossendale object

The Uppermill object

(Source: Jenny Randles, Lancashire Round-up, *Flying Saucer Review, Volume 21,* Number 6)

DECEMBER 1974

1st December 1974 – Triangular object seen over Somerset

During a 'sky watch' by members of a UFO organisation, held on the early morning of the 1st December 1974, at Beckington, Frome, Somerset, a bright object appeared in the sky. With the aid of binoculars, a triangular object was seen within the light. It was then plotted as heading north-west for four seconds, before dropping downwards for six seconds, followed by a 90 degree turn to south-east for four seconds – these movements being repeated three times, until it disappeared from view. From calculations carried out, it was established that the object was seen

> *"at an angle of100 degrees elevation,- height 1.4104 miles- distance 8.1235 miles- downward speed 846.24mph -diameter of object 384 feet,- lengths of sides adjacent to acute angle of a triangle 190-190 feet".* (**Source: Lawrence W. Dale, BUFORA**)

Winter 1974 – Wales: Police sight UFO over Ben Nevis

Police Constable David Dawson, of the Strathclyde Police, and his companion – both veteran climbers – were descending Ben Nevis after a gruelling climb lasting 16 hours, in winter 1974. The two men decided to stop and take a break at the Red Burn, halfway down the Mountain.

David:

> *"I was lying down, exhausted. Kerr shouted out in an alarming tone, 'Look at that Dave!' I forced myself up and looked outwards, seeing an object the size of a full moon approaching, increasing in size as it grew closer. It was about the size of a Double- Decker bus and silver all over, making a noise like an electricity transformer, moving at about 30 miles per hour, barely a hundred yards just above the ground. I studied it, trying to determine a regular shape or windows to it – there were none. We watched as it headed towards Polldubh, where we lost sight of it."*

(Source: Personal interview)

December 1974 – Animal mutilation in the United States

Following a spate of reports of animal mutilations, centred on Meeker County, Minnesota, NICAP researcher – Jack Bostract (who lived 100 miles away) went out to investigate. He discovered that Sherriff Mike Rogers had received a complaint from cattle owner Frank Schiefelbein, at North Kingston Township, on 1st December 1974, after discovering that one of his female Black Angus calves had been mutilated. Rogers drove out to the scene and examined for himself the deceased animal which was being examined by vet Dr. Nelson, who performed an autopsy and took samples which were later sent to the University of Minnesota, Veterinary School for further analysis.

> *"The lips of the animal had been cut off one inch above the nose to behind the rear of the left jaw bone. The tongue was cut out deep in the throat, and the jugular vein was slit. One cup of blood was found at the scene which indicated that the majority of the blood have been collected and moved from the scene. The edge of the left ear and the reproductive organs had been removed."*

The location where this had happened showed a perfect circle, with no traces of footprints in the snow.

4th December 1974 – Cone shaped UFO over London

Andrew Robert Worboys was then aged 15 and living in Antlers Hill Chingford in the London borough of Waltham Forest North east London. He had just arrived home from school when his Mother asked him to pick something up from the local shop. As he went outside to comply he saw at 4.25pm a . . .

> *"Flash of blue light cross the sky in the south direction moving very quickly and at some distance away. I made my way to Sewardstone Road and looked up again when I was stunned to see two cone shaped objects which merged and then separated one heading off towards the forest the other towards the reservoir. Ten seconds later I lost sight of the second one but the first was by now heading under the electric cables crossing the road above me .I heard what sounded like a high pitched sound like a fizzing or hissing. I ran to the shop but by then it had gone"*

Andrew contacted the Waltham Forest Guardian newspaper but never received any reply or confirmation they would publish his sighting. A few years later he contacted Dan Goring.

(Source: Essex UFO Study Group)

5th December 1974 – UFO over Colchester, Essex

A UFO was sighted over Colchester by a local resident, who had this to say at the time:

> *"I saw it approach initially from the south-west direction, stop, and reverse away from me without running around. It went behind some trees and then rose to the west and just 'messed about' in the sky, before disappearing. A few minutes later the 'light' reappeared, this time showing a cluster*

of red lights around it. These faded away – then it proceeded to go through a series of aerobatics, accelerating and slowing down, silently and gracefully. Finally, it shot off towards the west."

(**Source:** *Colchester Evening Gazette*, 6.12.1974)

16th December 1974 – 'Bright light' in the sky ... did the RAF respond?

A couple were driving along the A2, towards London, near the Dartford Heath turn off, at 8am on the 16th December 1974, when they saw a 'bright light', stationary in the sky, which then disappeared but reappeared further down the A2 – now grey in colour – at which point they *"...noticed a RAF jet overhead, at high altitude"*.

After turning off at the Danson Interchange, they saw the object and RAF jet heading off towards the direction of London. (**Source:** BUFORA)

21st December 1974 – Silver 'ball of light' over Essex

John Saville (38) – GPO engineer, and his wife, of Raydon Road, Dagenham, Essex, were travelling back home to Dagenham from London, when they saw:

"...a brilliant 'ball of silver light', moving slowly over the top of a block of high-rise flats, outside the town; we stopped the car over a bridge and got out. It was in view for five minutes, about a third of a mile away, and then dropped down behind the flats."

(Source: Dan Goring Essex UFO Study Group)

26th December 1974 – 'Red light' over Dyfed

A curious 'ball of red light' was seen descending through the sky, at about 9.55pm, over Hook, Dyfed, by a number of villagers, who rejected the suggestion, later made, that they had seen a flare. A search of the locality by Mr Randall Jones Pugh of Roch, near Haverfordwest, on Boxing Day, accompanied by a number of villagers, failed to locate anything of value.

(Source: *Western Mail*, 30.12.1974/ *Western Mail*, 6.1.1975/ *Western Telegraph*, 9.1.1975)

Dec 1974

Mystery red ball seen in the sky

HAVERFORDWEST garage proprietor, Mr. Cyril Hughes was still searching today (Tuesday) for mysterious red fireball which he saw falling from the sky near his Hook home on the evening of Boxing Day.

Mr. Hughes, proprietor of the Merlin Motor Company at Merlins Bridge, claims he saw the object fall either into the wood or the water near the Old Hook Quay - but its identity continues to baffle him and the police.

Police and Mr. Hughes, who lives at Oakhurst, Pill Road, Hook, have spoken to house-holders in the vicinity but it appears that Mr. Hughes is the only one who saw the object - a red ball which fell at medium speed from the sky.

TERRIFIC GLARE

It was about 10.00 p.m. when Mr. Hughes was driving to Haverfordwest to pick up his wife that he first saw the U.F.O. "I had got to Cottage Corner when I distinctly saw a red ball. It gave off a terrific red glare and fell behind some houses.

"I turned the car round and drove to Woodside Back and searched the shore line but found nothing. The tide appeared to be right in so it could well have fallen into the water. The shame is that

there wasn't a soul about, but I definitely saw it," he explained.

Sixty-four-year-old Mr. Hughes went back to the place where he claims the object landed on Friday but found nothing. He has continued his search and today planned to look through the wood in a bid to find some trace of the mysterious 'fireball'.

COULD HAVE BEEN METEOR

Mr. Hughes confesses that he is clueless as far as the object is concerned. "I have never seen a meteor but I suppose it could have been one. The whole thing is a complete mystery but I have no doubt that I saw the object. It was distinct and gave off a terrific glare," he said.

Because the RAF base at Brawdy was closed for Christmas the object could not be tracked on the radar screens, so it is likely that unless Mr. Hughes finds some trace the 'fireball' will remain a mystery for all time.

Updates

Further update for 1971 re: 16th November 1971 –
page 144 – Photo of two boys now shown.

Further update for 1971 re: 14th December 1971 –
page 186 – Newspaper cutting now available.

Mr. Paul Beckenham's picture (above) being examined (below) by Mr. F. Mountain at Birmingham Airport today.

U.F.O. photograph 'impressive,' says air traffic man

BIRMINGHAM EVENING MAIL 14-12-71

Evening Mail Reporter

THE latest and possibly clearest picture of an Unidentified Flying Object was examined today by a senior air traffic controller.

His verdict: "Impressive and interesting."

Mr. Paul Beckenham, a 22-year-old packer, of 62, Rochester Way, Twyford, Banbury, says he took a sequence of five pictures at 3.30 p.m. on Saturday when he was alone in the vicinity of the Burton Dassett Hills—scene of a recent unsuccessful "sky watch."

STANDARD EQUIPMENT

He said today: " The U.F.O. came in from the south and I had it in view for about 12 seconds.

"It made no noise and after coming in very fast it slowed almost to a standstill, then came round in an arc and disappeared in the direction from which it had come.'

Mr. Beckenham said he took his sequence of pictures using standard photographic equipment.

Mr. Beckenham is a member of the Banbury-based International U.F.O. Research Association, whose organiser is Mr. Keith Palmer.

Mr. Palmer said: "After examining the sequence of pictures we are convinced they are genuine.

"Numerous sightings were reported to us on Saturday, particularly from the South Midlands."

'CLEAREST'

Today, one of Mr. Beckenham's pictures was shown to Mr. F. Mountain, senior supervisor in the Air Traffic Control department of Birmingham Airport.

Mr. Mountain said that if the pictures were authentic it was the clearest picture of a U.F.O. taken so far.

The Air Traffic Control Department at the airport collects information from members of the public about sightings and sends it to the Air Ministry.

Further updates for 1972 re: 11th November 1972 – see page 181 – Newspaper cutting available.

Further updates for 1974:

Air Force Jets chase Ufo over New York City.

UFO's sighted in area

East Flatbush, N.Y. 12-9-74

While I was waiting for a bus in the evening I looked up in the sky and noticed a light flying along. I watched it as it moved along until it was obscured by a telephone pole. I waited for it to appear on the other side of the pole, but it just did'nt appear. There were no low clouds for it to get lost in. I'm sure it was not a plane, but I'm positive it was a solid object! Date of sighting 6:30 P.M. 12-9-74 The object was yellow-white, moving from north-east to sout-west. The rate of speed 150 Milms per hour
Your Friend   Inge

Late News Flashes

Otto Binder the famous UFO cartoonist has passed on-his photo is on display in our book store at Flying Saucer News- Be there! and see the latest and the largest selection of flying saucer books in U.S.A. Fast - Friendly - Service ! --- F R E E sample of top quality stick incense with your purchase- ask for it BUT BE THERE !

690-6016

BERNIE MACKEY
GUITARIST AND VOCALS MUSIC FOR ALL OCCASIONS
ALL KINDS OF MUSICAL INSTRUMENTS AND AMPLIFIERS

872 ST. NICHOLAS AVE., APT. 2   SALE REPRESENTATIVE OF
NEW YORK, N.Y. 10030   SORKIN MUSIC CO. INC.

Mercury Staff Reporter

Sunday Mercury 12-11-72

POLICE were last night investigating reports of an Unidentified Flying Object sighting over a lonely stretch of Midland countryside.

The sighting was reported at Beoley, near Redditch, when a housewife and a young farmworker claimed to have seen three lights hovering about 600 feet in the air over a belt of woodland for a period of four hours.

Police from Henley-in-Arden visited the scene twice, and a spokesman said: 'Two of our officers also saw these lights. They are still investigating the matter.''

Saw three lights

Last night, the farmworker, 15-year-old Keith Harris, of Ullenhall Lane, Beoley, said that he went to see the lights from the home of Mrs. Rita Tallis, who lives half-a-mile further up the lane, when she telephoned him.

"I saw three lights — apparently from three separate vehicles—hovering backwards and forwards about 600 feet up half-a-mile from the back of Mrs. Tallis's house," said Keith.

"They were like radiating lights and kept changing colour from red to white and back again. They kept hovering backwards and forwards—disappearing over the horizon and reappearing again.

No sound at all

"Sometimes they were travelling very quickly and at other times quite slowly. We were watching them from the back garden and there was absolutely no sound from them."

Keith said that the lights were most active early in the evening, but they kept flying about over the area for more than four hours.

He added: "I am certain they were not planes other-wise we would have heard the noise from the engines. I am quite satisfied that they were UFO's."

What's new?

In our last issue of October, 1974 we reprinted an article from the Psychic Observer '' Route To The Stars. However we would like to make a correction and that is Dr. Dan Fry is now the leader, Rev. Enid Smith is retired and the new center will open shortly. For a complete up-to-date story of this project write to Dr. Dan Fry,   Star Route 595, Tonopah, Arizona 85354

A new U F O magazine '' World Of The Unidentified '' will be ready soon. This magazine will definately be an exciting reading experience which will present a clear and honest insight into the world of the unidentified (UFOs). Write Gilbert J. Ziemba Box 515
----------- Joliet, Ill. 60434
Paris Flammonde - UFOs EXIST ! This is his next book which will be released this fall of 1975. It will have 32 pages of illustrations with up- to-the minute '' true citings. However, he does have a recent release '' THE MYSTIC HEALERS '' Cloth 252 pages $8.95 In this book the tone is objective, its style popular, its material well-researched, fascinating and provocative. He covers so much and so many people such as Mary Baker Eddy, Oral Roberts, Kathryn Kuhlman, Harry Edwards and Dr. John Lee Baughman: Church Of The Truth. On sale no at Flying Saucer News, 359 West 45th St., New York, N.Y. 10036 Telephone 212- 582-6380
Blessings!

U.S. AIR FORCE HIDING BODIES OF 12 MEN FROM OUTER SPACE

The Incredible Story of 25-Year Coverup Nears an End as Two Witnesses Describe Bodies

The article on these pages is incredible beyond belief. It may well be the most important article ever published on the phenomena some call "flying saucers."

TATTLER Special Projects Editor John Moulder, Managing Editor Bill Sloan and Correspondent Taris Savell spent weeks putting the story together. But the two researchers upon whose work it is largely based have spent, between them, most of a human lifetime collecting the startling array of facts presented here.

If you start reading this article, the odds are you won't be able to stop reading until you've finished it. It reads like the scenario for a science-fiction classic. But it is not science-fiction. It is true.

Over a period of more than 25 years, the U.S. Air Force has seized crashed spacecraft and their dead occupants and kept them a closely guarded secret, while intimidating, ridiculing and harassing civilian witnesses who tried to reveal the truth.

This is the stunning charge made by two leading researchers of unexplained flying objects, and a TATTLER investigation has turned up concrete evidence to bear it out.

A Tampa, Fla., space seminar was jolted recently by one expert's claim that an alien spacecraft crashed in New Mexico in February, 1948, and the Air Force seized the ship and its 12 deceased tiny occupants. The expert, Robert Carr, southern director of the National Investigations Committee on Aerial Phenomena, claims the bodies are still at Wright-Patterson Air Force Base in Ohio.

C.M. TENNEY, a retired Businessman, happened to witness the crash of a UFO in 1953 in Montana. He was summoned to the nearest Air Force base, closely questioned, and saw spacemen's bodies in laundry bags before he was shooed away.

ROBERT CARR, southern director of the National Investigations Committee on Aerial Phenomena, says the Air Force is still holding the bodies of 12 men from outer space from a craft that crashed in 1948 in New Mexico.

The Air Force, in a statement, denied the report with a trace of ridicule.

Five years after the New Mexico incident, a Montana businessman saw a UFO crash in a ball of fire and when the word spread he was ordered to appear at an Air Force base, where he was brusquely interrogated and saw laundry bags containing bodies of men who obviously died in the UFO crash.

THE BUSINESSMAN, C.M. Tenney, who now is retired and living in Delta, Colo., told his story exclusively to TATTLER and Robert D. Barry, director of the 20th Century UFO Bureau of Collingswood, N.J.

The treatment he received by high-ranking Air Force officials is typical of the military bullying of civilians who have reported experiences involving UFOs.

The Air Force officially closed its books on investigating UFOs in 1968 after a report by the late Professor E.U. Condon concluded UFOs are not extra-terrerrial. Many scientists have called the famed Condon Report a whitewash.

"I am convinced the Air Force knows more than they are telling about UFOs," Tenney told TATTLER.

He wrote to Prof. Condon about his experience, but Condon didn't even acknowledge the correspondence, let alone investigate it.

At the time of the incident, Tenny operated a flower shop at Conrad, Mont. He made frequent trips to Great Falls, 40 miles away, to acquire greenhouse supplies.

During one trip, he saw smoke coming from a nearby mountain. He passed it off as a forest fire, but the next day, returning to Conrad from Great Falls, he had a terrifying experience.

ON A BRIGHT, sun-filled afternoon, a shadow passed over his car. He looked up and saw a dirigible-shaped object "entirely covered with a gas or smoke that seemed to be pulsating." Dirigible-shaped UFOs are among the more common types reported.

The UFO followed Tenney's car. Becoming terrified, he accelerated, "but it followed right alongside of me."

As he neared an intersection, Tenney said, "I felt a swoosh, similar to a big truck passing, and balls of fire fell all over the road, fields and car."

Two other approaching autos were bathed in the fireballs, but the vehicles didn't stop.

"I looked in the rear view mirror and was shocked to see their exhaust tail pipes had a long trail of fire coming from them and mine was also on fire," said Tenney.

Arriving at the town of Brady, Tenney related his experience to a friend who said Tenney was "white as a ghost and his hair was standing straight up."

LATER THAT DAY, arriving back at his flower shop, his telephone was ringing. It was a colonel at Malmstrom AFB at Great Falls.

The colonel ordered him to return to the base at Great Falls "to make out a report in no uncertain terms." The base officials had heard of the incident from a Montana state trooper.

The colonel told Tenney if he didn't report to the base at 10 a.m. the next day, Air Police would be dispatched to bring him in.

When he arrived at Malstrom, Tenney was escorted to a building that "was like going inside a jail." The two-story building, surrounded by a wire fence, had no windows.

By a Team of TATTLER Reporters

He was met by three men, one an Air Force officer, who led him to the colonel's office, instructing him to keep his "eyes straight ahead and not do any looking around." Tenney saw officers carrying packages and letters all stamped "TOP SECRET."

IN THE COLONEL'S OFFICE, Tenney was grilled extensively about his experience. His interview was typed and he had to sign it before a notary.

Four officials then led Tenney down the stairs to the front door of the jail-like building.

Tenney then saw two men "staggering in with large laundry bags" – laboring under their great weight. One of the men accidentally dropped one of the bags directly in front of Tenney.

Tenney looked down at the bag and was shocked at what he saw.

"I could make out the outline of a body. It appeared to be doubled up." Tenney saw its head, knees and feet.

"The two men grabbed me and the officer opened the door and they threw me out," Tenney said.

He added that the officer yelled at him to get out of the building immediately.

AT THIS POINT, TENNEY WAS confident his experience was over. But a day later, between Great Falls and Conrad, he saw "a ball of fire and smoke coming toward me high in the sky and also heard a noise like several locomotives or a roaring noise."

This was near where the other incident occurred.

"When it (the UFO) passed me, the fire, smoke and noise stopped and I observed a shiny object," said Tenney. "It was travelling at terrific speed. It seemed to be going in a sort of climb away from the earth."

He didn't report this to the Air Force.

"Once down there was enough for me," he recalled.

Tenney is convinced the smoke he saw from the mountain was from a downed spacecraft and the bodies in the laundry bags were from the craft.

"Otherwise, why was I thrown out so fast?" he asks.

He thinks the dirigible-shaped object he saw the second day was a spacecraft looking for its downed companion.

"I am 74 years old," Tenney said in relating his experience. "I was 53 when I saw the UFO. I don't smoke or drink and have good eyesight. I was able to pass my driver's test without wearing glasses."

IT WAS THAT SAME YEAR, in Montana near the Canadian border, that Air Force Staff Sgt. William B. Kelly, radar specialist, saw six blips on his radar screen.

"The objects seemed to keep coming right in toward our station," Kelly told a TATTLER reporter.

When the formation was 18 miles from the radar base, the UFOs performed unusual maneuvers – changing directions five times in one minute.

The objects were tracked at speeds between 1,400 and 1,600 miles per hour.

Sergeant Kelly described the radar appearances of UFOs in 1953 as "a seige."

"Three different times we had these objects and all three times very similar and very characteristic," he said. In the second and third incidents, four objects were tracked on the radar screens. In the last case, the four UFOs were clocked at 1,800 miles per hour.

The UFOs "give a better return, have a better reflecting surface, than a plane does," Kelly said.

OTHER RADARMEN throughout the country have also reported tracking UFOs on their screens.

NICAP official Carr, who retired in June after teaching mass communications for nine years at the University of Southern Florida, claims air intelligence at Wright-Patterson AFB has in its possession a 31-foot-in-diameter spacecraft that crashed three miles west of Aztec, N.M., near the Colorado state line, in 1948.

"At that time, I owned and operated a ranch in the high mountains," Carr told TATTLER. "It happened in my neighborhood.

"All major law enforcement officers were rushed to the scene and planes were flown from the nearest major Air Force base, which was Edwards. And as they landed, there was a silvery, gleaming disc-shaped spacecraft leaning on a tripod landing gear. Apparently it made an automatic landing after its occupants had died.

The craft was undamaged, Carr said, except for a small hole in the transparent plastic dome which covered the cockpit.

Because of an accident in space, Carr added, 12 small human-like beings in the spaceship died of decompression.

"THEY WERE NOT SHOT DOWN by our fighter planes," said Carr. "They suffered an operational loss. It was very fortunate that our alert radar net in the western states had the UFO on screen. In fact, three radar stations were tracking it when it fluttered out of control and fell circling toward the earth."

When officials surrounded the downed spacecraft and peered inside, Carr said, they found "slumped over and motionless 12 small men."

Airmen managed to get the door of the craft open, he added, and medical officers found the bodies were still limp and warm. The bodies were flown to Edwards, which has a refrigerated morgue.

"The President was notified, but he didn't come," said Carr. "No one knew quite what to do. The bodies were carefully preserved. They weren't green ... they were fair-skinned. All were males. They were between three and four feet in height. All had light hair, blue eyes, perfect teeth. They were superb physical specimens."

Carr said one body was selected for autopsy by a group of government physicians.

"Six doctors performed the autopsy and it was photographed and motion pictures were made," Carr said. "He (the UFO occupant) was found to have the same organs as a human being. The blood type was human. Genes and chromosomes would match up with earth women. We are somehow related and they came here because they are oxygen-breathing."

THE RETIRED PROFESSOR SAID the body appeared to be that of a man about 30 years old, but the brain – when the skull was opened – was that of somebody several hundred years old.

"Brain specialists said they had never seen a brain with such intricate convolutions," said Carr.

"It could have been a man several hundred years old who had been spared the infirmities of age ... one who had never known senility. What a gift if they could tell us how to do it!"

Carr said authorities have drawn a veil "over the most important development in the history of our time.

The cover-up, he said, has been going on since June 24, 1947, when Kenneth Arnold sighted a fleet of disc-shaped craft flying at incredible speeds in the Pacific Northwest and coined the term "flying saucer."

The Air Force's position, Carr noted, has been to treat inquiries about UFOs as something funny.

"That's the nature of man, to protect himself from the unknown by ridicule," said Carr.

"**THE EVIDENCE** is piling up and up; filing cabinets are bursting with photographs; the vaults of U.S. Air Intelligence have hundreds of feet of motion pictures of UFOs flying close to U.S. planes," said Carr. "In some cases when the U.S. pilot waved, the occupant of the UFO waved back ... surely not a hostile act."

Regardless of this, numerous attacks have been made on UFOs.

"It's been documented that over 1,000 planes have been scrambled to attack harmless UFOs with deadly weapons to try to shoot one down, but they've never succeeded," said Carr.

Carr has personally checked out hundreds of UFO sightings.

"Most of them have been misunderstandings and misinterpretations of natural phenomena," Carr told TATTLER. "There have been a few outright frauds, and then there are those few hard-core cases that could not be explained by conventional means. Even the Air Force claims seven to 10 per cent of the reported cases do not yield to any conventional interpretation."

The respected and usually accurate Gallup Poll showed last year that more than half the American people take UFOs seriously and 15 million Americans admit to having seen unidentified flying objects.

RUSSIA, THE NICAP OFFICIAL SAID, is taking the UFO phenomena much more seriously than American armed forces.

He said Russians, like the U.S. Government sometimes treat UFO reports as a farce publicly, but that "they have highly trained teams of scientists and engineers studying this."

"For a while they thought they (the UFOs) were American, but they've stopped thinking that," Carr said. "They know now they're extra-terrestrial."

Carr's information is based on many interviews and years of investigation. He said the source of his detailed information on the New Mexico case "is a biologist who participated in it."

The Air Force is withholding its documentation on the New Mexico affair on the pretense "it is for our own good" so the American people wouldn't panic.

"A second disc was found near Farmington, N.M.," said Carr. "It was half-burned with decayed bodies in there ... it had little scientific value."

Like the Aztec disc, said Carr, the Farmington disc was removed and is being kept at Wright-Patterson.

WHEN TATTLER ASKED CARR if any other spacecraft are in custody of the U.S. government, the NICAP official replied:

"There was a crash in Mexico and investigators tried very hard to find what became of the material evidence. Apparently, the Central Intelligence Agency was so well-organized in Mexico that they were able to remove the entire evidence ... to some place other than Wright-Patterson. Wright-Patterson is a sort of cover for the second-rate stuff. The really first-rate stuff is someplace in Virginia at a location I've never been able to pinpoint."

UFO researchers have been provided with additional information about the craft downed in New Mexico by a retired security guard at Wright-Patterson.

On the bodies of each of the dozen occupants of the downed spacecraft, the security guard told Carr, were manuals written in an alphabet the military has not been able to decipher.

"If the Air Force would release this, there are men on earth who would be able to do it," Carr said.

"In one body that was autopsied there were a few traces of a light meal. There were food supplies on board (the craft) in the form of a white square biscuit wafer. They were analyzed and found to be very wholesome and nutritius and fed to guinea pigs who thrived on them."

MANY INCIDENTS of Air Force coverup or disregard for UFO sightings have been reported through the years, but none are more dramatic than the incidents detailed for TATTLER by Carr and Tenney.

Dr. J. Allen Hynek, Northwestern University astronomer and one of the nation's most respected authorities on unidentified flying objects, cited examples in his book, "The UFO Experience" – serialized two years ago in TATTLER – of Air Force officials trying to shoot down the credibility of persons who had sighted UFOs.

The sources of these sightings were highly respected individuals, including police officers.

With a majority of the American public believing in the existence of UFOs, and with the widespread belief that intelligent life exists on other planets, the government may finally be ready to lift its cloak of secrecy and tell what it knows about the phenomena.

Carr predicts that the Defense Dept. is ready to "loosen up" on its position about flying saucers.

A similar prediction was made to TATTLER recently by L. J. Lorenzen, executive director of the Aerial Phenomena Research Organization (APRO), one of the nation's most respected and conservative UFO research groups.

If and when this happens, a quarter of a century of official military devvil may at last be proved beyond the shadow of a doubt.

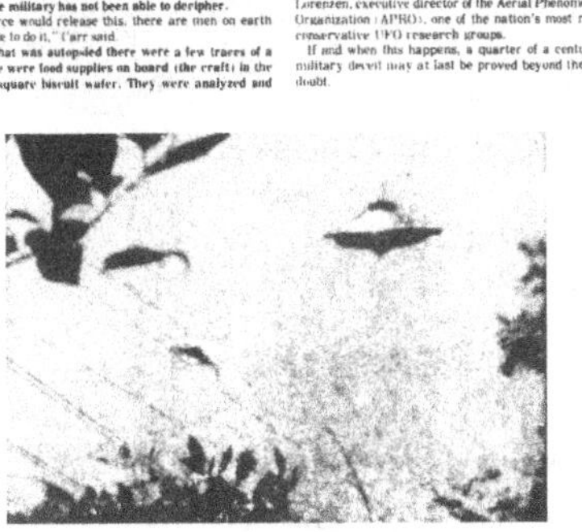

9th July 1974 – Police Officer encounters UFO at Ulster County, USA

In the same month, New York Police Officers – James Wallace and Richard Ramsell (26) – were out on patrol in Kingston Park, Ulster County (91 miles away from New York City), when they saw what at first they believed to be a plane.

The officers stopped the car and saw something very strange hovering in one spot, about 200 feet above a softball field.

The officers said that they could hardly see the outline of the football-sized object, estimated to be 30-40 feet in diameter, showing a row of alternating red and green lights around it and a hazy white light in the centre.

Ramsell edged the police car feet further, but jammed the brakes on when the object began to move towards them. The officers got out and stood watching. When the object was some 500 feet away, Ramsell turned on the spotlight and directed it at the UFO, but the beam did not reach. As it began to close in on them, the officers decided to make good their escape. As they were doing so, a beam of brilliant white light shot out from the base of the UFO and bathed them in light. Before the officers could leave, the object turned off its light and shot off at fantastic speed.

Further updates for 1974 re: additional information on page 278

Light display over New York

We learned that the UFO was one of several brilliant but slower moving objects which appeared over the faming community of Round Lake (12 miles north of Albany), at 8pm on the 20th August 1974. The mysterious object shot past a USAF Jet, before vanishing from the radar screens of six Air Traffic Controllers on duty at Albany Airport.

Air Traffic Controller Jim Mature (32)

One of them – Jim Mature, said:

> "I've never seen anything move so fast. We've received all kinds of UFO reports here over the tower at Albany Airport, but this time were able to detect something on the radar screens; it was an amazing experience, and we were as mystified as the police about what it was up there. It was uncanny that the policemen were watching what seemed to be the same object that appeared as a blip on our radar screens. I saw it split into two separate targets, then later into as many as four."

US pilot describes what he saw

About an hour after the event, Jim contacted the Air Force pilot, who had been on a training flight 20 miles north of Albany.

He told Jim:

> "I saw some lights in the south that were stationary. Shortly afterwards I saw an object, moving across my path from north to south in a blaze of orange light, travelling so fast I was shouting with excitement on the radio."

Jim:

"*I picked up the object on radar south of the military jet, heading towards the airport, at an estimated speed of 3,600 miles per hour. When it got to the airport it vanished.*"

Air Traffic Controller John Guzy (33):

"*It came straight for the airport at an unbelievable speed. I was watching my radar screen and just couldn't believe my eyes.*

There was no explanation for what happened next – the object seemed to be heading right for the control tower, but once it seemed to get above us it just vanished."

Air Traffic Controller Tom Lawson (33):

"*The military pilot was really excited. He said he'd never seen anything move so quickly in his life and neither have I.*"

Robert King – Supervisor (54):

"*The objects were visible on all four radar screens and we observed them for two hours.*"

State Trooper Warren Johnson:

"*I just couldn't believe my eyes. I saw one object hovering in the sky – then I saw another come out of the north at a hell of a speed.*

It was red or orange and it flashed right overhead. I don't know of any aircraft that could travel that fast and it sure wasn't a meteor."

Trooper Michael Morgan:

"*I saw three or four objects, moving at heights of between 500 and 1,500 miles. At times they moved slowly, and at other times they were real fast. It was strange. I've never seen anything like it.*"

Some photos and further information on Professor John Taylor, shown here with a young Uri Geller!

Scientist Says He Has Found Key To Uri Geller's Metal Bending Powers

By CLIFF LINEDECKER
Of the Tattler Staff

PROF. JOHN TAYLOR (left), scientist who teaches mathematics at King's College in London, claims to have discovered the secret behind Uri Geller's power to bend metal objects, such as the fork Geller is showing at right.

A mathematics instructor at King's College in London believes he has solved the riddle of Uri Geller's amazing power to bend metal with his mind.

"The most satisfactory explanation contemporary science can offer ... is that it is achieved by an electromagnetic field of force," says Prof. John Taylor.

Radioactivity, gravity and a force between sub-nuclear particles inside the nucleus of atoms – the other three natural forces now known to science – were ruled out by the mathematician after months of experiments and study.

Prof. Taylor tells of his search for the source of the power used in what has become known as "the Geller effect," in "Superminds: A Scientist Looks at the Paranormal," Viking Press.

The King's College instructor experimented with Geller, as well as more than a dozen others who have been able to emulate the metal-bending feats.

PROF. TAYLOR concedes there is a possibility that a completely unknown force could be behind the Geller effect, but he believes the chances of that are extremely slim. There is now no hint from science that such a force exists, he says.

He also dismisses deception, although he admits that without proper controls such as he and other scientists have used in their experiments, that the effect can be duplicated by trickery. He says however:

"In my view, the whole question of deception, either intentional or unconscious, can be dismissed as a factor, at any rate in the majority of instances.

"I have myself observed many cases of the results achieved both by Geller and by

children. Other people whose word one may trust have also been witnesses."

ELECTROMAGNETISM, Taylor explains, is a combination of the forces of electricity and magnetism.

Science now has a theory, Taylor writes, that metal-bending is made possible by low frequency electric fields emitted by various parts of the body, "these fields being amplified by stresses in the materials themselves.

"Evidence has already been presented in support of this hypothesis."

The researcher says there are, of course, still many questions to be answered before science has a full understanding of the Geller effect.

But continued investigation is important for many reasons, including the very strong possibility that the power behind the Geller effect is also used in psychic healing.

Taylor says, in fact, that it is quite possible that research could eventually lead to development of a healing machine.

"This conjecture can be put to a clear test by measuring the radiation coming from healers during the healing process," Taylor says.

"IT WILL BE DONE in the near future and let us hope it will be successful. If so, it might lead to the building of a healing machine, which could perhaps intensify the effects produced by the human 'psychic' healer."

Some of the children who have been able to reproduce the Geller effect have begun to also show an ability to perform psychic healings, Taylor points out.

The preponderance of children among those who have been able to duplicate Geller's feats is one of the more puzzling aspects of the research.

Several women have also been able to bend metal by stroking it lightly or from a distance using apparently only the powers of the mind. But few men have been able to do so.

"And what is one to make of the several Swedish women who have attributed their pregnancies to the fact that, as a result of a Geller programme transmitted on videotape, their contraceptive loops had

become too distorted to function efficiently?" Taylor asks.

Three consecutive appearances on British television programs by Geller, beginning in 1973, set off a rash of spoon-bending all over England.

"SCORES OF people suddenly discovered themselves to be metal-benders and hundreds claimed they could start or stop watches at will."

People who claim, and often demonstrate, Geller-effect powers, are still showing up. Prof. Taylor warns, however, that use of the metal-bending abilities is not without potential danger.

"Whatever force field is in operation causing cutlery or other metal objects to bend may well affect tissue, blood or bone.

"At this stage too little is known properly to assess the dangers associated with metal-bending," he says, "although in one case I have had to advise the parents to put a stop to it; both the son and the daughter appeared to be getting out of control."

"Superminds: A Scientist Looks at the Paranormal," by John Taylor. $10.95. Viking Press, 625 Madison Ave., New York, N.Y. 10022.

Professor John Taylor

CHAPTER 6 – 1975
COVER UP BY THE MEDIA CONTINUES –
WHEN WILL WE EVER LEARN?

JANUARY

2nd January 1975 – Formation of triangular lights sighted over the United States

4th January 1975 – Was it a UFO?

5th January 1975 – Lancashire schoolchildren sight UFO

7th January 1975 – Orange UFO seen to land on the River Dart, at Devon, by dozens of people

10th January 1975 – UFO sighed by glider Pilot over Lancashire

12th January 1975 – Bright light over Kent

14th January 1975 – Inverted 'saucer' seen in the sky over Lancashire

14th January 1975 – UFO Display over Doncaster

16th January 1975 – Pulsating UFO over Brighton and Oldham, Lancashire

17th January 1975 – Three 'lights' over the Downs

20th January 1975 – Pike, Illinois, USA

21st January 1975 – Strange 'figure', Southsea, Hampshire

28th January 1975 – Strange 'light' over Epsom and Yorkshire

31st January 1975 – 'Silver discs' seen over Kent

31st January 1975 – Triangular UFO, Reading

'Flying Saucer' landing at Liverpool- Fact or fiction?

FEBRUARY

7th February 1975 – UFO display over Harlow

8th February 1975 – Underwater surface object sighted

10th February 1975 – Disc shaped UFO sighted over Annandale, New York

10th February 1975 – UFO over RAF Uxbridge …?

February 1975 – Secret report of UFO film released

17th February 1975 – Strange 'lights' in the sky

18th February 1975 – Diamond shaped UFO sighted

23rd February 1975 – UFO over Kent – reported to SIGAP Omar Fowler

24th February 1975 – Mystery object sighted near Atomic Power Station, Suffolk

25th February 1975 – Diamond-shaped UFO sighted over Middlesburgh

26th February 1975 – UFO tracked on radar

27th February 1975 – Diamond-shaped 'lights'

28th February 1975 – UFO display, Jersey

MARCH

2nd March 1975 – UFO terrifies occupants of car at Elmwood, Wisconsin

6th March 1975 – Youths sight glowing object over Barking, Essex

APRIL

6th April 1975 – Humming UFO over Bournemouth

10th April 1975 – Triangular UFO sighted over Essex

3rd-9th April 1975 – V'-shaped UFOs over North Carolina

MAY

4th May 1975 – Bright 'light' over Sussex

18th May 1975 – UFO landing, Rainhill, Merseyside

1975 – Yellow 'orb', Scotland

Summer 1975 – UFO sighting, Cumbria, mid-1970s

31st May 1975 – UFOs sighted in Lancashire

JUNE

9th June 1975 – UFO display over Fire Station, London

12th June 1975 – Police Officer sights UFO

June 1975 – UFO over Birmingham

18th June 1975 – Did RAF chase UFOs?

Summer 1975 – 'Flying Hovercraft', Gloucester

1975 – UFO over Cley Hill, Warminster

18th June 1975 – Did RAF chase UFOs?

22nd June 1975 – UFO over Southampton

Summer 1975 – UFO over Warminster

Summer 1975 – UFO landing marks found in Worcestershire

Summer 1975 – Police sighting over Cleeve Hill, Gloucestershire

Mid-1970s – UFO sighted over Binfield, Berkshire, by policewoman

JULY

1st July 1975 – Were the RAF scrambled?

4th July 1975 – UFO sighted over New Jersey

6th July 1975 – Cigar-shaped UFO seen over Glastonbury Tor

8th July 1975 – *National Enquirer* releases details of UFO sighting, 10 months later!

6th July 1975 – Cigar-shaped UFO seen over Glastonbury Tor

9th July 1975 – Police Officer encounters UFO

10th July 1975 – Strange 'figure' on the A55

1975 – UFO display, Wales

22nd July 1975 – UFO landing on the Welsh Hills

July 1975 – Strange incident befalls motorist

AUGUST

2nd August 1975 – UFO sighted

5th/6th/7th August 1975 – Silver 'ball' seen in sky over Wanstead, London

8th August 1975 – Flying saucer seen Bristol

12th August 1975 – Green 'discs' over Cambridge

15th August 1975 – Police sight UFO

24th August 1975 – Crescent-shaped UFO over London

26th August 1975 – Hexagonal UFO sighted over Barking, Essex

27th August 1975 – UFO over Reading, Berkshire

SEPTEMBER

2nd September 1975 – 'Castle' shaped UFO sighted

5th September 1975 – Was it Jupiter?

6th September 1975 – UFO display over Michigan … NORAD contacted!

9th September 1975 – Flashing lights over Cleveland

15th September 1975 – UFOs over Reading, Berkshire

16th September 1975 – 'Red light' circles over Caterham

18th September 1975 – 'Flying Saucer' reported over Yorkshire Moor

20th September 1975 – Was it a meteor?

23rd September 1975 – Shining object over West Sussex

September 1975 – UFO over Southampton

1975 – UFO over Nottinghamshire

1975 – Close encounter with UFO over Essex

UFO over Cradle Hill, Warminster

OCTOBER

4th October 1975 – US Police Officer sights cigar-shaped UFO over New Jersey

6th October 1975 – Rectangular UFO over Huddersfield

8th October 1975, *Worthing Gazette* – 'Analyzing UFOs – by a councillor'

9th October 1975 – *Daily Telegraph* – 'UFO to a better life' leaves 20 missing

11th October 1975 – British Groups make TV appeal for Scientific Ufology

12th October 1975 – UFO seen over football field, Essex

14th October 1975 – Small UFO seen, Hay-on-Wye

18th October 1975 – Red pulsing 'light' over Reading

18th October 1975, 10.50pm – Yellow and white UFO seen, Worcester

22nd October 1975 – Luminous orange UFO over Liverpool

27th October 1975 – Loring AFB, Maine. UFO circles airbase

28th October 1975 – Cylindrical UFO over Manchester

28th October 1975 – UFO seen over Birmingham City Centre – no others details

31st October 1975 – 'Fairground' UFO sighed in sky over Essex

31st October 1975 – Mystery 'circle of light' in the sky

October/November 1975 – NORAD on high alert. UFOs plotted over Atomic weapons storage bases

Winter 1975 – Police Officer sights UFO

NOVEMBER

1st November 1975 – BUFORA lecture, London

2nd November 1975 – UFO over East Grinstead, West Sussex

5th November 1975 – Schoolchildren sight UFO

5th November 1975 – Three UFOs over Dade County, USA

7th November 1975, 5.55pm – Two purple and red UFOs seen over A449, Penkridge

9th November 1975 – 'Silver discs' seen over Hertfordshire

10th November 1975 – Police chase UFOs over USA and Canada

11th November 1975 – Travis Walton encounters a UFO … later allegation of abduction

13th November 1975 – Strange 'aircraft' over Preston, Lancashire

14th October 1975 – Small UFO seen, Hay-on-Wye

18th November – UFO display over Barnsley, Yorkshire

18th November 1975 – UFO over Basildon, Essex

19th November 1975 – 'Flying Cobra' UFOs sighted

22nd November 1975 – WATSUP Lecture, Southampton

27th November 1975 – Two 'red lights' reported over Essex

27th November 1975 – *Southern Evening Echo*, 'After Nessie, what about UFOs says Ernie'.

November 1975 – Motorist reports UFO landing, Cornwall

DECEMBER

2nd December 1975 – Into the Unknown

Southampton Echo published article on Warminster

5th December 1975 – UFO over Essex

6th December 1975 – Spectator – 'Loch Ness … the ageing hypothetical'

13th December 1975 – Silver domed UFO over Greater Manchester

19th December 1975 – UFO over Essex

21st December 1975 – Half-moon shaped UFO sighted over Basildon, Essex

21st December 1975 – Motorists paced by car in the United States

1975 – Frightening encounter on Lickey Hills, Worcestershire

Mid 1970s – Ghostly disturbance in Devon

JANUARY 1975

2nd January 1975 – Formation of triangular lights sighted over the United States

Between 7pm and 8pm, a number of people reported sighting unusual objects in the night sky. The first sighting occurred just west of the Baltimore Beltway, near Route 83 (leading to York, PA) and involved ex-USAF serviceman John Goode, and his family.

They saw four bright white 'lights', at 7.35pm, gliding slowly through the sky. John pulled up the car so they could obtain a closer look at the lights (each group contained three, forming a triangle) – now about 300 yards away from them. Although no structure was seen, an impression was received of a structure within the light source.

At 7.45pm, Kenneth C. Ryan – electrical engineer and private pilot – went to the back door to let the dog in, when he saw four bright 'lights', about 10 degrees above the horizon. Further scrutiny revealed they were moving. As the lights came closer, he saw that there were twelve in total, at a height of between 4-10 thousand feet. As they passed overhead, he saw the lead one only showed three red, blue, and white lights. Five minutes later, they were out of sight in the north-west sky.

The same phenomenon appears to have been witnessed by Timonium, Baltimore couple – Mr and Mrs Christie, at 9.20pm. This went on for an hour and, not unsurprisingly, the 'lights' were seen heading back along the way they had come.

(Source NICAP *UFO Investigator*, February 1975, Mr Millard F. Kirk)

4th January 1975 – Was it a UFO?

Veteran UFO/Paranormal investigator Paul Glover was taking part in a night watch at Cisbury Ring. He said:

> *"It was a little windy but the sky was clear. At 10.45pm, an object was seen travelling in a south to north direction. It looked like a meteor, at first, but was moving very slowly and had no tail; it was round and slightly orange in colour and seen for 10 seconds."*

5th January 1975 – Lancashire schoolchildren sight UFO

Two young children out playing, at Uppermill, told of having sighted a disc-shaped object, with a flickering yellow rim and flashing red light, heading across the moors making a humming sound. They were not the only ones; a group of eleven older boys also saw it. This was one of a number or sightings reported to the Manchester UFO Research Association that had taken place over the moorland regions north and east of Oldham. **(Source: Jenny Randles/MUFORA/*Flying Saucer Review*, Volume 21, Number 6)**

7th January 1975 – Orange UFO seen to land on the *River Dart*, at Devon, by dozens of people

In early January 1975, a number of residents living on the side of the *River Dart*, at Dartmouth, telephoned the police to report having seen a bright orange object, hovering over the Britannia Royal Naval College. The object was then seen to change direction and land on the river, for several minutes, before taking off again and heading towards Torbay. **(Source: *Western Morning News*, exact date not known)**

8th January 1975

The Waltham Forest Guardian carried a story about a '*Flying Saucer*' detector, invented and manufactured by cab driver Malcolm Jay of Nelson Road, Highams Park, for £7.80.

10th January 1975 – UFO sighed by glider pilot over Lancashire

An object showing red, orange, and blue lights, was seen low in the sky at Lees, Oldham, by a glider pilot and his wife.

12th January 1975 – Bright light over Kent

A bright light was seen motionless in the sky over the Kent area and subsequently recorded by the schoolboy concerned, who wrote a letter to the MOD. It was brief but very much to the point and packed with information.

14th January 1975 – Inverted 'saucer' seen in the sky over Lancashire

Two girls were walking home along a dark lane, after stabling their horse at Moorside, in the Rossendale Valley of Lancashire, when they were astonished to see an object resembling:

> "...an inverted 'saucer' showing a steady green light, with a red flashing one, hovering over nearby cottages. We shone our torch at it, and it appeared to rock to and fro in a gentle motion. We were frightened and ran away."

14th January 1975 – UFO display over Doncaster

At 6.30pm on the same day, three 14 year-old schoolboys were playing in a field close to Bentley Colliery, Doncaster, when the field became illuminated by a 'bright light', hovering in the sky above them. Looking upwards, they were astonished to see a diamond shaped object, about the size of an A4 sheet of paper (held at arm's length). According to one of the boys:

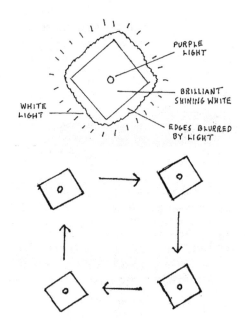

> "It seemed to get bigger and we thought it was going to land. It did a sort of 'square' dance, five or six times, each 'square' taking two to three minutes to complete. After about ten or fifteen minutes, the object just switched-off – like a TV going out."

The investigator in this matter – Mr Thrower, from BUFORA – told that one of the boys was so frightened, he had to be carried away to his home by friends. (**Source: *BUFORA Journal*, Volume 6, July/August 1977**)

16th January 1975 – Pulsating UFO over Brighton and Oldham, Lancashire

At 7.30am, Mr Clifford of Balsdean Road, Woodingdean, Brighton, was driving to work past Brighton Racecourse, when he saw a bright white and blue pulsating object in the sky, about 3 miles away over Devil's Dyke.

> "It was in sight for about four minutes, before disappearing in clouds seconds later."

At 8.55am, Darren Eggerton (9) was in the playground of St Anne's Roman Catholic School, Greenacres Road, Oldham, in Lancashire.

> "I was talking to my friend – Christopher Oakes (9) – and looking across the sky, when I saw a silver object spinning towards Mossley. We only saw it for two minutes and it was spinning fast. I think it was about 150 feet high in the sky." (**Source: Paul Glover**)

17th January 1975 – Three 'lights' over the Downs

Claire Davey (12) of Church Walk, Worthing, in Surrey, wrote to UFO researcher – Paul Glover, on the 5th April 1975, after seeing an article on UFOs in the local newspaper.

> *"At 7.40am I looked out of my bedroom window, towards the Downs. It was dark and I noticed three 'lights', close together, towards the Downs. I thought this was peculiar as there are no buildings anywhere in that area.*
>
> *As I watched, the centre 'light' grew blindingly bright while the other two began to fade. The object rose vertically into the sky, for a short distance – then veered off at an angle towards the south-east. As it neared I could see it was not an aeroplane, but just a saucer-shaped object. It then disappeared into a black cloud and a lightening sky."*

20th January 1975 – Pike, Illinois, USA

Housewife Marjorie Nighbert was awoken at 5am by a 'bright light', shining into the bedroom. Thinking there was a fire, she rushed to the window to see:

> *"...a large red 'ball' of silent light – larger than a 'washtub' – moving slowly from the north, low down in the sky, in a south-easterly direction. It was tadpole in shape, with lights blinking off and on in a constant pattern. It moved in the direction of the high school, made a U-turn, and came back toward her home. It then veered off in an easterly direction and disappeared from view."*

(Source: NICAP)

21st January 1975 – Strange 'figure', Southsea, Hampshire

Malcolm Handley from Southsea, in Hampshire, then a member of WATSUP – a UFO organisation ran by Nicholas Maloret – was discussing the day's events with his wife, Brenda, following his return home at teatime, when, out of the corner of his eye, he sighted a 'figure' standing about eight feet to his left. When he turned to have a look, there was nothing to be seen.

He told Brenda what he had just seen, at which point the 'figure' became visible again.

> *"She asked me to look directly at it, now moving its head from side to side in a negative manner. I waited several seconds and then looked straight at it, but saw nothing. When I looked out of the corner of my eye again, it was now visible but raising its right appendage. I can't say 'hand', because it wasn't clear enough – then it faded away.*
>
> *The 'figure' was dressed in a long black robe, without any apparent opening, and had a white face, bushy eyebrows, and a fairly substantial growth of white hair, pushed to one side of its head. Although the robe reached to the floor, I never saw any feet."*

Ufology!
WHY PETER'S LIFE IS LOOKING UP

❝RELIABLE reports indicate that there are objects coming into our atmosphere at very high speeds, and controlled by thinking intelligences.❞

ALTHOUGH that SOUNDS like something your kids might have heard Mr. Spock say in "Star Trek," it is, in fact, a quote from the Head of the Ballistic Missile Department of the United States Navy.

Mention U.F.O.'s (Unidentified Flying Objects) to some people of course, and they will fall about laughing, regaling everyone with tales of Little Green Men, or Take - Me - To - Your - Leader stories.

"In fact," said 46-year-old Peter Hill, "one usually finds that criticism and ridicule is based on ignorance of facts, figures, and carefully analysed statistics."

Conceited

And, let's be honest, many people reject the idea of U.F.O.'s because they prefer to believe that ours is the only intelligence in the Universe. Which is a rather conceited assumption.

For nearly 30 years, Peter Hill, District Medical Records Officer for Southampton and S.W. Hampshire, has been convinced that there is something behind the various reports of unexplained phenomena.

"In fact," he said, "if U.F.O.'s DON'T exist, then people responsible for the defence of their countries are hallucinating on a mass scale . . . which is a mystery in itself."

Away from the relatively normal routine of hospital life, Peter is concerned with the abnormal. He is Chairman of the Wessex Association for the Study of Unexplained Phenomena (WATSUP), and a member of the British Unidentified Flying Object Research Association. The President of this latter organisation is a hospital Consultant in Wessex.

Special

Ufology, the study of U.F.O.'s, is a serious business these days. Many leading scientists, astronomers, military and aviation experts are convinced of their existence.

Governments throughout the world, including the French, Canadian, West German, Brazilian and American Governments, have been ploughing a considerable amount of money into investigations into the subject. After a large number of sightings in France in the 1950's, the French Gendarmerie was given special instructions about the steps to take if a U.F.O. was spotted.

U.F.O.'s of course, have been around for a long time.

In 1173, the following report was recorded: "A large body of fire moved over the town, and remained in the Southeast, and all the people rose from their beds, for they thought it was the day."

In 1361, a frightened Briton recorded, "In this year, on the 25th February, at midnight, in the rarefied air, there appeared a certain luminous cloud like fire, and in the brightness of it, were seen men."

To bring things up to date a bit, a Hampshire couple driving along the Romsey Road, near Hursley, in September last year, reported a white flashing light in the sky ahead of them. The object was hovering about 100 feet from the road, over some open fields. It had five V-shaped

Peter Hill . . . 'A fascinating pastime'

angular lights. The phenomenon was totally silent.

Peter Hill, who is married with five children, was just 19 when he first became interested in his fascinating hobby.

Famous

"I was struck by headline newspaper reports of a famous sighting by a business man in America. He was flying his own aircraft when he saw a number of objects which he described as saucers skimming over the water.

"The press took it up, and coined the flying saucer name. They probably didn't know at the time that in the 19th Century, a farmer in Texas had reported a U.F.O. which looked like an inverted saucer."

From those early days, Peter began avidly reading literature on mysterious events, and he started to study various reports, and accounts of U.F.O. sightings.

"It soon became apparent that there was a lot of rubbish in the reports of sightings," he said. "Most of the people were genuine, but mistaken."

Today, Peter agrees with most leading authorities on the subject, that about 90 per cent. of all reports can be readily explained.

His associations spend much of their time investigating reports and eliminating those which COULD have a rational explanation.

U.F.O.'s, said Peter, can turn out to be many things . . . aircraft, weather balloons, satellites, ball lightning, stars, comets, meteors, space debris burning up, and even the reflection of car headlights on clouds!

"They can also be the result of wishful thinking, hoaxes, hallucinations, hysteria, and floating cells on the eyes!" he added.

But ten per cent. of all sightings still remain completely unexplained . . . and those are the ones Peter and his fellow members are interested in.

In an analysis of the first 31 reports of 1974 in the U.K., he said, three were genuinely unknown — the others were explained.

But what of this ten per cent.? "These," said Peter, "are phenomena which have been seen, heard, photographed, tracked on ground and air radar, and reported by civil and military aircraft, police and astronomers.

"Most of the best sightings have been reported by highly reliable people."

To study ufology, one needs a good working knowledge of astronomy, aircraft and meteorology. "This is because we approach the subject on a scientific basis," said Peter, "we are not cranks, following some sort of peculiar cult.

"We need to know about all these things so that we can recognise the normal phenomena and eliminate them from investigations.

"This is why," he added, "we often hold sky watchings at night. From time to time, members spend the whole night watching the sky. It gives us experience in determining what is a normal happening. It is also a fascinating pastime!"

Peter's particular interest lies in the formation of statistical analyses of sightings.

He has proved that sightings are not random; there seems to be some sort of pattern.

Although he wouldn't recommend that anyone dashes out to scan the skies, it appears that Thursdays between 11 p.m. and midnight, in May or October, are good for sightings.

Strange

A high peak of sightings does not occur, strangely enough, at times when more people are likely to be out and about i.e. during the holiday period, or at weekends.

Wessex, of course, is one of the areas in the world where there have been more sightings than anywhere else.

The best spot is at Warminster where Peter has met many enthusiastic U.F.O. spotters from all over the world, including New Zealand. A group of Soviet scientists have even visited there once.

For Peter, the fascination of his hobby is the Big Unknown.

"I am convinced there is something unexplained going on," he said. "The little - green - men - from - Mars hypothesis is naive and now disproved by space research. And as for the extra terrestrial hypothesis, there is no hard evidence to support it, but it cannot be ruled out.

"We now know more about U.F.O.'s than ever before, even though our knowledge is in rather negative terms, in that we have ruled out certain ideas. We used to think they could come from Mars, for instance, but now we know they don't."

What then, is Peter's ambition with his hobby? . . . "Well," he replied, "if I could shed some light on what is behind all these U.F.O. sightings, then I'd be happy."

January 28th 1975 – Strange 'light' seen over Epsom and Yorkshire

At 4pm, several girls from Rosebery County Grammar School, in Epsom, sighted what looked like a *"burning flash, heading across the sky"*.

At 9.30pm, an amber 'light' with a 'fuzzy edge' was seen in the sky over the Halifax area of Yorkshire, by a railwayman from Hebden Bridge, Yorkshire, who said:

> *"After moving fast through the sky, it suddenly stopped and hovered for a few seconds, before shooting away at right angles to its original course."* (**Source: Mr John Beresford**)

28th January 1975 – UFO over London

At 6.15am on 28th January 1975, Mrs Joan Stuart from Southwood Road, New Eltham London, happened to look out of the window, when she saw:

> *"...a huge, pulsating, globe of brilliant pale yellow light, with a slightly flattened top and bottom, hovering one to two hundred feet above trees; it was over the Mottingham area, about half a mile away. In comparison to a tiny star, it was the size of a tangerine. Suddenly, it moved in a straight line swiftly westwards along the horizon – gone in ten seconds."*

Mrs Stuart telephoned the *Eltham and Kentish Times* and explained what had happened. Her sighting was later published, the following week. At 9.30pm the same date an amber light, with 'fuzzy edge', was seen in the sky over the Halifax area of Yorkshire, by a railwayman from Hebden Bridge...

> *"After moving fast through the sky, it suddenly stopped and hovered, for a few seconds, before shooting away at right angles to its original course."* (**Source: John Beresford**)

31st January 1975 – 'Silver discs' seen over Kent

Chatham News (31.1.1975), told of 'two silver 'discs' seen over Temple School, Strood, in Kent, by many pupils and staff, during the morning break, 31st January 1975'.

We contacted two of the teachers – retired Deputy Headmaster Peter Bonney, (in 2006), and after discussing the nature of our enquiry, he forwarded a comprehensive report to us, in which he disclosed the school had received a number of letters written by obvious cranks, including one from a man who spoke Venusian!

> *"I was on playground duty, at 10.15am, when two boys approached me and directed my attention skywards, where a pair of vapour trails could be seen heading straight for each other across the sky; one from the north-east, the other south-east. To everybody's relief, the aircraft passed each other. Imagine my shock when a boy shouted and pointed upwards into the sky. I looked and saw two 'silver discs', motionless in the sky under cloud cover (despite a strong wind blowing, which was sending the clouds scudding across the sky). After about five minutes a crowd of about 150 pupils had gathered to watch the UFOs – still immobile in the sky – when the bell went for end of break. Nobody moved. Ten minutes later they were still there – then one of them moved away, gradually getting smaller as it became lost in the distance, heading up the Thames Estuary towards London, giving an impression it was climbing.*
>
> *A few minutes later the second one started to shrink and disappeared while still in the same position – unlike the behaviour of its companion."*

At lunchtime, Mr Bonney telephoned the police and asked the officer if they had received any other reports, but received a baffled response.

Contacted by the local newspaper

A short time later, the local newspaper rang the school and asked him a number of questions about what had been seen.

The following morning, Mr Bonney was contacted by another newspaper – this time from Folkestone. The reporter told him that *"exactly the same thing had been seen"* over Folkestone, 30 minutes before the Strood sighting.

Similar UFO seen over Canterbury and Yorkshire

Further information was then brought to his notice from another journalist, who explained a similar UFO(s) had been seen over Canterbury, fifteen minutes before the Strood sighing.

Incredibly some months later, a member of staff told Mr Bonney of a UFO sighted on the same day – this time over Halifax, West Yorkshire, at 2.30pm, which means that the objects were seen initially at Folkestone at 9.45am, then over Canterbury at 10am, before moving over to Strood at 10.15am, and last seen at 2.30pm over Halifax. We also tracked down former Arts teacher at the school – Ron Dutnall – who confirmed what had taken place.

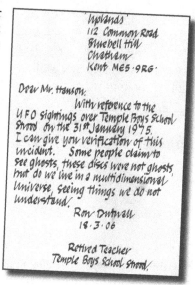

'Uplands'
112 Common Road
Bluebell Hill
Chatham
Kent ME5 9RG.

Dear Mr. Hanson,

With reference to the UFO sightings over Temple Boys School, Strood on the 31st January 1975, I can give you verification of this incident. Some people claim to see ghosts, these discs were not ghosts, but do we live in a multidimensional Universe, seeing things we do not understand.

Ron Dutnall
18.3.06

Retired Teacher
Temple Boys School Strood.

31st January 1975 – Triangular UFO, Reading

On the 31st January 1975, Mr Alan Edwin Lott – Civil Engineer by occupation, employed at the Atomic Weapons Research Establishment at Aldermaston, living in Richmond Road, Caversham Heights, Reading, in Berkshire – was out walking his dog, at 10.20pm.

> *"The dog stopped just outside the front gate and I casually looked up into the night sky. I was surprised to see some very bright 'lights' to the east, beyond the bungalow next door. After studying them for perhaps ten or fifteen seconds, I realised I was watching something extraordinary. I alerted my wife, Clarice, and picked-up a pair of binoculars, through which I could see the 'lights' moving slowly in a straight line, almost exactly east to west, directly above the house. It was clear to the naked eye that these were three extremely bright 'lights' – orange/yellow in colour, forming a large equilateral triangle with two other very small lights, one red and one white. All of the lights were steady with no flashing, without any beams of light – just the steady brilliant glare. The sighting from start to finish lasted about five minutes, in contrast to the movement of aircraft that are usually out-of-sight in fifteen seconds.*
>
> *I wrote to a Mr Appleby, at the MOD, explaining what had happened. They wrote back to me saying they were only interested in collecting information and were not prepared to comment."*

(Source: Personal interview)

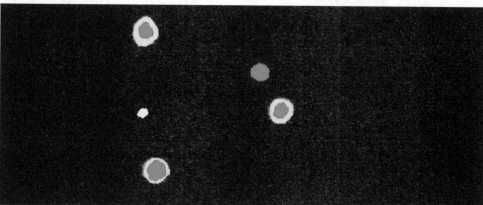

Dear Miss Holloway,

Further to your request in the Reading Evening Post of November 30th for reports of sightings of UFOs in the early 1970s my wife and I had a sighting in 1975. I submitted this report to:-

        Branch S4F (Air),
        Room 8249,
        Main Building,
        Ministry of Defence,
        Whitehall,
        LONDON. SW1A 2HB.

When I had heard nothing from them after about three months I wrote and enquired as to what this phenomena was. They replied that they only collected information and were not prepared to comment. So much for cooperation!

I enclose a copy of my report for your interest.

        Yours sincerely,

        A. E. Lott.

Ms D. Holloway,   12th January, 2001
Mr. J. Hanson.
PO Box 6371,
BIRMINGHAM,
B48 7RW

Dear Both,
    Thank you for your letter of December 2000, (no day) and the enclosure from the Sunday Mercury of December 19th 1999. I am unable to find a mention of Reading in this enclosure as you stated.

    I have no objection to the inclusion of my report in your chronological manuscript or my name but not my address being mentioned. However I do not wish any conclusions to be attributed to me because I have never come to any. I am still greatly puzzled by the experience.

    My wife and I can not understand your report that when you dialed our telephone number a lady stated that she had never heard of me. The number I typed was correct, as repeated above. We have lived here since 1956 and are well known through social contacts and membership of voluntary groups.

    There was a progamme on Channel 4 some time last year (I think) that suggested in America many strange sightings are the result of high electric charges built up in the atmosphere as a result of extreme stresses between shifting tectnic plates. However this would not explain my sighting.

    Some years ago I did attend some meetings of a UFO group in London, I've forgotten their name now, but left after a few months because there was an increasing tendency to go "all religious" which I thought was not a scientific approach.

        Yours sincerely,

        Alan E. Lott.

    C. Eng. FIEE (retired) F.A.C.I.

'Flying Saucer' landing at Liverpool – Fact or fiction …?

Reminiscent of the sort of fake news and disinformation which bombards the social media in 2017 by the on-line newspapers, whose respectability was once assured as they vied with each other to offer the most ridiculous of UFO stories, was unsigned notes from *Viewpoint* – a journal telling of a report of a *'Flying Saucer'* landing at Norris Green, Liverpool, which alleged that following TV interference, large numbers of residents watched from their doorsteps as 'space beings' materialised inside several rooms of the buildings. The simple truth is that it is highly unlikely any of this is true. If there had been reports of UFO activity or paranormal manifestations, there would have been a paper trail – so at the moment, we regard the story as highly dubious.

FEBRUARY 1975

7th February 1975 – UFO display over Harlow

Paul Sheering of Brockles Road, Harlow, was playing football in early February, when he noticed two strange lights circling the sky above him.

> *"All of a sudden, about five others appeared from nowhere and stopped at the bottom of Brockles head, and then another two appeared over Kennings Garage. I was amazed and ran home to tell my dad. Dad grabbed a pair of binoculars. He told me he thought he had seen two planes after the lights went out. They just faded away."* (**Source: *Harlow Citizen*, 7.2.1975/*UFO News*, 8.3.1975**)

8th February 1975 – Underwater surface object sighted

At 3.30am, Blythburgh resident – Keith Payne, was awoken by a deep humming noise. On going out to investigate, he saw what he took to be the source of the noise, *"…a strange 'red light' hovering approximately 40 feet above the* River Blythe *half-a-mile away"*. As the noise increased in volume, Mr Payne noticed the water under the object was illuminated by a white light, although he could see no sign of any beam of light being projected from underneath the red lights, which may lead us to consider there was a secondary object under the surface. Next morning Keith estimated that the light lay on a line between the Churches of Blythburgh and Southwold.

(**Source: Peter Johnson, BUFORA/*Flying Saucer Review,* Volume 21, No. 5, Blythburgh & Sizewell UFOs**)

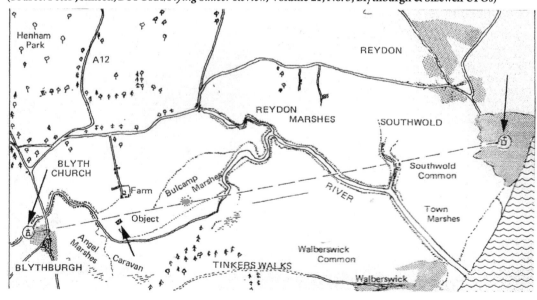

During the evening of the same day, several people sighted a large yellow sphere hovering in the sky, at low attitude, over a field close to the M10 flyover in Hertfordshire, before heading away at speed minutes later.

10th February 1975 – Disc-shaped UFO sighted over Annandale, New York

At 7pm, two teenagers sighted a 20 metre diameter 'disc' hovering low above the ground, for ten minutes, before it shrank away to nothing. Examination of the site revealed snapped tree branches and scorched earth.

(Sources: CUFOS files, report dated February 27, 1975; NICAP *UFO Investigator*, April 1975; *Skylook*, December 1975, p. 16; Margaret Sachs, *Celestial Passengers*, p. 108)

10th February 1975 – UFO over RAF Uxbridge?

In the enormous files of reports and letters obtained from the Essex UFO Research Group was one dated August 1977, from Jonathon Johnson (24) from Brentwood, Essex, who was interviewed about his knowledge of an incident which took place in 1975 at RAF Uxbridge, Middlesex (non-flying base).

> "I was talking to a friend of mine in the RAF, who was a radar operator at West Drayton Radar. He told me about a UFO sighted over the airbase, one Friday. That same evening I received a visit from my friend, who told me there was a UFO over the base. We went outside and I said to him, 'that's just a star'. He replied, 'No way have the RAF sent up aircraft', but each time they approached the object it flew away. I didn't see any craft – just the 'star', but I remained curious about this incident, as my friend said they believed 'it' was listening into radio transmissions from Heathrow Airport five miles away."

February 1975 – Secret report of UFO film released

The *Tatler* Journal, in February 1975, released details of a UFO sighting that was kept secret for nine years, involving the filming from a helicopter of a metallic sphere on the 15th April 1966, seen flying low over the mountains near Santa Catalina Island, some 25 miles from Long Beach, California. The TV cameraman said:

> "We were out there to shoot scenic serials for television documentaries, using an Arriflex camera equipped with a 12-5-120mm zoom lens, loaded with 16mm Ektachrome colour film. A 15 second colour film was taken of a metallic looking sphere, flying over the mountains at a distance of some five to six miles away. I first thought it was a tethered balloon, to start with."

The film was later tested by a California research group of 35 noted scientists and engineers.

Neil Davis (38) – a physicist who works for the Navy and Research and Development Laboratory, in San Diego – is convinced the film is genuine. He said:

> "The object was travelling between 150-190 miles per hour, and was 30 feet in diameter. Shadows seen on the object are consistent with the shadows on the island with the time of the day taken."

Comparison cases for that month from *Haunted Skies* Volume 2 Revised

10th April 1966 (UK) – UFO seen

At 9.15am, a newspaper employee – Mr Robert Peacock of Cheyne Walk, Kettering, Northants – was sat in his living room when he saw a brilliant, circular, whitish-yellow object flash by, visible for a couple of seconds, heading in a south to north direction.

Other witnesses were teenage cyclists – John Panther and Ian Houghton – who were riding along Cheyne Walk, Kettering, Northamptonshire, at 9.30am, when they observed:

> "...several flashes of brilliant light in the eastern part of the sky, moving towards the south-east.

Through a break in the clouds, we saw a white 'ball of light' with strange edges, moving parallel to the ground, heading south to north."

At about the same time, two girls from Wellingborough noticed what they presumed to be lightning in the sky, after a bright 'flash of light' revealed *"four horizontal red straight lines – the phenomenon being repeated four times, at 3-4 minute intervals"*.

Fifteen minutes later, two girls from Kettering were cycling along Cheyne Walk, when they saw *"several flashes of light"* in the eastern part of the sky, followed by the sighting of a 'fuzzy white ball' seen heading northwards. (**Source: Mr R.A. Jahn**)

Another witness was a police officer and his wife from Parr, St. Helens, Lancashire, who sighted:

"...six oval objects moving in formation across the sky, at 10.30am; they halted for about fifteen seconds before moving on". (**Source Birmingham University Group**)

An amateur photographer – Mr W. Parker of Kendray, Barnsley, in Yorkshire – was in his van outside the house, when he saw:

"...three objects, one larger than the other two, glinting with sunlight, climbing into cloud, about twelve miles away, towards the direction of Wakefield – far too fast to have been aircraft, and only in view for five seconds".

(**Source: Isle of Wight UFO Society/Mr J.M. Steer, BUFORA, Halifax/Cambridge UFO Society**)

13th April 1966 (USA) – Three UFOs seen

At Western Michigan University, in Kalamazoo, Michigan, several students and a policeman watched an unidentified flying object in the sky for more than 20 minutes, after 1am, and described it as star-like. They said it moved in angles around two stationary stars. Matt Kurz – a freshman from Chicago – watched the object through binoculars and said:

"It looked like an elongated football with an orange tip, like on a cigarette."

Others described it as showing red, green, and white colours, moving around two stars, before then suddenly shooting straight upwards and disappearing.

17th April 1966 (USA) – Police chase UFO

An incident took place in Portage County, Ohio, on the morning of the 17th April 1966, following a call to the police by a member of the public, reporting having seen a UFO.

The facts

This has parallels with a series of UFO sightings in October 1967, when police officers also gave chase in Devon, UK, and were later told they had been chasing Venus!

On this occasion, the officers were Deputy Sheriff Dale P. Spaur – a full time member of the Portage County, Ohio, Sherriff's Department.

It all began with a report from a woman in Summit County, who told of having seen a strange object – as big as a house – flying over the neighbourhood. No doubt the incident was treated with much scepticism by the officers, who continued on their patrol westwards along Route 224, when they noticed a car parked on the side of the road and decided to investigate further.

Dale Spaur: *"Neff gets out the right side; I got out of the left. He goes to the front corner of the cruiser and I went to the left rear of the vehicle. I turned around and looked to see if anyone had gone into the woods to 'take a leak' or something, when I saw this thing coming up the rise of the hill. I looked at Barney and saw he was still watching the car and then told him to look over his shoulder.*

He looked and just stood there with his mouth wide open for a minute. I started looking down at my hands and my clothes as it stopped over us, flooding the area with bright light, and this humming noise – like a transformer being loaded or overloaded."

"I was pretty scared for a couple of minutes – as a matter of fact I was petrified, so I moved my right foot and everything seemed to work. We then got back into the car and sat there, seconds, minutes, (who knows?), as it continued to hover over us, before moving eastwards and halting in mid-air. I punched the microphone and told Bob (the radio controller) about what we were seeing. He told me to shoot it first, and then Sergeant Schoenfelt (who was off duty at the station) told us to follow it and keep it under observation while they tried to get a photo unit to the scene – which is what we did."

Officer Wayne Huston joins the chase – Jets scrambled

The officers chased the UFO for 70 miles, at speeds up to 105 miles per hour, through Ohio and into Pennsylvania. Police Officer Wayne Huston of East Palestine, Ohio, situated near the Pennsylvania border, had been monitoring the radio broadcasts and was parked at an intersection he knew the Portage County officers would he passing soon. Shortly afterwards, he saw the UFO pass by with the Sheriff's cruiser in hot pursuit. He swung out and joined the chase. At Conway, Pennsylvania, Spaur spotted another parked police car and stopped to enlist his aid, since their cruiser was almost out of gas. The Pennsylvania officer called his dispatcher. According to Spaur, as the four officers stood and watched the UFO (which had stopped and was hovering) there was traffic on the radio about jets being scrambled to chase the UFO, and …*"we could see these planes coming in"*.

Another witness was Conway Officer Frank Panzanella, who saw a plane taking off from Pittsburgh Airport and pass underneath the UFO, which then took off vertically and disappeared from view.

Close Encounter of the Third Kind

This UFO encounter earned significant mainstream publicity, and probably inspired a scene in Steven Spielberg's *Close Encounters of the Third Kind*, where three Indiana police cruisers are depicted chasing several UFOs into Ohio, eastbound across state lines.

After interviewing one of the police witnesses, Project Blue Book (the official UFO investigative arm of the US Air Force) determined that the witnesses had chased a communications satellite, then the planet Venus. This conclusion was rejected by the officers involved as ridiculously inadequate, and was furthermore subject to some wider criticism, contributing to the opinions of some observers that Blue Book was a failure as an investigative project. The UFO chase was one of the cases that contributed to the creation of the Condon Committee, ostensibly an independent scientific investigation of UFOs.

Courage rewarded by ridicule

Unfortunately, after having had the courage to report what took place, the Deputy Sheriff was later subjected to ridicule and became a virtual outcast, suffered a disrupted home and was made to bear outrageous personal embarrassment. He was accused of gross incompetence, hallucination, and even insanity. We hope that our books will vindicate people like Dale Spaur, and others, whose lives have often been inexorably changed by a single event of monumental proportions, and that history will record the truth and not the lamentable explanations offered by those who are fearful of confronting something, or someone, who continues to makes its appearance known to us.

17th February 1975 – Strange lights in the sky

At about 7.10pm, a Hartlepool resident was cycling up Park Road, when he saw:

> "...what appeared to be a very large star in the sky, with a smaller start to the right – also very bright; looking towards the sea I saw another light in the sky, showing a flashing light beneath it, which was moving in very tight circles and occasionally standing still."

18th February 1975 – Diamond-shaped UFO sighted

Mr R. Harris was driving up Fore Street, Chard, in Somerset, at 8am, when he saw:

> "...a large object travelling across the sky, at speed, before disappearing from view. It looked like a species of a shimmering monster seagull sitting on its tail."

According to the *Teeside Gazettee*, in their edition of 25th February 1975, a diamond-shaped UFO was sighted hovering in the sky over Great Ayton and Middlesbrough, for about half an hour on the evening of 18th February. One of the unnamed witnesses said:

> "There were lights at the corner of the 'diamond', which appeared to be rotating."

(The newspaper disclosed that they had covered 30 separate UFO incidents since Christmas)

At 1.45am on 20th February 1975, a brightly-lit object, shaped like a bowl, was reported to have pursued a car being driven by a farmer's wife near Tern Hill, Shropshire, "*swinging from side to side before moving away*".

23rd February 1975 – UFO over Kent – reported to Omar Fowler, SIGAP

Peter Paul Walsh (20) of St. Pauls Cray, in Kent – a machine operator by trade – was driving his mini car, at 6.41pm, and approaching the junction of Marlings Park Avenue and Petts Wood Road, when he sighted something very odd in the car and shortly afterwards contacted BUFORA representative – Lawrence Dale, who asked him to point out where he had seen it. Both men then made their way to the location, arriving there at 8.41pm.

Lawrence:

> "We proceeded through the forest at the firebreak, which was 10 yards wide and leads to a subway under the four track railway line. Frequent aircraft made their appearance overhead on the approach to London airport, their navigation lights being clearly visible. Suddenly, in comparison to the aircraft, a small but faint orange 'light' appeared lower in the sky than the aircraft.
>
> I brought this to Mr Walsh's attention. It gradually increased in size and seemed to be on a course heading towards us, now four times in brightness of an aircraft landing light. Mr Walsh exclaimed 'it's going away... it's going to leave, I can feel it'. It then headed away towards the north- east and, seconds later, was out of sight. We waited for a couple of minutes and noticed that three aircraft were circling much lower than the others. Two seemed paired, while the other (which looked like a Vulcan bomber) was on its own. We left at 10.30pm."

24th February 1975 – Mystery object sighted near Atomic Power Station, Suffolk

At 6.55pm, postal worker – Mr Thomas Meyer from Aldringham, Suffolk, was exercising his dog 'Titus' along the beach at Sizewell, approximately one and a quarter miles from Sizewell Nuclear Power Station, on what was a clear night with the moon beginning to rise over the sea. He said:

> "I noticed what appeared to be a shooting star approaching from the north-eastern direction. Within seconds it was near me, close enough to see what looked like a big pumpkin – green and yellow in colour, with a luminous glow like a TV set. It was about 20 yards away from me and hovering about six feet above the ground. After 30 seconds it sped away as quickly as it had arrived, and soon

FORM R.I. 1.

BRITISH UNIDENTIFIED FLYING OBJECT RESEARCH ASSOCIATION

RESEARCH SECTION

AIMS

(1) To encourage and promote unbiased scientific investigation and research into Unidentified Flying Object Phenomena.

(2) To collect and disseminate evidence and data relating to Unidentified Flying Objects.

(3) To co-ordinate UFO research on a nation-wide scale and co-operate with persons and organisations engaged upon similar research in all parts of the world.

REPORT FORM FOR U.F.O. SIGHTING

Investigator's Ref. SB7a....

Report No........

Please write your story below and make a drawing of what you saw and then complete the questionaire overleaf.

I was driving my car (mini 1275 GT) approaching the junction of Marlings Park Ave and Petts Wood Rd. accompanied by my fiancé when I noticed, and brought to her attention, a very bright object in the sky. Time 18.41. I thought originally that it was a flare, but reconsidered when I noticed that it did not burn like a flare. I stopped the car and we both got out to get a better view. I have an Omega Chronostop watch (first to be worn on the moon), and began the 'stop' timer and noted that the object hovered for 30 secs. It then descended slowly at ± 30 m.p.h. ± 5mph (using tachymetric scale on watch) for 5 secs. It moved from view by going either into or just beyond the small forest known as Petts Wood.

The object was very bright > full moon on a clear night with a faint pink colour. I would have had to hold a football at arms length to just cover the object. It did not change shape Elevation was ± 60° and view was lost at ± 35° The evening was clear with a bright moon and stars clearly visible.

I proceeded immediately to L. Dale.

If there is insufficient space for your story above, please continue on an additional sheet.

PLEASE USE BLOCK CAPITALS AND PREFERABLY A BALL-POINT PEN

Name in Full.(Mr.,Mrs.,or Miss)...PETER..PAUL..WALSH............

Address:...

Telephone Number:.........................Age:......20...............

Occupation.....MACHINE..OPERATOR...............................

Professional/Technical/Academic qualifications:.....NONE................

disappeared from sight. During the time that it had hovered in front of me, I experienced a warm feeling and noticed a pungent acid smell. The object made no noise and I had an impression it was rotating – its outlines were quite clear and it appeared to be some sort of machine."

Mr Meyer told UFO researcher – Mr M.K. Howe, of Bury St. Edmunds, that his dog was trembling and had cowed behind him during the sighting. After the object went away, the dog bolted and he found him waiting at the Power Station.

(**Source:** *Blythburgh & Sizewell UFOs*, by Peter Johnson, *Flying Saucer Review*, Volume 21, No. 5)

25th February 1975 – Diamond-shaped UFO sighted over Middlesburgh

The *Teeside Evening Gazetter* told its readers about a diamond-shaped UFO seen during the evening, hovering in the sky between Great Ayton and Middleburgh for about half an hour. According to an eyewitness:

"There were lights at each corner of the 'diamond', which appeared to be rotating." [The sighting was one of 30 separate incidents since Christmas.]

27th February 1975 – Diamond-shaped lights

Sunderland man – Mr R A Freake, and three others, were outside 'sky watching'. Mr Freake was looking through his telescope into the night sky, when he saw:

"...an object, showing six lights on it, set in a diamond formation – not flashing like an aircraft, but perfectly still – over Hylton Castle. We kept observations on it for about three minutes."

28th February 1975 – UFO display, Jersey

On the late evening, amateur astronomer – William Kerr of Trinity Hill, Jersey, sighted an object in the sky,

"...several times larger than a Jumbo Jet, which moved about through the sky in various manoeuvres, all in the space of ten seconds, before moving away and out of sight."

Mr Kerr contacted the Air Traffic Control, who reported it to the military, in London, after being unable to explain what it could have been. (**Source:** *Jersey Evening Post*, 28.2.1975)

MARCH 1975

2nd March 1975 – UFO terrifies occupants of car at Elmwood, Wisconsin

At 8pm, an unidentified flying object – disc in shape, the size of a car, white in colour, showing lights all around it, with what looked legs or landing gear – attempted to land in front of a car with the Forster family inside, while the children in the car screamed. They repeatedly pressed their car horn – which alerted farmer Roger Weber, who came out of his farmhouse and guided the family home. The UFO flew off.

(**Source:** Jay Rath, *The W-Files: True Reports of Wisconsin's Unexplained Phenomena*, p. 67)

6th March 1975 – Youths sight glowing object over Barking, Essex

Barking, Essex youths – Stephen Sawkins (14), Peter Hawkley (19), and Stephen Esterhai (16) – were outside, at 8pm, when they saw a glowing object pass overhead, as a result of which it was reported to Roy Lake – Chairman of the Essex UFO Study Group, based in Parsloes Avenue, Dagenham – and the *Barking and Dagenham Post*.

"Barking & Dagenham Post", 12-3-75

DAY, MARCH 12, 1975

Youths see a UFO in the night sky

THREE YOUTHS were startled when they spotted a "round glowing object" in the night sky on Thursday evening.

It was like nothing they had ever seen before and they believe the hovering object over Barking was a UFO.

The lads were Peter Hawkley, 19, Stephen Esterhai, 16 and Stephen Sawkins, 14.

STORY: BARRY BOLTON

Stephen Esterhai, of Pelham Avenue, Barking, said: "I was shocked and a bit frightened really. I didn't think there was anything like it anywhere.

"I didn't believe until I saw it. It wasn't like an aeroplane one of those went past while this thing was there."

HOVERED

The lads were near Eastbury House, Barking, when they saw the UFO.

Stephen Sawkins, of Blake Avenue, Barking, described what he saw: "It was between 8 p.m. and 8.30 and was just a big glow in the sky. It hovered and then shot across the sky and hovered again. "It was there for about 20 minutes."

The glowing UFO definitely wasn't a star or an aeroplane, say the lads. "It was too bright and it moved in circles."

Roy Lake, chairman of the Essex UFO Study Group, who lives in Parsloes Avenue, Dagenham, said of the siting: "It sounds like a cellular saucer. The description seems genuine enough but we will look into it."

And another skywatcher, Mrs. Pamela Cliff, of Rainham Road South, Dagenham, who spotted a UFO in January has reported another siting since.

Mr. Lake says of Mrs. Cliff's siting: "We have examined her case very thoroughly and it is fine."

The Essex Study Group held a meeting in Harts Lane Hall on Monday to discuss all recent sitings in the area.

STEPHEN
ESTERHAI

I WAS. STANDING By ESTBREY HOUSE AT ACBOUT 8oCLOCK,
WHEN I SOUR a BRITE LITE IN THE SCLY, I TEREND
To MY FREND STEVEN HE LOOLT UP LNTOW THE SCIEy IN AMASEMENT
I, WAS, SCRED I RAN TO PEATER'S HOUSE, AND PEAT KAM OUT
IT SErKELD, THE SCLY & THEN THE THING LET OUT 3. RED THINGS
A CLOWD, WENT By THE THING SHON THROO THE
CLOWD, THEN WEN THE CLOWD PAST THEIV IT DIOERPEAD

Date: Thursday, 6th March, 1975   Stephen Guy Sawkins
Time: 8.00 to 8.30 p.m.   10/3/75
Location: Nr. Eastbury House, Barking, Essex   1975-3-2

On 6th of March at 8.30 my friend Stephen saw a U.F.O. It was a spotlight shaped and it hovered very slowly over the rooftops, then my friend ran to our maters house so we could have another witness, and to see if we still had our senses. Peter our friend came out and saw it circle the sky in a matter of a second and in the process passed a passing plane. After 10mins it disappeared and reappeared in another spot in the sky, and 3 little "Scout craft came from under it. I wasn't sure it and the 3rd went off over a few mins, which inturn neither made no noise. Two minutes later it totally disappeared.

16th March 1975 – Silver object over Oldham, Lancashire

DARREN EGERTON March 19th 1975
SIGHTING JAN 1975.
Dear mr blaver
At 8.55am on Thursday 16.1.75 I was in the Playground I was talking to my friend Christopher who is 9. And I was looking across the sky and I saw a silver object spinning across towards Mossley. And we only saw it for about 2 minutes and it was spinning very fast. I think it was about 130 ft high in the sky.

Thank you for the letter
Darren Egerton.

St Annes RC School
Greenacres rd
OLDHAM
Lancashire.

APRIL 1975

6th April 1975 – Humming UFO over Bournemouth

Mr Alan Radford from Wentworth Avenue, Southbourne, Bournemouth, was at home with his wife, Lesley, at 11.10pm, watching TV, when they a loud humming.

> *"We put up with it for five or six minutes, then realised it was coming from outside. We rushed out of the house in time to see a bullet-shaped object heading up into the sky, which disappeared within seconds. The hum then stopped. It had a green and yellow trail coming from behind it."*

(**Source:** *Scan/Evening Echo*, 7.4.1975 – 'Take-off hum was not TV')

10th April 1975 – Triangular UFO sighted over Essex

At 5.10am, a triangular formation of three white lights, with a larger red one in front, was seen moving north-west across the sky over Thunderley, in Essex, before disappearing from sight, a couple of minutes later.

It appears another witness was Mari 'J' (25) of Rose Road, Canvey Island, in Essex. She was in a car, heading northwards along Kent Hill Road, with two others, around 5am.

> *"We saw a circle of lights (four in total) – three forming a triangle, with a smaller red one apparently leading the other three – heading slowly through the sky.*
>
> *We stopped and got out of the car, to ensure this wasn't reflection of something else. It crossed overhead but not above us and moved northwards, before being lost from view as it dropped down behind houses a couple of minutes later."* (**Source:** **Barry King**)

3rd to 9th April – 'V'-shaped UFOs over North Carolina

There were over 29 separate, independent UFO sightings involving 'V' shaped UFOS and close encounters made from Robeson, Hoke, Sampson, Bladen, Pitt, and Columbus Counties, in the early morning hours, and again in the evening, centred on Lumberton, North Carolina.

(**Sources:** NICAP, *UFO Evidence II, Section VIII*/Dwight Connelly, *Skylook,* May 1975, p. 3/Jennie Zeidman, *Lumberton Report: UFO Activity in Southern North Carolina,* pp. 5-8/*Raleigh News Observer,* 6.4.1975)

MAY 1975

4th May 1975 – 'Bright light' over Sussex

A UFO was seen over Sussex, at 10.19pm and 11.35pm, by 'sky watchers' from Hove and Crowborough, including Mr Paul Glover, who described it as a 'bright light' in the western sky. The police were told and said they were unable to explain it.

18th May 1975 – UFO landing, Rainhill, Merseyside

Three pulsating objects – resembling tennis balls in shape, forming a triangular pattern – were seen moving through the sky over Rainhill, Merseyside, at 10.10pm, and then apparently descend in a small copse, illuminating trees and ground with an orange light.

A search of the area with torchlight, by local residents – Mr and Mrs Scothern – who had witnessed the phenomenon, failed to reveal anything of significance, although the next morning four boot marks, measuring 14 inches long by 6 inches wide, with a stride of 46 inches between the impressions, were found in mud next to a duck pond – which may or may not be connected.

(**Source:** *UFOs: A British Viewpoint,* by **Jenny Randles & Peter Warrington/Personal interview**)

1975 – Yellow 'orb', Scotland

Instances involving mysterious 'globes of light' which appear during thunderstorms, commonly referred to as ball lightning, which can penetrate solid walls – sometimes described as red, orange or blue in colour, making a hissing or crackling noise, before exploding in mid-air – still forms the subject of scientific controversy. Unlike flashes of lightning, which last a fraction of a second, ball lightning is of much longer duration.

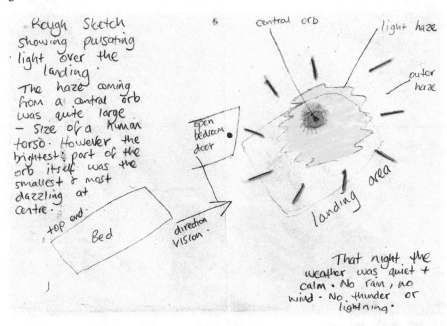

Is this what Melanie Cunningham and her boyfriend saw while on holiday, staying for the weekend in Newton Wamphray – a small community, 5 miles south of Beattock, Dumfries and Galloway – or was there another explanation?

> *"I was awoken by my boyfriend; one look at his face told me he was terrified. He directed my attention towards a bright yellow 'orb of light', two to three inches in diameter, hovering silently 3-4 feet above the landing floor carpet. The glare given off by the object was so bright and dazzling it lit up the bedroom – then switched off, plunging the room into darkness, and switched back on.*
>
> *We watched it, feeling that we were being observed in some way. After four or five minutes, it stopped flashing and disappeared – never to be seen again. The next morning I examined the carpet most carefully but found nothing unusual, such as burns or damage.*
>
> *The weather that night had been calm, clear and dry, without any thunder or lightning.*
>
> *I believe what we saw was some kind of paranormal event, rather than any example of alien intelligence."*

(Source: Personal interview)

31st May 1975 – UFOs sighted in Lancashire

At 2.40am, Rochdale resident Edward Kerringham – then living in Park Way, Greave, employed as a security guard – was in the kitchen, making himself a cup of tea. He happened to glance through the window, when he saw six or seven strange lights in the back garden. Knowing that this was highly unusual, he picked up a Polaroid camera and went outside, where he took one photograph. While removing the film, in order to take another shot, the lights went out – as if 'switched off', about a minute later.

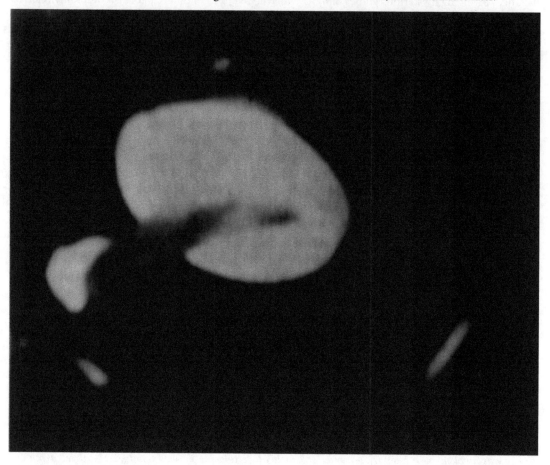

Mr Kerringham telephoned the local newspaper, the next day, and told them what had happened, but they didn't seem interested. However, he did receive a visit from a freelance reporter from the *Manchester Evening News*, who wrote-up a story entitled: "Saucers at the bottom of his garden", (4.6.1975).

Bill Skellon of DIGAP (Direct Investigation Group for Aerial Phenomena) visited Mr Kerringham and subsequently interviewed him about the incident, which involved the sighting of six or seven lights, surrounding a saucer-shaped object.

Many years later we spoke briefly to Edward, who had moved to Cumbria. He maintained the photograph was genuine. He never said that he had seen any 'Flying Saucers' – just what had taken place.

(Source: As above/Jenny Randles/DIGAP, Bill Skellon/*Flying Saucer Review*, Volume 22, No. 12, 1976/www.2012)

Summer 1975 – UFO sighting, Cumbria

Geoff Grundhill was aged 15 and living with his parents in Workington, Cumbria, and alone at the time when the sighting took place, in summer 1975.

> *"It was early evening; the sky was a beautiful blue colour with one or two clouds about. I was in the bedroom, looking at some books, when without any prior warning or sound, a dark shadow*

fell across the room as the window was blotted out by the appearance of an object resembling an aircraft, but unlike any plane I had seen before that floated into view around the gable end of the house."

"It had a bright shining metallic surface, glistening as it caught the sun. I went towards the window and was horrified to see that it was hovering. It was almost as if it seemed alive and was watching me – like something out of a science fiction film.

I moved slowly to where my camera was lying; my heart was thumping with excitement and fright. Suddenly, it shot away from the window and took up a position over the rooftops, opposite, discharging what looked like vapour or smoke, and then – like chocolate melting in a heat – vanished. I noticed that long after the object had gone, the birds refused to fly anywhere near that portion of the sky."

(Source: Personal interview/Jenny Randles)

JUNE 1975

9th June 1975 – UFO display over Fire Station, London

The entire staff at Heston Fire Station (16 members in all) at Isleworth, London, watched in astonishment when a strange parade of white star-like objects were seen moving through the sky, at 1.15am. They varied in direction and luminosity, and seemed at high altitude; their speed ranged from slow to very fast, one crossing the horizon in 8-10 seconds. A special phone link was set up with the police, but they reported nothing seen from their location. Heathrow Airport were contacted and confirmed nothing was showing on their radar, or that any flights were moving in or out of the airspace.

A report was later sent to the MOD who responded with, *"that they could not undertake to pursue research, other than for defence implications, to a point where positive correlation with a known object is established."*

(Source: *BUFORA Journal*, Volume 4, Number 11, January/February 1976)

10th June 1975 – UFO display, Kent

At 1.30am, Mr B. Douglas (34) of Farley Close, Chatham, Kent, were out stargazing on what was an exceptionally clear night, with his wife – V. Douglas, and son John.

"We noticed a pulsating blue flash of light, high in the sky. Suddenly, a white glowing 'light' shot across the sky and stopped dead in its tracks. Another series of pulsating flashes occurred, and a second white 'light' appeared on a different bearing. This pattern of behaviour was repeated many times."

Five minutes later, the phenomena moved away and out of sight. (**Source: Essex UFO Study Group**)

12th June 1975 – Police Officer sights UFO

At 10.30pm, on a woman, from Walthamstow, London, accompanied by her 20 year-old son, and 11 year-old daughter, sighted a yellowish light, motionless in the western sky . . .

"It was about 1,000ft high, and changed colour and flashed. One such flash seemed to strike a van, parked outside our house, and for several days afterwards, the radio would only give static. We called the Police and a young policewoman arrived, who observed the phenomenon as it moved silently, towards the north-east, fading and descending. She estimated it was about twenty miles away and, in her opinion, was a lighted balloon."

As a result of that telephone call, Woman Police Constable 830 Deacon of Leyton Police Station, Essex, went to Chelmsford Road, Walthamstow, where she met up with Mrs Brennan, who reported having sighted a UFO on two consecutive evenings.

WPC Deacon:

"I saw an object above the rooftops in the western direction. It emitted a yellowish light, which varied in intensity. I estimated it was about 1,000 feet high and two miles away. Over the next hour it receded towards the north-west, growing fainter as it did so, before being obscured by cloud and lost sight of." (**Source: Barry King, BUFORA**)

June 1975 – UFO over Birmingham

Paul Hunter from Redditch, Worcestershire, still remains completely baffled what it was he and his friends saw while visiting the Swan Recreation Ground, Acocks Green, close to the A45 Swan Island, Birmingham, during summer 1975.

BLACK/GREY IN COLOUR WITH RED & BLUE LIGHTS IN A CIRCLE UNDERNEATH. POSSIBLY GREEN? AS WELL BUT NOT 100% SURE.

"I was playing with friends, watching a kite being flown over a group of trees, one morning, when out of nowhere appeared this black, huge, saucer-shaped craft.

I shouted out to my friends, 'Look, it's a Flying Saucer!' ... some of them screamed with fright. I stood watching, noticing it had red and blue pulsing lights under its base, seemingly oblivious of the strong wind blowing – then, in a split second, it disappeared completely, leaving me very frightened and unable to comprehend what I had seen." (**Source: Personal interview**)

18th June 1975 – Did RAF chase UFOs?

Unconfirmed sources tell of two RAF Phantom Jets chasing flat circular 'discs' over Newcastle to Clayton and Keele.

We were told that many people contacted the authorities about this. A spokesman at RAF Coningsby (Lincoln) denied the intercept had taken place.

Summer 1975 – 'Flying hovercraft', Gloucester

Dave Cosnett, from Gloucester, was 8 years of age (then), and living at Hardwicke (about four miles from the City), when he happened to glance up into the sky, one summer's evening of 1975, and saw a 'red light' hovering there – a matter to which he paid little attention to at the time – until the following evening, when he was flabbergasted to see what resembled:

> "...a 'flying hovercraft'; I could see windows with lights revolving inside, and a red light at each end. I rushed to the front of the house as it passed behind the building. When I arrived, there was nothing to be seen."

26 THE CITIZEN, TUESDAY, MARCH 8, 2011   CIT-E

'More truth out there on UFOs'

By Chris Campbell
chris.campbell@glosmedia.co.uk

UFO experts in Gloucester are calling for more sightings to be released to the public in the wake of 35 files being published by the Government.

More than 8,500 pages of UFO discussions, sightings and reports have been released by the National Archives, the largest single batch so far.

But Churchdown's Dave Cosnette, who co-founded UFO and paranormal website Cosmic Conspiracies, called for more to be published.

Dave, 43, said: "The release of these files puts more credibility into the subject. When you take into consideration that people from all walks of life are reporting sightings, it's clear at least some are credible.

"We want more files to be disclosed."

Freedom of information requests and letters from 'persistent inquirers' led to the Ministry of Defence opening the UFO files for the first time.

One of the files shows 15 unidentified aircraft were detected on radar approaching the UK between January and July 2001 in the months leading up to 9/11.

Thousands of encounters

■ **SIGHTINGS:** Dave Cosnette.

are listed including an "alien abduction" in London and an unidentified aircraft shadowing a Lancaster bomber.

Other highlights include claims that the Home Office had emergency procedures for dealing with landed and crashed satellites and UFOs.

Details in the files show how the workload of the UFO desk at the MoD increased by 50 per cent during 1996 and 1997, due to media interest in the subject around the 50th anniversary of the Roswell incident.

In Gloucestershire, Steve Sparkes thought he saw a UFO when orange discs flew across the sky above Gloucester in 2009.

Mr Sparkes, 49, of Hempsted, said he saw red and orange circular objects in the sky when walking out of The Regal pub in St Aldate Street. They later turned out to be Chinese lanterns.

Cosmic Conspiracies said it receives hundreds of e-mails a day with sightings from all over the world.

Dave said he created the website after witnessing a very large triangular UFO in December 1999.

To view their site visit www.ufos-aliens.co.uk.

The National Archives files are available to download for free for a month from the website:
www.nationalarchives.gov.uk/ufos

Have you seen a UFO? Email us at citizen.news@glosmedia.co.uk

The next day he read a story in the newspaper about UFOs being seen over the Forest of Dean, some ten miles away. (**Source: Personal interview**)

1975 – UFO over Cley Hill, Warminster

Gary Lanham – a UFO researcher from Birmingham, with a wealth of information retaining to his many investigations carried out both in the UK and Canada, over the years – decided to visit Cley Hill, Warminster, in 1975, together with a group of friends, hoping to see something himself, rather than relying on what had been published in the press.

Gary Lanham

"By about 10.30pm the temperature had dropped, so we prepared some soup while looking out over the Wiltshire landscape, towards Frome, still partially illuminated by the rays of the setting sun.

As darkness settled, I watched the occasional aircraft moving overhead and, in the distance, the eerie intermittent light flashes from a distant train. On an impulse I turned around, facing east, and saw a large blue coloured 'light' that appeared to 'blink on', just hanging in the sky. I shouted out to the others and we watched as it shot off across the sky, disappearing from our view behind a hill. Within seconds, or so, the same or identical light blinked on again, exactly in the same area of sky where we had first seen it.

This sequence of actions was repeated at five second intervals, before it performed an amazing manoeuvre from a standing start. It flew horizontally at terrific speed, but as it neared the point of a hill where it had previously disappeared, it stopped and began to move backwards and forwards at high speed, reminding me of a sparkler being waved in the air. At the end of the 'display' the 'light' made a sudden change to the vertical, ascending at breathtaking speeds until the human eye was unable to catch it." (**Source: Personal interview**)

Here is a photo of Whitley Strieber who has himself visited the location some years ago now shown on Cradle Hill.

22nd June 1975 – UFO over Southampton

At 3pm on 22nd June 1975, Mr Monty Warlock and his wife from Hill Lane, Southampton, were sat in the back garden, enjoying the sunshine, when they were disturbed by the sound of the children next door, shouting excitedly. At first they took no notice, but then heard their next door neighbour – Harry – shout out. They looked up to see him pointing upwards into the sky.

> *"We saw a bright object, hovering overhead; it resembled a glass chandelier and seemed to be at a height of about several thousand feet. We could see some extremely bright lights around its main body, although this could have been caused by the sun's rays reflecting off its body. It seemed to be pulsating slowly. My wife came dashing out with her camera, and took several photographs of the object."*

At this stage, the couple reported it to the local newspaper. Unfortunately, the reporter failed to take the call seriously.

After about ten minutes, the object suddenly turned on end and began to climb upwards, the pulsating effect increasing rapidly as it did so. (Source: Frank Marshall)

On the 24th June 1975, a silvery oval object, surrounded in haze, was seen over Belfast, moving west to east, above vapour trails left by aircraft. On the same day, two Belfast schoolboys reported having sighted a pear-shaped UFO in the south-east part of the sky. The object was seen to move towards them slowly, discharging what looked like sparks from its right side, and then hover briefly for a few seconds, before disappearing over houses to the north-east.

Summer 1975 – UFO over Warminster

Battlesbury Camp, Warminster – one of the most important Iron Age Hill Forts in Britain – was the source of a completely different kind of interest, during summer 1975, according to Major A.L. Smith (retired), who wrote to us about what he saw, while returning to the Camp on Imber Road, late one evening.

> *"There were four of us – the Garrison Chaplain, and the two wives. It was just before midnight, as I recall, when, as we approached the main entrance, we all saw this UFO travelling fast and low in the sky, emitting a glow – like the exhaust of a Jet aircraft, from what looked like a rectangular vent in its rear (except this was totally silent), before disappearing over Battlesbury Barracks.*
>
> *The next morning, I rang the Met. Office and told them what I had seen. They couldn't help, other than confirming no aircraft were in the air at the time."*

Summer 1975 – UFO landing marks found in Worcestershire

Painter/Decorator Geoffrey Tandy of Malvern, Worcestershire, was out walking over the Worcestershire Beacon, Malvern Hills, in summer 1975, when he noticed a luminous object, travelling from left to right across the night sky.

> *"It suddenly stopped in mid-air, at a height of about 500 feet, and dropped into the ground. The next morning, I went over to have a look and found three marks in the bushes, forming a triangle, as if something like a three-wheeler car had been resting there."* (**Source: Crystal Hogben,** *Magic Saucer*)

Summer 1975 – Police sighting over Cleeve Hill, Gloucestershire

During the summer of 1975, Police Constable Trent Davis of the Gloucestershire Constabulary, who was to serve 30 years with the Force before going on to work at GCHQ as a civil servant for another 12 years, was on patrol one evening, at about 11.30pm. He was directed to a report of an unusual 'white light' seen hovering above the radio transmission masts, situated on top of Cleeve Hill on the outskirts of Cheltenham. The fact that the Force sent a number of officers to investigate this sighting was because of IRA fears.

GCHQ

> *"As I drew level with the masts, the 'light' drew level with me. It then followed me, keeping a parallel distance from me until I neared a village, on my left, where it stopped. I turned to look at the light, which was immense in size. I stared at the 'light', trying to work out what it was, and then felt some pressure on the back of my neck and heard what I thought was a whisper; 'communicate' – so I thought 'what the hell', and flashed my headlights at it. In one second it must have travelled hundreds, if not thousands, of miles away from me, at fantastic speed. By this time other police officers had arrived, and we continued to look at it until we got bored and left the scene. For the next month or so, the police in the Gloucestershire area were being alerted about strange 'lights' in the sky. Some of the officers attempted to pursue the 'lights'."*

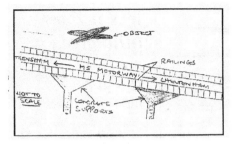

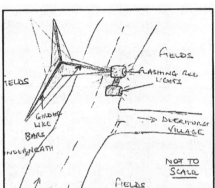

In an email conversation with Trent, during April 2012, Trent was to claim that *'he had been plagued by these beings to the present day'*.

We emailed him back, explaining that reports of recurring manifestations, whether deemed paranormal or otherwise, had often been found in the background history of people – presumably caused through exposure to the fields of energy surrounding the UFO – and that, in our opinion, we did not believe he was suffering from any form of mental degeneration. We learned that another officer who attended was Sergeant David Thompson, from traffic – now retired.

We traced David and explained the reason for contacting him. He promised to get in touch, but we never heard anything.

PC Trent Davis

Trent with late wife Veronica

Trent also told us that PC Nick Dean (retired) saw a UFO in Cheltenham and believes he lives in Stroud, Gloucestershire. Likewise, we also contacted him but haven't heard anything either.

This was not to be the last time that Trent was to sight UFOs, as the reader will see for themselves as time goes on. **(Source: Personal interviews)**

Mid-1970s – UFO sighted over Binfield, Berkshire, by policewoman

Another officer who sighted something strange was Special Police Constable Janet Burrell, after hearing of her sighting that took place in Binfield, Berkshire, during the early to mid-1970s.

We contacted her, and this is what she told us:

> *"I was having trouble sleeping at the time, and looked out of the window, when I noticed an unusual flickering 'bright light', many miles away on the horizon, which caught my attention. I watched, mesmerized, and then became aware that it was moving closer. Suddenly, in the space of a short time, it was outside the window – not close enough to touch it, but close enough to see that it was near to the house. It then dropped down and turned away. I was so amazed at what I had witnessed, I told everybody about it but nobody believed me."* **(Source: Personal interview)**

JULY 1975

1st July 1975 – Were the RAF scrambled?

4th July 1975 – UFO sighted over New Jersey

College students – Miss Tiger and her friend, Mr Cahill from Parsippany, New Jersey – were driving home from the movies, at 12.05am, when they saw a huge object, estimated to be 60-80 feet in diameter. The UFO was seen to travel from a south-west direction and cross over the vehicle. The couple, who were able to observe it well after it halted in mid-air and was stationary for eight minutes, said:

> *"It was unlike any light we had ever seen before and that, although it illuminated the surrounding area, it did not create a glare; no matter what direction we observed the light it appeared to be directed away from us. When we first sighted it we saw lights shining from the front and rear, and that there was a green light on the top of the turret .The interior was lit by a dull green light. There were also red and green lights at the end of the object. After we had observed it for a few minutes, now a 100 feet high off the ground, we noticed a bright white light emitting from the front and bottom, which appeared to be sweeping the area – almost as if it was looking for something(?)"*

A second later and it had shot away into the sky.

The couple telephoned the Parsippany –Troy Hills Police to report the matter.

Enquiries conducted into the incident revealed other residents had also witnessed this occurrence, including a pilot – Jim Quodomine. Jim told of landing at 10pm on the 4th July on Caldwell Field, New Jersey, after having been flying over the area watching firework displays with his fiancée. While tying the aircraft up, Jim was approached by a couple who seemed

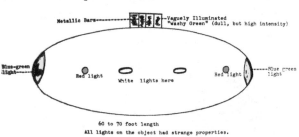

distressed and pointed out a 'bright light' in the sky. (Was this Tiger and Cahill, or another couple?) The couple told him it had been hovering over them about an hour ago, which would have been 9pm. Jim and his fiancée took off in his Cessna 150 and climbed to 3,000 feet, closing in on the object. When 4-5 miles away, Jim saw the object (estimated to be 60-80 feet in diameter) and attempted to move closer, at a speed of 100 miles per hour. As he did so he saw it change brightness, but it moved away at speed and was out of sight. **(Source:** *UFO Investigator* **(NICAP), September 1975)**

6th July 1975 – Cigar-shaped UFO seen over Glastonbury Tor

At 3am on 6th July 1975, members of a 'sky watch', at Glastonbury Tor, sighted a cigar-shaped object, flashing white, green, and red colours in the southern sky. Five similar objects then appeared, showing the same colour changing pattern of lights. One was seen heading in a south to north direction, while another appeared to land in a field.

As dawn broke, at 4.30am, the first object moved away and out of sight. **(Source: BUFORA)**

Was it those little green men in the sky?

THOSE LITTLE green men in outer space have been stirring things up again, according to Herald reader Mr Nicholas Churcher of Roedean Road, Worthing.

Ice-cream worker Mr Churcher spotted 'a strange shape' in the sky over Collingwood Road, on Tuesday at 11 p.m., showing a greenish light. 'Then three lights came on and off. It shot across the sky. It didn't make a noise,' said Mr Churcher.

He said he saw two helicopters over in another direction. 'They were going across the sky in zig-zags. They seemed to be looking for something.'

It wasn't only Mr Churche who saw it. His girl friend and her mother saw the shape as well.

Now he wants to know if there were any other sightings of his UFO.

FRIDAY 4 JULY 1975

8th July 1975 – *National Enquirer* releases details of UFO sighting, 10 months later!

Why it took so long to release this information is a mystery. Was there a clampdown on the sighting by the Authorities?

On page 286 we outlined a report from Dorset, involving a parachute-like object, seen by Michael John Byatt on the 24th September 1974. What would he have made of this report, which took place on the same day but many thousands of miles away in the United States?

Police Officers – Deputy William Medary (44), of the Cumberland County Sheriff's Department, and Walter Butcher (49) – were patrolling an isolated area on Bailey Island, across the channel from the Wiscasset Nuclear Power Station, Maine.

William, with over 7,000 hours of flying time and served in the Navy and Air Force, said:

> "Walter was the first to see it just hanging there in the sky, motionless. We watched it for several minutes and then suddenly it rose straight up, without a sound, moving at incredible speed to about 15,000 feet."

The two men watched it through a pair of binoculars.

Walter:

> "As it reached the top of its climb, red lights started glowing at the centre and then greenish lights began pulsating at its end. It was shaped something like a football and metallic in appearance, about the size of a Jumbo Jet or even bigger."

As the officers continued their observations, two smaller 'lights' were seen to break away from the larger object and sweep away in an arc across the sky, before merging back into the UFO, and shot away and out of sight.

Enquiries made with Police Dispatcher – Harold Page, with the nearby Brunswick Naval Air Station, as to whether anything had been tracked on radar, met with a negative result.

(Source: *National Enquirer*, 8.7.1975 – 'Police with thousands of hours flying experience watch UFOs)

10th July 1975 – Strange 'figure' on the A55

On the 10th July 1975, Mr and Mrs Taylor were driving along the A55, at Ewloe, Clwyd, in broad daylight, when they were surprised to see a tall 'figure', wearing something that resembled a diving suit or boiler suit, with a balaclava helmet, stood at the front of a nearby embankment, with its arms stretched upwards. As they drove past the strange 'figure', it turned to face them and then bent down – as if to pick something off the ground. **(Source: *Northern UFO News*, Volume 41, Ron Sargeant)**

1975 – UFO display, Wales

In 2011, we were contacted by Geoffrey Mason (63) – a gas fitter by employment, living in the Kinswinford area – who wanted to tell us about what he witnessed around 1975.

> "I was aged 28, at the time, and staying in a caravan belonging to friends in Towyn, with Dave, his girlfriend, myself and partner.
>
> On the Saturday night Dave (who had just left the RAF, with experience of working on 'Jump Jets'), left the two 'girls' behind and suggested we go out for a walk on the beach, to stretch our legs, after the long drive. We were looking out to sea; it was a clear night, when I saw an object moving around, high in the sky, which I brought to Dave's attention. We stood watching it, for at least ten minutes, until it began to descend. It then stopped and did a right-hand

turn, went across the sky and stopped again, before travelling very slowly over towards the horizon. The next thing was it headed towards us and came close enough for us to see that it was shaped like an upside-down street lamp, oval in shape with a flat bottom, giving off a pale green light. As it came across the sea, it suddenly accelerated from its position, which we estimated was two and-a-half miles away. It then lifted itself over the mountains and was gone in a flash."

The next day, Geoffrey telephoned his mother, in Stourbridge, to tell her they had arrived safely.

On returning home from holiday, he was surprised to learn, in conversation with this mother, of a UFO sighted over Clent, by a chef working at Belbroughton, which had been published in the *Express and Star* – 'Waitresses see UFO fly over Clent' – on the same evening as his sighting.

Discussing the UFO subject can be detrimental to career prospects!

Geoffrey believes that this was the same UFO (from the description given to him) that he had seen over the Welsh coast, a short time before. Although the impact of the sighting was of great curiosity to Geoffrey, it raised considerable concerns with his friend, Dave, who told him:

"Whatever you do, don't ever mention my name as it could affect my RAF pension."

22nd July 1975 – UFO landing on the Welsh hills

We learnt of a disturbing encounter, involving the appearance of a mysterious dome-shaped 'craft', seen during a holiday visit to the Cambrian Mountains, at Machynlleth, by a young boy, referred to as Trevor 'P' by Andrew Collins and Barry King.

Andy and Barry conducted a thorough investigation into the matter, after having been contacted originally by Jenny Randles, following a letter received from the boy's parents, expressing their concern about a very strange version of almost unbelievable events.

On the 22nd July 1975, the parents went to view a cottage for sale at Dovey Vale, located on the road near Wylfa Hill, close to Machynlleth, and arrived there at 5pm. (˙Ordnance survey map 135, ref. 738999)

Trevor decided to go for a walk while negotiations were taking place, and strolled up to the top of a 250 feet hill which lay to the south. Glancing forward, over the ridge, he saw something which puzzled him as to what it was he was looking at. Realising that he was in a vulnerable position, he ducked down behind some boulders and watched carefully.

Object seen resting on the ground

In front of him, not more than 50 feet away, was an object resting on the ground. It had a large base – like a paddling pool. It was about 40 feet in diameter and some 7-8 feet high, showing a number of large circular lights, approximately 5 feet in diameter, positioned around the base. Each was shining brightly and of a colour he didn't recognise, and were not casting any light on the ground. Between each light (about seven in view), Trevor could see deep grooves or curves set into the base, which was silvery in colour.

On the base 'sat' a hemispherical transparent dome which, if viewed from a horizontal plane, rose vertically from the base and then arched over into the hemisphere. At the central apex of the dome was another large light, which seemed to be fitted to the apex from the inside and not interfering with the curvature of the hemisphere. The dome seemed to be lesser in diameter than the

base. In the centre of the base, inside the dome, was a big 'metal unit', about 15 feet long and 7 feet tall. This consisted, from left to right, of a vertical side, eventually sloping away towards the right, at a 45° angle – then levelled out into a horizontal top, which stepped down in an irregular pattern. This appeared to be constructed of metal, being silver in colour. No marks, switches, knobs, or instruments, could be seen inside the 'craft'.

Trevor:

> *"Inside the dome were two 'forms', looking like massive pieces of jelly – irregular in appearance and about seven feet across.*
>
> *They were a translucent white in colour. Inside 'them' were hundreds of white discs – like doughnuts – each about six inches in diameter. The masses were constantly changing shape to a considerable degree, although from the movement of the white discs, it seemed the centre of each of the masses remained inactive. One of the 'forms' was positioned in front of the metal unit, while the other was half obscured behind it."*

Trevor waited about 20 seconds, frightened but inquisitive, trying to come to terms with what he was witnessing.

> *"I noticed a panel, or section, which was beginning to open, about 7ft x 7ft on the right-hand side of the base, which slowly pivoted downwards towards the ground. This took about seven seconds, then one of the 'forms' – now in full view – began to start floating towards the ground, gradually lowering itself out of the 'craft'. At this stage I ran, and made my way back to where my father was. I said something to him and then ran back to have a look. By this time, the 'form' was back in the object and the hatch was closed. I heard a strange constant noise – like a car revving up, but quieter – and then a large circular disc of light on the object's side, together with the light on the top of the apex, began to flash simultaneously in the colours of the surrounding countryside – green grass, brown soil, blue sky – increasing in speed until almost enveloping the 'craft', until it blended into the background – just like a chameleon."*

The wealth of information obtained from the interview is most impressive and reflects the professionalism of Andrew Collins. He took part in many important investigations, over the years, involving close encounters, and their occasional perceived occupants. This is, without doubt, one of the strangest ones we have ever come across and, while bordering on the unbelievable, was considered genuine by Andrew and Barry King, who interviewed Trevor on the 29th March 1978, accompanied by Graham Philips – a parapsychologist and trained hypnotist.

Father interviewed

Trevor's father was also interviewed. He confirmed his son had approached him and said, quite calmly:

> *"You won't believe me, come on."*

… and ran back towards the ridge (witnessed by his father), who then saw him lie down for a short time, then get up and run back down the hillside, tripping over his father's feet (clearly petrified), where he then said:

> *"A jelly man got out of it."*

His father asked him to show him the scene – which he did, but by then there was no sign of the 'craft' and its weird occupants. Initially, the family thought the story was due to a figment of their son's imagination, and just got on with their holiday. In the absence of any physical evidence, what else could they do?

Lost use of vocal chords

The day afterwards, Trevor lost the use of his vocal chords and went to see a doctor, who examined both Trevor and his brother. His prognosis was tonsillitis.

Blind in one eye

After arriving home, a week later, Trevor went back to school and had only been there for 14 days, when he became blind in his left eye, which continued for some time. He also complained of a thumping headache and was unable to sleep, spending time downstairs, drawing. He was taken to an eye specialist and also a psychiatrist, who were told of the experience in Wales, but his medical condition worsened.

Trevor became blind in his right eye and then the left again – and then totally blind. Fortunately, this condition cleared up. From being a quiet introverted boy he became short-tempered, aggressive and argumentative.

We do not know what Trevor saw, but even without having ever met him and relying on the judgement of Barry and Andrew, it is painfully obvious that this is a genuine matter, rather than any vivid imagination or fabrication. Sightings of objects like these, which are rarely photographed, leaves one feeling perplexed. Ironically, with the growth of the internet and 'YouTube', photographs and films which are uploaded and presented as genuine, often fall short of any such thing.

July 1975 – Strange incident befalls motorist

In the same month (exact date not known), Company Executive – Derek Hutchinson (44), was driving his Ford Cortina Mk 3 saloon near to Gerpins Lane, Rainham, near Ockendon, when he noticed a Datsun van parked on one side of the road with its back doors open. In the back of the vehicle was seen what appeared to be large amount of electrical equipment. Standing by the vehicle were two men, dressed in short jackets (ski type); one was holding a box with a long wire. Derek drove past the van, which to be best of his memory was showing the following foreign – plate [??419? 22] [D plate] and turned into Gerpins Lane. He had only gone a few yards when:

> *"I saw a small silver disc-shaped object moving in front of me, and braked sharply, and sat there initially observing the object through the windscreen and then opening the door to get a better view."*

Now feeling frightened, Derek turned the car around and drove away. To his horror the 'disc' began to follow his car for a distance of about half a mile, before returning to where he had first seen it.

Somewhat as a footnote to this very mysterious sighting was an even more disturbing incident, which took place the same night. After arriving home, he went up to bed but was shocked when:

> "I looked out and saw the same object, hovering outside my bedroom window; it was that close and almost up against the glass." The object was seen again, the next night. Derek awoke his wife Maureen, but by the time she had rushed to the window it had gone.

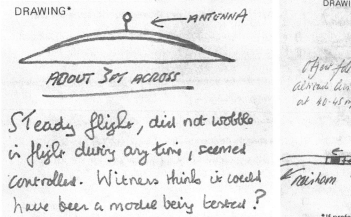

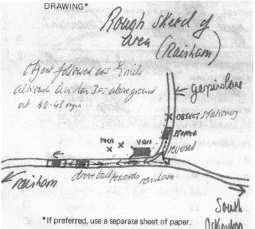

AUGUST 1975

2nd August 1975 – UFO sighted

Mr David Clark (40) – a truck driver – of Verney Gardens, Dagenham, was in his rear garden, at 11.30pm, when:

> "I saw an amber coloured object pass overhead, shaped like a very large bird. My wife also witnessed this. Thirty seconds later it was out of view."

5th/6th/7th August 1975 – Silver 'ball' seen in sky over Wanstead, London

Russell Spencer Smith (13), of Nine Acre Close, and his mother – Joan, father – Ernest, and neighbours, sighted a pulsating star-shaped silver 'ball of light', which appeared in the clear sky at 10pm, for at least five to six minutes, over three days duration.
(Source: Mr Ron Markwick)

8th August 1975 – 'Flying Saucer' seen, Bristol

The activity for early August continued with a report from a retired BAC employee, who was

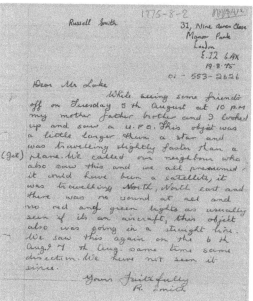

living at Soundwell, Bristol. He told of being awoken by his cat that growled and jumped onto the window, at 4.30am on the 8th August 1975. On looking out he saw:

"...a saucer-shaped object, with a rotating edge. It glittered and made a sound like a generator. A 'trap door', opened, and light seemed to radiate from the inside – then a small shape appeared to come out and move slowly southwards. It returned, 20 minutes later; the 'trap door' closed, and the object vanished. The object remained stationary in the sky until dawn, when it faded away.

I saw the object the next night, but no sign of any 'trap door' opening." (**Source: BUFORA**)

12th August 1975 – Green 'discs' over Cambridge

At Wisbech, Cambridge, three people were outside at 10.10pm, when they saw three greenish 'discs' move across the sky, rotating as they did so, heading northwards. One of them was seen to fly underneath the other two and then move back erratically to its original position. Five minutes later a cluster of about 16 'globes', in tight formation, swept across the sky following the same flight path as the previous objects had taken.

15th August 1975 – Police sight UFO

At 3.30am, two uniformed police officers in different police vehicles – one north of Bury, Greater Manchester; the other, in the town itself – observed a brightly-lit UFO, heading in the direction of Heywood. They were not the only witnesses. The UFO was also sighted by a member of the public.
(**Source:** *Flying Saucer Review*, Volume 23, No. 2)

24th August 1975 – Crescent-shaped UFO over London

Incredibly, Mr and Mrs Smith and their two sons of 9 Acres Close, Manor Park, London E12, were getting ready for bed, at 10pm, when a strange large 'bright light' in the sky was seen through the window. They looked out to see: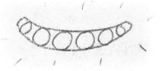

"...a crescent-shaped object, showing small round windows along its side, motionless for a few minutes, before heading northwards towards the Wanstead area."

26th August 1975 – Hexagonal UFO sighted over Barking, Essex

Mrs Elizabeth D. Lynch (69) of 16, Levine Gardens, Barking, and her daughter – Sheila, were at their home address, at 10.45pm.

Elizabeth:

"I was closing the bedroom door, when I saw a large orange object moving slowly through the sky, in movements of forward then sideways and then forward again. It then halted in mid-air for about 15 minutes. It was octagonal-shaped and had a slightly flat top; the bottom was almost cone in shape. We watched it for about 15 minutes and then closed the window and curtain."

(**Source: Barry King, Dagenham Paranormal Research Group**)

27th August 1975 – UFO over Reading, Berkshire

Thanks to *Scan* Magazine editor and Bournemouth-based UFO Investigator – Leslie Harris, we learnt of his investigation into a number of UFO sightings that took place on this evening. The first to sight something unusual was Jill Bodman and her husband – then a reporter for the local newspaper.

The couple were driving along the A.32 Wokingham Road, in Surrey, when Jill noticed an object,

"...bell-shaped, metallic in colour, and the surface was covered with what looked like small indentations and had a flashing green and red light on its top."

We spoke to her husband, Bob – the photographer for the *Reading Chronicle* (now the picture editor of a National daily newspaper) – who confirmed knowledge of the sighting, but told us his view of the object was restricted due to his position as driver.

(Source: *Reading Chronicle*, 29.8.1975 – 'A Wokingham women claims she has seen what may have been a visit from Outer Space by Flying Saucer')

It appears a similar craft was seen over Winnersh during the same evening, by other members of the public, although the local police denied receiving any UFO reports from the public for that evening.

Leslie:

> "I was able to establish that the UFO had commenced a low approach in the sky over Winnersh, and hovered for a few minutes, before moving north over the town centre at a fairly low speed, towards Caversham, where it was seen to move at tremendous speed over Emmer Green, described as '...changing colours to bright orange, as it accelerated away in a flash of blue light'. In addition to these reports was a sighting made by a woman driving along Henley Road, Caversham, towards Shiplake, who had just passed the 'Flowing Spring', when she saw an 'object' hovering over the hedge, only a few feet off the ground – inky-blue in colour, rounded at the bottom with a domed top, and flashing a very bright yellow and white light.
>
> The woman, who admitted she was very frightened at the time, noticed that neither the hedge nor the grass underneath the 'object' were being disturbed in any way, despite the appearance of the unidentified object – which she estimated to be about twelve feet in diameter – hovering over the ground."

According to the Meteorological Office at Bracknell, who was contacted, it could not have been a weather balloon!

> "The ones we used were constructed of reflective plastic and, sometimes, had a small lantern attached to them, and generally speaking, such devices were only used in the daytime."

A spokesman at RAF Odiham, in Hampshire, said:

> "It was highly unlikely it could have been a helicopter, but it may have been a light Jet aircraft, showing intensely bright lights been moving quickly."

At 10.30pm, Mr David Stringer and Pail Glover, of National UFO Research, sighted a red/orange pulsating object with a glow around it, heading due south-west across the sky, before changing course to North. Two to three minutes later, it inexplicably vanished from sight.

SEPTEMBER 1975

2nd September 1975 – 'Castle' shaped UFO sighted

Robin Goodwin (9) of Portland Close, Eaglescliffe, Stockton-on-Tees, was cycling home from his friend's house, at 8.30pm, when he saw a glowing 'red light' in the sky, heading in the direction of Yarm.

When he arrived home, he told his mother – Marie, what he had seen. She said:

> "The picture he drew looked like a sandcastle with a square on top."

(Source: North East Evening Gazette, 3.9.1975 – 'Watch the skies')

5th September 1975 – Was it Jupiter?

An egg-shaped object was reported, by two people, moving through the night sky over Cleveland, according to Mr David McGroarty – Press officer for the Cleveland UFO Group. Another witness was Thornaby mechanic – Richard Leroy, of Stainsby Hill, who said:

> *"I was coming through Leven, near Yarm, when I noticed a stationary flashing light, high up in the sky. I phoned the Evening Gazette and they told me 50 people had contacted them about this already."*

One explanation was that they (apart from the first report) had seen Jupiter, which was high in the western sky and could appear to blink when certain cloud conditions prevailed.

(Source: Cleveland UFO Group)

6th September 1975 – UFO display over Michigan ... NORAD contacted!

At 9.30pm, Campground owner – Carl Bailey, from Port Austin, Michigan, contacted the police after sighting what looked like 'batwing-shaped UFOs in the sky.

> *"There were a lot of them – it seemed like a whole fleet; it was amazing. They were floating up and down, left and right, in the sky." Carl telephoned NORAD (The North American Aerospace Defense Command) of the 754th Radar Squadron, at Port Austin, and reported the incident. He was then connected with the 23rd NORAD Region HQ, at Duluth, Minnesota, and described what he was still seeing to the senior officer in charge. He listened and then said:*

> *"Well the Air Force doesn't investigate UFOs anymore, Mr Bailey."*

Later, Major William Frensley – an information officer at NORAD, Colorado Springs, told newsmen that the Radar Squadron at Port Austin had tracked five unknown objects for about 30 minutes on the morning of the 7th September, and that two policemen and a civilian had been questioned. He admitted they didn't know what the objects were. The officers were Huron County Sheriff's deputies – Greg Gordon (24) and Gary Krugh.

Air Defense Chiefs Admit: We've Tracked UFOs on Radar–For a Second Time in Less Than a Year

For the second time in less than a year the North American Air Defense Command (NORAD) has admitted tracking UFOs.

"Radar operators of the 754th Radar Squadron at Port Austin Air Force Station in Michigan reported tracking five unknown objects for about 30 minutes early on the morning of September 7," Maj. William Frensley, an information officer at NORAD headquarters in Colorado Springs, Colo., told The ENQUIRER.

He also confirmed that two policemen and a civilian who observed the UFOs from the ground were questioned by NORAD.

On Nov. 11, 1975, NORAD admitted scrambling two F-106 jet fighters in an unsuccessful attempt to intercept a UFO over Sudbury, Canada. But no jets were dispatched in the Port Austin sighting because the objects did not pose a threat to national security, Maj. Frensley said.

"Determining whether an unknown object is a threat is based on certain criteria, such as point of origin, direction and speed and a number of other things I cannot discuss for security reasons," he said. The UFOs were first reported to the police at 4:30 p.m.

EYEWITNESS Carl Bailey described UFOs as "a fleet of floating objects shaped like batwings."

September 6, by Carl Bailey, 28, one of the eyewitnesses questioned by NORAD. He said the objects were shaped like "batwings."

"There were a lot of them. It seemed like a whole fleet. It was amazing. They were moving up and down and left and right, just sort of floating."

Bailey said he got a phone call at home from the radar base at about 2:30 a.m., September 7. "They asked me to go outside and see if I could still spot something. I took a look and they were still up there."

When Bailey, who manages a campground, reported what he saw, he was connected with the senior officer in charge at the 23rd NORAD Region Headquarters in Duluth, Minn.

"He asked me what the objects looked like. I told him and he asked a couple more questions and then said: 'Well, the Air Force doesn't investigate UFOs anymore, Mr. Bailey,' and he thanked me."

But Huron County sheriff's deputies Greg Gordon and Gary Krug were also interviewed about what they saw. Gordon, 24, reported: "We observed one object that was a very bright light in the sky. It would descend very rapidly, looking as though it was going to land. It would then return to its original height. It moved so quickly it was unbelievable.

"At one point, one of the objects was over Lake Huron and the next instant it was

over the Port Austin Shores Campground. It moved so quickly our eyes were unable to follow it.

"At 5 a.m. two men from the 754th Radar Squadron came out to the scene.

Maj. Frensley said it's not unusual for NORAD to question people who've reported seeing unidentified flying objects.

"We like to talk to as many people as possible so we can correlate these sightings, if possible, with something like a straying aircraft or flares that are dropped."

But the Port Austin UFOs remain a mystery. "We don't know what the objects were," Maj. Frensley admitted.

— BOB PRATT

RADAR ROOM of 754th Radar Station, Port Austin, Mich., where five unknown flying objects were tracked for 30 minutes on September 7.

MAP shows where five UFOs were tracked by radar and seen by two sheriff's deputies and a campground manager.

A host of Reading sure they saw flying

IT NOW SEEMS almost certain that Reading was visited by something from outer space last week.

Many accounts of sightings of the unidentified flying object indicate that what passed over Reading on Wednesday night last week was definitely not an aircraft or a helicopter.

One popular theory is that the round or oblong object that shone brightly, hovered and moved at astonishing speed could have been a meteorological balloon. But there were no balloons in the area at the time.

The report by Mrs. Jill Bodman of a bell-shaped craft hovering over Winnersh was followed by a host of reports to the "Chronicle" of a strange craft seen in various parts of the town at about the same time.

Though descriptions differed in several respects there were startling similarities in every case.

From the reports it appears that the U.F.O. began its low pass at Winnersh. There it hovered for some minutes before moving in a northerly direction, travelling over the town centre at a fairly slow speed.

It continued north over Caversham and then picked up a "tremendous" speed by the time it reached Emmer Green. An eye witness to its spectacular departure from the sky said it went a bright orange as it accelerated and disappeared in a flash of blue light.

All those who saw it said it was moving quite slowly or hovering just above the roof tops. They all agreed there were very bright lights shining from it and that at no time did it make any noise.

Each witness stated categorically it was not an aeroplane or a helicopter or like anything they had ever seen before.

Mrs. Bodman saw the object over Winnersh and said it was a dull metallic grey in colour and shone brightly when it reflected light.

It was next seen passing over Earley and a few minutes later it was seen by three members of the Ryde family of Downshire Square, Reading.

"Three of us all saw it from

'Chronicle'

our garden," said Mrs. Rose Ryde. "It looked like a falling star at first but it had a little light on top of it. It is hard to describe but it was going very fast and moving to the north west.

"It did not look like a balloon or an aircraft. It must have been a flying saucer. At first I laughed it off but when I saw the article in the paper I realised I had seen the same thing."

Mrs. Ryde's two grandchildren, Steven and Philip, also saw the visitors from space.

Two young planespotters, who were on the lookout for Concorde, got quite a shock when all they saw was a flying saucer.

Ian Cox and Mark Huntley, both 12, of Valentine Crescent, Caversham, said the object was moving so fast they only saw it for a few seconds.

"It was round and oblong in shape and made no noise at all," Mark explained. "It was travelling very fast, much faster than a plane. In fact it went right under a plane that was going over.

"It was a dull silvery grey colour and it came up from the south. It was going too fast to be a helicoptor or balloon."

The last sighting was made by Mrs. Denise Palmer, of Eccles Close, Caversham, who described how the strange object vanished into the night sky over Emmer Green.

"All I got to see of it was the light—it was a bit like a star. It made no noise and I thought that was strange. I kept my eyes on it and it hovered for a while.

"It was completely quiet but it suddenly picked up tremendous speed. As it did it turned a bright orange and started to go up. There was a flash of blue light and it was gone," said Mrs. Palmer.

"I think it was probably some sort of U.F.O. It was very uncanny because nothing could travel at that speed and it went in different colours."

Neil Shepherd, aged 12, saw the U.F.O. from his home at Hartland Road, Reading. He suggested he saw more than one of them travelling north.

He told me he spotted five flying saucers in formation. All were bright white and flying in a staggered pattern.

Mark Huntley and Ian Cox with the drawing Mark made of the objects they say they saw last week flying beneath Concorde.

Unidentified flying objects—or just people's imaginations playing tricks?

Reading Chronicle, Friday, September 5th, 1975

Mrs. Rose Ryde— "Like a falling star."

Mrs. Denise Palmer— "Very uncanny."

eople are saucers

Investigation by Mark Prior

"They were going much faster than a plane and going just above the rooftops. I saw them for about a minute before they flew out of sight. They were very low down and did not make any noise," said Neil.

THE flying saucer has been seen again this week just north of Caversham hovering only a few feet above the ground, writes Mark Prior.

An Emmer Green woman saw the saucer, which was domed, while driving her car along the Henley Road on Tuesday evening. She came within feet of the inky-blue coloured object, but sped away in fright at what she saw.

It was rounded at the bottom with a domed top. There was a very bright flashing light at the top—which fits other descriptions. It was quite small, perhaps only 12 feet in diameter.

She told me: "It was only a couple of feet off the ground. If I had got out of my car I could quite easily have touched it but I was so scared I drove straight off. It gave me a big fright."

What was more strange was that though it was hovering there was no air disturbance and the hedges and grass were still. She was not sure whether it made any sound—she was more interested in getting away quickly.

The whole Shepherd family are keen skywatchers and are always on the lookout for anything strange. Mr. Alan Shepherd claimed to have seen about 12 U.F.O.s in the past three years.

"I think there is definitely life on other planets—there cannot be just us. We go to the moon and try to get to other stars so I do not see why someone else should not try to come here and have a look at us," said Mr. Shepherd.

A spokesman for the Meteorological Office at Bracknell said they were not using any weather balloons at the time, although the plastic ones they used reflected light and sometimes had a small lantern on them.

Most of their balloon ascents were made during daylight hours.

And at the R.A.F. base at Odiham in Hampshire a spokesman said it was highly unlikely that what was seen was a helicopter.

"We do have aircraft on night flying but I very much doubt if it was a helicopter. There were none in that area." He thought it could have been a light jet aircraft which have intensely bright lights and are very quiet.

Mr. Jim Betts, of the Reading Astronomical Society, said there was always an element of doubt in sightings of U.F.O.'s. "There are many that have been explained but the few that have not are the ones that are most interesting.

"I do no think there are little green men on Mars. But there is still a big area of doubt and we are not qualified to dismiss the whole thing."

Mr. Alan Shepherd and his son, Neil, who says he saw "five flying saucers in formation."

He continued that a lot happened in the sky every night and he was anxious to see a U.F.O. himself. "We do not scoff at it but the majority can be explained."

Greg Gordon:

> *"We observed one object that was a very bright light in the sky. It would descend very rapidly, looking as though it was going to land. It would then return to its original height. It moved so quickly it was unbelievable. At one point one of the objects was over Lake Huron and the next instance it was over the Port Austin*

9th September 1975 – Flashing lights over Cleveland

Other reports from this period in time included reports of a bright flashing light, seen by a number of people living in the Berwick Hills area of Cleveland on this date, appearing at half-minute intervals – definitely not lightning, according to the witnesses. (**Source: David McGroarty**)

15th September 1975 – UFOs over Reading, Berkshire

Carol Ward from Ufton Nervet, near Burghfield Common, Reading, sighted what looked like *"eight floodlights, or a train hanging in the sky"*, before they slowly moved away towards Winnersh. Later, the same evening, William Crowley (then aged 15) was out fishing near Burghfield Bridge, at Holybrook, with a number of other youths.

> *"Without any warning a white light appeared behind a nearby bush, on the opposite side of the river. I shouted to the other boys, and we watched as it dropped downwards and then rose back into the air followed by a red flash, revealing six or seven objects motionless in the sky. After a short time they suddenly disappeared, just as an aircraft came over."*

Rita Noyes

Another witness to UFO activity occurring in the Reading area that month was Rita Noyes.

> *"We had been to a photographic club meeting at the Abbey Gateway, Reading, and were about to get into the car when we saw a 'bright light' in the sky. We stood watching as it began to move from side to side, at which point we could clearly see that it was dome-shaped, with brighter top than base – almost as if it was lit from inside. Within a few minutes it was out of sight."*

(**Source: Personal interviews**)

16th September 1975 – 'Red light' circles over Caterham

At about 2am on 16th September 1975, Jack Hennequin was walking home with his girlfriend, along Eldon Road, in Caterham, when they saw an unidentified object rotating in the sky, showing bright red, white, and green lights. Within minutes, the object descended below tree level and was then lost from view. Mr Hennequin contacted the police at Caterham, who telephoned the airports but told him nothing else had been reported. (**Source:** *Caterham Times*, **19.9.1975**)

In mid-September 1975, a British Aircraft Corporation 1-11 aircraft was travelling between London and Glasgow when, at a height of 27,000 feet, while passing over Lichfield, in Staffordshire, the crew sighted two 'bright lights' moving away from them.

Enquiries made later, revealed the UFO had been tracked on radar.

18th September 1975 – 'Flying Saucer' reported over Yorkshire Moor

Two 'flying saucer' shaped objects, showing red lights underneath, were seen hovering over the Yorkshire Moors by a woman motorist, parked at the side of the road at Harden Moss, Between Holmfirth and Greenfield, at 10.30pm.

(**Source:** *Huddersfield Examiner*, **19.9.1975** – '**Woman claims she spotted flying objects**')

Many of these sightings were brought to the attention of Halifax residents.

BUFORA UFO investigators Trevor Whittaker and his wife – Doreen, pictured here.

1975: A 'cone' or triangular-shaped object, seen by spectators at Hall Green Stadium, Birmingham, at 8.30pm, for one minute. Original file sent to BUFORA mislaid – no other details.

20th September 1975 – Was it a meteor?

At daylight, Eric Briggs of Saltersgill Avenue, Middlesbrough, reported having sighted a bright red 'ball' moving across the sky, with what looked like a 'grey saucer-shaped object' inside it – later explained away as a meteor.

(**Source:** *North East Evening Gazette*, 20.9.1975 – 'UFO could have been a meteor')

23rd September 1975 – Shining object over West Sussex

Hayley Dickson and Karen Dickson – both young girls of Tower Road, Lancing – wrote up about what they witnessed. It took place at 8.50pm and involved the sighting of a round object in the sky, hovering over the nearby railway line. About an hour later it moved over, near to a big chimney, and inexplicably vanished into thin air. Their aunty – Jayne Guile, also enclosed some brief details about what she saw, after being alerted by the two girls.

> *"The first thing I did was to look out of the window. I saw something shining. I said to Karen to call her mum, and uncle Bob, to come upstairs. After this, they went outside and saw the object was going up and down in the sky. At about 8.50pm, a 'shooting star' went past into some clouds. It was silver and star-shaped and had come from the 'shining thing'."*

September 1975 – UFO over Southampton

Andrew Paglia (then aged 14), was visiting Southampton Sports Centre with a friend – Michael Gatrell – and sat on a bench near the cricket pitch, bordered by a wooden chain-link fence, at 9pm, when, out of the corner of his eye, he saw a huge translucent elliptical set of multicoloured red, green, and blue lights, roughly half the size of the pitch – (like the blue gas flame in the British Gas advert on TV) – approaching through the air towards them.

> *"I looked at my friend, speechless, as whatever they were came to a halt ten feet off the ground in front of us, about a hundred feet away. At this point we decided to run away, feeling very uneasy,*

and made our way home, a short distance away from the Centre itself, where we summoned up the courage to look behind us, seeing the elliptical ring change to circular, momentarily, and then back to elliptical (as though banking in a turn) and move along Dunkirk Road, down the side of the Sports Centre – now fifty feet above the ground. It then turned and actually moved over our heads, where it stopped for a brief second before accelerating away into the sky." Andrew told us, some years later, that he came across a report in *The Unexplained* magazine, which outlined a UFO report from a man living in Coxford Road, Southampton, just half a mile away from his house, which he believes (from the description) to have been the same UFO he saw. (Source: Personal interview)

1975 – UFO over Nottinghamshire

Mrs Edson from Skegby, Nottinghamshire, (then in her late 80s), was walking the family dog along Buttery Lane, one evening in the same year.

"All of a sudden I felt an uneasy feeling creep over me. I looked upwards and was astonished to see an object in the sky similar in appearance to the old style vacuum cleaner, showing a number of small red and yellow flashing lights, hovering just above me.

I watched in amazement as it slowly moved towards the direction of King's Mill Hospital, Mansfield, making a low humming noise. Despite the years that have passed, I have never forgotten this singular incident which was to leave such an indelible impression on my memory."

(Source: Personal interview)

1975 – Close encounter with UFO over Essex

Steven Smith – a part-time soldier from Queen's Park, Billericay, in Essex – was motorcycling with two other friends, along the Wickford road, near Burnham-on-Crouch, just before 9pm, when he saw two 'lights' in his rear view mirror. After a few minutes had elapsed, without any sign of being overtaken, Steve shouted to Jackie (his pillion passenger) to take a look behind. One look at her horrified face, told him something was wrong. Instinctively, he took immediate action by slewing the machine into a ditch.

"Looking up I was astonished to see a bullet-shaped object, showing a single flashing light underneath, pass silently over our heads, moving southwards. I later reported this incident to the police and my regiment, and tried to forget about it until I received a visit from two plain clothes men, who identified themselves as military. They asked me to accompany them to my army base, where I was interviewed and told, in no uncertain terms, that the incident had not happened."

A week after the event, he noticed the paint had begun to peel off the tanks of the motorcycles. He told the regiment what had happened, who replaced the tanks with new ones. **(Source: Ron West)**

UFO over Cradle Hill, Warminster

Brian Savory from Cheltenham, in Gloucestershire, was on Cradle Hill, Warminster, in September 1975, when he noticed a cylindrical object appear over a copse, near the military firing range, approximately two hundred feet off the ground, at 10.30pm.

"It came to a halt and just hung in the sky, for about three minutes, before moving slowly away. I managed to take a photograph of the object, using a Zorkji 4K, 35mm camera, on a time exposure f4, at about eight seconds."

Although we could vaguely make out the object on the photograph that Brian sent us, it was only by using a filter that we were able to extract a much sharper and clearer visual image of the object concerned, which shows a *cylindrical or drum shaped object*. Unfortunately, the image is still not good enough quality to include.

OCTOBER 1975

4th October 1975 – US Police Officers sight cigar-shaped UFO over New Jersey

At 2.55am, Ramsey, New Jersey Police Officers – Francis J. Gross and Ragazzo – were on duty when they received a call about strange looking 'lights' in the southwestern sky. Both officers then saw for themselves,

> *"...lights in a straight line formation, heading slowly across the sky. They appeared solid and were reddish in colour. The rear sections of the objects were blurred, but the rest of the cigar shape was outlined. We watched them until out of sight."*

6th October 1975 – Rectangular UFO over Huddersfield

Mrs Mary Taylor of George Avenue, Birkby, and her husband – Ronald, along with their two children, watched a rectangular object in the sky for over an hour and-a-half on the evening. Through binoculars it was clearly seen as being no aircraft, or explained logically.

This was not the only occasion the family saw this UFO. About a fortnight later they were accompanied by a friend, who had driven over from Newsome, when the oblong spinning UFO was sighted once again, over the Emley Moor direction.

Mary:

> *"Initially it was green on top and red underneath, but then the colours began to alternate."*

(**Source:** *Huddersfield Daily Examiner*, 15.10.1975 – 'Birkby couple again claim seeing UFOs')

8th October 1975, *Worthing Gazette* – 'Analyzing UFOs – by a councillor'

Councilor Ivan Robinson for the Marine Ward, Worthing, wrote an interesting letter to the *Worthing Gazette*, which was published, telling of his own sighting that took place on the 24th June 1960, when he and some other witnesses saw seven brilliant 'points of lights' hovering in the sky above them. He telephoned Gatwick Airport and spoke to the radar unit. An official told him that because the cross channel radar angle prevented a high altitude scan, and also of having received a report of this, he would be switched to Heathrow.

> *"Heathrow confirmed visual contact, but were too busy with night traffic to follow it up. I was transferred to a military radar unit in the south. I was surprised to learn, in conversation with the duty officer there, that as they had picked up so much satellite garbage floating around at different heights, he was doubtful if his operators could differentiate between that and an ICBM attack." Ivan contacted the observatory at Herstmonceux. The answer was simple – at that time of the year the sun was just below the horizon at midnight, and at that time, on that date only, the path of seven satellites were converging over Sussex, their flight path high enough to reflect the unseen sunlight. A salutary lesson, if nothing else!*

9th October 1975 – *Daily Telegraph* – 'UFO to a better life leaves 20 missing'

Sheriff's officers at Newport, Oregon, said that all twenty individuals had vanished without trace, after being told to give away all of their possessions, including children, so that they could be transported in a 'Flying Saucer' to a better life, tells of 20 people who went missing after a UFO lecture by a man from outer space.

This bizarre story and outlines the disappearance of twenty people from small coastal communities of Oregon, following reports of an imaginative fraud scheme involving a 'Flying Saucer' and hints of mass murder.

An investigation launched revealed that there had been a meeting on the 14th September 1975, at the

Bayshore Inn, Waldport, Oregon, when about 100 people turned up to hear an advertised speech by a person from outer space. It was later ascertained that the speaker did not claim to be from outer space, but told the audience how their souls could be saved through a UFO. The hall was reserved for a fee of $50 by a man and woman, who gave false details. Chief Criminal Investigator for the surrounding Lincoln County – Mr Ron Sutton, said that he had been told by some people who went to the meeting that:

> "...they would be assassinated in a very short time and then reincarnate; others would be selected to go to a special camp at Colorado for life on another planet and would be picked up by a UFO in the next ten years. They were told they would have to give everything away, even their children. I'm checking a report that one family gave away a 150 acre farm and their three children. We don't know if it's a fraud, or whether these people were killed. There are all sorts of rumours, including human sacrifice, and that it was sponsored by the Charles Manson family."

(Source: *Daily Telegraph*, 9.10.1975 – 'UFO to a better life leaves 20 missing')

10th October 1975 – White/red UFO seen over Essington, Wolverhampton

(Source: UFOSIS original report missing)

11th October 1975- British Groups make TV appeal for Scientific Ufology

According to Jenny Randles there was something of a minor breakthrough for British Ufology, when members of the Northern UFO Network (NUFON) were allowed nine and-a-half minutes of TV time on the 11th October 1975.

Jenny tells in her report, published in an edition of *Flying Saucer Review* (Volume 21, Numbers 3 & 4, 1975) that the aims of this production was to inspire confidence in the public to come forward with their sightings, bearing in mind that prior to the screening, the group were receiving *50 new sightings a week,* subsequent to the programme going out. We are not sure how many weeks this was, but presume it was few rather than many. Jenny also explained how local groups operated.

Others who took part were Trevor Whittaker of BUFORA, Peter Warrington – Chairman of the Manchester Research Association, and Michael Dean of the Wirral UFO Society. As a result of the programme being screened twice, they received over a hundred letters and a similar amount of telephone calls – which continued to flow in for a number of weeks.

In a letter sent to David Procktor by Jenny Randles, and subsequently published, a different picture emerged which, if nothing else, shows that little has changed – now over 40 years later!

DEAR UFO NEWS....(Letters of importance and interest relating to this journal).

Dear Sir,

Many thanks for the recent copy of UFO NEWS which I was most pleased to receive. It is good to know that you are still in business, making, as ever, a valuable contribution to British Ufology.

Personally I have been a BUFORA member for about five years and have throughout, been unhappy about the way we 'out of Town' members are left out. When the new policy of Regional Investigations began in late 1972, I was hopeful that things would improve. For a while this did and the RIC Gordon Clegg visited me a couple of times but he eventually formed a loose group of non-BUFORA members together, signed them up, and that was that! I made one of two investigations on my own (particularly in early '73 since I was a Crewe Teachers'Training College, which was close to the scene of the Winsford UFO flap). I sent long reports in but never got an acknowledgement. Since that time I have continuously suggested that we organise a BUFORA branch in the area since I feel it needs the backing of a group to fully investigate reports. At first his reply was "No time!" After that he didn't give any answer. In the past two years I must have written a dozen or more times to him, and Dave Rees has tried often enough too.

Of course I reported the situation to BUFORA HQ. I got the reply from both recent RICs (Richard Colborne and Ken Phillips)"Be patient. We are not happy with your region." They began telling me that over a year ago but despite many suggestions they have not done a thing to improve the situation. By summer '73 I was pretty frustrated. I had several copies of several reports I had submitted to BUFORA but I wanted to be in a group. I answered an ad in FSR for a new group and was told..."There are not enough replies (only 34) to try to organise a group yourself!" I had a letter printed in the Manchester Evening News and the response was good. It was from this I found Dave Rees. He had answered the FSR nd., but despite living only a few miles apart they had not put in much touch.

The point is that BUFORA DO exist and so we must try for mutual co-operation. I see no real value in blindly criticising them but often on behalf of NUFON, made severe yet constructive criticism. There is a change in the wind but I (and other northern groups) will not be satisfied until we get more positive action from them.

Yours Sincerely,
Jenny Randles, Northern UFO Network.

EDITOR'S REPLY: Although this letter is an amalgam of two letters from Miss Randles (which I hope is ok) readers can perhaps appreciate the dissatisfaction that groups outside London are experiencing with BUFORA. I don't get very far, and I'm IN London! However things do seem to be moving slowly, and perhaps if the conference hosted by BUFORA(Staffs) works out well, an improvement will be the outcome. I am personally interested in speaking to many BUFORA people, including the editor of their journal, who seemingly has no intention of exchanging UFO NEWS, and also Lionel Beer who has the wrong idea about WHY I complain (to their faces, not behind) about the standards they maintain. See this issue's editorial for an example. My best wishes to NUFON for the work they continue to undertake, and to Dave Rees for the MAPIT journal he never fails to send me.

12th October 1975 – UFO seen over football field, Essex

Barry King interviewed the witness here – Steven Wheeler (10) and his father, at their home address in Waveney Drive, Springfield, Essex.

Steven:

> "I was playing football with some of my friends at Pollards Meadow, around 7.30pm, when we heard a humming noise.
>
> Craig, my next door neighbour, looked up and caught sight of an object hovering just above some trees. I looked up and saw a grey metallic looking object – round, with colored lights on the bottom. I'm not sure how many ... two or three red and orange.
>
> We were all scared – then it moved away from us."

POLLARDS MEADOW, SPRINGFIELD PLACE OF SIGHTING 12-10-75

Stephen Wheeler draws his impression of the flying saucer while Paul Macgregor helps to jog his memory.

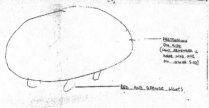

Did flying saucer men spy on boys' soccer match?

ESSEX CHRONICLE 17-10-75

By ALAN GEERE

A BUNCH of Springfield youngsters just couldn't believe their eyes when a spectator turned up to watch their Sunday evening soccer match.

Who he was or where he came from is still a mystery, but the boys do know how he arrived . . . in a FLYING SAUCER.

The petrified lads looked on as the flying saucer, a blaze of flashing lights, droned over the trees at Pollards Meadow.

"We thought it was going to come down and land right in the middle of our pitch," said 11-year-old Paul Macgregor.

"But it hovered over the trees and finally went."

PICTURES

The boys rushed home only to find disbelieving parents, who dismissed the idea as a childish fantasy.

"But we certainly did see something," said nine-year-old Stephen Wheeler.

And to prove their point they drew pictures of how the object looked to them.

"It was quite big and had a lump on each side just like the UFOs on TV, but what we noticed most was all the flashing lights," explained Paul.

The Essex Chronicle has not had any other reports of this object, but aviation authorities say they often have reports of strange objects seen in the sky.

The most common theory is that they are either helicopters or 'planes which are distorted by the evening lights.

Steven showed Barry the location, from which he was able to deduct that the distance from the boys to the tree was 143 feet, angle from ground to object was 30 degrees, distance to object from witnesses 164 feet, height of tree 86 feet, width of trees 56 feet.

The object was seen in the east and last seen moving south-east.

Another witness was Paul McGregor, of the same road, but he chose not to make any statements due to the ridicule aimed at him.

14th October 1975: Small UFO seen, Hay-on-Wye

18th October 1975 – Red Pulsing light over Reading

A family from Tilehurst, Reading, was driving home near to the traffic island at Theale, when they noticed what looked like two pairs of car's headlights, low down in the sky, which slowly faded from view revealing a red pulsing light. On reaching their destination, they were shocked to see the same four lights hovering over a nearby house. **(Source: Ken Rogers)**

18th October 1975, 10.50pm: yellow and white UFO seen, Worcester (Source: UFOSIS)

22nd October 1975 – Luminous orange UFO over Liverpool

At 8.45pm, B.A. graduate – Marilyn Parkes from Westvale, Kirkby, Liverpool, was driving away from Parsons Walk, Springfield, after having visited her aunt (who lived in Barnsley Street) on her way to pick up her boyfriend from the Wigan College of Technology.

> "It was drizzling slightly, so I switched on the headlights and windscreen wipers. I was about to pull out when, for some inexplicable reason, I glanced up in into the sky and saw a luminous orange, perfectly spherical object, moving slowly across the road. It then disappeared over the houses and I drove on to see if I could find it, but lost sight of it."

(Source: *Wigan Observer*, 31.10.1975 – 'A 'flying saucer' has been spotted hovering over Wigan')

27th October 1975 – Loring AFB, Maine … UFO circles airbase

At 8.45pm, Sgt. Grover K. Eggleston, of the 2192nd Communications Squadron, was on duty at the tower when he received a call from the Command Post of an unknown aircraft reported. Six minutes later, while watching his radar screen, Eggleston noted the 'unknown' appeared to be circling approximately ten miles east-north-east of the base.

Object disappears off radar screen – emergency situation declared

Forty minutes later the object suddenly disappeared from the screen, indicating either the object had landed, or dropped below the radar coverage. The Wing Commander arrived at the weapons storage area, seven minutes after the initial sighting was made. Immediately, other units of the 42nd Police began pouring into the area. Security vehicles with blue flashing lights were converging from all over the base.

Air Support requested

Through the Loring Command Post, the Wing Commander requested fighter coverage from the 21st NORAD Region at Hancock Field, New York, and the 22nd NORAD Region at North Bay, Ontario, Canada. However, fighter support was denied by both regions. The Wing Commander then increased local security posture and requested assistance from the Maine State Police in trying to identify the unknown craft, which they presumed was a helicopter. A call was made to local flight services for possible identification, without results. The 42nd Security Police conducted a sweep of the weapons storage perimeter inside and out. An additional sweep was made of the areas that the craft had flown over. All actions produced no results.

Suspicious object heads away towards Canada

The craft broke the circling pattern and began flying toward Grand Falls, New Brunswick, Canada. Radar contact was lost in the vicinity of Grand Falls, bearing 065 degrees, twelve miles from Loring. Canadian authorities were not notified. No further unusual events occurred throughout that night. Priority messages were sent to the National Military Command Center in Washington, D.C., the Chief of Staff of the US Air Force, the USAF Forward Operations Division at Fort Ritchie, Maryland, and Strategic Air Command headquarters at the 8th Air Force and the 45th Division, informing them of what had taken place. The base remained on a high state of alert for the rest of the night and into the early morning hours of 28th October.

28th October 1975 – UFO seen over Birmingham City Centre – no others details
(Source: UFOSIS)

28th October 1975 – Cylindrical UFO over Manchester

A silver-white, smooth, cylindrical object, described as resembling Concorde, showing a pointed nose, drooped at the front, was seen low down in the sky by a motorist and his two companions, while driving along the A57 road towards Barton, near Manchester, at 10.45pm.

(**Source: Phil Whitehead and Jeff Porter/***BUFORA Journal***, Volume 5, No. 4, November/December 1976**)

31st October 1975 – 'Fairground' UFO sighted in the sky over Essex

An Essex man wrote to the *Independent on Sunday* about his UFO sighting, enclosing some images. The same man had already been interviewed by Ron West, many years previously, but declined to be identified. On that date he was glancing up at the night sky, when he saw a bright 'red light' moving erratically, at a speed which ruled out any aircraft.

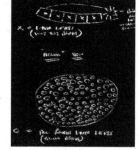

> *"Suddenly the 'red light' seemed to turn in flight – as if to reveal its top. As it did so, it changed into a mass of white lights.*
>
> *It resembled an aerial view of a fairground merry-go-round with masses of light bulbs glowing."*

31st October 1975 – Mystery 'circle of light' in the sky

Ballantrae local Librarian – Mrs Jeanette MCulloch – was at her home address, at 2am, when she saw:

> *"...a 'circle of lights' in the sky, about 10-15 miles away in the direction of Larne, some 400 feet off the ground. I watched it for an hour before it disappeared from view."*

The next morning, she discovered that her neighbour's daughter – Miss Lorna Brown – had also seen the same UFO.

Sightings of the mysterious 'circle of light' were reported over the Ayrshire coast, Belfast and Donaghadee County, where it was claimed some of the residents had seen orange egg-shaped objects in the sky.

(**Source: *Carrick Herald*, 13.11.1975 – 'UFOs seen at Ballantrae? Woman reports strange sights'**)

One of those mysterious 'circle of lights' was even seen hovering over Alvechurch, Redditch, and Barnt Green, Worcestershire, in 2016, by a number of people that contacted us. A similar phenomenon was even photographed by a Scottish man, during the same period. The sketches made at Alvechurch and other parts of Worcestershire appear identical.

Coincidently Peter and Pauline Leek, friends of ours who emigrated to Minneapolis, a couple of years ago, photographed a 'circle of lights' over Chanhassen, Minnesota, on the 8th May 2017. During a previous visit to the United States, we had even visited Rachel, Nevada – home of the *Little ÁlÉ Inn*. We hope the readers will enjoy the photos….lovely memories, including hot rum and intoxicating company.

On the 9th August 2015, again at Minneapolis, Minnesota, multiple witnesses observed a peculiar *'ring of 12 white lights'*, which hovered in the night-time sky for up to an hour. At least one person reported that the lights were visible for up to an hour.

Sometimes these lights were seen to fade away on one occasion, when an aircraft moved overhead.

October/November 1975 – NORAD on high alert – UFOs plotted over atomic weapons storage bases

Over a period of about three weeks in October and November of 1975, several Strategic Air Command (SAC) bases in the northern tier states were placed on a high priority (Security Option 3) alert, because of repeated intrusions of unidentified aircraft flying at low altitude over atomic weapons storage areas. The Commander-in-Chief of North American Air Defense Command (NORAD) sent a four-part message to NORAD units on 11th November 1975, summarizing the events:

> *"Since 28 Oct 75 numerous reports of suspicious objects have been received at the NORAD CU; reliable military personnel at Loring AFB, Maine, Wurtsmith AFB, Michigan, Malmstrom AFB, Mt, Minot AFB, ND, and Canadian Forces Station, Falconbridge, Ontario, Canada have visually sighted suspicious objects."*

A teletype message to the National Military Command Center in Washington, D.C., said:

> *"The A/C [aircraft] definitely penetrated the LAFB [Loring Air Force Base] northern perimeter and on one occasion was within 300 yards of the munitions storage area perimeter."*

NOVEMBER 1975

1st November 1975 – BUFORA lecture, London

Rudy De Groote, the editor of the Dutch edition of *UFO-INFO*, addressed a BUFORA meeting – *UFO scene in Belgium and the EEC* – at Kensington Library, Campden Hill Road, London, to talk about Flemish UFO cases and contacts.

1975 – UFO over Normanton

At 4am one winter's morning, in 1975, Police Constable Robert Tomlinson was driving a police vehicle along Wakefield Road, near Normanton, when he saw a huge UFO hovering low on his left. He estimated the object's altitude as being in the region of 200-300 feet. He said:

> *"It was shaped like a kid's spinning top and looked to be 100 feet in diameter. There were lights all around the lower rim, where there were a number of rectangular windows. I stopped the vehicle in the middle of the road and watched it for several minutes, before the object streaked off in the direction of Wakefield, and out of view."* (**Source: Graham Birdsall,** *UFO Magazine*)

Could there have been any connection with a spectacular sighting in the same town by local resident Mrs. Jones and her children during 1979 – investigated by Philip Mantle?

2nd November 1975 – UFO over East Grinstead, West Sussex

Shortly after midnight, Alison Read (then age 21) of Hammerwood, East Grinstead, was in the process of getting out of the passenger seat of a car, after a night out with her boyfriend, when she noticed a powerful light in the eastern part of the sky.

> *"It seemed to be the centre of a big oval of light, surrounded by a grey-green haze. Although it appeared very low in the sky, just above treetop level, it was difficult to judge its size but it was immense – perhaps as big as a house. We stayed in the car and, even with the windows closed, could hear a loud engine noise coming from the direction of the light. Suddenly it shot across the sky, at tremendous speed – faster than any plane. As it travelled northwards in an arc, the light flashed on and off several times, before it plummeted out of sight behind trees."*

The next day Alison learnt that her boyfriend had seen what looked like a large battery of light on his left-hand side, (while driving home after having dropped her off), when driving along the Hammerwood-East Grinstead road, adjacent to the Holtye Golf Course.

Presuming it was the lights of a house, he looked out for the building the next day, while driving along the same stretch of road.

Alison reported the incident to the police and then the MOD.

(Source: Roma Browne/*Flying Saucer Review*, Volume 21, No. 6)

5th November 1975 – Schoolchildren sight UFO

Christopher Gardiner (9) of Langley Hills, Laindon, Essex, was on the school playing field, at 12.30pm, with several other friends, when they sighted a cigar-shaped object in the sky, which changed to 'disc' and then 'cigar' again.

Chris later drew a sketch and contacted Barry King and the *Basildon Recorder* newspaper.

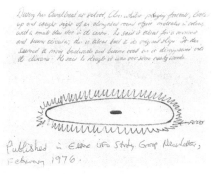

5th November 1975 – Three UFOs over Dade County, USA

At 4.39am, six Dade County Police officers sighted three UFOs in the sky at 4.39am. Over the space of the following few days, the police radio stations and newspapers were inundated with hundreds of calls from the public, reporting having sighted cone-shaped objects. The Air Force denied the existence of UFOs over Dade County, but admitted they had no planes up at the time and that nothing had showed on radar.

7th November 1975, 5.55pm – Two purple and red UFOs seen over A449, Penkridge
(Source: UFOSIS)

9th November 1975 – 'Silver discs' seen over Hertfordshire

At 11.15am, two shining 'silver discs' were seen over Letchworth, in Hertfordshire, by a local housewife, who noticed *"...that they were invisible when moving, but visible when hovering"*. A few seconds later they vanished from sight, after being seen to move in a north-westerly direction. **(Source: Mr R. Everett)**

9pm, the same date

Amateur astronomer – Mr Wilhem Weiner of Hough Green, Chester, was observing the four moons of Jupiter in the southern sky, when he saw:

> *"...two objects, pink in colour moving very fast – twice the speed of a satellite. They showed as faint pink spots with the naked eye, but through binoculars two 'discs' were seen. When overhead in the constellation of Andromeda, I saw them clearer; the pink colour was the most beautiful I had ever seen before in my life. When they were in the northern area they separated."*

(Source: *Chester Courant*, 11.11.1975 – 'Were they men from another world?')

10th November 1975 – Police chase UFOs over USA and Canada

On the 10th November, six Florida County police officers reported seeing strange objects, with flashing lights, hovering around 2,000 feet over Dade County. It appears this was the same evening when four unidentified 'blips' were plotted on radar screens at Falconbridge, Ontario, crossing over from the United States into Canada.

Two Jet fighters were then scrambled from the NORAD Selfridge, National Airbase, Michigan, but they failed to see the objects, although police at Sudbury, Ontario, saw them a short time later, described as: *"...three bright circles with two black dots, and a separate white object"*.

One of the officers was John Marsh, of Sudbury, and police radio dispatcher – Fred Sauve, at Haileybury, 90 miles north, who said:

> *"It was bright and stationary. I've never seen anything like it before."*

11th November 1975 – Travis Walton encounters a UFO. Later allegation of abduction

Travis Walton, and five other men, sighted a 'Flying Saucer' while driving home from the Sitgreaves Apache National Forest, in Arizona.

Wikipedia 2017 tells us the following: *The Travis Walton UFO Incident* refers to an American logger who claims he was abducted by a UFO on November 5, 1975, while working with a logging crew in the Apache-Sitgreaves National Forest in Arizona. Walton reappeared after a five-day search. The Walton case received

Travis Walton circa 1975

mainstream publicity and remains one of the best-known alleged alien abduction stories, although skeptics consider it a hoax.

[Walton wrote a book about it in 1978, called *The Walton Experience,* which was adapted into the film *Fire in the Sky* in 1993, written by Tracy Tormé.]

LIE TEST FOR WITNESSES

E. STAR Nov 10 1975

Man vanishes in UFO mystery

SEE ALSO
NEXT PAGE

SIX forestry men are to be given lie detector tests on their story that a seventh worker vanished after being struck down by a blue ray from a flying saucer.

The men, working in the Apache National Forest in Arizona, said they were driving home at dusk when they saw an object like a flying saucer hovering over the road ahead.

Travis Walton, 22, jumped from the truck and ran forward to get a closer look.

Navaho County Sheriff Marvin Gillespie said the men claimed Walton was struck by a beam of blue light from the hovering object and fell to the ground.

Frightened

The men were so frightened that they drove away, leaving Walton lying there, the sheriff said. When they returned about 15 minutes later their companion and the flying saucer had disappeared.

Sheriff Gillespie told reporters the six men would be given lie detector tests, but added, "I am not a total disbeliever in their story".

WE ARE NOT ALONE... Day 4 of the great Express

Walton...abducted by aliens?

THE CASE OF THE KIDNAPPED LUMBERJACK

By GEOFFREY LEVY

LIE TEST FOR UFO MEN

NAVANO COUNTY: Six forestry men are to be given lie detector tests on their story that a seventh worker vanished after being struck down by a blue ray from a flying saucer.

The men, working in the Apache National Forest in Arizona, said they were driving home at dusk on Wednesday when they saw an object like a flying saucer hovering over the road ahead.

Travis Walton, 22, jumped from the truck and ran forward to get a closer look.

Navano County Sheriff Marvin Gillespie said the men claimed Walton was struck by a beam of blue light from the hovering object and fell to the ground.

The men were so frightened that they drove away, leaving Walton lying there, the sheriff said. When they returned about 15 minutes later their companion and the flying saucer had disappeared.

Sheriff Gillespie told reporters the six men would be given lie detector tests, but added: "I am not a total disbeliever in their story."

Space story that's out of this world

Ivor Davis SNOWFLAKE Arizona

APART from the name there was nothing remarkable about Snowflake, Arizona, until the night of November 5. Since then the little town with a population of only 3,000 has become famous throughout the world with a story bizarre even by American standards, which tells of the five-day kidnapping of one of its citizens, 22-year-old Travis Walton—by a flying saucer.

In Britain the immediate reaction would be to put it all down to a Guy Fawkes night stunt. But whatever you may have heard about American gullibility the Arizonans are a hard headed bunch. In fact the local sheriff immediately suspected a hoax. But after he had ordered the six witnesses to take a lie detector test he was not so sure.

Even in America the tale would have been met with scepticism were it not for the whole question of unidentified flying objects being given added validity by the report this week from Professor J. Harder of California University.

He claims that taped conversations during the Gemini IV and XI flights and the Apollo XII flight reveal astronauts had to take evasive action to avoid other space vehicles.

I went to Snowflake to talk to eye witnesses and investigators and finally to Walton himself. This is what he told me:

IT WAS the most terrifying period of my life. It seemed like three hours—but it was really five days.

I know people may not believe me. They call me a freak or a crackpot, but I knew it happened, that I was in their spaceship and I met those creatures.

It wasn't a dream—but days in my life that seemed like hours. We all saw the saucer that night. I knew what it was right away. I was excited as the truck slowed down, and I just jumped out of the truck and ran towards the orange-white glow. I had no fear.

I wanted to take a closer look, and some of the guys from my works crew screamed at me to stop. I got close and something hit me. It was like an electric blow to my jaw and I fell backwards. I was

Travis Walton

still, and everything went black.

When I woke up there was a strong light in my eyes and I had problems focusing. I was panicky because there was a terrible pain in my head and chest. My mind cleared a little and I thought I was in hospital. I was on a table on my back and as I focused I saw three figures. It was weird. They were not human. I closed my eyes and opened them again. They were creatures looking around. They were ... strange.

They looked like a well developed foetus to me about five feet and they had on tan brown robes, tight fitting. Their skin was white like a mushroom and they had no clear features.

Terrified

They made no sound, their faces had no texture or colour. I could see they had no hair, their foreheads were domed and their eyes were very large and darted around the expressionless face. Their ears were tiny. I guess I panicked I didn't want to go into the spaceship ... I just wanted to talk to them.

I was terrified and still had bad pains and they were ugly. I jumped up knocking a clear plastic tray from my chest to the floor. I was in a big room and I grabbed a transparent tube and tried to smash it to use as a weapon. But it wouldn't break, I was petrified but I screamed "Who are you ... what do you want

from me?" There was no answer. I wanted to attack them but they scampered away.

I was alone ... I looked around and as I did a man came in or suddenly appeared a few feet away. He was human but he just smiled at me through a kind of helmet—it was like a fishbowl. He was dressed in a tight-fitting blue uniform. He smiled when I asked him who he was. He led me through a corridor into another big, bright room. There was a high-backed chair in the middle of the room with buttons on one arm and a lever on the other. I sat down. I was in a planetarium. Outside it was dark but I recognised some galaxies.

The man left as suddenly as he had appeared and I began to play with the buttons. When I pushed a button a small screen attached to the chair changed, the line patterns changed and it didn't mean anything. I pushed the lever and the scene outside suddenly changed. I felt we were moving.

I knew I was in a spaceship but I didn't want to experiment with the lever. I was scared I might destroy or damage the ship.

The man in blue, still smiling, reappeared. He ignored my questions and led me down a ramp about 40 paces, and suddenly I was in bright sunlight. I was hot and sticky and it was a kind of hangar, because I saw some small space saucers sitting nearby. Then I saw three other people. They looked human. They wore helmets and in blue and one of them was a woman.

I think I must have shrieked "Am I on earth?" I asked the trio. But they just looked at me. The man who brought me in walked out through a sliding type door. The place was huge. It was round and there were no corners or edges. It felt like sleepwalking ... only I made a sound.

The three people looked normal and then took me to a table and eased me on to it. I didn't struggle. They put a mask on my face. It was like an oxygen mask and had a big black ball, like a golf ball, off the top. Then things went black again.

When I woke again I was shaky. I was on the highway. It was black but the trees were lit up because just a few feet away was their saucer. I saw no one. Suddenly the saucer lifted straight up. There was a warm gust just in my direction, then it was gone.

Deranged

I went to my mother's house in Snowflake and I ate everything I could get my hands on. And I had a terrible thirst.

I slowly told them my story. My mother and Duane believe me. They believe there are other forms of life. Many people are too scared to believe it. I know people will say I'm deranged or I'm on drugs or fantasising. But I know what I saw. I still shudder when I think of it and those weird creatures.

I guess most of all I am angry. I wanted to communicate with them. If only they'd answered my questions.

Night of the UFO

BOSS of the tree trimming crew, Mike Rogers, 28, a level headed family man, was driving the crew home in his truck before the incident. He told me what he had told the sheriff while taking a lie detector test.

"Someone said 'There's a U.F.O.' and everyone got excited. Even before I stopped Travis was out of the cab. I just sat there with the rest of the guys looking and not believing my eyes. 'What in the hell do you think you're doing ' I shouted at Travis.

"I saw this greenish blue flash, it bounced off my windshield and lit everything up real bright. You could see the forest even though it was almost pitch black.

"I saw Walton falling backwards. No one went to help him, in fact they wanted to do the opposite. I hit the gas and took off at about 20 miles an hour, which is fast for the dirt

road. A quarter of a mile away after we turned a curve we looked back and saw blackness. We stopped. I was icy and chilled. My stomach was all watery. My eyes were blurry and I could hardly see."

Navajo County Sheriff Marlin Gillespie, 41, is in charge of the case, which was on his book as "missing person." This is his version :

"The Wednesday night my deputy Chuck Elison phoned me. He said he didn't want to put a flying saucer kidnap message on the radio. Naturally my first reaction to Chuck was 'Okay, so pull the other one'

"But we rounded up a posse and made a search of the area. Later we called in helicopters and had men on horseback, but there was no sign of Travis. So we decided to give them all lie detector tests—and they all passed.

"I'm still baffled and puzzled and maybe we'll give Travis a lie detector test as well.

The guys screamed... I hit the gas

EXPRESS FOOTNOTE NOV 15 1975

TREE-TRIMMER crew boss Mike Rogers, 28, a level-headed family man was driving the crew home in his truck before the incident. He told me what he had told the sheriff while taking a lie-detector test :—

Someone said : "There's a UFO" and everyone got excited. Even before I stopped, Travis was out of the cab: I just sat there with the rest of the guys looking and not believing my eyes. "What in the hell do you think you're doing ?" I shouted at Travis.

Suddenly I saw this greenish-blue flash. It bounced off my windshield and lit everything up real bright. You could see the forest, even though it was almost pitch black. The guys screamed.

I saw Walton falling backwards. Nobody went to help him—in fact they wanted to do the opposite. I hit the gas and took off at about 20 miles an hour which is fast for the dirtroad. A quarter of a mile away after we turned a curve, we looked back and saw blackness. We stopped. I was icy and chilled. My stomach was all watery, my eyes were blurry and I could hardly see.

I gotta say they passed the lie tests

SEE PREVIOUS PAGE

NAVAJO County Sheriff Marlin Gillespie, 41, is in charge of the case, which was on his book as " missing person." This is his version :—

On the Wednesday night my deputy Chuck Elison phoned me. He said he didn't want to put a flying saucer kidnap message on the radio. Naturally my first reaction to Chuck was: " Okay, so pull the other one."

But we rounded up a posse and made a search of the area. Later we called in helicopters and had men on horseback but there was no sign of Travis. So we decided to give them all lie-detector tests—and they all passed.

When I heard from Duane that Travis had turned up, I told him that I had to see and talk to Travis personally. I said there was a suspicion of obstructing justice.

I'm still baffled and puzzled and maybe we'll give Travis a lie-detector test as well. A hoax ? Who can say ? I think the six witnesses who were given lie-detector tests did see something they believed was a UFO, and I gotta say they did pass the tests.

What days right

APART from the name there was nothing remarkable about Snowflake, Arizona, until the night of November 5.

Since then the little town (population 3,000) has become famous across the United States with a story bizarre even by American standards.

Nothing less than the five-day kidnapping of one of its citizens, 22-year-old Travis Walton—by a flying saucer.

Even in America his tale would have been met with scepticism were it not for the whole question of Unidentified Flying Objects being given

Arizona Man Captured by UFO

In one of the most baffling cases ever recorded, a young laborer was taken aboard a UFO — in full view of six terrified co-workers — and held for five days.

The stunned witnesses readily agreed to take lie-detector tests. Five passed, proving they were telling the truth. The sixth was so nervous that the results of his test were inconclusive.

The abducted man, 22-year-old Travis Walton of Snowflake, Ariz., suddenly disappeared when struck by a dazzling ray from the strange hovering, saucer-shaped object, his fellow workers told police and The ENQUIRER.

In gripping detail, the witnesses described the chilling incident:

Dwayne Smith, 21: "It was a spaceship, there's no doubt of that — and Travis went on it. He got out of our truck, walked toward it — and just vanished!"

Kenneth Peterson, 25: "I saw a bluish light come from the machine and Travis went flying — like he'd touched a hot wire."

Alan Dalis, 21: "It sent out a blue ray, and the last we saw of Travis was his silhouette outlined, arms outstretched. We couldn't believe what was happening — the horror was unreal!"

Mike Rogers, 28: "We were

By TONY BRENNA, JOHN M. CATHCART, CHRIS FULLER, PAUL JENKINS, NICK LONGHURST, ROBERT G. SMITH and JEFF WELLS

SKETCH of hovering UFO drawn by Mike Rogers and Dwayne Smith.

tree trimmers were heading home at dusk along an isolated mountain road. Crew member Dwayne Smith said they were about 12 miles from Heber when they suddenly spotted the saucer hovering in a clearing beside the road.

"I was numb with disbelief and terrified!" said Smith.

just vanished! Mike Rogers, who was driving the truck, screamed 'Shut the door!' and gunned past the saucer.

"When we could see the saucer wasn't following us, Mike stopped the truck and we all got out, shouting and screaming at each other with fear in our faces and terror in our hearts. Then we saw a flash in the trees, and figured the saucer was leaving.

"We went back to the spot where the saucer had been . . . but Travis was gone. He went on the spaceship, there's no doubt of that.

"We went and reported what had happened. We didn't expect anyone to believe us, and nobody did — until we took lie detector tests."

Because Walton wasn't able

EXPERTS QUIZ abducted man, Travis Walton (center). At left is Dr. Jean Rosenbaum, at right Dr. James Harder.

Dr. Harder that as he approached the craft for a closer look, he was hit by something and suddenly everything went black.

"When I woke up, there was a strong light in my eyes and I had problems focusing. I was panicked because there was a terrible pain in my head and chest," he told Dr. Harder.

"My mind cleared a little and I thought I was in a hospital. I was lying on a table on my back, and these figures were standing over me.

"It was weird. They weren't human — they were creatures.

"They looked like well-developed fetuses to me — they were about 5 feet tall and wore tight-fitting tan-brown robes. Their skin was white like a mushroom and they had no clear features. They made no sounds.

"Their faces had no texture or color, and there was no

SHERIFF Marlin Gillespie: "I'm sure they saw UFO."

ing aboard the craft — and his description of the creatures he

taken off by the saucer."

John Goulette, 21: "I know what I saw — and it wasn't anything from this earth!"

Steve Pierce, aged 17, of Snowflake said: "I was just as frightened as the others when we saw the UFO.

"It hovered, rocking slightly, just 25 yards away from us and emitted this yellow light."

And Navajo County (Ariz.) Sheriff Marlin Gillespie stated: "The results of the polygraph examinations show there's no doubt they're telling the truth — right down the line.

"I thought at first there was a very good possibility it was a hoax — but not now. I've been in law enforcement over 18 years and I've never known anything like this. I feel sure that all 6 of them saw a UFO."

Dr. James Harder, professor of engineering at the University of California was elated: "This is the first abduction I know of that was witnessed by other people."

Walton abruptly turned up five days after his disappearance — dehydrated, bewildered and with a curious puncture mark on his right arm.

"I remember waking up on a road about eight miles from where I was picked up by the saucer," the stunned man told The ENQUIRER. "It was near the town of Heber.

"I ran into town as fast as my legs would carry me. I was terrified.

"I rushed into the first phone booth I came to and called my mother, who sent my brother Duane to pick me up. On the way to my mother's home, I told Duane what had happened . . . and to my relief, he believed me."

Walton had disappeared Nov. 5 as he and a crew of

orange light.

"We watched it in shock a few seconds, then suddenly Travis jumped out of our truck and started walking toward the saucer. We all shouted: 'Get back, you fool!' But he just kept going.

"He walked beneath the saucer — then a blue ray shot down from the saucer and he

MAP shows the area where, witnesses say, Travis Walton was taken aboard a flying saucer.

The Spot Where Witnesses Say Travis Walton Vanished

be interviewed under hypnosis by Dr. Harder, a member of The ENQUIRER's prestigious Blue Ribbon Panel on UFOs.

The hypnotic session was witnessed by three Phoenix physicians, Drs. Robert Ganelin, Joseph Saltz and Howard Kandell, as well as psychiatrist Dr. Jean Rosenbaum.

Under hypnosis, Walton told

very large. They had long fingers — but no fingernails.

"I panicked and jumped up, knocking a clear plastic tray that was lying on my chest to the floor. I grabbed a transparent tube and tried to smash it, to use it as a weapon. But it wouldn't break."

Dr. Harder said Walton was knocked out again — and when he awoke he was lying on the pavement about a quarter of a mile from Heber.

"Travis said he remembers seeing the craft take off into the sky," the scientist said.

Dr. Harder, who spent eight hours interviewing Walton and another three hours talking to the witnesses, told The ENQUIRER that "after considering all the known facts" he's convinced Walton was taken aboard an alien craft.

"This is supported by Travis' description of the creatures, which exactly matches a description given in another, unpublicized UFO encounter a few hundred miles away three months earlier," he said. "My conclusion is that we must add this case to the dozen or more cases of reported abductions."

Details of the other UFO encounter to which Dr. Harder referred were revealed to The ENQUIRER by Jim Lorenzen, head of the Aerial Phenomena Research Organization.

"It happened in New Mexico," said Lorenzen. "A man was out alone on the desert watching a meteor shower when a saucer-shaped craft suddenly dropped out of the sky near him.

"The man later said he remembered be-

"There's been no publicity about this case because the man feels it would jeopardize his job to discuss it."

Dr. Jean Rosenbaum, a psychiatrist, was asked by The ENQUIRER to interview Walton and evaluate his story.

"As a result of extensive examinations, I concluded that the boy was not lying," declared Dr. Rosenbaum, chairman of the Southwest Psychoanalytic Assn.

"There was no hoax involved. He really believes he was abducted by a UFO.

"But my evaluation of the boy's story is that although he believes this is what happened, it was all in his own mind. I feel he suffered from a combination of imagination and amnesia — that he did not go on a UFO, but simply was wandering around during the period of his disappearance.

"But I'm unable to account for five witnesses having the same story and passing the lie-detector tests."

Dr. Howard Kandell, who examined Walton 15 hours after his reappearance, expressed doubt that the young man had simply been wandering around.

"Although he lost weight from water evaporation, he was obviously well-nourished when he was brought to my office," said the physician.

"A sample of urine I tested supported this fact. Also, his condition was not that of a man who'd been wandering about the woods for 5 days.

"And there was a small puncture wound on the inside of his right arm — the kind you get from a blood test. But he said that nobody had stuck a needle in his arm.

"The entire thing is very puzzling."

EYEWITNESSES: Left to right are Dwayne Smith, Kenneth Peterson, Alan Dalis, Mike Rogers and John Goulette. All say that they saw Walton walk toward a flying saucer and vanish.

Award winners: Travis Walton (foreground), who told of being abducted by a UFO, shows off a cheque for $2,500. Six others who saw the incident share $2,500. Left to right are Allen Dalis, Kenneth Peterson, Mike Rogers, Dwayne Smith and John Goulette. Absent is Steve Pierce. Below: Travis shown with David Young.

Dawn Holloway displaying one of 'Modo's' paintings in the company of Philip Mantle

Philip Mantle on Travis Walton

We spoke to Philip Mantle, who is a veteran UFO researcher from Pontefract, Yorkshire, now publishing UFO books under the FLYING DISK PRESS label, about his knowledge of Travis Walton.

"I first met Travis Walton in 1993. I had been hired to help promote the movie 'FIRE IN THE SKY' upon its release in the UK.

One of the many things I did was to organise an evening lecture at the London Business School. The lecture was presented by Travis Walton and Mike Rogers. They were both accompanied by their wives and this was the first time I had met Travis Walton. After their presentation they took questions from the sell-out audience and this was then followed by a press conference for the national media.

I later got to meet Travis again at a conference in Rome, and again the 2000 seat theatre was sold out. During both these events I had the opportunity to see Travis in front of a live audience and be questioned by the news media, and then at the hotel afterwards I got to speak to him on a one-to-one basis. I must admit that I found Travis to be a quiet, intelligent man. I played the devil's advocate at one point, asking him if he had made a lot of money from the movie. He smiled and said he'd made so much money that he had to go back to work on Monday. We also went on to discuss a variety of possibilities of what may have been the nature and origin of his encounter and he was very willing to talk about this and did not dismiss anything out of hand. I must admit that I did find Travis a very personable man. His book, in my opinion, answers all of his critics, so there's no need for me to do that here."

(**Sources:** *Evening Star*, **Suffolk** – 'Lie test for witnesses – man vanishes in UFO mystery', 10.11.1975/ *Sunday Express*, 26.6.1977 – 'What really happened in the five days that Travis Walton vanished right off the face of the earth?')

11th November 1975 – Ohio police officers sight triangular UFOs

Madison, Ohio, Patrolman – Zachary Space, and three civilians, including Lester Nagle and Kenneth Ohtola of Madison, Ohio, sighted a flashing object, described as two triangular clusters of red and green lights, during the early morning, and gave chase for over 20 minutes.

> "Space said there are high-tension wires going through town and one hovered over the towers, about treetop level. That's when it glowed white. Then it started to rise and glowed red and green and it went up like a flash – whoosh! – Like somebody blew a match out. The five of us saw it rise up, disappear, then come back again. We couldn't decide whether it was the same one or another one. Then we heard more radio traffic. A Lake County sheriff's deputy saw something.
>
> I have a telescope in my unit. It's not very powerful, but I got it out and looked at it. That's when I got the triangular effect.
>
> The village police car has an aircraft landing light as a spotlight and we shined it at the thing. It would come closer. I was not too crazy about being that close to it – maybe within a quarter mile, it was hard to tell. We couldn't determine the size just that it would have to be awfully large."
>
> We watched the object hovering level with high-tension wires near the Ashtabula County line. It came down above the wires for 15-20 seconds, and then it would rise up slowly out of sight and appear again. When it was hovering it was a big bright light; when moving (red and green), it did not – gone in a flash."

(Sources: *The Logan Daily News,* **from Logan, Ohio, 12.11.1975/Unknown newspaper:** 'Flashing UFO chased by 2 fighter planes'/ *The Bryan Times*)

Huge Glowing UFO Hovers Over High Tension Tower and Follows Police Spotlight

A brightly glowing UFO that showed a strange fascination for a high tension tower frightened a policeman when it suddenly became attracted to his squad car spotlight.

The UFO was one of two that swept in off Lake Erie and cavorted over the Madison, Ohio, area for 90 minutes early on the morning of November 4.

"It was an eerie feeling," said Patrolman Lester Nagle, 24, who turned his spotlight on one of the UFOs to get a better look at it. "It was as though someone or something was watching us, checking us out."

For nearly an hour and a half Nagle and Patrolman Zachary Space, 26, watched the UFO sweep in time after time to hover over a 125-foot-tall power line tower 6 miles northeast of Madison.

"The first time I cut the spotlight on, the object moved away," said Nagle.

"Then I flicked it on and off a few more times — and the glowing object actually started to move toward the spotlight, as if it were attracted to it.

"It was astounding! It seemed to be intrigued by the light. I didn't know what to do — so I turned the light off real quick!"

The two UFOs, glowing red and green, had flown in over Lake Erie about 3:45 a.m., Patrolman Space told The ENQUIRER.

"It was incredible," he said. "They were in formation and then they broke off. One hovered over Madison and the other headed northeast.

"The one near the tower leveled off and slowly approached as though it was maneuvering carefully to get as close to the tower as possible.

"When it was directly over the tower, the reddish-green lights faded and the object began to glow pure white, so bright I couldn't see if it was actually touching the tower.

"I was about half a mile away and I couldn't estimate how large it was. When I held up my hand at arm's length to judge its size, it was larger than my hand. It was huge.

"Just as the white light reached its peak, the object streaked off across the sky so fast you couldn't see it move. Then it approached again, glowing red and green.

"I didn't know what to make of it. I spent 5 years in the Air Force as a mechanic and I've never seen a plane that can maneuver like that.

"It made about 20 passes at the tower, each time approaching the same way and then zipping off into the darkness."

Nagle, a 6-year veteran Air National Guard crew chief, decided to return to Madison to investigate the other UFO. "As I left the area, the object moved along above my car for a while *and for some mysterious reason my* radio wouldn't work."

Walt Rogers, an auto wrecker, had the same experience when he met Nagle on the highway not far away.

"My two-way radio wouldn't work either," Rogers said. "Whatever that thing was, it seemed to be attracted to lights and power."

Nagle said he had a camera in his squad car — "but I just didn't think about taking a picture.

"I was just too spellbound by the sight of the object."

The other UFO hovered over Madison the entire time.

"We received at least a dozen calls on it," said Police Dispatcher Gerry Bowers. "I could see it from my window and I went outside once, but I got scared and didn't go out again."

Both objects vanished after about an hour and a half, Patrolman Space said.

"I had a strange feeling that as we were watching the objects we ourselves were being watched — the way we would watch a colony of ants."
— FRANK ZAHOUR

THEY SAW IT: Patrolman Lester Nagle (left) discusses drawing of UFO with fellow officer Zachary Space. Spotlight on patrol car is one Nagle trained on UFO.

13th November 1975 – Strange 'aircraft' over Preston, Lancashire

Mr Frederick Iredale from Preston, in Lancashire, was driving to work along the Ringway, at 8.20am, on a clear day, heading northbound, when he noticed an odd-looking aircraft flying at about 500 feet off the ground on an eastbound course.

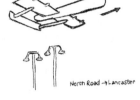

North Road →Lancaster

> *"I'm obviously used to seeing aircraft flying over, but this was completely different. There was no registration letters or identification on the outer body, which was silver, no tapered fuselage, no windows or doorway, not even a cockpit, or undercarriage. In fact, the overall image was of a long 'cigar' shape, rounded at both ends. The wing was parallel sided, and joined by two struts to a tail plane."*

Mr Iredale was so curious that he telephoned Ringway Airport and BAC Warton. The latter suggested he may have seen an Armstrong Whitworth Argosy, which he disputed, and has yet to see another example of this aircraft, despite nearly 35 years having elapsed since the event. (**Source: Personal interview**)

18th November – UFO display over Barnsley, Yorkshire

At 5.10pm John Brook was walking home with his friend – Ken Bagley, near Barnsley, South Yorkshire, when they heard a high-pitched humming or whistling noise.

Looking upwards, they saw a 'ball' of fluorescent blue light, moving erratically across the sky in a zigzag motion, south-westwards. The object, rotating along its axis, was seen to vanish suddenly, for seconds, and reappear in an unexpected position of the sky, several times. Suddenly, there was a silent flash of light and the object separated into two 'balls' of violet light, which moved away from each other at 90 degree angles. These vanished instantly, but after a few moments reappeared and moved together, impinging with another silent explosion and flash of light, before finally dropping out of sight.

(**Source: David Strickland, BUFORA**)

18th November 1975 – UFO over Basildon, Essex

At 7.20pm, Leslie Scotting – a 28 year-old probation officer and amateur pilot from Chapel North Estate, Laindon, Basildon, in Essex – was walking back home with her young son. As they cut through from Falstones into Great Knightleys, the son brought his mother's attention to a strange 'light' in the sky. In an interview held later with Ron West, she had this to say:

> *"I looked up and was startled to see the 'light' was now moving towards us, roughly 500 feet away. Quickly I*

urged my son and started to run homewards, but when I looked back was dismayed to see it was gaining on us. We crossed Laindon Road and started to run along the footway, crossed by a number of arches connecting houses on each side. As we passed the fourth arch, I was horrified to see it was now hovering above our heads. I banged on the door and screamed for my husband to open it. When he let us in, I switched all the lights out and explained what had happened. We peered out of the window and now saw it about 300 feet up in the air – luminous yellow in colour, shaped like a pear but flattened at the larger end, with what looked like flames coming-out of the one end."*

After contacting the MOD she received a visit from two men, who asked her to fill out a number of comprehensive forms. A MOD spokesman later stated that his department were only interested in matters of Defence significance, but disclosed the MOD had received a total of 201 UFO sightings for 1972, five of which remained unexplained.

Another sighting, some hours later the same day

Another witness was Derek Beal, well-known freelance photographer, living in Stanford-le-Hope, Basildon, in Essex. He was watching an eclipse of the moon, at 10pm the same day, with his son.

> *"We saw a very ghostly massive object in the sky. It was completely silent and was showing three long, huge, orange lights along the side. We rushed around the side of the house and saw it heading towards Southend, accompanied by a two-tone whistling noise."*

(Source: *Basildon Recorder,* 12.12.1975 – 'Two more say: We saw that jumbo-saucer'/Andrew Collins)

Witness Intimidation

Dan Goring, who kept in touch with Leslie Scotting for a number of years after the event, was to tell him the following information.

> *"In March 1977, she told me that she had received up to 20 telephone calls from an unidentified man each week, for some months after the sighting. On two occasions a muffled voice was heard. Initially the calls were made at midday; however, they then started at 1am. She complained to BT (she was ex-directory) and they attempted to trace the caller, but met with no success. She also told me that she had seen, on at least 3-4 occasions, UFOs during the hours of darkness, mostly in the same place over open space, in the direction of Langdon Hill, between 7.45pm-10.45pm. They were much smaller that the UFO she had seen on the 18th November 1975 – somewhat domed and dark yellow in appearance."*

Saudi Arabian cheques arrive at the house

Very oddly, following a telephone call on the 6th January 1977, mystyerious cheques began to arrive at the house, which were made out to Leslie. The first was £50, the second £250, and the third, £300, (last on the 7th March 1977) – all from Saudi Arabia, but no covering letter. Leslie asked her solicitor to check this out, but he was unable to identify the sender. In addition to this she saw what she referred to as a 'ghostly man', which manifested on two occasions about two feet away from her.

On the 11th February 1977, she was going out to a dinner dance with her husband, when, as he locked the door of the car, she turned around to see the 'man' again, described as being 6 feet, 6 inches tall, well built, chin length hair at sides, cropped evenly, a glowing face. He was wearing a silver suit. In the place of the belt was a glow – like a buckle; hands were also lit up and glowing. He never walked but seemed to glide backwards – apparently as solid as anyone else, rather than 'ghostly'. On the other occasion he was in possession of a white box, about the size of a pocket transistor, which he held up. Leslie had the impression the 'man' wanted her to take the 'box', but she became frightened and declined. She tried speaking to him but with no response.

SIGHTING 18-11-75

The night I saw a UFO —scared wife talks

A LAINDON housewife is scared to go out alone at night since she encountered a pear-shaped UFO last week.

The woman — "I won't reveal my name because people will think I'm crazy" — told the Recorder she, her husband and seven-year-old son all saw the object hovering over Lee Chapel North on Wednesday week.

"I've never been so frightened in my life," she said.

Next day she plucked up courage to ring the Ministry of Defence, Southend Airport, and the police, but was told that there were no planes, helicopters, air balloons or other objects in the area at the time, about 7.30 p.m.

"Even more baffling," said the woman, a very articulate and intelligent 28-year-old, "was the strange reply I got from the Ministry. I gave them details and a man phoned back about an hour later, confirmed there were no planes or anything over the area, and then added: 'We've checked it out, but we can't tell you what we think it is'."

Interview

A Ministry representative is now coming to interview the woman for further details.

She said: "I know it all sounds very far-fetched, but my son saw it first. He said: 'Look, mum, there's a spaceship.' We were in Ballards Walk.

"It was a flattened pear-shape with flames out the back, but the most frightening thing was that it was silent. I reckon it was about the size of a Jumbo-Jet and about 500 feet up. I have a good idea of these things because I used to fly light aircraft myself.

"It seemed to stay with us till my son and I got home. I ran and when we got there I switched off the lights and called my husband. He saw it too. We watched it through the kitchen window for what seemed to be about half-an-hour.

"I know it was the night when the moon eclipsed, but I can assure you we weren't looking at the moon. It doesn't move that fast!

"I've never been so frightened in my life. People may think I'm daft but I'm not going out on my own at night.

A spokesman for the Ministry of Defence told a reporter: "We are only interested in UFO sightings as far as defence implications are concerned. The last year in which figures were kept was 1972, when there were 201 sightings.

"Of these seven turned out

YES, THERE REALLY WAS A FLYING SAUCER

We saw it, too, say readers

THERE REALLY was a flying saucer over Basildon last week.

Following our report that a Lee Chapel North woman, her husband and young son had seen an unidentified flying object, the Recorder received a succession of calls last Friday from people who confirmed the sighting.

The UFO was seen on the same night that the moon was eclipsed — Wednesday, November 19. But callers were adamant that what they saw was not the eclipse.

One 18-year-old reported seeing a pear-shaped object over Whitmore Way a week after the earlier sighting.

"It was oval and bright," he said. "A light aircraft was following about a mile or so behind, but although we heard the plane's engines there was no noise from the UFO.

A seven-year-old Vange boy told his parents — before our report of the sighting by the Lee Chapel North housewife — that he had seen a UFO. It was the same night as the sighting we reported and his description tallied. But until our report was published nobody took any notice of his claim.

Vanished

Said Neil Davey of Gambleside: "I saw it for a few seconds and then it disappeared.

"It was very high, yellow and shaped like an egg with fire coming out of it. I didn't hear any noise.

"My mum and dad didn't believe me at first and I didn't tell anyone else in case they thought I was making it up.

"It was nothing like a plane or a firework."

Whitehall

Our original informant, an intelligent and articulate housewife, with experience of flying light aircraft, reckoned the UFO was the size of a jumbo jet and hovering at about 500 feet.

In an attempt to make sense of what she had seen she contacted the police, Southend Airport and the Ministry of Defence.

This week a man from the ministry visited her to discuss the sighting, as promised.

"The man said he was from a separate department inquiring into these things. Then he produced forms for me to fill in. I've never seen so many forms in my life. And though he wouldn't really commit himself, I did gather he was aware that something was going round.

"I am very grateful that poeple took the trouble to get in touch with your paper. Seeing something like that is so unbelievable it puts your mind at rest knowing someone else saw it as well."

● BACK in March 1974 the Recorder published a feature on UFOs by staff reporter Peter Biscoe. In it he reported a prediction by Contact UK, which logs UFO sightings.

They said sightings seemed to come in a four-year cycle and that autumn was a favourite time. The next "flap" was due in autumn 1975, they added.

TV Interference – Items going missing

Following the sightings, the colour TV began to switch itself off – normally this occurred just prior to the appearance of the 'man'.

Her wristwatch still continues to stop each day at 11.25am, and domestic household items, like hairbrushes and makeup, continues to go missing but apparently reappears later. In March 1978 Dan spoke to Leslie, who told him the following information:

> *"The phone calls had slowed down, generally died away, still considerable interference on the TV but no UFOs seen, or further strange manifestations of the 'phantom man'."*

19th November 1975 – 'Flying Cobra' UFOs sighted

We were to learn of an even stranger sighting, which occurred the morning after Mrs Scotting's experience, when a local resident sighted three *'cobra' shaped translucent objects* were seen moving low down across the sky, between Wareham and the coast, just before 8am.

"It was a mild and dry day; visibility was good, cloud was high and thin, with patches of varying shades of grey, brown, and yellow. The sun was beginning to rise on the horizon. I saw these 'cobra' shaped, yellow-grey objects (not particularly bright) heading east towards Wareham at just below cloud height, at about the speed of an aircraft, moving in a line astern formation straight along the sky. They seemed composed of a tenuous vaporous substance and their shapes never altered."

At 8.05am, he was shocked to see another UFO of similar substance, but different shape, travelling a little slower than the first three, heading north-east.

"This one appeared smoky-grey and silhouetted against the bright background of the horizon. Suddenly it appeared to intersect the previous course of the other UFOs and actually altered course eastwards". (**Source: Frank Marshall**)

21st November 1975 – *Manchester Evening News* – 'Flying Saucer' hunt

22nd November 1975 – WATSUP Lecture, Southampton

The Wessex Association held their first UFO meeting at the Cotswold Hotel, Southampton. Mr Peter Hill gave a talk on *'Flying Triangles'*, WATSUP Secretary – Mr Roy Goutte on *'The Bermuda Triangle'*, and Mr Ron Weighell on the theory of *'Ley lines, psychic, and other mysterious phenomena'*, while Mr Cerris Francis spoke about *'Yeti', 'Nessie', and the Surrey Puma'* – last but not least, Mr David Almond on *'psychic phenomena'*.

(**Source:** *Southern Evening Echo* – 'Phenomenal crowd at Watsup')

27th November 1975 – Two red lights reported over Essex

A faint green 'light', followed by two red lights, was seen in the north-eastern part of the sky over Halstead, accompanied by a droning noise, during the late evening. (**Source:** UFOLOG)

27th November 1975

Bizarrely, the *South East London and Kentish Mercury* ran a story under the headlines – 'UFO kids land in lecturer Tim's bad books'. This was about a number of youngsters who had attended one of Timothy Good's talks at the Library in Bromley, Greater London a couple of weeks ago; after picking up some of his books with promises to pay later, they scarpered and presumably, after not having come forward and settled up with Timothy, he felt honour-bound to contact the Press. Tim was out of pocket to the amount of £13.05 pence, and it is doubtful that they ever paid!

27th November 1975 – *Southern Evening Echo,* 'After Nessie, what about UFOs says Ernie'.

Ernie Sears – a long-standing veteran of the UFO subject and previously a member of the Southampton Group, (SUFOG), run by Steven Gerrard, was out walking, in March, 1958, when he noticed a cigar shaped UFO hovering over the experimental Radar Base, on Portsdown Hill, Portsmouth.

"It was a blustery morning. I watched the object for a full minute, assuming it was an aircraft fuselage caught in the sun. Approximately thirty minutes later, two RAF Fighter jets raced over the town at low

2 7 NOV 1975

After Nessie, what about UFOs says Ernie

NOW that the experts have decided that the Loch Ness Monster (or monsters) really exists, and the stories of sightings over the years aren't pooh-poohed any more, perhaps scientists will pay more attention to another controversial phenomenon.

Southampton reader Ernie Sears, who lives in Westridge Road, Portswood, hopes so.

Ernie, still full of regrets that he didn't play a hunch and follow that Scotsman's example who put a £100 bet on the existence of the monster just hours before these photographs were announced last week, reckons now that those people who have reported flying saucers deserve more serious attention.

"I wonder, hopefully, with all those witnesses and photographs of strange things in the sky, and all the reports by obervers, pilots and astronomers, will now be taken seriously.

"After all, for years, the so-called "myth" of the Loch Ness Monster has been used to disprove the existence of unidentified flying objects."

And a closer study of UFOs would help to take our minds off terrestrial problems for a while, Ernie adds.

MYSTERIOUS UFOS SPOTTED IN HAMPSHIRE SKIES

STAR GAZERS: UFO experts Ernie Sears (left) and Andy Phillips.

The truth is over here . . .

altitude. As an ex-RAF man, I knew their actions were very unusual. I watched as they climbed in a gradual curve, towards the gleaming 'cigar'. As they closed in, it slowly turned on end and vanished, leaving the aircraft circling the area. I rushed to a telephone box and rang the Control Tower, at Thorney Island Airbase, (where the 'Meteor' jets were based) and asked the official what the object was which the 'Meteor' jets were chasing? He replied, "You didn't see any jets!" (**Source: Personal interview**)

November 1975 – Motorist reports UFO landing, Cornwall

Just before midnight, John Porrit – a miner by occupation – was driving home to Sussex from Chacewater, in Cornwall, on a cold and foggy evening. At a point between Blackwater and Goonhaven, the engine cut out inexplicably and the lights then failed. While stood by the side of the road, examining the battery leads, he noticed a 'light' moving towards him, accompanied by a humming noise.

> *"My first thoughts were that it was an oncoming motorcycle, but then I realised it was displaying a red light instead of a white light and was travelling not on the road but over a field to my left. I stood there peering through a patch of fog, trying to determine what it could possibly be. Suddenly there was a blinding flash of colours, a few feet off the ground. I summoned up my courage and moved closer.*
>
> *I have to admit to being shocked to see an object resembling an upside-down haystack, covered with lights of different colours, continually flashing on an off, and the external surface of the UFO seemed to comprise of metal with what looked machine like parts in comparison with the rest of the structure. It then began to pulse with a faint glow, at which time I decided to leave fearing an explosion. As I opened the car door and tried the ignition, it burst into life as the object rose quickly upwards into cloud cover.* (**Source: Personal interview**)

DECEMBER 1975

2nd December 1975 – *Into the Unknown*

On December the 2nd and 9th Southern ATV screened *Into the Unknown* – a two hour long ATV programme about the paranormal. One of them featured an interview with Astronaut Dr Edgar Mitchell, who said his moon walk profoundly changed his outlook on life. His psychic investigations are featured in the first film. (**Source:** *The News*, Portsmouth, 7.11.1975 – 'Explaining the inexplicable')

A few years ago I had the pleasure of meeting Edgar Mitchell, at the NEC in Birmingham, thanks to David Bryant. While on the subject I asked David (in 2017) what he thought of another UFO report made by Russian Astronaut Leonov, in 1975.

2nd December 1975 – *Southern Evening Echo* – 'Outer Space and a dying hitchhiker'

A discussion about the ATV documentary *Into the Unknown* (which went out on the same night) mentions Dr. Edgar Mitchell, who underwent what he calls:

> "...*a very profound internal change of state that allows you to see things that you've overlooked before and to feel things that you haven't felt before ...perhaps a momentary glimpse into the secrets of the Universe.*"

A reference is made to other witnesses in the programme, which included a charge nurse at a psychiatric hospital, who claims his life was saved on the motorway by a young girl, hitchhiking in old-fashioned clothes. She turned out to be an old woman who was dying at the hospital.

2nd December 1975 – *Glasgow Herald* – 'Now its Nessie Monster from Mars'

Also covered the theory about intelligent beings crash- landing into Loch Ness hundreds of years ago, quoting conversation from Mr Richard Lawrence – secretary of the British UFO Society, who oddly said he did not believe in UFOs but admitted he had joined the group because he was sceptical, and while he was still sceptical two years later, although he now accepts that UFOs are possible! The same newspaper also informs its readers of a symposium to be held in Edinburgh on the Loch Ness Monster, later the same month, the speakers being Dr. Gordon Corbet of the British Museum, London, and Sir Peter Scott.

This programme was to spark off huge media interest, in comparison to the daily reports of strange objects which continued to make their appearance, night and day, over the skies of this planet.

Russian astronaut claims UFO sighting in 1975

David Bryant:

> "*The Apollo/Soyuz Joint Mission was 1975, and the Soviet invasion of Afghanistan began in earnest in 1979; I suspect that's the dateline for the news story. Incidentally, I chatted to Leonov at some length about the phenomenon and he did mention the 'barn door' sighting. He reckoned it was booster debris – he always denied that he'd ever seen anything in space that couldn't be explained, although he confirmed that a number of cosmonauts claimed to have had very close encounters!*"

Moon shots

John Hanson: Something else that sparked off my interest was some photographs taken by David Bryant recently of the Moon, which showed a very strange anomaly.

David Bryant:

> "*On September 17th, 2017, I got up early to photograph the crescent moon near Venus in the dawn sky. As luck would have it, the Moon was exhibiting a terrific degree of 'earthshine', where the unilluminated portion of the Moon's disc is lit up by reflected light from the Earth; I began taking*

images of the phenomenon with my Pentax K-3 dslr, using a 300mm Pentax prime lens and 1.4 x converters. Photographing the bright Moon but capturing the earthshine is quite fiddly, involving adjustments of f-stop, ISO and backlight settings; under these circumstances I check the images on the back screen until I see I've got things set up correctly. The first image I took at 6.07am showed an anomalous bright object above the Moon's North Pole, which I cropped in on. I was sufficiently intrigued to take a couple more images before whatever it was departed south at high speed."

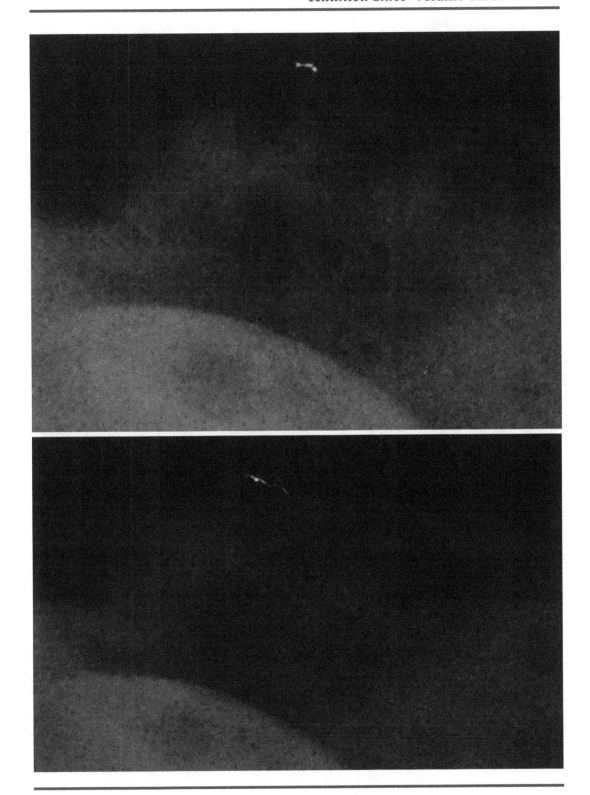

Aleksei A. Leonov (right) with David Bryant

Saucers and Soviets:
UFOs MONITOR
AFGHANISTAN
INVASION!

(continued from page 27)

Highlights

As a result of flying to the moon, Dr Ed Mitchell now devotes himself to the investigation of psychic phenomena. He explains why in *Into The Unknown* (ITV, 10.30)

Cosmonaut Aleksei A. Leonov, commander of Apollo-Soyuz mission in 1975, reportedly saw "flying barn door" in space — a flat, rectangular UFO with yellow glow.

a blue-white saucer that moved in abrupt spurts of speed.

Whatever the objects are—apparently the KGB is still far from finding out — they're viewed as a threat to Soviet manned and unmanned spacecraft alike. The sudden appearance of unexplained nocturnal lights was blamed, in 1978, for the malfunction of an SS-18 missile that went astray and had to be destroyed by remote control.

Whatever the Russians are doing, they obviously intend to keep quiet about it. "I won't be able to provide insights on this much longer," says Kathy Soderlund,

who will soon be departing her Stockholm watchpost and returning with her husband to the U.S If Dr. Soderlund has one wish, it's that the Russians wouldn't be so secretive.

"They could admit that they're bamboozled by UFOs. They could appoint a study group of academic experts, rather than using professional spies. The could share data on UFO sightings, rather than locking them away in KGB vaults ..."

They could. But they won't.

"The reason we don't have a billion-dollar UFO research project in the U.S. is that there

isn't public support for it. In Russia, they do it regardless. And since the public doesn't matter, the public isn't told about it."

If UFOs really are visitors from space, and if they are hostile, the day may come when the KGB will want its leaders to share its findings on the Moscow-Washington "hot line." In fact, if flying saucers really do turn out to be a danger, they could bring Russians and Americans closer together. But until then, the KGB can be expected to keep a tight lid on its research into unidentified flying objects. Whatever they know, their lips are sealed.

IDEAL'S UFO MAGAZINE 57

■ **Into The Unknown (ITV, 10.30)** Do you believe in ghosts, flying saucers, life after death, reincarnation or telepathic powers? Answer yes to any of these questions, and, according to Dr Christopher Evans, you join the vast majority of mankind. The first of two programmes examines our belief in the paranormal. The programmes are written and narrated by Dr Evans, who is sceptical and produced by Lawrence Moore, who believes in the occult.

In a series of filmed interviews they talk to people with first-hand experience of mysterious encounters, who describe how their lives were changed as a result. One of these is American astronaut Ed Mitchell, the sixth man to walk on the moon. As a result of his experience on the moon, Mitchell now devotes himself to the investigation of psychic phenomena and extra sensory perception and has written a book called Psychic Exploration.

Dr. Edgar Mitchell displays a copy of 'Haunted Skies', with author and researcher John Hanson

Edgar Mitchell
(1930-2016)

5th December 1975 – UFO over Essex

At 3.45pm, Christopher Gardner was to find himself witnessing an even stranger object passing through the sky, over Laindon – this time described as being:

> *"...circular, with a metallic sheen; on its left-hand edge was a blue circle with what looked like webbing across it, inside this was a circular light surrounding a star with a further circle inside the star. It appeared to hover – then rose slightly, making a humming sound, before moving away towards a wooded area."*

(Source: *Evening Echo* Newspaper and the *Basildon Recorder*, 28.11.1975/ Barry King/Brenda Butler/Ron West/ BUFORA/Norman Oliver)

12th December 1975

The Kent and Sussex Courier – 'Keep watch' – told their readers that the recent UFO sightings over East Grinstead had captured the interest of the British UFO Society.

The Chairman – Ken Rogers, asked the readers to keep their eyes on the sky.

Ironically, Robert Wood (21) from Leek, in Staffordshire, was driving his car along the main A54 road from Holmes Chapel, towards Congleton, at 5pm, when he saw flashing lights in the sky.

> *"As I drew closer I saw a conical object, showing what looked like seven or eight portholes, about 100 yards from the road and some 150 feet in the air. I could see a green light at one end and flashing white lights, giving a stroboscope effect. Five minutes later it vanished from sight."*

INFLATION'S TO BLAME

The Thing ain't what it used to be

LIKE the magic dragon in the song, which sadly retired to his cave when nobody believed in him any more, the Warminster "Thing" seems to have lost interest and flown away.

The "Thing" you must know by now, is the weird flying object which for years has favoured the skies above the Wiltshire town, coming in from nowhere and getting folks all of a flutter.

Arthur Shuttlewood, the Warminster journalist who followed up scores of sighting stories back in the 60's and later produced a book about the "Thing" with what former colleague Gordon Sewell called "a lot of sound reporting" took such an interest in the object that he became a world expert on Unidentified Flying Objects.

And not every UFO expert could boast of his own home-town UFO to study, as Arthur had.

But the great days of the "Thing" appear to be over. I'm told by Ken Rogers, of the British UFO Society, that they have only received two good sightings this year, compared with several hundred in previous years.

One, I'm told, came from a Royal Marine Commando, who said his car was chased by an orange ball of light, and the other was by a local photographer.

What's caused the demise of the "Thing," and why has its loyalty to Warminster waned?

The answer, depressingly prosaic, is: money.

The UFO men say high fares and petrol prices are discouraging people from converging on Warminster to see for themselves.

And perhaps the crew of the "Thing," who certainly have a flair for the theatrical, reckon it's a waste of time playing to an empty house.

12th December 1975 – Roy Stemman

2011, Roy Stemman:

"A Happy New Year to you and Dawn. I have just been sorting through some papers in preparation for a book (on reincarnation), which I need to write before the end of June, and I have come across the photo of myself which I mentioned to you on the phone. This was taken around 1958 or 1959, after I had reported on George Adamski's lecture at London's Caxton Hall on his claimed contacts with extraterrestrials. Although the headline is not readable (the photograph has faded over the years), I'm pretty certain that it is my account of that lecture, published in Psychic News, that I am holding (it was my first published story, so I was very proud of it!). Incidentally, I was living at home at that time, in Islington, North London, and I am pictured standing on the flat's balcony. It was from this very vantage point that I saw a 'red light' moving across the night sky on 29th April 1957 and posted a report of the sighting to Flying Saucer Review (which carried it, along with others)."

RAF Jets scrambled

"Next day, on 30th April, the London evening newspapers carried front-page stories about the jets scrambled from RAF Odiham to chase a UFO and also carried eyewitness accounts from people in and around London, who described seeing much the same as I did; one described it as 'like a red golf ball'."

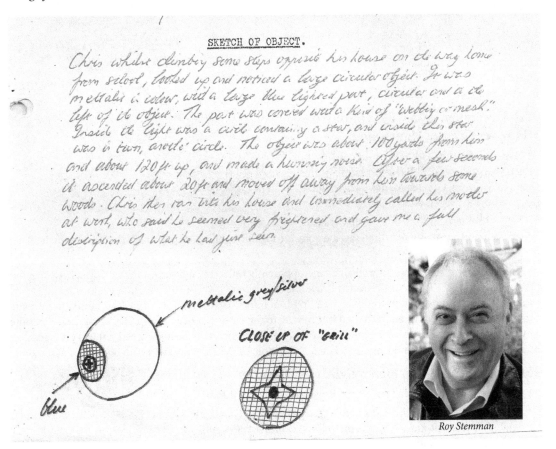

Roy Stemman

Roy Stemman with his book and the sea horse said to have been regurgitated by a medium

ROY'S RESEARCHES TAKE HIM DEEP INTO THE UNKNOWN

By ROSALIND RENSHAW

THINGS that go bump in the night, hauntings by moonlight, and messages from the dead: All these and more are the stock in trade of author Roy Stemman.

Roy (33), has just published his latest book, "Spirits and Spirit Worlds," in which he presents evidence for and against Spiritualism—the belief that the dead can and do make contact with the living.

Roy, who works from his home in Regent Street, Fleet, is a confirmed Spiritualist.

"But he came to the belief via an interest in flying saucers and other UFOs—he is a founder member of the London UFO Research Organisation. As a youth in North London, he wrote to the journal "Psychic News" and offered to submit an unbiased report of flying saucer developments.

"I had neither shorthand nor training," said Roy, "but my offer was accepted."

That was 15 years ago. Roy joined the magazine as a staff reporter and was later assistant editor for eight years.

Soon after starting work at "Psychic News," editorial policy changed and UFOs were removed from the schedules.

Checking

Roy, a sceptic, found himself covering Spiritualist assignments.

Then he was persuaded to go to a medium called Bertha Harris in Golders Green. "It was the best sitting I have ever had," Roy recalled. "I was given a great deal of information from my father—who had died the year before."

Roy was also told things which he did not and could not know at the time. Subsequent checking showed the facts to be accurate.

Scepticism vanished. Roy believes that he was luckier than many who first seek Spiritualism. "I had lost my father after first becoming interested," he said. "But there are people who turn to it in the shock of bereavement and they will believe anything."

He still feels there is nothing sadder than grieving people who go to Spiritualist services every week in the hope of getting a message from a loved one.

He himself has been in touch, via mediums, with several people who have died. But he added: "I am not remotely psychic myself. I am a straightforward reporter."

His belief in Spiritualism is such that he now rarely attends seances or visits mediums—"although if there is a new medium I'll pay a visit as a kind of consumer research."

And he infrequently attends Spiritualist church services, which he describes as "mainly fairly orthodox religion with hymns and prayers plus some clairvoyance stuck on the end. Sometimes there is healing too."

Proof

Roy and his wife Patricia (30), are both firm believers in the power of Spiritualist healing. Both claim they have recently had slipped discs cured instantaneously by the touch of a psychic.

He is not interested in witchcraft or astrology. One feels he has turned to Spiritualism as a practical step; "Spiritualism incorporates the knowledge that this is not the only life," he explained. "This is not a unique belief and many other religions have it."

"Spiritualism differs because it also believes that this life can have communication with other planes of existence.

"It provides tangible proof—tangible evidence of a continuing existence. Faith itself is not enough for me—I have to have proof as well."

The subject of proof is one on which Roy is a leading exponent. He has had more than his share of exposing fakes and he is expert on cases brought under the little known Fraudulent Mediums Act (1952).

Some of his stories on cunning hoaxes could fill a book—and undoubtedly will at some future date. But disbelief is all very well—belief is what matters. Table thumping, ouija boards, poltergeists and perfectly ordinary ghosts—especially the sort that died violently and return to haunt the place on the anniversary of their death—are everyday stuff in the Stemman household.

"Yes I believe in ghosts," said Roy.

His enthusiasm for things spiritual is unmistakable.

He has a wonderful collection of things produced in evidence—for example a genuine sea horse regurgitated by a medium in a heavy trance.

A fake? "I had my doubts," said Roy. "On the other hand it is not a trick I'd fancy doing myself." He can also produce a knife used by a medium to carry out an eye operation.

Among Roy's previous books is "Medium Rare," the biography of the famous psychic Ena Twigg. She was the minister who married the Stemmans in a Spiritualist church ceremony.

Invisible

Luckily there was a conventional registrar in attendance who spotted that a crucial part of the wedding service had been left out, and finished off marrying Roy and Patricia before they left on honeymoon.

One of the brightest stars in the literary occult, Roy looks forward to the future.

Not least to seeing sons Paul (5), and Mark (3), grow up—both have exhibited remarkable signs of being psychic, to the extent of seeing and being terrified by a man invisible to everyone else in a Bournemouth hotel last year.

In the shorter term, more books and writings are planned. Roy particularly hopes to return to his first love, flying saucers.

And in the longer term there is the certainty of a fate more birth than death.

● "Spirits and Spirit Worlds," by Roy Stemman published by Aldus Jupiter, 288pp. 120 illustrations, £4.95 net.

Southampton Echo published article on Warminster

A sceptical, somewhat cynical, overview presented in this article from yet again journalists, who in all probability have never been to Warminster or examined for themselves a plethora of inexplicable sightings – then no doubt in the tens of thousands – and here we are in 2017, some 40 years later, and none the wiser!

13th December 1975 – Silver domed UFO over Greater Manchester

At 4.45pm on the 13th December 1975, the fifteen year-old son of the Dutton family – then living in Swinton, Greater Manchester – alerted his parents and sister, after sighting something unusual in the sky.

When the family went outside, they saw a mysterious white 'light' moving towards them from the western direction.

As it approached closer they saw a silver dome, apparently reflecting light from the setting sun, displaying red, white and blue, lights underneath. It then passed silently overhead, showing a bluish tinge, at an estimated height of a few hundred feet, heading in a north- eastwards direction. The family then made their way to the front door and watched it hovering in the air over a nearby road, for about half a minute – until without warning, it accelerated away south-eastwards, at incredible speed, taking on a reddish hue as it did so. (**Source: Jenny Randles & Peter Warrington,** *UFOs: A British Viewpoint,* **Book Club Associates**)

15th December 1975 – Silver 'light' over Lancing

Paul Glover was walking along Western Road, Lancing, at 5.20pm.

> *"I saw a flashing silver 'light' stationary in the clear sky, about 3,000 feet high. I then saw it move towards the south-west direction – gone from view ten minutes later."*

19th December 1975 – UFO over Essex

Linda (26) and Brian Haspineall (25) of Eastwood Road, Raleigh, in Essex, were driving on the A2 road (Stock Road, near Ingelstone) towards Margaretting, in a south-east to north direction. The couple were already late for their dinner dance and were looking out for the venue – the *Haybridge Moat House*. Linda looked out to see a pinkish light through the windscreen and mentioned it to Brian. As it approached closer to the vehicle, they were astonished to see a circular object with two white beams protruding from the rear – like 'headlamps'. The couple stopped the car and looked out, watching it for a couple of minutes as it passed overhead.

> *"The pinkish light was much more intense in the middle. After it headed away and over the horizon in a few minutes, we decided to move on as we would have been late for our appointment. As we did so, we noticed another car had stopped and two people were also watching it. When we reached out destination, we explained what we had seen and why we were late. People just ridiculed us so much that we decided to keep quiet."* (**Source: Andrew Collins and Barry King, BUFORA**)

21st December 1975 – Half-moon shaped UFO sighted over Basildon, Essex

Miss Gloria Francis of Whitmore Way, Basildon, Essex – a bank clerk by employment – was in the process of picking up her colleague – Deborah Gardner, at 8.05am.

Deborah:

"We usually go to work on the bus, but this time she showed me an object in the sky. At first I thought it was the sun, but its shape was wrong. It was motionless in the sky above some trees and was half-moon with the flat piece on top – a bright red- orange in colour. It then slowly grew smaller, until only a thin line in the sky, before disappearing from sight."

(Source: Barry King)

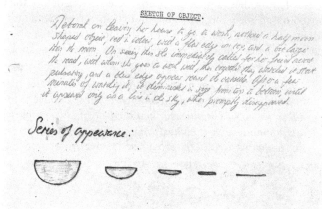

21st December 1975 – Motorists paced by car in the United States

At 10pm, a woman and her sister were driving along Route 19, north of Weeki Wachee Springs, Florida, at 65 miles per hour, when they saw a 'bright light' to the right of their car, which was moving slightly faster than they were. They stopped the car and saw:

"...it circled – then moved straight up in a 'flip flop' motion. It was shaped like a large mushroom and was off-white in colour." **(Source: *UFO Investigator*, NICAP, January 1976)**

On the 31st of May 1981, a motorist was driving homewards in the same locality heading east near Bayport Inn when a dark, smooth and flat round object moved up from behind him and settled in the air above his car *'close enough to touch'*. At this stage the headlights dimmed and the ignition cut out . . .

"I heard a 'woosh' and it took off north on US19, before coming to a complete stop and then heading west towards the gulf gone in a matter of seconds. I reported it to the sheriff's office and they said it was probably the military testing aircraft off the coast. This was a flying saucer that I witnessed."

(Source: MUFON)

1975 December 1975 – Frightening encounter on Lickey Hills, Worcestershire

A few days before Christmas, Michael Farrell from Romsley, Worcestershire, was walking along a narrow forest path at the foot of the Lickey Hills – an area of natural beauty, covering 500 acres, situated 11 miles from Birmingham City Centre.

"I became aware of some movement in front of me, about ten yards away. As it was getting dark, closer inspection revealed a glowing 'white mist', about 8 feet in height, hovering a few feet off the forest floor. I stood mesmerised, watching as it changed into something resembling a 'figure', although the bottom half was very indistinct.

To my utmost fear it began to move in what looked like some leisurely dance, the 'head' slowly beginning to bend forwards, then lifting its 'arms' above its head, all in slow motion – as if it was struggling to get out of something. At this stage I ran away, fearful of my own safety."

We were to learn of another identical sighting, involving Tom Dongo and Linda Bradshaw, who were to write a book – *Merging Dimensions* – relating to strange phenomenon that occurred in the Sedona area of Arizona towards the end of the 20th Century.

Tom:

> "We saw a white 'mass of light' (the size of an average person), which took on human form, extending what appeared to be 'arms' outstretched, and then bending at the waist – a cycle of action that was constantly repeated before 'it' changed into a 'ball of light' and disappeared." (Source: Personal interviews)

Mid 1970s – Ghostly disturbance in Devon

Ghostly encounters are common to many localities, but something far more frightening happened to Crediton Police Sergeant – Derek Davis (whose previous account of what transpired, one evening in 1968, has already been published in a previous edition of *Haunted Skies*).

Derek was in the process of booking off duty, at 1.40am, when the telephone rang. On answering it, a woman (in a clearly agitated tone) said to him:

> "Is that the police? Please come quick, I've got some real trouble out here."

Derek asked her if it was of a domestic nature. She replied,

> "Please hurry".

Derek jumped into the police car and made his way to the house concerned, which lay 7-8 miles away from the town in Morchard Road, Morchard Bishop.

Two Saxon bookends on the mantelpiece

> "When I arrived at the terraced house, a feeling of uneasiness crept over me when I realised I had been there some years previously, but couldn't remember the reason why. I knocked on the door and was greeted by a middle-aged woman, who thanked me for attending. As I walked into the house, I felt a presence surround me; it was like a black, thick, swirling thing. I felt my hairs go up on the back of my neck. As I entered the room, the first thing I saw was two Saxon head bookends on the mantelpiece, complete with helmets and horns. I thought maybe they were the root cause of my uneasiness. How wrong I was to be."

Derek asked the woman (a schoolteacher) where her husband was, thinking it was a domestic dispute. She replied:

> "I live all alone here; there is an evil presence that overwhelms me. Please sit down and I will put the kettle on and tell you all about it."

As the woman moved towards the kitchen, she suddenly stopped and exclaimed "Oh no, it's here again!"

Swirling blackness

Derek felt the same invisible swirling blackness surrounding him for the second time, the hairs on the back of his neck standing up. He felt a shiver of fear course through his body and said a prayer. Immediately, whatever it was had gone. Unable to know what to do, he suggested to the woman that the next time she felt 'it', she should say a prayer. Relieved, the woman nodded in approval, but then in a mind-boggling second, it was back. Frightened, the woman held out her hand and touched Derek. Straightway she let out a yell, as if an electric current had passed through her body.

Derek:

> "*I was mystified as to what this source of power was and said the following prayer:*
>
> '*Oh God, our Father, fill our hearts and our homes with thy Holy Spirit, more and more, until we come to thy everlasting Kingdom.*'"

The next morning, when Derek arrived at the police station, he was shocked to discover that the woman had been found wandering in the early hours of the morning, outside a bus depot, some 12 miles from her home address. Such was her mental state that she was taken to Digby Mental Institution and admitted for care and treatment. We have no idea what happened to the woman.

Seeks advice

Derek pondered on what was the best course of action and went to see the local vicar at Morchard Bishop, who told him that it was his day off! Derek persisted and the vicar listened to him with an attitude of indifference, and then thanked him and bade Derek goodbye, without asking any questions about the incident. Derek told us:

> "*I felt very dissatisfied about his apparent lack of interest and went to see the vicar of Newton St. Cyres, the Reverend Scott, who decided to contact the Bishop so that an exorcism could be carried out. A few nights later, I was awoken by low moaning noises, coming from inside my house. I had a look around but couldn't find the cause. This went on for over a week at the same time; the only thing I could do was to say a prayer, which helped, but more was to come! One evening, I was awoken by a brilliant light that filled the room. I shook with fear, and hid my head under the pillow. It made no difference. Suddenly, it extinguished. I told my wife about what I had witnessed. She began to feel very apprehensive about what had taken place.*"

Apparition of the Virgin Mary

About a week later, Derek was reading in bed when, suddenly, what he took to be the apparition of the Virgin Mary appeared in the doorway. He said:

> "*The colour of her robes was brilliant; there was clarity beyond belief. I was so amazed I just stared – then she was gone.*"

Some weeks later Derek dealt with a car accident, involving two vehicles, and as was the police custom then, conveyed one party to their house with the promise of a cup of tea. As he entered the house he saw, from the pictures on the wall, that they were Roman Catholics. During conversation with the woman, he plucked up his courage and told her about his experience. She then showed him a sketch of the Virgin Mary that her daughter had done recently.

> "*I was astounded to see that it was perfect in every detail to what I had seen.*"

In 2012, we emailed the Bishop of Exeter asking him if they could confirm that an exorcism had been carried out at an address in Morchard Bishop, during the 1970s. His personal assistant, Sarah, replied:

> "*Thank you for your email to Bishop Michael. I am sorry, but we do not have any records that might help you.*
>
> *Yours sincerely,*"

It is still a case that Derek remembers vividly, despite the many years that have passed; he sees no reason to disbelieve the woman's account, not forgetting his own experience at the house, which, according to Derek:

"...was first left at the Church, and a short distance down the road."

Derek is a credit to the Police Force. He was involved in no less than five firearms' incidents and retired from the Force in 1984. He is a member of the Church choir and has sung at Exeter Cathedral. We wish him and his wife the best for the future.

According to local legend it is said that a ghostly black dog haunts the lanes, and is celebrated on 18th October each year with a ceremony known as the *'Running of the black dog'*.

It always seems odd to us that accounts like those given by Derek Davis, and others, seem far more frightening in contrast to reports of UFOs and their occasional occupants. We suppose that this is because while UFOs have far more substance (radar returns and ground traces) ghostly encounters which take place mostly in the dark of the night, when our imagination can run riot, appear to lack any physical parameters. Whether this is due to our own belief system, which identifies reports of ghosts as a manifestation of the spirit, or soul of a dead person that has remained on Earth after death, and UFOs as Alien 'visitors' to our planet, is, of course, a speculative one.

Below: Birmingham UFOSIS Group. These files were mislaid years ago by BUFORA – their current whereabouts are not known.

Unidentified Flying Object Studies Investigation Service, U.F.O.S.I.S.					
UB/61	25-8-54	8.55pm	Erdington	Pink/Y	
ONE/14	1960	9.00pm	Moxley	R	–
UB/100	1962?	12.30am	Stone Cross	S/R-G	20m
UB/43	196$\frac{7}{8}$	Late	Sparkhill	O	4s
UB/30	196$\frac{8}{9}$	Pm	Marlow,Bucks	O/R	1m
UB/41	$\frac{Oct}{Nov}$ 72	8.00pm	Aston Rd,B.ham City	B	10m
UB/73	1973	8.00pm	Handsworth Wood	G	–
ONE/17	18-10-73	6.00pm	Shirley		–
		6.50pm	"	O/R	–
		7.30pm	"	S/Gr	15m
ONE/8	-11-74	7.30pm	Smethwick,Warley	R	25s
UB/21	5-8-74	10.50pm	Castle Vale	Gr	5s
ONE/1	28-10-75	11.53am	B.ham City Center	S/W	–
ONE/2	18-10-75	10.50pm	Worcester	Y/W	20s
ONE/3	7-11-75	5.55pm	A449,Penkeridge	Purple/R	20s
ONE/4	4-8-75	10.22pm	Cley Hill,W'minster	W	12s
ONE/6	27-9-75		Smethwick,Warley	O	–
ONE/7	$\frac{4}{7}$-10-75	9.30pm	Smethwick	W	–
ONE/9	8-10-75	Late	Essington,W'hampton	W/R	15m
ONE/10	19-12-75	7.50am	Redditch	Y/Gold	3m
ONE/12	9-8-75	10.15pm	Devils Bridge,Wales	Y	–
ONE/13	.................Hoax...................				
ONE/15	19-12-75	2.00pm	Redditch	Y	2m
UB/25		75 2.15pm	Rotten Park Rd,B.ham	Radiant	–
UB/50	-11-75	Pm	Hay-on-Wye,Here'shire	S	15s
UB/81	14-10-75	Pm	"	S/W	8s
UB/82		75 8.30pm	Hall Green Stadium	B/O	1m
UB/83		75 7.15am	Kingswinford	Purple/G	5m
UB/88	74or75	9.00pm	Smethwick,Warley	O/W	5m
	20-7-75	11.50pm	Oldbury Rd,Smethwick	W	1hr
UB/85		10.30pm	Tooting Common,London	–	30m

Missed case – apologies to the reader – here it is!

25th October 1974 – Bizzare close encounter for Wyoming man

Rawlings man – Carl Higdon (then aged 41) – a father of four children and, according to friends and relatives, not a man prone to flights of fancy – was to encounter something so strange during the afternoon of this day which would defy explanation. It is, without doubt, one of the strangest reports we have heard for many years – involving interaction between a human being and perceived aliens from another planet. We were to come across many websites which contained details of the incident, along with illustrations later obtained, although little acknowledgement was credited to Dr. Richard F Haines, who later wrote a book – *UFO Phenomenon and the Behavioral Scientist* – in which this incident was thoroughly examined, along with the assistance of Dr. Leo Sprinkle.

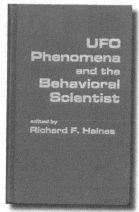

Carl was preparing for his second shift at the AM Wells service company, at Riverton, as foreman with 20 years service, when he received a call from one of the men reporting sick. Carl decided, in view of the circumstances, to take a day off and hunt for elk.

He loaded his gear into the company vehicle and headed towards McCarthy Canyon in nearby Canyon County.

While on his way, Higdon sighted a pair of stranded motorists working on their broken down van and pulled over to assist them to repair the vehicle. During the course of their conversation the duo told him they were also hunters and knew of a place where there was much more game than Higdon's current destination. Higdon recounted the conversation:

Dr. Richard Haines
Aerospace Researcher – NASA, Retired

> *"I pulled in front of them and helped them. During our chat, they told me the hunting was much better farther back in a remote section of the Medicine Bow National Forest."*

Medicine Bow National Park

Higdon decided to change his course and begin driving toward the northern region of Medicine Bow National Park, located just 40 miles south of where he lived, arriving at the park in the late afternoon.

> *"Around four o'clock, I parked my two-wheel-drive on a knoll. An old friend, Gary Eaton, walked over and together we surveyed the area. After a few minutes, Gary told me he was going on higher up into the forest. Jokingly he suggested he might scare down some elk for me."*

Sights a small herd of elk

Higdon then separated from Gary and picked up his brand new Magnum rifle and loaded it with powerful 7mm bullets, after deciding to explore an area concealed behind a hill and set off… never imagining what would happen next. A few minutes later, out of the corner of his eye, he caught a flash of movement and then saw a small herd of elk. Higdon silently raised his heavy rifle, put his eye to the sight and took aim at the largest male.

> *"I fired my rifle. It can give your shoulder a mean whack if you're not careful. As soon as I pulled the trigger I was astounded by the fact that I felt no kick back from the rifle. Even more perplexing, the detonation was absolutely silent; it was as if the entire world had fallen still. I actually watched the bullet leave the barrel of my rifle and soar forward so slowly it looked as if it were travelling through a wall of invisible 'Jello'. The bullet glided about 50 feet, before it plummeted to the snow*

Carl Higdon with his wife, Margery, in November 1974

speckled ground in front of me. I was awestruck. I froze. All around me there was a painful silence. Not a chirping bird or the rustling of leaves on nearby trees could be heard. The only sensation I could detect was a tingling feeling which crawled up my spine. This was similar to the feeling you often get before a fierce thunderstorm, when the air is full of static electricity."

Still immersed in the eerie, static charged silence, Higdon cautiously retrieved the bullet and inspected it closely. He immediately noticed that the lead portion of the 7mm had disappeared and only the oddly misshapen case remained.

Entity appears

He placed the bullet into his pocket and took a few perplexed steps forward. That was when the deathly silence surrounding him was abruptly broken by the sound of a twig snapping. Higdon spun around and was confronted by a sight that he instantly knew was not of this Earth.

"Turning to my left, I saw a 'man' standing there. At first I thought he was just another hunter, so I lowered my gun. Then he moved out of the shadows, into the light, and immediately I realized something was terribly wrong ... My heart skipped a beat and my knees were shaking so badly I could hardly stand. I thought, 'Hell, I should have stayed in McCarthy Canyon like I'd originally planned!"

Standing before the trembling hunter was what appeared to be a humanoid being clad in a skintight, black, one-piece outfit that Higdon claimed was: *"similar to a wet-suit scuba diver's wear."*

Description – Metallic belt adorned with a large, yellow, six-pointed star seen

Atop the suit was a pair of harness-like straps that criss-crossed its chest, below which was a metallic belt adorned with a large, yellow, six-pointed star. Beneath the star was an insignia that the outdoorsman could not identify. Higdon described the (at least what he presumed to be) masculine entity in detail.

"It was definitely a male... The visitor had no detectable ears. His eyes were small and lacked eyebrows... The dome of his skull was covered with the coarsest hair imaginable. It looked as if he had straw growing out of his head...[His complexion was] very similar to an Oriental's... He was definitely man-like in height. I'd estimate he stood well over six feet, and weighed around 180 pounds. This was definitely no ghost! Good Lord, he was flesh and blood. Amen."

Description – Three exceptionally large teeth seen

Higdon would go on to depict this creature's oddly upsetting facial features, including a lipless, slit-like mouth that concealed three exceptionally large teeth — not entirely unlike the notorious Fanged Humanoids of Kofu — on the top and bottom, a pair of antennas and, most alarmingly to Higdon, a face that blended directly into its neck.

Carl:

"Personally, it took getting used to, in order for me to look at him without getting a queasy feeling in the pit of my stomach. No chin was visible. His face just seemed to blend right into his throat. He had no jaw bone! Stranger still was the fact that this long armed, bow-legged, jaundice skinned creature had a pointy, almost drill bit-like appendage sticking out of its wrist where its right hand ought to have been and nothing at all on the left."

'Alien' approaches the witness

The 'being' slowly approached the terrified Higdon and asked him:

"How are you doing?"

The bewildered hunter, trying to stay calm, weakly responded,

"Pretty good"

Package containing pills levitated towards the witness

'He' asked Higdon if he was hungry, but before he could respond the creature sent a small, clear cellophane package floating toward him.

The entity: Ausso One'

"He waved a pointed object where his right hand should have been, and it levitated over to me. I opened the packet and found four pills inside. He told me, in English, to take one of them; that it would last four days. Now normally I don't like taking pills, not even an aspirin, but something happened. It's as if I had no control over my actions, so I just swallowed one of them and put the other three into my jacket pocket."

'Ausso One'

The humanoid then introduced himself as 'Ausso One'. It was at this point that Higdon sighted a strange box-like object, catching the sun's rays in the clearing behind the being.

Cube-shaped object on the ground

"There, not far from us, was a transparent, cube-shaped object resting on the ground. To me it looked like a huge

Christmas package. You know — flat on all sides, like a box. I couldn't see any landing gear or entrance… It was much smaller than any of our commercial or military planes. In fact, you're going to think I'm crazy, but this thing couldn't have been more than five feet high, seven feet long, and four and a half feet wide. Tiny is the only word I can think of to accurately describe its size!"

Inside the craft

The 'alien' asked the hunter, *"Do you want to come along?"*

Higdon, fully aware of the fact that he was in no position to refuse, lamely shrugged his shoulders in assent. It was at this point that time appeared to leap forward, as Higdon's next recollection was of being inside the cube-like craft.

"Before I was able to move a muscle, I found myself inside this contraption. It was instantaneous. How I was able to fit inside remains a riddle. They must have shrunk me – the only explanation that seems plausible. I wouldn't venture how they accomplished this feat. 'Ausso One' just pointed, and we were where he wanted us!"

At this stage Higdon started to panic.

"My memory fails me, here. I recall my head starting to reel. My hands were sweating. Somehow the pill this fellow gave me must have deadened at least some of my senses; otherwise, I'm positive I would have been crying and perhaps even fainted. I may be strong, but I'm only human!"

Not on his own … elk also present!

At this point Higdon noticed that all five of the elk he had been stalking, just moments before, were also in the cube behind what he perceived to be an invisible barrier. The hunter marveled at the creature's ability to incapacitate the untamed animals.

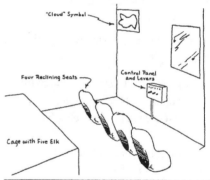

"I'm kind of fuzzy as to how they managed to contain such wild beasts. They were motionless; paralyzed."

It would seem that the elk were not the only things paralyzed, because at virtually the same moment as he saw the frozen beasts, Higdon claimed that he became abruptly aware of the fact that he was now sitting in a high-backed "bucket seat" with what he described as restrictive "bands" securing his arms and legs.

"As we took off, I found myself strapped down to this seat with my hands held fast to the armrests of the chair. My legs were similarly bound."

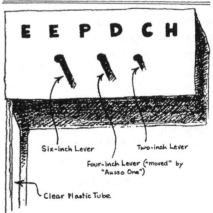

Resisting what must have been an overwhelming urge to panic, Higdon watched in growing horror as another jawless, straw-haired being appeared out of nowhere, at which point he and his genial partner strapped a bizarre, wire-smothered, football helmet-like device to his head, prompting the hunter to state:

"I felt like the monster in an old Frankenstein movie."

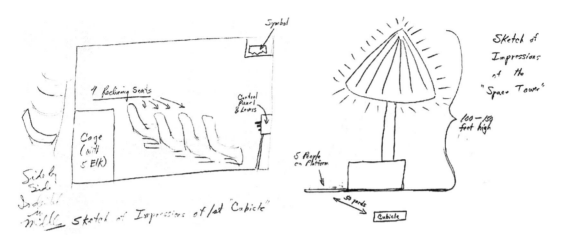

Higdon then observed a console with three dissimilar levers, which 'Ausso One' used to control the craft. The alien pointed its 'hand' at the longest lever and seemed to move it telepathically. It was then that the peculiar, transparent cube that Higdon would later describe as a *"flying box car"* took off.

UFO hovers over truck

'Ausso One' manipulated the vehicle so that it hovered above Higdon's truck. With a point of his conical hand the vehicle vanished before his eyes.

> *"When we got above the trees, 'Ausso' aimed his arm at my pick-up and it disappeared — poof — vanished into thin air!"*

Mysterious sphere seen aboard the 'craft'

Higdon then tells of seeing, just as suddenly as they left terra firma, an ominous, planet-like sphere — *"shaped similar to a basketball"* — through the clear floor of the box-like craft... a planet he maintained was not Earth!

Higdon later recalled from his impromptu tour of this alien world a colossal tower that loomed above the surface comparing it to Seattle's Space Needle, but the huge, umbrella-like structure was covered in rotating lights so blinding they hurt his eyes. In addition, his hearing was overwhelmed by a sound that he compared to an electric razor buzzing. The second 'humanoid' commented they had similar problems on their home world, saying: *"Your sun burns us, too!"*

The craft lands on an alien planet

The odd 'craft' then landed about 150 feet away from the platform at the base of the tower – the second being vanishing just as abruptly as 'it' had arrived. Through the transparent walls of the 'ship', Higdon saw what he claimed were:

> *"...five human beings, dressed in average Earth fashions, talking to one another. The individuals consisted of one brown-haired girl who appeared to be about 11 years-old, a blonde girl who was just*

Carl Higdon's drawing

Sketch by Carl Higdon drawn on Saturday, November 2, 1974

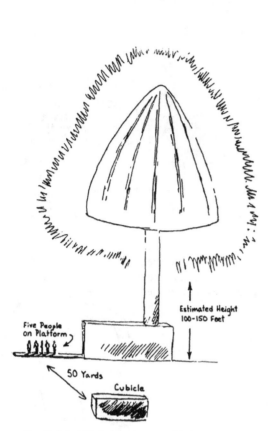

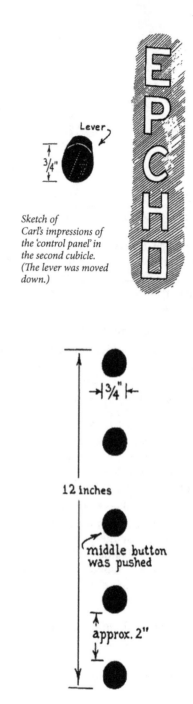

Sketch of
Carl's impressions of
the 'control panel' in
the second cubicle.
(The lever was moved
down.)

*Sketch of Carl Higdon's impressions of the 'space tower'.
Drawn by Nelson R. Sprinkle*

*a few years older, and a teen couple who seemed to
be about 17 or 18. The group was rounded out by a
man who seemed to be in his 50s. The people seemed
to be talking to one another and did not notice me."*

163,000 'light miles' from Earth

'Ausso One' explained they had touched down on a planet
that was 163,000 'light miles' from Earth.

[Higdon was quick to elucidate that the creature did not
say "light years", which to him indicated in no uncertain
terms that: *"To them the passage of time is different than it
is to us."*]

Into the tower

'Ausso One' escorted Higdon into the dazzling tower. The
pair ascended in an elevator, which deposited them into a
room where the hunter was instructed to stand on a small
platform. Higdon noted that he and the alien never actually

*Sketch of Carl's impressions about the 'elevator buttons'
in the space tower*

walked anywhere, but seemed to be floating just above the ground. While they hovered toward their destination, 'Ausso One' explained there were no fish on his planet and that these 'finned critters' were one of his peoples' favourite things about Earth.

A glassy shield appears

At this point an odd device — that Higdon described as resembling a *"glassy shield"* — slipped out of the wall and paused in front of him and 'scanned' him for almost five minutes, before it disappeared back into the wall.

Back inside the cube

His 'captor' informed Carl he was going to return him to the spot where they had first met because the examination had shown that he did not *"suit their purpose"*. Higdon then realised that he and his alien companion were now back inside the clear cubicle. 'Ausso One' was admiring the human's rifle and, with a tinge of regret, admitted that as much as he would like to he would not be able to keep the *"primitive"* weapon as a souvenir.

'Ausso One' telepathically handed the rifle back to Higdon, then removed the food pills from his pocket – a fact that dismayed the hunter, as it

Photograph shows the approximate location of the alleged encounter with a humanoid

represented the only piece of concrete evidence he had of this weird event.

Once again the alien pointed at the longest lever. Higdon realised he was no longer hovering above an alien world, but that his alien comrade and his miraculous 'cube' had apparently instantaneously transported him back to Earth.

Carl says that his truck had been inexplicably transported some five miles from the glade where it had been parked two and a half hours before. The hunter later considered the situation.

> *"Since I was in a state of mental stress, this fact did not have any impact on me until sometime later. I know that I could never have driven over that impossible terrain — even if I had been physically capable of driving, which I most certainly was not!"*

Back on Earth

At this point the 'being' said: *"We'll see you"*.

Carl was overwhelmed by a floating sensation and without warning found he was standing on the edge of a steep, rocky slope. The loose stones could not support his weight and he suddenly found himself plummeting down the nine foot decline, severely impacting against the hard ground and injuring his head, neck and shoulder.

The next thing he recalled was staggering nearly three miles down an old, dirt road, rifle in hand, freezing and in a state of nearly hysterical amnesia:

> *"I didn't know what had happened, who I was, or where I was, for that matter. The only thing I could think of was to get out of there as fast as possible and find someone who could help me."*

Higdon was in such a state of shock that he walked past his pick-up without even recognising it. When he realised that he was utterly alone on the dirt road he backtracked to the vehicle.

> *"There I stood, shivering, eyes filled with tears and not knowing my own identity. I saw a truck parked off the road between some trees, and decided to crawl into it for shelter and to keep warm. I didn't realize the truck belonged to me."*

Higdon was startled by a feminine voice that suddenly crackled over the CB radio.

> *"There was a two-way set under the dashboard, so I picked up the microphone and held it close to my mouth. I managed to blurt out that I was sick and lost and desperately in need of assistance. When the voice on the other end asked me where I was, I told them I had seen a sign down the road which read, 'North Boundary National Forest'. This didn't seem to be much help, however, as there was absolutely no indication as to what forest the sign was referring to."*

Richard F Haines:

> *"On Tuesday, October 29, 1974, I received two telephone calls: from Rick Kenyon, art teacher in the Rawlins, Wyoming, public schools, and from Robert Nantkes, vocational rehabilitation counselor of Riverton, Wyoming. Each man is known to me personally and each is a person of high intelligence and integrity. The telephone calls dealt with the same topic: the alleged UFO experience of Carl Higdon, as reported to Sue Taylor of the Rawlins Daily Times (vol. 87, no. 204), Tuesday, October 29, 1974: According to the newspaper article, Carl Higdon (a 40-year-old oil driller for the AM Well Service of Riverton, Wyoming) had been hunting elk on the north edge of the Medicine Bow National Forest (40 miles south of Rawlins) at 4:00 p.m., Friday, October 25. Then, approximately at 6:30 p.m., he placed a call on the radio of the pickup truck he had been driving to his boss, Roy Fleming, and gave directions about the approximate location of the pickup truck.*

> He said that it was parked approximately three miles from where he parked it initially; it was in a "mud hole" where no one would normally take a two-wheel-drive vehicle (as this one was). A rescue party (Sheriff Ogburn, Deputy Sheriff Ed Tierney, Roy Fleming, Bob Rosacker, Dave Martin, and Harold Schurtz) drove several four-wheel-drive pickup trucks into the area. With difficulty, they found Carl and the truck (at approximately 11:40 p.m., October 25). The truck was towed out by the four-wheel-drive vehicles. Mrs Margery Higdon, Carl's wife, was with Mr and Mrs Don James; they were waiting about two or three miles from the area where Carl was located. During the rescue operation, they observed a flashing light for about 20 minutes --changing from red to green to white, in a pulsing pattern, and moving in an arc which was described as "three feet," at arm's length. When Carl was found, he was described as dazed and confused; he had difficulty in talking and recognizing his wife."*

Margery Higdon:

> *"When I first got to him, I opened the pickup door, and he just looked at me like, well, like you were just looking right straight through him. And the first thing I could think of to say to him that would maybe make him think or anything, I said, Oh, Honey, did you get any elk? And the minute I said*

Photographs of the bullet fired and recovered by Carl Higdon. The mono photos show bullet from opposite sides.

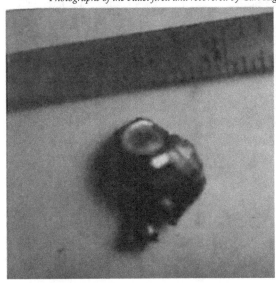

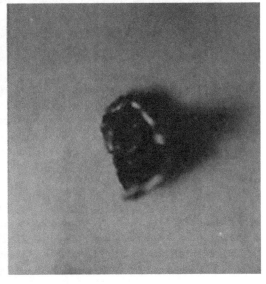

'elk,' he started looking out the windshield like this – I just figured he was looking into the tree line, you know, I mean. the look he had on his face scared me, though. Don was on the other side of the pickup. The other guys-- the pickup was just about out of gas, and we had got plenty of gas with us; so they were out filling the tank. 1 said to Don, "Get that gun out of the rack, because 1 didn't know what 'buck-fever' is, but this is the only thing I could imagine he had, you know. So I told him to get the gun out of there, and he was shaking. So I took my coat off and tried to put it around him. "Don't you dare touch me I Don't you dare touch me" I That's all he would say. And 1 just kept telling him, it's all right, it's all right. I went ahead and put the coat around him, and he went ahead and let me put it around him, but 1 was not to touch him. And after that, well, with having the doors open and shaking like that and being in shock, well, we figured maybe it would be better if maybe he just stayed warm, so we just shut the doors. Then 1 just stood there by the pickup until after they got it gassed up and got going"

Dr Richard F Haines:

"He has said he was taken to Carbon County Memorial Hospital, approximately at 2:00 a.m., Saturday, October 26, for observation, and released around 10:00 a.m., Monday, October 28. During his hospitalization, Carl said, the physician, Dr. Tongco, had X-rays taken. Carl was told that the films were OK. (However, he had been hospitalized for tuberculosis at one time in Kimball, Nebraska. Chest X-rays in 1958, and 1970, had indicated there was scar tissue on his lungs, according to a Kimball physician.) During his recent hospitalization, the physician, Dr. Tongco, told Carl that he was 'OK,' and his blood was 'OK'--in fact, it was 'super,' 'very rich.' Carl is hopeful that information can be obtained from medical personnel which will support these statements. However, the Sheriff has made some public statements which raise questions about his acceptance of the report. Rick Kenyon said that he had interviewed Carl Higdon and obtained the basic description of his experience, plus some drawings of the 'man'. Carl agreed to other interviews, plus the use of hypnotic techniques, for the purpose of obtaining further information about his experience."

Other witnesses included two residents of Rawlins, Wyoming, Don and Marliyn James, who told of having sighted an unusual radiance in the vicinity of Medicine Bow Forest at the same time that the Police officers were conducting a search for the missing hunter.

Margery claimed that she never once doubted the sincerity of her husband's strange tale, later telling reporters from the *Star-Tribune*:

"I believed him because it was him and because I was out there and saw a lot of different things that went on that night."

Bullet found

Within days of her husband's hospitalization, Margery discovered a crushed 7mm bullet hidden in his canteen patch. Higdon: *"I'd never seen anything like it before, to compare it to. Soon as I could I took it to the Carbon County Sheriff's Department where the officer in charge of ballistics analysis examined it through a microscope. He told me it was from a 7mm Magnum rifle, which is the caliber of my gun. Returning the chunk of metal, he noted that he had never seen a bullet in that shape or condition commenting it looks as if it has been turned inside out by a superhuman being!"*

APRO arrange for tests on the bullet

The Aerial Phenomena Research Organization (APRO) sent metallurgy consultant, Dr. Walter Walker, to inspect the 'bullet' jacket. After a rigorous examination of the object he testified that it had collided with and exceptionally solid surface with immense force. This assertion is not to be underestimated as a 7mm bullet travels at such a fantastic rate of speed it would have been well nigh impossible to track the casing down had it not hit something incredibly hard — much harder than a rock or a tree.

[In the *APRO Bulletin, Vol. 23 No. 5,* which was published in March, 1975, investigators were planning on organizing a search party in order to find the lead slug of the 7mm in the hopes that it might produce additional evidence of what it had impacted against. Unfortunately a search carried out was unsuccessful.]

On October 29, 1974, the *Rawlins Daily Times* published an account of Higdon's extraordinary experience and from there the story spread like wildfire.

Higdon, still a nervous wreck about the whole affair, claimed that for weeks following the *"trip"* he was followed by a colossal *"green light"* in the sky.

Underwent lie detector test

Higdon was subjected to what was then one of the most advanced polygraph tests available, the PSE (Psychological Stress Evaluator) device. The test was presided over by a technical consultant for LAPD, Dr. Greenberg and his colleague Dr. Sidney Walter. The scientists ascertained that the former hunter was giving a truthful account of what happened and Greenberg concluded: *"I am forced to admit that something utterly fantastic did happen in this man's life. The test proves it beyond doubt."*

Rawlins man describes
hunting experience

Oct. 25, 1974

By SUE TAYLOR

"Everyone will think I'm a quack, but it really happened," Carl Higdon said Monday.

He was referring to his elk hunting trip Friday which turned into a bizarre experience for him.

Higdon was hunting south of Rawlins on the north boundary of the national forest about 4 p.m. Friday when his "experience" began to unfold.

"I walked down over this hill and saw five elk," Higdon said. "I raised my rifle and fired, but the bullet only went about 50 feet and dropped. I looked over to my right and there in the shadow was this sort of man standing there."

Higdon said the "man" was about six-foot-two and weighed 180 pounds. He was dressed in a black suit and black shoes and wore a belt with a star in the middle and a yellow emblem. He was quite bowlegged and had a slanted head. His forehead and facial features were similar to humans but he had no chin. His hair was thin and stood straight up on his head, Higdon said.

"He asked me if I was hungry and I said yes," Higdon said, "So he tossed me some pills and I took one. I don't know why I did it — I never take pills of any kind unless a doctor prescribes them, not even asprin."

Higdon said the "man" then pointed, what resembled a long finger at him and the next thing he knew, he was in a seven by

seven foot cubicle with two "men" and the five elk.

"He asked me if I wanted to go with him and I said 'yes', Higdon said. "I told my wife a long time ago, when these stories about UFO's and strange creatures were coming out, that if I ever got a chance, I would talk with them or go with them."

Hidon said the "men" placed a helmet on him with a strap around his neck. Six wires were sticking out from it on three sides, Higdon said. The "men" then told him they were going "home" which was 163,00 miles away.

"In no time we arrived at this tall tower similar to a rotating restaurant like the Seattle Space Needle," Hidgon said. "The lights there were so intense and hurt my eyes a lot and the "men" said our sun affects them in the same way."

Higdon noted that the "men" were never in the sunlight but always in the shade.

Because the light was so intense on his eyes, Higdon said the "men" said they would take him home.

"The next thing I remember is talking to Roy Fleming on the radio," he said.

Fleming is manager of the Maddox Well Service and Higdon is employed by AM Well Service of Riverton.

—Rawlins

(Continued on Page 14)

(Continued from Front Page)

"My truck was about three miles from where I parked it," Higdon said. "It's only a two-wheel drive and was in a mud hole where no one without a four-wheel drive would attempt to go."

After Higdon was rescued by the Carbon County Sheriff's officers, he was taken to Carbon County Memorial Hospital for observation.

"My doctor said there were no bruises on me and I wasn't bleeding anywhere, but I'm still suffering from headaches and a backache," Higdon said.

Higdon's wife said she and two friends went looking for her husband when he failed to return home on time and as they approached the area they saw a bright red, white and green light resembling a large star. Mrs. Higdon said it was too high for a helicopter but too low for an airplane.

Higdon said he does not drink and does not take drugs of any kind.

I WAS KIDNAPED

By FRANK BOURNE

'Life is not the same since I met

Carl Higdon's truck, found in a different place to where he had left it

Authors

Due to lack of space we are unable to include the full statements made by Margaret and so many others witnesses who were involved in this matter. What impressed us was the incredible amount of detail remembered by Carl about what had taken place and what had been said to him during conversations held with his captors…The case bears many similarities to other incidents involving close encounters we had come across over the years and instinct indicates there is no reason to dispute the account given rather than fabrication. One thing is assured these confrontations will continue! Our hearts go out to people whose lives are changed for forever by experiences of this nature which are still incomprehensible to understand over 40 years later!

Additional information obtained during research into this book

Ref: Page 110 – Original UFO sketch

away.   Its direction towards the coast.
     Huge . Original colour –
silver grey.
Sodium lighting coming out of the
windows
The light from the windows appeared
to bleed around the aircraft
giving it, its bright orange colour.
At the front from each side
what looked like fins, corrugated.
Like this. : —   Very thick

could this
thickness be
fat when it settles
on the ground ?

The impression I had was that the
windows must have had something
to do with its' lifting power. They
were right from the nose to
the tail.   The motors (or whatever
they were) in the side pods or fins.

Ref: Page 231 – Alan Shepherd

Unidentified flying objects—or just people's imaginations playing tricks?

Reading Chronicle, Friday, September 5th, 1975

Mrs. Rose Ryde— "Like a falling star."

Mrs. Denise Palmer— "Very uncanny."

eople are saucers

nvestigation by Mark Prior

"They were going much faster than a plane and going just above the rooftops. I saw them for about a minute before they flew out of sight. They were very low down and did not make any noise," said Neil.

THE flying saucer has been seen again this week just north of Caversham hovering only a few feet above the ground, writes Mark Prior.

An Emmer Green woman saw the saucer, which was domed, while driving her car along the Henley Road on Tuesday evening. She came within feet of the inky-blue coloured object, but sped away in fright at what she saw.

It was rounded at the bottom with a domed top. There was a very bright flashing light at the top—which fits other descriptions. It was quite small, perhaps only 12 feet in diameter.

She told me: "It was only a couple of feet off the ground. If I had got out of my car I could quite easily have touched it but I was so scared I drove straight off. It gave me a big fright."

What was more strange was that though it was hovering there was no air disturbance and the hedges and grass were still. She was not sure whether it made any sound—she was more interested in getting away quickly.

The whole Shepherd family are keen skywatchers and are always on the lookout for anything strange. Mr. Alan Shepherd claimed to have seen about 12 U.F.O.s in the past three years.

"I think there is definitely life on other planets—there cannot be just us. We go to the moon and try to get to other stars so I do not see why someone else should not try to come here and have a look at us," said Mr. Shepherd.

A spokesman for the Meteorological Office at Bracknell said they were not using any weather balloons at the time, although the plastic ones they used reflected light and sometimes had a small lantern on them.

Most of their balloon ascents were made during daylight hours.

And at the R.A.F. base at Odiham in Hampshire a spokesman said it was highly unlikely that what was seen was a helicopter.

"We do have aircraft on night flying but I very much doubt if it was a helicopter. There were none in that area." He thought it could have been a light jet aircraft which have intensely bright lights and are very quiet.

Mr. Jim Betts, of the Reading Astronomical Society, said there was always an element of doubt in sightings of U.F.O.'s. "There are many that have been explained but the few that have not are the ones that are most interesting.

"I do not think there are little green men on Mars. But there is still a big area of doubt and we are not qualified to dismiss the whole thing."

Mr. Alan Shepherd and his son, Neil, who says he saw "five flying saucers in formation."

He continued that a lot happened in the sky every night and he was anxious to see a U.F.O. himself. "We do not scoff at it but the majority can be explained."

Ref: Page 267– Original Illustration

DIRECTOR'S MESSAGE

BY CHARLES J. WILHELM

As director of O.U.F.O.I.L.,INC., I would like to introduce myself especially to the readers who don't know me. I've been interested in the UFO phenomena for twenty years,but have recently become actively involved. In this short time,I've had a world of experiences open up to me and I have come in contact with some fantastic people through the exploration of this great phenomena.

People have asked how I became interested in the study of UFO's. It all started at the age of six when I witnessed one of the most famous sightings of all time, being that of Capt. Mantell in pursuit of a UFO. However, it was years later and through research that I found this out.

The reason for starting our organization is to keep the public informed on an up-to-date basis about UFO activity. There are many fine organizations,but I feel that ours is unique,in that, it is devoted to the people and run by the people. Although I am the director,I don't make the final decisions because they are voted upon by the members. I feel that this is very important because the people become involved, informed,and prepared on the subject. After all,it takes the public to cause a break through in the UFO field.

Many may not agree with this hypothesis,but stop and think! Who are the people that report these sightings,not to speak of the legitimate contacts with the UFOnaut? How many famous UFOlogists can you name in the public's eye have had a good UFO experience? Think about this!

I am proud to have "THE OHIO SKY WATCHER" as our official publication. It will take some time to develop a good publication as we are not experts and we have a lot to learn. However,we are fortunate to have excellant men to head and produce our quarterly publication. They are: John Michael and Bill Benesch,and we are confident that they'll do an excellant job. They are in the process of developing a new format geared specifically for our readers,which will include current UFO sightings;articles by noted UFOlogists;a little humor; and a running story in cartoon form from time to time. Many other ideas will be discussed in future issues.

Concerning the continuation of this publication,it will depend solely on the generosity of the readers. Our organization is still in its infancy,and therefore we have little operating expenses. We hope to obtain enough subscriptions to take care of the cost of printing.

We wish it were possible to send the publication to anyone who wishes to receive it free,but at this time it is not possible. After all,that would fulfill our purpose in helping people to become aware of the UFO phenomena and inspire them to become active in the field.

In closing,I urge the readers to send in their UFO experiences, newspaper clippings from your area and especially your letters of comments about our publication. Until the next issue,I remain...

      Sincerely,
      (Signed)
      CHARLES J. WILHELM
      Executive Director

MYSTERY OBJECT OVER NEW HAMPSHIRE

An "unidentified flying object" reported by a family in South Hampton, stirs New Hampshire. The UFO mystery is alive again.

While driving home after attending a PTA meeting on Route 150 at 9:30 p.m., Mrs. Stevens, her son and daughter saw a red beacon like light in the sky ahead of them. The light got larger and they saw a large red illuminated dome , there was a bright white rectangular-shaped opening with something like blades spinning round inside. The blades seemed to protrude outside as well. White, blue and yellow sparks spewed out at opposite sides around the base of the dome. However, then they realized it was noiseless and very unusual, they became frightened and sped off.

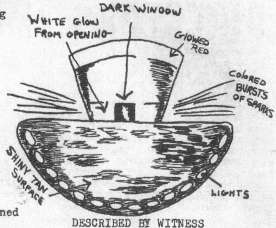

DESCRIBED BY WITNESS

When they reached Locust Street, the UFO hovered with a bobbing, fluttering motion. It was over a 90-foot elm tree in an adjoining field. A band of soft glowing colored lights like a "string of beads" flickered on and off. After they watched the multicolored lights flickering on and off for several minutes, all of the lights would go on at once with just one solid color. First red, then blue, and then green.

WITNESS DRAWING

All of a sudden a low-flying aircraft came over the east side of Route 150, seemingly heading directly for the hovering object. As soon as the plane approached, the object began to move about with jerky motions and descended in a step-by-step motion into a swampy area where it seemed to settle on or near the ground. A red glow could be seen for a short time, then it too faded away.

This was not the first time that New Hampshire has had UFO activity. In 1965 in Exeter, several people claimed to have seen an enormous UFO with pulsating, brilliant red lights. It was low enough that a police officer dropped to the ground and drew his gun.

In September of 1961, occurred the biggest UFO incident until the Mississippi one of 1973, that of Betty and Barney Hill. The incident occurred along Route 3 near Lincoln, where the couple claimed they saw a UFO ringed with windows in the front through which they saw figures looking at them.

Is this area a hot spot for UFO's? There seems to be a lot of action over the years. Lets keep looking and see if anything happens.

Ref: Page 317– Photo of Malcolm Handley and his wife

THE NEWS (PORTSMOUTH) 1974.

In search of the truth about those mysteries

Have you ever seen a ghost or a flying saucer? Do things go bump in the night? If so, a young Southsea couple would like to hear from you.

Mr. Malcolm Handley and his attractive wife, Brenda, of 9, Norman Road, have, with several others interested in the unusual, formed an association called W.A.T.-S.U.P., standing for the Wessex Association for the Study of Unexplained Phenomena.

The association has Mr. Peter Hill, of Southampton, as its Chairman and Mr. Richard Nash, of Cosham, is treasurer.

Mr. Handley, assisted by his wife, is Secretary.

"There is so much going on for which there is no logical explanation — particularly in the U.F.O. (unidentified flying object) field," said Mr. Handley.

STRANGE SHAPE

He said that a couple of years ago he and his wife saw a strange shape in the sky when walking in Southsea.

"There just does not seem any likely explanation for this. It was not an aircraft, hovercraft, or helicopter. It must have been some sort of flying saucer," said Mrs. Handley.

She said it was furthest from her or her husband's minds to try to fit an unusual explanation to what could be a logical answer.

"We are trying to seek the truth," she added.

So far the membership of W.A.T.S.U.P. stands at more than 20.

"In a few weeks' time, we are going to spend a week-end at Warminster, Wiltshire, and as there have been some inexplicable happenings there," said Mr. Handley, a trainee manager for a finance company.

His wife added: "We should like people to come forward who have previously been scared of doing so for fear of being laughed at."

It is hoped that W.A.T.-S.U.P. will hold monthly meetings to discuss — shall we call it — what's up?

6754-1

Mr. and Mrs. Malcolm Handley, helping to run W.A.T.S.U.P.

Ref: Page 330 – Re-Landing at Rainhill

The author

The area of the Rainhill landing case

One of the strange bootmarks found at the Rainhill landing site. A small stone inside the print was seemingly scuffed by metal inlays in the boot.

Ref: Page 330 – UFO (USA) sighting on the 4th of May 1975

JULY 1975

UFO INVESTIGATOR

NATIONAL INVESTIGATIONS COMMITTEE ON AERIAL PHENOMENA

NICAP

NICAP ■ 3535 UNIVERSITY BLVD. WEST, SUITE 23 ■ KENSINGTON, MARYLAND 20795 ■ A NONPROFIT CORPORATION FOUNDED 1956

SCIENTIST PUZZLED BY SIGHTING

NICAP comment: *The following report is presented in the form received with, omissions made of comments that were not pertinent. This report illustrates that good observers and "non-believers" often see objects which are not identifiable. As the report is reviewed you will note that the speed of the object is too slow for a fixed wing aircraft. The pattern and sequence of lighting is not characteristic of aircraft, including helicopters. The sound heard is not characteristic of aircraft with the possible exception of a jet helicopter. However, there were no jet helicopters operating at the time of the sighting.*

First of all, I should state that I am a scientist, a sociologist by profession, and that I have never been a believer in UFOs. I have, in fact, scoffed at such reports, and the subject has not even seriously held my interest. I have always thought that the reported "sightings," all without exception, could be explained by naturalistic phenomena. And I still do. It is for the purpose of securing a satisfactory explanation of the following experience that we are writing this account in as accurate detail as possible.

At 11:15 p.m. on Sunday, May 4, 1975, my wife and I were returning home along a road we frequently travel. Shortly after we turned north off Illinois Highway 16 onto the country road (approximately a mile and a half east from where Illinois 159 dead ends into 16), we saw a bright light to the right. It appeared to have about the brightness of a farm light or yard light commonly found in this area. This was about two miles north of 16. We could not figure out what the light was, as we recalled no such light in that location.

As we drove further, we came closer and closer to the light, as we would if it were a light on top of a building. When we were about 200-500 feet from it, with

the light about 60 to 100 feet in the air, we saw there was no building beneath it. We then saw a searchlight go on, from approximately the same point as the original light. The searchlight was directed southwards and parallel to the ground. We then stopped the car, turned off the car lights, and got out. The white light and the searchlight remained stationary for about five seconds, off on our right (east of the road we were on). The light began moving slowly southwards, in the direction to which the searchlight was focused. A red flashing light then appeared, followed about five seconds later by a green flashing light. The red and green lights appeared to be on the side nearest us, with the original white light farther from us. When it became apparent that the lights were going to continue moving, we got back in our car, backed up about fifty feet, turned around in a driveway on the west side of the road, and followed the moving object. The lights moved slightly faster than we did, continuing on a straight path in a southwestern direction. We were travelling about 25-30 miles per hour, and I estimate the speed of this airborne vehicle to be approximately 35 to 45 miles per hour. We continued following the vehicle until we reached Highway 16. We then crossed 16 and parked. The vehicle continued on a straight course in a southwestern direction. We watched it until it was out of sight.

The red and green lights were blinking, while the white light was constant. The red and green lights never appeared simultaneously. One could see them only one at a time. The blinking was not an alternate blinking in a completely regular pattern, i.e. there was an "unevenness" about the length of the appearance of the green and red lights. Perhaps "flashing" or "flickering" is a more accurately descriptive term than blinking. The red light was more highly pronounced than the green light, i.e., it was brighter.

The sound of the object was low and smooth. It was not "choppy" like a helicopter. We could not hear the sound until we turned off our own car engine.

We then turned around to continue home. We backtracked on the same road. We drove approximately two miles north and had not yet come to the place where we had first seen the bright light when a moving white light caught our attention. It was now 11:35 p.m. We stopped the car, again turned off our lights and motor and got out of the car. The moving light followed a course approximately parallel to that which the first vehicle had traversed, but it was higher and perhaps a thousand feet or so farther east of where the first had been. There was neither a searchlight nor flashing colored lights. This light continued its course, travelling out of sight. We observed it for approximately three or four minutes.

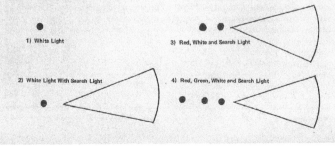

1) White Light

2) White Light With Search Light

3) Red, White and Search Light

4) Red, Green, White and Search Light

Haunted Skies **Volume Three Revised**

UFO INVESTIGATOR/JULY 1975

We then stood alongside the car and searched the skies. Within a minute we saw a third object. This one was farther east and about the same height as the second one. It also travelled southwards, but its course was due south, thus not being quite parallel with the first two. This one showed neither a white light nor a searchlight. Only red and green lights were visible, with the same flashing pattern as previously observed on the first object. No sound of a motor was audible.

As we were watching this third object, a fourth appeared to the south and east of us. This fourth object followed a curving direction from the east toward the west, continuing northward. We watched this object at the same time as we were observing the third one. It also had red and green flashing lights, and no searchlight. We cannot remember whether or not it had a white light. It also continued out of sight, going northwards.

While we were watching the third and fourth objects, a plane flew over, flying approximately from the northeast to the southwest. There was the regular sound of a plane engine at this time, and regular flashing red and green lights. The "regularity" of the flashing of the airplane's lights was in marked contrast to the flashing pattern of the other objects. The sound of the engine of the first object we had seen was also different from the sound of the airplane's engine.

After the plane flew over, no objects were visible for about one to two minutes. We then saw a distant white light to the northwest of us, more north than west. This fifth object appeared to be stationary, and we could not tell for sure whether or not it was a star. We could dimly make out flashing red and green lights, however. We watched this fifth object for about fifteen minutes, and it appeared to make up and down and circular movements. We could not be certain about its movements, however, because of the distance of the object from us and the autokinetic effect. The object did, however, gradually become dimmer, as though it had moved farther from us.

While we were watching this fifth object, we saw a sixth. This sixth object came directly from the north going due south. It was about the same altitude as the plane we had just seen, perhaps somewhat lower. It had red and green lights also, and we were certain that it

was a second plane. It became apparent that the lights were not flashing, when the object was closer to us. They were constant. The object flew directly over us, continuing its southward flight. When this sixth object was directly overhead, the green and white lights disappeared and were replaced by a white light. The change in lights was simultaneous, that is, at no time was there no light visible to us. The object maintained its altitude and speed, continuing on the same straight course until it was out of sight. There was no sound of an engine on this sixth object, as there had been with the airplane, although the altitude did not appear to be much different from that of the airplane.

We then got back in the car and continued driving. We would stop from time to time and watch the distant fifth object, but it appeared to be stationary. As we were driving, we saw a stationary white light over a field, but we could not make out anything else. The light was perhaps a couple of thousand feet distant. There were no blinking lights, and no searchlight was visible.

At 12:45 a.m. we arrived at the farm. When we pulled up to the house, we saw a white light above our pasture. We stopped the car and cut the lights and motor. We got out and looked toward the light. This again was a single white light. A searchlight then came on, directed downwards. This object was to the southwest of where we were standing. It remained stationary for about two to three minutes. No motor sound was audible, although the object was only approximately 500 to 1000 feet from us and only about 20 to 50 feet off the ground.

The object then began flying slowly, with flashing red and green lights coming on. It appeared to be flying toward us, and we moved under the cedar tree in the corner of the pasture so as not to be in the path of the searchlight. A motor became audible at this time. There was no choppy sound to the motor, but it was smooth and low, as had been the motor sound of the first object we had seen. If we had been in the house we would have been unable to hear it. The best description we can come up with for this sound is a low, smooth, soft, humming sound.

I then called the Carlinville police department and asked them if they knew of an air search being conducted in our

area. The man reported that he knew of no such search, and after I described what we had seen fly over our land, he told me that one of the Carlinville police officers had phoned him and said he had seen a helicopter and had been "flashed back." He said he would check on it. It was perhaps 12:55 a.m. when I made this call. At 1:45 a.m. I again called the Carlinville police department and the man who answered the telephone said that someone else had called in and said that a helicopter was flying over the railroad tracks with a searchlight. A second police officer had also called in about a flying object.

At about 2:05 a.m. I called the Illinois State Police in Litchfield to see if they could provide an explanation for what we had seen. They could not, but they said they would do some checking.

Sometime that morning the Illinois State Police telephone and stated that what I saw was probably a helicopter and that I did not hear a choppy noise because it was moving away from me. I told him that the object had been moving toward us, not away from us.

The next day, Monday, May 5, I called the Federal Aviations in Springfield, Illinois, and asked if they could shed some light on this matter. The man there suggested that I call Scott Air Force Base, which I did. I was put in contact with a Colonel Vaughan who took down some basic information and called me back in a couple of hours. He reported that the military did not conduct any maneuvers in the area on Sunday night, and he could locate no other group that did. He took down more information and said he would pass along this information. When I asked if he knew of an air vehicle that could match the description I gave, he suggested a jet-powered helicopter to account for not hearing the choppy noise. But it did not sound like a jet, and the military did not have any operations in the area.

We are still at a loss how to satisfactorily account for the objects we observed.

Coming next month... Special Book offer: *The UFO Controversy in America.*

Ref: Page 331– Melanie Cunningham UFO Photo

FLYING TRIANGLE OVER DERBYSHIRE, JUNE 1999

We feel that our presentation of Miss Melanie Cunningham's photo of the big Flying Triangle seen by her over Derbyshire, and reported by our Director/Consultant Omar Fowler in FSR 44/4 (front cover and page 3) was not entirely satisfactory, so we are running it again here. As readers will see, the relative position of the Moon in the picture is now made clear. -G.C.

'A visit to the Nazca lines' by Omar Fowler

Bob Dean (left) with Omar Fowler, 1994

A VISIT TO NAZCA

By Omar Fowler, FSR Consultant

Our colleague Omar Fowler, who used to live in Surrey and ran the S.I.G.A.P. UFO Investigation Group (now taken over by another FSR Consultant, Paul Whitehead), is currently living near Barcelona, in Spain. He has just returned from a trip to South America, where he was able to fulfil a life-long dream of seeing the Nazca Lines and Figures, and where he also met the famous German lady Dr. Maria Reiche, who has devoted her entire life to the study of all these strange forms and markings on the Peruvian Desert. Omar has sent us this very interesting account of what he saw.

EDITOR

I was fortunate recently in being able to fulfil one of my life-time ambitions when I visited Peru in May of this year (1988), and had the opportunity to explore and fly over the famous "Lines" and "Figures" of the Nazca Plain (around 14° 53 S., 74° 54 W.)

The road journey from Lima to Ica and then on to Nazca turned out to be a hair-raising adventure on tracks that rapidly deteriorated as the trip progressed. White crosses at the side of the road marked particularly dangerous points where various persons had been killed in accidents. At one bad corner up in the mountains, seven black crosses showed a spot where seven people had apparently misjudged the bend and disappeared into the rocky valley below.

Finally the battered old Peruvian V8 "*Chevvy*" taxi arrived on the Nazca Plain, and we pulled up next to an observation tower that had been constructed beside the highway. This tower is some fifteen metres in height and gives a panoramic view of the desert. It was possible to make out a number of distant lines and part of a geoglyph figure nearby, but it was not until later in the day, when I flew over the Plain, that the figures and lines were completely visible.

The first impression was of the large number of lines that criss-cross over the desert, far more than I had expected. The famous figures became visible one after another, as the pilot flew over them in his *Cessna* for probably the umpteenth time this year. The figures were far duller than they appear in many photographs, and were a little difficult to distinguish. There were now car-tracks showing up, crossing over many of the Lines and some of the Figures. I was later to learn from Dr. Maria Reiche that these tyre-tracks were some fifteen years old, and had been caused by

an influx of tourists after the sensational treatment given to the Lines and Figures in the books by Erich von Däniken.

The careless drivers had badly damaged several of the lines, and their tyre-tracks would probably stay there for another two or three hundred years. I photographed numerous figures, mainly for my own interest, as they have been professionally taken by aerial cameramen many times. The desert was criss-crossed

with dried up river-beds meandering across the Plain. Although these old river-beds looked as though they had only been formed a year or so ago, they pre-date the lines and figures and are probably over 1500 years old. The whole scene was quite remarkable. Who had made the lines and figures, and for what purpose?

I had booked into the Nazca Tourist Hotel for a few days, and as soon as we landed, I intended to try and find the whereabouts of Dr. Maria Reiche. I had meanwhile already heard various theories about the lines and figures from Dr. Javier Cabrera Darquea, a person that I had travelled many miles to see. He had his own ideas, one of which was the fact that the "runway" lines on the Nazca Plain were old launching sites for spacecraft! It was not so bizarre as one might think, for Dr Javier Cabrera produced pieces of iron and other ores from the Nazca Plain to explain his

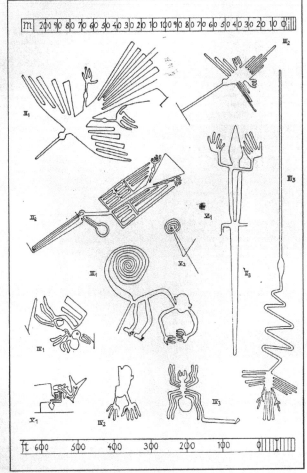

Some of the bird and animal drawings from Maria Reiche's book.

15

theory. When held close together, the opposite poles of the materials repelled each other. Had the inhabitants of Nazca discovered linear motive power thousands of years ago? He next showed me a model clay vessel closely resembling a "UFO" (see photo). This had been found along with many other artifacts some year ago, and the original was now in the Aeronautical Museum of Peru. The Nazca people reproduced all of their feelings and thoughts in their pottery, ranging from the birth of man, to the feelings expressed in facial features and depicted on various artifacts. In this instance, the dome shaped object appeared to be a craft. Its flight capability was signified by the bird emblem portrayed around the dome, and stars appear to be shown around the circumference lower down.

Could this have been their interpretation of a UFO seen many thousands of years ago? Had the craft landed and contacted the people of Nazca, and were the huge figures in the desert and on the hillsides a signal to bring down the UFOs? We know that many of the old Andean folklore tales speak of "Gods coming down from the sky". There are theories that they taught the people the rudiments of agriculture, and certainly the weaving of cotton, grown in the area, has been depicted in some of the oldest line drawings visible on the desert.

Finally one evening, I was fortunate in meeting Dr. Maria Reiche. I had requested an interview, and this took place in her hotel room, with her sister Renate and a young Peruvian companion nearby. I was sorry to learn that Dr. Reiche, who was now aged 85, had a stroke fairly recently. She was now almost completely blind and could only take her evening walk with the

assistance of two companions to support her. Fortunately she was still in complete command of her senses, and we chatted about her work over the past forty years, her meticulous study of the figures and lines, and her mathematical work on trying to find the unit of measurement used by the ancient Nazcans. This subsequently turned out to be what Dr. Reiche has called "the elb," a measurement taken from the elbow to the end of the fingers. (A unit of measurement used within recent memory by old people in various parts of the globe.) The Nazca lines, she believed, were mainly astronomical in importance, but the figures were, even now, still a mystery. She had calculated that one abstract design had 365 angles in it, one for every day of the year, but there was still so much work and research to be done.

The damage to the lines and figures was discussed, and Dr. Reiche pointed out the difficulty in keeping the figures clear and undamaged. It was far too easy for a driver to turn off the road across the Plain and to damage the lines and figures. The road was unfenced, and completely open. There were indeed large notices, warning of dire consequences if you strayed from the road: imprisonment and large fines. But who was there to enforce the security of the figures on the Plain? I was amazed to learn that although Dr. Maria Reiche has been honoured by the Peruvian Government and now has a home for life at the Tourist Hotel, she alone is striving to protect the ground drawings of Nazca. She employs three motorcyclists to patrol the road in an effort to stop people defacing the figures. The cost of this operation is paid for solely by the

(continued on Page iii)

(continued from Page 16)
money collected from the sale of her book, *"Mystery On The Desert",* * and although a 2 dollar tax is levied on each person flying over the Nazca Plain "for the protection of items of archaeological interest", not one cent has been spent on the protection of the figures. It has all been up to Dr. Reiche and her own private crusade.

Fortunately, Dr. Maria Reiche has now named a successor to carry on her work. She is an American scientist, Phyllis Pitlugar. Armed with all the latest technology and computers (something that Maria Reiche never had), Phyllis will try and unravel the secrets of the Nazca Plain. We wish her luck!

*NOTE BY THE EDITOR OF FSR.
I had the good fortune to meet Dr. Maria Reiche in London about twenty years ago, when she lectured to a small audience in a room at London University on the marvels of her beloved Nazca, and to secure a copy of her book, which is entitled GEHEIMNIS DER WÜSTE/MYSTERY ON THE

DESERT/SECRETO DE LA PAMPA. It is richly illustrated with photographs, coloured as well as black and white, and has the entire text in German, English and Spanish. It was published in 1968 by NAZCA PERU SA, Lutzweg 9, Stuttgart-Vaihingen, Germany. — G.C.

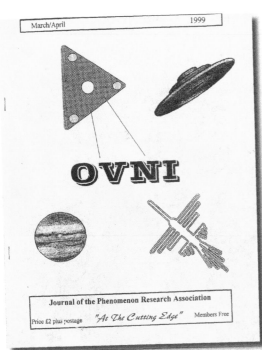

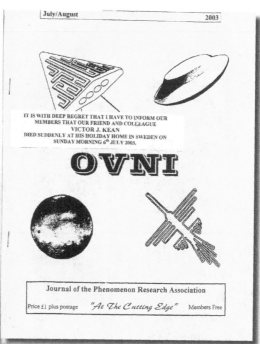

TALE ENDERS

VIVIENNE OLBISON BIRDSALL : We were all stunned to read the terrible news in the 'UFO Magazine', that Vivienne died on the 26th January. The wife of Mark Ian Birdsall, she was a popular figure at many 'Quest International' conferences and always added an aura of brightness to the proceedings. Her presence will be sadly missed and our thoughts and condolences go to Mark, his son and daughter.

PRA THANKS go to Claire Upton who has been our efficient Secretary for many years and has now handed over the job to Deb' Hollis (see leading page).

SAD NEWS from our Australian member Bernadette Pattison. Regular readers will have read about the deadly snakes around her home. We have just heard that 'Bella', her favourite Labrador dog has died as the result of being bitten by a deadly 'Eastern Brown' snake.

ALL UFO GROUPS ARE INVITED TO PARTICIPATE IN "PROJECT FT". At present there are 33 UFO groups assisting in this 'Flying Triangle' research and the database (Director: Victor J.Kean) has over 7,000 FT sighting reports (Aug.1942 - to the present day). See: http://ourworld.compuserve.com/homepages/Tspurrier/ufosight.htm. Send your data to: Tony Spurrier, 18 Argyle Road, Edmonton, London, N18 2PP, or E-Mail Victor J.Kean: 100545.1505@Compuserve.com

THE MILLENNIUM YEAR will mean nothing to at least a quarter of the World's population. There is one correction to the last OVNI (Jan/Feb), we are now in the Chinese year of the 'Rabbit'!

"CAR PAIR IN A BALL OF LIGHT ENCOUNTER" was the headline in the ECHO (Loughborough). 26 February 1999. A couple were driving on the A46 going towards the A6, when a ball of light flew past their car. "It flew past the car, towards the roundabout and then disappeared." The sighting comes after what was thought to be an Alien encounter in the area on February 8, by local woman Sarah Rushbrook.

BETTY CASH DIES: Betty Cash was one of three people injured in a UFO close encounter near Huffman, Texas, on December 29 1980. She died on the 18th anniversary of the event, in Birmingham, Alabama.

Betty had been in poor health ever since the encounter, which involved a huge UFO accompanied by military helicopters on a dark road in the east Texas Pitney Woods. The car occupants were exposed to radiation from the object which caused extreme medical problems such as burns, eye damage and hair loss, etc. (Source: MUFON)

EARTH CHANGES continue in Australia according to our PRA contact Bernadette Pattison, a regular contributor to the OVNI. "We have floods here in Queensland, the worst ever recorded in some areas. It has certainly been the worst summer I can ever remember", says Bernadette. "The grass is high, the tanks (water) are full and I can see changes everywhere."

MINISTRY OF DEFENCE documents on unexplained phenomena are to be declassified and released to the public, according to the Daily Express 5 March 1999. BUFORA has been fighting to gain access to the documents for years. (*We will still only see what they will allow us to see...Ed.*)

NEXT MEETING

Will be held at the Allenton, Derby, Royal British Legion at 8pm on Tuesday 23rd March.
Video presentation direct from the U.S.A. (shown on TV 17th Feb.)
'Conformation' Hard Evidence of Aliens!
Includes unique new footage of an 'implant' being medically removed, with electron microscope analysis.
Non-members welcome: £1 on the night.

*OVNI articles may be reproduced by other organisations, with due credit to the source.
Articles and opinions printed in this journal do not necessarily reflect the views of the P.R.A.*

Ref: Page 369 – Travis Walton-another newspaper cutting shown- insert 369

y MIRROR, MON OCT 10. 1977

THE HELLICAR REPORT
EXAMINES THE UNACCOUNTABLE MYSTERIES OF...

THIS WEIRD WORLD

the improbable happens, modern science shrugs impossible. When the impossible happens, it is phenomenal. But, as a new book points out, the the impossible and the phenomenal are happen-time. Today the Mirror looks at the weird world plained—and the unexplainable...

HE A PRISONER PACE?

TRAVIS WALTON

by MICHAEL HELLICAR

Adopted from "Phen-homena; A Book of Wonders," by John Michell and Robert J. M. Rickard. To be published by Thames and Hudson Ltd. on October 17. Price £1·95.

tle truck bumped slowly along orest path, the six young men looking forward to a bath after their long day's work ees.
k; chilly night and no one felt much

e silence
by an
from
passen-
tlying
ove the

eched to
an near-
year-old
jumped
others
or from
greenish-
from the
Walton

driven
ut when
d to the
es later,
sign of
brightly-

mber 5,
Snow-

appear-
gated by
sheriff,
who im-
ected a

on was
a miss-
Gillespie
osse of
routine
area,
d
nesses
counter
were
detector
passed,
now
ed, or-
search.

This time, hundreds of men combed the country-side on foot, horseback and in helicopters. But in vain.

Then, five days after his strange disappear-ance, Walton turned up in the village of Heber, a few miles from Snow-flake.

He was pale, shocked and 10lb. lighter in weight.

The story he told was incredible. ...

"As I got near to the UFO in the forest some-thing hit me," he said. "It was like an electric shock in my jaw, and everything went black.

"When I awoke I thought I was in hospi-tal. I was on a table in a big room with a bright light in my eyes. Then, as my eyes focussed, I saw three figures. They weren't human.

"They were about 5ft. tall and wore tight-fitting brown robes. Their skin was white, they had domed foreheads, no hair, and their eyes were very big. They just peered at

me and nobody made a sound.

"A man in a blue uni-form appeared and led me into another room. He seemed human, but he wore a helmet like a fish-bowl.

"I sat in a high-backed chair with buttons on one arm and a lever on another. Outside it was dark and I could see only stars.

"I pushed the lever and the scene changed. I was scared to touch any-thing else in case we were in a spaceship.

"Eventually, I was led down a ramp into a kind of hangar, with some small living saucers

nearby. Three more human-looking people appeared, one of them a woman.

"I was angry and shouting questions, but they never spoke. They laid me on a table and put a mask on my face. It was like an oxygen mask with a big black ball on top. I seemed to lose consciousness.

"When I awoke, I was on the side of the road.

"I ran and ran until I came to a phone booth. I realised I was in Heber."

Was it an illusion, a joke — or the incredible truth?

INDEX

DISCLAIMER

Should we have inadvertently missed anybody, we unreservedly apologise and will credit the copyright in *Haunted Skies*, Volume 12.

Thanks go to many people who assisted us with putting this book together. They include Nick Pope for the foreword, David Sankey, Steven Franklin, David Bryant and Wayne Mason for their illustrations. Bob Tibbitts for the design and typesetting of this volume. Philip Mantle for his assistance. Not forgetting those whose sightings and reports are contained within the pages of this book, some of whom have sadly left us.

All statements made by the people involved in the book are opinions expressed by them and should be treated as such.

The publisher/author John Hanson and the co-authors Dawn Holloway and V. J. Hyde do not accept liability or responsibly for statements made by the participants involved. All rights are reserved.

This book or parts thereof may not be reproduced in any form, stored in any retrieval system or transmitted in any form by any means – electronic, mechanical, photocopy, or otherwise – without permission from the publisher or co-authors.

These books have cost us a great deal of money to produce, but we strongly believe that this information forms part of our social history and rightful heritage. It should therefore be preserved, despite the ridicule still aimed at the subject by the media.

If anyone is willing to assist us with the preparation of any illustrations, it would be much appreciated. We can be contacted by letter at **31, Red Lion St, Alvechurch, Worcestershire B48 7LG**, by telephone **0121 445 0340**, or email: **johndawn1@sky.com** • Website: **www.hauntedskies.co.uk**

John Hanson's daughter and co-author of 'Haunted Skies' . . . Victoria Jane Hyde

Volume 1 of *Haunted Skies* 1940-1959 *(Foreword by Timothy Good)*

We present sightings from the Second Word War. They include many reports from allied pilots, who describe seeing unidentified flying objects, while on bombing missions over Germany. Some pilots we interviewed told of being ordered to intercept a UFO; one pilot was even ordered to open fire! In addition to these are reports of early close encounters, involving allegations of abduction experiences.

Another report tells of strange 'beings' seen outside an RAF Base. We also outline a spectacular sighting, in 1957, that took place in Bedfordshire, which appears identical to that seen over Oregon by employees of the Ames Research Laboratory, San Francisco. There are also numerous reports of 'saucer', 'diamond' and 'cigar-shaped' objects seen during these years.

Volume 2 of *Haunted Skies* 1960-1965 *(Foreword by Jenny Randles)*

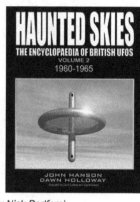

We re-investigated what may well be one of the earliest events, involving mysterious crop circles discovered in June 1960, at Poplar Farm, Evenlode. A 'V'-shaped UFO over Gloucestershire, and an example of a early 'Flying Triangle' over Tyneside in early September 1960. This type of object attracted much media interest in the early 1980s, following attempts by the Belgium Air Force to intercept what became labelled as 'Triangular' UFOs. This book contains many reports of saucer-shaped objects, and their occasional effect on motor vehicles. We also, wherever possible, include numerous personal letters and interviews with some of the researchers. We should not forget the early magazines, such as UFOLOG, produced by members of the (now defunct) Isle of Wight UFO Society.

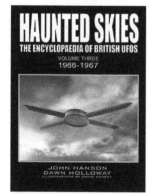

Volume 3 of *Haunted Skies* 1966-1967 *(Foreword by Nick Redfern)*

This was two years before manned landings took place on the Moon. In October 1967, there was a veritable 'wave' of UFO sightings which took place in the UK, involving cross-shaped objects, reported from Northumberland to the South Coast, with additional reports from Ireland and the Channel islands. (The police in the USA also reported sightings of 'Flying Crosses'). The sightings took place at various times, mostly during the evening or early morning hours, and involved an object which was manoeuvrable, silent – and at times – apparently flying at a low altitude. Attempts were made by the police and various authorities to explain away the sightings as Venus, based on the fact that the planet was bright in the sky during this period, which is clearly, in the majority of sightings, not the answer.

Volume 4 of *Haunted Skies* 1968-1971 *(Foreword by Philip Mantle)*

This book begins with a personal reference to Budd Hopkins, by USA researcher – Peter Robbins.

We outline a close encounter from Crediton, in Devon, which was brought to the attention of the police. Further police sightings of UFOs have been tracked down from Derbyshire, and a police chase through Kent. Multiple UFO sightings occur over the Staffordshire area, which are brought to the attention of the MOD. UFO researchers – Tony Pace and Roger Stanway – travel to London to discuss the incidents with the MOD. Close encounters at Warminster are also covered. A domed object at Bristol and further UFO landings are covered. They include a chilling account from a schoolteacher, living near Stratford-upon-Avon, and a 'flying triangle' seen over Birmingham.

Volume 5 of *Haunted Skies* **1972-1975** *(Foreword by Matt Lyons, Chairman of BUFORA)*

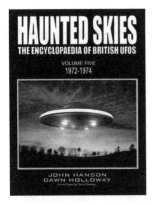

Further examples of UFO activity at Warminster, involving classic 'sky watches' from such locations as Cradle Hill, was the focus of worldwide attention during this period. In addition to this are reports of mysterious footsteps heard. A visit from the 'Men in Black', and other amazing stories, form just a tiny part of some amazing material collected by us, over the years, during personal interviews with the people concerned. UFO fleets are seen over Reading, and a landed saucer-shaped object is seen at Lancashire.

A UFO, containing aliens, is seen at close range over Worcestershire. A local councillor also described seeing what he believes was an alien spaceship, with occupants. There is also an investigation into the famous Berwyn Mountain incident, when it was alleged, by some, that a 'craft' had landed.

Volume 6 of *Haunted Skies* **1976-1977 Jubilee edition** *(Foreword by Kevin Goodman)*

Strange globes of light, seen moving in formations of three (often referred to as triangular in overall shape). Warminster, Wiltshire – reports of mysterious black shadows, flying globes of light and a triangular-shaped UFO seen over Cleeve Hill, near Cheltenham by police officers. There is also an investigation into a number of reported landings of alien craft around the Dyfed area, in February 1977. We present some original illustrations, drawn by children at the local school (which will be reproduced in colour, in a later edition of Haunted Skies). A triangular UFO is seen over Stoke-on-Trent. Comprehensive details were also obtained, regarding Winchester woman, Joyce Bowles – who was to report many encounters with UFOs and their alien occupants.

Volume 7 of *Haunted Skies* **1978-1979** *(Foreword by David Bryant)*

The famous debate into UFOs, held at the United Nations, is covered. A UFO landing at Rowley Regis, West Midlands – involving housewife Jean Hingley – labelled by the Press as the 'Mince Pie Martian' case. Many original sketches and additional information supporting her claims are offered. Another classic UFO sighting is re-investigated, following interviews held with Elsie Oakensen – a housewife from the Daventry area – who sighted a dumb-bell shaped UFO while on the way home from work. Thanks to Dan Goring, editor of EarthLink we were able to include a large number of previously unpublished sighting reports from Essex and London. We also include a close encounter from Didsbury, Manchester involving Lynda Jones, who is known personally to us.

Volume 8 of *Haunted Skies* **1980** *(Foreword by Philip Mantle)*

This book covers the period of just one year and is now, for the first time in the *Haunted Skies* series of books, published in colour. Unfortunately, due to the increase in pagination and the use of colour, the price has been raised, but still represents extremely good value. The first part of the book covers the period from January to November 1980. This includes numerous reports of UFO sightings and encounters. In addition to this, we outline our investigation into the Zigmund Adamski death, and the UFO sighting involving Todmorden Police Constable Alan Godfrey. In the second part, which covers December 1980, we present a comprehensive overview of the events that took place in Rendlesham Forest, thanks to the assistance of retired Colonel Charles Halt and long-standing UFO researcher, Brenda Butler.

Volume 9 of *Haunted Skies* 1981-1986 *(Foreword by Nick Redfern)*
Over 450 pages, many in colour

The authors point out that the majority of the information contained within the *Haunted Skies* series of books will not be found in declassified UFO files, catalogued in the Public Records Office, Kew, London.

This book contains:

UFO sightings over RAF Woodbridge, Suffolk – the scene of much interest during the previous month; a landed UFO at South Yorkshire; UFOs seen over Kent – harrowing close encounters between UFOs and motorists are outlined. These include a report from three women, driving home along the A5 in rural Shropshire (UK), which can be contrasted with a similar allegation made by three women from Kentucky, USA. A close encounter over the M50 Motorway, Gloucestershire; a couple from Hampshire tell of their roadside encounter – which left the husband with some strange marks on his body; a man out fishing, in Aldershot – who was approached by aliens; mysterious apports of stones that occurred, over a number of years, at Birmingham, West Midlands, involving the police – who staked out the locality in a bid to catch the offender. In addition to this, falls of coins and stones in other parts of the world are also outlined.

Although primarily covering British UFO sightings – wherever space permits (always in short supply) – we now include other forgotten worldwide cases of interest, brought to the attention of the reader. One such incident tells of a triangular UFO, seen over Arizona; another of a UFO sighted by a Russian astronaut.

A bizarre story involving David Daniels, who approached a number of prominent worldwide UFO researchers during the early 1980s – he alleged he was from the Pleiades and claimed to be able to metamorphosise from a human body to a reptilian. While it is difficult to believe rationally that this could be true, the authors tell of visits made to influential people, such as the head of the MOD, and The Lord Hill-Norton. Fact is stranger than fiction!

Volume 10 of *Haunted Skies* 1987-1988 *(Foreword by Nick Pope)*
632 pages, many in colour

Includes a focus on UFO cases reported from USA, Australia and New Zealand, 1940-1962.

Volume 10 of *Haunted Skies* catalogues the results of over 20 years research into reported UFO activity by the authors. The majority of those sightings and personal experiences will not be found in any declassified MOD files. Despite promises by their department to release specific individual files from 1971 (which we brought to their notice), the situation remains unchanged.

This volume covers the period of 1987-1988; which documents not only British UFO activity but also UFO activity from New Zealand, Australia and the United States, and forms an ongoing process by the authors to document such matters. In addition, a number of historical UFO cases between the periods 1940 and 1962 is also presented.

The book contains over 600 pages – many in colour – including numerous original illustrations relating to increased UFO activity over the Essex area. In addition to this, the authors outline a mysterious incident in 1987, involving claims of a UFO crash-landing in Nottinghamshire, and a spectacular sighting of goblin-like creatures that invaded a farm in Kentucky. A number of thought-provoking images, captured on camera, are shown from locations such as Cumbria, Rendlesham Forest and the Sedona area of the United States.

Volume 11 of *Haunted Skies* 1989-1990 *(Foreword by Charles I. Halt, USAF Col. Ret.)*
756 pages, many in colour

Includes a focus on UFO cases reported from UK, USA, Australia and New Zealand, 1963-1964.

Volume 11 contains over 750 pages with a foreword written by retired USAF Colonel Charles Halt – then the Deputy Base Commander of RAF Woodbridge – during the now famous UFO incident that has attracted worldwide attention, which took place in late December 1980. In this Volume the the authors continue their examination of further chronological reports of UFO activity over Great Britain, USA, Australia, New Zealand and Tasmania, for the period 1989-1990.

They also include previously unpublished material from the late Essex UFO researcher Ron West, which shows that the Essex area, like its Belgium and European counterparts, was the source of much UFO activity involving sightings of the Flying Triangle .

There is also an examination of historical UFO reports covering the period of 1963-1964, which includes sightings from the archives of Project Blue Book for the first time. In addition, the Volume outlines the valuable commitment made by the researchers themselves and their efforts to preserve what forms part of our important social history, rather than relying on other dubious sources of information.

The authors point out that very few of the UFO sighting reports published in the *Haunted Skies* books will be found in any declassified MOD files.

Volume 1 Revised – *Haunted Skies* 1939-1959 *(Foreword by Timothy Good)*
628 pages, many in colour

The original Volume 1 of *Haunted Skies* (320 pages) covered the period 1940-1959, with a foreword submitted by Timothy Good, and was published in 2010.

Due to the early books being removed from sale in late October 2015 by our ex-publisher, we were obliged to republish the book ourselves, which then gave us full control – now the volume has twice as many pages as the early one.

This is not a reproduction of the original black and white book. It includes many additional UFO reports from RAF servicemen, accompanied by photos and images, wherever possible, in colour.

We have now gone even further into the past and presented sightings of strange objects from the turn of the Century.

In this unique book you will read of numerous inexplicable close encounters, some involving humanoid figures, red glowing objects, ghostly figures, a number of reports of landed 'craft', allegations of abduction, dogfights with UFOs, gremlins – and our review is only up to the first 100 pages!

People asked us to publish in colour; we have done that. People asked us to document as much as we could; we have also done this to the best of our ability.

No one else (as far as we know) has ever compiled such an incredible amount of UFO social history – which should be preserved for posterity. Make of it what you will.

Haunted Skies Wiltshire *(Foreword by Nick Pope)*
Over 700 pages, many in colour

Haunted Skies Wiltshire is another in a series of unique books on the UFO subject, co-written by retired Police Officer John Hanson and his partner – Dawn Holloway. The couple have made many personal visits, over a period of 20 years, to interview members of the public living in the Wiltshire area, in order to preserve the history of reported UFO activity. This volume contains approximately 1,000 images in over 700 pages – in colour and black and white. They include photographs, sketches, private letters and illustrations, many of which have not been previously published.

Whether it's 'sky watching' from the now famous Cradle Hill, outside the lovely town of Warminster – host to some incredible UFO sightings back in the halcyon days of the 1960s/1970s, recorded by local journalist Arthur Shuttlewood – or perhaps a visit to the famous *Barge Inn* at Honey Street, Alton Barnes, overlooking the famous 'White Horse', or the magic of nearby ancient sites, such as Silbury Hill, Avebury Stone Circle, Adam's Grave, West Kennet Long Barrow, or Stonehenge, the authors have been there and enjoyed every fascinating moment.

Whatever the reason, no one can deny the breathtaking beauty of what this wonderful magical county has to offer in exceptional landscapes, and the possibility that strange objects may be captured on film or photograph.

The locality is rich with not only legends and myths but reports of UFO sightings – along with their occasional occupants – and a huge number of mysterious crop circles which abound each year, attracting tourists from all over the world, eager to see for themselves the intricate, dazzling formations which have been the subject of so much media interest over the years.

We hope you enjoy this book, as much as we have putting it together.

John & Dawn
www.hauntedskies.co.uk

The Halt Perspective *(Foreword by Nick Pope)*
Over 780 pages, many in colour

Over three nights running, in December 1980, a series of UFO encounters occurred at RAF Bentwaters and United States Air Force Woodbridge – twin bases, in Suffolk.

"As the Deputy Base Commander in a senior management position, I knew most of the main witnesses to the reported sightings, and was involved in investigating these incidents. Additionally, as many of the readers will know, I was a witness myself to UFO activity taking place in the nearby forest. I wasn't sure what to make of what I and the other airmen saw. Other than briefly reading a book as a teenager, I never gave any thought to UFOs, although I had read one or two out of interest.

I asked UK retired Police Officer, John Hanson, to assist me with the publication of this book in order to set the record straight, instead of relying on the continuing rumours about what did or didn't take place. Ironically, when initially confronted with the unexplained, I did everything in my power to keep the events quiet. Over the years there has been so much rubbish and sensational accounts given in the media surrounding the allegations made, who talk of missing time, alien beings meeting with the base commander, and so forth – more in keeping with science fiction than reality! I decided it was time to let people know exactly what took place and then make up their own minds, rather than trusting assessments made by people who weren't there and continuing publication of so much misinformation over the last 36 years. My own personal perspective on what took place needs to be told for posterity's sake." **Colonel Charles I. Halt USAF Retired**

Volume 2 Revised – *Haunted Skies* **1960-1969** *(Foreword by Nick Pope)*
622 pages, many in colour

Haunted Skies Volume 2 Revised – The history of the UFO presence on Earth – the files that Governments don't want you to see! Foreword by Nick Pope, endorsement by Irena Scott, Ph.D. John and Dawn along with V.J Hyde proudly present their latest unique book, which covers the now forgotten period of UFO history spanning 1960-1969. Many people have given us support over the years; some of them include, Betty and Freda Turpin of Coronation Street fame (aka Betty Driver), Bill Chalker, Colin Andrews, Colonel Charles Halt, Colonel Wendelle C. Stevens, Edgar Mitchell, Ex-Canadian Defence Minister – Paul Helyer, Gordon Creighton, Graham Shuttlewood, Kevin Goodman, Steve Wills, Bob Tibbitts, Malcolm Robinson, Moira McGhee, Nick Pope, Philip Mantle, Robert Hastings, Roy Lake, 'Busty' Taylor, Maria Wheatley, Polly Carson, Pat Delgado, Mathew Williams, Robert Salas, Jenny Randles, Tim Good, Trevor James Constable and many more. This revised *Haunted Skies* book represents another colossal undertaking of work, involving the spectacular presentation of hundreds of forgotten UFO sightings from police officers, RAF pilots, and members of the public, following over 20 years research by the authors – and, of course, the valuable contributions made by the researchers themselves. This book is not about us but about them and our joint efforts to ensure that this information is preserved for future generations. Our journey of discovery covers various peaks of UFO activity, including the short-lived phenomena that became labeled as the 'Flying Cross', which was to plague the later part of the UK in 1967. This book, like the others, is published in colour and includes reports from the United States. It contains approximately 600 photos, sketches, illustrations, images and supporting witness testimonials.

RECOMMENDED READING

CPSIA information can be obtained
at www.ICGtesting.com
Printed in the USA
BVHW011727130620
581343BV00001B/2